GESELLSCHAFT
FÜR INFORMATIK

C. Hoffmann, A. Stein,
A. Ruckelshausen, H. Müller, T. Steckel, H. Floto (Hrsg.)

Informatik in der Land-, Forst- und Ernährungswirtschaft

**Fokus:
Resiliente Agri-Food-Systeme**

**Referate der 43. GIL-Jahrestagung
13.-14. Februar 2023
Osnabrück, Germany**

Gesellschaft für Informatik e.V. (GI)

Lecture Notes in Informatics (LNI) - Proceedings
Series of the Gesellschaft für Informatik (GI)

Volume P-330

ISBN 978-3-88579-724-1
ISSN 1617-5468

Volume Editors

Dr. Christa Hoffmann
oeconos GmbH
73265 Dettingen, Germany
Email: christa.hoffmann@oeconos.de

Jun.-Prof. Dr. Anthony Stein
Universität Hohenheim
Institut für Agrartechnik & Computational Science Hub (CSH)
70599 Stuttgart, Germany
Email: anthony.stein@uni-hohenheim.de

Prof. Dr. Arno Ruckelshausen
Hochschule Osnabrück
49090 Osnabrück, Germany
Email: A.Ruckelshausen@hs-osnabrueck.de

Dr. Henning Müller
Deutsches Forschungszentrum für Künstliche Intelligenz GmbH (DFKI)
& Agrotech Valley Forum e.V.
49163 Bohmte, Germany
Email: henning.mueller@hof-fleming.de

Dr. Thilo Steckel
Claas E-Systems GmbH
49201 Dissen a.T.W., Germany
Email: thilo.steckel@claas.com

Helga Floto
GIL-Geschäftsführung
73730 Esslingen, Germany
Email: gil.floto@gmail.com

Series Editorial Board
Andreas Oberweis, KIT Karlsruhe,
(Chairman, andreas.oberweis@kit.edu)
Torsten Brinda, Universität Duisburg-Essen, Germany
Dieter Fellner, Technische Universität Darmstadt, Germany
Ulrich Flegel, Infineon, Germany
Ulrich Frank, Universität Duisburg-Essen, Germany
Michael Goedicke, Universität Duisburg-Essen, Germany
Ralf Hofestädt, Universität Bielefeld, Germany
Wolfgang Karl, KIT Karlsruhe, Germany
Michael Koch, Universität der Bundeswehr München, Germany
Peter Sanders, Karlsruher Institut für Technologie (KIT), Germany
Andreas Thor, HFT Leipzig, Germany
Ingo Timm, Universität Trier, Germany
Karin Vosseberg, Hochschule Bremerhaven, Germany
Maria Wimmer, Universität Koblenz-Landau, Germany

Dissertations
Rüdiger Reischuk, Universität Lübeck, Germany
Thematics
Agnes Koschmider, Universität Kiel, Germany
Seminars
Judith Michael, RWTH Aachen, Germany

© Gesellschaft für Informatik, Bonn 2023
printed by Köllen Druck+Verlag GmbH, Bonn

This book is licensed under a Creative Commons BY-SA 4.0 licence.

Vorwort

Die 43. Jahrestagung der Gesellschaft für Informatik in der Land-, Forst- und Ernährungswirtschaft (GIL) steht im Jahr 2023 unter dem Leitthema **„Resiliente Agri-Food-Systeme: Herausforderungen und Lösungsansätze"**. Sie findet statt in einer Zeit, in der die globalen Agri-Food-Systeme besonderen Herausforderungen ausgesetzt sind. Externe Einflüsse wie Krieg auf europäischem Boden, die anhaltenden Auswirkungen des globalen Corona-Pandemiegeschehens und zunehmende Cyber-Angriffe stellen tagtäglich die Resilienz unserer Agri-Food-Systeme auf den Prüfstand. Rohstoffe oder Betriebsmittel für die Produktion können nicht geliefert, oder fertige Produkte nicht versandt werden, weil ganze Lieferketten zusammenbrechen. Zunehmend müssen auch Verbraucher immer häufiger erfahren, dass Produkte des alltäglichen Lebens zeitweise nicht verfügbar sind. Die digitale Transformation nimmt in diesem Kontext eine Doppelrolle ein: So hat die Digitalisierung vieler Prozesse auf der einen Seite zu vielen Erleichterungen in der Produktion und Verarbeitung von Lebensmitteln geführt. Auf der anderen Seite ermöglicht sie eben durch den Aufbau sog. Cyber-Physischer Systeme auch in diesem Sektor eine neue Dimension von Angriffen auf Agri-Food-Systeme. Die Digital-Branchen-Community steht aus diesem Grund aktuell an einem Scheideweg. Die Anzahl an Faktoren, welche die Resilienz der Systeme bedrohen, wächst täglich. Im gleichen Atemzug ist jedoch noch nicht zufriedenstellend definiert, wie Resilienz überhaupt systematisch ermittelt und bewertet werden kann. Wichtig für die Branche wird es sein, geeignete Konzepte und Lösungen zu schaffen, um den Grad der Resilienz von Agri-Food-Systemen zu erhöhen. Bestehende Ansätze und mögliche zukünftige Lösungswege sollen auf der diesjährigen Tagung diskutiert werden. Daneben stehen wieder aktuelle, wissenschaftliche Entwicklungen in den Bereichen Informatik, Künstliche Intelligenz & Robotik, Sensortechnik sowie das Datenmanagement im Fokus.

Wie auch in den vergangenen Jahren bietet die 43. Jahrestagung der GIL eine Plattform für die vom Bundesministerium für Ernährung und Landwirtschaft geförderten „Digitalen Experimentierfelder". In einem Diskussionsforum bekommen die eingeladenen VertreterInnen der Experimentierfelder, sowie VertreterInnen der Swiss Future Farm und der Innovation Farm die Möglichkeit die Ergebnisse der ersten Projektphase vorzustellen und diese kritisch zu reflektieren.

Der vorliegende Tagungsband enthält 66 wissenschaftliche Beiträge, die aus 98 eingereichten Abstracts nach einem zweistufigen Begutachtungsverfahren (peer review) hervorgegangen sind. Von den 66 Beiträgen fallen 21 Beiträge in die Kategorie Long Paper, die einer zusätzlichen dritten Begutachtungsphase unterzogen wurden. Unser Dank gilt allen, die sich aktiv an der Vorbereitung und Durchführung der Tagung mit großem Engagement beteiligt haben. Abschließend danken wir allen Sponsoren für ihre finanzielle Unterstützung.

Osnabrück, im Januar 2023

Dr. Christa Hoffmann, oeconos GmbH, 1. Vorsitzende der GIL
Jun.-Prof. Dr. Anthony Stein, Universität Hohenheim, 2. Vorsitzender der GIL
Helga Floto, GIL-Geschäftsführung
Prof. Dr. Arno Ruckelshausen, Hochschule Osnabrück
Dr. Henning Müller, DFKI GmbH & Agrotech Valley Forum e.V.
Dr. Thilo Steckel, Claas E-Systems GmbH und GIL-Beirat

Wir danken der Landwirtschaftlichen Rentenbank für die freundliche Unterstützung.

Wir danken den folgenden Unternehmen und Institutionen für die Unterstützung der Tagung (PREMIUM).

Wir danken den folgenden Unternehmen und Institutionen für die Unterstützung der Tagung (SUPPORTER).

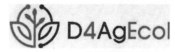

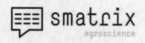

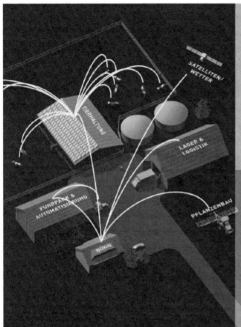

LEBENSMITTEL-PRODUKTION VERNETZEN

mit standardisierten Schnittstellen

Helfen Sie dabei, diese Vernetzung durch Normung zu realisieren.

Ihr Ansprechpartner:
Johannes Lehmann
Leiter Geschäftsfeldentwicklung Smart Farming, DIN e.V.

johannes.lehmann@din.de

SmartFarmingDays.com

DEIN GRATIS TICKET IN RICHTUNG ZUKUNFT

- Erlebe Smart Farming Lösungen, die du heute und morgen zur Optimierung deines Betriebes einsetzen kannst.

- Informiere dich zu am Markt verfügbaren Produkten von zahlreichen Maschinenherstellern, Soft- und Hardwareanbietern.

- Gewinne neue Erkenntnisse in Fachforen und Live-Demos zu vielfältigen generellen Smart Farming Themen.

- Tausche dich mit Experten aus Industrie und Wissenschaft zu Smart Farming Themen von morgen aus.

DAS NETZWERK-EVENT FÜR DIE LANDWIRTSCHAFT.

14.-16. JUNI 2023
Gut Arenshorst, Raum Osnabrück

BLOCK	BEREICH	REIHE
1A	A	1

Making farming a piece of (strawberry) cake

A robot as a harvest helper – IAV is working on this in a pioneering project together with large agricultural enterprises in Germany.

www.iav.com/ernteroboter

RICHTUNGSWEISENDE DIGITALE LANDWIRTSCHAFT

Mit den John Deere Technologien für die Präzisionslandwirtschaft setzen Sie ganz neue Maßstäbe für Ihren landwirtschaftlichen Betrieb. Heute, morgen und auch übermorgen.

NOTHING RUNS LIKE A DEERE

Programmkomitee

Dr. Thomas Anken	Agroscope, Tänikon, Ettenhausen, Schweiz
Prof. Dr. Sonoko Bellingrath-Kimura	Leibniz-Zentrum für Agrarlandschaftsforschung e.V., Müncheberg
Prof. Dr. Frank Beneke	Universität Göttingen
Prof. Dr. Heinz Bernhardt	Technische Universität München, Freising
Karsten Borchard	Christian-Albrechts-Universität zu Kiel
Prof. Dr. Michael Clasen	Hochschule Hannover
Dr. Marianne Cockburn	Agroscope, Schweizer Nationalgestüt, Avenches, Schweiz
Dr. Nadja El Benni	Agroscope, Tänikon, Ettenhausen, Schweiz
Dr. Andreas Gabriel	Bayerische Landesanstalt für Landwirtschaft (LfL), Freising
Prof. Dr. Hans W. Griepentrog	Universität Hohenheim, Stuttgart
Prof. Dr. Joachim Hertzberg	Universität Osnabrück & DFKI Niedersachsen
Andreas Heiß	Hochschule Geisenheim University
Constanze Hofacker	act GmbH, Kiel
Dr. Dieter von Hörsten	JKI, Braunschweig
Dr. Timo Korthals	Claas E-Systems GmbH, Dissen a.T.W.
Jun.-Prof. Dr. Christian Krupitzer	Universität Hohenheim, Stuttgart
Daniel Martini	KTBL, Darmstadt
PD Dr. Andreas Meyer-Aurich	Leibniz-Institut für Agrartechnik und Bioökonomie e.V. (ATB), Potsdam
Dr. Viktoria Motsch	BOKU, Wien, Österreich
Dr. Henning Müller	DFKI GmbH & Agrotech Valley Forum e.V., Bohmte
Dr. Matthias Nachtmann	BASF, Limburgerhof
Prof. Dr. Dimitrios Paraforos	Hochschule Geisenheim, University
Johanna Pfrombeck	Bayerische Landesanstalt für Landwirtschaft (LfL), Freising
Heinrich Prankl	Josephinum, Wieselburg, Österreich
Prof. Dr. Guido Recke	Hochschule Osnabrück
Prof. Dr. Arno Ruckelshausen	Hochschule Osnabrück
Olivia Spykmann	Bayerische Landesanstalt für Landwirtschaft (LfL), Freising
Dr. Thilo Steckel	Claas E-Systems GmbH, Dissen a.T.W.
Prof. Dr. Stefan Stiene	Hochschule Osnabrück
Prof. Dr. Heiko Tapken	Hochschule Osnabrück
Dr. Torben Toeniges	Claas E-Systems GmbH, Dissen a.T.W.
Prof. Dr. Uta Wilkens	Ruhr-Universität Bochum
Prof. Dr. Andreas Wübbeke	Fachhochschule Südwestfalen, Soest

Organisationsteam

Dirk Bock	Agrotech Valley Forum e.V., Bohmte
Robert Everwand	Agrotech Valley Forum e.V., Bohmte
Prof. Dr. Joachim Hertzberg	Universität Osnabrück & DFKI Niedersachsen
Julia Ludger	Hochschule Osnabrück
Dr. Henning Müller	DFKI GmbH & Agrotech Valley Forum e.V., Bohmte
Tim Oeljeklaus	Hochschule Osnabrück
Prof. Dr. Arno Ruckelshausen	Hochschule Osnabrück
Dr. Thilo Steckel	Claas E-Systems GmbH, Dissen a.T.W.
Dr. Michaela van Eickelen	Agrotech Valley Forum e.V., Bohmte
Dr. Christa Hoffmann	1. GIL-Vorsitzende, oeconos GmbH, Dettingen
Jun.-Prof. Dr. Anthony Stein	2. GIL-Vorsitzender, Universität Hohenheim, Stuttgart
Helga Floto	GIL-Geschäftsführerin, Esslingen

Long Paper

Hans Bethge, Thomas Mählmann, Traud Winkelmann, Thomas Rath
Remote plant sensing and phenotyping – an e-learning tool in higher education 29

Sebastian Bosse, Karsten Berns, Johannes Bosch, Jörg Dörr, Frederick Charles Eichhorn, Peter Eisert, Christoph Fischer, Eike Gassen, Michael Gerstenberger, Heike Gerighausen, Jonathan Heil, Anna Hilsmann, Jochen Hirth, Christopher Huber, Mortesa Hussaini, Martin Kasparick, Peter Kloke, Hartmut Krause-Edler, Lukas Mackle, Jannes Magnusson, Felix Möhrle, Markus Möller, Peter Pickel, Clemens Rautenberg, Hans Dieter Schotten, Slawomir Stanczak, Lars Thiele, Henrik Ücdemir, Annett Wania, Anthony Stein
Nachhaltige Landwirtschaft mittels Künstlicher Intelligenz – ein plattformbasierter Ansatz für Forschung und Industrie 41

Jonas Credner, Peter Rehrmann, Waldemar Raaz, Thomas Rath
Blue Apple – an algorithm to realize agricultural classification under difficult light and color situations 53

Andreas Gabriel
Farmers' attitudes towards data security in agriculture when using digital technologies 65

Laura Sophie Gravemeier, Anke Dittmer, Martina Jakob, Daniel Kümper, Oliver Thomas
Conceptualizing a holistic smart dairy farming system 77

Jonathan Heil, Juan Manuel Valencia, Anthony Stein
Towards crop yield prediction using Automated Machine Learning 89

Lukas Hesse, Maik Fruhner, Heiko Tapken, Henning Müller
Computer-Vision-basierte Aktivitätserkennung bei Schweinen 101

Saskia Hohagen, Niklas Obermann, Uta Wilkens
Antecedents of organizational resilience and how these can be transferred to agriculture 113

Naeem Iqbal, Justus Bracke, Anton Elmiger, Hunaid Hameed, Kai von Szadkowski
Evaluating synthetic vs. real data generation for AI-based selective weeding 125

Jana Käthner, Karuna Koch, Nora Höfner, Volker Dworak, Mostafa Shokrian Zeini, Redmond Shamshiri, Woj Figurski, Cornelia Weltzien
Review of agricultural field robots and their applicability in
potato cultivation 137

Christoph Manss, Kai von Szadkowski, Janis Bald, David Richard, Christian Scholz, Daniel König, Matthias Igelbrink, Arno Ruckelshausen
Towards selective hoeing depending on evaporation from the soil 149

Mary-Rose McGuire, Hans Schulte-Nölke
Verträge über smarte Landmaschinen nach der Umsetzung der Warenkauf-
und der Digitale-Inhalte-Richtlinie 159

Marvin Melzer, Nishita Thakur, Florian Ebertseder,
Sonoko Bellingrath-Kimura
Identifizierung kleinräumiger Erosionshotspots unter Berücksichtigung
aquatischer Ökosysteme zur Etablierung von Erosionsschutzstreifen 171

Frank Nordemann, Ralf Tönjes, Heiko Tapken, Lukas Hesse
Kooperative Agrarprozesse resilient gestalten und dynamisch optimieren 183

Maren Pöttker, David Hagemann, Simon Pukop, Thomas Jarmer,
Dieter Trautz
Kartierung des Bedeckungsgrads von Cirsium arvense im Mais (Zea mays L.)
mithilfe Neuronaler Netze in UAV-Daten 195

Marian Renz, Mark Niemeyer, Joachim Hertzberg
Towards model-based automation of plant-specific weed regulation 207

Andreas Schliebitz, Henri Graf, Tobias Wamhof, Heiko Tapken,
Andreas Gertzen
KI-basiertes Computer-Vision-System zur Qualitäts- und Größenbestimmung
von Kartoffeln 219

Redmond R. Shamshiri, Volker Dworak, Mostafa Shokrian Zeini,
Eduardo Navas, Jana Käthner, Nora Höfner, Cornelia Weltzien
An overview of visual servoing for robotic manipulators in
digital agriculture 231

Olivia Spykman, Stefan Kopfinger, Andreas Gabriel, Markus Gandorfer
Erste Praxiserfahrung mit einem Feldroboter – Ergebnisse einer
Fokusgruppendiskussion mit early adopters 243

Olivia Spykman, Andreas Roßmadl, Johanna Pfrombeck,
Stefan Kopfinger, Axel Busboom
*Wirtschaftlichkeitsbewertung eines Feldroboters auf Basis erster
Erfahrungen im Praxiseinsatz* 255

Henning Wübben, Raphaela Butz, Kai von Szadkowski,
Marco Barenkamp
*Instance-level augmentation for synthetic agricultural data
using depth maps* 267

Short Paper

Katharina Albrecht, Kristoffer Janis Schneider, Daniel Martini
*Vom RESTful Webservice für Pflanzenschutzmittelregistrierungsdaten
zur anwendungsunabhängigen Ontologie* 279

Tim Bohne, Gurunatraj Parthasarathy, Benjamin Kisliuk
*A systematic approach to the development of long-term autonomous
robotic systems for agriculture* 285

Fredrik Boye, Raghad Matar, Philipp Neuschwander
Data sovereignty needs in agricultural use cases 291

Sebastian Burkhart, Patrick Noack
Digital weed reduction 297

Michael Clasen, Jasmin Westermann
*Analyse und Klassifizierung von Digitalisierungsinitiativen
in der Landwirtschaft* 303

Daniel Eberz-Eder, Franz Kuntke, Gerwin Brill, Ansgar Bernardi,
Christian Wied, Philippe Nuderscher, Christian Reuter
*Prototypische Entwicklungen zur Umsetzung des Resilient
Smart Farming (RSF) mittels Edge Computing* 309

Santiago Focke Martinez, Joachim Hertzberg
Route-planning in output-material-flow operations using side-headlands 315

David Hagemann, Tim Zurheide, Dieter Trautz
*„CognitiveWeeding": Entwicklung von Entscheidungsregeln für ein
kontextbezogenes KI-Expertensystem auf Einzelpflanzenbasis
– pflanzenbauliche Aspekte* 321

Ludwig Hagn, Johannes Schuster, Martin Mittermayer, Kurt-Jürgen Hülsbergen
Satellitengestützte Analyse der räumlichen Variabilität für die Ableitung von Ertragszonen und deren Ursachen 327

Jens Harbers
Erhöhung der Biodiversität von Graslandbeständen mittels p-Wert-korrigierter Assoziationsregeln 333

Andreas Heiß, Dimitrios S. Paraforos, Galibjon M. Sharipov, Hans W. Griepentrog
Nutzerzentrierte Entscheidungstools und dynamische Steuerungsalgorithmen für eine differenzierte mehrparametrische N-Düngung 339

Daniel Herrmann, Jan-Philip Pohl, Steffi Rentsch, Daniel Jahncke, Nina Lefeldt, Dieter von Hörsten
Digitales Assistenzsystem zur Applikation von Pflanzenschutzmitteln 345

Niklas Hilbert, Jens-Peter Loy, Karsten Borchard
Metaanalyse zum aktuellen Stand der Digitalisierung in der Landwirtschaft 351

Stefan Hinck, Daniel Kümper
Automatisierte Verarbeitung von heterogen aufgelösten Datenquellen zur Berechnung einer teilflächenspezifischen Flüssigmistapplikationskarte 357

Joschka Andreas Hüllmann, Hauke Precht, Carolin Wübbe
Configurations of human-AI work in agriculture 363

Tobias Jorissen, Silke Becker, Konstantin Nahrstedt, Maren Pöttker, Guido Recke, Thomas Jarmer
Ökonomische Bewertung zum Spot-Spraying durch Drohnentechnik 369

Jascha Daniló Jung, Daniel Martini
Horticulture Semantic (HortiSem) 375

Jan Christoph Krause, Jaron Martinez, Henry Gennet, Martin Urban, Jens Herbers, Stefan Menke, Sebastian Röttgermann, Joachim Hertzberg, Arno Ruckelshausen
Konzeption und Realisierung einer feldbasierten landwirtschaftlichen Versuchsumgebung zur dynamischen Umgebungswahrnehmung 381

**Priska Krug, Adriana Förschner, Tobias Wiggenhauser,
Hansjörg Nußbaum, Jonas Weber**
*Different methods of yield recordings in grassland
– how accurate are they in practice?* 387

Alexander Kühnemund, Guido Recke
*Automatisierte Erkennung von Gruppenaktivitätsverhalten von Schweinen
in der Aufzucht mithilfe von KI-Kamerasystemen* 393

Marie Lamoth, Heiko Neeland, Christina Umstätter
*Beurteilung von Use Cases zur Tierortung nach dem Grad
des Informationsgehalts* 399

Greta Langer, Sarah Kühl, Sirkka Schukat
*IoT in der Milchviehhaltung am Beispiel von Gesundheitssensoren
– Akzeptanzbarrieren im Adoptionsprozess* 405

**Lukas Meyer, Andreas Gilson, Franz Uhrmann, Mareike Weule, Fabian Keil,
Bernhard Haunschild, Joachim Oschek, Marco Steglich, Jonathan Hansen,
Marc Stamminger, Oliver Scholz**
*For5G: Systematic approach for creating digital twins
of cherry orchards* 411

Marius Michels, Hendrik Wever, Oliver Mußhoff
Understanding German foresters' intention to use drones 417

**Ariane Moser-Beutel, Luisa Kiesecker, Andreas Meyer-Aurich,
Kristian Möller**
*Chancen der Remote-Zertifizierung im Agrar- und Ernährungssektor
am Beispiel ausgewählter IFA-Zertifizierungsaudits von GLOBALG.A.P* 423

**Konstantin Nahrstedt, Tobias Reuter, Maria Vergara Hernandez,
Dieter Trautz, Thomas Jarmer**
*Multilokale Modellierung der Bestandesentwicklung von Kleegrasgemengen
mittels Leaf Area Index (LAI) und multispektralen Drohnendaten* 429

**Eduardo Navas, Volker Dworak, Cornelia Weltzien, Roemi Fernández,
Mostafa Shokrian Zeini, Jana Käthner, Redmond Shamshiri**
*An approach to the automation of blueberry harvesting
using soft robotics* 435

**Burawich Pamornnak, Christian Scholz, Eduard Gode, Karen Sommer,
Timo Novak, Steffen Hellermann, Benjamin Wegmann, Arno Ruckelshausen**
*"Ready for Autonomy (R4A)": concept and application
for autonomous feeding* 441

Sara Anna Pfaff, Michael Paulus
Investitionsförderung für Agrarsoftware? 447

Frederick John Phillips, Marc-Alexandre Favier, Jörg Dörr
FarmBot-based-ISOBUS demonstrator for research and teaching 453

Jan-Philip Pohl, Axel Dittus, Lorenz Berhalter, Dieter von Hörsten
*Digitalisierung im Weinbau am Beispiel der
Pflanzenschutzmittelapplikation* 459

**Sandra Post, Ingmar Schröter, Eric Bönecke, Sebastian Vogel,
Eckart Kramer**
Modellierung des organischen Kohlenstoffs in Ackerböden 465

Sebastian Pütz, Malte Kleine Piening, Lars Schilling
*Interactive waypoint navigation for autonomous monitoring
of vegetables in complex micro-farming* 471

**Nils Reinosch, Alexander Münzberg, Daniel Martini, Alexander Niehus,
Liv Seuring, Christian Troost, Rajiv Kumar Srivastava, Thomas Berger,
Thilo Streck, Ansgar Bernardi**
*SIMLEARN – Ontologiegestützte Integration von Simulationsmodellen,
Systemen für maschinelles Lernen und Planungsdaten* 477

**Robert Rettig, Marcel Storch, Lucas Wittstruck, Christabel Edena Ansah,
Richard Janis Bald, David Richard, Dieter Trautz, Thomas Jarmer**
*A coupled multitemporal UAV-based LiDAR and multispectral
data approach to model dry biomass of maize* 483

**Tobias Reuter, Juan Carlos Saborío Morales, Christoph Tieben, Konstantin
Nahrstedt, Franz Kraatz, Hendrik Meemken, Gerrit Hünker, Kai Lingemann,
Gabriele Broll, Thomas Jarmer, Joachim Hertzberg, Dieter Trautz**
*Evaluation of a decision support system for the recommendation of
pasture harvest date and form* 489

**Vadim Riedel, Andreas Möller, Matthias Terhaag, Thomas Meyer,
Daniel Mentrup, Hendrik Kerssen, Elena Najdenko, Frank Lorenz, Tino Mosler,
Heinrich Tesch, Walter Peters, Stefan Hinck, Arno Ruckelshausen**
*Datenfluss bei der Applikation der Bodenbeprobung mit dem
mobilen Feldlabor „soil2data"* 495

Christof Schroth, Patricia Kelbert, Anna Maria Vollmer
*A data quality assessment tool for agricultural structured data as
support for smart farming* 501

Freddy Sikouonmeu, Martin Atzmueller
Active-learning-driven deep interactive segmentation for cost-effective labeling of crop-weed image data 507

Katrin Sporkmann, Heiko Neeland, Christiane Engels, Maria Trilling, Marten Wegener, Steffen Pache, Wolfgang Büscher
Evaluierung eines Funktionsmusters für ein Tracking-Referenzsystem in der Rinderhaltung 513

Astrid Sturm, Oliver Schöttker, Karmand Kadir, Frank Wätzold
Wann, wo und wie? Ein softwarebasiertes Mehrebenen-Informationssystem zur Optimierung von Beweidungssystemen 519

Beat Vinzent, Franz-Xaver Maidl, Markus Gandorfer
Analyse ausgewählter digitaler Lösungen zur N-Düngung 525

Lucas Wittstruck, Heike Gerighausen, Annelie Säurich, Markus Möller, Knut Hartman, Michael Steininger, Simone Zepp, Thomas Jarmer
Räumliche Erfassung des organischen Kohlenstoffgehaltes von Böden einer landwirtschaftlichen Intensivregion aus Sentinel-2-Daten 531

Martin Wutke, Clara Lensches, Jan-Hendrik Witte, Johann Gerberding, Marc-Alexander Lieboldt, Imke Traulsen
Entwicklung eines automatischen Monitoringsystems für die Geburtsüberwachung bei Sauen 537

Mostafa Shokrian Zeini, Redmond R. Shamshiri, Volker Dworak, Jana Käthner, Nora Höfner, Eduardo Navas, Cornelia Weltzien
Overview of control systems for robotic harvesting of sweet peppers and apples 543

Remote plant sensing and phenotyping – an e-learning tool in higher education

Hans Bethge[1], Thomas Mählmann[2], Traud Winkelmann[3] and Thomas Rath[4]

Abstract: Within the consortium "Experimentation Field Agro-Nordwest", a practical concept for knowledge and technology transfer of digital competence in agriculture was created. For this purpose, the web-based e-learning system "SensX" was set up, consisting of videos, presentations and instructions. In addition, the classical e-learning concept was extended by data sets, student experiments and sensor data of plants acquired by a remote phenotyping robot. This resulted in a massive open online course (MOOC), which was tested with agricultural and biotechnology students in higher education at the University of Applied Sciences Osnabrück over two years. The evaluation process of "SensX" included an empirical survey, qualitative interviews of the participating students by an external institution and an evaluation of the concept by the lecturers.

Keywords: agriculture, digital competence, e-learning concepts, remote experiments, sensors in teaching

1 Introduction

In higher education, the number of teaching modules based on e-learning systems, blended learning systems (traditional teaching combined with e-learning) or MOOCs (massive open online courses) is steadily increasing, both nationally (Germany) and internationally [Lü20; Al18]. The majority of these (approx. 30%) are offered in the computer sciences, but almost 6% are part of the agricultural and life sciences curricula, worldwide [Al18]. The COVID19 pandemic has caused further acceleration in the use of e-learning, blended learning approaches or MOOCs in higher education [Be21]. Yet the terms used to describe the use of computer technologies in education (here e-learning, blended learning, MOOCs) vary widely and are not coherent. In many publications and reports, the methods are

---

[1] University of Applied Sciences Osnabrueck, Laboratory for Biosystems Engineering (BLab), Oldenburger Landstr. 24, D-49090 Osnabrueck, h.bethge@hs-osnabrueck.de, https://orcid.org/0000-0002-3487-9725
[2] University of Applied Sciences Osnabrueck, Laboratory for Biosystems Engineering (BLab), Oldenburger Landstr. 24, D-49090 Osnabrueck, thomas.maehlmann@hs-osnabrueck.de
[3] Leibniz Universität Hannover, Institute of Horticultural Production Systems, Woody Plant and Propagation Physiology Section, Herrenhaeuser Str. 2, D-30419 Hannover, traud.winkelmann@zier.uni-hannover.de, https://orcid.org/0000-0002-2509-1418
[4] University of Applied Sciences Osnabrueck, Laboratory for Biosystems Engineering (BLab), Oldenburger Landstr. 24, D-49090 Osnabrueck, t.rath@hs-osnabrueck.de, https://orcid.org/0000-0001-7277-7335

grouped under terms such as "digital education" or "e-learning". Defined competences should be specified and consolidated. In contrast to the original intention of the Bologna process to focus academic education very strongly on vocational training, digital education in particular is based on four (or even more) areas of competence acquisition: (i) self-competence: ability to act on one's own responsibility, (ii) subject-matter competence: the ability to be able to make judgments and take action in specific areas, (iii) time competence: the ability to plan and carry out actions and intellectual achievements in a chronological sequence, (iv) social competence: ability to make judgements and act in a complex society [Ar18]. When evaluating digital education with regard to the criteria and competences listed above, digital education is sometimes seen as having a disruptive character [Ki19], since universal access makes it possible to support any university. Thus knowledge and methods are, at least in theory, available to many institutions and locations. On the other hand, difficulties are also seen that ultimately cause high dropout rates, e.g. with MOOCs [Ki19]. Empirical studies do not show a uniform picture of the educational success of digital higher education. In an analytical-theoretical study, it was demonstrated that there is only a slight correlation between digital and classic teaching methods in higher education with regard to learning success [Sc20]. In contrast, specific digital evidence-based and tested teaching concepts in the agricultural sector showed the superiority of digital teaching concepts to classical teaching in terms of learning success [We22; Ke16].

Of course, it should also be noted that the use and success is largely dependent on the users, i.e. the learners themselves. Thus, Kahan et al. differentiated users of MOOCs into five categories: (i) tasters, (ii) downloaders, (iii) disengagers, (iv) offline engagers and (v) online engagers [Ka17]. Each of these groups handles digital education differently and presumably, this leads to strong dispersion in learning success or in other evaluation parameters of digital teaching. On closer inspection, the teaching concepts and methods used in digital education or e-learning are also complex, and the terms used for them are multifaceted, not clearly demarcated, and only partially defined (see the comprehensive table of terms in [Lü20]). [Ca20] distinguished only three teaching approaches: (i) e-learning by distributing, (ii) e-learning by interacting and (iii) e-learning by collaboration. They were able to show that e-learning in higher education is still largely dominated by e-learning by distribution (uploading texts, graphics, PDFs, etc.), while more far-reaching approaches such as e-learning by interacting or e-learning by collaboration often remain largely unexplored [Ca20]. Approaches that go beyond this, such as e-learning supported by self-performing experiments, do not appear at all in the considerations and therefore, seem to be so far unconsidered in digital education and literature. The need to develop educational concepts that go beyond the three approaches of [Ca20] in order to provide efficient and successful academic training in as many areas of competence as possible is becoming increasingly evident.

In agriculture, the field of sensor technologies is very suitable for this purpose, as it is a subject with constantly evolving contents. Additionally, it is gaining increasing importance in all areas of agribusiness, and already plays a dominant role in practice, research, and development (see [Ha19] and [Yi21]). Moreover, students of agricultural sciences usually have little affinity for sensor technologies prior to their studies. So for many of them, a deeper engagement in sensor topics with new e-learning methods can lead to new knowledge, skills and competences. Therefore, the aim of our project is to establish and explore the use of sensor technology in agriculture using an interactive e-learning approach in order to provide students with in-depth digital competence.

2 SensX

2.1 Concept and categories

Within the consortium, "Experimentation Field Agro-Nordwest" a proof-of-concept project called "SensX" was initiated to promote and establish the use of sensor technology in the plant sector at university and college level. For that purpose, a MOOC e-learning system was developed that extends classical e-learning concepts by using sensor data, sensor kits, and, as a future perspective, fully remote and collaborative teaching with a robotic sensor demonstrator (Fig. 1). We have structured the features of the e-learning system into four categories, as described in detail in the following subchapters.

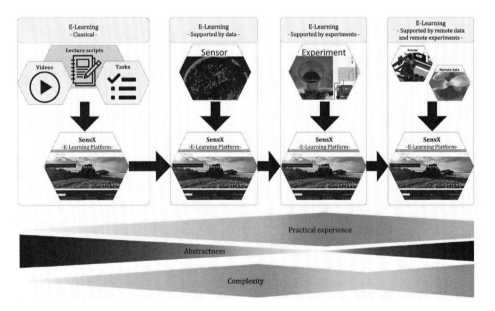

Fig. 1: Supported e-learning concepts of the MOOC platform "SensX"

Classical e-learning

Up to now, SensX contains 12 sessions (see Tab. 1 at the end of this chapter), four of which were structured according to basic/classical e-learning concepts following e-learning by distribution. The transfer of knowledge took place through the exchange of information by uploading lecture scripts, explanatory videos and exercises about agricultural engineering topics, for instance operating principles of specific sensors used in crop production and research, such as ultrasonic and spectral sensors, RGB, NIR and IR cameras, fluorescence spectroscopy, LIDAR (light detection and ranging), soil moisture, temperature and humidity sensors.

E-learning supported by sensor data

Two of the 12 SensX sessions (see Tab. 1) were conceptualized according to e-learning supported by RGB sensor data sets to demonstrate the measurement of spatially resolved data and their processing with current approaches of artificial intelligence. Based on this, image-processing algorithms were developed to evaluate the generated feature vectors with a neural network.

E-learning supported by sensor experiments

Since SensX is a hands-on online course, each participant received a sensor kit (worth about € 30) for the session categorized as e-learning supported by experiments at the beginning of the module. The kit consisted of a microcontroller platform, electronic components and various sensors. This enabled the participants to carry out their own experiments at home and to collect data of plants and other real objects. In addition, for specific tasks, participants carried out exercises with smartphone-based sensors.

E-learning supported by remote sensor data and remote sensor experiments

In order to also enable multisensory applications at a high academic level, the novel low-cost demonstrator "Phenomenon" was developed [Be22], by which different sensory information from real plants was obtained (Fig. 2). It consists of exclusively low-cost hardware and open-source software components, which were selected to construct a xyz-scanning system with an adequate accuracy for consistent data acquisition and total costs of around € 3000. The developed device allows remote control via HTTP of all the functions such as motion control, data acquisition and access of sensor data due to its unique software design. We have installed four different sensors inside the robot, (RGB and thermal camera as imaging sensors, laser-based depth sensor and spectrometer as point measuring sensor) that correspond to the current sensor technologies used in modern agriculture. The resulting data sets provide students with multisensory data acquired remotely from real phenotypic experiments that they learned to handle and process. We already included the resulting data sets of the system in two modules of SensX.

Remote plant sensing and phenotyping 33

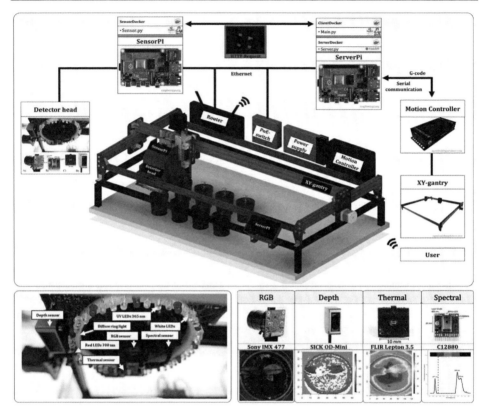

Fig. 2: Demonstrator "Phenomenon" for multisensor technology

Agritechnical content	Category	Hardware
Analog sensor data acquisitions	Basic/Classical	PC
Thermodynamics in greenhouses	Basic/Classical	PC
CO_2-tracer gas method	Basic/Classical	PC
Computer vision (CV) and machine-learning	Basic + data sets	PC + RGB data
Plant classification, CV and neural networks	Basic + data sets	PC + RGB data
Optoacoustic signals	Basic + experiments	PC + Microcontroller
Radiometry & spectroscopy	Basic + experiments	PC + Smartphone
Temperature and spectral data acquisition, analysis and visualization with R/Rstudio	Basic + (rem.) exp. + (remote) data sets	PC + Demonstrator + MCont. + sensor data

Tab. 1a: Sessions and categories in SensX for *Sensor control and analysis*

Agritechnical content	Category	Hardware
Randomization of experiments in controlled environment	Basic/Classical	PC
Moisture sensor data acquisition	Basic + experiments	PC + Microcontroller
Determination of crop performance traits	Basic + experiments	PC + Smartphone
Spectroscopic Methods and data visualization	Basic + (remote) experiments + (remote) data sets	PC + Demonstrator and Microcontroller sensor data

Tab. 1b: Sessions and categories in SensX for *Applied technology in crop experimentation*

2.2 Evaluation methods and statistics

The 12 application sessions of SensX were evaluated internally with surveys within two university lectures ("Sensor control and analysis" with 18 participants and "Applied technology in crop experimentation" with 16 participants) addressing agriculture and biotechnology students over two semesters (winter 20/21 and summer 21) at the University of Applied Sciences Osnabrück. Within the surveys, the students have to rank a) the different sessions in general (scale: very good, good, average, bad, very bad) and b) the difficulty level of the sessions (scale: very easy, easy, average, heavy, extreme heavy). Because of different semesters, different survey years, different studies and different prior knowledge of the students, the results were not statistically condensed. Additionally, the students were asked to rank every session, which was integrated into their course, with a German grading scale from 1 (excellent) to 6 (very poor). These rankings were combined with categories (see above) and statistically analysed with Kruskal-Wallis rank sum test with Fisher's Least Significant Difference using R.

In the following year (summer semester 22, "Sensor control and analysis" with 9 participants), the courses were evaluated externally as qualitative interview by the Institute for Futures Studies and Technology Assessment IZT, Berlin.

3 SensX evaluation

3.1 Internal empirical survey

The internal empirical survey with the participating students revealed that over 90% rated SensX as very good, good or average. However, only 65-70% of the students were satisfied with the clarity and design of the Moodle-based web interface of SensX (data not shown). Participants were highly satisfied with subject-specific content of SensX in general, regardless of the teaching concept (Fig. 3) and there was no significant difference in the overall rating of SensX in terms of the defined teaching concepts (Tab. 2).

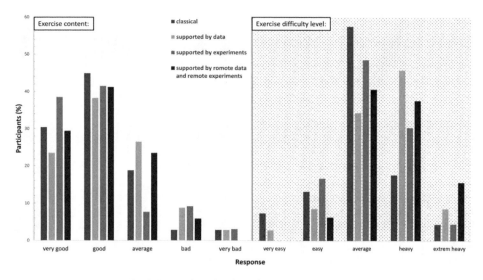

Fig. 3: Internal evaluation of SensX by participants

Concepts	Mean±sd	Median	Count	Rank
Classical	2.13±0.95a	2	70	94.6
Supported by data	2.34±1.19a	2	35	103.1
Supported by experiments	2.27±1.13a	2	66	99.4
Sup. by rem. data and rem. experiments	2.68±1.25a	2	31	119.6

(German grading scale, Kruskal-Wallis rank sum test with Fisher's Least Significant Difference, $\alpha = 0.05$)

Tab. 2: Statistical summary of participants' overall rating of SensX by in the internal evaluation

Further analyses by the students regarding the developed sessions showed that there were no difficulties with regard to the usability and the clarity of the presentation of the individual subject contents. This was of great importance, as it was the basic prerequisite for quantitatively evaluating the students' further statements regarding the sessions. In terms of difficulty level, the optimum was exceeded for some participants, in particular when complexity and abstractness (Fig. 1) were increased due to the teaching method. Nevertheless, that also indicated the need for specific teaching tools addressing those skills. This was particularly evident in the sessions with remote data of the "Phenomenon" robot, where 70% of the participants rated the content of the sessions as very good to good (Fig. 3), but at the same time 70% of the participants rated the difficulty level as heavy to very heavy.

The motivation of the students to engage with the sessions of SensX as well as the results achieved in the exams were rated as very good by the lecturers. These evaluations showed that especially the e-learning sessions, which were based on the analysis of data and simple experiments, received very good ratings from the students. The more complex the applications became, the more critically the students rated the individual sessions (see Tab. 2). These evaluations are understandable, as individual modules with a high degree of complexity demanded a lot from the students, especially methodological and procedural expertise and competence orientation.

3.2 External qualitative interview by IZT

The post hoc analysis of the interviews, conducted and reported by the IZT, revealed that participants rated SensX an average of 7.9 in terms of overall satisfaction on a scale from 1 (low satisfaction) to 10 (high satisfaction). It should be noted that this survey was conducted a year later with other participants of the module and slightly optimized contents of the sessions. The students surveyed the gain in their own digital competence particularly positive being achieved through the independently performed experiments with microcontrollers and sessions regarding computer vision. However, the surveys also indicated that there is a strong desire for more collaboration.

Representative statement from students:

- "I would definitely also say that I was able to take away a lot of digital skills in this module and that will continue."
- "What disappointed me a little bit: I thought we would be standing together more in the greenhouse looking at plants."

3.3 Evaluation by lecturers

In the first six columns, Figure 4 shows the main characteristics and criteria of the developed sessions in relation to the four e-learning categories (lines) that were considered and implemented in the module design.

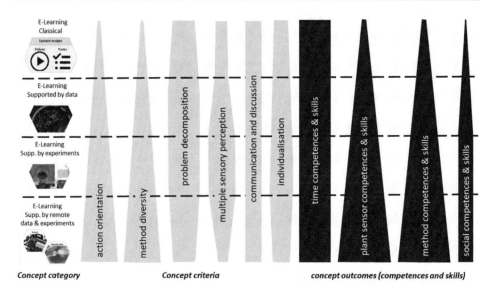

Fig. 4: Criteria of SensX sessions based on experiences of module creators and lecturers and the competence output profile within two years (four semesters) of application

It should be emphasized that the information on the module properties in Figure 4 refers exclusively to the sessions created and the concepts behind them. Nevertheless, Figure 4, columns 1 to 6 provide important information about the general concept of SensX. In contrast, the last four columns represent the actual competences achieved within the sessions based on the evaluations (see chapters 3.1 & 3.2), but also based on the oral and written examination results and the statements made by the students. A summary of the different evaluations indicated that the new e-learning concept supported by experiments and data analysis mainly raised plant sensor expertise and methodological competence and skills of the participants.

3.4 General discussion

The SensX system presented in this study goes beyond the **classical e-learning concepts** [see Ca20] and uses technical tools that meet today's digital potential and requirements for higher education. Our teaching concept successfully demonstrated the proof-of-concept that an extension of classical e-learning systems by action-oriented methods in the field of agricultural engineering is possible and reasonable.

However, the extension of e-learning requires considerable additional technical and financial effort for higher education institutions. The hardware used (microcontrollers, sensors) must be provided as a kit to each student for home work and should be in the low-cost range so that students can **experiment** with it freely and without prior knowledge.

The additional more complex systems required, such as the "Phenomenon" robot in our case, which enables remote experiments at the educational institution, must also meet low-cost conditions. Our "Phenomenon" system fulfils this criterion, costing less than € 3000 [Be22]. It should be noted, however, that remote access to "Phenomenon" requires an open IT structure of the educational institution that is freely accessible from outside. Usually this is not the case, or only to a limited extent. Also in our case, we had to provide students with the data collected on site without direct students' access to the sensor system. Although this limitation can be reduced by video presentations (in our case) or similar documentation, a free **remote access** from outside is actually necessary, or at least desirable, for the complete implementation of our teaching concept. We were therefore only able to show the perspective of our remote experimental concept, where students will be taught how to remotely program, control and use a remote robot to phenotype a small biological experiment through a collaborative online programming workshop. We are convinced that this will address the identified students' demand for collaborative work.

At this point, we would like to once again highlight the different e-learning types of students [Ka17]. Possibly, here lies a problem of the created system: due to the high technology employment, for individual students, e.g. the group designated as downloaders, the study within a technical unknown field (developing circuits, calling sensor data with programmed scripts etc.) may need too much time and self-initiative so that no new knowledge or new method competences can be gained. On the other hand, the complex sessions forced students to interact with each other, which is otherwise considered difficult and critical in e-learning systems [Ca20]. Despite the very high content-related, methodical and self-organizational requirements, the students rated our new e-learning concept as efficient and useful in the overall evaluation. Understandably, sessions with their own (easy) experiments tended to score best. Analysis of **complex remote data sets** was rated as very difficult and was obviously at the learning limit of the students involved. Nevertheless, these sessions were generally not devalued significantly, supporting that an appropriate methodological teaching approach was chosen. A direct comparison of the final grades of SensX participants with the final grades of students from the previous five years, which had the same content but no e-learning components, showed a better final grade on average (data not shown). In the evaluations of our overall concept, it is essential to take into account that the newly designed teaching units have so far only been used in the period affected by the COVID19 pandemic, where the boundary conditions were difficult due to the temporary closure of the university and were uncharted territory for all involved. The clarification of possible correlations is still pending and can only be answered after several runs of SensX in different study programs and at different educational institutions.

4 Conclusions

In this article, we have demonstrated the feasibility of a new e-learning approach that addresses the need of modern agriculture for high digital competences in higher education. We propose that a deep understanding of sensor technologies and methods of digital data processing can only be obtained when higher education, which has been dominated by e-learning concepts in the last 2 years due to pandemic circumstances, includes hands-on sessions and is supported by self-performing experiments. Further expansion of SensX will accommodate even more collaborative opportunities for participants and forces to prepare tomorrow's plant sciences students for the challenges of digitized modern agriculture.

Acknowledgements: We would like to thank the participating students of University of Applied Sciences Osnabrück and the Federal Ministry of Food and Agricultural (BMEL, Grant No: 28DE103F18).

Bibliography

[Ar18]   Arnold, P.; Kilian, L.; Thillosen, A.; Zimmer, G.M.: Handbuch e-learning: Lehren und lernen mit digitalen Medien. Vol. 4965. UTB, 2018.

[Al18]   Al-Rahmi, W.; Aldraiweesh, A.; Yahaya, N.; Bin Kamin, Y.: "Massive open online courses (MOOCS): Systematic literature review in Malaysian higher education." International Journal of Engineering & Technology 7, no. 4 (2018): 2197-2202.

[Be21]   Bedenlier, S.; Händel, M., Kammerl, R; Gläser-Zikuda, M.; Kopp, B.; Ziegler, A.: „Akademische Mediennutzung Studierender im Corona-Semester 2020: Digitalisierungsschub oder weiter wie bisher?." MedienPädagogik: Zeitschrift für Theorie und Praxis der Medienbildung 40 (2021): 229-252.

[Be22]   Bethge, H; Winkelmann, T.; Lüdecke, P.; Rath, T.: Low-cost and automated phenotyping system "Phenomenon" for multi-sensor in situ monitoring in plant in vitro culture. Manuscript submitted, September 2022 in Plant Methods.

[Ca20]   Cammann, F.; Hansmeier, E., Gottfried K.: Möglichkeiten und Szenarien einer durch digitale Medien gestützten Lehre – zentrale Tendenzen des aktuellen E-Learning-Einsatzes im Hochschulsektor. In: Vom E-Learning zur Digitalisierung - Mythen, Realitäten, Perspektiven. Medien in der Wissenschaft, Band 76, Waxmann Verlag, Münster https://doi.org/10.31244/9783830991090; 2020.

[Ha19]   Halachmi, I.; Guarino, M.; Bewley, J.; Pastell, M.: "Smart animal agriculture: application of real-time sensors to improve animal well-being and production." Annu. Rev. Anim. Biosci 7, no. 1: 403-425, 2019.

[Ka17]   Kahan, T.; Soffer, T.; Nachmias, R.: "Types of participant behavior in a massive open online course." International Review of Research in Open and Distributed Learning: IRRODL 18, no. 6: 1-18, 2017.

[Ke16]   Kersebaum, A.: „Bewertung von hochschulübergreifendem eLearning unter Berücksichtigung von statischer Lerner-Adaptivität und Lernstilen." PhD diss., Hannover: Gottfried Wilhelm Leibniz Universität Hannover, 2016.

[Ki19]   Kirchner, K.; Lemke, C.: „MOOCs als disruptive Innovation für die akademische Bildung." In Hochschulen in Zeiten der Digitalisierung, pp. 239-263. Springer Vieweg, Wiesbaden, 2019.

[Lü20]   Lübcke M., Wannemacher K.: Digitalisierung ohne Wandel? Der hochschuldidaktische Diskurs in Schlüsseljournals. In: Bauer R., Hafer J., Hofhues S., Schiefner-Rohs M., Thillosen A., Volk B., Wannemacher K. (Hrsg.) 2020: Vom E-Learning zur Digitalisierung - Mythen, Realitäten, Perspektiven. Medien in der Wissenschaft, Band 76, Waxmann Verlag, Münster https://doi.org/10.31244/9783830991090.

[Sc20]   Schaper, N.: „Entwicklung und Validierung eines Modells zur E-Lehrkompetenz." MedienPädagogik: Zeitschrift für Theorie und Praxis Der Medienbildung 37: 313-342, 2020.

[We22]   Wernecke, A.: „E-Learning: Das Schwein in Tiermedizin und Landwirtschaft – Patient und Schnittstelle zwischen tierärztlicher Praxis und landwirtschaftlichem Betrieb." PhD diss., LMU, 2022.

[Yi21]   Yin H., Cao Y., Marelli B., Zeng X., Mason A. J., Cao C.: Soil Sensors and Plant Wearables for Smart and Precision Agriculture. Advanced Materials, 33, 20; 2021; https://doi.org/10.1002/adma.202007764.

Nachhaltige Landwirtschaft mittels Künstlicher Intelligenz – ein plattformbasierter Ansatz für Forschung und Industrie

Sebastian Bosse[1], Karsten Berns[2], Johannes Bosch[3], Jörg Dörr[2,4], Frederick Charles[3] Eichhorn, Peter Eisert[1], Christoph Fischer[5], Eike Gassen[2], Michael Gerstenberger[1], Heike Gerighausen[6], Jonathan Heil[7], Anna Hilsmann[1], Jochen Hirth[8], Christopher Huber[3], Mortesa Hussaini[7], Martin Kasparick[1], Peter Kloke[1], Hartmut Krause-Edler[9], Lukas Mackle[3], Jannes Magnusson[1], Felix Möhrle[2], Markus Möller[6], Peter Pickel[3], Clemens Rautenberg[10], Hans Dieter Schotten[2,5], Slawomir Stanczak[1], Lars Thiele[1], Henrik Ücdemir[10], Annett Wania[11] und Anthony Stein[7]

Abstract: Digitale Technologien gelten als möglicher Schlüssel zur Verknüpfung von Nachhaltigkeit, Klimaanpassung und wirtschaftlicher Effizienz in der Pflanzenproduktion. Die Heterogenität und Dezentralität des landwirtschaftlichen Systems stellt besondere Anforderungen an den Entwurf datengetriebener Lösungen: Daten entstehen lokal in landwirtschaftlichen Betrieben unterschiedlicher Größe; ihre Erhebung und Auswertung erfolgt meist multimodal, dezentral und durch Dritte; landwirtschaftliche Stakeholder stellen als Dateneigentümer hohe Ansprüche an die Datensouveränität. Das Forschungsprojekt „Nachhaltige Landwirtschaft mittels Künstlicher Intelligenz" (NaLamKI) entwickelt einen plattformbasierten Ansatz, um diese Anforderungen zu adressieren und setzt hierzu auf Cloud-Edge Services zur 1) Erhebung divers strukturierter landwirtschaftlicher Daten, 2) KI-gestützte Fusion und Auswertung dieser Daten sowie 3) nutzerorientierte Haltung und Bereitstellung der erzeugten Datenprodukte in einem digitalen Farm-Twin unter Wahrung der Datensouveränität, Schaffung von (Daten-)Interoperabilität sowie GAIA-X-Konformität. Dieser Beitrag leitet die Notwendigkeit dieses Forschungsansatzes her, erläutert dessen zugrunde liegende Konzepte und diskutiert wissenschaftliche Ansatzpunkte und Ergebnisse sowie offene Herausforderungen und Chancen dieses integrierten Ansatzes.

Keywords: Künstliche Intelligenz, Plattform, nachhaltige Landwirtschaft, Sensorik, Geodaten

---

[1] Fraunhofer HHI, Einsteinufer 37, 10587 Berlin, sebastian.bosse@hhi.fraunhofer.de
[2] Technische Universität Kaiserslautern, Gottlieb-Daimler-Str. 47, 67663 Kaiserslautern
[3] John Deere GmbH & Co. KG, Straßburger Allee 3, 67657 Kaiserslautern.
[4] Fraunhofer IESE, Fraunhofer-Platz 1, 67663 Kaiserslautern
[5] Deutsches Forschungszentrum für Künstliche Intelligenz, Trippstadter Str. 122, 67663 Kaiserslautern
[6] Julius Kühn Institut, Bundesallee 69, 38116 Braunschweig
[7] Universität Hohenheim, Fachgebiet für Künstliche Intelligenz in der Agrartechnik, Garbenstraße 9, 70599 Stuttgart, anthony.stein@uni-hohenheim.de
[8] Robot Makers GmbH, Merkurstraße 45, 67663 Kaiserslautern
[9] NT Neue Technologien AG, Peterstraße 1, 99084 Erfurt
[10] OptoPrecision GmbH, Auf der Höhe 15, 28357 Bremen
[11] Planet Labs Germany GmbH, Kurfürstendamm 22, 10719 Berlin

1 Einleitung

Nachhaltig, ressourcensparend, intelligent und vernetzt: Im Forschungsvorhaben Nachhaltige Landwirtschaft mittels Künstlicher Intelligenz (NaLamKI) wird eine intelligente und interoperable Software-as-a-Service (SaaS) Plattform für die Digitale Landwirtschaft entwickelt. Hierzu werden Daten aus konventionellen und autonomen Landmaschinen, Satelliten und Drohnen in digitalen Abbildern landwirtschaftlicher Betriebe zusammengeführt und mit weiteren externen Daten- und Informationsquellen verknüpft. Künstliche Intelligenz (KI) bereitet die multiskaligen Daten auf, wertet diese aus und stellt intelligente Tools für das Datenmanagement bereit.

Landmaschinen zeichnen bereits heute fortlaufend Daten auf, die zur Prozessoptimierung herangezogen werden. KI-Verfahren versprechen hierbei, Wegbereiter der Landwirtschaft von morgen zu sein: Von einem verbesserten Nährstoff- und Pflanzenschutzmanagement oder der Überwachung der Bodenfeuchte sowie der Ertragsentwicklung bis hin zur Erkennung von Pflanzenerkrankungen und phänologischen Merkmalen mittels Fernerkundung [Mi20]. KI verspricht Mehrwerte in allen Stadien von Acker- und Gartenbau. Die gesteigerte Transparenz ermöglicht es dem Anwender, Prozesse wie Düngung und Schädlingsbekämpfung nachhaltiger und effizient zu gestalten. Um die Potentiale durch intelligente Systeme in der Landwirtschaft ausschöpfen zu können, müssen einerseits die KI-Methoden auf landwirtschaftliche Anwendungsfälle angepasst werden. Andererseits müssen domänenspezifische Daten für das Training der Modelle aufbereitet und zugänglich gemacht werden.

Durch Aggregierung und Fusion von Sensor und Maschinendaten, die mittels Fernerkundung, Bodensensorik und Robotik gewonnen werden, entsteht ein wertvoller Datenpool. Durch den Aufbau eines International Data Space for Agriculture (IDSA) und GAIA-X-konformer Dienste wird die NaLamKI-Plattform interoperabel zwischen verschiedenen zentralen und dezentralen Cloud-Anbietern und Anwendern agieren.

In diesem Beitrag werden zunächst ausgewählte Aspekte der digitalen Landwirtschaft dargestellt (Abs. 2). Die Notwendigkeit eines neuartigen, integrierten Ansatzes für die KI-gestützte digitale Landwirtschaft ergibt sich unmittelbar aus den Limitierungen des State-of-the-Art: Eine weitreichende Prozessoptimierung erfordert ein systematisches Zusammenführen, Aufbereiten und Verfügbarmachen von abgeleiteten Kennzahlen. In Abschnitt 3 werden die Lösungsstrategien präsentiert, die die NaLamKI Plattform hierfür bereitstellt. Abschließend werden die Ergebnisse diskutiert (Abs. 4).

2 KI in der digitalen Landwirtschaft

Precision Farming bezieht sich in der agrartechnischen Forschung im weiteren Sinne auf alle Systeme für das Management der Produktion, die zum Ziel haben, die Ertragsleistung und Umweltqualität durch die Nutzung und Steuerung der räumlichen und zeitlichen Variabilität im Anbau zu optimieren [PL17]. Einerseits bestehen unabhängige

Einzelsysteme, wie KI-Verfahren zur Steuerung einzelner Anbaugeräte, andererseits übergeordnete zusammenhängende Smart Farming und Digital Farming Systeme [SR20].

Ein charakterisierendes Merkmal der Landwirtschaft ist die Heterogenität durch natürliche standortabhängige Faktoren wie Bodenbeschaffenheiten und (mikro-) klimatische Bedingungen sowie sozioökonomische Umstände hinsichtlich der Struktur landwirtschaftlicher Betriebe mit unterschiedlichen Ansprüchen an Datenschutz bzw. gering ausgeprägte Technologieadoptionsbereitschaft. Bechar et al. [BV16] klassifizieren die Landwirtschaft in die komplexeste Kategorie für Robotikanwendungen, was durch die räumliche und zeitliche Variabilität der Umgebung und der Objekte begründet wird. Das Einsatzspektrum von KI rangiert hierbei von intelligenten individuellen und kollektiven Robotikszenarien auf dem Acker [BV16], über die Optimierung von Bewässerungssystemen [Su17], Bodenbeprobungsmustern [Is19] und Fahrspurplanungen [HBS11], bis hin zur nicht-destruktiven Erfassung und zum Monitoring von Prozess- und phänologischen Parametern in der Außenwirtschaft [Sr22]. Der Einsatz von KI in der Landwirtschaft stützt sich auf die Verfügbarkeit von Daten zum Training der Modelle. Diese müssen dabei hinreichend repräsentativ sein, damit die Modelle über Heterogenität und Dynamik der Umweltbedingungen generalisieren. Umfragen dokumentieren allerdings eine klare Zurückhaltung der Landwirte, Daten zu teilen [RM22]. Gleichsam sind erhebliche Mengen an Daten implizit erfasst und verfügbar: Maschinendaten, die über fahrzeugeigene Telemetriesysteme aufgezeichnet werden, aber auch agronomische Daten über Einsatzzeiten, Ausbringungsmengen und Ertragsdaten, die über Dokumentationsschnittstellen der Fahrzeug- und Anbaugerätehersteller bereitgestellt werden. Zur Ergänzung der Maschinendaten wird anwendungsspezifische Sensorik, wie Kamerasysteme oder NIR-Sensoren, in Verbindung mit hochgenauen GNSS-Systemen eingesetzt. Diese Daten werden zur (Teil-)Automatisierung weiterer Arbeitsschritte wie der Spurführung genutzt und dienen als Rohdaten für landwirtschaftliche Informationssysteme wie 365FarmNet, GeoBox Viewer, Nevonex, Operation Center und xarvio Field Manager.

Für die explizite Datenerhebung kommen spezielle Sensorträger wie Drohnen oder Satelliten zum Einsatz. Insbesondere im Hinblick auf eine echtzeitfähige oder auch breitbandige Datenübertragung kann im ländlichen Raum die Dateninfrastruktur ein limitierender Faktor für zukünftige Technologieanwendungen darstellen.

Im Rahmen der Weiterentwicklung der Anwendungssysteme von Precision Farming über Smart Farming wie teilflächenspezifische Applikation zu Digital Farming [SR20] hat sich in der Landtechnik hierbei der ISOBUS, eine Datenbus-Anwendung konform zu der Norm ISO 11783, durchgesetzt. Sie definiert physikalische Eigenschaften und Datenformate für die Maschinenkommunikation. Für Anforderungen wie sie von KI-Anwendungen ausgehen ist ISOBUS nicht ausgelegt. Ein vergleichbarer Standard, der die Interoperabilität von impliziter und expliziter Datenerhebung, KI-Diensten, Modellen oder Daten ermöglicht, ist in der Landwirtschaft nicht verfügbar. Herstellerübergreifende

Schnittstellen verfügbarer Farm Management Information Systeme (FMIS) erlauben nur begrenzt, Datenpunkte auszutauschen.

Einzelne KI-Anwendungen sind bereits in der Landtechnik implementiert. Beispiele sind autonom operierende Traktoren (z. B. John Deere 8R) oder die Feldspritze See and Spray™ (John Deere). Diese Technologien sind weder interoperabel noch können auf die Bedürfnisse eines einzelnen Landwirts angepasst werden. Weitere Anwendungsfälle wurden bislang nur durch Studien z.T. unter Laborbedingungen demonstriert. Beispiele sind die Erkennung bestimmter Pflanzenerkrankungen [MHS16], Ertragsschätzungen ausgewählter Feldfrüchte [Ma20] oder bestimmte Aspekte der autonomen Feldnavigation [AKK20]. Die entsprechenden Verfahren sind jedoch wegen zu geringer Robustheit, hoher Kosten und großer Komplexität nicht marktreif. Integrierte Smart Farming Lösungen sind nicht vollumfänglich, haben nur teilweise offene Schnittstellen und ein diskriminierungsfreier Zugang fehlt üblicherweise. NaLamKI adressiert beide Herausforderungen. Zu den besonderen Herausforderungen zählen Fragen der Interoperabilität, Standards für Schnittstellen und der Verwaltung der Daten sowie anwendungsspezifische Aspekte bei der Adaption von KI-Methoden und der Datenakquise.

3 Lösungsansatz

NaLamKI begegnet den im vorherigen Abschnitt dargestellten Herausforderungen mit einer Plattform, die 1) eine informierte und semi-automatisierte Bestandsführung in Obstbau, Grünland und Ackerbau durch raumzeitlich hochaufgelöstes Monitoring realisiert, 2) dabei der Heterogenität und Dezentralität des landwirtschaftlichen Systems in einem Cloud-Edge-basierten Ansatz in Kombination mit einem Digitalen Zwilling Rechnung trägt und 3) unter Wahrung der Datensouveränität KI in föderierten und automatisierten Diensten auch kleinen Betrieben zugänglich macht. Dieser Abschnitt gibt einen Überblick über die wissenschaftlichen Konzepte und Methoden und stellt erste Ergebnisse des Ansatzes dar. In Abs. 3.1 erläutern wir Aspekte der multimodalen und multiskaligen Datenerhebung für eine raumzeitlich hochaufgelöste Bestandsführung und skizzieren die hierfür entwickelte verteilte Sensorik. Die Architektur des Cloud-Edge-Systems und die Struktur des Digitalen Zwillings zur Organisation der Sensordaten wird in Abs. 3.2 dargestellt. Abs. 3.3 stellt die entwickelten KI-Dienste und ihre föderierte Integration vor.

3.1 Informierte Bestandsführung mittels erhöhter Automatisierung

NaLamKI ermöglicht eine raumzeitlich hochaufgelöste Bestandsführung im Obstbau, im Grünland und im Ackerbau auf der Basis multimodaler und multiskaliger Sensordaten. Als Trägerplattformen dienen Traktoren, autonome Roboter, Drohnen und Satelliten. Die Systemarchitektur (Abs. 3.2) ermöglicht beliebige Ergänzungen weiterer Sensorträger und -modalitäten.

Autonome Roboter als intelligente bodengebundene Sensorträgerplattform: Zur Datenerhebung von Plantagen- und Feldfrüchten werden in NaLamKI mehrere autonome Roboter als Sensorträger entwickelt und im Obstbau konzeptionell vorgestellt. In Apfelplantagen sind das Erkennen der Umgebung zum autonomen Navigieren und das Inspizieren der Pflanzen wesentlich. Eingesetzt wird ein kettengetriebenes Fahrzeug, das mit einem Autonomie-Kit (Row Crop Pilot der Firma RobotMakers) ausgestattet wurde. Es erweitert das Fahrzeug um einen LiDAR, ein GPS und eine Recheneinheit und ermöglicht das autonome Fahren und Arbeiten in Reihenkulturen. Zur Datenerhebung werden zwei Stereokameras und ein weiterer LiDAR verwendet. Die Kameras können die gesamte Höhe des Apfelbaums aufnehmen.

Robuste in-situ Bestandsdatenerhebung auf Landmaschinen: Um Nebeneffekte wie Bodenverdichtung und Schädigung der Bodenstruktur möglichst zu vermeiden, ist es sinnvoll, Sensorik für die Bestandsdatenerhebung auf Traktoren anzubringen, die Acker oder Grünflächen ohnehin überfahren. Moderne Landmaschinen sind zunehmend mit Sensoren zur Maschinenautomatisierung ausgestattet, die ebenfalls zur Bestandsdatenerhebung geeignet sind (Abs. 2.1). Für das Projekt NaLamKI wurde ein Serientraktor John Deere 6155M für die Aufnahme mehrerer Stereokameras und weiterer Sensorik am Frontkraftheber, am Zugpendel sowie am Heck umgebaut. Über die Vegetationsperioden hinweg werden in Durchfahrten über Testfelder und regulär bewirtschaftete Schläge Daten aufgenommen. Die Position wird dabei mit Hilfe eines serienmäßigen John Deere StarFire™ 6000 RTK-GNSS-Systems erfasst. Auf diese Weise entsteht ein Datensatz georeferenzierter Stereo-Bildgruppen, der alle Wachstumsstadien u.a. von Mais, Weizen und Zuckerrüben in variablen Umweltbedingungen abdeckt.

Drohnen-basierte Datenerhebung: Im Gegensatz zur bodengebundenen Datenerhebung ist die Datenerfassung durch tieffliegende unbemannte automatische Systeme nicht invasiv. In NaLamKI erfolgt die Datenerfassung durch eine, an Sentinel-3 angelehnte, Kamera mit multispektralen Wellenlängen sowie durch RGB-Sensorsysteme im Kontext der Bestimmung von Blattflächenindex und der automatischen und frühzeitigen Pflanzenkrankheitserkennung.

Satellitengestützte Datenerhebung: Eine systematische Akquisitionsstrategie von Satellitenkonstellationen wie die der Sentinels des europäischen Raumfahrtprogramms Copernicus und die ca. 200 sogenannten Doves des privaten Unternehmens Planet Labs erlauben den Aufbau kontinuierlicher, hochauflösender Zeitreihen. Die Satelliten ergänzen sich gegenseitig, da sie aufgrund ihrer spezifischen räumlichen und zeitlichen Auflösung und der verwendeten Sensorik unterschiedliche Prozesse und Zustände an der Erdoberfläche erfassen. In NaLamKI wird diese Komplementarität zur Schaffung einer Datengrundlage genutzt, welche die Durchführung eines flächendeckenden Monitorings des Pflanzenzustandes und der Bestandsentwicklung ermöglicht.

3.2 Cloud-Edge basierter Ansatz

5G-basierte Vernetzung von Sensorträgerplattformen und Datenübertragung: Mögliche Echtzeitanforderungen an die Übertragung der Sensordaten stellen besondere Ansprüche an die Vernetzung. Um die Daten in eine Cloud oder auf eine separate lokale Datenspeichereinheit zu übertragen, setzt NaLamKI 5G ein. Vor dem Hintergrund der eingeschränkten Verfügbarkeit des öffentlichen 5G Netzes im ländlichen Raum werden dazu private Campusnetze errichtet. Sie sind Alternativen wie WLAN in Bandbreiten, Reichweiten und Zuverlässigkeit überlegen. NaLamKI untersucht Möglichkeiten direkter Vernetzung von Landmaschinen und Sensoren mittels 5G-Sidelinks. KI-Methoden ermöglichen eine intelligente Vernetzung, die Übertragungstechnologie und -infrastruktur im Betrieb an die Anforderungen und Umgebungsbedingungen anzupassen [AF20].

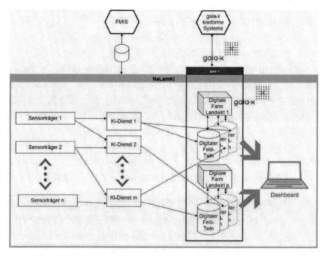

Abb. 1: Systemarchitektur von NaLamKI

Systemarchitektur: Die Plattform stellt die Verbindung zwischen der Datenerhebung und -speicherung und den KI-basierten Auswertungen innerhalb des NaLamKI-Systems dar (Abb. 1). Eine GAIA-X-konforme Schnittstelle des Digital Farm Twin (s.u.) gewährleistet die Einbindung NaLamKIs in das GAIA-X-Ökosystem. Die von Sensorträgern erfassten Daten (Abs. 3.1) werden zur Verarbeitung und Analyse an KI-Dienste (Abs. 3.3) übergeben. Die Datenprodukte der KI-Dienste werden in einem Digitalen Feld-Twin gespeichert. Mehrere Feld-Twins werden durch einen Digital Farm-Twin zusammengefasst (Abb. 1). Dieser ist je Landwirt personalisiert. Zusätzlich erlaubt das NaLamKI-System die Einbindung von FMISs und neben Web-Diensten die Anbindung von und an GAIA-X konforme Systeme. Deutschlandweite Satellitenbild- und Geodatenzeitreihen werden analysefertig verfügbar gemacht [Ba21]. Dazu gehören Wetterzeitreihen des DWD und phänologische Zeitreihen [MBS20]. Die gespeicherten Daten aus dem Digitalen Zwilling können vom Nutzer abgerufen und in einem Dashboard angezeigt werden (Abb. 3).

Föderierte Dienste und GAIA-X: Die GAIA-X-konforme Schnittstelle NaLamKIs (s. Abb. 1) dient als zentraler Knoten für alle Betriebsdaten, sowohl für den Landwirt als auch für externe Datenproduzenten. Die Datenhoheit liegt allein beim Landwirt. Dienstleister, die z. B. Agrardaten auf dem Feld erheben oder Ertragsprognosen erstellen, können mit dem digitalen Zwilling interagieren und die Datenprodukte sicher an den Landwirt zurückspielen. Die NaLamKI-Plattform leistet somit einen Beitrag, um Landwirten die Teilnahme am GAIA-X Ökosystem ohne technisches Know-how zu ermöglichen.

3.3 Föderierte und automatisierte KI-Services

KI zur Beikraut-, Pflanzenkrankheits- und Wachstumserkennung: Um auf der Basis der Sensordaten (Abs. 3.1) den Zustand der Nutzpflanzen abzuleiten, bietet NaLamKI den Nutzern KI-Dienste zur Erkennung von Schadpflanzen, von Pflanzenkrankheiten und des Pflanzenwachstums. Die hierbei entstehenden Prozessketten setzen Verfahren zur 3D-Rekonstruktion einzelner Pflanzen oder Schläge, semantischer Segmentierung und Klassifikation zur Detektion, Erkennung und Lokalisation von Früchten, Unkräutern und Krankheitsbefall, sowie zur Bestimmung pflanzenphysiologischer Eigenschaften ein. Zur Erstellung von Wachstumsprognosen werden multimodale Daten über die Zeit fusioniert und koreferenziert. Zur Frucht- und Beikrauterkennung werden YOLO-, und Faster-RCNN Netze verwendet und vergleichend getestet [Ge21]. ResNet-Autoencoder und U-Net [RFB15] Architekturen kommen bei der semantischen Segmentierung zum Einsatz. Zusätzlich werden prototypenbasierte Verfahren zur Erklärung relevanter Features angepasst. Die Klassifikation von Qualität, Reifegrad und möglichem Krankheitsbefall wird durch ResNet und VGG-Netze erreicht. Um die Nutzung von KI-Methoden nutzerfreundlich zu gestalten, stützt sich NaLamKI auf Automated Machine Learning [HVS23]. Die 3D-Rekonstruktion von Pflanzen in der Landwirtschaft erfordert Methoden, Robustheit gegen schnell wechselnde Licht-, Wind- und Wetterverhältnisse. Die Aufnahme von Trainings- und Testdaten darf landwirtschaftliche Produktionsprozesse nicht einschränken. Aktuelle Methoden rekonstruieren Bäume ohne Blattwerk [Wu14] oder werden auf alleinstehende Pflanzen angewendet [Gu20]. NaLamKI demonstriert die Anwendbarkeit am Beispiel der Apfelbaummodellierung. Bäume werden mit prozeduralen Modellierungsmethoden aus den Bilddaten rekonstruiert. Dabei wird die Überführung der Bilddaten in ein Lindenmayer-System untersucht, um einen digitalen Zwilling der Bäume zu erstellen, der u.a. eine zeitliche Modellierung und Wachstumsschätzung als Planungs- und Entscheidungshilfe für Landwirte ermöglicht [MP96].

Raumzeitliche Datenfusion zur Ableitung phänologischer Daten: Schlag- und teilschlagspezifisches Monitoring erfordert Zeitserien biophysikalischer Parameter mit einer hohen geometrischen (< 30 m^2) und zeitlichen Auflösung (< 7 d). NaLamKI nutzt Datenfusionsalgorithmen zur Kombination von Satellitenbildern komplementärer raumzeitlicher Auflösungen (Abs. 3.1) [Gh19]. Die Fusionsgenauigkeit ist abhängig von der Anzahl und zeitlichen Distanz, sowie deren phänologischer Repräsentativität der für die Fusion notwendigen Bildpaare [Mö17]. Diese fusionierten Daten sollen genutzt werden, um Parameter, wie die räumliche Verteilung des Blattflächenindex (Abb. 2, links), zu schätzen. Ein weiteres Anwendungsbeispiel ist die Erkennung von Wachstumsphasen. Abbildung 2 rechts zeigt die Übergänge zwischen den Phasen, abgeleitet aus den täglichen Zeitreihen des Vegetationsindex (oben) und dem Biomasse-Proxy (unten). Diese Datensätze werden für das Training von KI-Modellen genutzt.

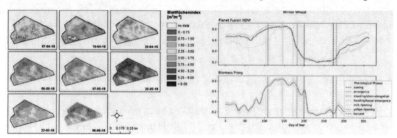

Abb. 1: Links: räumlich differenzierter Blattflächenindex [Ar21]. Rechts: Zeitreihe (1 Jahr) des Vegetationsindex (*NDVI*) und abgeleiteter Biomasse

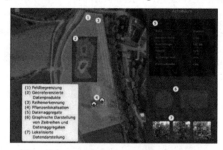

Abb. 2: Dashboard Prototyp zur Visualisierung der Datenprodukte (Satellitenbild: Planet Labs.)

Interaktion zwischen Nutzer und KI: NaLamKI entwickelt innovative, intelligente und interaktive Benutzeroberflächen, um Analyseergebnisse und Datenprodukte nutzergerecht zu visualisieren und Möglichkeiten zu geben, dem System explizites und implizites Domänenwissen zur Verbesserung der KI- Verfahren zur Verfügung zu stellen. Damit schafft NaLamKI ein Framework zur Erforschung von Technologien der Datenvisualisierung und interaktiven Lernansätzen im heterogenen System „Landwirtschaft". Zur Ergebnisvisualisierung erlaubt eine interaktive Dashboard-Anwendung (Abb. 3) den Zugriff auf die Datenprodukte der KI-Dienste. Sie implementiert kein FMIS, sondern trägt zu deren Weiterentwicklung bei, indem sie auf die Darstellung spezifischer Ergebnisse auf Grundlage der implementierten NaLamKI-Systemarchitektur fokussiert. Sie dient als zentrale Anlaufstelle für alle vom Nutzer gebuchten Dienste. Das Dashboard erlaubt die Darstellung von räumlichen Ansichten, Zeitreihen und multivariaten Datenaggregaten. Das zentrale Geografische Informationssystem erlaubt die Integration und Darstellung von Daten externer Provider. NaLamKI begegnet der Daten- bzw. Annotationsknappheit in der Landwirtschaft mit einem eigens entwickelten aktiven intelligenten Annotationstool. Der Aufwand zur Abfrage expliziten Domänenwissens wird so reduziert. In einem human-in-the-loop-Ansatz wird Nutzern weiterhin die

Möglichkeit gegeben, implizites Domänenwissen zu integrieren, in dem sie Rückmeldungen und Hinweise zur Inferenz geben [Ge22].

4 Diskussion

4.1 Erwarteter Nutzen

Der NaLamKI-Ansatz strebt nach einer interoperablen, datensouveränen und intelligenten Software-as-a-Service Plattform. Diese Plattform soll Akteure der Landwirtschaft und der nachgelagerten Wertschöpfungsbereiche zusammenbringen. Dazu gehört auch die IT-Branche, die auf die digitale Landwirtschaft angepasste KI-Lösungen als Software-Dienste anbieten und Landwirten niedrigschwellig zur Verfügung stellen kann. So wird KI zur Optimierung landwirtschaftlicher Prozesse und zur Entscheidungsfindung jedem landwirtschaftlichen Betrieb bereitgestellt. NaLamKI treibt auf diese Weise den informationstechnologischen Fortschritt in der digitalen Landwirtschaft mit an. Technologisch gibt es weitere Nutzen: Der Cloud-Edge-Ansatz ermöglicht auch den Einsatz von KI "on-the-edge", also lokal bei den Betrieben oder sogar auf den eingesetzten Landmaschinen. In-situ-Erhebungen von Pflanzenstress oder anderen physiologischen Merkmalen mittels unbemannter oder bemannter Landtechnik haben das Potential, die raumzeitliche Auflösung der Informationsakquise zu erhöhen. Gezielte Analyse und visuelle Aufbereitung informationsdichter Daten ermöglichen dem Landwirt informierte Entscheidungen zur Erträgeerhöhung. Ein weiterer Nutzen einer föderierten Service-orientierten Plattformlösung wie NaLamKI ist die Interoperabilität zwischen Datenerzeugern und Datenkonsumenten. Konsumenten können neben den Landtechnikherstellern und Behörden auch KI-Serviceprovider sein, die auf neu verfügbare Daten zurückgreifen können, um die angebotenen KI-Modelle kontinuierlich zu verbessern. Dies erfordert die Bereitschaft der Datenerzeuger zum bedenkenlosen Teilen ihrer Daten – unter Wahrung ihrer Datensouveränität. In NaLamKI trägt dazu neben der GAIA-X-Konformität auch der Einsatz des föderierten maschinellen Lernens bei, da hier keine zentrale Stelle auf die betriebseigenen Daten zurückgreifen muss (Abs. 3.3). So ermöglicht NaLamKI indirekt, lokale bzw. verteilte Datenbestände zu nutzen und dadurch für KI-Servicenutzer direkte Vorteile im Sinne verbesserter KI-basierter Lösungen für die Landwirtschaft zu stiften.

4.2 Offene Herausforderungen

NaLamKI adressiert die in Abs. 2 skizzierten Herausforderungen auf technologischer Ebene. Um Dienste und Anwendungen zum Landwirt oder KI-Entwickler zu bringen, muss es auf (betriebs-)wirtschaftlicher Ebene möglich sein, diese anzubieten, zu bepreisen und bei Bedarf zu buchen. NaLamKI stellt diese wirtschaftliche Perspektive nicht explizit in den Fokus, denkt sie aber mit und steht dazu in engem Austausch mit dem Schwester-projekt AgriGAIA [AG20]. Synergien werden in naher Zukunft genutzt, damit die Konzepte und Technologien NaLamKIs Aussicht auf eine erfolgreiche Etablierung in der landwirtschaftlichen Praxis haben. Zur Gewährleistung der Datensouveränität setzt NaLamKI auf föderiertes maschinelles Lernen, gekapselte Digitale Zwillinge und GAIA-X. Letzteres ist für die Anknüpfung an externe Teilnehmer und Systeme wesentlich. Allerdings läuft die Entwicklung des GAIA-X-Vorhabens zeitgleich zu NaLamKI. Dieser Herausforderung wird mit einer nach innen GAIA-X-agnostischen, über die NaLamKI-Grenzen hinweg (Abb. 1) GAIA-X-konformen Schnittstellenstrategie begegnet, um eine frühzeitige Entwicklung der NaLamKI-Systemarchitektur zu ermöglichen. Die Dynamik und Heterogenität des landwirtschaftlichen Systems erschwert die Akquise großer Datenmengen mit hoher Qualität. Zugleich erfordert das Training robuster KI-Modelle hinreichend große und überwiegend annotierte Datensätze [BV16]. Hier wird ein grundsätzliches Problem KI-orientierter Forschungsprojekte in der Landwirtschaft deutlich: Typischerweise reichen Projektlaufzeiten nicht aus, adäquate, d.h. repräsentative Datenmengen zu erheben, die die Komplexität und Heterogenität abbilden können. Die Annotation landwirtschaftlicher Daten setzt Domänenwissen voraus. Zur Erleichterung der Datenannotation entwickelt NaLamKI nutzerfreundliche interaktive Benutzerschnittstellen. Hybride Ansätze aus KI-basierter und manueller Annotation stellen eine vielversprechende Forschungsrichtung dar. NaLamKI stellt hohe Ansprüche an die Sensortechnologie und ihre Verfügbarkeit; der Betrieb erfordert geschultes Personal und investitionsfähiges Kapital. Vor diesem Hintergrund ist es unklar, ob und wie die NaLamKI-Technologien von sehr kleinen landwirtschaftlichen Betrieben implementiert und genutzt werden können, die vom hohen Potential der digitalen Landwirtschaft besonders profitieren könnten, insbesondere in weniger entwickelten Regionen [CC20].

5 Zusammenfassung

Wir haben einen plattformbasierten Ansatz für die Etablierung moderner digitaler Technologie in der Landwirtschaft für Forschung und Industrie vorgestellt, zugrundeliegende Konzepte erläutert und Chancen und Herausforderungen diskutiert. Zentrales Element ist dabei die Kombination von Künstlicher Intelligenz mit digitalen Abbildern landwirtschaftlicher Betriebe. Diese Digital Farm Twins werden auf Basis multimodaler Daten aus in-situ-Erhebungen im Feld, Fernerkundung mittels Satelliten und Drohnen, sowie der Verknüpfung mit externen Informationsquellen kreiert und haben das Potential, die Arbeitsplanung und Entscheidungsprozesse von Landwirten signifikant zu verbessern. Die identifizierten Kernherausforderungen aus wissenschaftlicher und industrieller Perspektive stellen gleichzeitig die technologischen Hauptaugenmerke des NaLamKI-Konzepts dar. Hierzu zählen eine fundamental verbesserte Datengrundlage im Sinne eines räumlich-zeitlich hochaufgelösten Monitorings der bewirtschafteten Flächen, die Berücksichtigung der Dezentralität und Heterogenität des landwirtschaftlichen Systems, sowohl in ökologischer als auch ökonomischer Hinsicht, sowie die Wahrung der Datensouveränität landwirtschaftlicher Akteure. Erste Schritte und erzielte Ergebnisse wurden dargestellt und der erwartete Nutzen sowie offene Herausforderungen für eine zukunftsträchtige digitale Landwirtschaft aus wissenschaftlicher Perspektive diskutiert.

Förderhinweis: Das NaLamKI-Projekt wird vom Bundesministerium für Wirtschaft und Klimaschutz unter den Fördernummern 01MK21003[A-J] gefördert.

Literaturverzeichnis

[AKK20] Adhikari, S. P.; Kim, G.; Kim, H.: „Deep neural network-based system for autonomous navigation in paddy field". In: IEEE Access 8, S. 71272-71278, 2020.

[AF20] Arjoune, Y.; Faruque, S.: „Artificial intelligence for 5g wireless systems: Opportunities, challenges, and future research direction." In: Comput. And Commun. Workshop and Conf. (CCWC), S. 1023-1028, 2020.

[AG20] https://www.agri-gaia.de/, abgerufen 9.12.2022.

[Ar21] Arnold, J.; Brandt, P.; Gerighausen, H.: Erprobung der satellitengestützten Ertragsschätzung für die Agrarstatistik – Projekt SatAgrarStat. In: WISTA. Statistisches Bundesamt, Wiesbaden, 2021 (6): 43-53.

[Ba21] Baumann, P.: „A general conceptual framework for multi-dimensional spatio-temporal data sets". In: Environ. Model. Softw. 143, S. 105096, Sep. 2021.

[BV16] Bechar, A.; Vigneault, C.: „Agricultural robots for field operations: Concepts and components". In: BioSyst. Eng. 149, S. 94-111, 2016.

[CC20] Chandra, R.; Collis, S.: „Digital Agriculture for Small-Scale Producers: Challenges and Opportunities". In: Communications of the ACM. 64.12, 2021.

[Ge21] Ge, Z. u. a.: „Yolox: Exceeding yolo series in 2021". In: arXiv:2107.08430, 2021.

[Ge22] Gerstenberger, M. u. a.: „But that's not why: Inference adjustment by Interactive prototype deselection". In: arXiv:2203.10087, 2022.

[Gh19] Ghamisi, P. u.a.: „Multisource and Multitemporal Data Fusion in Remote Sensing: A Comprehensive Review of the State of the Art". In: IEEE Geosci. Remote Sens. Mag. 7.1, S. 6-39, März 2019.

[Gu20] Guo, J. u.a.: „Realistic Procedural Plant Modeling from Multiple View Images". In: IEEE Trans. on Vis. and Compu. Graph. 26.2, S. 1372-1384, Feb. 2020.

[HBS11] Hameed, I. A.; Bochtis, D.; Sorensen, C.: „Driving angle and track sequence optimization for operational path planning using genetic algorithms". In: Appl. Eng. Agric. 27.6, S. 1077-1086, 2011.

[HVS23] Heil, J.; Valencia, J. M.; Stein, A.: „Towards Crop Yield Prediction using Automated Machine Learning". In: 43. GIL-Jahrestagung (Feb. 2023).

[Is19]   Israeli, A. u.a.: „Statistical Learning in Soil Sampling Design Aided by Pareto Optimization". In: Proc. Genet. Evolut. Comput. Conf. GECCO '19. Prague, Czech Republic: ACM, S. 1198-1205, 2019.

[Ma20]   Maimaitijiang, M. u.a.: „Soybean yield prediction from UAV using multimodal data fusion and deep learning". In: Remote sens. environ. 237, S. 111599, 2020.

[MBS20]   Möller, M.; Boutarfa, L.; Strassemeyer, J.: „PhenoWin – An R Shiny application for visualization and extraction of phenological windows in Germany". In: Comput. Electron. Agric. 175, S. 105534, Aug. 2020.

[MHS16]   Mohanty, S. P.; Hughes, D. P.; Salathé, M.: „Using deep learning for image-based plant disease detection". In: Frontiers in plant science 7, S. 1419, 2016.

[Mi20]   Misra, N. u. a.: „IoT, big data and artificial intelligence in agriculture and food industry". In: IEEE Internet Things J., 2020.

[Mö17]   Möller, M. u.a.: „Coupling of phenological information and simulated vegetation index time series: Limitations and potentials for the assessment and monitoring of soil erosion risk". In: CATENA 150, S. 192-205, März 2017.

[MP96]   Měch, R.; Prusinkiewicz, P.: „Visual models of plants interacting with their environment". In: Proc. Conf. Comput. Graph. Interact. Tech. - SIGGRAPH '96. ACM Press, S. 397-410, 1996.

[PL17]   Pedersen, S. M.; Lind, K. M. u.a.: Precision agriculture: Technology and economic perspectives. Springer, 2017.

[RFB15]   Ronneberger, O.; Fischer, P.; Brox, T.: „U-net: Convolutional networks for biomed. image segmentation". In: Int. Conf. on Med. image comput. comp. assist. interv. Springer, S. 234-241, 2015.

[SR20]   Saiz-Rubio, V.; Rovira-Más, F.: „From smart farming towards agriculture 5.0: A review on crop data management". In: Agronomy 10.2, S. 207, 2020.

[Sr22]   Srivastava, A.K. u. a.: „Winter wheat yield prediction using convolutional neural networks from environmental and phenological data". In: Scientific Reports. 12.1, S. 1-14, 2022.

[Su17]   Sun, L. u. a.: „Reinforcement Learning Control for Water-Efficient Agricultural Irrigation". In: Symp. on Parallel Distrib. Process. Applic. and Int. Conf. on Ubiquitous Comput. Commun. IEEE, S. 1334-1341, 2017.

[Wu14]   Wu, C. u.a.: „3D reconstruction of Chinese hickory tree for dynamics analysis". In: BioSyst. Eng. 119, S. 69-79, März 2014.

Blue Apple – an algorithm to realize agricultural classification under difficult light and color situations

Jonas Credner[1], Peter Rehrmann[2], Waldemar Raaz[3] and Thomas Rath[4]

Abstract: Computer-image processing becomes more and more important in the analysis of data in biological and agricultural research and practice. However, robust image processing is highly dependent on the histogram analysis algorithms used and the quality of the data being processed. The algorithm presented here aims to improve the accuracy of the classification of image data generated under complex boundary situations and inconsistent lighting conditions. Using the example of the determination of nitrogen content of tomato leaves and the qualitative determination of starch content of apples on the basis of color image processing, we showed that the developed algorithm is able to perform a robust classification and represents an improvement to simple histogram analysis.

Keywords: classification, histogram analysis, color image processing, starch detection apples, N-analysis plants

1 Introduction and objectives

Spatial data or images are the most important data sources in biology and agricultural science in practice and research. Today, image processing algorithms that analyze different color spaces with different color channels are mainly used to evaluate such data [HCR18; NAA21; PR18]. By using standard cameras, the number of color channels is limited to three. Newer sensor data sets often also contain a higher number of different color channels (multispectral data) [Ra17]. The evaluation of such data is usually done in such a way that first the objects are separated that are of importance (foreground-background separation or binarization), then the objects are analyzed by color, shape and other morphological properties and compared with existing (calibrated) data sets. At the end, the previously unknown dataset (image) is classified into one or more reference data. Histograms of the color channels are often used in this process [HLE18]. These histograms are evaluated additively, multiplicatively or by artificial intelligence methods. The special problem is that the histograms are usually not normally distributed, since they originate

---

[1] Biosystems Engineering Laboratory (BLab), Osnabrück University of Applied Sciences, Oldenburger Landstr. 24, 49090 Osnabrück, Germany, j.credner@hs-osnabrueck.de

[2] Biosystems Engineering Laboratory (BLab), Osnabrück University of Applied Sciences, Oldenburger Landstr. 24, 49090 Osnabrück, Germany, p.rehrmann@hs-osnabrueck.de

[3] Biosystems Engineering Laboratory (BLab), Osnabrück University of Applied Sciences, Oldenburger Landstr. 24, 49090 Osnabrück, Germany, waldemar.raaz@hs-osnabrueck.de

[4] Biosystems Engineering Laboratory (BLab), Osnabrück University of Applied Sciences, Oldenburger Landstr. 24, 49090 Osnabrück Germany, t.rath@hs-osnabrueck.de, https://orcid.org/0000-0001-7277-7335

from a natural image or a natural environment. Thus, they are skewed, contain an unknown number of zero values, and, above all, are often provided with several peaks. Therefore, statistical methods that assume a normal distribution of the histograms cannot be used. Likewise, it significantly complicates the use of deep learning methods, since essentially the results depend on the infinitely possible combination of input data. In addition, different lighting situations in the reference data set and (or) within the test image complicate the evaluation, so that today the evaluation of biological color images under different natural lighting conditions is a major challenge [JTZ11]. Figure 1 illustrates the problem described above with a simple example. An algorithm should assign a test image in the RGB color space with the help of a simple histogram comparison to one of three images in a reference database; namely to the image which comes closest to one of the reference images. Due to the skewness of the histograms of the reference images and the many zeros in the histograms, the algorithm does not succeed in assigning the test image (although from the optical impression a clear assignment would be possible).

In order to be able to solve the presented problem of the histogram evaluation in biological images with high variability, new procedures are necessary, which

- consider the non-statistical distributions of histograms,
- take into account the histograms of all available color channels,
- are independent of the number of color channels and color spaces,
- are independent of the compression of the original images and
- compensate lighting differences as far as possible.

2 Methods and algorithms developed

The Blue-Apple algorithm was developed with the image processing software Halcon (MVTec, Munich, Germany) with the intention to enable difficult color classifications of biological-agricultural objects and to improve or support previous mentioned procedures and methods. It can be divided into three sections.

Section 1: In a first binarization step, all image parts except for the "region of interest" are removed in order to use only relevant image information for the subsequent classification process. This includes at least the removal of the background as in the first example in chapter 3 (determination of the nitrogen content of tomato leaves). In the second example of starch analysis of apple halves, the removal of the apple core housing is also required. Thus, as defined in the test procedure, only the fruit flesh is analyzed in the discoloration reaction and false conclusions or pseudo-correlations due to the apple core housing are avoided. The corresponding algorithms are strongly based on the use of classical morphological operators and shape factors. They are briefly presented in sections 3.1 and 3.2, and the implemented Halcon code with the corresponding operators can be downloaded from [Re22] and [Cr22].

Section 2: The main procedure of the developed analysis algorithm is the subsequent conversion of the relative histograms of the individual color channels into Gaussian-like distributions. In the following, these converted histograms are referred to as pseudo-Gaussian histograms. This should demonstrate that they are not Gaussian distributions, since a statistically clearly defined Gaussian profile cannot be generated from data with arbitrary (non-normal) distribution. However, the following criteria are imposed on the pseudo-Gaussian histograms generated with our algorithm:

- There are no zeros in the entire definition range of the histogram, i.e. no element of the histogram vector may contain the value 0.
- The histogram values decrease towards the edges. Whether these decreases are still visible in the finally generated histogram or lie outside the definition range of the histogram is irrelevant.
- The peaks and data distributions present in the original histogram are taken into account as much as possible when creating the pseudo-Gaussian histograms.
- The pseudo-Gaussian histograms are normalized to a vector length of 1.
- The pseudo-Gaussian histograms consist of interpolation points between which the vector elements are linearly interpolated.
- The pseudo-Gaussian histograms are composed of two half-sided histograms (right side and left side), so that extremely skewed distributions can also be modelled through different histogram halves. The separation between the right and left halves does not have to be exactly in the middle of the histogram. Rather, it depends on the initial data set and its distribution.

If $H_{i,z}$ is a histogram with v values h_i of a color channel i of the image z, first a relative input histogram $H_{rel,i,z}$ with $h_{rel,i} = h_{abs,i}/\sum h_{abs,i}$ is generated from the absolute input histogram $H_{abs,i,z}$. Subsequently, the relative input histogram is extended at the beginning and at the end by at least x (default: x >= 256) values each. The new $h_{arb,i}$ values are set to 0. The histogram $H_{arb,i,z}$ formed in this way is called the working histogram and contains $v = 3x$ numerical values, whereby the middle third contains the original relative histogram $H_{rel,i,z}$. Subsequently, interpolation points for the new pseudo-Gaussian histogram $H_{Gau,i,z}$ are derived from the working histogram separately for left and right sides. For this purpose, the expected value for the maximum of the working histogram is first determined by calculating the center of gravity line of the histogram area. Then linear interpolations are carried out between interpolation points in the working histogram.

The following steps were used: Coming from the left, the point µL is determined in the histogram where the partial sum of h_1 to $h_{µL}$ exceeds 50% of the total area of the histogram above the x-axis. In the same way coming from the right, with the partial sum h_{max} to $h_{µR}$ the point µR is determined. The indices of the important points of the working histogram, namely the peak h_p, $h_{µR}$, $h_{µL}$, are then recalculated by

$$p = \text{trunc}((µR + µL)/2) \qquad (1)$$
$$µL = p \qquad (2)$$
$$µR = p + 1 \qquad (3)$$

In addition to the important histogram points, the total histogram area HF is calculated from the sum of all vector elements of the working histogram.

The value of the histogram vector at the point p is calculated with

$$h_p = (h_{\mu R} + h_{\mu L}) \cdot 0.5 \tag{4}$$

The area below the histogram to the left of p is calculated with

$$F_{uL} = h_p \cdot 0.5 \tag{5}$$

It is thus simulated that the pseudo-Gaussian histogram initially consists of a straight line at the level of half of the theoretical peak at the value p. For further calculations, the increases of the area fractions are calculated according to one side of the Gaussian distribution at 1σ - coming from h_p - with $F_1 = 0.34135 \cdot HF$. At 2σ the further increase in area is $F_2 = 0.13590 \cdot HF$, at 3σ correspondingly $F_3 = 0.02140 \cdot HF$ and at 4σ correspondingly $F_4 = 0.00135 \cdot HF$.

In a next step, 8 interpolation points (4 (L1 to L4) to the left of p and 4 (R1 to R4) to the right of p) are determined for the pseudo-Gaussian histogram. Starting from the point μL to the left, the working histogram values are added until the sum value reaches or exceeds F_1. This point is noted as the first interpolation point left = L1. In case the F_1 limit is not reached, L1 is assigned to the first number of the input histogram but positioned in the working histogram. In the second step, the procedure for determining L2 is carried out similarly, with the difference that now the area $F_1 + F_2$ is tested for. Since the original histogram is not Gaussian distributed, nothing can be predicted about the location of L1 to L2, so the following query is of great importance afterwards:

If L2 >= L1 then L2 is set to L1 (6)

This means that L2 can in any case not lie to the right of the grid point L1. However, the markers L1 and L2 can fall on the same work histogram element. The interpolation points L3 and L4 are determined in the same way. The test areas are increased by F_3 and then by F_4 and the test from equation 6 is of course always carried out with the grid point determined in the previous step. The determination of the interpolation points to the right of μR is done analogously, except that if the area is not reached, the position of the last element of the input histogram is noted in the working histogram as the interpolation point. Additionally the test in equation 6 is carried out with <=.

At the end of the interpolation point determination, an average distance on the left and right side of the histogram is calculated from the distances of the determined points (Eq. 7 & 8). Afterwards, the interpolation points LN and RN are calculated (see Eq. 9 & 10).

$$DL = ((L1 - L2) + (L2 - L3) + (L3 - L4)) / 3 \tag{7}$$
$$DR = ((R2 - R1) + (R3 - R2) + (R4 - R3)) / 3 \tag{8}$$
$$LN = L4 - DL \tag{9}$$
$$RN = R4 + DR \tag{10}$$

Because of the extending of the input histogram to the working histogram, LN or RN may well lie within the range of the original data of the input histogram. They are then either set to the first digit before the range of the input histogram in the working histogram (left-hand side) or after the last digit of the input histogram in the working histogram (right-hand side). This later guarantees that no zero values appear within the pseudo-Gaussian distribution.

The values at the grid points should be based on the original histogram, but at the same time there is also the requirement that the new histogram should ultimately have a Gaussian distribution. This requirement was implemented by assuming for each interpolation point the histogram value that would result from the distance to the next grid point and the area sizes F_1 to F_4 according to Gauss. For example, for L1 the vector value is calculated from the distance from L1 to µL in relation to the area of Gaussian distribution F_1. The following calculations result in the same way for the other interpolation points:

$$h_{L1} = F_1 / (µL - L1) \tag{11}$$
$$h_{L2} = F_2 / (L1 - L2) \tag{12}$$
$$h_{L3} = F_3 / (L2 - L3) \tag{13}$$
$$h_{L4} = F_4 / (L3 - L4) \tag{14}$$
$$h_{LN} = 0 \tag{15}$$

In the case that the distance between the grid points is 0, i.e. that both grid points lie on the same histogram element, the respective area value without divisor is taken as the histogram value. This results in the histogram values h_{L1} to h_{L4}:

$$\text{if } (µL - L1) = 0 \quad \text{then} \quad h_{L1} = F_1 \tag{16}$$
$$\text{if } (L1 - L2) = 0 \quad \text{then} \quad h_{L2} = F_2 \tag{17}$$
$$\text{if } (L2 - L3) = 0 \quad \text{then} \quad h_{L3} = F_3 \tag{18}$$
$$\text{if } (L3 - L4) = 0 \quad \text{then} \quad h_{L4} = F_4 \tag{19}$$

Analogous equations result for the right-hand working histogram.

In this step, the values of the working histogram are calculated by interpolation between the neighboring interpolation points. In the case that two interpolation points occupy the same histogram point, no calculation is carried out and the previously calculated value is left. Otherwise the pseudo-Gaussian histogram results from the linear interpolations between the grid points (LN,0) and (L4,h_{L4}), (L4, h_{L4}) and (L3,h_{L3}), (L3,h_{L3}) and (L2,h_{L2}), (L2,h_{L2}) and (L1,h_{L1}), (L1,h_{L1}) and (R1,h_{R1}), (R1,h_{R1}) and (R2,h_{R2}), (R2,h_{R2}) and (R3, h_{R3}), (R3,h_{R3}) and (R4,h_{R4}), (R4,h_{R4}) and (RN,0). Note that both LN and RN are definitely outside the original input histogram at any points in the working histogram.

Finally, the middle third of the working histogram is extracted and the vector values are normalized to a total length of 1. This histogram then represents the relative pseudo-Gaussian histogram with which further calculations can be carried out. These steps of the procedure were implemented under Halcon in H-Develop and can be downloaded as source code under [Ra22].

Section 3: The classification of the data sets is done by simple difference formation of the vectors involved (or histograms of the color channels). For each channel, the Hamming distance between the test histogram and every of the reference histograms is first determined individually. Since these are relative histograms, the maximum distance (S_{max}) between two histograms can be 2. If several histograms are considered, the individual distances of each histogram are simply added. If three color channels are taken into account, S_{max} is 6 and if there is perfect agreement, S_{real} will be 0. If S_{real} is the distance between the histograms resulting from the calculations, the numerical agreement value U* results in

$$U^* = (1-(S_{real}/S_{max})) \cdot 100 \, (\%) \tag{20}$$

The image that achieves the highest U* value from the reference data set can be considered the best match. Optionally, pseudo-Gaussian histograms and rel. original histograms can be used together in the algorithm for the classification process. Both histogram types are treated equally in the classification process. In this case, a maximum distance value of 2 times 2 = 4 results per color channel. For example, with three color channels, a S_{max} of 6 times 2 = 12 is possible. The principle of the evaluation process always remains the same, regardless of how many or which color channels from which color space are entered into the classification algorithm. In the same way, the image data can be compressed to a low color or pixel resolution before analysis.

Figure 1 demonstrates the effect of the Blue Apple algorithm by using a simple example, created manually with a computer. On the top of the figure the images A to C are given as the reference data set. The Image D is the test image which should be classified into one of A, B or C. The original histograms of the red-channels (of RGB) of A, B and C are shown in the bottom left part of Figure 1. One sees immediately that with our U*-calculation (Eq. 20) none of the images could be chosen as a result, because the U*-values are always 0. Converting the histograms into a pseudo-Gaussian distribution leads directly to the result that Image D is closest to C. Of course, this theoretical example is very extreme, but it is only meant to explain how the Blue Apple algorithm works. In the next chapter, concrete applications will demonstrate the applicability in complex situations.

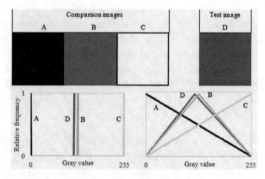

Fig. 1: Example for using the Blue Apple algorithm by means of 4 manually created easy images (top) and their responding histograms (bottom left: original, bottom right: pseudo-Gaussian distribution after conversion). For more explanations see text

3 Evaluation and examples

3.1 N-analysis tomato leaves

With this experiment we tested the practical use of the Blue Apple algorithm in a specific plant based task like plant nutrition.

Solanum lycopersicum 'Hoffmanns Rentita' were sown in week 14/20 in sand and they were transplanted in week 18/20 in nutrient solution Ferty Basis 1 plus calcium nitrate, EC 1.5. The experimental variants were 0.5, 1.0, 2.0, 4.0, 8.0 and 16 mmol NO_3 or NH_4 in the nutrient solution. Cultivation was done in 2 L vessels with 3 plants per pot. For the studies, 3 leaves were taken from each N stage from different plants in the middle area. Leaves were photographed under standardized conditions in artificial light using a Go-Pro 8 camera (Go-Pro Inc., San Mateo, USA) with the following settings: photo / fov linear / superphoto off / protune on / shutter 1/125 ......(Auto) / iso min 100 /iso max 3200 / ev comp 0 / white balance 2800 K / sharpness high / color flat / no magnification. The total nitrogen content was determined in the dry mass by dry combustion (DIN EN 16168). The image files were prepared by selecting the green content with the image processing software Halcon. The code can be downloaded under [Re22].

Results and discussion example 1

An increasing nitrogen content was observed in the leaf samples corresponding to the increase in concentration in the nutrient solution, which was also visually recognizable by a more intense green coloration. (see Figure 2)

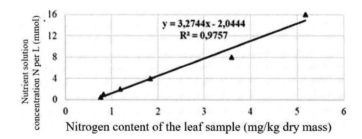

Fig. 2: Increasing nitrogen content in leaf samples of *Solanum lycopersicum* 'Hoffmanns Rentita' as a function of nitrogen concentration in the nutrient solution. The triangle dots are the values of 6 reference images

The images (Fig. 2 and see for examples Fig. 3) of the gradient experiment were analyzed with the Blue Apple methods in different color spaces which results in the reference data sets. The same procedure was done with randomly taken test samples. These were also photographed under the standardized conditions and the images were subsequently analyzed with the Blue Apple method. After digital capture, the leaves were dried and then the nitrogen content was determined.

standard 1 standard 6 sample 1

Fig. 3: Reference leaves (standard 1 and standard 6) and test sample 1

RGB color space		Nutrient Solution	Test Sample 1	Test Sample 2	N-content measured reference data	N-content measured test samples
		mmol N/L	Match with reference		mg N/kg dry mass	mg N/kg dry mass
			%	%		
Image 1	Standard 1	0,5	48,2	73,4	0,76	
Image 2	Standard 2	1,0	45,2	69,7	0,82	
Image 3	Standard 3	2,0	63,7	80,1	1,18	1,21
Image 4	Standard 4	4,0	83,2	71,7	1,83	
Image 5	Standard 5	8,0	87,9	57,9	3,59	2,71
Image 6	Standard 6	16,0	77,7	53,1	5,18	

Tab. 1: Matching results of two test images comparing with the reference images in the RGB color space and relating N-content and measured N-content of best matches

Image analysis using the Blue Apple program demonstrated a sufficient correlation between leaf coloration and nitrogen content. The best agreement was provided by the analysis in the RGB color space. The data for other color spaces are not shown.

3.2 Starch-analysis apples

In the second example we wanted to validate the Blue Apple algorithm in complex outdoor situations with different lightning conditions. To do this, we choose an example in the field of fruit analyses. A total of 42 apples were collected on October 5, 2020 at the Osnabrück University of Applied Sciences. Twelve apples of the 'Elstar' variety, nine apples of the 'Topaz' variety, seven apples of the 'Jona Gold' variety and 14 apples of the 'Braeburn' variety were selected. The apples of the 'Elstar', 'Topaz' and 'Jona Gold' varieties were taken from a ULO (Ultra-Low-Oxygen) store (harvest season 2019) and the 'Braeburn' variety was harvested unripe from an apple tree.

Subsequently, the starch-iodine index of 28 apples (nine apples each of the varieties 'Elstar' and 'Braeburn' and five apples each of the varieties 'Topaz' and 'Jona Gold') was determined in the laboratory using the ART-LB light box 3.0 (UP GmbH, Ibbenbüren, Germany). For this purpose, the apples were cut in half and the cut surface of one half of the apple was immersed in a Petri dish containing iodine solution. The apple halves were set aside with cut side facing up and after 15 minutes excess iodine solution was dabbed off. The starch-iodine index of the colored apple halves was determined using the ART-LB light box 3.0. Subsequently, the apple halves were photographed individually on a black background under a cloudy sky and under standardized lighting conditions in the laboratory using a mobile phone (HTC, One M9, Taoyuan, Taiwan). Photographs were taken with automatic white balance and exposure time. The remaining 14 apples were stored at room temperature for four weeks and on November 2, 2020, the starch-iodine index was determined as described above and the colored apple halves were photographed. The total sample size was 42 apples and 84 image files.

By pre-processing the image files with the Halcon image processing software, the apple halves were isolated from the black background and the core was removed with specific algorithms from the image (see following chapter). The pre-treated image files were evenly divided into a test data set and a reference data set. 21 image files were assigned to both the test and the reference data set. Each image file in the test data set was compared to all image files in the reference data set and the image file with the highest match was selected from the reference data set. Only image files photographed under the same lighting conditions were compared.

Results and discussion example 2

Figure 4 shows the individual steps of image processing pre-treatment of the image files. In the untreated image, the half of the apple is selected and isolated from the black background. The image is reduced to the region of the apple half. Then the core housing is automatically recognized and removed from the image file. For more information about the Halcon code developed for this see [Cr22]. The image files pre-treated in this way can be processed with the Blue Apple algorithm.

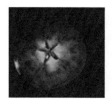

Fig. 4: Pre-treatment of the image files using the example of an apple of the 'Braeburn' variety. Left: Untreated image file of the apple on a black background. Middle: Isolation of the apple from the background. Right: Core removal from the image file

Figure 5 shows the results of assigning the starch-iodine index of the test images by the Blue Apple algorithm when comparing the unmodified histograms.

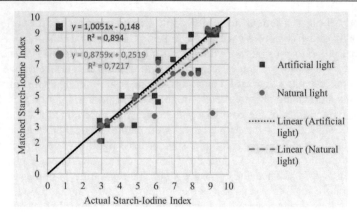

Fig. 5: Results of the assignment of the starch-iodine index by the Blue Apple algorithm when comparing the unchanged histograms of test and reference images under different lighting conditions

Figure 6 shows the results of assigning the starch-iodine index of the test images by the Blue Apple algorithm using the pseudo-Gaussian histograms.

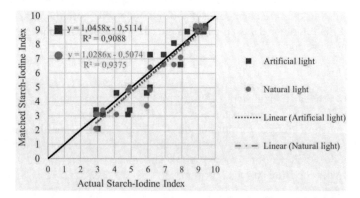

Fig. 6: Results of the assignment of the starch-iodine index by the Blue Apple algorithm when comparing the pseudo-Gaussian histograms of the test and reference images under different lighting conditions

Figure 7 shows the results of assigning the starch-iodine index of the test images by the Blue Apple algorithm using unmodified and pseudo-Gaussian histograms together.

Table 2 shows the summarized results of all comparisons performed by the Blue Apple algorithm and the manual index assignment.

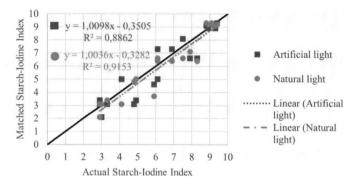

Fig. 7: Results of the assignment of the starch-iodine index by the Blue Apple algorithm in the combined comparison of the pseudo-Gaussian and unmodified histograms of the test and the reference image files under different lightning conditions

Test variant	Light condition	Difference between actual and matched starch-iodine index	
		Mean deviation	Standard deviation
Pseudo-Gauss. histogram	Artificial light	0.63	0.51
	Natural light	0.46	0.53
Original histogram	Artificial light	0.61	0.55
	Natural light	0.83	1.15
Pseudo-Gauss. and original histogram	Artificial light	0.69	0.57
	Natural light	0.52	0.57

Tab. 2: Summarized results of the comparison of test and comparison images with different test variants and lighting conditions. Values rounded to two decimals

It could be shown that the Blue Apple algorithm is basically able to match an apple to a reference apple with similar starch-iodine index. The mean deviation from the measured starch-iodine index was 0.83 with a standard error of 1.15 in the worst case and 0.46 with a standard error of 0.53 in the best case. The natural light experiments had the clearest effects, while the artificial light experiments gave different results. Furthermore, looking at the level of index fluctuations, the result of the assignment could be improved when using the pseudo-Gaussian histogram compared to using the unmodified histogram under both lighting conditions. The coefficient of determination increased from 0.72 to 0.94 under natural light conditions and from 0.89 to 0.91 under standardized light conditions.

4 Discussion and outlook

The newly developed Blue-Apple algorithm was designed for a better image processing in RGB or similar color spaces in the field of agriculture and horticulture. In the case of using manually generated extreme color channel histograms, we were able to show that the algorithm achieves a clear improvement in classification tasks. Its use in biological and agronomic practice was successfully confirmed by the example of nitrogen determination of plant images. The comparison with conventional histogram evaluation based on the starch determination of apples showed that classification improves with Blue-Apple even under diverse boundary conditions (degree of ripeness, apple variety). The algorithm performed particularly well under difficult natural lighting conditions. Blue-Apple is knowledge based and statistical data driven. Therefore, conversion of grey-scale histograms into so-called pseudo-Gaussian histograms and thus the quality of Blue-Apple's success always depends on the distribution of the histograms to be evaluated. The use of the method appears to be promising, especially for color classifications in the field of plant cultivation. In addition to histogram evaluations in image processing, the use of Blue-Apple is also conceivable for processing other types of sensor data (e.g. fluorescence data or laser distance data). Likewise, one could use it as a pre-processing step of deep learning methods. Blue-Apple thus represents a viable and promising extension of evaluation tools in biological and agricultural research and practice.

Bibliography

[Cr22]   Credner, J., Fadami, M., Rehrmann, P., Rath, T.: Blue Apple – Isolation and removal of apple core housings in color images. BLab Code No. 20222, http://www.blab-osnabrueck.de/blue-apple2.txt, 2022.

[HCR18] Hameed, K., Chai, D., Rassau, A.: A comprehensive review of fruit and vegetable classification techniques. Image and Vision Computing, 80, 24-44, 2018.

[HLE18] Hassanein, M., Lari, Z., El-Sheimy, N.: A new vegetation segmentation approach for cropped fields based on threshold detection from hue histograms. Sensors, 18(4), 1253, 2018.

[JTZ11] Jeon, H. Y., Tian, L. F., Zhu, H.: Robust crop and weed segmentation under uncontrolled outdoor illumination. Sensors, 11(6), 6270-6283, 2011.

[NAA21] Ngugi, L. C., Abelwahab, M., Abo-Zahhad, M.: Recent advances in image processing techniques for automated leaf pest and disease recognition–A review. Information processing in agriculture, 8(1), 27-51, 2021.

[PR 18] Patrício, D. I., Rieder, R.: Computer vision and artificial intelligence in precision agriculture for grain crops: A systematic review. Computers and electronics in agriculture, 153, 69-81, 2018.

[Ra17]   Ravikanth, L. et. al.: Extraction of spectral information from hyperspectral data and application of hyperspectral imaging for food and agricultural products. Food and bioprocess technology, 10(1), 1-33, 2017.

[Ra22]   Rath, T., Credner, J., Fadami, M., Rehrmann, P.: Blue Apple – Transformation of histograms to Gaussian distributions. BLab Code No. 20223, http://www.blab-osnabrueck.de/blue-apple3.txt, 2022.

[Re22]   Rehrmann, P., Credner, J., Fadami, M., Rath, T.: Blue Apple – Object green free. BLab Code No. 20221, http://www.blab-osnabrueck.de/blue-apple1.txt, 2022.

Farmers' attitudes towards data security in agriculture when using digital technologies

Farmers' attitudes towards data protection guidelines

Andreas Gabriel[1]

Abstract: This article explores the question of which farmers are aware and also trust the current data protection guidelines for the sharing of agricultural data when using digital technologies. A decision tree analysis was used to identify the characteristics of group segments that differ in their attitudes (awareness, confidence) towards current data protection guidelines. Although a large proportion of respondents said they were aware of the current data protection guidelines, most farmers are skeptical and do not trust their effectiveness. Three segments were identified that are more open to monetary or information-based compensations in return for sharing their farm data with third parties.

Keywords: data protection guidelines, data sharing, digital farming technologies, segmentation

1 Introduction

Advances in digital technologies and Big Data applications in agriculture have the potential to help address current challenges such as yield security, productivity, labor support, and sustainability [Wo17]. However, these promising goals can only be achieved if farmers trust the exchange and sharing of data with other actors (e. g., producers, extension agents, service providers) [Am22]. Utilizing digital tools that are interconnected and remotely accessible raises concerns related to (farm) data privacy and therefore reduces farmers' motivation to engage in data collection activities [Am22]. Previous studies on issues of data security and data sharing have shown that many farmers still have reservations and are reluctant to share operational data with third parties [Ja19]. This may be due to a lack of transparency in the terms and conditions of producer licenses [Wi19], a lack of knowledge about their own data rights, or the fear of smaller farms of an unequal distribution of benefits from sharing data with bigger players of the industry [Ma18]. In general, the European General Data Protection Regulation, in effect since 2018, also has an impact on the private spheres of farmers' lives, thus generally increasing the awareness of privacy and data protection [Wi19]. Furthermore, farmers' mixed feelings can also be explained by the fact that they assume that a generally unclear legal situation does not

---

[1] Bavarian State Research Center for Agriculture, Digital Farming Group, Kleeberg 14, 94099 Ruhstorf a.d. Rott, andreas.gabriel@lfl.bayern.de, https://orcid.org/0000-0001-5736-1593

sufficiently support their rights to data protection [Va20]. The fact that the farming sector in Germany is increasingly confronted with data security issues is evident in many areas. One indication of growing awareness of farm data protection issues is the changing reporting of barriers to acceptance of digital technologies in widely read German agricultural trade journals [Ga21]. While topics of data sovereignty and data security of sensitive data were rarely mentioned in journal articles and short reports about digital technologies in the period from 2008 until 2013, these are barriers that were mentioned dominantly between 2014 and 2018 [Ga21].

The present article uses information from Bavarian farmers collected via an online survey to assess their attitudes towards data protection guidelines and policies when interconnected digital technologies are used on their farm. The research approach follows the general and established agreement of researchers that attitude is an evaluative response of an individual to an object that is influenced by cognitive, affective, and behavioral inputs [EC93]. Regarding this framework, farmers' self-assessed awareness of data guidelines (cognitive input), their confidence in their protective effectiveness (affective-emotional input), and their actual on-farm experience and use of interconnected digital technologies including associated issues of data security and potential farm data sharing (behavioral input) are considered. A decision tree analysis helps to identify characteristics of group segments that differ in their attitudes (awareness, confidence) towards current data protection guidelines and rights when sharing farm data. Decision tree methods are widely used to classify objects and to support decision problems. They are applied for both a concise display of formal rules, but also for diverse applications in data mining, e. g., in the segmentation of customers or target groups based on their characteristics or behavior. Assuming that farmer segments with less awareness and trust in their own rights require more effort to reduce barriers of investing in interconnected farm technologies, a decision tree algorithm is employed to predict profit performance of identified group segments (end nodes). A better knowledge of the composition and characteristics of these farmer segments can provide advice to actors such as technology and software manufacturers, agricultural extension services, or policymakers to better understand the concerns of farmers in adopting digital technologies and to provide information focused on how to handle farm data when using interconnected technologies. A review of the literature indicates that no study has yet investigated how farmers' and farm characteristics affect farmer awareness and confidence in data protection guidelines when using digital technologies. This article intends to fill this gap.

2 Material and methodology

The data used for this study originates from an online survey conducted in spring and summer 2020 among farmers in Bavaria to inquire about the use of and experiences with digital technologies on their farms. In 2020, the population of 103,552 Bavarian applicants were accessed via the support and funding platform of the Bavarian State Ministry of Food, Agriculture and Forestry (StMELF). Applications for EU agricultural subsidies in Bavaria are mandatory to be submitted via this platform during a fixed time period each year. The link to the online survey was prominently displayed and promoted in the application portal. Thus, every Bavarian farmer applying for EU direct payments in 2020 had the option to participate in the survey (for more details on data collection procedure see also [GG22]). This access to the entire population of Bavarian farmers enabled a broad data base to be obtained with a complete sample of 2,390 farms including all farming production categories (arable farming, forage production/grazing, livestock farming, and specialty crops). The respondents were given the option to provide information on a total of 30 digital technologies in crop and livestock production, insofar as these were already in use. Thus, structure and characteristics of the farms and farm management as well as the digital technologies already in use are known. A number of studies have investigated the acceptance and adoption of digital technologies in German agriculture (e. g., [Mi21]; [MK21]), although the actual use in practice is difficult to assess. A special methodological feature of the present survey is the distinction between whether farmers "have purchased and are using" or "have purchased and are not using" a technology. This allows for better conclusions about technology users and not only about adopters.

In addition to technology-specific inquiries, general questions on farm data security issues, sovereignty of farm data, and data sharing were answered. In one question, the farmers indicated whether they a) are aware of and confident in the current data protection guidelines, b) are aware of these guidelines but do not expect them to protect them from misuse, or c) are not aware of them. These three options form the target variable to classify group segments using a stepwise decision tree procedure ("Chi-squared Automatic Interaction Detection" = CHAID algorithm) (Table 1).

Sample size: n=1,949	Scale level	Categorial levels; span, mean of metrics
Target variable		
Awareness and confidence in data protection guidelines	categorical	(1) awareness & confidence; (2) awareness & no confidence; (3) no awareness of data protection rules
Segmentation variables		
Type of farm operation	categorical	(1) full-time; (2) part-time
Type of management	categorical	(1) conventional; (2) organic
Farmer's vocational education level	categorical	(1) skilled worker; (2) master, technician, university degree; (3) vocational training program part-time farming, lateral entrants
Number of digital technologies used on farm	metric	0-15; mean: 1.98 technologies/farm (number of farms with no digital technology in use = 730 (37.5%))
Farm size (total production acreage in ha)	metric	5-880 ha; mean: 96.49 ha/farm; including missing values

Tab. 1: Structural influence parameters used for the CHAID segmentation procedure

The Chi²-based procedure can be used exploratively and generates a tree-structured classification model, whereby the dependent target variable categories (a-c) are predicted on the basis of independent segmentation variables. The pre-selection of five segmentation variables was based on literature (e. g., [Ma18]; [Wi19]; [Ga21]) and on own considerations. The non-parametric CHAID algorithm carries out merging and splitting processes in several segmentation steps based on contingency tables. For the independent (segmentation) variables, it determines which categories of these variables can be merged with minimal loss of information to show the least significant difference with respect to the dependent (target) variable. Thus, the decision tree algorithm classifies a population into inverted tree-like constructs with root nodes, and end nodes (segments) [SY15]. Predefined categories of categorial variables are merged if they are not significantly different with respect to the dependent variable. The algorithm can handle different data categories, thus allowing to combine metric variables with categorical variables to perform stepwise segmentation. With metric data, the optimal cut-off thresholds for a statistical division of segments are automatically carried out (e. g., a cut-off value for the subdivision of production acreage). The composition of the final segments then allows the calculation of the response rates for the selected target category of the dependent variable as well as the estimation of the profit performance of the individual segments in the model. The modelling was carried out using IBM SPSS Decision Trees 28.

3 Results and discussion

3.1 Self-assessment and confidence in farm data protection

Farmers were asked about their self-assessed knowledge of and confidence in the protection by current guidelines and data protection laws when sharing farm data. Their opinion on that question varies greatly in the overall sample of farmers surveyed in Bavaria (Fig. 1a).

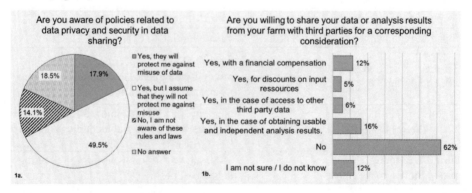

Fig. 1a: Distribution of total sample on data protection guidelines awareness (n=2,390) and Fig.1b: Share of responses on compensation options for data sharing (percentage of cases, n=2,390)

Less than 18% of the 2,390 respondents stated that they were aware of the data protection guidelines and felt sufficiently protected by them. The majority of farmers feel that they are aware of the guidelines, but that these do not protect their data from misuse (49.5%). 14.1% of the respondents stated that they do not know much about data protection guidelines. A further share of 18.5% could not provide any concrete information on this question – these were excluded from the sample, resulting in a total of 1,949 data sets for the further analyses. Figure 1b illustrates the farmers' responses on whether they would be willing to share farm data with third parties for different options of compensation. For almost two thirds of the sampled farmers, this is out of the question, and around 12% did not want to or could not comment on this. Among those who are willing, the greatest interest was shown in direct financial compensation (12%) or in exchange of usable analysis data with other parties (16%). The distribution between farmers who admit to not being aware of protection guidelines, those who trust them, and the skeptical counterparts can also be analyzed at single technology level (Fig. 2).

Question: Are you aware of policies related to data privacy and security in data sharing?

Technology	Yes, they will protect me against misuse of data	Yes, but I assume that they will not protect me against misuse	No, I am not aware of these rules and laws
Fleet management systems (21/1,490)*	48%	43%	10%
Drones (47/1,490)*	36%	53%	11%
Automatic basic feed supply (28/1,121)*	36%	36%	29%
NIR sensors harvest quality (25/1,490)	32%	56%	12%
Variable rate - sowing (35/1,490)	31%	63%	6%
Yield mapping (51/1,490)	29%	55%	16%
Variable rate - basic supply (48/1,490)	29%	63%	8%
Geo-referenced soil sampling (54/1,490)	28%	48%	24%
Barn cameras (205/1,121)	26%	59%	16%
Forecast models, & apps (749/1,949)***	26%	61%	13%
Maps from satellite data (217/1,490)	25%	62%	13%
FMIS livestock farming (196/1,121)	24%	61%	15%
Variable rate fertilizer - nitrogen (59/1,490)	24%	61%	15%
Variable rate plant protection (64/1,490)	23%	66%	11%
Robotic feed pushing (64/879)	23%	61%	16%
Communication platform (470/1,949)	23%	63%	14%
FMIS crop farming (208/1,490)	23%	61%	16%
Digital field records (330/1,490)	22%	65%	13%
Automatic milking system (111/879)	22%	61%	17%
Robotic slat cleaner (63/879)	21%	57%	22%
Section control (191/1,490)	18%	63%	18%
Behavior monitoring sensors (137/1,121)	18%	62%	20%
Automatic steering systems (252/1,490)*	17%	62%	21%
Lightbar systems (157/1,490)	15%	69%	16%

Fig 2: Distribution of responses on data policy awareness (absolute number of users/absolute numbers of respondents per technology, depending on production categories); Asterisks show significant differences of distributions between users and non-users of an individual technology (Pearson- Chi^2; *<0.01; ***<0.001)

The online survey contained a total of 30 queried technologies, a subset of which was shown to each survey participant. The subset was individually adapted based on their responses to initial questions identifying the arable farming category (crop production, feed production and grazing, specialty crops) and animal categories in which they are currently active.

Three categories of technology that have a high number of farmers with confidence in data protection and a relatively low proportion of skeptics are fleet management systems, drones, and automated basic feed supply in livestock production. However, the proportions of users are rather low, with absolute numbers of 12, 28 and 47 users of these technologies, respectively, in the sample. However, it is noticeable that in these categories, the proportion of trusting farmers is significantly higher than among the non-users of the technology. High proportions of skeptics of data protection effects (>60%) can be seen in supporting technologies such as automatic steering systems and lightbar systems, but also in variable rate applications. In the case of information-intensive variable rate technologies, the shares of users who stated that they are not aware of data protection laws is relatively low, which indicates that these user groups are also more aware of the effects of data networking. Independently from production categories, all respondents were asked about their use of forecast models and apps (e. g., weather prognosis and pest pressure forecast models). Here, the proportions of users who said they were aware of the data protection laws (with or without trusting them) are significantly higher than those who do not use such model and apps on their farm.

3.2 Decision tree segmentation and segment profits assessments

Regardless of the use of single or multiple digital technologies on the farms, structural influences on the above statements on awareness of and confidence in the protection of farm data were analyzed employing the CHAID segmentation procedure. The modelled decision tree with the respective breakdowns of the target variable shows that four of the five influencing variables play a role in the segmentation process (Fig. 3). Only the type of management, conventional or organic, has not turned out to be a relevant separating characteristic in the model. The number of terminal nodes was determined by the default settings of the decision tree model (maximum tree level depth of 3, minimum numbers of 100 cases in the parent node and 50 in the child node). These six end nodes form the identified segments to be evaluated later.

The categorization into full-time and part-time farms is the segmentation variable with the strongest influence on the responses provided by the farmers on their awareness and confidence on data protection guidelines when sharing data. The distribution into these two root segments also roughly mirrors the distribution of part-time and full-time farms in Bavaria [BS20]. It is already evident at this first tree level that part-time farmers are more likely to agree that they have enough knowledge about current data protection guidelines and also have more confidence in them. In the next tree level, both types of farm operation are split by the variable "number of digital technologies used on farm". The algorithm thereby provides the optimal separation threshold for the metric variable, which here is the use of no technologies on the one side and the use of one or more technologies on the other side. This low threshold can be explained by the fact that the percentage of Bavarian farms that do not use any digital technologies is already relatively high at 37.5% of the total sample.

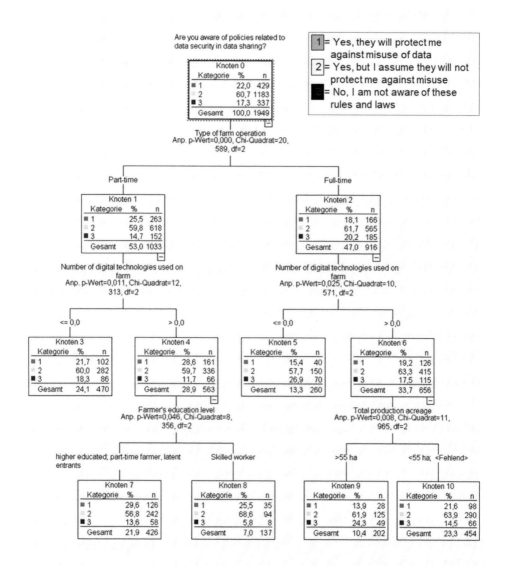

Fig. 3: Decision tree diagram based on the target variable

In the case of part-time farmers who already use digital technologies, there is a further distinction at the third tree level based on the specification of vocational education of the respondents. Among farmers with higher education (e. g., master, technician, university degree) merged with part-time farming educated and lateral entrants, the share of the respondents that have confidence in the data protection guidelines is the highest of all segments (29.6%). Among the farmers with basic agricultural education ("skilled worker"), the group of those who stated that they are not aware of any data protection guidelines is the smallest of all segments identified (5.8%). Among full-time farmers using digital technologies, it is the farm size (measured in the total acreage of the production area) that causes a separation into two further end nodes on the third tree level. The CHAID algorithm sets the optimal separation threshold at 55 ha. In segment 9, the proportion of farmers that are aware and trust data protection guidelines when data sharing is the lowest of all segments (13.9%). The underlying reasons why part-time farmers show a higher self-assessed knowledge than their full-time counterparts and also seem to have a higher overall confidence in the data protection guidelines cannot be read directly from the data. In the case of the full-time farmers with less acreage, it can be assumed that owners of smaller farms have to engage even more intensively with the investment in new technologies and therefore also familiarize themselves with data protection rules and then also learn to understand them better. This is also an important point, as it is often more difficult for farmers of smaller businesses to negotiate standard terms and conditions of data licenses with suppliers [Ca16].

The CHAID method is a popular segmentation method in business marketing as it makes it very easy to attribute a "response rate" to identified customer segments. The response rate is determined by an above- or below-average allocation to a target category in a segment compared to the total number of cases. Assuming that the category "Yes, they will protect me against misuse of data" is to be determined as the intended target category, the six segments can be ranked according to their response rate (Table 2). The index value shows to what extent the observed percentage for the target category in each of the segments differs from the expected percentage for the target category. An index value of more than 100% means that the target category has more cases than the total sample percentage in the target category (in our case 22% of 1,949 farmers). Conversely, an index value of less than 100% means that there are fewer cases in the target category than the total percentage.

Segment	Node (abs)	Node (%)	Gain (abs)	Gain (%)	Response (%)	Index (%)
7	426	21.9	126	29.4	29.6	134.4
8	137	7.0	35	8.2	25.5	116.1
3	470	24.1	102	23.8	21.7	98.6
10	454	23.3	98	22.8	21.6	98.1
5	260	13.3	40	9.3	15.4	69.9
9	202	10.4	28	6.5	13.9	63.0

Tab. 2: Response rate per segment in relation to the selected target category

In the case of the six identified end nodes, segments 7 and 8 (part-time farmers already using digital technologies) in particular are the segments that have the highest gain rates in their current composition, as they hit the target variable most frequently (29.6% and 25.5%). In contrast, the skeptics and those who know little or nothing about data protection guidelines are overrepresented among segments including full-time farmers and farms that do not yet use digital technologies. This is where leverage can be applied in technology design, sales, and also in the service of digital technologies to better inform these segments and to prepare the prevailing data protection guidelines in a more comprehensible way.

In addition, the CHAID method enables the calculation of profits and return of investment (ROI) per segment by considering the probabilities of all categories of the segmentation variable through predefined revenues and efforts. For these revenues and efforts, experience or monetary amounts can be entered in the model, but also dimensionless levels. If one sets the value 1 as revenue for all three segmentation categories (corresponding to the adoption of a digital technology as revenue target), then different efforts are to be applied to each of the three subgroups of the target variable in order to attract them as technology users. For farmers who say they know data protection guidelines but do not trust them, the highest efforts are to be expected, as they first and foremost have to be convinced to use data sharing technologies (effort = 1). Farmers who know little about data protection can be convinced more easily with appropriate information offers (0.5). Farmers who are aware of these rules and are also confident with them do not require any significant effort (0).

Segment	Description	Number (%)	Profit rate	ROI (%)
7	Part-time, technology use, higher vocational education & lateral entrants	21.9	.364	57.4
3	Part-time, no technology in use	24.1	.309	44.6
10	Full-time, technology use, < 55 ha	23.3	.289	40.6
5	Full-time, no technology in use	13.3	.288	40.5
8	Part-time, technology use, skilled farmers	7.0	.285	39.8
9	Full-time, technology use, > 55 ha	10.4	.260	35.1

Tab. 3: Segments' profit performance

Applying these predefined levels of revenues and efforts to the model results in a revised order to the previous response rates in relation to a target category (table 3). Segment 8, with its major proportion of skeptics (69%), is associated with a higher effort to convince them of the data protection guidelines. Therefore, the calculated profit rate (= revenues minus efforts) and ROI are relatively low (<41%). The other two segments including part-time farmers have the highest average profits and ROI in their current compositions (57% and 45%).

3.3 Compensation opportunities

Now that the six identified end nodes have been evaluated in terms of their target variable composition with regard to attitudes towards data protection, it is interesting to find out how the obstacles to these topics can be reduced in a targeted manner. One option of convincing skeptical farmers, or at least raising their awareness for protection guidelines and handling of their own data, is to offer them compensation opportunities in return for sharing their farm data. Figure 1b already illustrated that various compensation offers are only considered by a smaller proportion of the farmers surveyed (62% of the total sample reject such deals; 12% have not yet an opinion on that). Nevertheless, it can be shown for some segments that they are more open to such compensations for the provision of farm data (Fig. 4).

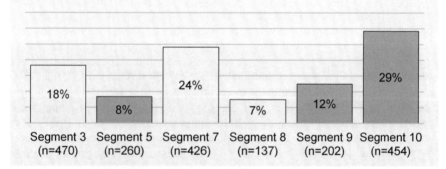

Fig. 4: Agreement shares per segment on data sharing for any kind of compensation (white pillars = part-time farmer segments, grey pillars = full-time farmer segments)

Regardless of the type of compensation offered, segments 3, 7 and 10 show a higher willingness to consider counteroffers (18%, 24%, 29%) than the average of the total sample. The first two segments comprise a higher proportion of farmers who are confident in data protection guidelines. Here, a reasonable explanation would be that compensations provide an additional incentive for them and that the trade-off with data security concerns does not weigh too heavily. Segment 10, however, shows the highest willingness for compensation options (29%), although it is the strongest segment in terms of profit performance. As it is the numerically second largest segment, including full-time farmers with total production areas under 55 ha, this group of farmers – in contrast to other segments – is worth addressing with respective compensation offers.

4 Conclusions

This article explores the question of which farmers are aware of and confident in current data protection guidelines for the sharing of agricultural data when using digital technologies. The application of a decision tree segmentation method to an online survey sample of Bavarian farmers yielded the following main findings: First, although a large proportion of respondents said they were aware of the current data protection guidelines, most farmers are skeptical and do not trust their effectiveness. Second, there is only a handful of individual technologies for which differences between users and non-users in terms of awareness and confidence in data protection policies could be detected. Users of some digital technologies (e. g., fleet management, drones, automated feed supply) show higher levels of confidence in data protection guidelines. Third, the application of the segmentation method showed that particularly the type of farm operation (part-time), the level of experience with digital technologies at the farm (at least one technology used), the type of vocational training (skilled worker), and the size of the production area (in this case, less than 55 ha) had an influence on the target variable. In particular, the characteristics of the segmentation variables highlighted here increase the shares of the target category ("Yes, they will protect me against misuse of data") and are responsible for a high "profit" performance of the respective segments, when a general trust in data protection guidelines is the goal. Fourth, the possibility of using monetary or data-related forms of compensation to mitigate farmers' concerns on data sharing and data exchange has so far been rejected by most of the Bavarian farmers surveyed. Nevertheless, there are individual identified segments that are open to such compensation variants and expect own benefits. Such offers represent only one way of overcoming concerns of data protection and sharing farm data. Essential strategies to facilitate the use of interconnected technologies are to assure the protection of farm data, a commonly understandable elaboration of guidelines, and provision of pinpoint information for farmers. The target variable used in the decision tree model so far gives little background on why farmers do not engage with guidelines and what influences mistrust in their effectiveness. In order to better understand these backgrounds, qualitative studies such as focus group discussions or information sessions with farmers would be useful. The presented segmentation process characterized individual groups of farmers to be targeted for inclusion in such qualitative studies.

Bibliography

[Am22]   Amiri-Zarandi, M. et al.: Big Data Privacy in Smart Farming: A Review. Sustainability 14(15), 9120, 2022.

[BS20]   Bayerisches Staatsministerium für Ernährung, Landwirtschaft und Forsten: Bayerischer Agrarbericht, 2020. https://www.agrarbericht.bayern.de/politik-strategien/index.html

[Ca16]   Carbonell, I.: The ethics of big data in agriculture. Internet Policy Review 5(1), 2016. https://doi.org/10.14763/2016.1.405

[EC93]   Eagly, A.H.; Chaiken, S.: The psychology of attitudes. Harcourt Brace Jovanovich, Fort Worth, 1993.

[Ga21]   Gabriel, A.; Gandorfer, M.; Spykman, O.: Nutzung und Hemmnisse digitaler Technologien in der Landwirtschaft. Berichte über Landwirtschaft - Zeitschrift für Agrarpolitik und Landwirtschaft 99(1), 2021.

[GG22]   Gabriel, A.; Gandorfer, M.: Adoption of digital technologies in agriculture – an inventory in a european small-scale farming region. Precision Agriculture, 2022. https://doi.org/10.1007/s11119-022-09931-1

[Ja19]   Jakku, E. et al.: If they don't tell us what they do with it, why would we trust them? Trust, transparency, and benefit-sharing in Smart Farming. NJAS-Wageningen Journal of Life Sciences 90, 100285, 2019.

[Ma18]   Maru, A. et al.: Digital and data-driven agriculture: harnessing the power of data for smallholders. F1000Research 7(525), 2018.

[Mi21]   Michels, M.; Bonke, V.; Musshoff, O.: Understanding the adoption of smartphone apps in crop protection. Precision Agriculture 21, 1209-1226, 2021.

[MK21]   Mohr, S.; Kühl, R.: Acceptance of artificial intelligence in German agriculture: an application of the technology acceptance model and the theory of planned behavior. Precision Agriculture 22, 1816-1844, 2021.

[SY15]   Song, Y.Y.; Ying, L.U.: Decision tree methods: applications for classification and prediction. Shanghai archives of psychiatry 27(2), 130-135, 2015.

[Va20]   Van der Burg, S.; Wiseman, L; Krkeljas, J.: Trust in farm data sharing: reflections on the EU code of conduct for agricultural data sharing. Ethics and Information Technology 23(3), 185-198, 2020.

[Wi19]   Wiseman, L. et al.: Farmers and their data: An examination of farmers' reluctance to share their data through the lens of the laws impacting smart farming. NJAS-Wageningen Journal of Life Sciences 90, 100301, 2019.

[Wo17]   Wolfert, S.; Ge, L.; Verdouw, C.; Bogaardt, M.J.: Big data in smart farming – a review. Agricultural Systems 153, 69-80, 2017.

Conceptualizing a holistic smart dairy farming system

Leveraging sensor fusion and AI to the benefit of humans and animals

Laura Sophie Gravemeier [1], Anke Dittmer [1], Martina Jakob[2], Daniel Kümper[3] and Oliver Thomas[1,4]

Abstract: With the increasing use of sensor technology and the resulting diverse data streams in dairy farming, the potential for the use of AI rises. Beyond the AI-based solution of individual problems, a holistic approach to smart dairy farming is necessary. In this contribution, we identify and analyse a set of diverse use cases for smart dairy farming: lying behaviour analysis, heat stress monitoring, work diary, barn and herd monitoring, and animal health tracking. These focus both on animal health and welfare as well as assistance for farmers. Based on the requirements of these use cases, we design a holistic smart dairy farming system in an iterative development process.

Keywords: sensor integration, computer vision, assistance system, dairy cow monitoring, animal welfare

1 Introduction

Dairy farming entails many challenges for both humans and animals. On the one hand, farmers must perform physically demanding tasks, ensure the profitability of their farms and bear responsibility for the health of their animals [Ko13]. On the other hand, dairy cows achieve peak performance while exposed to risks of disease [Vo09] or hot weather periods [We03]. To meet these challenges, there has been an increase in technology adoption ranging from automatic milking and feeding systems [Ma19] to ruminal bolus sensors [HKV22] and activity trackers [ZWV19]. Thus, an artificial intelligence (AI)-based data analysis of the generated data streams has high potential. To ensure that this does not solely solve individual use cases in isolation, a holistic approach to the digital barn is called for. This constitutes the main motive of our research project, which integrates multiple sensor streams and tackles a diverse set of use cases. These use cases

---

[1] German Research Center for Artificial Intelligence GmbH, Smart Enterprise Engineering, Parkstr. 40, 49080 Osnabrück, Germany, laura.gravemeier@dfki.de, https://orcid.org/0000-0002-2306-1477; anke.dittmer@dfki.de, https://orcid.org/0000-0002-9122-3271; oliver.thomas@dfki.de
[2] Leibniz Institute for Agricultural Engineering and Bioeconomy (ATB), Max-Eyth-Allee 100, 14469 Potsdam, Germany, mjakob@atb-potsdam.de
[3] iotec GmbH, Albert-Einstein-Straße 1, 49076 Osnabrück, Germany, daniel.kuemper@iotec-gmbh.de
[4] Osnabrück University, Information Management and Information Systems, Parkstr. 40, 49080 Osnabrück, oliver.thomas@uni-osnabrueck.de

were selected based on consortium expertise as well as expert input and include *(A) lying behavior analysis* and *(B) heat stress monitoring* in terms of analyzing specific animal behavior. On top of that, we focus on providing a *(C) work diary* and a *(D) barn and herd monitoring* solution for the farmers. Lastly, we tackle overall *(E) animal health tracking* to provide extensive documentation and a starting point for multivariate predictions to support farm management. These use cases require the analysis of various data and sensor inputs as well as sophisticated means to extract relevant actionable knowledge. Thus, we define the following research question:

How can a holistic smart dairy farming system be conceptualized?

In order to address this research question, we analyze the five use cases tackling animal health and welfare, support for the work of farmers as well as documentation of the animals' condition. Our system design concept is comprised of a technical architecture including hardware as well as software. It is geared towards integrating the analyzed use cases, handling vast data streams from multiple sensors including cameras and microphones as well as delivering relevant information and support to the farmers.

In the following, we will first present related work regarding assistance systems in livestock farming and AI-based dairy farming solutions. We then describe our research methodology, the design science research approach. Next, we provide a systematic analysis of the five use cases followed by the derived concept for a holistic smart dairy farming system. Finally, we discuss our results and provide an outlook for future work in research and practice.

2 Related work

Current scientific discourse recognizes the potential of AI – for agriculture in general and dairy farming in particular – and drives innovation by developing relevant AI-based solutions. Not only the analysis of structured data, but especially the evaluation of image and video data – namely, computer vision – has a major impact in this domain. For example, the prediction of body weight and body condition scores can be automated [Ru20]. On top of that, different approaches for tracking cow activities have been proposed. Among these are solutions that focus on tracking the animals' position in different areas of the barn [SK21], the animals' feeding time [PF18], their lying behaviour [Po13] and their rumination activity [So19]. But the analysis of social interactions within the herd is also of interest [SK20]. Another current research problem in this domain deals with cow identification in order to track the behaviour and state of individual cows. Approaches range from face recognition [We22] and muzzle characteristics [KC18] to methods based on coat patterns in spotted cattle [Ta21]. A major concern in AI-based animal monitoring is animal health. For example, lameness can be detected early when using anomaly detection on pedometer data compared to visual inspection by farmers [By19]. For dairy cows, particular health-related developments are especially important to understand. These include the detection of heat stress [Be21] and the gain of reproductive health information such as diagnosing mastitis [Ka22], predicting calving [Ca08] and detecting oestrus [Gu19]. Of course, information related to economic efficiency is also relevant, such as predicting milk yield [Li20]. In order to obtain the necessary data for AI-based dairy farming, research is using cameras and especially depth cameras, microphones, as well as sensors placed on and inside of the cows. The methods for data analysis range from decision trees to deep convolutional neural networks.

However, as sophisticated as these solutions are becoming, they need to be integrated into a holistic system for smart dairy farming to reach their full potential. On the one hand, this requires the integration of diverse data sources as they provide the best results for specific use cases, e.g., when detecting diseases in cows [La21]. On the other hand, this should include the integration of diverse use cases in order to provide a truly useful and easily manageable tool to farmers. This issue will be addressed in our contribution as we selected a set of five diverse use cases to be analysed by experts and integrated within a technical framework.

3 Research approach

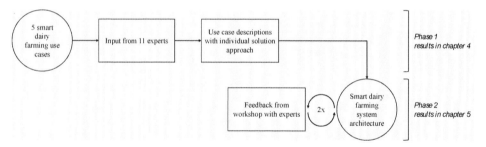

Fig. 1: Research approach

To analyse use cases and design a solution approach, we carried out our research in two phases that are visualized in Figure 1. In phase one, we conducted interviews with 11 experts. The experts, their company or institution and expertise as well as the content of the interviews are described in Table 1. Based on these interviews, we identified relevant use cases as well as the current practice regarding the use cases, and requirements for an AI-based solution as well as a solution approach. In phase two, we developed a hardware and software architecture for a holistic dairy farming system over the course of an iterative development process. The first draft was designed based on the interviews and evaluated with a group of four experts for AI engineering and assistance systems. The resulting draft was evaluated in turn by two experts currently engaged in developing other smart dairy farming solutions. This evaluation resulted in the final architecture presented in this article.

No.	Company or Institution	Expertise	Content of the interview
1	Research Institution A	Expert for digital monitoring of human health	Interface design, handling of streaming data, potential for explainability
2	Research Institution A	Expert for intelligent assistance systems	Interface design, potential for learning purposes
3	Farm B	Animal husbandry worker	Current practice and potential for AI in daily activities, requirements for assistance system
4	Farm B	Herd manager	Current practice and potential for AI in daily activities, requirements for assistance system
5	Farm C	Herd manager	Current practice and potential for AI in daily activities, requirements for assistance system
6	Public Institution D	Official Veterinarian	Current practice and potential of AI for detecting health problems in cows, application of assistance systems with the involvement of veterinarians
7	Public Institution E	Work scientist and expert for digitilization in animal husbandry	Current practice of AI in farming and work science, requirements for management support
8	Farm F	Animal husbandry worker	Current practice and potential for AI in daily activities, requirements for assistance system
9	Farm F	Herd manager, advisor for projects in animal husbandry	Current practice and potential for AI in daily activities, requirements for assistance system
10	Farm F	Expert for digitalization in animal husbandry	Current practice and potential for AI in daily activities, requirements for assistance system
11	Farm F	Expert for digitalization in animal husbandry	Current practice and potential for AI in daily activities, requirements for assistance system

Tab. 1: Description of the interviewed experts

4 Primary use cases in the smart dairy farming system

Five use cases have been identified as most relevant and realistic for achieving a smart dairy farming system. The selection was based on the expertise of the consortium as well as the input from the experts described in Chapter 3. Table 2 describes the five use cases, names the proposed area of support for the farmer, and gives examples for the expected output. As a result, dashboard visualisations of events and recommendations for action will support the farmer to detect health problems earlier and make farm management more efficient. Use case (A) for example is aiming to analyse the lying behaviour of the cows. The process of lying down gives information about the barn design, but also if the animal has health problems such as pain in the joints or lameness. The smart farming system aims to monitor the process continuously and send an alarm in case of abnormal behaviour.

Conceptualizing a holistic smart dairy farming system   81

Use Case	(A) lying behaviour	(B) heat stress monitoring	(C) work diary	(D) barn and herd monitoring	(E) animal health tracking
Brief description	Analyzing lying process, deriving information on barn design, comfort, hygiene and indicators for health problems	Recognition of heat stress indicators in animal behaviour and recommendations for counter measures	Record of productive times and ancillary for efficient management, monitoring of health and safety issues of workers	Review of current activities and status of the barn, visual barn representation for the farmer with added information from other use cases	Recording health parameters for each animal and the herd continuously, relevant data is bundled in one place, automatically forwarded when necessary and used for predictions
Area of support	Animal health	Animal health	Farmer assistance	Farmer assistance	Documentation, animal health
Solution approach	Determine the lying times, aggregate information on lying time and lying-down process	Tracking animal locations and activities in the barn, measuring temperature and humidity	To do list, anonymized recognition and registration of task fulfilment, visual representation of completed activities	Animal tracking, barn evaluation to support task management, temperature control or health care issues	Interfaces to existing systems, track individual animals, aggregate herd health, manual entry of relevant data if necessary, contact to veterinarians for emergencies
Output	Dashboard with lying times and duration	Dashboard showing heat stress indicators	Record of work activities, entry in database, visualization for the user	Dashboard showing live position of animals, warning in case of abnormal events	Dashboard, digital health record for the individual animal/herd, warning system
AI functions	Cow detection, pose estimation, pose classification, ergonomic analysis and anomaly detection of lying behaviour, box detection, box status classification	Cow tracking and identification, activity classification, anomaly detection of activity patterns, classification of heat stress behaviour, weather data analysis, heat stress prediction	Human pose-estimation, anonymization, ergonomic analysis during tasks, recognition of performed tasks, time analysis, classification of human-animal-interaction	Cow detection and tracking, cow identification, activity classification, anomaly detection of activity patterns, herd interaction recognition, anomaly detection of herd interaction	Ergonomic analysis of cow movement, anomaly detection of activity patterns, anomaly detection of health parameters, illness prediction

Tab. 2: Use case descriptions

5 Designing a holistic smart dairy farming system

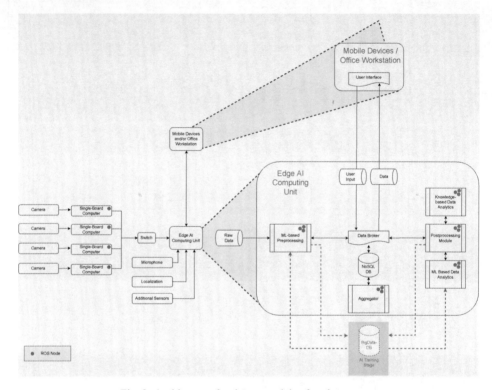

Fig. 2: Architecture for the smart dairy farming system

The derived architecture of our holistic smart dairy farming system divides itself into hardware and software components. Figure 2 gives an overview of the system, where hardware components can be seen on the left side of the figure and software components are depicted in relation to the corresponding hardware parts in the right of the figure. Overall communication between components will be realised with the Robot Operating System (ROS). Below, first the software and then the hardware components of the architecture are described in detail.

In terms of software, the first module of our ROS-based implementation is the Machine-Learning-based pre-processing, consisting of several ROS-nodes used for the pre-processing of raw input data of all sensors. This includes the sensor integration of the used sensors, Machine Learning algorithms for cow detection and tracking as well as cow identification, activity classification of cows, box condition classification, pose estimation of animals and humans as well as tracking human-cow and cow-cow interaction. The refined information generated by the Machine-Learning-based pre-processing will be passed over to a data broker handling all information flows of the edge AI computing unit. The data broker administrates communication with a NoSQL database, a post-processing module, and a user interface. Incoming information is stored in the NoSQL database, and requests from the user interface are followed by the provision of relevant information stored in the database. An aggregator module is continuously running on the data stored in the database and provides temporal aggregation. For example, a summary of information on the position of animals resulting in overall length of stay by the drinking trough, walkways, lying boxes and feeding table for different time intervals like days, weeks, or months. The post-processing module administers both the knowledge-based data analytics and Machine-Learning-based data analytics. The post-processing is responsible for all data analytics on refined data relying on the knowledge-based data analytics for expert knowledge, and on Machine-Learning-based data analytics for predictions or anomaly detections. While analytics of lying times of specific cows or the whole herd would be compared with desired lying times for cows in the knowledge base, an anomaly detection of lying times would be conducted in the Machine-Learning-based data analytics. As no raw data is stored in the NoSQL database, a second database is needed for the training stage of all Machine Learning algorithms. The big data database is depicted in light grey in Figure 2 to illustrate that it will not be part of the operative smart dairy farming system but rather be used for training purposes. The Flutter-based user interface will be able to run on any mobile or stationary device the user chooses, offering the opportunity to use the system while walking through the barn or from a desktop PC sitting in the office.

In terms of hardware, the project utilizes the Intel RealSense D455 Depth Camera to obtain a live picture stream of red, green, blue and depth (RGB-D) information in the barn. It captures RGB images at a resolution up to 1280 x 800 at a frame rate of max. 30 frames per second (fps). The depth data has a resolution of 1280 x 700 and a frame rate of max. 90 fps. It is created by an infrared emitter, which projects a pattern into the barn. Thereby, the stereoscopic depth camera can reconstruct a depth image. The RealSense vision processor D4 merges the RGB and depth images and provides data via a SuperSpeed USB 3.1 interface. For high data rates, the USB 3.1 specifies cable lengths up to 3m or max. 5m. Active extension cables or optical USB extension cables can overcome this limitation but need an energy supply at the devices' end of the USB cable i.e., at the cameras in the barn. Due to deployment limitations in the barns, which are constantly populated with living cattle, the project aims at using low-voltage installation. Therefore, we decided on the distribution of camera nodes via Power over Ethernet (PoE+ IEEE 802.3at) connection, which provides a low voltage, 48V/25W energy provision whilst enabling gigabit ethernet connection. For integration into the Architecture, every camera node is equipped with a Raspberry Pi 4 single-board computer (SBC), which enables the provision of the USB-based camera functionality in the network [Op22]. However, this solution results in a reduction of available RGB-D picture resolutions or a reduction of fps due to bandwidth limitations. Since the project is not aiming at high-speed object detection and since the cattle are moving at a limited speed, a framerate reduction seems feasible. For installation purposes, we developed a parameterized 3D-model that can be printed via fused deposition modelling (FDM) to provide a long-term reliable mount of the camera, a Power over Ethernet splitter and the SBC. It is designed in OpenSCAD and accepts parameters for camera position, pitch, roll and azimuth. Thereby, a customized mount can be printed after measuring this parameter set and cameras can be installed securely in any position. In addition to the image data, further heterogeneous sensors are used in the project. In particular, the localization of individual animals is provided by a bluetooth (BT) 5.1 angle of arrival (AoA) indoor localization solution. Depending on the size of the barn, a set of 4-8 BT AoA antennas is installed to track collar-mounted tracking tags that provide the location of individually identified cattle as a ground truth for the AI. Distributed microphones are used to monitor the noise level and to identify individual cattle sounds that may support the detection of situations like heat stress. To enable a holistic sensor fusion, we aim to develop interfaces to existing sensors and other technology in the barns, e.g., cooling fans, brushes, and milk robots. Ideally, this would include all available sensor information and result in a fully integrated assistance system.

6 Discussion and outlook

In order to address our research question – *How can a holistic smart dairy farming system be conceptualized?* – we selected a diverse set of dairy farming use cases, conducted expert interviews to analyze these use cases and subsequently developed a solution concept for an AI-based dairy farming system. This concept was derived through an iterative development process and illustrates the hardware and software architecture of the intended smart dairy farming system. The hardware architecture integrates different sensors ranging from cameras and microphones to localization tags and enables edge AI computing with an approach suitable to a barn. The software architecture consists of two main stages and is geared towards efficient data processing and combining both machine learning and expert knowledge. In stage one, raw sensor data is streamed and analyzed to obtain relevant metadata. Especially, computer vision techniques are utilized to extract structured data from images. For example, pose estimation is performed on images of cows during a lying-down process, and pose coordinates are saved. In stage two, high-level information and recommendations for action are derived from the obtained metadata. For example, machine learning can be used to recognize anomalies in lying-down behavior that might coincide with relevant issues such as lameness or unsuitable lying box conditions. On top of that, expert knowledge can be used to recognize issues in lying down time when certain stages of the lying down process exceed defined standards. Taking into account a set of diverse use cases enabled us to design a holistic concept for smart dairy farming systems. As opposed to optimizing a solution to an individual problem in dairy farming, this system is aiming to integrate multiple sensors and create a consolidated assistance system for farmers.

However, the objective of a holistic smart dairy farming system is accompanied by three major challenges. Firstly, the multi-sensor setting including depth cameras produces an extremely large amount of streaming data that needs to be handled. Analyzing such a large volume of image data through computer vision and integrating several camera perspectives requires efficient algorithms and sufficient computing power. Secondly, the process of multi-sensor integration itself is far from trivial [Zh18]. In terms of image data streams in our application scenario, cow movements must be tracked, poses estimated, and individual cows identified based on several cameras covering different areas of the barn, missing some parts of the barn entirely and overlapping on others. On top of that, the other sensor inputs such as microphones need to be integrated as well. Therefore, producing a consolidated set of metadata for the barn based on the sensor information is a crucial step in implementing an effective assistance system for the farmers. Thirdly, in order to fully deliver on the promise of a holistic smart dairy farming system, interfaces for the existing technical infrastructure already installed in the barn and software solutions already used by the farmer need to be established. Otherwise, farmers would still need to keep track of the unintegrated infrastructure by themselves and have to interact with a large number of applications. Tackling these practical challenges will be part of our future research and implementation process.

In the future, we plan to focus on the technical implementation as well as practical evaluation in an iterative process. The developed concept constitutes a blueprint for successively implementing individual functions that may each be utilized in multiple use cases. Naturally, implementation will start at stage one, i.e., extracting metadata and later advance to stage two when metadata streams are available for analysis. Initially, we will address the described use cases. In the long run, a smart dairy farming system would benefit from including an even broader range of use cases. In addition to the technical developments, there will be a continuous evaluation with the help of two farms using the provided solution and guiding its evolution. The application of the smart dairy farming system raises several research questions to be tackled in the future. For example, expert knowledge should not only be integrated into the system through domain standards translated into rules in the knowledge base. Ideally, farmers using the system and giving feedback on recommended actions or correcting false predictions would also have an impact on future Machine-Learning-based outputs. At this point, only few approaches to human-in-the-loop systems and feedback learning exist in the domain of dairy farming [Ta20]. On top of that, providing a personalised interaction for different farmers would be an important feature of the smart dairy farming system [MFH09]. As users might have varying experience levels in farming as well as with AI-based assistance systems, their needs for detailed information and their amount of time available when interacting with the system might differ. Another success factor of smart dairy farming systems is user acceptance. This might be impacted by numerous design choices and needs to be prioritized in the development process. For example, providing the farmers with relevant and easily understandable explanations for the AI-based recommendations and predictions might help to reduce negative attitudes towards AI and improve farmers' decision-making process [Ha22]. On top of that, the interviews revealed that installing cameras in the barn might negatively impact farmers acceptance as this could be interpreted as a measure of surveillance. Thus, human-centered strategies are necessary that ensure privacy and still enable the extraction of data used to help the farmers manage their tasks. These topics are important areas of research we will take into account during the further development of our smart dairy farming system.

Acknowledgements: The project is supported by funds of the Federal Ministry of Food and Agriculture (BMEL) based on a decision of the Parliament of the Federal Republic of Germany. The Federal Office for Agriculture and Food (BLE) provides coordinating support for artificial intelligence (AI) in agriculture as funding organisation, grant number 28DK110A20.

Bibliography

[Be21]   Becker, C. A.; Aghalari, A.; Marufuzzaman, M.; Stone, A. E.: Predicting dairy cattle heat stress using machine learning techniques. Journal of dairy science, 104(1), p. 501-524, 2021.

[By19]   Byabazaire, J.; Olariu, C.; Taneja, M.; Davy, A.: Lameness Detection as a Service: Application of Machine Learning to an Internet of Cattle. In: 2019 16th IEEE Annual Consumer Communications & Networking Conference (CCNC), p. 1-6, 2019.

[Ca08]   Cangar, Ö.; Leroy, T.; Guarino, M.; Vranken, E.; Fallon, R.; Lenehan, J.; Mee, J.; Berckmans, D.: Automatic real-time monitoring of locomotion and posture behaviour of pregnant cows prior to calving using online image analysis. Computers and electronics in agriculture, 64(1), p. 53-60, 2008.

[Gu19]   Guo, Y.; Zhang, Z.; He, D.; Niu, J.; Tan, Y.: Detection of cow mounting behavior using region geometry and optical flow characteristics. Computers and Electronics in Agriculture, 163, p. 104828, 2019.

[HKV22] Hajnal, É.; Kovács, L.; Vakulya, G.: Dairy Cattle Rumen Bolus Developments with Special Regard to the Applicable Artificial Intelligence (AI) Methods. Sensors, 22(18), p. 6812, 2022.

[Ha22]   Harada, I.; Fauvel, K.; Guyet, T.; Masson, V.; Termier, A.; Faverdin, P.: XPM: An explainable-by-design pattern-based estrus detection approach to improve resource use in dairy farms. In: Proceedings of the 36th AAAI Conference on Artificial Intelligence, 2022.

[Ka22]   Kammler, P.; Heidemann, C.; Lingemann, K.; Morisse, K.: Digitaler Experte im Stall: ein Expertensystem am Beispiel des Eutergesundheitsmanagements. In: 42. GIL-Jahrestagung, Künstliche Intelligenz in der Agrar-und Ernährungswirtschaft, 2022.

[KC18]   Kusakunniran, W.; Chaiviroonjaroen, T.: Automatic cattle identification based on multi-channel LBP on muzzle images. In (IEEE): 2018 International Conference on Sustainable Information Engineering and Technology (SIET), p. 1-5, 2018.

[Ko13]   Kolstrup, C. L.; Kallioniemi, M.; Lundqvist, P.; Kymäläinen, H.; Stallones, L.; Brumby, S.: International Perspectives on Psychosocial Working Conditions, Mental Health, and Stress of Dairy Farm Operators. Journal of Agromedicine, 18:3, p. 244-255, 2013.

[La21]   Lasser, J.; Matzhold, C.; Egger-Danner, C.; Fuerst-Waltl, B.; Steininger, F.; Wittek, T.; Klimek, P.: Integrating diverse data sources to predict disease risk in dairy cattle—a machine learning approach. Journal of Animal Science, 99(11), 2021.

[Li20]	Liseune, A.; Salamone, M.; Van den Poel, D.; Van Ranst, B.; Hostens, M.: Leveraging latent representations for milk yield prediction and interpolation using deep learning. Computers and Electronics in Agriculture, 175, p. 105600, 2020.
[MFH09]	Măruşter, L.; Faber, N. R.; Haren, R. J. V.: Personalization for specific users: designing decision support systems to support stimulating learning environments. In: Symposium on Human Interface, pp. 660-668, 2009.
[Ma19]	Mattachini, G.; Pompe, J.; Finzi, A.; Tullo, E.; Riva, E.; Provolo, G.: Effects of feeding frequency on the lying behavior of dairy cows in a loose housing with automatic feeding and milking system. Animals, 9(4), p. 121, 2019.
[Op22]	Open-Source Ethernet Networking for Intel RealSense Depth Cameras, https://dev.intelrealsense.com/docs/open-source-ethernet-networking-for-intel-realsense-depth-cameras, Stand: 26.10.2022.
[PF18]	Pastell, M.; Frondelius, L.: A hidden Markov model to estimate the time dairy cows spend in feeder based on indoor positioning data. Computers and Electronics in Agriculture, 152, p. 182-185, 2018.
[Po13]	Porto, S. M.; Arcidiacono, C.; Anguzza, U.; Cascone, G.: A computer vision-based system for the automatic detection of lying behaviour of dairy cows in free-stall barns. Biosystems Engineering, 115(2), p. 184-194, 2013.
[Ru20]	Ruchay, A.; Kober, V.; Dorofeev, K.; Kolpakov, V.; Miroshnikov, S.: Accurate body measurement of live cattle using three depth cameras and non-rigid 3-D shape recovery. Computers and Electronics in Agriculture, 179, p. 105821, 2020.
[SK20]	Salau, J.; Krieter, J.: Instance segmentation with Mask R-CNN applied to loose-housed dairy cows in a multi-camera setting. Animals, 10(12), p. 2402, 2020.
[SK21]	Salau, J.; Krieter, J.: Predicting use of resources by dairy cows using time series. Biosystems Engineering, 205, p. 146-151, 2021.
[So19]	Song, X.; van der Tol, P. P. J.; Koerkamp, P. G.; Bokkers, E. A. M.: Hot topic: Automated assessment of reticulo-ruminal motility in dairy cows using 3-dimensional vision. Journal of dairy science, 102(10), p. 9076-9081, 2019.
[Ta20]	Taneja, M.; Byabazaire, J.; Jalodia, N.; Davy, A.; Olariu, C.; Malone, P.: Machine learning based fog computing assisted data-driven approach for early lameness detection in dairy cattle. Computers and Electronics in Agriculture, 171, p. 105286, 2020.
[Ta21]	Tassinari, P.; Bovo, M.; Benni, S.; Franzoni, S.; Poggi, M.; Mammi, L. M. E.; Mattoccia, S.; Di Stefano, L.; Bonora, F.; Barbaresi, A.; Santolini, E.; Torreggiani, D.: A computer vision approach based on deep learning for the detection of dairy cows in free stall barn. Computers and Electronics in Agriculture, 182, p. 106030, 2021.
[Vo09]	Von Keyserlingk, M. A. G.; Rushen, J.; de Passillé, A. M.; Weary, D. M.: Invited review: The welfare of dairy cattle—Key concepts and the role of science. Journal of dairy science, 92(9), p. 4101-4111, 2009.

[We22]   Weng, Z.; Meng, F.; Liu, S.; Zhang, Y.; Zheng, Z.; Gong, C.: Cattle face recognition based on a Two-Branch convolutional neural network. Computers and Electronics in Agriculture, 196, p. 106871, 2022.

[We03]   West, J. W.: Effects of heat-stress on production in dairy cattle. Journal of dairy science, 86(6), p. 2131-2144, 2003.

[ZWV19] Zambelis, A.; Wolfe, T.; Vasseur, E.: Validation of an ear-tag accelerometer to identify feeding and activity behaviors of tiestall-housed dairy cattle. Journal of dairy science, 102(5), p. 4536-4540, 2019.

[Zh18]   Zhang, L.; Xie, Y.; Xidao, L.; Zhang, X.: Multi-source heterogeneous data fusion. In: 2018 International conference on artificial intelligence and big data (ICAIBD), p. 47-51, 2018.

Towards crop yield prediction using Automated Machine Learning

Jonathan Heil[1], Juan Manuel Valencia[1] and Anthony Stein[1]

Abstract: Recently, several Machine Learning models for crop yield prediction have been introduced in literature. The models differ in the underlying methodological approaches and show variations in the temporal and spatial resolution of the databases. For the creation of the models, a deep understanding of Machine Learning is required. Therefore, Automated Machine Learning, which aims to automate the creation process of Machine Learning models, offers a promising solution as an easy entry point in Machine Learning for crop yield prediction to non-professionals. Based on publicly available data for weather, phenological and yield observations, in this work, we created a dataset for winter wheat and winter barley on Germany's regional districts level. Furthermore, an initial evaluation of four state of the art Automated Machine Learning frameworks and three baseline models has been conducted. The results showed almost always significantly better performance of models created by Automated Machine Learning.

Keywords: crop yield prediction, Automated Machine Learning, open source data, winter wheat, winter barley

1 Introduction

The prediction of crop yields can play an important role to prevent yield failures and therefore contributes to the second Sustainable Development Goal "Zero Hunger" of the United Nations [Un15]. For instance, farmers can make use of crop yield predictions as a decision support tool to recognise potential losses and take actions to save the harvest [Ru19]. Furthermore, an accurate prediction of crop yields enables the different levels in the value chain to react to potential yield shortages or bumper crops, for example with marketing activities [Sh20]. Moreover, crop yield predictions also serve for researchers to examine influential factors such as weather conditions on crop yields [We20]. Several Machine Learning models have been introduced for the prediction of crop yields [vKC20]. The models vary in their underlying methodological approaches as well as the used data, e.g. Convolutional Neural Networks [Sr22] or Random Forest models [Vo19], weather station data [We20] or satellite images [Pe22]. However, strong expertise in Machine Learning and a deep understanding of the data is required to build reliable models. Accordingly, a high amount of manual effort for constructing a crop yield prediction model is needed. Therefore, Automated Machine Learning (AutoML) is a suitable solution to overcome the problems of expertise and time-consuming model construction. The idea

---

[1] University of Hohenheim, Department of Artificial Intelligence in Agricultural Engineering, Garbenstraße 9, 70599 Stuttgart, jonathan.heil@uni-hohenheim.de; juanmanuel.valenciapineda@uni-hohenheim.de, anthony.stein@uni-hohenheim.de

behind AutoML is to automate the processes to build a Machine Learning model [Fe20]. This involves typical steps in the Machine Learning process, such as preprocessing of the data, model selection or the optimization of hyperparameters. AutoML frameworks showed promising results in benchmark tests on classification and regression problems [Er20].

The heterogeneous and sophisticated research area of crop yield prediction exposes as a well-suited use case for AutoML: (1) Open access databases for yield observations [St22], climate data [De22b; De22a] and satellite images [Pe22] are available. (2) Researchers pursue different aims in their studies. Some are using the Machine Learning models to search for influential factors on crop yields [We20], others try to improve the models' prediction accuracies [Sr22]. AutoML could help the researchers without a deep knowledge in Machine Learning to build prediction models and thereby to focus on their specific research task [Er20]. In addition, researchers with sufficient knowledge of Machine Learning can build prediction models for benchmarking or even improving their own models by means of AutoML. But not only researchers will profit. If AutoML exposes as an easy and well performing entry point for applying Machine Learning by non-professionals, farmers in the first place without a deep knowledge in Machine Learning will be enabled to build advanced prediction models. Therefore, the aim of this study is to reveal the potential and suitability of AutoML when applied to crop yield prediction. The next chapter provides an overview of crop yield prediction models using Machine Learning. Following, the data acquisition process, the data analyzation and the investigated AutoML methods are described in detail. The experimental setup and the results are presented in the fourth chapter and discussed in chapter five. Finally, we draw a conclusion in the last chapter.

2 Crop yield prediction using Machine Learning

The number of publications about the prediction of crop yields using Machine Learning increased since 2013 with a peak in 2018 [vKC20]. Subsequently, we describe several studies, subdivided in Shallow Learning and Deep Learning approaches.

Shallow Learning approaches: A global prediction of yields for spring wheat, maize, soybeans and rice was conducted in [Vo19]. The data set combined yield observations and climate data from 1961 to 2008. A special focus was on climate extremes such as anomalies in temperature and precipitation. A Random Forest model served for the prediction of the crop yields. A crop yield prediction with focus on the influence of weather, soil and phenological stages was carried out in [We20]. A crop modelling approach as well as a Support Vector Machine were implemented for the prediction task. The data set comprises on crop yield observations, phenological phases, weather data and soil structures on a scale of the regional districts of Germany in the period from 1998 to 2018. The authors extracted the years with the highest yield losses and analysed potential factors causing the deficits. The climatic features seem to have an impact on yield losses, especially in the Support Vector Machine. Nevertheless, some years showed an overall decline of yields, whereas in other years the yields varied depending on the crops and regions. In [Ka20], Sentinel 2 [EE22] data were used to calculate several Vegetation Indices such as Normalized Difference Vegetation Index and Enhanced Vegetation Index. The crop yields were predicted with the indices using an Ordinary Least Squares Regression. Likewise, vegetation indices by means of Sentinel 2 data were calculated and combined with soil data for the yield prediction of soybeans for Austria in [Pe22]. Afterwards five different models, e.g. a Random Forest model and a Support Vector Machine, were trained to predict the yields. A Stochastic Gradient Descent model showed the lowest Mean Absolute Errors and Root Mean Squared Errors. A crop yield prediction for Algeria was carried out in [Me21]. The authors used preprocessed satellite data from the Anomaly Hotspots of Agricultural Production program [Re17]. The yield observations were provided by the agricultural ministry of Algeria. For the prediction task, several Machine Learning models were tested against two non-ML benchmarks. The first benchmark stated a congruence between the yield for a specific county and the yield mean of all counties. The second benchmark model based on a linear correlation between the Normalized Difference Vegetation Index and the yield. The prediction accuracy of the Machine Learning models varied during the vegetation period and, especially in the beginning of the year, the difference in the prediction accuracy between the Machine Learning models and the first benchmark model were negligible.

Deep Learning approaches: In [KWA19], a combination of a Convolutional Neural Network and a Recurrent Neural Network is introduced for the prediction of corn and soybean yields within the spatial area of the US-Corn Belt. The data set consisted of weather data, soil conditions, agricultural treatments and yield observations from 1980 to 2018. The presented approach outperformed the baseline models significantly. Another Deep Learning approach on base of genotype, weather, soil and yield data is presented in [KW19]. The authors predicted the yield potentials for different corn hybrids. Therefore, two Neural Networks were trained. The first Neural network served for the prediction of the yield of all hybrid crops at different locations, the second Neural Network was specified for the yield prediction of one particular corn hybrid. The yield potentials of the different corn hybrids were estimated by the difference of the results from the two Neural Networks. In [NNL19], multispectral and RGB images of barley and wheat were taken at different dates in the vegetation period. The yield data was captured during the harvest with a sensor mounted at the harvest combine. The authors discussed various settings for the architecture of a Convolutional Neural Network and stuck to already implemented Convolutional Neural Networks such as in [KSH17]. Predictions based on RGB images showed a lower Mean Absolute Errors than predictions based on multispectral images. In [Ma20], an unmanned aerial vehicle was equipped with multispectral, panchromatic and thermal sensors. The features of the multimodal data were fused using a Deep Neural Network. The crop yields were predicted with another Deep Neural Network and compared with baseline models.

3 Materials and methods

3.1 Data acquisition

The dataset created in this work is inspired by [We20], where open access data were used to predict crop yields and examine influential factors on crop yield losses. The data stems from two main providers: The federal and state statistical offices, specifically from "Regionaldatenbank Deutschland" [St22], and the DWD German Weather Service [De22a; De22b]. The regional database contains information for yearly crop yields in dt/ha of the two selected crops winter wheat and winter barley and a spatial scale corresponding to the regional districts of Germany, e.g. "Landkreis Osnabrück". The selected time period ranged from 1999 to 2021. Two types of stations of the DWD were used: *weather stations* [De22a] and *phenological stations* [De22b]. The weather database provides historical observations of more than 1000 stations distributed all over Germany. Nevertheless, we used those stations (853) reporting data within the time period from 1999 to 2021. Six weather variables with daily resolution were selected: maximum temperature (°C), minimum temperature (°C), relative humidity (%), sunshine duration (hrs), wind speed (m/s) and precipitation (mm). The phenological stations were a total of 6503 and after filtering the specified time period, 1809 were selected for winter wheat and 1833 for winter barley. These stations provide the day of the year (DOY) for BBCH-stages which is referred as Phase ID.

For obtaining the final dataset for crop yield, a preprocessing step has been conducted. First, we considered only yields corresponding to the deeper division level in the regional database, i.e. for counties (or districts), and avoiding aggregated information present in the data in a city, state or national level. A five-digit code represents the district depth, with the first two digits corresponding to the state number, the next one the government district and the last two digits to the district number. A total of 471 districts were available. In sum 17.6% of the data was missing for the 23 years and the two selected crops. For dealing with missing values we applied two operations. Initially, an average of the surrounding districts that belong to the same government district and to the same year has been used to impute the missing values. This reduced the percentage of missing data to 5%. Second, the mean historical yield value per district was used to fill those remaining gaps, leaving 0.28% of missing values, which correspond to two districts that did not contain information, and therefore were removed from the final dataset.

For the case of weather data, after filtering the recording time range that fits the crop yield data, we resampled the data with a seven days (weekly) average for all the variables, except for precipitation, in which a weekly sum was performed. The 52nd week was calculated with eight or nine days to cover the whole 365 or 366 days of the year, depending on whether it was a leap year or not. Every week of each variable equals a different feature for the dataset. The number of official districts can change depending on the year of their definition. Therefore, we used a shapefile with the districts division of 2021 [Op22], representing the administrative areas within Germany [Bu22]. The total number of districts in the shapefile was 401. Using the metadata information of the DWD weather stations, the latitude and longitude of the selected weather stations were obtained. Then, we took the shapefile and assigned each weather station to a district. 347 districts had at least one weather station, and from the 853 stations, 842 were assign to a district. Some districts were assigned several stations. Four of the eleven stations, that were not assigned to a district, were located on the North Sea and therefore removed. The remaining stations were not assigned due to uncertainties of the order of decimals in the definition of the latitude and longitude of the stations with respect to the georeferencing of the districts shapes, or vice versa, resulting in the stations being at the boundary of a district. Therefore, the distance method of Pythons Geopandas module was used to assign them to the closest shape [Ke22]. Also, a mean operation was applied to those districts with more than one station to obtain a final value per district.

A similar process was carried out to assign the phenological stations with the same shapefile. Phenological stations are ascribed districts wherein volunteer workers observe BBCH-stages of crops. The metadata did not contain all the stations that were in the winter wheat and winter barley datasets. A total of 1852 stations were available in the winter barley dataset, 19 were not found in the metadata, and 3 were not assigned to any district. For winter barley, 349 districts had at least one phenological station. In the case of winter wheat, 1830 stations were available but 21 were not included in the metadata, and 3 not assigned into a district. 352 districts had at least one phenological station for winter wheat. Finally, we joined the crop yield observations with the weather and phenological datasets. The weather stations had also missing values, at least one missing value was found in approximately 55% of the weather dataset, meaning that at least one week of any variable did not have a recorded value. The phenological data for winter barley presented 26% of all rows with missing values, which accounts for the years in specific districts where no phenological data was recorded, while 5% contained at least one missing phase ID. For winter wheat 25% of the data was missing, and 7% had at least one missing value. Therefore, a five-year-mean value for each feature of the district was calculated for imputing the missing values to cover the regional characteristics without an overweighting of influences by climate change.

3.2   Data description

The yearly mean yield values on national scale for winter wheat oscillate around 62 dt/ha and 83 dt/ha, while for winter barley they vary between 51 dt/ha and 75 dt/ha. Even if there have been some years with a marked decrease in the production of both crops (e.g. 2003, 2007, 2011, 2018), the general trend is positive. The regression slope for winter wheat is less distinct with a value of 0.3, while the winter barley has shown a higher increase through the years with a slope of 0.48. The mean yield during this 23-years period is approximately 73 dt/ha for winter wheat and 65 dt/ha for winter barley, respectively. The mean temperature values range between 8 degree Celsius and 10.7 degree Celsius, showing with a minimum in 2010 and a maximum in 2018. The mean temperature does not exhibit a significant trend, with magnitude of 0.02 in the slope of the regression line. For the case of average precipitation over Germany, the values oscillate between 350 mm and 670 mm. The global minimum occurred in 2018. However, another significant local minimum happened in 2003. The maximum mean precipitation value occurred in 2002. Opposite to temperature, the trend for precipitation is evident, showing a decrease during the last two decades. The occurrence of the phenological stages for winter wheat and winter barley were time-displaced. For winter wheat the sowing period (phase 10) starts later (277-283) than for winter barley (260-267). Consequently, the rest of the stages also appear later. If the sowing happened later in the year, the rest of the stages are deferred as well and vice versa. This is the case for years like 2001, 2007, 2013 or 2014 in winter barley crops. The years 2003 and 2018 show the opposite behaviour for winter barley, having an earlier sowing period and nevertheless the steam elongation stage occurred later.

3.3 Automated Machine Learning methods

In agricultural sciences, few experiments with AutoML have been conducted, e.g. for the identification of weeds [Es21] or the identification of pest aphid species [Ha19]. AutoML aims to automate tedious tasks in the construction and optimization of Machine Learning models, e.g. the preprocessing of data, the selection of suitable models or the optimization of hyperparameters. Several frameworks have been introduced offering an end-to-end-solution for applying Machine Learning. Therefore, we compared four different state of the art AutoML frameworks: AutoGluon, Auto-sklearn, H2O and TPOT. For this study we made use of the 2020 introduced AutoGluon Tabular in the version 0.5.2 [Er20]. AutoGluon Tabular includes datatype specific preprocessing and an ensemble method with stacking of multiple layers which are trained sequentially. TPOT relies on the scikit-learn package and makes use of genetic programming for their algorithm and hyperparameter optimization [Ol16]. We used the version 0.11.7. Auto-sklearn was first introduced in 2015 [Fe19]. Meanwhile, an updated version with improvements, for example in the model selection process, is available [Fe20]. For our experiments, we used the currently latest version 0.15.0 [Ma22]. Auto-sklearn is based on Bayesian optimization methods. The framework provides 15 different models from the Python package scikit-learn. Auto-sklearn includes Meta Learning based on meta-features, which are computed for every input dataset. Moreover, the ensemble building process is conducted by the ensemble selection method [Fe19]. H2O AutoML is available since 2017 [LP20]. The H2O AutoML framework draws on models from H2O, which is a Java-based, in-memory machine learning platform [H222]. H2O makes use of fast random search for their algorithm selection and hyperparameter optimization. For our experiments, we used the currently latest version 3.38.0.1. All four frameworks have in common to offer different configuration parameters, for example for excluding specific machine learning models.

4 Experiments

4.1 Experimental setup

As we stated in the motivation that AutoML opens the opportunity to quickly construct Machine Learning models without the lengthy and knowledge intensive process of tuning, the configuration parameters of all AutoML frameworks have been left in the default settings with one exception. We restricted the time limit for training to 30 minutes per run due to limited resources. The experiments were carried out on a notebook equipped with an AMD Ryzen 9 5900HX CPU, 32 GB RAM and a NVIDIA GeForce RTX 3080 GPU. The AutoML frameworks investigated in this study make use of stochastic algorithms for the inner optimization process. Therefore, 30 runs for every framework per dataset were conducted to produce statistical expressive results. The datasets winter wheat and winter barley were split into a training set and a testing set. The AutoML frameworks include validation steps such as k-fold cross validation. Therefore, a separate validation set was not necessary. For training, the years from 1999 to 2018 were used. The hold-out periods from 2019 to 2021 built the testing set. For benchmark models, we followed the work of [Sr22], which published a crop yield prediction on an equal dataset [We20]. Therefore, we built a Random Forest model (RF), a Support Vector Regression model (SVR) as well as a Deep Neural Network (DNN) with the same hyperparameters as in [Sr22]. Other models, such as in the second chapter presented, showed too big differences in the time periods, the crop types, the research areas, the data and the evaluation to act as benchmark. For evaluating the models, we computed the metrics Root Mean Squared Error (RMSE), Mean Absolute Error (MAE) and the Concordance Correlation Coefficient (CCC). The results were tested on statistical significance by means of an analysis of variance and pairwise comparisons with f-tests. Few results were not normally distributed. Therefore, an additional Friedman-test and pairwise comparisons with Mann-Whitney-U-tests were conducted. The significance level was set to 0.05.

4.2 Results

In Tab. 1, the mean values over 30 runs of the evaluation metrics based on the predictions for the winter wheat testing dataset are presented. The small letters indicate whether the mean values for all 30 runs had significant differences (different small letters column-wise) or not (same small letters column-wise). The analysis of variance and the Friedman-test stated that within the evaluation metrics are significant differences. The SVR produced with an average RMSE of 10.90 and an average MAE of 8.60 the worst predictions. The CCC values for SVR were close to zero, so we rounded them. The lowest average RMSE and average MAE was achieved by H2O. In the pairwise comparison to the other three AutoML frameworks, H2O showed significantly lower RMSE and MAE values. Whereas the highest average CCC occurred for AutoGluon. The pairwise comparison confirmed, that AutoGluon has a significantly higher CCC than Auto-sklearn, H2O and TPOT.

Framework/Model	RMSE (+/- 1SD)	MAE (+/- 1SD)	CCC (+/- 1SD)
AutoGluon	8.88^a (+/- 0.24)	7.04^a (+/- 0.23)	**0.65^a (+/- 0.02)**
Auto-sklearn	8.92^a (+/- 0.33)	7.00^a (+/- 0.32)	0.50^b (+/- 0.03)
H2O	**8.59^b (+/- 0.12)**	**6.68^b (+/- 0.10)**	0.52^c (+/- 0.02)
TPOT	9.34^c (+/- 0.62)	7.28^a (+/- 0.60)	0.54^d (+/- 0.05)
Benchmark RF	9.63^d (+/- 0.04)	7.55^c (+/- 0.04)	0.28^e (+/- 0.01)
Benchmark SVR	10.90^e (+/- 0.02)	8.60^d (+/- 0.02)	0.00^f (+/- 0.00)
Benchmark DNN	10.16^f (+/- 0.68)	8.01^e (+/- 0.64)	0.43^d (+/- 0.04)

Tab. 1: Means of the evaluation metrics of all 30 runs based on the winter wheat testing dataset

The average evaluation metrics for the predictions based on the winter barley training dataset are displayed in Tab. 2. The two benchmark models SVR and DNN showed again a significant difference to the AutoML frameworks. The benchmark SVR model had the highest average RMSE and average MAE as well as the lowest CCC. In the pairwise comparison, the MAE values did not significantly differ between RF and Auto-sklearn. The lowest RMSE and MAE values as well as the highest CCC were provided by H2O.

Framework/Model	RMSE (+/- 1SD)	MAE (+/- 1SD)	CCC (+/- 1SD)
AutoGluon	10.22^a (+/- 0.29)	8.40^a (+/- 0.29)	0.41^a (+/- 0.02)
Auto-sklearn	10.44^b (+/- 0.44)	8.57^{ab} (+/- 0.46)	0.39^b (+/- 0.04)
H2O	**9.57^c (+/- 0.15)**	**7.70^c (+/- 0.15)**	**0.43^c (+/- 0.03)**
TPOT	10.07^a (+/- 0.33)	8.11^d (+/- 0.34)	0.32^d (+/- 0.05)
Benchmark RF	10.63^d (+/- 0.06)	8.60^b (+/- 0.06)	0.20^e (+/- 0.01)
Benchmark SVR	12.49^e (+/- 0.03)	10.13^e (+/- 0.03)	0.00^f (+/- 0.00)
Benchmark DNN	12.03^f (+/- 0.63)	9.81^f (+/- 0.58)	0.31^d (+/- 0.03)

Tab. 2: Means of the evaluation metrics of all 30 runs based on the winter barley testing dataset

5 Discussion

The results show significant differences in the evaluation metrics of the different AutoML frameworks for both datasets. Especially H2O performed well on the evaluation metrics RMSE and MAE. A reason for the superior results of H2O is deemed to the internally used and automated algorithm and hyperparameter selection process. H2O is based on a fast random search method [H222]. Auto-sklearn uses Bayesian Optimization and Meta-Learning [Fe19], TPOT an evolutionary method for the algorithm and hyperparameter selection process [Ol16]. The experiments with AutoGluon did not have a hyperparameter optimization because it is disabled in the default settings [Er20]. AutoGluon reached for winter wheat the highest CCC between the predicted and true values for the yield. In Fig. 1, the distribution of the true and predicted yields by H2O and AutoGluon for winter barley are displayed. Even though there was a significant difference in the pairwise comparison between H2O and AutoGluon for the CCC, the visual difference is not easy to recognize.

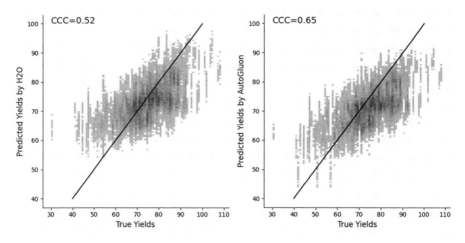

Fig. 1: Distribution of true and by H2O (l.) and AutoGluon (r.) predicted yields for wheat

A comparison with prediction results of the above-mentioned publications in the second chapter is difficult to realize because of differences in the time periods, the crop types, the regional areas, the data types and structures as well as the evaluations of the models. The experimental setup with a 30-minute time limit only delivers a first indication. Therefore, further experiments with a wider range of time limits should be examined. As the frameworks base on different algorithm selection and hyperparameter optimization processes, the prediction results could vary on various run time limits. Additionally, the AutoML frameworks offer different configuration parameters for adjusting. In this study we did not change the default settings to examine an off-the-shelf usage of AutoML for non-professionals in Machine Learning. Further experiments with different settings of the configuration parameters are worth considering. The benchmark models revealed almost for every evaluation metric a significantly inferior result than the AutoML frameworks. Due to the lack of knowledge about the detailed preprocessing steps of the database in [Sr22], where we extracted the hyperparameters of the benchmark models, it is expectable that the benchmark models will have problems to fit our datasets. Surprisingly, the MAE for the predictions on the winter barley dataset did not significantly vary between RF and Auto-sklearn. Although we used the same initial data as in [Sr22], the preprocessing of the data captured a high amount of manual effort due to missing values, discrepancies in the regional districts compared to the third level of the nomenclature of territorial units for statistics (NUTS-3), which are used in [Sr22], and the assignment of the weather stations data to the corresponding districts. Therefore, we decided to elaborate on the data acquisition part in detail. The section about related work on crop yield prediction using Machine Learning exposed that several more open access databases, such as satellite images [Pe22], are available for crop yield prediction. For further studies these databases could serve for experiments with AutoML frameworks.

6 Conclusion

The aim of this work was an initial investigation of the suitability of AutoML for crop yield prediction. Thus, we created a dataset with winter wheat and winter barley yields, weather data and phenological data. Subsequently, we predicted the crop yields by means of four AutoML frameworks and three benchmark models. The experimental results showed a significantly improved performance in terms of RMSE, MAE and CCC for AutoML methods in comparison to hand-tuned RF, SVR and DNN models. There are two main contributions this study reveals: (1) AutoML can offer an easy entry point for the application of Machine Learning in crop yield prediction. But configuration parameters, such as the restriction of the runtime, have to be taken in consideration. Therefore, further experiments with changes in the configuration parameters are worth considering. (2) The data acquisition and preprocessing part played an important role in this study. Several challenges with the data, such as many missing values or the assignment of the weather stations, occurred. Therefore, we offer in this study a detailed description how we created and manipulated the data.

Acknowledgements: The research was conducted within the scope of NaLamKI [Bo23] and funded by the Federal Ministry for Economics and Climate Action with the funding code 01MK21003[A-J].

Bibliography

[Bo23]   Bosse, S. et al.: Nachhaltige Landwirtschaft mittels Künstlicher Intelligenz – Ein plattformbasierter Ansatz für Forschung und Industrie. 43. GIL-Jahrestagung, 2023.

[Bu22]   Bundesamt für Kartographie und Geodäsie: Verwaltungsgebiete 1:250000. https://gdz.bkg.bund.de/index.php/default/verwaltungsgebiete-1-250-000-stand-01-01-vg250-01-01.html, accessed 19 Oct 2022.

[De22a] Deutscher Wetterdienst: Historische Klimadaten. https://opendata.dwd.de/climate_environment/CDC/observations_germany/climate/daily/kl/historical/, accessed 19 Oct 2022.

[De22b] Deutscher Wetterdienst: Phänologische Beobachtungen. https://opendata.dwd.de/climate_environment/CDC/observations_germany/phenology/annual_reporters/crops/historical/, accessed 19 Oct 2022.

[EE22]   European Union; European Space Agency: Copernicus Open Access Hub. https://scihub.copernicus.eu/, accessed 30 Oct 2022.

[Er20]   Erickson, N. et al.: AutoGluon-Tabular: Robust and Accurate AutoML for Structured Data, 2020.

[Es21]   Espejo-Garcia, B. et al.: Testing the Suitability of Automated Machine Learning for Weeds Identification. AI 1/2, pp. 34-47, 2021.

[Fe19]	Feurer, M. et al.: Auto-sklearn: Efficient and Robust Automated Machine Learning. In (Hutter, F.; Kotthoff, L.; Vanschoren, J. Eds.): Automated Machine Learning. Methods, Systems, Challenges. Springer, Cham, pp. 113-134, 2019.
[Fe20]	Feurer, M. et al.: Auto-Sklearn 2.0: Hands-free AutoML via Meta-Learning, 2020.
[H222]	H2O.ai: Welcome to H2O 3. https://docs.h2o.ai/h2o/latest-stable/h2o-docs/welcome.html, accessed 19 Oct 2022.
[Ha19]	Hayashi, M. et al.: Automated machine learning for identification of pest aphid species (Hemiptera: Aphididae). Applied Entomology and Zoology 4/54, pp. 487-490, 2019.
[Ke22]	Kelsey Jordahl et al.: geopandas/geopandas: v0.12.1. Zenodo, 2022.
[KSH17]	Krizhevsky, A.; Sutskever, I.; Hinton, G. E.: ImageNet classification with deep convolutional neural networks. Communications of the ACM 6/60, pp. 84-90, 2017.
[KW19]	Khaki, S.; Wang, L.: Crop Yield Prediction Using Deep Neural Networks. Frontiers in plant science 10, p. 621, 2019.
[KWA19]	Khaki, S.; Wang, L.; Archontoulis, S. V.: A CNN-RNN Framework for Crop Yield Prediction. Frontiers in plant science 10, p. 1750, 2019.
[LP20]	LeDell, E.; Poirier, S.: H2O AutoML: Scalable Automatic Machine Learning. 7th ICML Workshop on Automated Machine Learning, 2020.
[Ma20]	Maimaitijiang, M. et al.: Soybean yield prediction from UAV using multimodal data fusion and deep learning. Remote Sensing of Environment 237, p. 111599, 2020.
[Ma22]	Machine Learning Professorship Freiburg: auto-sklearn. https://automl.github.io/auto-sklearn/master/, accessed 19 Oct 2022.
[Me21]	Meroni, M. et al.: Yield forecasting with machine learning and small data: What gains for grains? Agricultural and Forest Meteorology 308-309, p. 108555, 2021.
[NNL19]	Nevavuori, P.; Narra, N.; Lipping, T.: Crop yield prediction with deep convolutional neural networks. Computers and Electronics in Agriculture 163, p. 104859, 2019.
[Ol16]	Olson, R. S. et al.: Automating Biomedical Data Science Through Tree-Based Pipeline Optimization. In (Squillero, G.; Burelli, P. Eds.): Applications of Evolutionary Computation. Springer International Publishing, Cham, pp. 123-137, 2016.
[Op22]	Opendatasoft: Shapefile Germany. https://data.opendatasoft.com/explore/dataset/georef-germany-

kreis%40public/export/?disjunctive.lan_code&disjunctive.lan_name&disj
unctive.krs_code&disjunctive.krs_name&disjunctive.krs_name_short&ref
ine.lan_code=04, accessed 19 Oct 2022.

[Pe22] Pejak, B. et al.: Soya Yield Prediction on a Within-Field Scale Using Machine Learning Models Trained on Sentinel-2 and Soil Data. Remote Sensing 9/14, p. 2256, 2022.

[Re17] Rembold, F. et al.: ASAP - Anomaly hot Spots of Agricultural Production. 9th International Workshop on the Analysis of Multitemporal Remote Sensing Images (MultiTemp), 2017.

[Ru19] Rupnik, R. et al.: AgroDSS: A decision support system for agriculture and farming. Computers and Electronics in Agriculture 161, pp. 260-271, 2019.

[Sh20] Sharma, R. et al.: A systematic literature review on machine learning applications for sustainable agriculture supply chain performance. Computers & Operations Research 119, p. 104926, 2020.

[Sr22] Srivastava, A. K. et al.: Winter wheat yield prediction using convolutional neural networks from environmental and phenological data. Scientific reports 1/12, p. 3215, 2022.

[St22] Statistische Ämter des Bundes und der Länder: Erträge ausgewählter landwirtschaftlicher Feldfrüchte. https://www.regionalstatistik.de/genesis//online?operation=table&code=41241-01-03-4&bypass=true&levelindex=0&levelid=1662987040832#abreadcrumb, accessed 19 Oct 2022.

[Un15] United Nations: Transforming our World: The 2030 Agenda for Sustainable Development. https://sdgs.un.org/sites/default/files/publications/21252030%20Agenda%20for%20Sustainable%20Development%20web.pdf, accessed 13 Sep 2022.

[vKC20] van Klompenburg, T.; Kassahun, A.; Catal, C.: Crop yield prediction using machine learning: A systematic literature review. Computers and Electronics in Agriculture 177, p. 105709, 2020.

[Vo19] Vogel, E. et al.: The effects of climate extremes on global agricultural yields. Environmental Research Letters 5/14, p. 54010, 2019.

[We20] Webber, H. et al.: No perfect storm for crop yield failure in Germany. Environmental Research Letters 10/15, p. 104012, 2020.

Computer-Vision-basierte Aktivitätserkennung bei Schweinen

Lukas Hesse [1], Maik Fruhner [2], Heiko Tapken [3] und Henning Müller[4]

Abstract: Die Sicherstellung des Tierwohls ist einer der Kernaspekte in der modernen Nutztierhaltung. Da sich durch den steigenden Bedarf an Lebensmitteln und dem steigenden Kostendruck immer mehr Landwirte dazu gezwungen sehen, immer größere Tierzahlen zu halten, fällt es vor dem Hintergrund des Fachkräftemangels schwieriger, diesem Aspekt nachzukommen. Aus diesem Grund müssen Technologien zur Unterstützung von Landwirten entwickelt werden, welche datenbezogene hochwertige Entscheidungshilfen geben können. Einen solchen Ansatz erarbeitet das Team des Forschungsprojektes SmartTail, bei dem unter anderem eine Computer-Vision-basierte Aktivitätserkennung erarbeitet wird. Durch die nicht-invasive und kostengünstige Hardware können so potenziell flächendeckend Systeme zur Unterstützung der Landwirte implementiert werden. Innerhalb dieser Arbeit wird sich mit der videobasierten Aktivitätserkennung bei Schweinen beschäftigt. Besonders betrachtet wird dabei das Problem des Schwanzbeißens. Dieses ist in der Schweinehaltung bekannt, aber aufgrund der multifaktoriellen Ursachen existiert bisher weder ein System zur Vorhersage noch zum Erkennen solcher Attacken. Aus diesem Grund werden innerhalb dieser Arbeit mehrere state-of-the-art Modelle zur bildbasierten Aktivitätserkennung betrachtet und miteinander verglichen, um so ein effektives System zur Aktivitätserkennung bei Schweinen zu entwickeln.

Keywords: Computer Vision, Aktivitätserkennung, Künstliche Intelligenz, Mastschweine

1 Einleitung

Ein in der Schweinemast immer wieder auftretendes Problem, zu dessen eindeutigen Ursachen nur wenige Informationen vorliegen, ist das Schwanzbeißen. Dies ist eine Verhaltensstörung bei Schweinen, bei denen sich die Tiere gegenseitig die Ringelschwänze verletzen. Dies kann zu entzündeten Wunden und einem stagnierenden Wachstum führen. Zudem breitet sich dieses Verhalten nach einmaligem Auftreten schnell auf weitere Tiere der Gruppe aus, weshalb eine frühzeitige Erkennung oder sogar eine Vorwarnung von größter Bedeutsamkeit wäre.

---

[1] HS Osnabrück, Fakultät IuI, Albrechtstr. 30, 49076 Osnabrück, lukas.hesse@hs-osnabrueck.de, https://orcid.org/0000-0001-5247-7537

[2] HS Osnabrück, Fakultät IuI, Albrechtstr. 30, 49076 Osnabrück, m.fruhner@hs-osnabrueck.de, https://orcid.org/0000-0002-9094-6996

[3] HS Osnabrück, Fakultät IuI, Albrechtstr. 30, 49076 Osnabrück, h.tapken@hs-osnabrueck.de https://orcid.org/0000-0002-0685-5072

[4] Hof Fleming, Ehrener Kirchweg 6, 49624 Löningen, henning.mueller@hof-fleming.de

Aktuell wird eine solche Attacke erst während der regelmäßigen Bonitur erkannt, indem ein lädierter Schwanz festgestellt wird. Zu diesem Zeitpunkt ist allerdings nur noch das Opfer der Attacke identifizierbar und der Aggressor kann nicht von der Gruppe getrennt werden. Durch die multifaktoriellen Ursachen solcher Beißattacken existiert bis heute kein Vorhersagesystem und die Informationen zum eigentlichen Beißvorgang sind minimal.

Da keine Methode zur sicheren Eindämmung des Schwanzbeißens besteht, wird in der konventionellen Tierhaltung oft auf das Kupieren zurückgegriffen. Hierbei werden den Ferkeln die Ringelschwänze abgeschnitten, bevor andere Artgenossen diese abbeißen können. Dieses Vorgehen wird allerdings scharf von Tierschützern kritisiert und der „Aktionsplan Kupierverzicht" [AkKu18] plant eine schrittweise Eindämmung dieser Praktik.

Ausgehend von diesem Problem wurde die von einem Landwirt geleitete Projektgruppe SmartTail gegründet, um ein technisches System zur automatischen Erkennung von Schwanzbeißen zu entwickeln. Durch ein solches System soll zum einen dem Landwirt das Auftreten von Schwanzbeißen in Echtzeit mitgeteilt werden, zum anderen soll es dabei helfen, die existierende Datenlücke für den Vorgang des Schwanzbeißens zu schließen. Der im Projekt gewählte Lösungsansatz beruht auf einer videobasierten Aktivitätserkennung, bei der durch eine dauerhafte Überwachung sowohl Aggressor und Opfer als auch das Auftreten von Schwanzbeißen erkannt werden sollen.

Um einen weiteren Schritt zur Ursachenforschung des Schwanzbeißens zu erreichen, werden verschiedene Deep-Learning-Architekturen erarbeitet, um eine generelle Aktivitätserkennung bei Schweinen zu erreichen. Hierfür wurde in einem ersten Schritt ein umfangreicher Datensatz geschaffen, bevor verschiedene state-of-the-art Architekturen auf unterschiedlich detaillierten Aktivitätskatalogen trainiert wurden.

2 Stand der Forschung

Videobasierte Ansätze zur Aktivitätserkennung von Schweinen sind ein aktuelles Thema in der Forschung. Eine Vielzahl von vergleichbaren Arbeiten nutzen Deckenkameras, um eine möglichst gute Übersicht über einzelne Buchten zu erhalten [Na19]. Zudem kann ein Fokus auf Computer-Vision-basierte Ansätze festgestellt werden, was mit der generellen Transition im Feld der Aktivitätserkennung einherzugehen scheint. Bisherige Arbeiten zu diesem Thema lassen sich meist an zwei Faktoren unterscheiden. Der Erste bezieht sich auf die erkannten Aktivitäten. Da es bisher keine allgemeingültige Auflistung von Schweineaktivitäten gibt, werden auch bei Arbeiten mit einem ähnlichen Erkennungsziel verschiedene Aktivitätskataloge gewählt. Der zweite Faktor verweist auf die genutzten Techniken. Obwohl eine allgemeine Verschiebung hin zu Computer Vision mit neuronalen Netzen basierten Ansätzen erkennbar ist, gibt es keinen Konsens zur optimalen Architektur.

So untersuchen beispielsweise Zheng et al. [Zh18] die Körperhaltung von Schweinen mithilfe von Tiefenkamerabildern und einem Faster R-CNN Modell. Analog zu diesem

Ansatz untersuchen Nasirahmadi et al. [Na19] die Performance verschiedener Objektdetektoren zur Erkennung von drei verschiedenen Körperhaltungen. In einer Arbeit von Alameer et al. [AKB20] wurde sowohl mit YOLO- als auch mit Faster R-CNN-Detektoren gearbeitet, um komplexere Aktivitäten zu erkennen.

In verschiedenen Arbeiten von Yang et al. [Ya18] [Ya20] wurden ähnlich komplexe Aktivitäten untersucht. Hierbei wurde sich jedoch nicht auf einfache Objektdetektoren verlassen. Stattdessen wurde eine einfache Two-Stream-Architektur genutzt, bei der ein separater Input zur Analyse des optischen Flusses angewandt wird. Auf diese Weise werden in zwei Streams jeweils die zeitlichen und örtlichen Merkmale verarbeitet.

Andere Arbeiten nutzen bereits modernere Architekturen, welche die direkte Verarbeitung von Videos erlauben. So nutzen Zhang et al. [Hu20] ein I3D-Modell zur Erkennung von fünf verschiedenen Aktivitäten, während auf dem gleichen Datensatz eine SlowFast-Architektur von Li et al. [Zh20] trainiert wurde. In einer Arbeit von Chen et al. [Ch20] wurde eine abgewandelte Two-Stream Architektur mit einem CNN- und einem RNN-Pfad zur binären Erkennung von aggressivem Verhalten genutzt.

Zum speziellen Ziel der spatio-temporalen Erkennung (ST-Erkennung) liegen bisher wenige Vergleichsarbeiten vor. In einem Versuch von Liu et al. [Li20] wird ein Netzwerk zur Erkennung von Schwanzbeißen trainiert. Dieses ermöglicht eine binäre Klassifikation, wobei jeweils Paare von Schweinen betrachtet werden.

Generell ist in den hier beachteten Arbeiten ein Trend hin zu komplexeren End-to-End Modellen erkennbar, wie beispielsweise dem I3D [CaZi17] oder dem Slowfast-Netzwerk [Fe19]. Allerdings liegen speziell für die ST-Erkennung kaum Arbeiten vor und für eine solche Aktivitätserkennung in Kombination mit Multi-Object Erkennung sind keine Arbeiten bekannt. Bei der Verfolgung des Trends ist ein solcher Ansatz jedoch der logische nächste Schritt, welcher bessere Ergebnisse verspricht.

3 Versuchsaufbau

Der in dieser Arbeit genutzte Datensatz beruht auf dauerhaften Videoaufnahmen einzelner Buchten, welche innerhalb des Projektes SmartTail aufgenommen wurden. Hierzu wurden in verschiedenen Ställen insgesamt fünf Buchten mit IP-Kameras überwacht. Diese Kameras verfügen sowohl über einen Farb- als auch einen aktiven Infrarotmodus und sind mit einem orthogonalen Blickwinkel unter der Stalldecke angebracht, sodass durch eine Kamera eine gesamte Bucht abgedeckt wird. Die für dieses Paper genutzten Kameras besitzen eine Auflösung von 3840 * 2160 Pixeln und nehmen mit einer Framerate von 30 FPS auf, wobei eine leichte Fish-Eye Verzerrung existiert.

Durch diesen Aufbau liegen projektintern inzwischen mehrere komplette Mastzyklen vor, was einem rohen Datenmaterial von mehr als 15 TB entspricht. Während eines Zyklus kann die Anzahl der Schweine pro Bucht variieren, wobei jedoch bei einem Großteil der

Aufnahmen 13 Schweine pro Bucht zu sehen sind. Dies entspricht der maximalen Auslastung einer Bucht ihrer Größe unter Berücksichtigung der rechtlichen Vorgaben.

4 Methodik

In diesem Kapitel werden sowohl der für dieses Paper gewählte Ansatz zur Datenvorverarbeitung als auch die genutzten künstlichen neuronalen Netzwerke, welche zum Vergleich herangezogen wurden, vorgestellt. Hierbei wird auf die Besonderheiten dieser Netzstrukturen hingewiesen und ihre Vor- und Nachteile werden aufgezeigt.

4.1 Datensatz

Bei einem Vergleich verwandter Arbeiten zur automatisierten Erkennung von Schweineaktivitäten fällt auf, dass bei diesen die genutzten Ethogramme zur Aktivitätsdefinition oft bewusst klein gewählt sind, um für den jeweiligen Use Case die besten Ergebnisse zu erhalten. Bei dem hier angegangenen Problem geht es jedoch um eine generelle Erkennung von Aktivitäten, weshalb die verwandten Arbeiten nicht die benötigte genaue Unterteilung von Aktivitäten mitbringen.

Aus diesem Grund wurde auf ein Ethogramm aus der lange etablierten Schweineforschung zurückgegriffen. In der Arbeit von Zonderland et al. [Zo11] geht es im Besonderen um die ausgeführten Aktivitäten von Schweinen vor einer Schwanzbeißattacke. Innerhalb dieser Arbeit wurden 33 verschiedene Aktivitäten definiert, welche ein Schwein zu jeder Zeit ausführen kann.

Ein weiterer Vorteil dieses Ethogramms ist die bereits existierende Unterteilung dieser feingranularen Aktivitäten in allgemeinere Oberkategorien. So existieren beispielsweise fünf übergreifende Klassen: „Posture", „Performed Behavioural States", „Received Behavioural States", „Performed Behavioural Events" und „Received Behavioural Events".

Diese umfassen die Körperhaltung eines Tieres, welche zu jedem Zeitpunkt zugewiesen werden kann. Zusätzlich werden hier längere ausgeführte oder aufgezwungene Verhaltenszustände festgelegt. Ein Tier befindet sich immer in mindestens einem ausführenden Zustand und kann zu jedem Zeitpunkt gleichzeitig auch Teil einer aufgezwungenen Aktivität sein. Hierzu zählen beispielsweise das Untersuchen von Spielzeug in der Bucht, zu dem es keine aufgezwungene Aktivität gibt, als auch das Manipulieren eines anderen Schweins, zu dem eine zugehörige aufgezwungene Aktion existiert.

Zusätzlich zu den länger andauernden Aktivitätsklassen existieren die ausgeführten und aufgezwungenen Events. Diese sind im Gegensatz zu Zuständen lediglich kurzweilig und müssen nicht zu jeder Zeit von einem Tier ausgeführt werden. In diese Kategorie fällt beispielsweise das Schwanzbeißen und das Gebissenwerden. Zu diesen fünf

Oberkategorien existieren teilweise weitere Unterkategorien, bevor die einzelnen elementaren Aktivitäten definiert werden. Diese hierarchische Unterteilung ist bei den hier angestellten Untersuchungen besonders hilfreich, da zu Beginn nicht bekannt ist, wie genau ein automatisiertes System die einzelnen von Schweinen ausgeführten Aktivitäten unterscheiden kann. Auf diese Weise wird eine zusätzliche Untersuchung zur Feinheit der definierten Aktivitäten ermöglicht.

Eine Herausforderung dabei, den so definierten Aktivitätskatalog innerhalb eines automatisierten Systems mit Computer Vision zu nutzen, ist die Erstellung eines gelabelten Datensatzes zum Ermöglichen des Trainings eines Netzwerks. Innerhalb des Projekts wurde sich dafür entschieden, einen Ansatz zur Analyse des Gesamtbildes der Bucht zu verfolgen.

Eine Alternative bietet der Einzeltieransatz, bei dem die einzelnen Tiere aus dem Gesamtbild ausgeschnitten werden und diesen Ausschnitten daraufhin eine oder mehrere Aktivitäten zugewiesen werden. Hierbei fällt die örtliche Zuweisung weg, da diese bereits in einem vorgelagerten Schritt durch das Ausschneiden des Tieres aus dem Originalbild geschieht.

Ein Vorteil der Gesamtbildanalyse besteht darin, dass hier für alle Schweine einer Bucht potenziell nur ein Netzwerk genutzt werden muss. Dieses kann den Rechenaufwand reduzieren. Bei einem Einzeltieransatz müssten in dem hier vorliegendem Versuchsfall bis zu 13 verschiedene Schweine pro Frame erkannt, ausgeschnitten und analysiert werden, was auch bei einem potenziell leichtgewichtigerem Analysenetzwerk einer Vervielfachung des Rechenaufwands entspricht. Da eine solche Analyse allerdings langfristig auf einem Edge-Gerät im Stall durchgeführt werden soll, wurde in dieser Arbeit darauf geachtet, die allgemeinen Rechen- und Hardwareanforderungen möglichst gering zu halten.

Zusätzlich ermöglicht die Nutzung des gesamten Bildes voraussichtlich bessere Rückschlüsse auf Aktionen mit mehreren Akteuren. Eine Vielzahl interessanter Schweineaktivitäten besitzen einen Aggressor und ein Opfer, bei denen das Zusammenspiel dieser beiden Tiere besonders interessant ist. Bei einem Einzeltieransatz könnten so bereits vor der Analyse durch ein neuronales Netzwerk wichtige Informationen verworfen werden.

Wie bereits erwähnt, erfordert der hier gewählte Ansatz zur Analyse des Gesamtbildes eine ST-Annotation des Datensatzes. Hierzu wird in diesem Paper eine eventbasierte Keyframe-Annotation mit einem unterstützenden YOLO-Netzwerk genutzt. Im Detail bedeutet dies, dass die zugrunde liegende Daueraufnahme in einzelne, kurze Events unterteilt wird. Diese Events werden von Hand ausgewählt und beinhalten ein möglichst aktives Verhalten von Schweinen innerhalb der Bucht. Diese Auswahl wird so durchgeführt, um eine möglichst große Vielfalt an Aktionen innerhalb eines Events und auch übergreifend über alle ausgewählten Events zu erhalten.

Um die so ausgewählten Events innerhalb eines Deep-Learning Netzwerks nutzen zu können, muss jedem Schwein eine Bounding Box zugeordnet sein, welcher dann wiederum eine Auswahl an Aktivitäten angeheftet sind. Zusätzlich müssen für das Training alle Events die gleiche Dauer besitzen. Um diese Uniformität der Länge zu erreichen, wird jedes Event in einzelne gleichlange Clips zerlegt, deren Dauer durch den Keyframeabstand festgelegt wird. Hierbei muss dieser Abstand möglichst groß gewählt werden, um überflüssigen Annotationsaufwand zu verhindern. Gleichzeitig dürfen die Abstände nicht zu groß gewählt werden, um mögliche Aktionswechsel einzelner Tiere innerhalb eines Events nicht zu verpassen. Hierzu wurde in einer vorausgehenden Masterarbeit ein optimaler Keyframe-Abstand von 90 Frames ermittelt.

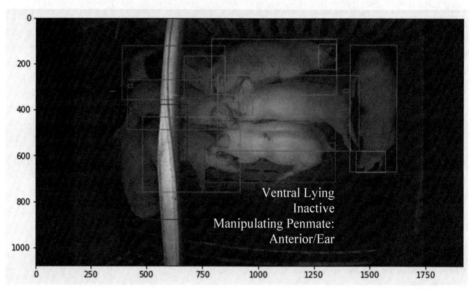

Abb. 1: Beispielbild der Daueraufnahme mit generierten Bounding Boxen und beispielhaft angefügten Aktivitätslabeln für die blaue Bounding Box

Um im eigentlichen Labeling-Prozess jeden Clip zu labeln, wird auf eine Kombination von Keyframes und einem trainierten YOLO-Netzwerk zur Schweineerkennung gesetzt. In einem ersten Schritt werden alle Frames der ausgewählten Events durch das YOLO-Netzwerk vorannotiert, wodurch für jeden Frame bereits Bounding Boxen der Schweine vorliegen. Im Folgenden können dann für jeden Keyframe die einzelnen Aktivitäten den ermittelten Bounding Boxen zugewiesen werden. Eine vereinfachte Darstellung eines so annotierten Frames mit Labeln für eine Box kann in Abb. 1 gesehen werden. Der hierdurch entstandene Datensatz besteht aus 349 Events und zugehörigen Keyframes, die eine Unterteilung in Clips ermöglichen. Alle Daten wurden im AVA-Format [Gu18] annotiert.

4.2 Genutzte Netzwerk-Architekturen

In diesem Abschnitt werden die in dem Projekt betrachteten Netzwerk-Architekturen vorgestellt, mit denen Untersuchungen zur Machbarkeit einer generellen Aktivitätserkennung durchgeführt wurden. Hierbei handelt es sich um drei spezielle

Implementierungen von state-of-the-art Ansätzen zur Aktivitätserkennung bei Menschen, welche von der Facebook Research Group erstellt wurden. Im Speziellen wird das X3D Netzwerk, beruhend auf 3D-Convolution, das SlowFast Netzwerk, basierend auf Two-Stream Architekturen und das MViT Netzwerk aus der Gruppe der Transformatoren genutzt.

Nachfolgend werden lediglich die grundlegenden Funktionsweisen sowie Vor- und Nachteile der Architekturen aufgezeigt. Generell konnte ausgehend von der existierenden Literatur nicht darauf geschlossen werden, welches Netzwerk die besten Ergebnisse erzielen könnte, da alle Benchmarking-Messwerte von menschlichen Aktionen ausgehen und Tiere generell außer Acht gelassen wurden.

Die sogenannten 3D-Convolution Networks (3D-CNN) bilden einen direkten Übergang der klassischen Bildanalysemethoden, wie CNNs, hin zur Videoanalyse. Hierbei wird ein Video als eine Reihe an Bildern aufgefasst, die neben den räumlichen Dimensionen Höhe und Breite auch eine temporale Dimension besitzen [Tr15]. Hierzu müssen die typischen Filter eines CNNs um eine dritte, zeitliche Dimension erweitert werden, sodass dreidimensionale Bildfilter entstehen. Diese Erweiterung bringt einige Vorteile mit sich.

So ist es möglich, bereits bekannte, erprobte Netzwerk-Architekturen aus der Bildanalyse direkt in den 3-dimensionalen Raum zu überführen. Hierbei können zusätzlich bereits vortrainierte Gewichte der einzelnen Schichten erweitert und übernommen werden [CaZi17]. Da das Feld der Videoanalyse mit neuronalen Netzwerken noch nicht so weit fortgeschritten ist wie die Bildanalyse, lohnt es sich oft, diese Gewichte zu übernehmen.

Ein Problem dieser Architekturen ist allerdings die Lokalität der Filter. Da die genutzten Filter nur eine begrenzte räumliche Dimension abdecken können, sind 3D-CNNs nicht gut in der Lage, zeitlich oder räumlich voneinander entfernte Merkmale in einen Zusammenhang zu bringen. Ob dieses Merkmal auch im Bereich der Schweineforschung zum Tragen kommt, ist jedoch fraglich, da sich die Tiere räumlich oft wenig bewegen und die Aktionen zeitlich direkt zusammenhängen. Das hier genutzte X3D Netzwerk [Fe20] ist eine optimierte Form eines 3D-CNNs, welche sich während des Trainingsprozesses den genutzten Trainingsdaten anpasst, um so ein möglichst effizientes Netzwerk zu bilden.

Neben 3D-CNNs gibt es in der Literatur einen weiteren vorherrschenden Ansatz zur Verarbeitung der zeitlichen Dimension in einem Video, die sogenannten Two-Stream-Architekturen. Bei diesem Modell werden zwei Netzwerke parallel genutzt, um jeweils den räumlichen Zusammenhang innerhalb eines Frames und den temporalen Zusammenhang mehrerer Frames zu ermitteln.

Der sogenannte „Spatial Stream" oder auch „Slow Pathway" einer solchen Architektur arbeitet auf individuellen oder wenigen Frames eines Videos und führt eine Aktivitätserkennung aus. Es hat sich dabei gezeigt, dass bereits statische Bilder Rückschlüsse auf Aktivitäten erlauben und sich hier die Nutzung eines 3D-CNNs als Pathway lohnt.

Dem gegenüber liegt der „Temporal Stream" oder auch „Fast Pathway". Ziel dieses Pfades ist es, eine möglichst genaue Repräsentation der temporalen Dimension zu verarbeiten, was durch eine möglichst hohe Bildrate erreicht wird. Auch hier wird wieder ein 3D-CNN als Pathway genutzt. Um bei dieser höheren Framerate die Rechenanforderungen vergleichbar mit dem „Spatial Stream" zu halten, werden innerhalb dieses Pfades nur wenige Filter innerhalb einer Schicht verwendet.

Diese Struktur der zwei Pfade bringt einige Vorteile mit sich. Zum einen wird durch den dedizierten Pfad ein besseres temporales Verständnis erreicht, zum anderen können für beide Pfade vergleichbar einfache 3D-CNN Architekturen genutzt werden, da diese nur eine Art von Merkmalen erkennen sollen. Das hier genutzte SlowFast Netzwerk [Fe19] zeichnet sich zudem über einige Querverbindungen aus, durch die temporaler Kontext an die Aktivitätserkennung weitergegeben werden kann, schon bevor die beiden Pfade endgültig zusammengeführt werden.

Einen grundsätzlich anderen Ansatz verfolgen die Visual Transformer Networks (ViT) [Do20]. Diese basieren auf dem Prinzip der Self-Attention und kommen ursprünglich aus dem Bereich des Natural Language Processing. Hierbei wird die ursprüngliche Encoder-Decoder-Architektur an die neue Aufgabe der Bilderkennung angepasst, indem zum einen der Decoder entfernt und durch eine Klassifikation ersetzt wird. Zum anderen muss der Input angepasst werden.

Da die vorliegende Architektur eine Sequenz an Wörtern erwartet, muss die Bildsequenz in ein passendes Format gebracht werden. Hierzu werden einzelne Bilder fragmentiert und begradigt, wodurch die einzelnen Farbwerte eines Bildausschnitts als Token-Input des Netzwerks genutzt werden können.

Generell bietet der Ansatz der ViT eine Möglichkeit zur Erkennung besonders weit auseinanderliegender Zusammenhänge, egal ob örtlich oder zeitlich. Das hier genutzte Netzwerk der Multiscale Visual Transformer (MViT) [Fa21] bietet eine Architektur mit mehreren verschiedenen Skalierungsebenen, wodurch kleine bildliche Merkmale nach und nach in einen größeren temporalen Zusammenhang gebracht werden können.

5 Ergebnisse und Diskussionen

Vor einer Beurteilung der einzelnen Netzwerkgenauigkeiten muss der zugrunde liegende Datensatz dargestellt und mögliche Schwachpunkte müssen erläutert werden. Tab. 1 stellt eine vereinfachte Auflistung der Aktivitäten mit ihren jeweiligen Häufigkeiten dar. Hierbei ist zu erwähnen, dass nicht alle elementaren Aktivitäten dargestellt werden konnten. So bilden die Punkte „Manipulating", „Manipulated", „Performed Aggressive Behaviour" und „Received Aggressive Behaviour" weitere Oberkategorien, zu denen es einzelne elementare Aktivitäten gibt. Für diese Kategorien wurden die Häufigkeiten der darunterliegenden Aktivitäten akkumuliert. So stellt diese Tabelle die zweite von drei möglichen Ebenen auf, in die dieser Datensatz unterteilt werden kann. Elementare Aktivitäten, für die keine Events im Videomaterial vorhanden sind, wurden nicht berücksichtigt.

Aktivität	#Events	#Keyframes	#Label
Posture	--	--	--
Lateral Lying	346	2112	11444
Ventral Lying	240	1623	6144
Sitting/Kneeling	102	676	2141
Standing	316	1772	6857
Performed Behavioural States	*793*	*5630*	*20526*
Inactive	287	2075	14364
Locomotion	75	369	2019
Playing	26	201	267
Mounting	6	39	39
Manipulating	*399*	*2946*	*3837*
Received Behavioural States	*261*	*1908*	*2265*
Mounted	6	39	39
Manipulated	*255*	*1869*	*2226*
Performed Behavioural Events	*162*	*990*	*990*
Tail Biting	23	118	118
Ear Biting	42	260	260
Performed Aggressive Behaviour	*97*	*612*	*612*
Received Behavioural Events	*162*	*990*	*1046*
Tail Bitten	23	118	118
Ear Bitten	42	260	260
Received Aggressive Behaviour	*97*	*612*	*668*

Tab. 1: Übersicht des Aktivitätskatalogs mit zugehörigen Events, Keyframes und Labeln

Ausgehend von diesem Datensatz wurden die drei verschiedenen Modellarchitekturen angelernt und hingehend ihrer Genauigkeit verglichen. Hierzu wurden für alle Modelle vortrainierte Gewichte des AVA-Datensatzes [Gu18] genutzt und alle Modelle wurden auf allen drei möglichen Verallgemeinerungsstufen des Aktivitätenkatalogs getestet.

Modell	Trainings-mAP	Test-mAP
MViT	0.1534	0.1198
SlowFast	0.1294	0.1043
X3D	0.0953	0.0523

Tab. 2: Genauigkeiten der verschiedenen Netzwerke für alle möglichen Aktivitäten

In einem ersten Versuch wurden die Netzwerkarchitekturen auf allen zur Verfügung stehenden Aktivitätsklassen getestet, um herauszufinden, ob diese bereits bei der feinsten Aktivitätsgliederung hinreichend genaue Ergebnisse liefern. Hierbei wurde als Basis zur Bestimmung der Genauigkeit die mean Avergage Precision (mAP) gewählt. Anhand von Tab. 2 kann erkannt werden, dass alle Netzwerke ähnliche Genauigkeiten erreichen, wobei MViT mit 11,98% Testgenauigkeit am besten funktioniert. Allerdings muss gesagt werden, dass diese Genauigkeit nicht als akzeptabel gewertet werden kann, obwohl die erreichte Genauigkeit bei 30 Aktivitäten für ein kontextbasiertes Lernen spricht.

Modell	Trainings-mAP	Test-mAP
MViT	0.6320	0.5270
SlowFast	0.5821	0.5194
X3D	0.5443	0.5054

Tab. 3: Genauigkeiten der verschiedenen Netzwerke für die acht Oberkategorien

In einem weiteren Versuch wurden die maximal zusammengefassten Aktivitäten getestet, bei denen lediglich die Körperhaltungen und restlichen Oberkategorien genutzt werden. Hier zeigt sich eine klare Steigerung der Genauigkeit bei allen Netzwerken, wobei MViT auch hier am besten abschneidet, wie in Tabelle 3 gesehen werden kann.

Der Grund für diesen Genauigkeitsverlauf zwischen den verschieden genauen Aktivitätskatalogen lässt sich erkennen, wenn die erreichten Genauigkeiten pro Aktivität betrachtet werden. Hier zeigt sich, dass außer den Körperhaltungen keine elementare Aktivität mit mehr als 6 % Genauigkeit erkannt werden konnte. Dies bedeutet, dass die Netzwerke für diese keine kontextbasierten Merkmale lernen konnten und lediglich zufällig entscheiden. So lässt sich auch der Genauigkeitssprung bei einer Reduzierung auf acht Klassen erklären, da hier die hohen Genauigkeiten der Körperhaltungen die schlechten Genauigkeiten der restlichen Klassen ausgleichen.

Für dieses Verhalten kann es zwei mögliche Folgerungen geben. Zum einen ist es möglich, dass der hier verfolgte Ansatz der Gesamtbilderkennung nicht zielführend ist. Zum anderen kann es sein, dass durch die spärlich vertretenen Aktivitäten im Datensatz kein effektives Training ermöglicht wurde und der Datensatz zunächst ausbalanciert werden muss.

6 Schlussfolgerungen und Ausblick

Innerhalb dieses Papers konnten neben einem effektiven Weg zur Erstellung eines ST-annotierten Datensatzes für Schweine mehrere trainierte Netzwerke miteinander verglichen werden. So konnte eine automatisierte Erkennung von Aktivitäten bis zu einem gewissen Grad erreicht werden. Jedoch entsprechen diese Ergebnisse noch nicht der im Projekt angestrebten Genauigkeit. Die Verallgemeinerung einzelner Aktivitäten in allgemeine Oberkategorien verbesserte die Ergebnisse leicht, wobei jedoch nur für verschiedene Körperhaltungen eine echte Erkennung erreicht werden konnte. Aus diesem

Grund war die Ermittlung eines am besten geeigneten Netzwerks nicht möglich, weshalb alternative Ansätze verfolgt werden sollten.

Aktuell werden im Projekt Untersuchungen zur Nutzung von Positions-Heatmaps und Ellipsenrepräsentationen von Einzeltieren durchgeführt. Hierbei wird langfristig versucht, über diese Heatmaps Rückschlüsse auf den generellen Aktivitätslevel eines Tieres zu schließen.

Ein anderer Ansatz ist die Erkennung von paarweisen Interaktionen. Aggressive Verhaltensweisen unter Schweinen besitzen sowohl ein Opfer als auch einen Täter. Daher liegt der Gedanke nahe, diese paarweisen Interaktionen genauer zu untersuchen, um eine Erkennung von aggressivem Verhalten zu ermöglichen.

Fördernhinweis: Wir danken der Europäischen Innovationspartnerschaft „Produktivität und Nachhaltigkeit in der Landwirtschaft" (EIP Agri) für die Förderung des Projektes SmartTail, im Zuge dessen diese wissenschaftliche Veröffentlichung entstehen konnte.

Literaturverzeichnis

[AKB20] Alameer, A., Kyriazakis, I., & Bacardit, J.: Automated recognition of postures and drinking behaviour for the detection of compromised health in pigs. Scientific reports, 10(1), S. 1-15, 2020.

[AkKu18] Aktionsplan Kupierverzicht, https://www.ringelschwanz.info/weitere-infomationen/-aktionsplan-kupierverzicht.html, Strand: 28.10.2022

[CaZi17] Carreira, J.; Zisserman, A.: Quo vadis, action recognition? a new model and the kinetics dataset. In proceedings of the IEEE Conference on Computer Vision and Pattern Recognition, S. 6299-6308, 2017.

[Ch20] Chen, C. et al.: Recognition of feeding behaviour of pigs and determination of feeding time of each pig by a video-based deep learning method. *Computers and Electronics in Agriculture*, *176*, 105642, 2020.

[CZN21] Chen, C.; Zhu, W.; Norton, T.: Behaviour recognition of pigs and cattle: Journey from computer vision to deep learning. Computers and Electronics in Agriculture 187, 2021.

[Do20] Dosovitskiy, A. et al.: An image is worth 16x16 words: Transformers for image recognition at scale. arXiv preprint arXiv:2010.11929, 2020.

[Fa21] Fan, H. et al.: Multiscale vision transformers. In Proceedings of the IEEE/CVF International Conference on Computer Vision, S. 6824-6835, 2021.

[Fe19] Feichtenhofer, C. et al.: Slowfast networks for video recognition. In Proceedings of the IEEE/CVF international conference on computer vision, S. 6202-6211, 2019.

[Fe20] Feichtenhofer, C.: X3d: Expanding architectures for efficient video recognition. In Proceedings of the IEEE/CVF Conference on Computer Vision and Pattern Recognition, S. 203-213, 2020.

[Gu18]   Gu, C. et al.: Ava: A video dataset of spatio-temporally localized atomic visual actions. In Proceedings of the IEEE Conference on Computer Vision and Pattern Recognition, S. 6047-6056, 2018.

[Hu20]   Huang, J. et al.: Automated video behavior recognition of pigs using two-stream convolutional networks. *Sensors*, *20*(4), S. 1085, 2020.

[Li20]   Liu, D. et al.: A computer vision-based method for spatial-temporal action recognition of tail-biting behaviour in group-housed pigs. Biosystems Engineering, 195, S. 27-41, 2020.

[Na19]   Nasirahmadi, A. et al.: Deep learning and machine vision approaches for posture detection of individual pigs. Sensors, 19(17), S. 3738, 2019.

[SiZi14]   Simonyan, K.; Zisserman, A.: Two-stream convolutional networks for action recognition in videos. Advances in neural information processing systems, 27, 2014.

[Tr15]   Tran, D. et al.: Learning spatiotemporal features with 3d convolutional networks. In Proceedings of the IEEE international conference on computer vision, S. 4489-4497, 2015.

[Ya18]   Yang, A. et al.: Automatic recognition of sow nursing behaviour using deep learning-based segmentation and spatial and temporal features. Biosystems Engineering, 175, S. 133-145, 2018.

[Ya20]   Yang, A. et al.: An automatic recognition framework for sow daily behaviours based on motion and image analyses. Biosystems Engineering, 192, S. 56-71, 2020.

[Zh18]   Zheng, C. et al.: Automatic recognition of lactating sow postures from depth images by deep learning detector. Computers and electronics in agriculture, 147, S. 51-63, 2018.

[Zh20]   Zhang, K. et al.: A spatiotemporal convolutional network for multi-behavior recognition of pigs. *Sensors*, *20*(8), S. 2381, 2020.

[Zo11]   Zonderland, J. J et al.: Characteristics of biter and victim piglets apparent before a tail-biting outbreak. Animal, 5(5), S. 767-775, 2011.

Antecedents of organizational resilience and how these can be transferred to agriculture

A systematic literature analysis

Saskia Hohagen[1], Niklas Obermann[1] and Uta Wilkens[1]

Abstract: The agricultural sector is increasingly characterized by national competition and a dynamic environment. The resilience concept, which is used in connection with farms, is based on the social-ecological perspective and primarily gives emphasis to a system. To this end, there is a research gap in the consideration of resilience from a management perspective in agriculture. Drawing on the literature on organizational resilience from a managerial perspective, this article examines resilience-enabling factors that can be used by operations managers to prepare for future challenges in agriculture. A systematic literature review was conducted from which four main categories of antecedents (leadership, individual factors, digitalization and strategic alignment) could be derived, consistent with a socio-technical perspective on organizations. Considering these factors can help farm managers to build resilient farms not only from a social-ecological, but also from an organizational (management) perspective.

Keywords: organizational resilience, antecedents, agriculture, farm manager

1 Introduction

Organizations are increasingly operating in a dynamic environment. The same applies to farms [PEG18]. In the agricultural sector change, economic uncertainties [Da14; Sl20] or global crises like the Covid-19 pandemic [Du23] pose enormous challenges. Against this background, the construct of resilience is regularly invoked to sustain business operations [e.g. Ha20]. The management literature adopted an organizational perspective, considering resilience at the organizational level. Resilience can be understood as a process "by which an actor […] builds and uses its capability endowments to interact with the environment in a way that positively adjusts and maintains functioning prior to, during, and following adversity" [Wi17, p. 742]. Resilience research has increased in this area since the beginning of the 21st century [Li17] and will continue to increase due to developments such as the Covid-19 pandemic [e.g. DL22]. In contrast, resilience research in agriculture has a stronger focus on social-ecological resilience [PEG18]. This perspective encompasses both the agricultural system and the farm [MD03]. Up to this point, there are only isolated approaches [e.g. Da21] that understand resilience more as a

---

[1] Ruhr-Universität Bochum, Institut für Arbeitswissenschaft, Lehrstuhl Arbeit, Personal und Führung, Universitätstraße 150, 44780 Bochum, saskia.hohagen@rub.de, niklas.obermann@rub.de, uta.wilkens@rub.de

process and thus move in the direction of the definition of organizational resilience according to Williams et al. [Wi17] or Duchek [Du20]. Research has taken multidisciplinary approaches to studying resilience, which have led to a psychological [WLX22], a social-ecological [Wa02] and a management [Li17] perspective, among others.

Particularly from the management perspective of resilience research (organizational resilience), decisive insights can be drawn for the management of farms. This is also reinforced by the fact that scientific studies show that farmers are increasingly becoming managers of their farms, which makes commercial skills more and more important [HWZ21]. Therefore, this article focuses on farms from an organizational resilience perspective. Aside from the growing body of work on organizational resilience, Linnenluecke [Li17] and Hartmann et al. [Ha20] draw attention to the fact that it is not yet fully understood which developmental parameters promote the emergence of organizational resilience. Barasa et al. [BMG18] addressed this issue, albeit tailored to the healthcare sector, and identified antecedents such as material resources, information management, governance processes, and management practices. Hartmann et al.'s [Ha20] study supplemented the antecedents of individual and team resilience. What is still missing in the research is a cross-sector overview of the antecedents of organizational resilience. This would help organizations find concrete starting points for developing organizational resilience. To fill this research gap, the present paper identifies antecedents of organizational resilience with a focus on working methods and behaviors as factors that influence organizational resilience. These factors are considered, because these resources reside within the organization and can be influenced, for example, by the managers themselves.

Using a systematic literature review based on Fink [Fi14], a literature review of the antecedents of organizational resilience is provided. By reviewing essential studies dealing with antecedents of organizational resilience, relevant insights are gained about the factors that promote the resilience in organizations. In the last section of this article, these insights are applied to the agricultural sector and concrete practical recommendations for farm managers are highlighted.

2   Theoretical background

Today's challenges impact how farmers do business. In view of this, questions about securing the harvest become less important. In this context, organizational measures that farmers can take to remain competitive in an increasingly dynamic environment gain importance. However, only a few studies have pursued this approach. As mentioned earlier, resilience in the agricultural context is still often viewed from a social-ecological perspective [PEG18]. From this point of view, resilience can be defined as "the potential of a system to remain in a particular configuration and to maintain its feedbacks and functions, and involves the ability of the system to reorganize following disturbance driven change" [Wa02, p. 19]. This understanding forms the basis of numerous studies [e.g. St21;

Du23; PMM20; Da19]. Some of them focus on the characteristics of social-ecological resilience, which Milestad and Darnhofer [MD03] and Darnhofer [Da14], following Carpenter et al. [Ca01], define as buffering capacity, self-organizing capacity, and adaptive capacity. Meuwissen et al. [Me19] tend to move away from the social-ecological focus and "define resilience of a farming system as its ability to ensure the provision of the system functions in the face of increasingly complex and accumulating economic, social, environmental and institutional shocks and stresses, through capacities of robustness, adaptability and transformability" [Me19, p. 1]. As can be seen from their definition, Meuwissen et al. [Me19] attribute the following capacities to resilient farms: robustness, adaptability, and transformability. In doing so, they laid the foundation for work by Slijper et al. [Sl20] or Kangogo et al. [KDB20]. While their work was an essential step in identifying the capacities of resilient farms, it is not yet clear how resilient organizational capacities like these can be developed. This, however, is an important aspect in order to provide farmers with concrete implementation proposals. Therefore, it seems promising to take a look at resilience research from an organizational perspective.

The concept of resilience is a comparatively new area of research in the working context [KNL16]. The beginnings of resilience research in the 1980s and 1990s were shaped by the concept of the reliability of internal processes in organizations. It was not until the September 11 terrorist attacks in the U.S. that the focus shifted to coping mechanisms and response strategies of organizations under conditions of great uncertainty [Li17]. While resilience generally means "a system's ability to continue to perform and meet its objectives in the face of challenges" [BMG18, p. 496], organizational resilience has been conceptualized in different ways i.e., as an outcome or a process [Du20]. This paper follows the definition of Williams et al. [Wi17] and defines organizational resilience as a process "by which an actor […] builds and uses its capability endowments to interact with the environment in a way that positively adjusts and maintains functioning prior to, during, and following adversity" [Wi17, p. 742]. This definition expands the understanding of resilience by looking at resilience from a process perspective and dividing it into three phases. Hartmann et al. [Ha20] and Linnenluecke [Li17] point out that one of the essential elements of the resilience process are resilience-promoting factors. Thus, they highlight the need to study the factors that promote resilience in each phase in more detail.

In order to do so, Duchek's [Du20] capability-based conceptualization of organizational resilience offers a solid starting point. Similar to Williams et al. [Wi17], Duchek [Du20] argues that organizations have to be able to anticipate unexpected events and minimize their impact, cope effectively with those events and adapt through learning, reflection and change after they overcome them. However, in addition to these capabilities supporting factors like the prior knowledge base of the organization, resource availability, social resources, power and responsibility and cognitive as well as behavioral skills positively influence the resilience process [Du20].

This implies a sound understanding of resilience-promoting factors (in the further course referred to as antecedents of resilience) in organizations. In her work, Duchek [Du20] lists several approaches from related research fields of how organizations can build the capabilities of anticipation, coping and adaptation. However, the direct link of these approaches like routines to acquire external information such as extensive market research to resilience in organizations has not yet been established [Du20]. This creates a significant difficulty for organizations to act and establish concrete working methods to promote their resilience.

To shed some light into what antecedents are already known to improve organizational resilience, the next section expands on the understanding of those methods by performing a literature review of antecedents of organizational resilience.

Antecedents are comprised of working methods and the ability to act in organizations that can be a promising approach to building more resilient organizations and farms. Especially given the serious impact of recent crisis, creating an understanding of the way organizations can build and sustain their resilience is more important than ever before. As Barasa et al. [BMG18] note, understanding the antecedents of organizational resilience can help organizations of any type to prepare for adversity and overcome future challenges without loss of performance.

3 Methodology

The methodological basis for this paper is a systematic literature analysis based on Fink [Fi14]. A literature search was carried out in the following three databases in October 2022: EBSCOHOST, ScienceDirect and Web of Science. *Organizational resilience* and *organisational resilience* were utilized as keywords to be used in the title, abstract, or keyword. After reviewing the EBSCOHOST literature list, the keywords used for the other two databases were further specified by putting the two keywords in quotation marks to search for these fixed terms. This approach was chosen because many publications have examined resilience in organizations, but the focus was, for example, on individual or supply chain resilience and not on organizational resilience. A total of 1592 publications were identified and screened in two steps.

In the first step, the title and abstract were considered. The main focus was to investigate whether papers examine organizational resilience from a management perspective. To be considered relevant for the second screening step, papers had to meet the following criteria: (1) peer-reviewed (2) written in English, (3) examine organizational resilience, (4) investigate the antecedents (working methods or behaviors) of organizational resilience, and (5) conduct a quantitative study. After this first screening step, 1493 publications were removed from the review (including 213 duplicates). A large number of publications were excluded because they did not consider organizational resilience from a management perspective. For this reason, studies from the agricultural context were also excluded. It was noticeable that no contributions in German were to be found, but e.g. Chinese-language papers. In addition, research on organizational resilience from a managerial perspective seems to be deeply rooted in the English community.

In the subsequent second screening step, the focus was on examining the papers in detail for the antecedents addressed and the underlying methodology used. Since access to all 99 full papers was not possible, only 60 contributions were analyzed in more depth. In the course of this, further 48 papers were excluded because they dealt with antecedents that did not focus on working methods or behaviors applied within the organization, or the empirical study was not considered to be representative. In total, the literature review includes 12 studies. The figure below (Fig. 1) shows the screening process in summary.

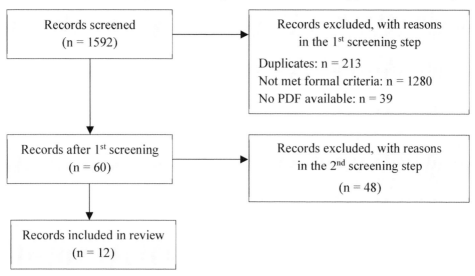

Fig. 1: Summary of the screening process

Two authors carried out this review process. Based on Fink [Fi14], a pilot test was also organized for the reviewing process. Only publications for which both reviewers agreed were excluded. In cases where the reviewers disagreed, a reassessment was made by the reviewers, which resulted in agreement in all cases considered.

4 Key findings: antecedents of organizational resilience

The literature review shows that various working methods and behaviors have already been examined that represent influencing factors for organizational resilience. A total of 12 studies were included in the review. The selected antecedents can be divided into four categories: (1) leadership, (2) individual factors, (3) digitalization, and (4) strategic alignment. The figure below (Fig. 2) provides a summary overview of the selected relevant antecedents from the literature review.

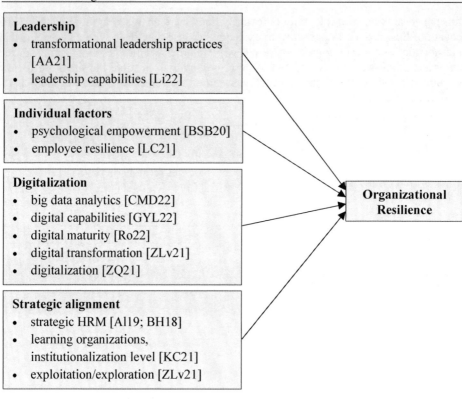

Fig. 2: Summary of the selected studies

The first category focuses on leadership antecedents. Abd-El Aliem and Abou Hashish [AA21] highlighted transformational leadership when examining leadership as an antecedent of organizational resilience. To that end, Liang and Cao [LC21] concentrated on leadership skills in a more general sense. Applied to farms, this means that managers (farmers) can help increase their farm's resilience and prepare it for crises. As has already become clear, studies show that farmers are increasingly becoming managers of their farms [HWZ21] and the task of managing employees falls within the remit of a farm manager. If they actively lead their employees and it is clear what is expected of employees, this can contribute to the resilience of the organization.

Another category, which deals more with human aspects, addresses individual factors. Beuren et al. [BSB20] examined psychological empowerment as a factor influencing organizational resilience. In the agricultural context, this means that when farmers give meaning or impact to their work, it can contribute to organizational resilience. Liang and Cao [LC21] focused on employee resilience. In their study, employees assessed their own resilience and the resilience of the organization. Looking at resilience at different levels enables a holistic view of an organization's resilience, as the levels are interrelated

[KNL16]. If farmers have high levels of resilience at the individual level, this can have a positive impact on resilience at the organizational level.

The literature review makes it clear that most studies relate to the topic of digitalization. These include the studies with the antecedents big data analytics capability [CMD22], digital capabilities [GYL22], digital maturity [Ro22], digital transformation [ZLv21], and digitalization [ZQ21]. The consideration of the operationalization of digital transformation shows that the studies focus on the use of digital technologies [e.g. GYL22], but also on the possibilities of digital transformation in the direction of new business processes, business models or customer acquisition [e.g. ZQ21]. On the one hand, the perspective of digitalization is directed at what is immediately available, but at the same time there is also a future perspective. Both perspectives show a positive correlation with organizational resilience. In a study by Hohagen and Wilkens [HW22], it became clear that farmers tend to focus more on the existing and less on the future possibilities offered by digitalization. Regardless of the understanding of digitalization, the study results considered illustrate that a focus on digitalization topics can add value to the resilience of organizations.

Another category relates to strategic alignment. Both exploitation/exploration [ZLv21] and strategic HRM [Al19; BH18] were considered. The strategic perspective on innovations that relate to adjustments or updates of existing products/services (exploitation) as well as innovations related to the development of new products/services (exploration) are positively related to the development of organizational resilience. This implies that companies, regardless of whether they focus on the existing in their company or alternatively look to future issues, can make a contribution to the development of organizational resilience. With a focus on strategic HRM, it is noticeable that various operationalizations were used. Al-Ayed [Al19] focused on strategic value of HR practices, HR analytics and high performance work practices, whereas Bouaziz and Hachicha [BH18] used the indicators staffing, training, participation, performance appraisal and compensation. This reveals that managers with a focus on strategic HRM can contribute to developing the resilience of their organization. Looking at the category of leadership and strategic orientation, it appears that larger farms that have hired several employees tend to benefit more from the antecedents shown than smaller farms, e.g. family-run farms. Furthermore, Bouaziz and Hachicha's [BH18] operationalization seems more appropriate for the farm use case. A complete strategic HRM requires comprehensive planning and monitoring. This cannot be considered realistic for farms with only a few employees, for example. However, facilitating individual aspects of strategic HRM, e.g., enabling participation in training courses on agricultural topics or involvement in decision-making, can contribute to the development of organizational resilience.

In summary, it can be said that there are various starting points for positively influencing the resilience of an organization. The results made it clear that three core levels emerged for the antecedents of organizational resilience: the levels of human, technology and organization. The categories of leadership and individual factors contribute to the human level, the category of digitalization to the level of technology and the category of strategic alignment to the level of the organization. In terms of a socio-technical system [e.g. Or92;

SU97], it appears that the interaction of individual ability, technological potential and organizational framework conditions is relevant. These three levels are interrelated and interdependent. This integrative approach provides a broad foundation for developing organizational resilience.

5 Discussion: implications for agriculture

In the literature review, it once again became clear that in agricultural research, organizational resilience is less considered from a management perspective. For farms, however, this perspective of resilience could create added value. The social-ecological perspective, which is widely used in the agricultural context, mainly focuses on approaches to sustain farm production under changing conditions [e.g. Wa02; PEG18]. The management perspective can be seen as complementary to this approach by looking at factors that contribute to maintaining farm operations and processes in a dynamic (market) environment [e.g. Du20]. Research in the agricultural context is already indicating initial approaches that broaden the view to include management-based factors of organizational resilience. For example, the definition of organizational resilience by Meuwissen et al. [Me19] shows a deviation from the social-ecological perspective. The management perspective can help improve operations and processes on farms and make them more resilient. To do this, farmers are encouraged to take a detailed look at their own organization in order to derive targeted measures that fit the characteristics of their farm.

In this context, the four categories highlighted (leadership, individual factors, digitalization and strategic alignment) can provide orientation. With the underlying antecedents, this study provides starting points with concrete practical implications for the development of organizational resilience in farms. Therefore, farmers now have a form of checklist that they can use to start building the resilience of their farm. However, it should also be noted that not all implementation support is equally relevant to all farms. Instead, farms should familiarize themselves with this topic and reflect on where there are suitable approaches for their farm. It is less about starting with the development of the farm's resilience in all aspects at the same time, but rather about filtering out the ones that are suitable for the farm and starting at these points. It is already known from a study by Hohagen and Wilkens [HW22] that farms are well positioned when it comes to interlocking the human and technology levels. To that end, however, there seem to be challenges in dovetailing into organizational management. Farms with fewer or no employees will hardly start with leadership or strategic HRM. Although the view of digitalization differs, there may be potential in this aspect. A digitalization perspective of farms towards the use of digital technologies, the marketing/sales of products via digital channels or the development of digital business models can offer an opportunity to react to future crises. A first step, for example, would be to start with the individual factors, since these are directly in the sphere of action of the farmers themselves, and to devote attention to other topics on this basis.

It appears that there are several starting points for developing organizational resilience. In terms of an integrative approach, however, it becomes apparent that the interaction of the factors of the three levels human, technology and organization can create a competitive advantage for organizations. If the focus is placed on only one of the levels, such as the human or the organizational, this view seems too short-sighted. Although not all identified antecedents are equally applicable to all organizations, this wide range of different aspects allows farmers to focus on selected aspects at the levels and develop them in a targeted manner, for example, through education or training opportunities. Farmers should be shown this possibility so that they have the chance to develop farm-specific approaches to promoting organizational resilience.

6 Conclusion and Outlook

This contribution represents an attempt to incorporate a new (different) perspective on resilience in agriculture. The main focus is on the added value that this perspective brings to farms. As has been shown, organizational antecedents of resilience can provide critical entry points for farmers to best prepare for future challenges. However, it must be pointed out as a limiting factor that this contribution is based on a conceptual basis. There is a lack of empirical support, which needs to be built up in the future in order to further develop and investigate this new research perspective.

Bibliography

[AA21] Abd-EL Aliem, S. M. F.; Abou Hashish, E. A.: The relationship between transformational leadership practices of first-line nurse managers and nurses' organizational resilience and job involvement: a structural equation model. Worldviews on Evidence-Based Nursing 18, 273-282, 2021.

[Al19] Al-Ayed, S. I.: The impact of strategic human resource management on organizational resilience: an empirical study on hospitals. Verslas: Teorija Ir Praktika/Business: Theory and Practice 20, 179-186, 2019.

[BMG18] Barasa, E.; Mbau, R.; Gilson, L.: What is resilience and how can it be nurtured? A systematic review of empirical literature on organizational resilience. International journal of health policy and management 7, 491-503, 2018.

[BSB20] Beuren, I. M.; Santos, V. D.; Bernd, D. C.: Effects of the management control system on empowerment and organizational resilience. Brazilian Business Review 17, 211-232, 2020.

[BH18] Bouaziz, F.; Hachicha, Z. S.: Strategic human resource management practices and organizational resilience. Journal of Management Development 37, 537-551, 2018.

[Ca01] Carpenter, S.; Walker, B.; Anderies, J. M.; Abel, N.: From metaphor to measurement: resilience of what to what? Ecosystems 4, 765-781, 2001.

[CMD22] Ciasullo, M. V.; Montera, R.; Douglas, A.: Building SMEs' resilience in times of uncertainty: the role of big data analytics capability and co-innovation. Transforming Government: People, Process and Policy 16, 203-217, 2022.

[Da14] Darnhofer, I.: Resilience and why it matters for farm management. European Review of Agricultural Economics 41, 461-484, 2014.

[Da21] Darnhofer, I.: Farming resilience: From maintaining states towards shaping transformative change processes. Sustainability 13, 1-21, 2021.

[Da19] Daugstad, K.: Resilience in mountain farming in Norway. Sustainability 11, 1-11, 2019.

[DL22] De La Garza, C.; Lot, N.: The socio-organizational and human dynamics of resilience in a hospital: The case of the COVID-19 crisis. Journal of Contingencies and Crisis Management 30, 244-256, 2022.

[Du20] Duchek, S.: Organizational resilience: a capability-based conceptualization. Business Research 13, 215-246, 2020.

[Du23] Durant, J. L. et al.: Farm resilience during the COVID-19 pandemic: The case of California direct market farmers. Agricultural Systems 204, 1-18, 2023.

[Fi14] Fink, A.: Conducting research literature reviews: From the internet to paper. Sage publications, Los Angeles, 2014.

[GYL22] Gao, Y.; Yang, X.; Li, S.: Government Supports, Digital Capability, and Organizational Resilience Capacity during COVID-19: The Moderation Role of Organizational Unlearning. Sustainability 14, 1-19, 2022.

[Ha20] Hartmann, S.; Weiss, M.; Newman, A.; Hoegl, M.: Resilience in the workplace: A multilevel review and synthesis. Applied Psychology 69, 913-959, 2020.

[HW22] Hohagen, S.; Wilkens, U.: Towards a digital maturity model for agriculture – Diagnosis instruments and measurement results from farming in Germany. European Academy of Management Conference 2022, Winterthur, 15.-17.06.2022, 2022.

[HWZ21] Hohagen, S.; Wilkens, U.; Zaghow, L.: Digitalisierung in der Landwirtschaft – Resilienz der Entwicklung aus arbeitswissenschaftlicher Perspektive. In (Meyer-Aurich, A. et al. Hrsg.): Informations- und Kommunikationstechnologien in kritischen Zeiten? Gesellschaft für Informatik, Bonn, p. 145-150, 2021.

[KC21] Kaçmaz, Y. Y.; Çevirgen, A.: The impact of learning organizations on organizational resilience through institutionalization: a study during the period of COVID-19. International Journal of Contemporary Economics and Administrative Sciences 11, 469-488, 2021.

[KDB20] Kangogo, D.; Dentoni, D.; Bijman, J.: Determinants of farm resilience to climate change: The role of farmer entrepreneurship and value chain collaborations. Sustainability 12, 1-15, 2020.

[KNL16] King, D. D.; Newman, A.; Luthans, F.: Not if, but when we need resilience in the workplace. Journal of organizational behavior 37, 782-786, 2016.

[LC21] Liang, F.; Cao, L.: Linking employee resilience with organizational resilience: the roles of coping mechanism and managerial resilience. Psychology Research and Behavior Management 14, 1063-1075, 2021.

[Li17]   Linnenluecke, M. K.: Resilience in business and management research: A review of influential publications and a research agenda. International Journal of Management Reviews 19, 4-30, 2017.

[Li22]   Lisdiono, P.; Said, J.; Yusoff, H.; Hermawan, A. A.: Examining Leadership Capabilities, Risk Management Practices, and Organizational Resilience: The Case of State-Owned Enterprises in Indonesia. Sustainability 14, 1-19, 2022.

[Me19]   Meuwissen, M. P. et al.: A framework to assess the resilience of farming systems. Agricultural Systems 176, 1-10, 2019.

[MD03]   Milestad, R.; Darnhofer, I.: Building farm resilience: the prospects and challenges of organic farming. Journal of sustainable agriculture 22, 81-97, 2003.

[Or92]   Orlikowski, W. J.: The duality of technology: Rethinking the concept of technology in organizations. Organization science 3, 398-427, 1992.

[PMM20] Perrin, A.; Milestad, R.; Martin, G.: Resilience applied to farming: organic farmers' perspectives. Ecology and Society 25, 1-17, 2020.

[PEG18] Peterson, C. A.; Eviner, V. T.; Gaudin, A. C.: Ways forward for resilience research in agroecosystems. Agricultural Systems 162, 19-27, 2018.

[Ro22]   Robertson, J. et al.: Fortune favours the digitally mature: the impact of digital maturity on the organisational resilience of SME retailers during COVID-19. International Journal of Retail & Distribution Management 50, 1182-1204, 2022.

[Sl20]   Slijper, T.; de Mey, Y.; Poortvliet, P. M.; Meuwissen, M. P.: From risk behavior to perceived farm resilience: a Dutch case study. Ecology and Society 25, 1-36, 2020.

[St21]   Stotten, R.: The role of farm diversification and peasant habitus for farm resilience in mountain areas: the case of the Ötztal valley, Austria. International Journal of Social Economics 48, 947-964, 2021.

[SU97]   Strohm, O.; Ulich, E.: Unternehmen arbeitspsychologisch bewerten. Ein Mehrebenenansatz unter besonderer Berücksichtigung von Mensch, Technik und Organisation. Zürich: vdf Hochschulverlag, 1997.

[Wa02]   Walker, B. et al.: Resilience management in social-ecological systems: a working hypothesis for a participatory approach. Conservation ecology 6, 1-18, 2002.

[Wi17]   Williams, T. A. et al.: Organizational response to adversity: Fusing crisis management and resilience research streams. Academy of Management Annals 11, 733-769, 2017.

[WLX22] Wut, T. M.; Lee, S. W.; Xu, J.: Role of Organizational Resilience and Psychological Resilience in the Workplace—Internal Stakeholder Perspective. International Journal of Environmental Research and Public Health 19, 1-14, 2022.

[ZQ21]   Zhang, J.; Qi, L.: Crisis preparedness of healthcare manufacturing firms during the COVID-19 outbreak: digitalization and servitization. International Journal of Environmental Research and Public Health 18, 1-23, 2021.

[ZLv21] Zhang, J.; Long, J.; von Schaewen, A. M. E.: How does digital transformation improve organizational resilience?—findings from PLS-SEM and fsQCA. Sustainability 13, 1-22, 2021.

Evaluating synthetic vs. real data generation for AI-based selective weeding

Naeem Iqbal[1], Justus Bracke[1], Anton Elmiger[1], Hunaid Hameed[1] and Kai von Szadkowski[1]

Abstract: Synthetic data has the potential to reduce the cost for ML training in agriculture but poses its own set of problems compared to real data acquisition. In this work, we present two methods of training data acquisition for the application of machine vision algorithms in the use case of selective weeding. Results from ML experiments suggest that current methods for generating synthetic data in the field of agriculture cannot fully replace real data but may greatly reduce the quantity of real data required for model training.

Keywords: synthetic images, plant detection, phenotyping, deep learning, agriculture

1 Introduction

As a response to the ever-rising demand for training data in Machine Learning (ML) applications, much research has been conducted on simplifying the process of data recording and labelling. This is also true for the agricultural domain, where e.g., various high-throughput field phenotyping systems for recording plant data have been developed in recent years [Bo21]. Different approaches have also been proposed to reduce the effort for data annotation, such as the deep interactive object selection method presented in [Xu16]. Given the laborious and costly nature of real data acquisition, it is no wonder that the use of synthetic data (SD) has become a popular alternative in recent years [Ni21].

However, synthetic data comes with its own pitfalls, first and foremost the inherent and sometimes subtle difference between reality and simulation, commonly referred to as the (simulation) reality gap. This special case of a domain gap between data from various sources is the deciding factor in how useful SD can be for a particular ML use case, its impact depending on the characteristics of the used data and algorithms. It is thus difficult to predict how well SD can be used for any particular use case or algorithm, as the relevance of different aspects of the data may vary between contexts and inference targets.

While synthetic data has been used in numerous applications, as reviewed by Nikolenko [Ni21], its application for machine vision tasks are of special interest in the context of agriculture, where current and future smart farming applications depend on the ability of

---

[1] Deutsches Forschungszentrum für Künstliche Intelligenz GmbH, Forschungsbereich Planbasierte Robotersteuerung, Berghoffstraße 11, Osnabrück, 49090; Contact: kai.von_szadkowski@dfki.de; naeem.iqbal@dfki.de; justus_felix.bracke@dfki.de; anton.elmiger@dfki.de; hunaid.hamid@dfki.de

agricultural machinery and robots to make sense of camera data, e.g., for crop row detection or selective weeding. Aggravating the laborious nature of real data acquisition, agricultural contexts pose additional problems such as uncontrollable external factors (e.g., weather conditions) or seasonality of the objects of interest. Due to the fractal nature and thus complex shape of plants, data annotation can also become more costly or error-prone in agricultural contexts, a point where ML models trained on SD could provide useful assistance even if their performance is not fully on par with models trained on real data.

It is thus of little surprise that a number of recent studies have used synthetic data for different machine vision applications in agriculture. Ubbens et al. used synthetic plant models created via a Lindenmayer system to generate relatively simple image data for a leaf counting task, discussing how various aspects of the data impacted model performance [Ub18]. Barth et al. created synthetic data of pepper plants in a harvesting scenario, using an elaborate mix of procedural generation and 3D-scanned parts and training a segmentation model to facilitate autonomous harvesting with promising results [Ba18]. Carbone et al. even produced both RGB and infrared using the Unity game engine[2], finding that the inclusion of synthetic near-infrared (NIR) data can improve segmentation results [CPN20]. Similarly using a game engine (Unreal Engine 4[3]), Di Cicco et al. explored the use of synthetic data for crop and weed detection in sugar beets [Ci17]. These (and other) studies show the potential benefit of using synthetic data for various applications in the agricultural domain, often finding that the best results can be achieved when synthetic and real data are combined.

In this study, we present our approaches for generating real and synthetic data for a simple selective weeding use case that requires differentiating between crop and weed plants in a maize field. Using state-of-the-art machine vision algorithms, we evaluate the benefits of synthetic data for future applications in this research area.

2 Data acquisition

2.1 Synthetic data

To create a synthetic data set of a maize field, we used *Syclops*, a modular software pipeline allowing to generate synthetic data for agricultural environments. Syclops is currently under development in the Agri-Gaia[4] project and is intended to be made available open-source over the course of the project. For the data used in this work, we utilized Syclops' module interfacing it with the open-source 3D software Blender[5]. This allowed rendering photorealistic images using Blender's raytracing engine *cycles*. Achieving a

---

[2] https://unity.com
[3] https://www.unrealengine.com
[4] https://www.agri-gaia.de/
[5] https://www.blender.org/

quality of synthetic data close to photorealism helps to minimize the simulation-reality-gap in the RGB data and realistically depict e.g., shadows or subsurface scattering (scattering of light in organic and other translucent materials such as plant leaves).

A combination of commercially available and free assets was used in the 3D environments generated with Syclops. Models from the Maxtree [Ma22] plant library were utilized for the maize plants, adapting them to match the desired growth stages of their counterparts in the real data (Fig. 1). The weed models stem from the Graswald [Ha22] library and were similarly adjusted to fit the scene. Using Syclops' tooling for generating agricultural scenes, the plant models were distributed on a virtual field environment in specific distribution patterns (rows for maize, scattering for weeds), using random transformations such as scaling and rotation to increase variability.

Fig. 1: Rendering of 3D-Models of the virtual maize plants

To simulate changing lighting conditions in real outdoor environments, lighting of the scene was set up using a large number of HDR (high dynamic range) images, randomly chosen for each output image. For this, HDR imagery was used that is freely available from Polyhaven [Za22]. Similarly, ground materials were varied for each image, also using Polyhaven assets, thus sampling from a collection of soil and dirt textures to reproduce realistic backgrounds for the plants. Additionally, an elevation map was used to create micro-displacements of the ground to better simulate ground structures such as pebbles, tire tracks, or clods of soil. Finally, a shadow caster object was created in the virtual scene representing the recording setup of the real data set (Section 2.2), further facilitating a close match of real and synthetic data.

Overall, the combination of these elements results in a data set with variable composition and illumination, as shown in Figure 2. In total, 6500 images were rendered (matching the resolution of the real data set, see section 2.2) with their associated bounding boxes for the two classes *Maize* and *Weed*, totaling 45997 and 119316 instances respectively.

Fig. 2: Example images from the generated synthetic data set, illustrating different lighting conditions for identical perspective (top), different ground textures for identical lighting with simulated shadows from hardware (middle) and overall variability (bottom row)

2.2 Real data

Several data sets of maize for ML applications have been published, e.g. [La22], [Li22], and [MS22]. However, existing data sets exhibit limitations such as low variability of growth stages, controlled constant lighting, missing annotations for weeds, low weed levels due to conventional herbicide treatments or simply small data set size. We therefore made use of an experimental field established at Hof Fleming (Löningen, Germany) within the Agri-Gaia project to record our own training and reference data. The experimental field consists of 32 rows of maize with a length of 40 m. Two measuring campaigns were conducted between May and August 2022, capturing early growth stages of maize following two seeding applications. Herbicide treatment was varied within the rows to create variable weed pressure.

A manually driven wheeled sensor carrier was constructed to serve as a non-invasive phenotyping platform, consisting of an aluminum frame mounted on bike wheels (Fig. 3). A sensor box is mounted at the center, containing a JAI FS3200T multispectral camera in nadir view and a processing unit running ROS Noetic. The overall carrier is lightweight and maneuverable and can be operated by a single person, while the large tires make it possible to leave taller crops undisturbed. Additional equipment includes a tablet to control the ROS setup, an RTK-GPS receiver for georeferencing and an LTE/WIFI router.

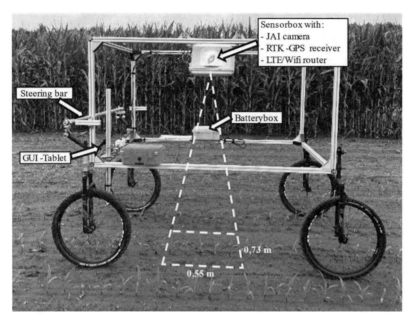

Fig. 3: The developed manually driven sensor carrier with various attachments

The image data was recorded with a resolution of 2047 x 1525 pixel, resulting in a spatial resolution at ground level of 0,36 mm/pixel. Data was captured on three time intervals after seeding (day 11, 15 and 17), covering different growth stages of the maize as well as environmental conditions such as weed coverage, soil texture or illumination (Fig. 4).

Fig. 4: Some example images of the recorded dataset showing the variability of the data regarding illumination conditions, weed intensity and growth stages

The open-source software CVAT [Cv22] was used for annotation. The data was labelled with bounding boxes of the same classes as the synthetic data, *Maize* and *Weed*. The labelled dataset contains 731 images with the two class IDs exported in both COCO annotation format and YOLO annotation format (Tab. 1). Most of the weed instances have areas of less than 30,000 pixels, while the maize instances have much larger areas, mostly around 100,000 pixels. It is intended to open-source this data set in the near future.

	Maize	Weed	Total
Day 11	1061	9743	10804
Day 15	696	14508	15204
Day 17	537	5435	5972
Total	2294	29686	31980

Tab. 1: Number of instances of Class IDs *Maize and Weed* across growth stages among Day 11, Day 15, and Day 17 after the initial seeding of the maize plants

3 Evaluation experiments

To conduct our deep learning experiments, we chose two state-of-the-art ML networks: Yolov5m (medium-sized) with ResNet50 backbone (see [Jo22], [RF18]) and FCOS with ResNet50 backbone (see [Ti20], [De22]). YOLOv5m uses anchors tuned to plant detection, while FCOS does not need any predefined anchors, thus comparing these models provides an insight into overall accuracy when there are no anchors involved. Both networks use a ResNet50 backbone which was pretrained on the ImageNet data set. We used the initialized weights from that pretraining as a starting point for all our experiments.

For each network, we ran eight experiments falling into four categories: training on synthetic data and testing on synthetic data (experiment Y1 and F1), training on real data and testing on real data (Y2/F2), training on synthetic data and testing on real data (Y3-7/F3-7), and training on a mix of synthetic and real data and testing on real data (Y8/F8).

The intention of experiments Y1/F1 and Y2/F2 was to establish a baseline of performance that could be achieved with our data sets and chosen models (with the added element of sanity-checking our synthetic data). Most experiments, however, are focused on evaluating how well the models performed when mainly or exclusively trained on synthetic data in this use case, thus exploring the impact of the domain gap between real and synthetic data. Following the recommendation of Nowruzi et. al. [No19], we implemented the idea of bootstrapping the network, i.e., first training the network only on synthetic data and then retraining it on a very small subset of the target domain data.

The networks were trained for at maximum 150 epochs, with some training cycles being stopped early when no progress was made on the loss values. We used the default hyperparameter values during training which are provided in the model repositories (see [De22], [Jo22]). Due to the small area of the weeds in the image, we downscaled the images to a resolution of 1312 x 1312 pixel. Any further downscaling compromises the detection accuracy by a large margin. Therefore, all of the following experiments are performed at a resolution of 1312 x 1312 pixel for both training and testing.

We split the synthetic data set into 5000 images for training and 1500 images for testing. For some of the experiments only the first 500 out of the 5000 images for training were used. The images were not shuffled in order to ensure comparability.

The 731 real images from all days were split into fixed subsets of 400 images for training, 150 images for validation and 150 images for testing. This was done as opposed to randomly picking subsets to prevent data leakage. For each day, images from different rows of the field were selected to exclude the possibility of individual plants re-occurring between days. Within these rows, data was spatially split between training and validation/test images to avoid overlap between consecutive images affecting separation of the data subsets. To ensure comparability, we used the same subsets of real data for all experiments. We combined training, validation and testing images into one subset for those experiments where the models were purely trained on synthetic images to increase the amount of available real images.

4 Results and discussion

Table 2 shows the results of all experiments, while Figure 5 shows an example output of a trained YOLO model. For training and validation on synthetic data, both YOLO and FCOS achieve high accuracy for both classes (see rows Y1 and F1), with higher values overall in the case of synthetic data. This establishes an upper bound on model accuracy in the absence of a domain gap and validates our synthetic data generation setup. Similarly, when the models are trained on real data, it yields high accuracies on the real validation data (see Y2/F2). The values of e.g., 95.6 and 90.5 on maize for YOLO and FCOS, respectively, are a high baseline to be reached for mixed training setups.

Overall, experiments with the models trained on synthetic data show a lower performance on the real test data compared to the experiments using only real data, indicating a substantial domain gap between the two data sets. This may indicate an insufficient level of realism in the synthetic data in some respects, e.g., the variability of the rendered plant models. However, it is also to be noted that the synthetic data contains a larger variability in backgrounds and illumination, given that the real data set was recorded on only a few days and on the same soil. This may also be an explanation for the observation that training on larger synthetic data sets does not lead to an increase in performance (see row Y3, Y4 and F3, F4), again also indicating the limited variability and thus number of features in the plant models.

Model	Exp	Training data set	Eval data set	mAP50 All	mAP50 Weeds	mAP50 Maize
YOLO v5m	Y1	5000 syn	1500 syn	97	98.1	**95.9**
	Y2	400 real	150 real	85.6	75.3	**95.9**
	Y3	5000 syn	700 real	52.4	29.6	75.1
	Y4	500 syn	700 real	61.8	44.6	**78.6**
	Y5	500 syn	304 real d11	63.1	37.2	89.0
	Y6	500 syn	240 real d15	62.3	51.2	72.3
	Y7	500 syn	187 real d17	53.9	42.8	65.0
	Y8	500 syn + 31 real	700 real	75.3	66.1	**84.5**
FCOS	F1	5000 syn	1500 syn	93.09	94.5	**92.05**
	F2	400 real	150 real	79.15	67.8	**90.5**
	F3	5000 syn	700 real	38.89	20.70	57.60
	F4	500 syn	700 real	47.33	24.00	**70.66**
	F5	500 syn	304 real d11	53.60	25.40	81.80
	F6	500 syn	240 real d15	49.76	26.23	73.28
	F7	500 syn	187 real d17	23.49	12.95	34.04
	F8	500 syn + 31 real	700 real	55.99	48.86	**63.12**

Tab. 2: Comparison of mAP50 for two object detectors trained on real and synthetic data sets and evaluated on different evaluation splits

Furthermore, the networks perform with varying degrees of accuracy on different growth stages of maize plants (Y5-7/F5-7), hinting at different degrees of accuracy to which the growth stages in the real data were reproduced with our set of 3D models. That performance is overall worse on weeds than on maize (best mAP 66.1 for YOLOv5m and 48.86 for FCOS) is an indicator for the higher variability in the weeds. The presence of grassy weeds (monocotyledons) in the real data which were not labelled and are part of the background may contribute to this, as they are both misclassified as weeds or maize, in both cases with low confidence values.

When the models are trained on synthetic data and then trained on a small subset of the real data set (see row Y8 and F8), the performance of training the model on large sets of real data (Y2/F2) is not reached. YOLO reaches higher accuracies compared to purely training on synthetic data and testing on the whole real data set (Y8: 84.5 vs. Y4: 78.6). Similar behavior is not observed for FCOS (F8: 63.12 vs. F4: 70.66). One possible explanation for this is the anchor-less architecture of the FCOS. Since FCOS has no prior knowledge of the target domain in terms of anchors, it needs more data to perform well on that data. Compared to FCOS, YOLO learns faster with a small number of data points, which could be explained by its use of anchors.

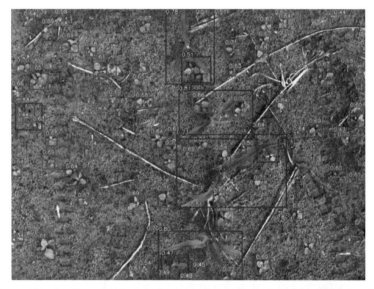

Fig. 5: Example image from real data set showing predictions for both Maize (blue) and Weeds (red) by YOLOv5m trained on 500 synthetic images, with the respective confidence values

5 Conclusion

We presented two data sets of a selective weeding use case, one obtained with established methods on a real field, the other generated using a synthetic data pipeline based on state-of-the-art 3D rendering tools. Our results show lower performance of current object detection models trained in a naïve way on synthetic data compared to models trained on real data, indicating a substantial reality gap. However, when using combinations of synthetic data with small sets of real data, accuracy can be improved, at least if the underlying model is able to adapt quickly to new data. It can be expected that reducing the domain gap apparent in the data from other experiments can further bolster performance, but more research is required to quantify the effects of the domain gap or the ratio of synthetic and real data in mixed data sets on the achievable results.

Future work in this area should focus on identifying adequate metrics to quantify the domain gap between synthetic and real data sets, as well as on developing methods to further eliminate it, e.g. by improving the utilized 3D models – work that is under way in the Agri-Gaia project. This may open the door to significantly reducing the effort to collect and label real data if the performance of mixed training setups can consistently reach the performance of models trained on large amounts of real data. Even if this cannot be reached, the level of accuracy demonstrated here already makes this approach useful for the purpose of assisting in labelling real data, thus reducing overall labelling effort.

Acknowledgements: We would like to thank Hof Fleming for their support during the field campaign and the data recording in the field. The assembly of the sensor carrier and the integration of the sensors into the ROS environment was supported by our Chief Technician Maik Ludwig and our Software Engineer Gurunatraj Parthasarathy. For their image annotation work we would like to thank our students Qalab Abbas, Vera Klütz, Reshma Khan, Lara Lüking, Dibyashree Nahak and Simon Zielinski.

This work was supported by the German Federal Ministry for Economic Affairs and Climate Action within the Agri-Gaia project (grant number: 01MK21004A). The DFKI Niedersachsen (DFKI NI) is sponsored by the Ministry of Science and Culture of Lower Saxony and the VolkswagenStiftung.

Bibliography

[Ba18]   Barth, R., Ijsselmuiden, J., Hemming, J., Henten, E.J.V.: Data synthesis methods for semantic segmentation in agriculture: A Capsicum annuum dataset. Computers and Electronics in Agriculture. 144, 284-296 (2018). https://doi.org/10.1016/j.compag.2017.12.001

[Bo21]   Botyanszka, L.: A Review of Imaging and Sensing Technologies for Field Phenotyping. Acta Horticulturae et Regiotecturae. 24, 58–69 (2021). https://doi.org/10.2478/ahr-2021-0011

[CPN20] Carbone, C., Potena, C., Nardi, D.: Simulation of near Infrared Sensor in Unity for Plant-weed Segmentation Classification. Presented at the January 1 (2020). https://doi.org/10.5220/0009827900810090

[Ci17]   Di Cicco, M., Potena, C., Grisetti, G., Pretto, A.: Automatic Model Based Dataset Generation for Fast and Accurate Crop and Weeds Detection, 2016.

[Cv22]   CVAT, https://www.cvat.ai/, last accessed 2022/10/13

[De22]   facebookresearch/detectron2, https://github.com/facebookresearch/detectron2, last accessed 2022/10/13

[Ha22]   Harling, J.: Graswald – State of the art 3D nature, https://www.graswald3d.com/, last

	accessed 2022/10/13
[Jo22]	Jocher, G.: YOLOv5 by Ultralytics, https://github.com/ultralytics/yolov5, (2020). https://doi.org/10.5281/zenodo.3908559
[La22]	Lac, L., Keresztes, B., Louargant, M., Donias, M., Da Costa, J.-P.: An annotated image dataset of vegetable crops at an early stage of growth for proximal sensing applications. Data in Brief. 42, 108035 (2022). https://doi.org/10.1016/j.dib.2022.108035
[Ma22]	Maxtree: Maxtree – 3D Plant Models	CG Assets, https://maxtree.org/, last accessed 2022/10/13.
[MS22]	Milioto, A., Stachniss, C.: Bonnet: An open-source training and deployment framework for semantic segmentation in robotics using cnns. Presented at the 2019 International Conference on Robotics and Automation (ICRA), 2019.
[Ni21]	Nikolenko, S.I.: Synthetic Data for Deep Learning, http://arxiv.org/abs/1909.11512, (2019). https://doi.org/10.48550/arXiv.1909.11512
[No19]	Nowruzi, F.E., Kapoor, P., Kolhatkar, D., Hassanat, F.A., Laganière, R., Rebut, J.: How much real data do we actually need: Analyzing object detection performance using synthetic and real data. CoRR. abs/1907.07061, 2019.
[RF18]	Redmon, J., Farhadi, A.: Yolov3: An incremental improvement. arXiv preprint arXiv:1804.02767; 2018.
[Ti20]	Tian, Z., Shen, C., Chen, H., He, T.: FCOS: A simple and strong anchor-free object detector, http://arxiv.org/abs/2006.09214, 2020.
[Ub18]	Ubbens, J.: The use of plant models in deep learning: an application to leaf counting in rosette plants. 10, 2018.
[Xu16]	Xu, N., Price, B., Cohen, S., Yang, J., Huang, T.: Deep Interactive Object Selection, http://arxiv.org/abs/1603.04042, (2016). https://doi.org/10.48550/arXiv.1603.04042
[Za22]	Zaal, G., Tuytel, R., Cilliers, R., Cock, J.R., Barresi, D., Mischok, A., Majboroda, S., Savva, D., Guest, J.: Poly Haven • Poly Haven, https://polyhaven.com/, last accessed 2022/10/13.

Review of agricultural field robots and their applicability in potato cultivation

Jana Käthner[1], Karuna Koch[1], Nora Höfner[1], Volker Dworak[1], Mostafa Shokrian Zeini[1], Redmond Shamshiri[1,2], Woj Figurski[1] and Cornelia Weltzien[1,2]

Abstract: This paper lists the potential, challenges and requirements of autonomous field robots for potato production. It presents an overview of existing autonomous field robots in arable farming, evaluates their suitability for potato production based on literature findings and gives an outlook on possible future solutions. The analysis was confined to the European market. In summary, 17 commercially available field robots, 4 robots in the test phase and 14 prototypes in the development phase were identified. The minimum requirements identified for field robots to enable their application in a potato field are primarily geometric due to the specific ridge structure and the habitus of potato plants. As a result, the field robot must have a track width of 0.75 m or a multiple of this dimension. In addition, a ground clearance between 0.35 m and 0.8 m must be ensured. The evaluation showed that two of the identified market-ready robot systems fulfilled the identified minimum requirements.

Keywords: autonomous field robots, market overview, potato production, technology evaluation, agriculture

1 Introduction

Agriculture faces numerous challenges like weather extremes, market fluctuations, and labour shortages. Furthermore, the sustainability of production systems depends largely on low production costs and high market prices to keep agricultural enterprises competitive. In order to achieve high market prices for table potatoes, for example, high yields that meet the quality standards of the market are required [UN17]. Reaching high product quality characteristics demands optimal plant health. Maintaining plant health, without increasing chemical treatments, in turn, involves numerous manual interventions. However, the demand for numerous manual cultivation measures is opposed by the shortage of skilled workers. The challenge therefore lies in finding solutions to execute more smaller interventions with high resource efficiency and ideally at low cost. Robotic technologies can help address this challenge as they can execute precise manoeuvres, are highly flexible and require less human labour. These advantages are also evident with respect to the optimization of organic potato production.

---

[1] Leibniz-Institut für Agrartechnik und Bioökonomie e.V. (ATB); Technik im Pflanzenbau, Max-Eyth-Allee 100; 14469 Potsdam, Deutschland, jkaethner@atb-potsdam.de
[2] Technische Universität Berlin, Fachgebiet Agromechatronik, Straße des 17. Juni 135, 10623 Berlin, Deutschland

Here, robots can assist with the complex steps of plant care such as maintaining the ridge structure and mechanically regulating weeds and pests. In the following, an overview of existing autonomous field robots (AFR) is presented and their suitability for potato production is analysed and discussed.

2 Materials and methods

An internet research was first carried out for commercially available robotic systems on the European market. In a second and third step, the literature searches considered common cultivation techniques in organic potato production as well as development cycles of potato plants in general. In order to back up the literature finding, in field measurements of plant and ridge height have been carried out during one season on a test field. The results of the research on cultivation measures and plant development were used to determine requirements for field robots in potato cultivation. Finally, these requirements were used to evaluate the applicability of the identified robots.

2.1 Internet research on European field robots

An analysis of AFR including prototypes, robots that are in the test phase and market-ready products was executed by means of an internet research. Search engines, such as Google Scholar and the Web of Science were used to find scientific publications regarding developed field robots. Furthermore, search queries were placed on the Google search engine to find commercial field robot systems. For the searches, the following keywords were used: field robot, autonomous, Europe, not vineyards, not orchards, not greenhouse, not viticulture, not drone, not unmanned aerial vehicle (UAV). Thus, the search was confined to autonomous field robots. In addition, the analysis was limited to products that are available on the European market, due to various current trade restrictions. Additional information was gathered through visits to robot field days and direct contact with the corresponding companies. The analysis considered all publications of robotic systems found up to and including October 2022 using the specified keywords. Based on the requirements formulated later, the essential features were identified for each robot.

2.2 Literature research on cultivation steps

The literature search on potato cultivation was conducted using search engines such as Google Scholar and Web of Science. The following keywords were used: potato cultivation, potato farming, potato growing, potato production, precision farming. Available publications over the period from 1950 to the present were reviewed. From the researched publications, a selection was made for an in-depth consideration. Then, the relevant regular work steps in organic potato cultivation have been identified. Tasks where robotics offer the greatest potential for improvement have been analysed in more detail.

Subsequently, requirements for a robotic system were derived based on these considerations.

2.3 Literature research on plant development stages

The literature research regarding the development stages of the potato plant was conducted in Google Scholar and Web of Science as well. The used keywords are: potato plant, development stages, potato model. The resulting articles were assessed for relevance and respective publications were analysed subsequently. With regard to the use of AFR, minimum requirements from plant development were identified.

2.4 Field observations and measurements

The results of the literature research with respect to potato development and cultivation steps were supplemented by general observations and random measurements executed on a test field during the season 2022. The plant height and ridge geometry were of particular interest. The test site is located in Schöneiche in the district Dahme-Spreewald (51°56'N, 13°29'E, 122 m above sea level) in Brandenburg. The soil in this area is attributed to the soil class slightly silty sand (Su2) [Na22]. The field is about 7.4 hectares in size. Various potato varieties were grown in this field during the 2022 season.

3 Results and discussion

3.1 Results web research of European field of robots

The analysis revealed 35 available field robots on the European market (see Tab. 1). It should be noted that this review does not claim to be exhaustive, due to the dynamic development of this sector. The determined robotic systems are divided into three categories: 17 field robots are available on the market, 4 robots are in the test phase and in field trials, besides, 14 prototypes.

3.2 Cultivation steps in potato production

Potato cultivation can be divided into six basic cultivation steps including stubble cultivation of the previous crop, fertilization, basic tillage, seedbed preparation and planting, plant care and harvesting [KH19]. After the basic soil preparation, depending on the soil type, bed separation is carried out to prepare the seedbed [KH19]. In dependence of the potato variety or their intended use, planting takes place between the end of March and mid-April [Ko12]. In addition to the basic functions of placing and covering the plant tubers, planters are increasingly taking on tasks such as preparing the seedbed, spreading fertilizer or building the final ridges [KH19]. With the formation of the ridges, planting is completed and the plant care phase begins. During plant development, the potato plant tolerates little competition from weeds in terms of biomass production. The aim is therefore to achieve freedom from weeds until full growth is reached. In organic farming,

Autonomous Field Robots (AFR)		
Market-ready	In field tests	Prototype development
AgroIntelli: Robotti LR	Dahlia Robotics: Dahlia 3.3/4.3	AI.Land GmbH: ETAROB
AgroIntelli: Robotti 150D	Naiture GmbH: "8-Spur Jätroboter"	Amazone (in cooperation with Hochschule Osnabrück and Bosch): BoniRob
Agxeed: AgBot 5.115T2	Small Robot Company: Dick	Continental: Contadino
Aigro: Up	Zauberzeug: Field Friend	Earth Rover: CLAWS
Carré: Anatis Co-Bot		Escarda
Elatec: E-Tract		Fraunhofer IPA: CURT (Crops Under Regular Treatment)
Exobotic: LAND-A1		Gentle Robotics: E-Terry
Exobotic: LAND-A3 (WTD4)		Innok Robotics: HEROS
Farmdroid: FD20		John Deere: Autonomous Field Sprayer
Farming Revolution: Farming GT		Strube (in cooperation with Naïo Technologies): PhenoBob® (adapted Dino)
Kilter: AX-1		Strube (in cooperation with Naïo Technologies and Fraunhofer): BlueBob® (adapted Orio)
Naïo Technologie: Oz		Small Robot Company: Harry
Naïo Technologies: Dino		Small Robot Company, COSMONiO, AV and N Lee, Crop Health Protection (CHAP): SlugBot
Naïo Technologies: Orio		TU Dresden, Fraunhofer IVI: Feldschwarm®
Pixelfarming Robotics: Robot One		
Sitia: Trektor		
Small Robot Company: Tom		

Tab. 1: Overview of the identified field robots divided into three categories: available on the market (white), robots in the test phase (light grey) and prototypes (dark grey)

direct weed control in young potato plants is usually carried out using mechanical methods like weed harrowing. Since the above-ground vegetation course of potatoes is hesitant, mechanical weed control can be carried out over a relatively long period of time. The mechanical weed control is followed by a re-ridging of the potato ridges. The ridge formation and its strong impact on the soil structure on the one hand as well as the high need for regular weed control on the other hand result in a very high erosion risk.

Requirements for field robots derived from potato cultivation steps

The requirements for field robots in crop care differ considerably from the requirements in stubble cultivation of the previous crop, fertilisation, basic soil cultivation, seedbed preparation and harvesting. These tillage steps require a high tractive force. Wide tires combined with a high dead weight are often used to realize the power transmission. Autonomous tractors, such as Agbot from Agxeed, could be suitable to manage these tasks. However, these qualities are disadvantageous for potato plant care, as the robot must move through the field without damaging the ridges or the plants. In addition, stubble cultivation of the previous crop, fertilization and basic tillage are not culture specific and are used for other crops as well. Therefore, an automation of these steps is not further considered in this context. Instead, the formulation of requirements for suitable field robots focuses on crop care steps.

After the initial ridge formation, plant care measures like mechanical weeding followed by re-ridging, irrigation and plant health measures require a high number of in-field measures. The usage of field robots performing these tasks thus have high saving potentials. However, such robotic systems must meet the basic requirements placed by the ridge geometry on a robot chassis. Standardized potato cultivators normally form ridges with a spacing of 0.75 m and a height up to 0.35 m [St17]. Thus, the track width of the robot should match with the intra-row spacing (0.75 m) or a multiple thereof. The ridge height of up to 0.35 m necessitate a minimum ground clearance of at least 0.35 m. Fulfilling these two dimensions avoids damaging the ridge structure when driving through the potato field.

Evaluation and discussion of field robot systems regarding their compliance with the cultivation step requirements

The evaluation revealed that 9 of the 35 available field robots listed in Table 1 meet the geometric requirements derived from the potato cultivation steps (see Tab. 2).

Multiple field robots were excluded because their track width and ground clearance were not available online or on request from the robot companies. Table 2 summarises the suitable robot systems and includes further information regarding integrated functionalities, track width and ground clearance. In a next step, these robotic systems are evaluated with respect to their integrated functions suitable for potato plant care measures. The provision of suitable functionalities are considered as optional as a robot with a fitting chassis can be expanded by integrating additional sensor systems or tools.

Autonomous driving represents an important function. As mentioned above, an autonomous robot would be beneficial to reduce the workload of farmers or to compensate for staff shortages. As autonomous driving was a selection criteria in the search for robotic systems, all listed robotic systems fulfil this requirement.

Status	Manufacturer / Research institution: Product name	Function	Track width	Ground clearance
Market-ready	AgroIntelli: Robotti 150D	Autonomous tool carrier for standard implements (seeding, weeding, spraying, ridging, mowing, rotovating) [Agr22a]	Adjustable from 1.66 m to 3.65 m [Agr22a]	0.9 m (personal communication with AgroIntelli)
	AgroIntelli: Robotti LR	Autonomous tool carrier for standard implements (weeding, seeding, spraying, ridging, etc. not requiring power take-off)	Adjustable from 1.80 m to 3.65 m [Agr22b]	0.9 m (personal communication with AgroIntelli)
	Agxeed: AgBot 5.115T2	Autonomous tractor [Agx22]	Adjustable from 1.5 m to 3 m or 3.2 m (depending on chassis and crawler track) [Agx22]	0.42 m [Agx22]
	Exobotic: LAND-A3 (WTD4)	Multipurpose tool carrier [Ex22]	Adjustable, typically 1.5 m [Ex22]	No data yet available
	Farming Revolution: Farming GT	Autonomous mechanical weed control, hoeing robot [Fa22]	Adjustable from 1.35 m to 2.25 m [Fa22]	0.5 m (personal communication with Farming Revolution)
	Naïo Technologies: Orio	Autonomous tool carrier on portal basis [Bö22]	3 track widths from 1.80 m to 2.25 m [Bö22]	0.6 m (personal communication with Naïo Technologies)
	Sitia: Trektor	Autonomous tractor	Adjustable from 1.08 m to 1.61 m (MINI) or 1.91 m to 2.44 m (MAXI) [Fu22]	Adjustable (no exact dimensions yet available) [Si22]

Prototype development	Amazone (Cooperation with Hochschule Osnabrück and Bosch): BoniRob	Targeted weed control by phenotyping, tamping in or precise spraying of liquid fertiliser or crop protection agent of individual plants [Ru09]	Adjustable from 0.75 m to 3 m [Ru09, Ra10]	Adjustable from 0.4 m to 0.8 m [Ru09, Ra10]
	Strube (in cooperation with Naïo Technologies Fraunhofer): BlueBob® (adapted Orio)	Hoeing robot (sugar beets)	Basis Orio: 3 track widths from 1.80 m to 2.25 m [Bö22]	Basis Orio: 0.6 m (personal communication with Naïo Technologies)

Tab. 2: Summary of the field robotic systems which meet the requirement for the processing steps in potato cultivation. The table is composed of researched data on the function, track widths and ground clearance. The field robots are divided according to their status into three categories: market-ready (white), in the test phase (light grey) and prototype development (dark grey)

In addition, for a robot to drive along ridges without damaging them, a precise steering system is required that autonomously adapts its path to the ridge structures as they change due to erosion or plant development. According to the product descriptions given by the manufactures, this feature is provided by the AgBot, FD20 and the Orio (see Tab. 2). The Robotti LR and the Robotti 150D navigate autonomously based on an input field plan.

As the mechanical weed control is a frequently repeated cultivation step, it would be particularly advantageous if carried out autonomously. Either by integrated tools on the robot (see FD20) or in form of a tool carrier (see AgBot, Orio, Robotti LR, Robotti 150D). However, based on its weeding method, the FD20 is probably not suitable, as it remembers the self-set seeding position and then bypasses these positions when weeding. Due to its crawler tracks with a minimum width of 0.3 m [Agx22], the AgBot could potentially injure the ridge structure. Therefore, the applicability of the AgBot would need to be tested in this regard. After weeding, preserving the ridge structure is crucial to prevent yield loss due to the occurrence of green potatoes [VVB12]. Thus, re-ridging after mechanical weed control is very important and should be performed by the robot as well. This can be realized by using AgBot, Orio or Robotti LR / 150D and a corresponding tool carrier.

To this point AgBot, Orio, Robotti LR and Robotti 150D would be suitable robot systems for potato cultivation. The increasing above-ground plant development places additional requirements on the robot systems and is therefore discussed in section 3.3.

3.3 Plant development stages in potato production

The development of a potato plant can be divided into 10 stages [Ko12]. The first stage 0 describes the germination of the mother tuber and underground shoots are formed. Stages 1-3 define the formation of an above ground shoot together with leaf development. The stages 4 and 5 begin at about the same time. Stage 4 describes the tuber formation until the complete ripening of the potato. Approximately, at the same time, stage 5 of flower formation begins above ground and continues with the stage of flowering (stage 6). While underground tuber development continues, aboveground development continues with fruiting (stage 7) and seed maturation (stage 8). In the following stage 9, leaves and stems begin to die and potato tubers ripen. Another characteristic of the potato plant is that its leaves form a canopy [Fl11]. Approximately in stage 3, the stems of the different mother tubers start touching, thus starting to develop plant closure [Ko12]. Under normal growing conditions, the height of the various potato species typically varies between 0.2 m and 1 m [Ta18; HBK20]. The potato requires a precipitation level between 500 mm and 700 mm. A significant part of the water requirement is met with normal local precipitation in Germany [BLE21]. However, supplementary irrigation can still improve the yield response by around 10 % to 20 % [Go22]. In addition, it is important to mention that organic potato production faces challenges with respect to diseases and pests [Pa03]. One of the most common diseases in potato production is late blight [Kr13]. This fungal disease causes significant damage to plants and potato tubers, up to complete crop loss [Es09]. In addition to plant diseases, potato cultivation also has to deal with pests that cause feeding damage and lead to yield reduction [Ka20]. The Colorado potato beetle and the wireworm attack the plants and the potato tuber, respectively [SPK10].

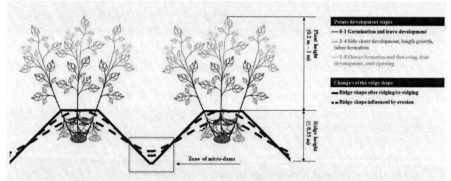

Fig. 1: Schematic representation of the potato plant development stages [Ko12], of geometrical changes of the cross-sectional area of a ridge structure and of the zone of micro-dams

Results of the measurements and observations in the test field

The observations on the test field complement the literature results proving that a robot is subject to a high degree of variance especially with respect to the different environmental factors. For example, different potato varieties were planted on the test field (i.a. Nixe, Ballerina, Mary Ann), which had different growing heights (high, small) and ripening times (early, very early, medium early) [Bu21]. Therefore, haulm height and plant closure were very inhomogeneous across the field. In a field measurement, the plant heights were determined on a random basis about 2.5 months after laying out the mother tubers. The extrema of the measured heights were 0.3 m and 1 m and thus evincing a height difference of 0.70 m (see Fig. 1). The measurement results confirm literature data [Ta18; HBK20]. In addition, as soon as the ridges are formed, weather conditions lead to soil erosion inevitably. Until plant closure starts (stage 3), mechanical weed control and a subsequent re-ridging was carried out several times, thus compensating for the erosion process to some extent. In order to determine the varying influence of erosion, measurements were performed on a random basis 4.5 months after planting the mother tubers. The ridge height was estimated by measuring the vertical distance from a linear connection between two contained ridges to the centre of the trench. For the ridge heights, minimum and maximum values of 0.14 m and 0.24 m were determined, respectively. In terms of ground clearance requirements, erosion cannot be considered a reliable factor reducing ground clearance requirements because it does not occur uniformly across the field. Measuring ridge spacing at the same points in the field showed minimum and maximum values of 0.75 m and 0.8 m, respectively. The deviations identified are considered minor and thus are not taken into account further.

Requirements derived from potato plant development

The basic requirements, arising from the potato plant and its development stages, are to avoid, as far as possible, hindering or interfering with the plant's growth or development, both above and below the ground. As the potato plant shows a comparatively slow development above the ground after laying out the mother tubers (stage 0-3) [Pr17], during this time period field robots, fulfilling the minimum requirements derived from the potato cultivation steps (see section 3.2 and Tab. 2) can be used in the field. With progressing plant growth, the demands on a robot become more stringent, as potato plants can reach heights in the range of 1 m [Ta18], show a variable growth to the side [Fl11] and tend to form canopies with their neighbouring plants. Since biomass injury can negatively affect photosynthetic rates, it can affect the potato quality as well. Moreover, if the ridge structure is damaged, potatoes may be exposed to light. As a result, green tubers may develop, leading to crop yield loss. Therefore, the robot must navigate precisely through the ridges and simultaneously pass the sprawling haulm unharmed. Possible plant heights of up to 1 m [Ta18, HBK20] require a ground clearance of at least 0.8 m. Since the stems are flexible to a certain extent, they could be deflected using baffles to prevent them from being damaged.

Evaluation and discussion of field robot systems regarding their compliance of the plant development requirements

The application of a field robot during the potato development stages 3-8 extends the minimum requirements to a minimal ground clearance of 0.8 m. The requirements regarding the track width remain. The comparison with the dimensions of the robot systems listed in Tab. 2 shows, only the Robotti 150 LR, Robotti 150 D and BoniRob meet these requirements. However, BoniRob is used exclusively for research purposes, no market launch is planned. Therefore, the BoniRob is not considered further.

An important optional function with regard to the plant development would be the monitoring of plant health in conjunction with adapted pest or disease control and fertilization according to the precision agriculture concept [Bl05]. Its automation would mean a strong reduction in workload for the farmer as well as a possible reduction of fertilizer or pesticides in the range of 25 % [Ke17]. This can be realized by integrated camera systems and corresponding data processing functions in combination with corresponding sprayers. The Robotti LR and the Robotti 150 D could provide this functionality if equipped with the corresponding carrier tool. It may be considered to suspend the application of a field robot during the period of plant closure especially formed by potato varieties reaching tall plant heights. During this time, plant damage may not be completely avoidable using a field robot, so drones could take over monitoring or local spraying tasks here.

In summary, Robotti LR and Robotti 150D fulfil the determined minimum requirements for an application for potato production. In addition, both systems meet optional requirements with regard to functions of autonomous driving, spraying and mechanical weed control if combined with the corresponding carrier tools.

4 Outlook

This review considers the basic applicability of the AFR available on the European market in potato cultivation, which places special requirements due to ridge and vegetation structure. Therefore, the focus of the evaluation was on the suitability of their geometric dimensions.

The evaluation showed that with Robotti LR, Robotti 150 D, an automation of certain cultivation steps along the entire vegetation period is possible. If the ground clearance of the BlueBob®, Orio, AgBot and Farming GT could be adjusted to the identified 0.8 m (see Tab. 2) they would be also suitable for all plant development stages. Adjusting the track width and ground clearance of those AFR identified in Table 1, which were not considered in more detail due to their dimensions, increases the choice of suitable robots for potato cultivation. With a small geometric change in the track width of 5 cm or an expansion of already existing geometric variability, e.g. Anatis from Carré, E-Tract from Elatec and Dino from Naïo Technologies also offer great potential for application in potato cultivation. For an expansion of potential field robots for potato cultivation, the global market could also be taken into account.

Whether a complete automation of all cultivation steps for potato production or other cultures in the field will be possible and if so, would be purposeful, remains to be seen in the future. In any case, the implementation of a complete digitalization of both the execution of cultivation steps as well as the harvest yields would be very useful and is realistic to achieve in the near future. In this way, optimization potentials could be easier identified and exploited. The foodChain project, launched in 2022, addresses the challenge of a further digitalization and automation in potato production by establishing a 5G campus network for real-time analysis of measurement data from the field in combination with real-time control of an autonomously driving robotic system.

Acknowledgements: This review was conducted as part of the project foodChain project funded by the Federal Ministry for Digital and Transport (BMDV).

Bibliography

[Agr22a] AgroIntelli: Robotti 150D Brochure. https://agrointelli.com/wp-content/uploads/2022/06/AI-Brochure-ENGLISH.pdf, accessed: 27/10/2022.

[Agr22b] AgroIntelli: Robotti LR Brochure. https://agrointelli.com/wp-content/uploads/2022/08/ROBOTTI-LR-ENGLISH.pdf, accessed: 30/10/2022.

[Agx22] Agxeed: Technical Specifications. https://agxeed.com/wp-content/uploads/2022/07/AgXeed_AgBot_5.115T2_Specifications-1.pdf, accessed: 27/10/2022.

[Bl05] Blackmore, S. et al.: Robotic agriculture - the future of agricultural mechanisation?. In Precision agriculture '05. Papers presented at the 5th European Conference on Precision Agriculture, Uppsala, Sweden, pp. 621-628, 2005.

[BLE21] BLE, Bundesanstalt für Landwirtschaft und Ernährung Anstalt des öffentlichen Rechts Referat 513: Bericht zur Markt- und Versorgungslage Kartoffeln. Bonn, 2021.

[Bö22] Böhrnsen, A.: Autonomes Arbeiten: die aktuellen Neuheiten. https://www.profi.de/technisch/elektronik/autonomes-arbeiten-die-aktuellen-neuheiten-29447.html, accessed: 30/10/2022.

[Bu21] Bundessortenamt: Beschreibende Sortenliste Kartoffel 2021. Hannover, 2021.

[Es09] Eschen-Lippold, L. et al.: Antioomycete Activity of γ-Oxocrotonate Fatty Acids against P. infestans. J. Agric. Food Chem. 57/20, pp. 9607-9612, 2009.

[Ex22] Exobotic, https://exobotic.com/products/L/58374093-d1cb-4127-a5ea-ccc7226a9385/, accessed: 08/12/2022.

[Fa22] Farming Revolution: Farming GT, https://farming-revolution.com/de/, accessed: 08/12/2022

[Fl11] Fleisher, D.H. et al.: Potato Stem Density Effects on Canopy Development and Production. Potato Res. 54, pp. 137-155, 2011.

[Fu22] FutureFarming, https://www.futurefarming.com/sitia-trektor-hybrid-robot-tractor/, accessed: 08/12/2022.

[Go22] Goffart, J.P. et al.: Potato Production in Northwestern Europe (Germany, France, the Netherlands, United Kingdom, Belgium): Characteristics, Issues, Challenges and Opportunities. Potato Res. 65, pp. 503-547 2022.

[HBK20] Harkel, J.t.; Bartholomeus, H.; Kooistra, L.: Biomass and Crop Height Estimation of Different Crops Using UAV-Based Lidar. Remote Sens. 12/1, pp. 17, 2020.

[Ko12] Kolbe, H. et al.: Kartoffeln im Ökolandbau 2012. Sächsisches Landesamt für Umwelt, Landwirtschaft und Geologie, Dresden, 2012.

[KH19] Köller, K.; Hensel, O.: Verfahrenstechnik in der Landwirtschaft. utb GmbH, Stuttgart, 2019.

[Ka20] Kadoić Balaško, M. et al.: Modern techniques in Colorado potato beetle (Leptinotarsa decemlineata Say) control and resistance management: history review and future perspectives. Insects, 11/9, pp. 581, 2020.

[Ke17]   Kempenaar, C. et. al.: Advances in Variable Rate Technology Application in Potato in The Netherlands. Potato Res. 60, pp. 295-305, 2017.

[Kr13]   Krebs, H. et al.: Kupferfreie Bekämpfung der Kraut- und Knollenfäule im Bio-Kartoffelbau. Agrarforschung Schweiz, 5/5, pp. 238-243, 2013.

[Na22]   Nagler, L. et al.: Der Einfluss der Fahrgassenpflege auf das Mikroklima in Schwarzen Johannisbeeren (Ribes nigrum L.). Erwerbs-Obstbau, pp. 1439-0302, 2022.

[Pa03]   Paffrath, A. et al.: Kartoffelanbau. Dokumentation 10 Jahre Leitbetriebe Ökologischer Landbau in Nordrhein-Westfalen, pp. 76-104, 2003.

[Ra10]   Rahe, F. et al.: First field experiments with the autonomous field scout BoniRob. *Proceedings 68th International Conference Agricultural Engineering*, pp. 419-424, 2010.

[Ru09]   Ruckelshausen, A. et al.: BoniRob – an autonomous field robot platform for individual plant phenotyping. *Precision agriculture*, 9(841), 1, 2009.

[SPK10] Schepl, U.; Paffrath, A.; Kempkens, K.: Regulierungskonzepte zur Reduktion von Drahtwurmschäden, 2010.

[Si22]   Sitia, https://www.sitia.fr/en/innovation-2/trektor/, accessed 09/12/2022.

[St17]   Steyn, F.: Understanding ridging to improve potato production. CHIPS, may/june, pp. 28-32, 2017.

[Ta18]   Tang, R. et al.: Physiological and growth responses of potato cultivars to heat stress. Botany, 96/12, pp. 897-912, 2018. https://doi.org/10.1139/cjb-2018-0125

[UN17]   UN, United Nations: UNECE-NORM FFV-52 für die Vermarktung und Qualitätskontrolle von Speisefrüh- und Speisekartoffeln. Genf, 2017.

[VVB12] Vučajnk, F.; Vidrih, M.; Bernik, R.: Physical and mechanical properties of soil for ridge formation, ridge geometry and yield in new planting and ridge formation methods of potato production. Irish Journal of Agricultural and Food Research, 51/1, pp. 13–31, 2012. http://www.jstor.org/stable/41756843

Towards selective hoeing depending on evaporation from the soil

Christoph Manss[1], Kai von Szadkowski[2], Janis Bald[3], David Richard[3], Christian Scholz[3], Daniel König[3], Matthias Igelbrink[3] and Arno Ruckelshausen[3]

Abstract: This paper presents how to generate an artificial dataset to test different hoeing rules. Therefore, images that have been obtained on two days of a field trial are analysed to infer weed and crop sizes. Then, weather data from 2021 and 2022 is gathered from open-source data for 100 synthetically generated fields. The generated dataset is then used to test hoeing rules that are conditioned to keep as much moisture in the soil as possible. The analysis with these hoeing rules indicates that much less hoeing would be applied if the proposed hoeing rules are used.

Keywords: weed control, data set generation, expert systems

1 Introduction

Water management is becoming increasingly relevant for sustainable agriculture. The world is facing more extreme weather events and their duration and succession becomes more unpredictable [SB21]. Consequently, farmers must change their usual practices to adapt to the new climate. One topic that will play a vital role in agriculture is water management [BBŠ22]. Heavy rain events need to be diverted and the field must be prepared for dry weather periods. It may thus be beneficial to implement rules for soil tillage that take its impact on water management of the soil into account.

Usually, soil tillage focuses on preparing the ground for seeding and weed management [Ge22]. Nowadays, zero tillage is considered as it might have better long-term effects on the soil regarding water management, e.g. evaporation [Bh17; Li22; Na21]. In the recent years, the effects of weed control in connection with tillage and zero tillage have been studied [Bu22; De20]. For tillage, the soil is cut deeply or turned over, but for weed control, only the surface of the soil (2.5 cm to 10 cm) is tilled to destroy unwanted weeds. In [BBŠ22], the authors show that weed control can reduce the soil moisture significantly. Depending on the current soil condition, this can lead to weaker plant growth. Yet, weed

---

[1] DFKI Niedersachsen, Marine Perception, Marie-Curie-Str. 1, 26129 Oldenburg, christoph.manss@dfki.de, https://orcid.org/0000-0003-4851-2622
[2] DFKI Niedersachsen, Planbasierte Robotik, Berghoffstraße 11, 49090 Osnabrück, kai.von_szadkowski@dfki.de
[3] Hochschule Osnabrück, Albrechtstr. 30, 49076 Osnabrück, {janis.bald@hs-osnabrueck.de, d.richard-guionneau@hs-osnabrueck.de, https://orcid.org/0000-0002-9072-7763, c.scholz@hs-osnabrueck.de, philipp-daniel.koenig@hs-osnabrueck.de, matthias.igelbrink@hs-osnabrueck.de, a.ruckelshausen@hs-osnabrueck.de}

control is also vital as the weeds compete with the crops among other things for water in the soil.

Thus, in this paper, rules for selective hoeing in maize are evaluated with the constraint to keep as much water in the soil as possible. Consequently, this approach looks not only at the size of the weeds, but also at additional circumstances in the field such as previous weather conditions, weather forecast, soil attributes, and the development stage of the crops. To evaluate these rules, a data set based on weather data of Lower Saxony (DE) and soil statistics is generated to evaluate rules of selective hoeing mechanisms.

2 Generation of a synthetic data set

Feature	Unit	Comment
GPS coordinate (latitude, longitude, height)	(°, °, m)	Random points to get weather data
Soil types	-	See Tab. 2
Seed date		Between mid-April and mid-Mai
Hoeing date		4 weeks after seeding
Max temperature when hoeing	[°C]	
Max temperature 3 days after hoeing	[°C]	
Sun hours {on the day of/two days after} hoeing date	[h]	
Statistics on maize size	[m^2]	Inferred from obtained data (mean and standard deviation)
Statistics on weed coverage	[m^2]	
Field size	[m^2]	
Rain 3 days {before/after} hoeing date	[mm]	

Tab. 1: Descriptive summary of the synthetic data set

To evaluate the decision system, a synthetic data set is generated. The data set is arranged in a tabular fashion and comprises the features as shown in Tab. 1. The assumptions and how the data has been generated are described in the following sections.

2.1 Assumptions and simplifications for the synthetic data set

To generate the synthetic data set the following is assumed:

- Maize is planted in between mid-April and mid-Mai. Then, the first hoeing application follows four weeks after seeding respectively, thus aligning with BBCH growth stages 12 to 16. Often a second hoeing application is applied six weeks after seeding, but this is not considered in this work.
- Fields in Lower Saxony were considered, where an agricultural holding has on average 73 ha of land [La22, Ni21]. Furthermore, it is assumed that this land is divided into 14 fields, which yields a field size of 5 ha. It is admitted that field sizes can vary according to a Gaussian distribution with a standard deviation of 0.3 ha.
- We assume only one soil type per field. The soil type is selected by the likelihoods in Tab. 2.

Sand	Clayey sand	Loamy sand	Strong sandy clay	Sandy clay	Clay
0.2	0.1	0.25	0.15	0.2	0.1

Tab. 2: The assumed likelihoods of the soil types, which might appear on the farmland

2.2 Plant Data

For the plant data, images of a maize field that has been recorded on two days in July 2021 were utilized. The system for the recording is presented in [Ko22]. The images have been manually labelled with the classes maize and weed (see Fig. 1). Crop rows, number of removable weeds, and coverage of the maize plants are inferred from the resulting box annotations as explained in the following. For the identification of the crop line, a regression is calculated based on the centre positions of the maize boxes. This regression

 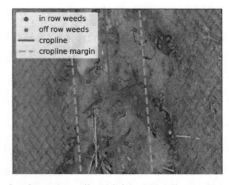

Fig. 1: Detected maize plants and weeds (left) and estimated cropline (right). According to the width of the maize, a margin is evaluated to identify in-row and off-row weeds. The off-row weeds can be removed with the hoe

represents the crop line, as shown in Fig. 1. To get the number of weeds that can be removed by selective hoeing, a margin from the crop line is calculated likewise. Subsequently, weeds that are not within the margins are removed.

This is computed for all labelled images. Then, the resulting data is used to predict the weed sizes per individual day by employing an exponential function

$$f(t) = a\, exp(bt) + c, \qquad (1)$$

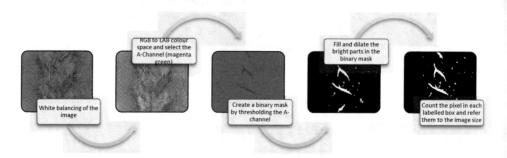

Fig. 2: Pre-processing of images to create a binary mask for detecting the weed and maize sizes. To detect the maize and weed sizes the number of pixels is counted, which have a known geometric resolution

where $a, b, c \in R$ are the parameters to be learned and $t \in N$ are the days. The parameters are inferred using a nonlinear least-squares optimization. To extract the data for both days, we make use of the Python package Plantcv [Fa15]. The pre-processing for the size determination of each plant is shown in Fig. 2. In this process, the image is first white balanced and converted into the LAB colour channel, where we only use channel A. Every value in the A channel is then set to zero if it is below a threshold and set to one if otherwise. This creates a binary mask. Then objects in the image are identified and filled with zeros, if they are below a certain size. Lastly, the remaining objects are dilated to reduce the gaps in the remaining objects. After the pre-processing, the bounding boxes are applied on the binary mask and the pixels equal to one in each bounding box are counted. The geometric size of the pixels is known such that a size in square metres can be computed.

For maize, another function $g(t)$, which uses the same model as in (1), is fitted to the size of maize. The results of both regressions are shown in Fig. 3 on the left together with the densities of the weed and maize sizes on the right. This regression is then used to extrapolate weed growth off row and maize growth for the synthetic data.

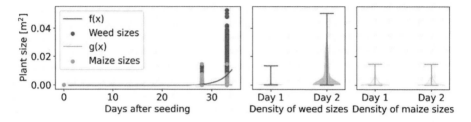

Fig. 3: Regression of the weed and maize sizes on the left. The middle shows a density of all calculated weed sizes, and the right shows the density for all maize sizes

2.3 Weather data

Now that the time for seeding and land tillage are determined, the weather data can be gathered. Therefore, the GPS position of each field instance is used to gather the actual weather of this position for the hoeing date. For this, we utilize the python package *Meteostat* [Ch22], which accesses multiple open data sources to get weather data.

3 Derivation of an expert system

In this section, decision rules are presented that decide according to the data if hoeing should be applied or not. In this paper, four rule systems are considered: conventional hoeing, selective hoeing, and two evaporation-optimized rule sets for hoeing. The rules are based on empirical studies as well as recommendations of agricultural societies. *Conventional hoeing* is basically the current standard in land tillage; the entire field will be tilled.

For *selective hoeing*, only the size of the maize and the weeds are considered. The following rules are considered:

- The BBCH of the maize must be within 12 and 16. This is measured by the size of the maize $s_{maize} \in R^+$ in [m²]. Therefore, s_{maize} must be in the range of 0.01 m² ≤ s_{maize} ≤ 0.3 m² for hoeing.

- The weed overage $c_{weed} \in R^+$ in [m²] must be large enough. Thus, $c_{weed} > 0.002$ m² to activate the hoe. That means that if all weeds are accumulated in a single patch, the patch has an edge length of 4.5 cm × 4.5 cm.

If all the rules are fulfilled, the hoeing is activated.

Evaporation-optimized hoeing considers rules that are chosen to maximize the water content in the soil or to minimize the evaporation according to the current literature. Soil evaporation in dependence of tillage has been looked at in [WB71] and for weed control in eucalyptus plantations in [De20]. However, for this scenario, the literature is sparse.

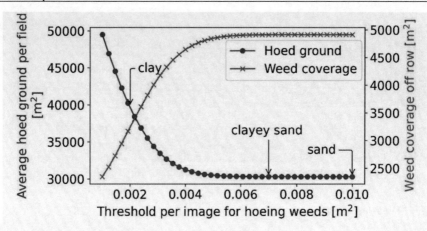

Fig. 4: After hoeing, this figure shows on the left y-axis the hoed ground and on the right y-axis the weed coverage, dependent on the threshold parameter for the weed size c_{weed}. Additionally, some of the soil dependent thresholds are annotated

Thus, the chosen values are based on educated guesses: sunny weather dries out the ground [BK15]. Loamier soils can hold the water better and can therefore be hoed even if there is less weed. If the weather is rainy, hoeing is not so harmful regarding the moisture in the soil.

This paper considers two rules for evaporation-optimized hoeing: *E-hoeing1* and *E-hoeing2*. For *E-hoeing1* we consider the same rules as for selective hoeing and the sun. Thus:

- The sun should not shine longer than 8h per day $s_t > 8$ h/d

For *E-hoeing2*, we consider a more complex rule-system, which takes the type of soil into account together with the weather conditions. The rules for E-hoeing2 are the following:

- The weed coverage c_{weed} is put into relation to the soil type. Here we assume that clay can hold water much better compared to sand. Consequently, clay will be hoed already if c_{weed} is small, and sand will be hoed if c_{weed} is large. For this rule, we chose a threshold $c_t > 0$ in [m²] that is linearly increasing in equidistant steps with the soil type. For clay $c_{t,\,clay} = 0.002$ m² and for sand $c_{t,\,sand} = 0.01$ m².

- Rainy days can influence how effective the hoeing can be. If it is rainy after hoeing, removed weeds might regrow. Thus, normally it is suggested that hoeing is applied before a period of dry weather. Here, we choose a different rule as we want to prepare the soil for the rain. Therefore, we set a threshold for the amount of rain within in the next three days $r_t > 7$ mm to activate the hoeing.

- Lastly, if the weather is sunny and hot, it is considered not to apply the hoeing because hoeing might increase the ground surface area such that more water evaporates. Therefore, the thresholds $s_t < 8$ h/d and $t_t < 27$ °C must be fulfilled for hoeing.

Hoeing is applied only if all these conditions are met.

This paper only evaluates these rules and does not put them into practice. However, the interested reader might look into [Ni21_2], where the authors present how to implement such an inference system.

4 Evaluation

All systems are compared regarding the removed weeds and the hoed ground. Furthermore, statistics on soil evaporation are utilized to estimate the water loss in the ground in each scenario. Fig. 4 shows the influence of c_{weed} on the hoed ground and the removed weeds. The crossing point of hoed ground and weed coverage after hoeing seems like a sweet spot for the selective hoeing.

Each rule set is evaluated for a relatively wet year (2021) and a relatively dry year (2022). Thus, two datasets were generated. In Tab. 3, the hoed ground, averaged over all fields, is presented for both years. Clearly, the hoeing optimized for less evaporation hoes less soil by design. Compared with conventional hoeing, selective hoeing reduces the hoed ground by 40% and the evaporation hoeing reduces the hoed ground by almost 92 to 99%.

	Weeding rule	Weeded ground [m²]	Weeded ground relative to *no-rules hoeing* [%]
2021	No-rules hoeing	50939	
	Selective hoeing	39662	77.86
	E-hoeing1	3988	7.83
	E-hoeing2	682	1.34
2022	No-rules hoeing	50908	
	Selective hoeing	39610	77.81
	E-hoeing1	2215	4.35
	E-hoeing2	643	1.26

Tab. 3: Averaged results from the hoeing rules for the considered parameters

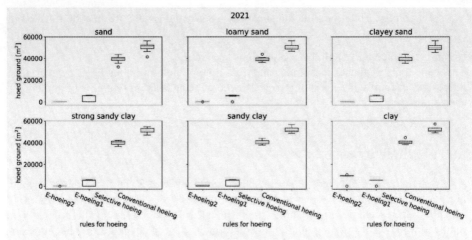

Fig. 5: The hoed ground for each field, based on the soil type based on the weather in 2021

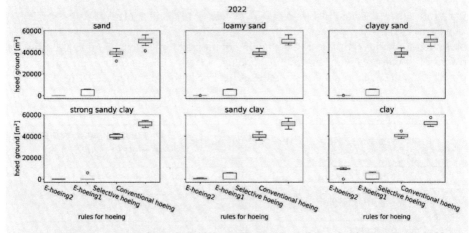

Fig. 6: The hoed ground for each field depending on the soil type for the weather in 2022

If the years are compared with each other, the hoeing rules for evaporation hoe a little more ground, if the weather conditions are more wet as in 2021 compared with dry weather conditions in 2022.

Next, we analyse the dependency of soil for each hoeing rule. Figure 5 displays the hoed ground depending on the soil for the weather in 2021 and Figure 6 for the weather in 2022. Comparing those figures, the E-hoeing2 is almost only applied if the soil is clay. For the other soils the weeds are not large enough. This can be seen as an artifact from the synthetic data set. The detected weed sizes are simply too small on those dates such that the threshold of weeds per image per soil type is too large. The E-hoeing1, on the other side, is more weather-dependent. In the wet year, it is applied more often than in the dry year. The reason why E-hoeing1 is more often applied for clayey soil is however a coincidence, as in the synthetic data soil and weather conditions are not linked.

5 Conclusion

This paper showed how to generate an artificial data set to test hoeing conditions for future smart agriculture applications in maize. For the data set, images from a field experiment were analysed to determine statistics of the maize and weed coverage. According to these statistics, multiple fields are generated with different soil properties and weather conditions on the date of hoeing. Given the simplicity of this artificial data set, first analyses can be applied regarding the conditions for hoeing. As test conditions, three expert systems are proposed that decide if the ground should be hoed or not based on the constraint to keep as much moisture in the soil as possible. The presented analysis shows that these systems hoe much less soil. The systems also have been tested against two datasets with dry and wet weather conditions. For the wet weather, the hoeing was activated much more often. Thus, this dataset can already provide a reasonable testing scenario for developing more sophisticated hoeing rules. These rules can then either be used on robotic platforms that decide to hoe the ground daily or as part of a farm management system, where the farmer wants to find the best day for hoeing. Additionally, these rules can be extended by a fuzzy system such that conditions that are almost met can be considered as well.

Acknowledgements: The German Research Center for Artificial Intelligence Lower Saxony (DFKI NI) is funded within the framework of Niedersächsisches Vorab by the Lower Saxony Ministry of Science and Culture and the Volkswagen Foundation. The work is funded by the Federal Ministry of Economics and Climate Protection (grant no. 01MK21004A).

Bibliography

[Bh17] Bhatt, R. ed: Zero tillage impacts on soil environment and properties. 10, 1-19 (2017).

[BK15] Bhatt, R., Kukal, S.S.: Soil Temperature, Evaporation and Water Tension Dynamics at Upper Vadose Zone During Intervening Period. Trends in Biosciences. (2015).

[BBŠ22] Bručienė, I., Buragienė, S., Šarauskis, E.: Weeding Effectiveness and Changes in Soil Physical Properties Using Inter-Row Hoeing and a Robot. Agronomy. 12, 7, 1514 (2022). https://doi.org/10.3390/agronomy12071514.

[Bu22] Budu, M., Atta-Darkwa, T., Amaglo, H., et al.: The Impact of Tillage and Weed Control Methods on Physical Properties of Sandy Clay Loam Forest Ochrosol in Cassava Cultivation. Applied and Environmental Soil Science. 2022, e6758284 (2022). https://doi.org/10.1155/2022/6758284.

[Ch22] Christian Lamprecht: Meteostat Python, meteostat.net. Version 1.6.5. 2022

[De20]   Deng, Y., Yang, G., Xie, Z., et al.: Effects of Different Weeding Methods on the Biomass of Vegetation and Soil Evaporation in Eucalyptus Plantations. Sustainability. 12, 9, 3669 (2020). https://doi.org/10.3390/su12093669.

[Fa15]   Fahlgren, N., Feldman, M., Gehan, M.A., et al.: A Versatile Phenotyping System and Analytics Platform Reveals Diverse Temporal Responses to Water Availability in Setaria. Molecular Plant. 8, 10, 1520-1535 (2015). https://doi.org/10.1016/j.molp.2015.06.005.

[Ge22]   Gerhards, R., Andújar Sanchez, D., Hamouz, P., et al.: Advances in site-specific weed management in agriculture – A review. Weed Research. 62, 2, 123-133 (2022). https://doi.org/10.1111/wre.12526.

[Ko22]   Koenig, D., Igelbrink, M., Scholz, C., et al.: Entwicklung einer flexiblen Sensorapplikation zur Erzeugung von validen Daten für KI-Algorithmen in landwirtschaftlichen Feldversuchen. Gesellschaft für Informatik e.V., 2022.

[Li22]   Liebhard, G., Klik, A., Neugschwandtner, R.W., et al.: Effects of tillage systems on soil water distribution, crop development, and evaporation and transpiration rates of soybean. Agricultural Water Management. 269, 107719, 2022. https://doi.org/10.1016/j.agwat.2022.107719.

[Na21]   Naveen-Gupta, Humphreys, E., Eberbach, P.L., et al.: Effects of tillage and mulch on soil evaporation in a dry seeded rice-wheat cropping system. Soil and Tillage Research. 209, 104976, 2021. https://doi.org/10.1016/j.still.2021.104976.

[Ni21]   Niedersächsisches Ministerium für Ernährung, Landwirtschaft, und Verbraucherschutz: Die_niedersächsische_Landwirtschaft_in_Zahlen_2021.pdf, 2021.

[Ni21_2] Niemann, N., Tieben, C., Lingemann, K., et al.: Wissensverarbeitung in der Landwirtschaft mit regelbasierten Inferenzsystemen und Begründungsverwaltung, 6, 2021.

[SB21]   Sheshadri, A., Borrus, M., Yoder, M., et al.: Midlatitude Error Growth in Atmospheric GCMs: The Role of Eddy Growth Rate. Geophysical Research Letters. 48, 23, e2021GL096126, 2021. https://doi.org/10.1029/2021GL096126.

[WB71]   Willis, W.O., Bond, J.J.: Soil Water Evaporation: Reduction by Simulated Tillage. Soil Science Society of America Journal. 35, 4, 526–529, 1971. https://doi.org/10.2136/sssaj1971.03615995003500040016x.

[La22]   Landwirtschaft, Forstwirtschaft, Fischerei Landesamt für Statistik Niedersachsen, https://www.statistik.niedersachsen.de/landwirtschaft_forstwirtschaft_fischerei, last accessed 2022/10/27.

Verträge über smarte Landmaschinen nach der Umsetzung der Warenkauf- und der Digitale-Inhalte-Richtlinie

Mary-Rose McGuire [1] und Hans Schulte-Nölke [2]

Abstract: Dieser Beitrag zeigt, wie eine Neuregelung im BGB, die eigentlich nur der Umsetzung von EU-Richtlinien zum Verbraucherrecht dient, auch für die Gestaltung der Rechtsbeziehungen zwischen Anbietern und Nutzern smarter Landmaschinen genutzt werden kann. Denn die neuen Vorschriften enthalten einzelne Normen, vor allem aber übergeordnete Rechtsgedanken, die auch auf Verträge unter Unternehmen angewendet werden können und wahrscheinlich auch werden. Sowohl die Vertragspflichten (z. B. Updates und Upgrades) als auch die Mängelrechte (z. B. Recht zur Beendigung und zum Anbieterwechsel) werden durch die Neuregelung beeinflusst. Zudem wird durch die gesetzliche Definition des Begriffs der „digitalen Güter" und der Öffnung des Kauf- und Mietvertragsrechts erstmals ein gesetzlicher Rahmen für Softwareüberlassungsverträge vorgegeben. Die Neuregelung gibt Anlass zur Überprüfung der Vertragsgestaltung bei smarten Landmaschinen mit dem Ziel, die Vertragspflichten und die Rechte an Software zu präzisieren. Zugleich gibt die Neuregelung Orientierung für die notwendige Anpassung der von den Anbietern verwendeten Terms & Conditions an die Vorgaben des Rechts der Allgemeinen Geschäftsbedingungen (AGB).

Keywords: smarte Landmaschinen, Terms & Conditions, Allgemeine Geschäftsbedingungen, digitale Produkte, Software, Mängelrechte, Gewährleistung

1 Einleitung

Smarte Anwendungen von Landmaschinen sind zunehmend nicht mehr eine bloße Zusatzfunktion, sondern zentral für deren Einsatz. Die hierfür erforderliche Software wird häufig, aber nicht notwendig vom Hersteller der Landmaschine angeboten. Gerade wenn es sich um eine bunte Landtechnik-Flotte handelt, setzt deren Zusammenspiel die Interoperabilität der Maschinen und Software voraus. Fehlt diese, sind auch für sich genommen mangelfreie Leistungen für den von den Vertragsparteien vorausgesetzten Zweck nicht brauchbar. Damit ist aus der Perspektive des Anbieters die Frage aufgeworfen, wie er sich gegen die Verantwortlichkeit für Mängel aus der Sphäre eines anderen Anbieters schützt, aus der Perspektive des Nutzers, welcher von mehreren Anbietern für dieses Defizit einzustehen hat und welche Rechtsbehelfe den Landwirten zustehen, z. B. um sich von einem – oder mehreren – Verträgen zu lösen.

---

[1] Universität Osnabrück, Institut für Unternehmens- und Wirtschaftsrecht, Katharinenstraße 13-15, 49076 Osnabrück, mmcguire@uos.de.

[2] Universität Osnabrück, European Legal Studies Institute, Süsterstraße 28, 49076 Osnabrück, schulte-noelke@uni-osnabrrueck.de, https://orcid.org/0000-0002-5535-8179.

Bisher waren diese Fragen kaum rechtssicher zu beantworten. Dieser Beitrag zeigt, welche neuen Begriffe und Regelungen nach der Reform relevant sind und wie eine Neuregelung im BGB dies erleichtern kann.

Folgende Beispiele für Verträge über smarte Landmaschinen sollen im Folgenden veranschaulichen, wie sich die Änderungen im BGB auswirken können:

- ***Beispiel (1):*** Kauf eines Feldroboters mit vorinstallierter eingebetteter Steuerungssoftware. Schuldner der beiden Leistungen ist jeweils der Hersteller/Verkäufer der Landmaschine, der die Software in-house programmiert hat.
- ***Beispiel (2):*** Kauf eines Mähdreschers und einer mit dieser kompatiblen KI-Softwarelösung zur Optimierung der Sortierung des Erntegutes. Schuldner der beiden Leistungen ist jeweils der Hersteller/Verkäufer der Landmaschine, wobei die Software von einem Dritten einlizenziert wurde.
- ***Beispiel (3):*** Kauf eines Feldroboters mit einem manuell steuerbaren Verschieberahmen für die Aufhängung der Hackwerkzeuge. Als gesonderte Leistung wird für eine Testzeit von 2 Jahren eine auf dem Roboter installierbare Software in Zusammenspiel mit einer hierfür eigens eingebauten zusätzlichen Kamera angeboten, welche den Verschieberahmen automatisch steuert. Um die Latenzzeit zu minimieren, wird Edge-Computing eingesetzt; nur große Abweichungen oder neue Parameter werden an den Hersteller übermittelt und dort verarbeitet, um nötigenfalls korrigierend einzugreifen, indem das Signal in Echtzeit an die Landmaschine übermittelt wird. Die Landmaschine wird von einem Händler geliefert, die Software unmittelbar vom Hersteller zum Download angeboten.

2   Kernelemente der beiden neuen EU-Richtlinien

Die zum 1.1.2022 in Kraft getretenen neuen Vorschriften des BGB, durch die die europäische Warenkauf- und die Digitale-Inhalte-Richtlinie in das deutsche Recht umgesetzt wurden, regeln explizit die Kombination verschiedenartiger Leistungen in einem oder mehreren Verträgen [Lo21; Ki21]. Da bei smarten Landmaschinen typischerweise mindestens zwei Leistungen, nämlich eine körperliche Sache und eine Software, kombiniert werden, können die neu in das BGB eingeführten Regelungen insbesondere unter drei Aspekten bei der Bewältigung der zahlreichen Rechtsfragen aus solchen komplexen Verträgen helfen.

Die erste hilfreiche Neuregelregung ist die Unterscheidung zwischen Paketvertrag, verbundenem Vertrag sowie Warenkauf mit digitalem Element und die Klarstellung, welche Rechtsfolgen für den jeweiligen Fall gelten sollen [Me22a; Sc21a]. Diese Unterscheidung kann auch für smarte Landmaschinen Orientierung geben (dazu sogleich unter 2.1).

Zum zweiten hat durch Umsetzung der Richtlinien der Begriff des digitalen Produkts Eingang ins BGB gefunden [Me22b; Sc21b]. Es handelt sich dabei um einen Oberbegriff für digitale Inhalte (z. B. Software) und digitale Dienstleistungen (z. B. Cloud). Damit hat der Gesetzgeber klargestellt, dass digitale Produkte auch als möglicher Gegenstand von Kaufverträgen und Mietverträgen in Betracht kommen und durch Verweisung auch die dann anwendbaren Normen festgelegt. Insbesondere bei Verträgen über Software entsteht nun mehr Klarheit, ob – je nach dem Leistungsversprechen – eine dauerhafte Überlassung einer Kopie zur eigenen Nutzung (Softwarekauf), eine zeitweise Überlassung einer Kopie zur eigenen Nutzung (Softwaremiete) oder die Gewährung eines Nutzungsrechts zur weiteren gewerblichen Verwertung (Softwarelizenz) vorliegt (dazu unter 2.2).

Bei der Beurteilung einer vertraglichen Vereinbarung ist drittens zu berücksichtigen, dass im Zuge der Neuregelung auch das Mängelgewährleistungsrecht verändert worden ist. Insbesondere sind neue Kriterien für die Festlegung der Leistungspflichten (z. B. für Updates und Upgrades) eingeführt worden, von denen der Zeitpunkt der Vertragsmäßigkeit, die Rechtsfolgen von Produkt- und Rechtsmängeln sowie die Möglichkeit abhängt, den Vertrag insgesamt zu beenden, falls nur eine der beiden Leistungen mangelhaft ist [Lo21; Wi21] (dazu unter 2.3).

2.1 Unterscheidung von Paketvertrag, verbundenen Verträgen, Vertrag mit digitalem Element

Für smarte Landmaschinen könnte die neu eingeführte Unterscheidung zwischen einem Paketvertrag, verbundenen Verträgen und einem Vertrag mit digitalem Element erhebliche Folgen haben. Zwar wird eine smarte Landmaschine kaum Gegenstand eines „Verbraucher"-Vertrags sein, trotzdem können die Regelungen des Verbraucherkaufs auch auf B2B-Verträge ausstrahlen [St21; Sc21d]. Denn die Vorschriften über den Verbraucherkauf können als Modell dafür dienen, welche Regelungen auf Verträge mit unterschiedlichen Leistungsinhalten anwendbar sind.

Das BGB enthält bisher keine Normen, ob für Leistungspflichten und Gewährleistung jeweils die Regeln des einschlägigen Vertragstypus anzuwenden sind oder ob – und unter welchen Voraussetzungen – eine der mehreren Leistungen Vorrang beansprucht und das Regime für den gesamten Vertrag festlegt. Auch die Frage der Auswirkungen der Beendigungsmöglichkeit für einen Teil auf den anderen Teil ist offen. Lehre und Rechtsprechung haben einzelne Fallkonstellationen etabliert, aber keine verallgemeinerungsfähige Regel entwickelt.

Diese Lücke könnte nun durch die neue gesetzliche Unterscheidung zwischen Paketvertrag, verbundenen Verträgen und Vertrag mit digitalem Element gefüllt werden. Ausdrücklich hat der Gesetzgeber damit das hier im Zentrum stehende Problem zu regeln versucht, also was gilt, wenn Sachen und digitale Produkte kombiniert werden. § 327a BGB unterscheidet dabei in drei Absätzen drei verschiedene Vertragsmodelle:

- Abs. 1 definiert sog. „Paketverträge", die folgende Eigenschaften haben müssen. Es muss sich um einen Vertrag zwischen denselben Vertragsparteien handeln, der neben der Bereitstellung digitaler Produkte die Bereitstellung anderer Sachen oder die Bereitstellung anderer Dienstleistungen zum Gegenstand hat. Darunter fällt etwa Beispiel (2): Kauf eines Mähdreschers und einer mit dieser kompatiblen KI-Softwarelösung zur Optimierung der Sortierung des Erntegutes.

- Abs. 2 definiert Verträge über Sachen, die digitale Produkte enthalten oder mit ihnen verbunden sind. Dies gilt auch für Verträge mit verschiedenen Vertragsparteien, wenn eine technische oder inhaltlich-funktionale Verbindung der Vertragsgegenstände besteht. Darunter fällt Beispiel (3): Kauf eines Feldroboters und Bereitstellung einer Software zur genaueren Einstellung des Verschieberahmens von verschiedenen Personen.

- Abs. 3 definiert „Waren mit digitalen Elementen"; das sind Kaufverträge über Waren, die in einer Weise digitale Produkte enthalten oder mit ihnen verbunden sind, dass die Waren ihre Funktionen ohne diese digitalen Produkte nicht erfüllen können. Darunter fällt Beispiel (1): Kauf eines Feldroboters mit vorinstallierter eingebetteter Steuerungssoftware.

Diese drei unterschiedlichen Definitionen von Vertragsmodellen dienen dabei zunächst als Wegweiser für die Bestimmung der anwendbaren Normen.

- Paketverträge nach Abs. 1 und verbundene Verträge nach Abs. 2 fallen unter §§ 327 ff. BGB, wobei diese Normen grundsätzlich nur auf diejenigen Bestandteile anzuwenden sind, welche die digitalen Produkte betreffen. Damit zeichnen die Normen eine Trennung zwischen den verschiedenen Pflichten vor (sog. Kombination).

- Verträge über Waren mit digitalen Elementen nach Abs. 3 fallen unter § 475a ff. BGB, sodass das digitale Element den Regelungen eines einzigen Vertrages, hier des Kaufvertrages, unterworfen wird (sog. Absorption).

Weiterhin löst die neu eingeführte „Durchschlagsbeendigung" nach § 327m Abs. 4 und Abs. 5 BGB auch die offene Frage, ob eine mangelhafte Teilleistung es dem Gläubiger erlaubt, sich vom übrigen Teil des Vertrags zu lösen. So ergibt sich für die Fallkonstellation der „Waren mit digitalen Elementen", dass der Mangel am digitalen Element einen Mangel der Gesamtleistung darstellt und – abhängig davon wie gravierend er ist – nach allgemeinen Regeln einen Rücktritt vom Gesamtvertrag erlauben kann. Für Paketvertrag und verbundenen Vertrag enthalten § 327m Abs. 4 und 5 BGB eine differenzierte Regelung, die eine Lösung unter unterschiedlichen Voraussetzungen erlaubt, nämlich wenn

- der Vertragspartner „an dem anderen Teil des Paketvertrags ohne das mangelhafte digitale Produkt kein Interesse hat" (Abs. 4)

- „aufgrund des Mangels des digitalen Produkts sich die Sache nicht zur gewöhnlichen Verwendung eignet" (Abs. 5) [Me22c].

Die Frage, in welche Kategorie ein konkreter Vertrag fällt, wird damit primär (d.h. vorbehaltlich evidenter Umgehungsversuche) durch das Geschäftsmodell und die Formulierung der Leistungspflichten bestimmt. Im Beispiel (3) kann der Käufer, wenn die Steuerungssoftware für den Verschieberahmen mangelhaft ist, also nicht vom Kaufvertrag über den Feldroboter zurücktreten, wenn ein Fall von § 327m Abs. 5 BGB vorliegt, weil sich der Feldroboter ohne die Software immer noch zur „gewöhnlichen Verwendung" eignet. Hier zeigt sich besonders deutlich, dass die Neuregelung neue Herausforderungen an die Vertragsgestaltung stellt, um die Rechte und Pflichten der Parteien an die Interessenlage und die Marktverhältnisse anzupassen (dazu sogleich unter 3.).

2.2 Unterscheidung von Softwarekauf, Softwaremiete und Softwarelizenz

Eine weitere wichtige systematische Änderung liegt darin, dass Software – wenn auch etwas versteckt – erstmals im BGB explizit genannt und systematisch verortet wird. In dem neuen § 327 BGB über den Anwendungsbereich des dort eingefügten Titels zu Verträgen über digitale Produkte findet sich in Abs. 2 eine Definition der digitalen Inhalte. Software, also ein Steuerungsprogramm, unter den Begriff des digitalen Inhalts zu fassen, liegt nicht unbedingt nahe. Allerdings regelt Abs. 6 Nr. 6 eine Gegenausnahme für Open Source Software. Daraus folgt jedenfalls im Umkehrschluss, dass „normale" Software ein digitaler Inhalt ist.

Dieser Begriff der solcherart definierten digitalen Inhalte findet sich nun auch in einer Reihe von Vorschriften, die nicht auf Verbrauchersachverhalte beschränkt sind. Dies sind insbesondere § 453 BGB über den Kauf sonstiger Gegenstände sowie § 548a BGB über die Miete digitaler Produkte. Letztere ist ein absolutes Novum und könnte zu weitreichenden Änderungen führen. Da nämlich Verträge über Software im BGB nicht geregelt waren, hat sich die Rechtsprechung bislang damit beholfen, auf den Datenträger und damit eine Sache i.S.v. § 90 BGB abzustellen Auf dieser Basis wird bislang zwischen zwei Typen unterschieden:

- Verträge über den Erwerb von Datenträgern, bei denen die auf dem Datenträger gespeicherte Software auf einem Gerät genutzt wird. Die Software wird dauerhaft zur Verfügung gestellt, hierfür als Gegenleistung ein Preis entrichtet. Nach herrschender Lehre und Rechtsprechung handelt es sich dabei um einen Kaufvertrag, weil Gegenstand des Vertrags nicht das Urheberrecht an der Software, sondern nur das Werkstück ist.[3] Praktische Bedeutung hat die Einordnung als Kaufvertrag insbesondere für zwei Fragen: Erstens für die Festlegung, zu welchem Zeitpunkt Mangelfreiheit vorliegen muss.[4] Zweitens für die Frage, ob der Vertrag beidseitig vollständig erfüllt ist. Letzteres ist insbesondere mit Blick auf das Schicksal von Verträgen in der Insolvenz des Softwareherstellers (§ 103 InsO) relevant [WB22].

---

[3] Bundesgerichtshof, 22.12.1999, Neue Juristische Wochenschrift (NJW) 2000, S. 1415; Bundesgerichtshof, 05.06.2014, Neue Juristische Wochenschrift – Rechtsprechungs-Report (NJW-RR 2014), S. 1204.
[4] Bundesgerichtshof, 22.12.1999, Neue Juristische Wochenschrift (NJW) 2000, S. 1415.

- Verträge über die zeitlich befristete Überlassung von Software. Je nachdem, ob man als Vertragsgegenstand den Datenträger bzw. die konkrete Vervielfältigung des Werkes oder das Urheberrecht ansieht, wurde der Vertrag als Mietvertrag, Rechtspacht oder als Lizenzvertrag eingeordnet [We23]. Praktische Bedeutung hatte diese vertragstypologische Einordnung einerseits für die Frage der Gewährleistung, weil die Anwendung des Mietrechts eine strenge Haftung begründet,[5] andererseits die Anwendung der Rechtspachtnormen eine Grundlage für eine ordentliche Kündigung nach § 584 BGB bieten könnte. Natürlich hatte die Einordnung als Dauerschuldverhältnis auch zur Folge, dass die Verträge nicht insolvenzfest sind.

Aus praktischer Sicht war problematisch, dass diese Einordnung den Vertragsgegenstand und Zweck nicht zutreffend erfassen kann. Für die eigene Nutzung einer Software bedarf es nur – vergleichbar einem Exemplar eines Buches – einer Kopie der Software, während die rechtmäßige Weiterentwicklung und Weitergabe (Unterlizenz) ein urheberrechtliches Nutzungsrecht am geschützten Werk erfordert.

Kernproblem bei der Anwendung des BGB war, dass sich eine Lizenz zwar unter den Wortlaut der Rechtspacht subsumieren lässt, die Regelungen über die Rechtspacht aber an der Grundstückspacht orientiert sind – etwa ordentliche Kündigung zu Ende des Erntejahres (§ 584 BGB) – und für die bei Lizenzen tatsächlich auftretenden Probleme (Sachmängel, Unterlizenz, Vertragsübernahme) keine passende Regelung enthalten [Mc12]. Die Anwendung des an sich besser passenden Mietrechts wurde von der Rechtsprechung nur bejaht, wenn dem Vertragspartner ein Datenträger (z. B. ein dezidierter Server, ASP) überlassen wurde.[6]

Beide Probleme hat die Umsetzung der Digitale-Inhalte-Richtlinie quasi stillschweigend erledigt. In § 548a findet sich die denkbar knappe Vorschrift, dass die Normen des Mietrechts auch auf die Miete digitaler Produkte anwendbar sind. Damit steht der Anwendung des Mietrechts auf die zeitlich befristete Softwareüberlassung kein Hindernis mehr im Wege.

Aus den neu eingefügten Regelungen in §§ 475a, 548a BGB folgt also, dass es keinen Softwarevertrag als Typus (mehr) gibt, sondern auch bei Software nach den Leistungspflichten zwischen Einmalschuldverhältnis (Kauf) und Dauerschuldverhältnis (Miete) unterschieden werden muss. Die Software in Beispielen (1) und (2) fällt unter den Fall Kauf, in Beispiel (3) unter Miete; zu den Folgen für die Vertragsgestaltung siehe sogleich unter 3.

2.3 Digitale Leistungspflichten und Mangelgewährleistung

Bedeutung hat das neue Recht schließlich für die Leistungspflichten bei smarten Landmaschinen. Die klassischen Regelungen des BGB sind um digitale Leistungspflichten ergänzt worden, insbesondere um Pflichten zu Updates und Upgrades

---

[5] Bundesgerichtshof, 15.11.2006, Neue Juristische Wochenschrift (NJW 2007), S. 2394.
[6] Bundesgerichtshof, 15.11.2006, Neue Juristische Wochenschrift (NJW 2007), S. 2394.

von Software. Zwar gelten diese Pflichten wiederum größtenteils ausdrücklich nur für Verbraucherverträge, bringen aber letztlich eine legitime Erwartung der Vertragsparteien zum Ausdruck, die – vorbehaltlich abweichender Vereinbarung – auch auf Verträge im unternehmerischen Verkehr übertragen werden kann.

Für Waren mit digitalen Elementen gibt es eine sog. Aktualisierungspflicht (auch Update-Pflicht genannt) für das digitale Element, die sich aus § 475b Abs. 3 Nr. 2 und Abs. 4 Nr. 2 BGB ergibt. Aktualisierungen sind danach, wenn nichts Abweichendes vereinbart ist, während des Zeitraums, den der Vertragspartner aufgrund der Art und des Zwecks der Ware und ihrer digitalen Elemente sowie unter Berücksichtigung der Umstände und der Art des Vertrags erwarten kann, geschuldet [Sa21]. Es müssen diejenigen Aktualisierungen bereitgestellt werden, die für den Erhalt der Vertragsmäßigkeit der Ware erforderlich sind. Dies gilt etwa für Beispiel (1). Wenn im Vertrag so versprochen, müssen digitale Elemente auch dauerhaft bereitgestellt werden, § 475e BGB.

Auch für Paketverträge und verbundene Verträge gibt das neue Recht Begriffsbestimmungen und Pflichten vor, die auf smarte Landmaschinen übertragen werden können. Hierzu zählen etwa die in den neuen Regelungen enthaltenen Begriffe – wie z. B. die Abgrenzung zwischen Aktualisierung (§ 327f BGB) und Änderung (§ 327r BGB) – und Regelungskonzepte wie z. B. die Interoperabilität als Kriterium für die Mangelfreiheit (§ 327e Abs. 2 BGB). Dies gilt sinngemäß für Beispiele (2) und (3).

3 Folgen für Geschäftsmodelle und Vertragsgestaltung

Das neue Recht kombinierter Leistungen mit digitalen Elementen strahlt nicht nur auf die Rechtslage bei smarten Landmaschinen aus. Er bietet auch Möglichkeiten, durch Gestaltung von Geschäftsmodellen und Verträgen deutlich mehr Rechtssicherheit zu schaffen. Klassische Kaufverträge über Landmaschinen ohne digitale Inhalte werden seltener. Zunehmend entstehen Dauerschuldverhältnisse, die eine Bereitstellung digitaler Inhalte vorsehen [Gs18; Ku20]. Die neuen Regelungen über die Bereitstellung digitaler Inhalte z. B. hinsichtlich Interoperabilität, Aktualisierung, Änderung oder Beendigung setzen einen Standard, der auch außerhalb des Verbraucherrechts Erwartungen schafft. An dieser Stelle wird zur Verdeutlichung exemplarisch auf einige Möglichkeiten zur Vertragsgestaltung hingewiesen:

Die Abgrenzung zwischen Kaufvertrag mit digitalem Element, Paketvertrag und verbundenem Vertrag kann durch Vertragsgestaltung beeinflusst werden. Insbesondere bei Test- und Betaversionen kann und sollte die Leistungspflicht durch eine – vorsorglich ausdrückliche und hervorgehobene – negative Beschaffenheitsvereinbarung beschränkt werden (zu Begriff und Funktionen von negativen Beschaffenheitsvereinbarung [Fa22], [Sc03], [Sc21e]). Ein Beispiel für eine weitgehende negative Beschaffenheitsvereinbarung ist etwa:

„Die Funktionen der zur Verfügung gestellten App sind Test-Funktionen, die nur als ‚As-is-Service' erbracht werden und jederzeit angepasst oder beendet werden können. Es wird keine Verpflichtung zur Erbringung von Leistungen übernommen."

Ebenso kann die Unsicherheit, ob eine smarte Funktion wesentlicher Vertragsgegenstand oder bloßes Add-On ist, durch Vertragsgestaltung verringert werden. Praktisch bedeutsam ist dies etwa für die Aktualisierungspflicht, da die Aktualisierung vom Händler im Gegensatz zum Hersteller oft gar nicht erbracht werden kann. Mit einer negativen Beschaffenheitsvereinbarung kann der Händler seine Aktualisierungspflicht eingrenzen, und zwar sowohl in zeitlicher als auch in inhaltlicher Hinsicht [Du22].

Jedoch ist zu bedenken, dass die Vertragsgestaltung auch im unternehmerischen Verkehr an die Grenzen des Rechts der Allgemeinen Geschäftsbedingungen (AGB) stößt. Ein Vorteil ist dabei, dass negative Beschaffenheitsvereinbarungen grundsätzlich nicht kontrollfähig sind, da es sich um Beschreibung der Hauptleistung handelt. Eine negative Beschaffenheitsvereinbarung kann deshalb wirksam sein, insbesondere wenn sie transparent ist. Dies ergibt sich inzwischen auch aus dem Zusammenspiel der objektiven und der subjektiven Anforderungen in der Definition des Mangels für Kaufverträge (§ 434 BGB) und für Verträge über digitale Inhalte (§ 327e BGB). Zu beachten ist aber, dass Werbeaussagen oder Anpreisungen im Verkaufsprozess (auch in der Lieferkette) im Widerspruch zu derartigen Klauseln stehen können. Die naheliegende Folge ist dann, dass Gerichte im Wege der Vertragsauslegung zu dem Ergebnis kommen können, dass die formularmäßige negative Beschaffenheitsvereinbarung wegen Widersprüchlichkeit oder abweichender Individualvereinbarung nicht zum Vertragsinhalt geworden und deshalb unwirksam ist.

Generelle Haftungsbeschränkungen (wie z. B. „Eine Haftung für Leistungen der App wird nicht übernommen.") sind grundsätzlich kontrollfähig und dürften ohnehin regelmäßig unwirksam sein, weil sie gegen die auch im unternehmerischen Verkehr geltenden Klauselverbote verstoßen [DSW21]. Dies gilt insbesondere für Vertragsklauseln, welche die Haftung für vertragswesentliche Pflichten, übernommene Garantien, Produktmängel, Personenschäden oder grobe Fahrlässigkeit einschränken [Fo22; Sc21c].

Bei Klauseln, die die Vertragsbeendigung beschränken, wenn z. B. nur eine App nicht ordnungsgemäß funktioniert, haben die Abgrenzungen in §§ 327a BGB und die Maßstäbe für eine Durchschlagsbeendigung in § 327m Abs. 4 und 5 BGB wahrscheinlich Indizwirkung. Eine Klausel, welche die Beendigung eines Vertrags über eine smarte Landmaschine ausschließt, wenn eine digitale Leistung fehlerhaft ist, dürfte deshalb unwirksam sein, wenn es sich um einen Paketvertrag handelt und der Landwirt an der Landmaschine ohne die digitale Leistung kein Interesse hat (so im Beispiel [2]).

Die neuen Normen in § 453 BGB und § 548a BGB lösen in zahlreichen Fällen Gestaltungsbedarf hinsichtlich der Software aus. So setzt die Anwendung des Mietrechts nach der Vorstellung des Gesetzgebers die Überlassung einer Kopie (einer statischen) Software auf einem Datenträger voraus. Andernfalls liegt ein Lizenzvertrag vor, für den neben den §§ 31 ff. UrhG nur die Regelungen des allgemeinen BGB-Schuldrechts gelten.

Daraus ergibt sich als gravierende Lücke die fehlende ordentliche Kündigung. Sie kann (und sollte) vertraglich vereinbart werden.

Die Neuregelung darf nicht den Blick dafür verstellen, dass Verträge weiterhin mit den zwingenden Vorschriften des Urheberrechts in Einklang gebracht werden müssen. Dabei kommt es darauf an, ob Gegenstand des Vertrags ein Datenträger/Werkstück ist (dann tritt Erschöpfung ein) oder nur das Nutzungsrecht (Lizenz) als solches ist. Im Fall der Lizenz empfiehlt es sich, deren Umfang ausdrücklich festzulegen. Lizenzen sind besonders fragil, weil der Vertragspartner wechseln kann (Übernahme des Softwareanbieters, z. B. eines Start Ups, durch ein anderes Unternehmen), sie gekündigt werden können (§ 314 BGB, § 42 UrhG) und nicht insolvenzfest sind (§ 103 InsO). Die Überlassung eines Datenträgers gegen Einmalzahlung bietet insoweit Vorteile.

Unabhängig von der Einordnung als Kauf, Miete oder Lizenz ist der Umfang der Nutzungsbefugnis an einer Software durch Gesetz begrenzt (z. B. Dekompilierung, Bearbeitung, Weiterentwicklung etc.). Abweichungen sollten explizit vereinbart werden, da eine konkludente Auslegung i.d.R. am sogenannten Zweckübertragungsgrundsatz scheitert [Sc22]. Praktische Bedeutung hat dies überall dort, wo die Software nicht zur bloßen Steuerung, sondern zur Weiterentwicklung oder Weitergabe an Dritte genutzt wird.

4 Zusammenfassung und Ausblick

Die aktuelle Reform des BGB hat durch die Erfassung von Verträgen, die physische und digitale Vertragsgegenstände kombinieren, ein Modell eingeführt, das zwar im Anwendungsbereich, nicht aber dem Konzept nach auf Verbraucherverträge beschränkt ist, und das für die rechtliche Bewältigung komplexer Verträge zweckmäßig erscheint. Durch die Einfügung des Begriffs der digitalen Produkte, die explizite Erfassung von digitalen Inhalten (Software) und Dienstleistungen (Cloud) und die Anforderung der Interoperabilität sowie an Updates und Upgrades wurde das BGB zugleich an die Realität angepasst.

Praktische Änderungen ergeben sich gerade beim Erwerb smarter Landmaschinen, wenn die Softwarekomponente nicht eingebettet ist, sondern als gesonderte Anwendung zeitlich befristet überlassen wird oder als Basis für die weitere Tätigkeit des Nutzers dient (Weiterentwicklung, Überlassung an Dritte).

Soweit es sich um den häufigen Fall statischer Software handelt, ist nach dem reformierten BGB zwischen einmaliger/dauerhafter Übertragung einer Kopie (Softwarekauf) und zeitlich befristeter Überlassung (Softwaremiete) zu unterscheiden. Die Öffnung des Mietrechts für digitale Produkte schließt insoweit eine lange bekannte Lücke und stellt für Gewährleistung und Kündigung nun gesetzliche Regelungen bereit, von denen aber durch Vertragsgestaltung abgewichen werden kann. Für den klassischen Lizenzvertrag enthält aber auch das reformierte BGB immer noch keinen geeigneten Rechtsrahmen. Hier erlangt die Vertragsgestaltung besondere Bedeutung.

Bei der Auslegung von Verträgen und der Anwendung des Gesetzesrechts ist zu beachten, dass die Neuregelungen des Verbraucherkaufs und der Verbraucherverträge über digitale Produkte Modellcharakter auch für Verträge über smarte Landmaschinen haben. Dies gilt etwa für den Mangelbegriff, die Unterscheidung zwischen Updates und Upgrades, die Pflichten zur dauerhaften Bereitstellung digitaler Dienstleistungen und insbesondere für die Fragen der Gesamtbeendigung bei Paketverträgen und verbundenen Verträgen.

Bei der Vertragsgestaltung ist folglich zu berücksichtigen, dass Regelungen des Verbraucherrechts, soweit sie verallgemeinerungsfähig sind, als (quasi-)dispositives Recht zur Lückenfüllung herangezogen werden können. In Verträgen zwischen Unternehmern besteht überdies bei Kombination von Sachen und digitalen Produkten die Möglichkeit, durch Vertragsgestaltung zu steuern, in welche der drei Kategorien des Rechts der digitalen Produkte die Verträge fallen sollen. Bei der Vertragsgestaltung ist weiter zu berücksichtigen, dass die neuen Regelungen über digitale Produkte auch als Maßstab für die AGB-Kontrolle herangezogen werden können, also potentiell eine Indizwirkung insbesondere für Klauseln zu Gewährleistung und Haftungsbeschränkungen in Verträgen zwischen Unternehmen haben.

Literaturverzeichnis

[DSW21] Duisberg, A.; Schweinoch, M.; Wollny, C.: Industrie 4.0 Recht-Testbed, Umsetzung und Teilnahmebedingungen im digitalen Experimentierfeld, Recht Digital (RDi), S. 249-259 (S. 256 f), 2021.

[Du22] Dubovitskaya, E.: Kauf von Waren mit digitalen Elementen, Multi-Media und Recht (MMR), S. 3-8 (S. 5), 2022.

[Fa22] Faust, F.: Beck Online-Kommentar BGB, 63. Edition (01.08.2022), § 434, Rn. 66-72.

[Fo22] Fornasier, M.: Münchener Kommentar zum BGB, 9. Auflage 2022, § 307, Rn. 83-88.

[Gs18] Gsell, B.: Der europäische Richtlinienvorschlag zu bestimmten vertragsrechtlichen Aspekten der Bereitstellung digitaler Inhalte, Zeitschrift für Urheber- und Medienrecht (ZUM), 75-82, 2018.

[Ki21] Kirchhefer-Lauber, A.: Verbraucherverträge über digitale Produkte, Die deutsche Umsetzung der Digitale-Inhalte-Richtlinie im BGB, Juristische Schulung (JuS) 2021, S. 1125-1129.

[Ku20] Kumkar, L.: Herausforderungen eines Gewährleistungsrechts im digitalen Zeitalter, Zeitschrift für die gesamte Privatrechtswissenschaft (ZfPW), 306-333 (S. 313 f.), 2020.

[Lo21] Lorenz, S.: Die Umsetzung der EU-Warenkaufrichtlinie in deutsches Recht, Neue Juristische Wochenschrift (NJW), S. 2065-2073 (S. 2070), 2021.

[Mc12] McGuire, M.: Die Lizenz: eine Einordnung in die Systemzusammenhänge von BGB und Zivilprozessrecht, S. 654 ff., 2012.

[Me22a] Metzger, A.,: Münchener Kommentar zum BGB, 9. Auflage 2022, § 327a, Rn. 3.

[Me22b] Metzger, A.,: Münchener Kommentar zum BGB, 9. Auflage 2022, § 327, Rn. 7.

[Me22c]	Metzger, A.,: Münchener Kommentar zum BGB, 9. Auflage 2022, § 327m Rn. 22.
[Sa21]	Saenger, I: Schulze et. al., BGB-Kommentar, 11. Auflage 2021, § 475b Rn. 9.
[Sc03]	Schulte-Nölke, H.; Anforderungen an haftungseinschränkende Beschaffenheitsvereinbarungen beim Verbrauchsgüterkauf, Zeitschrift für das gesamte Schuldrecht (ZGS), S. 184-188, 2003.
[Sc21a]	Schulze, R.: Schulze et. al., BGB-Kommentar, 11. Auflage 2021, § 327a Rn. 2.
[Sc21b]	Schulze, R.: Schulze et. al., BGB-Kommentar, 11. Auflage 2021, § 327 Rn. 7.
[Sc21c]	Schulte-Nölke, H.: Schulze et. al., BGB-Kommentar, 11. Auflage 2021, § 307 Rn. 9-14, 16-18.
[Sc21d]	Schreiber, K.: Ein neues Vertragsrecht für digitale Produkte, Multi-Media und Recht (MMR), S. 601-602, 2021.
[Sc21e]	Schöttle, H.: Software als digitales Produkt: Was bringen die gesetzlichen Neuregelungen, Multi-Media und Recht (MMR 2021), S. 683-690 (S. 684).
[Sc22]	Schulze, G.: Dreier, Schulze, Urheberrechtsgesetz, 7. Auflage 2022, § 31 UrhG, Rn. 110-113.
[St21]	Stiegler, S.: Indizwirkung der §§ 327 ff. BGB für den unternehmerischen Geschäftsverkehr?, Multi-Media und Recht (MMR), S. 753-754, 2021.
[WB22]	Wandtke, A.; Bullinger, W.: Praxiskommentar Urheberrecht, 6. Auflage 2022, § 103 InsO, Rn. 12.
[We23]	Weidenkaff, W.: Grüneberg, Bürgerliches Gesetzbuch, 83. Auflage 2023, Einführung vor § 581, Rn.7.
[Wi21]	Wilke, F.: Das neue Kaufrecht nach Umsetzung der Warenkauf-Richtlinie, Verbraucher und Recht (VuR), 283-293 (S. 266 f.), 2021.

Identifizierung kleinräumiger Erosionshotspots unter Berücksichtigung aquatischer Ökosysteme zur Etablierung von Erosionsschutzstreifen

Marvin Melzer[1, 2, 3], Nishita Thakur[1, 4], Florian Ebertseder[2] und Sonoko Bellingrath-Kimura[1, 3]

Abstract: Bodenerosion in der Landwirtschaft reduziert das Ertragspotential und schädigt gleichzeitig umliegende Ökosysteme, insbesondere Gewässer, durch Sediment-, Nährstoff-, und Pestizideinträge. Erosion muss daher dringend reduziert werden. Wirksame Maßnahmen sind z. B. Erosionsschutzstreifen, die im Zuge von Agrarumwelt- und Klimamaßnahmen gefördert und von Landwirten umgesetzt werden können. Für die Politik ist der Wirkungsgrad der Maßnahmen zur Festlegung leistungsorientierter Fördergeldzahlungen entscheidend. Für die Umsetzung dagegen ist eine präzise und praxistaugliche Verortung der Maßnahmen nötig. Im Projekt EROSPOT wurden daher Risikostandorte für Erosion (Hotspots) auf Teilflächenebene durch die automatisierte Verarbeitung von hochaufgelösten Geodaten identifiziert und hinsichtlich ihrer Schutzwirkung quantifiziert. Die erstellten Karten sind für die praktische Umsetzung von Erosionsschutzstreifen geeignet und lassen sich z. B. über digitale Schlagkarteien in den Präzisionspflanzenbau integrieren oder von Beratungsstellen zur gezielten Umsetzung von Agrarumweltmaßnahmen verwenden.

Keywords: EROSPOT, Gewässerschutz, Erosion, Präzisionspflanzenbau, Agrarpolitik

1 Einleitung

Bodenerosion in der Landwirtschaft wird neben natürlichen Einflussfaktoren (Klima, Relief, Bodeneigenschaften) insbesondere durch eine geringe Bodenbedeckung verursacht. Häufiger eintretende Extremwetterereignisse erhöhen die Schadwirkung durch Erosion [AU19]. Erosion reduziert langfristig das Ertragspotential landwirtschaftlicher Nutzflächen und schädigt gleichzeitig umliegende Ökosysteme. Siedlungsgebiete und Verkehrsflächen können durch Erosionsereignisse verschmutzt bzw. beschädigt werden. Insbesondere aquatische Ökosysteme werden durch Sediment-, Nährstoff- und Pestizideinträge belastet, mit weitreichenden negativen Auswirkungen auf nachgelagerte Wirtschaftssektoren (z. B. Fischerei, Tourismus) und die Gesundheit des Menschen. Erosionsschutz zählt deshalb zu den wichtigsten Ökosystemleistungen [SB18]. Daher besteht dringender Handlungsbedarf, Gewässer vor Bodeneinträgen aus

---

[1] Leibniz-Zentrum für Agrarlandschaftsforschung e.V., Eberswalder Straße 84, 15374 Müncheberg, marvin.melzer@zalf.de; belks@zalf.de; nishita.thakur@zalf.de
[2] Bayerische Landesanstalt für Landwirtschaft, Kleeberg 14, 94099 Ruhstorf a. d. Rott, marvin.melzer@lfl.bayern.de, florian.ebertseder@lfl.bayern.de
[3] Humboldt-Universität zu Berlin, Unter den Linden 6, 10099 Berlin
[4] Justus-Liebig Universität Gießen, Ludwigstraße 23, 35390 Gießen

landwirtschaftlichen Nutzflächen zu schützen. Erosionsschutzstreifen sind wirksame Maßnahmen zur Reduktion von Erosion, die im Zuge von Agrarumwelt- und Klimamaßnahmen (AUKM) gefördert und von Landwirten umgesetzt werden können. Durch eine Dauerbegrünung der Schutzstreifen wird zum einen der Bodenabtrag des Streifens selbst verhindert, zum anderen wirkt der Schutzstreifen als Barriere und Retentionsbereich für abfließendes Wasser und Bodenmaterial. Bekannte Beispiele sind Schutzstreifen am Feldrand entlang von Uferzonen (Gewässerrandstreifen), im Feld quer zum Hang oder in Talwegen (Talwegpuffer).

Mit Einführung der neuen Gemeinsamen Agrarpolitik (GAP) ab 2023 wird die Kulisse der als erosionsgefährdet eingestuften und damit für Erosionsschutzmaßnahmen förderfähigen Ackerflächen in Bayern etwa um den Faktor 2,5 ansteigen (Bayerische Landesanstalt für Landwirtschaft, unveröffentlicht). Eine präzise und praxistaugliche Verortung von kleinteiligen Maßnahmen ist daher zunehmend von Bedeutung. Die GAP wurde in der Vergangenheit für das Verfehlen von Umweltzielen kritisiert und zielt daher zukünftig auf eine ergebnisorientierte Vergütung von AUKM ab [BI17]. Aus diesem Grund sind flächendeckende und einheitliche Berechnungen der Maßnahmeneffekte nötig.

Um erosionsgefährdete Gebiete zu ermitteln, wurden Modelle entwickelt, die basierend auf Geodaten Erosionskarten berechnen. In Deutschland wird überwiegend die Allgemeine Bodenabtragsgleichung (ABAG) verwendet. Sie berechnet den jährlichen Brutto-Bodenabtrag pro Flächeneinheit basierend auf den Faktoren Bodenbedeckung (C), Bodentyp (K), Regenerosivität (R), Relief (LS) und Bodenbearbeitung (P). Detaillierte Informationen zur Bodenbedeckung lassen sich aus den InVeKoS-Nutzungsdaten[5] ableiten [ADS21]. Dazu wurden für Deutschland kulturartenspezifische, addierbare C-Werte (γ) berechnet [AU21]. Auch die Regenerosivität wurde für Deutschland neu berechnet [AU19]. Zudem wurde ein Geländemodell mit einer Auflösung von einem Meter (DGM1) erstellt, welches das Relief detailliert abbildet. Es ergeben sich somit neue Möglichkeiten für detaillierte und aktuelle Erosionsmodellierungen. Die ABAG kann Bodenverlagerungen nicht abbilden und somit die Schadwirkung von Erosion abseits landwirtschaftlicher Nutzflächen nicht quantifizieren [WLH05]. Das bereits erprobte Modell InVEST SDR dagegen kombiniert die ABAG mit einem "Sediment Delivery Ratio" (SDR) Modell, wodurch die Bodenverlagerung berechnet werden kann [HA15].

Im Projekt EROSPOT sollen für ganz Bayern hochaufgelöste Erosionskarten mit dem Modell InVEST SDR berechnet werden, die den Bodenabtrag aus landwirtschaftlichen Nutzflächen in aquatische Ökosysteme quantifizieren. Daraus sollen Hotspots identifiziert werden, die sich für teilflächenspezifische Erosionsschutzmaßnahmen eignen. Die Schutzwirkung der Maßnahmen soll quantifiziert werden. Abschließend soll eine serverbasierte, vollständig automatisierte Verarbeitung der Teilschritte und Datenverwaltung konzipiert werden.

---

[5] InVeKoS: Integriertes Verwaltungs- und Kontrollsystem

2 Material und Methoden

2.1 Funktionsweise des Erosionsmodells InVEST SDR

Das Modell InVEST SRD ist ein kostenloses Open-Source-Programm. Der Quelltext[6] basiert auf der Programmiersprache Python und ist frei zugänglich. Dadurch kann das Programm bei Bedarf für spezielle Fragestellungen, Datenbestände und Standortbedingungen angepasst werden. Das Modell verrechnet ortsspezifische Informationen, die in verschiedenen Rasterdateien hinterlegt sind. Die Auflösung der Modellergebnisse wird von der Auflösung der verwendeten Inputdaten bestimmt. Somit sind auch hochaufgelöste Analysen auf Feld- oder Teilflächenebene möglich. Für das Modell müssen die Layer i) „Relief", ii) „Gewässer", iv) „Regenerosivität", v) "Bodenerodierbarkeit", vi) „Landnutzung", sowie die Grenzen der untersuchten Einzugsgebiete bereitgestellt werden. Flächen im Layer „Landnutzung" sind über eine Objekt-ID mit einer Tabelle (Biophysical Table) verknüpft, in der die ABAG-Faktoren C und P hinterlegt sind. Der C-Faktor spiegelt den Effekt der sich verändernden Bodenbedeckung durch den Anbau einer Kultur innerhalb einer Fruchtfolge unter dem Einfluss der saisonal variierenden Regenerosivität dar. Der P-Faktor quantifiziert den erosionsmindernden Effekt durch eine Bodenbearbeitung quer zum Hang. Die Werte beider Faktoren liegen zwischen 0 und 1 und fungieren als Multiplikator. Je geringer der Wert, desto stärker reduziert er den errechneten Bodenabtrag im Modell.

Das Modell berechnet den natürlichen Verlauf von Gewässern basierend auf einer Reliefkarte. Der Gewässerverlauf definiert die Endpunkte der Sedimentation und beeinflusst daher die Ergebnisse der Erosionsmodellierung. Drainagen und unterirdische Kanäle werden im Relief nicht erfasst, wodurch das Erosionsmodell den tatsächlichen Verlauf von Bächen und Flüssen nicht ideal berechnen kann. Das Modell besitzt jedoch eine Schnittstelle, über die ein zusätzlicher Layer mit Informationen zu Drainagen und Kanälen ergänzt werden kann. Das Modell (Version 3.11) wurde für das vorliegende Projekt modifiziert, um den automatisch erstellten Gewässerverlauf vollständig durch eine externe Gewässerkarte zu ersetzen. Dazu wurde Zeile 968 im Quellcode umgeschrieben zu: „return drainage".

2.2 Auswahl und Verarbeitung von Geodaten für das Erosionsmodell

Die für das Erosionsmodell benötigten Layer wurden durch die Kombination und Verarbeitung von Geodaten erstellt, die in Einzugsgebiete[7] der Stufe 6 (n= 13050) unterteilt wurden. Die Einzugsgebiete waren durchschnittlich ca. 5,4 km² groß. Die Auswahl der für das Erosionsmodell benötigten Geodaten erfolgte unter folgenden Kriterien: i) die Daten sind für das gesamte Untersuchungsgebiet und möglichst flächendeckend verfügbar, ii) beständig und einheitlich in ihrer Struktur, iii) möglichst

---

[6] Quelltext und Modellbeschreibung: https://naturalcapitalproject.stanford.edu/software/invest
[7] Quelle: Bayerisches Landesamt für Umwelt

aktuell und iv) in einer hohen räumlichen und zeitlichen Auflösung. Die ausgewählten Geodaten wurden im Modelbuilder von ArcGIS Pro (Version 2.9) verarbeitet. Einzelne Verarbeitungsprozesse wurden zu Prozessabläufen verknüpft und automatisiert.

Informationen über das Relief wurden aus dem digitalen Geländemodell[8] mit einer Auflösung von einem Meter (DGM1) entnommen. Die Gewässerkarte wurde mit ATKIS-Daten[9] erstellt. Diese zeigen Gewässertypen als Flächen (z. B. Seen) oder Linien (z. B. Bäche). Die als Linien dargestellten Gewässertypen wurden in Flächen mit zwei bzw. fünf Meter Breite umgewandelt. Die Breite der Fließgewässer entspricht somit einem Vielfachen der Auflösung des DGM1, wodurch bei der Überlagerung der beiden Layer keine Informationen verloren gehen können. Unterirdisch verlaufende Gewässer wie z. B. Kanäle wurden ausgeschlossen, da sie von der Oberfläche isoliert sind und somit nicht als Senke fungieren können. Für den Layer „Regenerosivität" wurden die Ergebnisse von Auerswald et al. (2019) verwendet. Der Layer „Bodenerodierbarkeit" wurde von der Bayerischen Landesanstalt für Landwirtschaft zur Verfügung gestellt[10]. Der Layer „Landnutzung" wurde durch die Kombination von InVeKoS- und ATKIS-Daten erstellt. In den InVeKoS-Daten sind die jährlich angebauten Hauptfruchtarten sowie Agrarumweltmaßnahmen (AUM) und dazugehörigen nummerischen Nutzungscodes, schlagspezifisch hinterlegt. Die Daten müssen jährlich im iBALIS[11] als Voraussetzung für die Auszahlung von Agrarsubventionen im Zuge der GAP durch den Landwirt eingetragen werden und sind daher nahezu flächendeckend für landwirtschaftliche Nutzflächen verfügbar. Die Daten von 2015 bis 2021 wurden kombiniert, wodurch der mehrjährige durchschnittliche Einfluss von Fruchtabfolgen auf die Erosion berücksichtigt werden konnte. Um den spezifischen C-Faktor einer Fruchtabfolge zu bestimmen, wurden kulturartenspezifische C-Werte (γ) [AU21] einer Fruchtabfolge addiert und durch die Anzahl der Kulturjahre geteilt. Erosionsreduzierende Maßnahmen (Mulch- oder Direktsaat) wurden berücksichtigt, sofern die Information als AUM im iBALIS eingetragen wurde. Die Zuordnung der C-Werte erfolgte über die Nutzungscodes der Kulturarten und AUMs. Flächeninformationen zu nicht landwirtschaftlich genutzten Flächen, wie z. B. Wälder, Siedlungsgebiete und Straßen, wurden aus dem aktuellen ATKIS-Datensatz übernommen. Der ATKIS-Datensatz ist flächendeckend. Somit ist gewährleistet, dass alle im InVeKoS-Datensatz undefinierten Bereiche durch die Kombination mit den ATKIS-Daten lückenlos ergänzt werden. Somit kann das Modell auch diese an der Erosion beteiligten Bereiche berücksichtigen. Die C-Werte der ATKIS-Nutzungstypen wurden näherungsweise basierend auf der zu erwartenden Bodenbedeckung geschätzt und den ATKIS- Nutzungscodes zugeordnet. Für Waldgebiete wurde z. B. angenommen, dass aufgrund der dichten Bedeckung der Baumkronen und die Streu am Boden nahezu keine Erosion stattfindet (γ = 0,001). Straßen und Siedlungsgebiete wurden als versiegelt betrachtet, wodurch ebenfalls keine Erosion möglich ist. Der P-Faktor wurde für alle Flächen einheitlich mit dem Wert 1 festgelegt, da

---

[8] DGM1, Quelle: Landesamt für Digitalisierung, Breitband und Vermessung
[9] ATKIS-Basis-DLM, Quelle: Arbeitsgemeinschaft der Vermessungsverwaltungen der Länder
[10] Erstellt von Melanie Treisch, IAB1a
[11] iBALIS: integriertes Bayerisches Landwirtschaftliches Informations-System

in Bayern flächendeckend bisher keine Informationen über die Bodenbearbeitung verfügbar sind.

2.3 Erstellung der Erosionskarten mit InVEST SDR

Die erstellten Layer wurden mit dem Erosionsmodell verknüpft. Die in der Modellbeschreibung empfohlenen Modellparameter wurden übernommen: Borselli k (2), Borselli IC0 (0,5), Max SDR (0,8), Max L (122). Der Parameter „Threshold flow accumulation" ist durch die Modifikation des Modelles nicht mehr relevant. Das Modell kombiniert die Layer zu einer Rasterdatei, wobei jede Rasterzelle den örtlichen Bodenabtrag quantifiziert.

2.4 Identifizierung von Erosionshotspots

Für die Verortung von Hotspots wurde ein ortsabhängiger Schwellenwert auf Einzugsgebietsebene bestimmt. Dafür wurden die Erosionsrasterwerte (Abb. 1) eines Einzugsgebiets in einer Häufigkeitsverteilung betrachtet. Erosionswerte, die in der Häufigkeitsverteilung zwischen der einfachen und vierfachen Standardabweichung liegen, wurden als Hotspots definiert. Das Minimum wurde durch Versuche an verschiedenen Einzugsgebieten ermittelt und so festgelegt, dass möglichst gut abgrenzbare Bereiche in einer für kleinteilige Maßnahmen ausreichenden Größe identifiziert wurden. Ein Maximum wurde definiert um Artefakte auszuschließen, die bei der Erosionsmodellierung aufgrund von Fehlern in den Inputdaten hervorgerufen werden können. Aus den selektierten Rasterzellen (Abb. 2) wurde eine Vektordatei erstellt (Abb. 3). Durch Puffern der Vektordatei um 4 Meter (Abb. 4), gefolgt von einer negativen Pufferung um 5 Meter (Abb. 5), wurden kleine, aber nah beieinander liegende Polygone miteinander verbunden. Kleine, aber voneinander weiter entfernte Polygone wurden dagegen aus dem Datensatz entfernt. Polygone, die kleiner als 100 m² waren, wurden gelöscht, um die weitere Datenverarbeitung zu beschleunigen. Die verbleibenden Polygone wurden anschließend durch das Tool „Minimale Begrenzungsgeometrie" zu einfachen Geometrien umgewandelt (Abb. 6). Der Geometrietyp "convex hull" wurde gewählt, wodurch konvexe Polygone erzeugt wurden, deren Innenwinkel kleiner als 180° sind. Die erzeugten Polygone haben daher keine Einbuchtungen und sind besser für die Bearbeitung durch landwirtschaftliche Maschinen geeignet. Im nächsten Schritt wurden die Polygone mit den Schlaggrenzen (InVeKoS 2021) verschnitten, um deren Zugehörigkeit zu einzelnen Schlägen festzulegen. Die finale Hotspotkarte wurde durch eine abschließende Selektion erstellt, bei der Polygone kleiner 400 m² entfernt wurden. Zudem wurde der Bodenabtrag innerhalb der Hotspots durch das ursprüngliche Erosionsraster bestimmt.

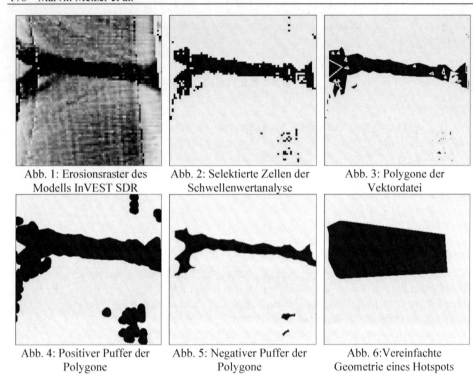

Abb. 1: Erosionsraster des Modells InVEST SDR

Abb. 2: Selektierte Zellen der Schwellenwertanalyse

Abb. 3: Polygone der Vektordatei

Abb. 4: Positiver Puffer der Polygone

Abb. 5: Negativer Puffer der Polygone

Abb. 6: Vereinfachte Geometrie eines Hotspots

2.5 Serverbasierte Automatisierung der Teilschritte (Konzept)

Um große Datenmengen zu verarbeiten, wurde ein serverbasierter Ansatz konzipiert. Die Geodaten zur Erstellung der Layer für das Erosionsmodell, die Erosionsraster und die Hotspotkarten sollen in einer POSTGIS Datenbank gespeichert werden. POSTGIS ist für räumliche Daten (Raster- und Vektordaten) konzipiert und eine Erweiterung des Datenbankmanagementsystems PostgreSQL. POSTGIS Datenbanken können durch die Erweiterung GeoPandas nahtlos mit Python verbunden werden. Somit kann InVEST SDR eingebunden werden, Daten abfragen und Ergebnisse wiederum abspeichern. Die im Modelbuilder erstellten Automatisierungen können von ArcGIS Pro als Python-Code exportiert und ebenfalls in die Serverumgebung integriert werden. Somit können alle Teilschritte zur Berechnung der Hotspotkarten in einem vollautomatisierten Ablauf verknüpft werden.

3 Ergebnisse und Diskussion

3.1 Prozessdauer, Systemanforderungen und Datenverwaltung

In mehr als 240 automatisierten Prozessen wurden Inputdaten zur Berechnung von Erosionskarten auf Einzugsgebietsebene im Modelbuilder verarbeitet. Durch weitere 30 Prozesse konnten Hotspots basierend auf den berechneten Erosionsrastern erfolgreich identifiziert werden. Die Inputdaten, die Erosionskarten und Erosionshotspots in Einzugsgebieten mit einer Größe von ca. 5 km² konnten in einer halben Stunde auf einem Office-Computer[12] berechnet werden. Erosionskarten von 25 km² großen Einzugsgebieten konnten dagegen nur auf einem speziell für rechenaufwendige GIS-Anwendungen konzipierten System[13] berechnet werden. Die Rechenzeit betrug ca. 10 Minuten. Das serverbasierte Konzept soll zukünftig eine noch schnellere Verarbeitung ermöglichen, insbesondere durch eine höhere Rechenkapazität und die Verknüpfung der bisher noch manuell ausgeführten Teilschritte. Bei einer geschätzten, durchschnittlichen Berechnungszeit von 5 Minuten pro Einzugsgebiet (n = 13050) würde die Hotspotanalyse für ganz Bayern ca. 45 Tage dauern. Für ein Einzugsgebiet von 24 km² werden ca. 3,14 GB an Rasterdaten erzeugt. Hochgerechnet auf ganz Bayern (70550 km²) würden ca. 9 TB Daten erzeugt werden. Hinzu kommen die benötigten Inputdaten und die Ergebnisse der Hotspotanalyse mit geschätzt 5 TB.

3.2 Bewertung der Erosionsmodellierung, Limitationen

Das Erosionsmodell InVEST SDR kann den Verlust von Boden auf einem Schlag ermitteln. Diese Kennzahl kann ein wichtiger Indikator für eine sinkende Bodenqualität und damit verbundene ertragsmindernde Effekte sein. Der Bodeneintrag in Gewässer kann ebenso berechnet und anteilig den Schlägen eines Einzugsgebiets zugeordnet werden. Er kann als Indikator für die von landwirtschaftlich genutzten Flächen verursachten Schäden am Gewässer genutzt werden. Beispielsweise wäre eine schlagspezifische Einstufung der Phosphoreinträge denkbar [AL21]. Des Weiteren kann die Wirkung einer Erosionsschutzmaßnahme (z. B. Dauerbegrünung) durch den berechneten Bodenabtrag innerhalb eines Hotspots oder auf Schlagebene quantifiziert und als Indikator für leistungsorientierte Fördergeldzahlungen genutzt werden. Förderfähige Maßnahmen würden somit nicht durch eine Pauschale vergütet werden, sondern aufgrund ihrer tatsächlichen Schutzwirkung vor Ort. Die Ergebnisse des InVEST SDR Modells sind jedoch kritisch zu bewerten, da sie von vielen Einflussfaktoren, wie den verwendeten Inputdaten, den Modellparametern und der zugrundeliegenden Berechnungsmethode abhängig sind. Der Open-Source-Charakter des Modells ist als Vorteil zu werten, da das Modell kontinuierlich durch eine gemeinschaftliche Nutzung und Entwicklung verbessert und an neue Erkenntnisse aus der Forschung angepasst wird. Das digitale Geländemodell spielt eine entscheidende Rolle in der Erosionsmodellierung, da es zur Bestimmung von

---

[12] Hardware Office-Computer: 16 GB RAM, i7-8550U CPU, 4 Kerne (1.80 GHz)
[13] Hardware GIS-Computer: 2x 64 GB RAM, 2x Intel Xeon Gold Scalable CPU, 28 Kerne (3.60 GHz)

Abflusswegen, Abtrags- und Sedimentationspunkten genutzt wird. Mit sinkender Auflösung sinkt der Detailgrad und somit die Variabilität des Reliefs, da Höhenpunkte aggregiert werden. Dadurch stieg bei höherer Auflösung die berechnete Erosionsmenge [WLH05] und ebenso die Fehleranfälligkeit ähnlicher Modelle [SKD19]. Sollte der berechnete Bodenabtrag zur Festlegung ortsabhängiger Fördergeldzahlungen verwendet werden, ist dieser daher zuvor zu validieren. Dafür sind aufwendige Feldversuche nötig, die den Bodenabtrag aus dem Schlag sowie die Bodeneinträge in Gewässer messen können [AL21]. Die hohe Auflösung des Geländemodells im Projekt war dennoch essentiell. Zum einen konnte damit der Verlauf schmaler Fließgewässer berücksichtigt werden, die an Ackerflächen angrenzen und einen bedeutenden Anteil an Sedimenten aufnehmen und abtransportieren. Zum anderen konnten so kleinteilige Hotspots von wenigen Metern Breite identifiziert werden. Hotspots dieser Größe sind in Bayern speziell im tertiären Hügelland aufgrund des Reliefs häufig und sollten nicht ignoriert werden.

3.3   Bewertung von Erosionsschutzmaßnahmen auf identifizierten Hotspots

Für ein repräsentatives Einzugsgebiet im tertiären Hügelland Bayerns wurden Hotspots verortet und quantifiziert (Abb. 7). Durch das Einzugsgebiet fließt ein Bach mit einer Breite von ca. einem Meter. Auf der westlichen Seite des Bachs befindet sich ein Gewässerrandstreifen (Dauergrünland), gefolgt von Ackerflächen, auf denen zwischen 2015 und 2021 überwiegend Silomais und Winterweizen bzw. Wintergeste im Wechsel angebaut wurden. In diesem Bereich befindet sich zudem ein vor Ort deutlich erkennbarer Talweg. Dort wurde basierend auf vorherigen Studien ein hoher Bodenabtrag erwartet [SB18]. Auf der östlichen Seite des Bachs hingegen befinden sich Wald- und Wiesenflächen. Innerhalb der Einzugsgebietsgrenze ist in Abb. 7 das berechnete Erosionsraster hinterlegt. Helle Bereiche zeigen einen hohen, dunkle einen niedrigen Bodenabtrag. Die hellen Bereiche befinden sich hauptsächlich in den Ackerflächen, während auf den Wald- und Wiesenflächen aufgrund der besseren Bodenbedeckung nahezu kein Bodenabtrag berechnet wurde. Die Rasteranalyse konnte deutlich abgrenzbare Hotspots identifizieren (schwarz umrandet). Der Hotspot H1 liegt längs zum Hang im Talweg, nur wenige Meter vom Bach entfernt. Das Erosionsraster zeigt auch im Gewässerrandstreifen am östlichen Ende von H1 einen erhöhten Bodenabtrag, vermutlich durch den Run-off, der sich im Talweg an dieser Stelle konzentriert. Weiter westlich im Hang befindet sich der Hotspot H2-5. Dieser liegt ebenfalls im Talweg. Er wurde aufgrund der vorliegenden Feldgrenzen und einem Feldweg in vier Teile aufgeteilt. Noch weiter westlich im Talweg wurde zudem der Hotspot H6 identifiziert, er liegt quer zum Hang. Der Bereich befindet sich auf einer Grenze von zwei Schlägen, die auf älteren Luftbildaufnahmen zu sehen sind. Im Grenzbereich wurden teilweise keine InVeKoS-Daten erfasst, weshalb mit einem C-Wert von 1 (Ackerbrache) gerechnet wurde. Dieser Wert könnte durch einen C-Wert der umgebenden Felder ersetzt werden, welcher die tatsächliche Bodenbedeckung besser repräsentiert. Der Bereich würde in einer wiederholten Analyse dementsprechend nicht als Hotspot definiert werden.

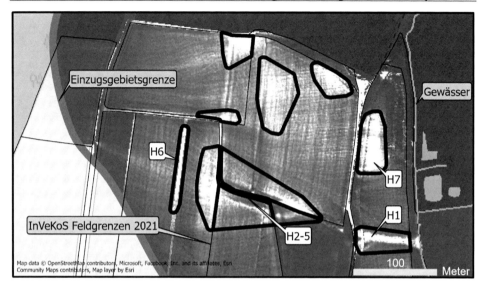

Abb. 7: Kartenausschnitt eines repräsentativen Einzugsgebiets mit identifizierten Hotspots (H1-7, schwarz umrandet). Die zugrundeliegende Erosionskarte zeigt den Bodenabtrag pro Rasterzelle, der in das östlich gelegene Gewässer eingetragen wird. Helle Bereiche zeigen einen hohen, dunkle einen niedrigen Bodenabtrag.

Die Ergebnisse zeigen, dass der angelegte Gewässerrandstreifen nicht in der Lage ist, den Bodeneintrag in den Bach aus darüber liegenden Flächen abzuhalten. Laut Modell wird z. B. aus H1 jährlich ca. eine halbe Tonne (3,16 t ha^{-1}) Boden in den Bach eingetragen (Tab. 1). Erosionsschutzmaßnahmen sollten hier deshalb am Entstehungsort umgesetzt werden. Der Bodenabtrag könnte z. B. durch einen Talwegpuffer mit Dauerbegrünung reduziert werden. Ein mit dem Modell errechnetes Szenario mit dauerhaftem Kleegras ergab z. B. eine Reduktion des Bodenabtrags um 83 % innerhalb von Hotspot H1.

Fruchtfolgeszenarien für einzelne Schläge und deren Wirkung auf die Erosion können durch Anpassungen in der Tabelle "Biophysical Table" (Kapitel 2.1) berechnet werden. Maßnahmen, die zur Reduktion von Erosion führen, lassen sich somit ortsspezifisch bewerten. Die einzelnen Kulturen innerhalb einer Fruchtabfolge wirken sich unterschiedlich auf den C-Faktor aus. Der Anbau von Silomais ($\gamma = 0{,}252$) im Vergleich zu einjährigem Kleegras ($\gamma = 0{,}039$) führt z. B. zu einer ungünstigen Bodenbedeckung [AU21]. Bei Betrachtung eines einzelnen Jahres wäre die errechnete Erosion laut ABAG auf einer Fläche unter Silomais daher bei sonst gleichen Bedingungen ca. sechs Mal höher als unter Kleegras. Da nur die Fruchtabfolge, aber nicht das wiederkehrende Muster einer Fruchtfolge ermittelt wurde, kann der mehrjährige C-Faktor eines Schlages über- oder unterschätzt werden. Werden z. B. nur die ersten vier Jahre einer fünfgliedrigen Fruchtfolge (Weizen-Silomais-Weizen-Roggen-Kleegras-Kleegras) erfasst, so wird der erosionsmindernde Effekt durch die zwei aufeinander folgenden Jahre mit Kleegras ignoriert und der C-Faktor größer. Werden nur die letzten vier Jahre erfasst, wird dagegen der erosionsfördernde Effekt durch Silomais vernachlässigt und der C-Faktor kleiner. Der

Einfluss eines Anbaujahres auf den durchschnittlichen C-Faktor der Fruchtabfolge wird jedoch kleiner, je mehr Fruchtfolgejahre betrachtet werden. Damit sinkt auch das Risiko, den C-Faktor zu unter- oder überschätzen. Durch die Betrachtung von sieben Anbaujahren konnte dieses Risiko also reduziert werden. Auch mehrgliedrige, insbesondere im Ökolandbau übliche Fruchtfolgen konnten angemessen erfasst und bewertet werden.

Hotspot	Größe (ha)	Aktueller Bodenabtrag (t ha^{-1} a^{-1})
H1	0,1685	3,16
H2-5	0,8601	8,68
H6	0,1022	2,23
H7	0,2141	3,11

Tab. 1: Größe und aktueller Bodenabtrag ausgewählter Hotspots des untersuchten Einzugsgebiets

Weitere Hotspots wurden im nördlichen Teil des Kartenausschnitts außerhalb des Talwegs identifiziert, z. B. H7. Die Erosion ist dort großflächiger verteilt, wodurch die Form der Hotspots weniger streifenhaft ist. Für diese Hotspots sind auch andere Erosionsschutzmaßnahmen denkbar. Besonders effektiv wäre aber auch hier eine Dauerbegrünung. Die generelle Eignung von Hotspots für Erosionsschutzmaßnahmen ist von verschiedenen betriebsspezifischen Faktoren (Maschinen, Entfernung zur Hofstelle, Wertschöpfungskette) abhängig. Kleinteilige Maßnahmen können einen Mehraufwand für den Landwirt verursachen, z. B. durch zusätzliche Arbeitsgänge und Fahrten zum Feld. Zudem können benachbarte Kulturen durch Randeffekte beeinflusst werden. Die Mindestgröße und Form für Hotspots sind daher schwer festzulegen. Die Selektionsparameter sowie die Formgestaltung der Hotspots können jedoch bei Bedarf an die Anforderungen einzelner Betriebe angepasst werden. Ein Erosionsschutzstreifen könnte z. B. durch eine Mindestbreite definiert werden, die an die verfügbare Maschinenbreite angepasst wird.

Der Wirkungsgrad einer flächigen Dauerbegrünung ist im Vergleich zu anderen Erosionsschutzmaßnahmen, wie Direktsaat, Mulchsaat oder dem Pflug quer zum Hang, deutlich höher. Die Opportunitätskosten (z. B. Mehrerträge anderer Kulturarten) aufgrund bestehender Betriebsstrukturen sind jedoch in vielen Fällen vermutlich zu hoch. Zudem rückt die Ernährungssicherung aufgrund globaler Krisen aktuell wieder stärker in den Fokus der Politik. Die Ernährungssicherung sollte durch die Aufrechterhaltung der inländischen Produktionsleistung landwirtschaftlicher Flächen gewährleistet werden. Erosionsschutzmaßnahmen innerhalb der analysierten Hotspots konzentrieren sich nur auf besonders erosionsgefährdete Bereiche, wodurch umliegende Flächen unverändert für die Lebensmittelproduktion genutzt werden können.

3.4 Verwertung der Hotspotkarten

Die Hotspotkarten sind für praxisorientierte Beratungsstellen und Projekte (Landschaftspflegeverbände, boden:ständig[14], Fairpachten[15]) hilfreich, um gezielte

---

[14] Projekt der Bayerischen Verwaltung für Ländliche Entwicklung, https://www.boden-staendig.eu/
[15] Projekt der NABU-Stiftung zur Beratung von Grundeigentümer, https://www.fairpachten.org/

Erosionsschutzmaßnahmen umzusetzen. Digitale Technologien in der Landwirtschaft gewinnen zunehmend an Bedeutung. Insbesondere Managementsysteme, wie digitale Schlagkarteien, werden immer häufiger in der Betriebsführung eingesetzt, um Maßnahmen zu planen und zu dokumentieren [GG22]. Dabei spielt die Nachweispflicht von Agrarumweltmaßnahmen gegenüber öffentlichen Stellen zur Freigabe von Fördergeldzahlungen eine entscheidende Rolle [MG21]. Über bestehende Schnittstellen können Hotspotkarten in digitale Schlagkarteien integriert werden. Die Übertragung der Karten auf GPS-gesteuerte Landmaschinen ermöglicht zudem eine präzise Umsetzung der Maßnahmen. Eine Schnittstelle zu iBALIS, zur Übermittlung von durchgeführten Maßnahmen auf den Hotspots, wäre ebenso denkbar. Unter Voraussetzung einer Validierung der Maßnahmeneffekte könnte damit eine leistungsorientierte Vergütung der Maßnahmen realisiert werden. Durch die Schnittstelle könnten die Feldgrenzen der Hotspots räumlich explizit in den InVeKoS-Datensatz überführt werden. Ein manuelles Einzeichnen der Feldgrenzen wäre dadurch überflüssig und würde die Antragsstellung erleichtern.

4 Fazit

Die Verortung, Umsetzung und Bewertung von Erosionsschutzmaßnahmen wird immer bedeutender. Schäden, die durch Erosion an aquatischen Ökosystemen entstehen, wurden bisher vernachlässigt. Durch die Verwendung hochaufgelöster Geodaten wurden kleinteilige Hotspots identifiziert, die sich für praxistaugliche Erosionsschutzmaßnahmen eignen. Durch den hohen Automatisierungsgrad der Verarbeitungsprozesse ließen sich Hotspots in wenigen Minuten berechnen. Die Wirkung ausgewählter Erosionsschutzmaßnahmen konnte bewertet werden, jedoch muss das Modell durch Feldversuche noch validiert werden. Die für Bayern verwendeten Daten stehen auch in anderen Bundesländern in ähnlicher Form und Qualität zur Verfügung, weshalb der Ansatz auf ganz Deutschland übertragen werden kann. In Talwegen kommt es zu einem besonders hohen Bodenabtrag durch konzentrierten Run-off. Gewässerrandstreifen bieten dort keinen ausreichenden Schutz vor Bodeneinträgen. Talwegpuffer mit Dauerbegrünung können dagegen die Erosion am Entstehungsort reduzieren, wobei umliegende Flächen unverändert für die Lebensmittelproduktion genutzt werden können. Die Hotspotkarten lassen sich in der Beratung einsetzen oder in digitale Schlagkarteien integrieren, um wirksame Erosionsschutzmaßnahmen umzusetzen. Sie sind damit eine hilfreiche Ergänzung bisheriger Konzepte, um die Landwirtschaft nachhaltiger zu gestalten.

Förderhinweis: Die Förderung des Vorhabens im Projekt EROSPOT erfolgte aus Mitteln des bayerischen Staatsministeriums für Ernährung, Landwirtschaft und Forsten. Förderkennzeichen: A/22/01.

Literaturverzeichnis

[AL21]   Allion, K. et al.: Use of Monitoring Approaches to Verify the Predictive Accuracy of the Modeling of Particle-Bound Solid Inputs to Surface Waters. Water 13/24, S. 3649, 2021.

[AU21]   Auerswald, K. et al.: Summable C factors for contemporary soil use. Soil and Tillage Research 213/12, S. 105155, 2021.

[AU19]   Auerswald, K. et al.: Rain erosivity map for Germany derived from contiguous radar rain data. Hydrology and Earth System Science 23/4, S. 1819-1832, 2019.

[ADS21]   Ayalew, D. A.; Deumlich, D.; Šarapatka, B.: Agricultural landscape-scale C factor determination and erosion prediction for various crop rotations through a remote sensing and GIS approach. European Journal of Agronomy 123/3, S. 126203, 2021.

[BI17]   Birge, T. et al.: Probing the grounds: Developing a payment-by-results agri-environment scheme in Finland. Land Use Policy 61, S. 302–315, 2017.

[GG22]   Gabriel, A.; Gandorfer, M.: Adoption of digital technologies in agriculture - an inventory in a european small-scale farming region. Precision Agriculture 19/1, S. 992, 2022.

[HA15]   Hamel, P. et al.: A new approach to modeling the sediment retention service (InVEST 3.0): Case study of the Cape Fear catchment, North Carolina, USA. The Science of the total environment 524-525, S. 166-177, 2015.

[MG21]   Melzer, M.; Gandorfer, M.: 105. Functions of commercial farm management information systems - a demand-oriented analysis in Bavaria, Germany. In (John V. Stafford Hrsg.): Precision agriculture '21. S. 877-883, 2021.

[SKD19]   Saggau, P.; Kuhwald, M.; Duttmann, R.: Integrating soil compaction impacts of tramlines into soil erosion modelling: A field-scale approach. Soil Systems 3/3, S. 51, 2019.

[SB18]   Steinhoff-Knopp, B.; Burkhard, B.: Mapping Control of Erosion Rates: Comparing Model and Monitoring Data for Croplands in Northern Germany. One Ecosystem 3, S. e26382, 2018.

[WLH05]   Wu, S.; Li, J.; Huang, G.: An evaluation of grid size uncertainty in empirical soil loss modeling with digital elevation models. Environmental Modeling & Assessment 10/1, S. 33-42, 2005.

Kooperative Agrarprozesse resilient gestalten und dynamisch optimieren

Die Modellierung, Ausführung und Optimierung von digitalisierten Agrarprozessen am Beispiel einer Flüssigmistausbringung im Projekt OPeRAtePlus

Frank Nordemann[1], Ralf Tönjes[1], Heiko Tapken[1] und Lukas Hesse[1]

Abstract: Die Digitalisierung von Arbeitsabläufen in der Landtechnik schreitet kontinuierlich voran. Arbeitsaufträge und Prozessdaten werden zunehmend digital ausgetauscht, verarbeitet und analysiert. Als Herausforderung hat sich jedoch die resiliente Gestaltung und Ausführung von kooperativen Agrarprozessen herausgestellt. Auf ländlichen Flächen können die Kommunikationsmöglichkeiten zwischen kooperativen Akteuren beschränkt sein, wodurch Prozessabläufe behindert werden oder fehlschlagen können. Auch Maschinenausfälle führen häufig zu Fehlern und Abbrüchen in den digitalisierten Prozessen. Am Beispiel einer kooperativen Flüssigmistdüngung aus dem OPeRAtePlus-Forschungsprojekt veranschaulicht dieser Beitrag, wie kooperative Agrarprozesse resilient gestaltet und zugleich hinsichtlich weiterer Kriterien (z. B. Genauigkeit/Kosten/Zeit der Prozessausführung) dynamisch optimiert werden können. Hierzu wird die Prozessbeschreibungssprache Business Process Model and Notation (BPMN) erweitert, um die Resilienz in unzuverlässigen Kommunikationsumgebungen zu verbessern. Die verbesserte Zuverlässigkeit wird durch Simulationen und Einsatz im Feld nachgewiesen.

Keywords: Prozesse in der Landwirtschaft, resiliente Modellierung von Geschäftsprozessen, unzuverlässige Kommunikationsumgebungen, Business Process Model and Notation (BPMN), Directed Acyclic Graph (DAG)

1 Einleitung

Die Digitalisierung hat ein großes Potential, die Effizienz von Arbeitsabläufen zu verbessern und Fehler zu reduzieren. Zudem erfordern gesetzliche Nachweispflichten, wie z. B. bei der Düngeausbringung, eine rechtssichere Dokumentation. Allerdings können im ländlichen Bereich die Kommunikationsmöglichkeiten zwischen den kooperativen Akteuren (Landwirt, Lohnunternehmer, Dienstleister, digitaler Vermittler, Behörde) beschränkt sein, wodurch Prozessabläufe behindert werden oder fehlschlagen können. Auch Maschinenausfälle führen häufig zu Fehlern und Abbrüchen in den digitalisierten Prozessen. Am Beispiel einer kooperativen Flüssigmistdüngung aus dem OPeRAtePlus-

---

[1] Hochschule Osnabrück, Fakultät Ingenieurwissenschaften und Informatik, Albrechtstr. 30, 49076 Osnabrück, info@franknordemann.de; {r.toenjes;h.tapken;lukas.hesse}@hs-osnabrueck.de

Forschungsprojekt untersucht dieser Beitrag, wie kooperative Agrarprozesse resilient gestaltet und dynamisch optimiert werden können.

Abb. 1 zeigt ein typisches Szenario zur Flüssigmistdüngung. Aufgrund der vielen Medienumbrüche und nicht einheitlichen Prozesssteuerung bestehen erhebliche Fehlerpotenziale. Daher soll, wie in Abb. 2 gezeigt, der Anwender durch automatisierte Prozesssteuerung bei der Prozessdurchführung sowie der Datenerfassung, Datenbereitstellung, Visualisierung und der Erzeugung der Prozessdokumentationen entlastet werden. Von der vereinfachten Auftragserstellung des Landwirts beim landwirtschaftlichen Dienstleister über die Einbeziehung von historischen und teilflächenbezogenen Daten, über die assistierte Ausbringung auf dem Feld bis zur exakten Dokumentation und Weitergabe der ausgebrachten Düngemengen an die zuständige Behörde, soll eine sehr breite Unterstützung für die betroffene Anwendergruppe geboten werden. Dabei soll der Düngeprozess ohne Medienbruch und unter Einhaltung der aktuellen rechtlichen Verordnungen durchgeführt werden. Hierzu wird die Prozessbeschreibungssprache Business Process Model and Notation (BPMN) erweitert, um den speziellen Anforderungen in der Landtechnik gerecht zu werden. Insbesondere sind Erweiterungen notwendig, um die Resilienz in unzuverlässigen Kommunikationsumgebungen zu verbessern und die Agrarprozesse hinsichtlich weiterer Kriterien (z. B. Genauigkeit/Kosten/Ausführungszeit) dynamisch zu optimieren.

Der Artikel gliedert sich wie folgt. Kapitel 2 analysiert den Stand der Technik und notwendige Erweiterungen. Kapitel 3 entwickelt ein Metamodell, um mittels BPMN-Erweiterungen die Resilienz von Prozessen zu verbessern. Anschließend wird am Beispiel der Flüssigmistausbringung demonstriert, wie Prozesse resilient beschrieben werden können. Kapitel 4 zeigt, wie mit Hilfe von Graphen die Resilienz von Prozessen geprüft und optimale Prozesspfade bestimmt werden können. Die Evaluation der Verfahren erfolgt in Kapitel 5. Kapitel 6 fasst die Ergebnisse abschließend zusammen.

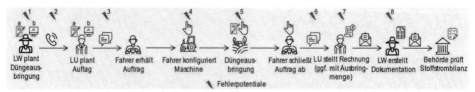

Abb. 1: Typisches Szenario eines aktuellen, fehlerbehafteten Prozesses zum Nährstoffmanagement

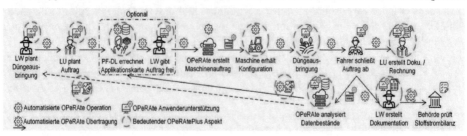

Abb. 2: Ganzheitliches Düngeszenario mit automatisierter Dokumentation in OPeRAtePlus

2 Stand der Technik

Aus der Literatur sind verschiedene Verfahren zur Beschreibung und Optimierung von Geschäftsprozessen bekannt. Für die Beschreibung von Geschäftsprozessen in Banken, Geschäften und Lieferketten in der Industrie wurde die *Business Process Model and Notation 2.0* [OMG11] entwickelt. Aufgrund ihres Umfangs und ihrer Flexibilität, kollaborative Arbeitsprozesse zu beschreiben, wird sie heute in vielen weiteren Bereichen eingesetzt. Eine Übersicht über die Eigenschaften verschiedener Prozessmodellierungssprachen findet sich in [Va13]. Die Veröffentlichung identifiziert drei Dimensionen für die Performanz (Zeit, Kosten und Qualität), berücksichtigt aber keine Nicht-Performanzspezifischen Kriterien. [BoDA11] berücksichtigt auch Kriterien wie Zuverlässigkeit und Performanz für BPMN. [Bo14] nutzt *Metadaten*, um die Zuverlässigkeit von Prozessen zu simulieren. Die Analyse der Zuverlässigkeit von BPMN-Prozessen steht im Fokus von [MaDo16] und [ReDo15], während [DRM16] den Einfluss personeller und anderer Ressourcen auf die Zuverlässigkeit untersucht. Zudem finden sich in der Literatur Ansätze zur Integration von Dienstgütekriterien (*Quality of Information (QoI)*), wie die Zuverlässigkeit von Geräten und Ressourcen im *Internet of Things (IoT)* [Bo16; DRM20; MaDo14].

In [Ch15] wird ein Algorithmus für die Auswahl von *Web Services* aufgrund multipler Kriterien vorgestellt. Die Autoren von [Ma17] präsentieren einen Ansatz zur Optimierung von Quality-of-Service-Aspekten in Cloud-basierten Umgebungen zur Prozessausführung. Inspiriert durch Optimierungstechniken für datenintensive Prozesse im Datenmanagement entwickelt [Go16] ein Konzept zur automatischen Optimierung der Performanz von BPMN-Prozessen. Es wird eine Minimierung der Kosten durch Umordnung und Parallelisierung der Teilprozesse angestrebt. Der Ansatz verwendet zwar *Directed Acyclic Graphs (DAGs, [Ev11])*, nutzt aber nur eingeschränkte Strategien, um aus Prozessbeschreibungen Graphen abzuleiten und Prozesse zu optimieren. [DDG09] nutzt Graphen, um die Ähnlichkeit verschiedener Prozesse bezüglich deren Steuerung und Komponenten zu bewerten.

Die Verbesserung von Geschäftsprozessen ist ein wichtiger Aspekt von *Process-Mining*. Dieses Feld kombiniert Prozessmodellierung und -analyse mit *Computational Intelligence* und *Data Mining Technologien* [Va11]. Allerdings erfordert Process-Mining historische Daten (Event Logs) für die Analyse. Dies kann helfen, geeignete Kriterien für Kantengewichte zu finden, ist aber für die Aufgabenstellung dieses Artikels ungeeignet. Viele der gelisteten Publikationen adressieren nur ein Kriterium zur Prozesssteuerung (z. B. Zuverlässigkeit), konzentrieren sich auf einzelne Performanzkriterien (z. B. Zeit, Kosten, Qualität) oder sind auf eine bestimmte Anwendung limitiert. Daher wird ein flexibler Ansatz für die Beschreibung von Geschäftsprozessen in unzuverlässigen Umgebungen sowie deren Optimierung anhand multipler Kriterien benötigt, der sowohl Unterstützung zur Design- als auch Laufzeit bereitstellt.

3 Modellierung resilienter Prozesse

3.1 Metamodell *rBPMN*

Die Metamodelerweiterung *resilientes BPMN (rBPMN)* ergänzt BPMN um neue Elemente zur Verbesserung der Resilienz bei Ausfällen von Kommunikationsverbindungen und Teilprozessen (s. Abb. 3).

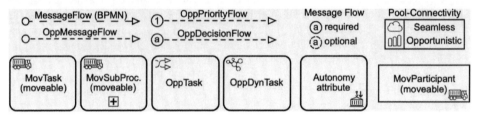

Abb. 3: Neue Modellierungselemente zur Unterstützung von Prozessresilienz gegen unzureichende Kommunikationsmöglichkeiten und Maschinenausfälle

rBPMN erweitert die bisherigen BPMN-Nachrichten um opportunistische Nachrichtentypen (*OppMessageFlows*) für unzuverlässige Verbindungen. Zugehörige Zuverlässigkeitsmaße, die entweder i) geschätzt oder ii) aus Statistiken vorhergehender Läufe bestimmt werden, charakterisieren die Verbindung. Die Zuverlässigkeitsmaße bilden die Basis für die Verifikation der Prozessresilienz. *Opportunistic Priority Flows (OppPriorityFlows)* und *Opportunistic Decision Flows (OppDecisionFlows)* sind Spezialisierungen von *OppMessageFlows* und ermöglichen die Definition von alternativen Verbindungen im Falle eines Verbindungsausfalls. Während *OppPriorityFlows* den Alternativen feste Prioritäten zuordnen, erlauben es *OppDecisionFlows* dynamisch die am besten geeignete Alternative basierend auf Charakteristika wie Resilienz, Genauigkeit, Kosten, etc. zu wählen.

Eine vollständige Vermeidung von Kommunikationsunterbrechungen ist in einigen Szenarien nicht möglich. Daher unterstützt *rBPMN* die Verschiebung von Funktionalitäten zwischen den Prozessbeteiligten, um Resilienz durch eine, ggf. leistungsreduzierte, lokale Ausführung herzustellen: Verschiebbare Aufgaben, Subprozesse und Teilnehmer (*MovTasks*, *MovSubProc.*, *MovParticipants*) bieten Funktionalität, die von *Opportunistic Tasks (OppTaks / OppDynTasks)* genutzt werden kann. *OppDynTasks* ermöglichen neu hinzukommende Teilnehmer dynamisch als Alternativen einzubinden. Mithilfe von Annotationen können lokal verschobene Funktionalitäten, Verbindungstypen der Teilnehmer und Nachrichtenflüsse als notwendig oder optional gekennzeichnet werden. *OppMessageFlows* enthalten szenariospezifische Verbindungsbeschreibungen wie Mindestbandbreite und maximale Unterbrechungszeit. Weitere Beschreibungen umfassen die Nachrichteneigenschaften (Größe, Sendeintervall, etc.) und erforderliche Dienstgüte (QoS mit Latenz, Fehlerwahrscheinlichkeit, etc.). Der Vergleich der Verbindungseigenschaften mit Nachrichtenanforderungen und QoS ermöglicht die Prädiktion der Erfolgs- bzw. Ausfallwahrscheinlichkeit einer Verbindung.

Kooperative Agrarprozesse resilient gestalten und dynamisch optimieren 187

Eine detaillierte Beschreibung der in Abb. 3 abgebildeten *rBPMN* Elemente findet sich in [NTP20] und [No20].

3.2 Beispiel: Prozessmodell für Flüssigmistausbringung

Abb. 4 zeigt beispielhaft ein *rBPMN*-Diagramm eines Prozesses S zur Flüssigmistausbringung. Der Prozess nutzt fortgeschrittene Precision-Farming-Methoden, um Flüssigmist umweltfreundlich auszubringen, und greift dafür auf Dienste unterschiedlicher Teilnehmer zu. OppDecisionFlows, die durch *die OppMessageGroups a, b, c* gruppiert werden, zeigen, dass nicht alle involvierten Verbindungen für eine resiliente Prozessdurchführung benötigt werden. Stattdessen ist nur eine Verbindung (für a, b) oder keine (für c) zwingend notwendig. Allerdings beeinflusst die Anzahl der möglichen Verbindungen zu Prozessteilnehmern Gütekriterien wie Robustheit, Genauigkeit, Kosten und Zeit. Der Prozess S gliedert sich in drei Teilprozesse S_a, S_b und S_c. In S_a entscheidet der Anwender, ob Precision Farming genutzt wird und ggf. ob die *Applikationskarte (AppMap)* für die Flüssigmistausbringung automatisch (aPF) oder manuell (mPF) mit erhöhter Genauigkeit erstellt wird. In S_b wird die Analysemethode für die Inhaltsstoffe des Flüssigmistes (Stickstoff, Phosphor, etc.) gewählt. Alternativ stehen *Laboranalyse (LAB)*, Nutzung des *NIR-Sensors (NIRS)* oder eine *Referenztabelle* für tierabhängige (Rind, Schwein, etc.) Inhaltsstoffe *(REF)* zur Verfügung, die jeweils unterschiedliche Genauigkeiten bieten. Letztendlich bietet S_c drei Optionen für die Ausbringung des Flüssigmistes mit unterschiedlicher Genauigkeit: ein *Global Navigation Satellite System (GNSS)* wie *GPS, Real Time Kinematik (RTK)* mit verbesserter Genauigkeit durch *Mobilfunkdienste (CELL)* oder *lokale Stationen in Feldnähe (LOC)*. Anhand dieses Prozessmodells sollen die folgenden Verfahren erläutert werden.

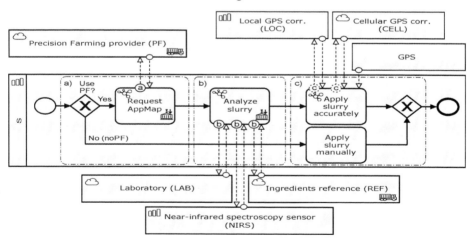

Abb. 4: Generalisierter Flüssigmistprozess S mit verschiedenen Optionen a) zum Precision Farming, b) zur Flüssigmistanalyse und c) zur ortsbezogenen Ausbringung

4 Graphbasierte Prozessoptimierung

Das Ziel der Prozessoptimierung ist es, den besten Pfad zur Prozessausführung zu finden. Die Prozessoptimierung beginnt mit der Definition der Kriterien anhand derer der Prozess optimiert werden soll. Als Kriterien für den Prozess S wurden solche gewählt, die auch für andere Prozesse typisch sind:

- Robustheit: Stabilität der Prozesskommunikation;
- Genauigkeit: Präzision des Ergebnisses der Aktivität;
- Kosten: monetärer Wert für Ausführung der Aktivität;
- Zeit: benötigte Dauer für Ausführung der Aktivität.

4.1 Erzeugung des Prozessgraphen

Dieser Abschnitt untersucht, wie Prozesse in Graphen, genauer DAGs, überführt werden können. Abb. 5 zeigt den resultierenden gerichteten Graphen für Prozess S, der im Knoten S beginnt und zum Endknoten S' führt.

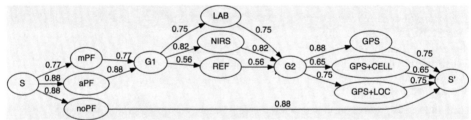

Abb. 5: Für die Resilienz- und Prozessanalyse in einen gerichteten Graphen überführter Flüssigmistprozess S

Der Prozessabschnitt S_a enthält drei Alternativen: Zuerst ist zu entscheiden, ob Precision Farming genutzt werden soll und wenn ja, ob die Applikationskarte automatisch oder manuell erstellt werden soll. Diese Alternativen werden durch drei Pfade (noPF, aPF und mPF) repräsentiert. Während die eine Applikationskarte nutzenden Prozesse im Knoten G1 enden, erfordert der Pfad ohne Applikationskarte noPF keine weiteren Entscheidungen und endet sofort in S'. Der Knoten G1 wird als Verbindungsknoten eingeführt, um alternative Pfade wieder zusammenzuführen. Der Prozessabschnitt S_b unterscheidet drei Alternativen zur Bestimmung der Inhaltsstoffe durch Laboranalyse (LAB), NIR-Sensor (NIRS) oder Referenztabelle (REF), die durch entsprechende Pfade dargestellt werden. Der folgende Prozessabschnitt S_c unterscheidet drei Alternativen zur Ortbestimmung, die entweder GPS (GPS) oder GPS mit Korrekturdaten über Mobilfunkdienste (CELL) oder von lokalen Stationen (LOC) nutzen. GPS ist ein notwendiger Teilprozess jedes Pfades. Die sich in CELL bzw. LOC aufteilenden Pfade können in GPS/CELL bzw. GPS/LOC Pfade fusioniert werden, um einen kompakteren Graphen zu erzielen. Hierzu müssen die Kantengewichte entsprechend umgerechnet werden (s. nächster Abschnitt). Ein detailliertes Regelwerk zur Erzeugung von Graphen aus Prozessmodellen beschreibt [NTP20].

4.2 Pfadmetriken

Der nächste Schritt ist die Bestimmung der Kantengewichte des Graphen. Das Gewicht beschreibt, wie gut ein Prozesselement das jeweilige Kriterium erfüllt. Um die Vergleichbarkeit verschiedener Szenarien zu unterstützen ist eine Normierung notwendig. Je nach Kriterium und Prozesselement kann ein Gewicht einer eingehenden, einer ausgehenden Kante oder dem Knoten selbst zugeordnet sein. So sind beispielsweise Genauigkeit, Kosten und Zeit Eigenschaften des RTK-basierten Dienstes und somit Knoten CELL im Prozess S. Dahingegen beschreibt Robustheit die Stabilität der Kommunikation und kann den Kanten, d.h. ein- und ausgehenden Nachrichten, zum Knoten CELL zugeordnet werden. Da viele Suchalgorithmen, wie beispielsweise Dijkstra's Shortest-Path [Ev11], auf Kantengewichten basieren, wird empfohlen, die Gewichte der Knoten zu Kanten zu verschieben. Dies kann durch i) Aufteilung des Knotens und Einfügen einer künstlichen Kante oder ii) Verschieben auf die eingehende oder ausgehende Kante erfolgen. Der letzte Fall erzeugt kompaktere Graphen und wird im Folgenden verwendet. Die Bestimmung der Kantengewichte ist in [No22] beschrieben.

Die Robustheit R, d.h. Zuverlässigkeit einer Kommunikationsverbindung, kann durch Wahrscheinlichkeiten $P^R_w \in [0, 1]$ ausgedrückt werden (s.a. Kap. 4.4). Auch die anderen Kriterien i wie Genauigkeit, Kosten und Zeit können durch eine entsprechende Kostenfunktion $C^i_w \in [0, 1]$ repräsentiert werden. Da üblicherweise Robustheit und Genauigkeit zu maximieren und Kosten und Zeit zu minimieren sind, wird empfohlen, die Funktion für letztere zu invertieren, um einheitliche Suchalgorithmen anwenden zu können.

Für die Analyse von Graphen mit mehreren Kriterien existieren zwei Möglichkeiten: 1. Der Graph wird für jedes Kriterium dupliziert und separat analysiert. 2. Die Kriterien werden gewichtet zusammengefasst und der Graph anschließend analysiert. Letzteres erfordert eine Normierung der Kriterien, ermöglicht aber, an jeder Verzweigung die Pfadentscheidungen basierend auf allen (zusammengefassten) Kriterien wahrzunehmen.

$$P_w = \alpha_0 P^R_w + \sum_{i=1}^{k} \alpha_i C^i_w \qquad mit \quad \sum_{i=0}^{k} \alpha_i = 1 \tag{1}$$

Teilprozesse in Graphen können für die übersichtliche Analyse zusammengefasst werden. Bei der Aggregation der Kantengewichte sind Reihen- (2) und Parallelschaltung (3) von Kanten zu unterscheiden:

$$P_{Reihe} = \prod_{i=1}^{n} P_i \tag{2}$$

$$P_{Parallel} = 1 - \prod_{j=1}^{m}(1 - P_j) \tag{3}$$

4.3 Graphbasierte Suchalgorithmen

Zur Identifikation des besten Prozesspfades können graphbasierte Suchverfahren eingesetzt werden. Dies erfolgt entweder durch Breitensuche [Ev11] oder Tiefensuche [Ta72], um alle möglichen Pfade zu ermitteln und anschließend den optimalen auszusuchen. Oder es wird ein Shortest-Path-Algorithmus wie Dijkstra [Ev11] und

Bellman-Ford [Be58] eingesetzt, um den Pfad mit den geringsten Kosten zu finden. Zudem kann mithilfe von Heuristiken, wie beispielsweise A*-Algorithmus, die Suche beschleunigt werden.

Allerdings erfordern die Suchalgorithmen eine bestimmte Metrik für die Kanten: Die Algorithmen basieren auf der Annahme, dass bessere Pfade ein kleineres Gewicht haben und das Gewicht des Gesamtpfades sich aus der Summe der Gewichte der Einzelpfade ergibt. Daher wird als Metrik für die Kanten ein Fehlerindex *I* wie folgt definiert:

$$I = -log_b P \tag{4}$$

Damit haben zuverlässige Verbindungen *(P=1)* den Fehlerindex *I=0* und fehlende Verbindungen *(P=0)* den Fehlerindex $I = \infty$. Der Fehlerindex I_G des gesamten Pfades ergibt sich zu

$$I_G = -log_b(\prod_{i=1}^n P_i) = -\sum_{i=1}^n log_b P_i = \sum_{i=1}^n I_i \tag{5}$$

Der Suchalgorithmus bestimmt den Pfad mit dem minimalen gesamten Fehlerindex $I_G \rightarrow min$ als optimalen Pfad.

4.4 Resilienzanalyse

Ein Maß für die Resilienz *R* einer Kommunikationsverbindung ist die Anzahl der möglichen Nachrichtenrahmen pro Zeitfenster. Damit wenigsten ein Rahmen gesendet werden kann, muss für eine resiliente Verbindung $R \geq 1$ gelten. Es wird eine Funktion gesucht, die $R\epsilon[0, \infty]$ auf $P\epsilon[0,1]$ abbildet. Eine Funktion, die diese Bedingung erfüllt, ist

$$P_i = 1 - b^{-R} \tag{6}$$

Damit eine Verbindung resilient, d.h. $R \geq 1$ ist, muss gelten $P_i \geq \frac{b-1}{b}$. Wählt man als Basis b=2 ergibt sich als notwendige Bedingung für eine resiliente Einzelverbindung $P_i \geq \frac{1}{2}$ bzw. $I_i \leq -log_2 P_i = 1$. Damit ein Prozess resilient ist, muss mindestens ein Pfad mit nur resilienten Einzelverbindungen existieren.

$$\exists I_G \; mit \; I_i \leq 1 \; für \; \forall \; I_i \epsilon I_G \tag{7}$$

Hiermit kann vorab die Resilienz eines Prozesses geprüft werden.

5 Evaluation

Dieser Abschnitt untersucht die Performanz der graphbasierten Suchverfahren zur Bestimmung der optimalen Prozesspfade und analysiert die Erfahrungen von Feldversuchen zur prozessgesteuerten Flüssigmistausbringung.

5.1 Performanz

Die Prozesse in der Landwirtschaft involvieren häufig eine Vielzahl von räumlich verteilten Akteuren. Die Leistungsfähigkeit der Kommunikationsverbindungen und der beteiligten Geräte ist oft eingeschränkt, was bei der Prozessoptimierung, insbesondere zur Laufzeit, berücksichtigt werden muss. Daher wird zur Leistungsbewertung der Suchalgorithmen ein Raspberry Pi Zero WH verwendet. Die Konfiguration des Raspberry Pi umfasst einen ARM-1GHz-prozessor (BCM2835 SOC) und 512 MB RAM. Die Software zur Performanzmessung wurde in Java geschrieben und nutzt das OpenJDK Runtime Environment 1.8. Die graphbasierten Suchalgorithmen stellt die JGraphT-Library [LVD09] bereit. Es wurden 1.000 Wiederholungen pro Simulation durchgeführt.

Zur Evaluation der Algorithmen wurde ein Generator für Prozessgraphen realisiert. Er erzeugt Graphen, indem er die Pfade an jedem Knoten aufteilt und den Kanten zufällige Gewichte zuordnet. Es können Graphen unterschiedlicher Größe erzeugt werden. Vertikale Schichten (V-Layer) geben die Anzahl der aufeinanderfolgenden Knoten an, bei denen eine Pfadaufteilung erfolgt, bis die Pfade wieder sukzessive zusammengefügt werden. Horizontale Schichten (H-Layer) bestimmen die Anzahl der ausgehenden Kanten an jedem Knoten.

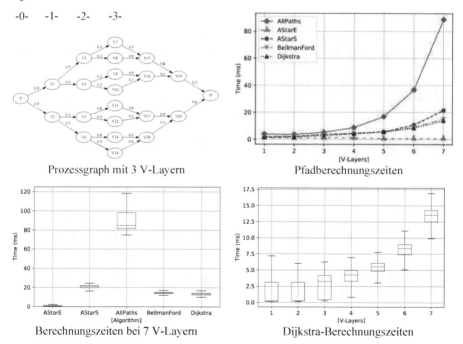

Abb. 6: Evaluation der Skalierung der Suchverfahren

Die Ergebnisse in Abb. 6 zeigen, dass ein Raspberry Pi Zero WH für die Suche optimaler Prozesspfade ausreichend ist. Die vollständige Suche (AllPaths) ist sehr aufwendig und sollte bei größeren Netzen aus Skalierungsgründen gemieden werden. Der Dijkstra-Algorithmus skaliert besser. Bei großen Netzen sind ggf. Heuristiken zur Suchbeschleunigung zu verwenden. Allerdings ist die Performanz des A*-Algorithmus abhängig von den Heuristiken: AStarS benutzt den Quellknoten als Heuristik und skaliert wesentlich schlechter als AStarE mit Endknoten als Heuristik [No22].

5.2 Feldtests

Zur Erprobung der prozessgesteuerten Flüssigmistausbringung auf dem Feld wurde eine App für ein ISOBUS-Terminal entwickelt, die ein Güllefass zur teilflächenspezifischen Ausbringung steuert. Das Workflow-Management-System Camunda BPM wurde um *rBPMN*-Elemente erweitert. Abb. 7 zeigt die Implementation des Prozesses *S*, der Bestandteil des Flüssigmistwagens ist und die Steuerung während der Ausbringung übernimmt. Mit Hilfe von sogenannten Micro-services können beispielsweise Funktionen zur Erstellung von Applikationskarten als auch zur Analyse auf die Maschine verschoben werden, falls eine Cloudanbindung nicht zuverlässig umgesetzt werden kann. Die Funktionen werden als Services definiert, nach denen dynamisch über angepasste Spring-Eureka-Service-Registries zur Laufzeit gesucht werden kann und der Prozess für die bestgeeignete Option rekonfiguriert werden kann. Die Kommunikation erfolgt über Mobilfunk und WLAN und nutzt als Protokoll MQTT mit Schnittstelle zu BPMN. Die prototypische Umsetzung demonstrierte erfolgreich eine resiliente Prozesssteuerung mit medienbruchfreier Datenhaltung.

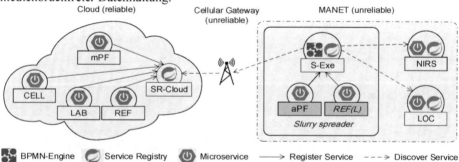

Abb. 7: Implementierung des Flüssigmistprozesses mittels BPMN-Runtime Engine und Microservices

6 Zusammenfassung

Dieser Artikel beschreibt, wie mit Hilfe von BPMN kooperative Prozesse modelliert und ausgeführt werden können. Um die Resilienz von Agrarprozessen und ihre optimale Ausführung zu gewährleisten, wurde die BPMN um zusätzliche Modellierungselemente und Analysemethoden erweitert. Für den Wegfall von Maschinen aufgrund unzureichender Kommunikation oder Maschinenfehler können Alternativen definiert und dynamisch identifiziert werden. Weiterhin können Funktionen zwischen Akteuren verschoben werden, um diese lokal auszuführen und den Prozessablauf fortzusetzen.

Zudem wurden Analysemethoden entworfen, die die Resilienz eines Prozesses zur Planungszeit überprüfen und die Prozessausführung optimal an die aktuellen Gegebenheiten anpassen. Ein Prozessmodell wird dazu in einen gerichteten, azyklischen Graphen transferiert und die Kanten gewichtet, um beispielsweise die Resilienz der im Prozess genutzten Kommunikationsverbindungen zu beschreiben. Mit einer anschließenden graphenbasierten Pfadsuche kann die Resilienz des gesamten Prozessmodells untersucht sowie der optimale Prozesspfad identifiziert werden. Bei Feststellung einer unzureichenden Resilienz kann das Prozessmodell vor der Ausführung angepasst werden, um einen Prozessabbruch zur Laufzeit zu verhindern. Auf Basis einer Multi-Kriterien-Prozessanalyse können neben der Resilienz weitere Aspekte wie Genauigkeit, Kosten und Zeit berücksichtigt und Prozesskonfiguration kontinuierlich zur Laufzeit überwacht und optimiert werden. Damit stehen erstmals aus der industriellen Prozessautomatisierung bekannte Werkzeuge für den Einsatz in fehleranfälligen, dynamischen landwirtschaftlichen Prozessen zur Verfügung.

Im praktischen Einsatz führt die digitalisierte Prozesssteuerung und -dokumentation zu effizienteren und fehlerunanfälligeren Arbeitsabläufen. Unterstützt durch eine Benutzeroberfläche für Landwirte und Lohnunternehmen, ein Modul zur Berechnung teilflächenspezifischer Applikationskarten, ein intelligentes Güllefass sowie ein via MQTT angebundenes ISOBUS-Terminal können Flüssigmistprozesse auf diesem Weg volldigitalisiert/medienbruchfrei ausgeführt und rechtssicher dokumentiert werden.

Literaturverzeichnis

[Be58]   Bellman, R.: On a routing problem. Quarterly of applied mathematics 16(1), S. 87-90, 1958.

[Bo14]   Bocciarelli, P. et.al: Simulation-based performance and reliability analysis of business processes. In: Proceedings of the 2014 Winter Simulation Conference, S. 3012-3023, 2014

[Bo16]   Bocciarelli, P. et.al: A BPMN extension to enable the explicit modeling of task resources. In: CIISE, S 40-47, 2016.

[BoDA11] Bocciarelli, P., D'Ambrogio, A.: A BPMN extension for modeling non-functional properties of business processes. In: Proceedings of the 2011 Symposium on Theory of Modeling & Simulation, S. 160-168, 2011.

[Ch15]   Chhun, S. et.al.: A multi-criteria service selection algorithm for business process requirements. arXiv preprint arXiv:1505.03998, 2015.

[DDG09] Dijkman, R., Dumas, M., Garcia-Banuelos, L.: Graph matching algorithms for business process model similarity search. In: International conference on business process management. S. 48-63, 2009.

[DRM16] Domingos, D., Respicio, A., Martinho, R.: Using resource reliability in BPMN processes. Procedia Computer Science 100, S. 1280-1288, 2016.

[DRM20] Domingos, D., Respicio, A., Martinho, R.: Reliability of IoT-aware BPMN healthcare processes. In: Virtual and Mobile Healthcare: Breakthroughs in Research and Practice, S. 793-821, 2020.

[Ev11] Even, S.: Graph algorithms. Cambridge University Press, 2011

[Go16] Gounaris, A.: Towards automated performance optimization of BPMN business processes. In: East European Conference on Advances in Databases and Information Systems. S. 19-28, 2016.

[LVD09] Lohmann, N., Verbeek, E., Dijkman, R.: Petri net transformations for business processes - a survey. In: Transactions on petri nets and other models of concurrency II, S. 46-63, 2009.

[MaDo14] Martinho, R., Domingos, D.: Quality of information and access cost of IoT resources in BPMN processes. Procedia Technology 16, S. 737-744, 2014.

[MaDo16] Martinho, R., Domingos, D., Respicio, A.: Evaluating the reliability of ambient-assisted living business processes. In: ICEIS (2). S. 528-536, 2016.

[Ma17] Mazzola, L. et.al: FCE4BPMN: On-demand QoS-based optimised process model execution in the cloud. In: 2017 International Conference on Engineering, Technology and Innovation (ICE/ITMC), S. 305-314, 2017.

[No20] Nordemann, F., Tönjes, R., Pulvermüller, E., Tapken, H.: A graph-based approach for process robustness in unreliable communication environments. In: 15th International Conference on Evaluation of Novel Approaches to Software Engineering (ENASE), 2020.

[No22] Nordemann, F.: Modeling and Execution of Resilient Business Processes in Unreliable Communication Environments, Dissertation, https://doi.org/10.48693/75, 2022.

[NTP20] Nordemann, F., Tönjes, R., Pulvermüller, E.: Resilient BPMN: Robust process modelling in unreliable communication environments. In: 8th International Conference on Model-Driven Engineering and Software Development (MODELSWARD), 2020.

[OMG11] Object Management Group (OMG): Business Process Model and Notation (BPMN) 2.0 Specification, https://www.omg.org/spec/BPMN/2.0/Beta2/About-BPMN/, Stand: 23.10.2022

[ReDo15] Respicio, A., Domingos, D.: Reliability of BPMN business processes. Procedia Computer Science 64, S. 643-650, 2015.

[Ta72] Tarjan, R.: Depth-first search and linear graph algorithms. SIAM journal on computing 1(2), S. 146-160, 1972.

[Va11] Van Der Aalst, W.: Process mining: discovery, conformance and enhancement of business processes, vol. 2, 2011.

[Va13] Van der Aalst, W.: Business process management: a comprehensive survey. ISRN Software Engineering 2013, 2013.

Kartierung des Bedeckungsgrads von *Cirsium arvense* im Mais (*Zea mays* L.) mithilfe Neuronaler Netze in UAV-Daten

Maren Pöttker [1], David Hagemann [2], Simon Pukop [3], Thomas Jarmer [1] und Dieter Trautz [2]

Abstract: Die Ackerkratzdistel (*Cirsium arvense* (L.) Scop.) verbreitet sich hauptsächlich über Wurzelausläufer, sodass sie gehäuft in Distelnestern auftritt. Diese können pro Jahr um bis zu 10 m im Durchmesser wachsen, sodass eine frühzeitige Erkennung neuer Nester und eine effektive Regulierung von hoher Relevanz ist. In dieser Arbeit wird *C. arvense* mithilfe hochaufgelöster Bilddaten aus UAV-Befliegungen, die in einem Zeitraum von vier Wochen erhoben wurden, durch ein Ensemble aus Convolutional Neural Networks (CNNs) kartiert und der Bedeckunsggrad abgeleitet. Die Ergebnisse zeigen, dass die Genauigkeit der Kartierung von Einzelpflanzen mit dem phänologischen Stadium der Pflanzen zusammenhängt, und bestätigen die Eignung von CNNs für eine artspezifische Erkennung von *C. arvense*.

Keywords: UAV-Daten, Neuronale Netze, teilflächenspezifische Beikrautregulierung, *Cirsium arvense*

1 Einleitung

Die Ackerkratzdistel (*Cirsium arvense* (L.) Scop.) ist ein perennierendes Wurzel- und Samenunkraut. Sie besitzt eine tiefe Pfahlwurzel und verbreitet sich primär vegetativ über Wurzelausläufer oder abgetrennte Wurzelausläuferteile, aber auch über im Frühjahr keimende Samen. Durch die Verbreitung über Wurzelausläufer tritt *C. arvense* gehäuft in Form von Distelnestern auf [Sö10]. Das Wurzelsystem eines solchen Distelnestes kann pro Jahr um bis zu 10 m im Durchmesser wachsen. Begünstigt wird ihr Wachstum unter anderem durch eine pfluglose Bodenbearbeitung und in zu frühen Wachstumsstadien stattfindende Herbizidapplikationen [Ba22]. Der optimale Behandlungszeitpunkt ist im 3- bis 4-Blattstadium, bei einer Blattfläche von etwa 200 cm² und einer Wuchshöhe von 13 cm [TVL19]. Zu diesem Zeitpunkt ist der Kompensationspunkt zwischen

---

[1] Universität Osnabrück, Institut für Informatik, Arbeitsgruppe Fernerkundung und Digitale Bildverarbeitung, Wachsbleiche 27, 49090 Osnabrück, maren.poettker@uni-osnabrueck.de, https://orcid.org/0000-0002-0711-732X, thomas.jarmer@uni-osnabrueck.de, https://orcid.org/0000-0002-4652-1640

[2] Hochschule Osnabrück, Fakultät Agrarwissenschaften und Landschaftsarchitektur, Arbeitsgruppe Agrarökologie und Umweltschonende Landbewirtschaftung, Am Krümpel 31, 49090 Osnabrück, david.hagemann@hs-osnabrueck.de, https://orcid.org/0000-0003-3896-2064, d.trautz@hs-osnabrueck.de

[3] Universität Paderborn, Heinz Nixdorf Institut, Fachgruppe Algorithmen und Komplexität, Fürstenallee 11, 33102 Paderborn, simonjp@hni.uni-paderborn.de, https://orcid.org/0000-0002-4473-5215

Photosyntheseleistung und Bedarf für Wachstum und Respiration erreicht, sodass die Distel empfindlich auf die Behandlung reagiert [NS11]. Eine frühzeitige Erkennung neuer Nester und effektive Regulierung zum passenden Zeitpunkt ist daher von hoher Relevanz. Zur Steigerung der Resilienz von landwirtschaftlichen Räumen und im Sinne einer nachhaltigen Landwirtschaft möchte die EU-Kommission im Rahmen der *Farm-to-Fork-*Strategie bis 2030 den Pestizideinsatz ihrer Mitgliedsländer um 50 % senken [EU20]. Um dies bei gleichbleibendem Ertragsniveau zu realisieren, sind Konzepte wie eine teilflächen- oder sogar einzelpflanzenspezifische Herbizidapplikation nötig. Je nach Kultur und Befallsstärke können bei einer teilflächenspezifisch durchgeführten Regulierung von *C. arvense* so 54 % [DGK04] bis 88 % [Ry21] Herbizid eingespart werden. Für die Umsetzung einer teilflächenspezifischen Herbizidapplikation sind vier Schritte notwendig: (1) die exakte Erkennung von Beikräutern, (2) Entscheidungssysteme und die Festlegung von Schwellwerten, (3) die präzise Herbizidapplikation und (4) die Kontrolle des Regulierungserfolges [Ch21]. Für eine exakte Erkennung von Beikräutern sowie die Kontrolle des Regulierungserfolgs eignen sich fernerkundliche Methoden, um große landwirtschaftliche Flächen effizient abdecken zu können. In der Erkennung von *C. arvense* wurden beispielsweise hochauflösende Satellitenbilder genutzt, um den Bedeckungsgrad anhand des *Patchyness-Indices* zu schätzen [RAN21]. Als *ground truth* für diese Klassifikation dienten hochauflösende UAV-Bilder, in denen die Einzelpflanzen erkennbar waren. Ebenfalls wurden UAV-Bilder als Klassifikationsgrundlage für die artspezifische Erkennung von *C. arvense* genutzt, um z. B. Applikationskarten für eine selektive Herbizidapplikation zu erstellen [Mi18] oder die Ertragsminderung zu schätzen [RN20]. Durch unterschiedliche Bedingungen während der UAV-Befliegungen, wie Wind oder wechselhafte Beleuchtung, ist die Qualität von UAV-Daten jedoch nicht gleichbleibend. Weiterhin können andere Beikräuter oder größer werdende Kulturpflanzen mit sich überlappenden Pflanzenteilen die Klassifikation von *C. arvense* erschweren. In dieser Studie wird *C. arvense* mithilfe von *Convolutional Neural Networks* (CNNs) in hochauflösenden UAV-Daten, welche unter wechselnden Bedingungen im Verlauf von vier Wochen erhoben wurden, detektiert. CNNs wurden in letzter Zeit vermehrt in der Analyse von fernerkundlichen Vegetationsdaten verwendet, da sie sich besonders für die Ableitung von räumlichen Merkmalen eignen [Ka21]. Architekturen unterschiedlicher Komplexität werden zurzeit für die Erkennung von Beikräutern verwendet. Neben reinen CNNs zur Bilderkennung werden beispielsweise *Region Proposed Networks* wie Yolo oder Mask RCNNs zur Objekterkennung bzw. Instanzsegmentierung oder *Fully Convolutional Networks* wie U-Net zur semantischen Segmentierung verwendet [Ha21]. Hohe Genauigkeiten in der Klassifikation von Beikräutern lassen sich vor allem mit komplexen, vortrainierten Architekturen sowie einer großen Menge Trainingsdaten erzielen [Ha21]. Da für diese Arbeit nur ein begrenzter Umfang an Trainingsdaten zur Verfügung steht, soll eine einfache Architektur verwendet werden. Um ein repräsentatives Ergebnis zu erzeugen, wird ein Ensemble aus 10 einfachen CNNs für die Klassifikation verwendet. Es sollen die Fragen beantwortet werden, (1) ob sich ein Ensemble aus CNNs mit einer einfachen Architektur für die Klassifikation von *C. arvense* eignet und (2) ob aus dem Ergebnis dieser Klassifikation der Bedeckungsgrad von *C. arvense* abgeleitet werden kann.

2 Material und Methoden

Auf der Versuchsfläche in Belm bei Osnabrück (52,321124°N, 8,153100°E) befinden sich mehrere Nester von *C. arvense* im Mais (*Zea mays* L.). Während des Untersuchungszeitraumes von Mitte Mai 2022 bis Mitte Juni 2022 wurden an fünf Terminen während unterschiedlicher Belichtungsverhältnisse Befliegungen (s. Tab. 1) mit einer DJI Matrice 210 V2 durchgeführt und multispektrale Bilddaten mit einer MicaSense Altum erhoben. Mithilfe dieses Kamerasystems wurden spektrale Informationen in den fünf Wellenlängenbereichen: Blau (459-491 nm), Grün (547-573 nm), Rot (661-675 nm), Red Edge (711-723 nm) und Nahes Infrarot (814-865 nm) in einer Flughöhe von 10 m und einer daraus resultierenden räumlichen Auflösung von rund 3,5 mm erhoben. Die Bilddaten wurden unter Verwendung der Software Agisoft Metashape (Version 1.7.2) prozessiert und mithilfe von in der Versuchsfläche ausgebrachten und mit einem differentiellen GNSS-Gerät (Stonex S9 III) eingemessenen Targets georeferenziert. Eine radiometrische Kalibrierung der Bilddaten wurde anhand eines im Gelände eingemessenen Reflexionspanels in Agisoft Metashape vorgenommen. Aus den Orthophotos wurden zu jedem der fünf Zeitpunkte zwei Bereiche mit Distelnestern extrahiert: Eine 110 m² große Trainingsfläche sowie eine 9 m² große Testfläche. Die Datensätze für beide Flächen wurden jeweils co-registriert und mittels des *nearest-neighbour*-Verfahrens auf eine einheitliche Pixelgröße von exakt 3,5 mm resampelt. Bedingt durch unterschiedliche Belichtungsverhältnisse während der Datenakquise weisen die Datensätze Differenzen in den Reflektanzen auf (s. Tab. 1). Für eine unabhängige Validierung wurden auf der Testfläche manuell Polygone für die Pflanzen der Klassen Mais, Distel und sonstiges Beikraut erstellt. Um die Daten (x) zu normalisieren, wurde mithilfe des arithmetischen Mittels (μ) und der Standardabweichung (σ) der Z-Score gebildet: $x_{norm} = \frac{x-\mu}{\sigma}$. Aus den fünf Datensätzen der Trainingsfläche wurden jeweils 200 Trainingsdaten in Form von 64 × 64 Pixel großen Samples für die beiden Klassen (Distel und Nicht-Distel) extrahiert (s. Abb. 1) und wie folgt augmentiert: Drehung um 90°, 180° und 270°, Spiegelung sowie die gelegentliche Verwendung eines Median-Filters, um Bildunschärfe hinzuzufügen [Pa17]. Für jede der beiden Klassen konnten so 13.000 Samples erzeugt werden, wovon randomisierte 75 % für das Training und 25 % für die Validierung des Modells während des Trainingsprozesses verwendet wurden.

Datum	Uhrzeit	BBCH	Belichtungsverhältnisse
12.05.2022	11:30	11-12	Sonne und Wolken im Wechsel
18.05.2022	12:00	14	wolkenlos
02.06.2022	11:30	15	Sonne und Wolken im Wechsel
07.06.2022	12:00	16-17	Sonne und Wolken im Wechsel
13.06.2022	15:30	18	geschlossene Wolkendecke

Tab. 1: Übersicht über die Datengrundlage. Die BBCH-Stadien beziehen sich auf den Mais

Als Modell für die Klassifikation wurde ein Ensemble aus 10 identischen CNNs gebildet [Ka21]. Der Trainingsprozess der CNNs unterschied sich dabei in der Verteilung von

Trainings- und Validierungsdaten; diese wurden bei jedem Modell neu randomisiert. Auf diese Weise konnte sowohl die gesamte Menge der Trainingsdaten genutzt, aber auch jedes Modell ausreichend validiert werden. Mithilfe eines *Moving-Window*-Ansatzes wurde die Testfläche von dem Ensemble aus CNNs klassifiziert. Für das Ergebnis der Klassifikation wurde der Median der 10 Klassifikationswahrscheinlichkeiten für die Klasse Distel genutzt. Weiterhin wurde die Standardabweichung der Klassifikationsergebnisse berechnet. Mithilfe der unabhängigen Validierungsdaten wurden die Klassifikationsergebnisse bei einem wechselnden Schwellwert für die Klassen Boden, Mais, Distel und Beikraut mithilfe einer Konfusionsmatrix validiert. Genutzte Metriken waren hierbei die Gesamtgenauigkeit und die Präzision der Klasse Distel sowie der Anteil der falsch klassifizierten Pixel der Klassen Boden, Mais und Beikraut [SL09]. Anhand der Betrachtung der sich verändernden Klassifikationsgüte bei wechselnden Schwellwerten wurde ein Schwellwert für die Ableitung des Bedeckungsgrads festgelegt. Der Bedeckungsgrad pro 0,25 m² wurde durch Zählen der Pixel der Klasse Distel sowohl im Klassifikationsergebnis als auch in den unabhängigen Validierungsdaten ermittelt und so der aus der Klassifikation abgeleitete Bedeckungsgrad dem tatsächlichen Bedeckungsgrad gegenübergestellt. Der Ablauf der vorgestellten Methodik ist in Abbildung 2 dargestellt.

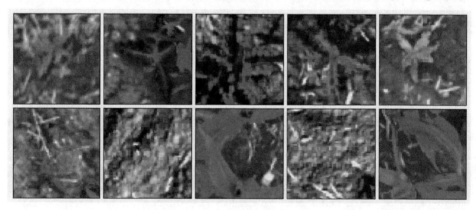

Abb. 1: Trainingssamples der Größe 64 × 64 Pixel nach der Z-Score Normalisierung, dargestellt in RGB. Obere Zeile: Klasse Distel, Untere Zeile: Klasse Nicht-Distel

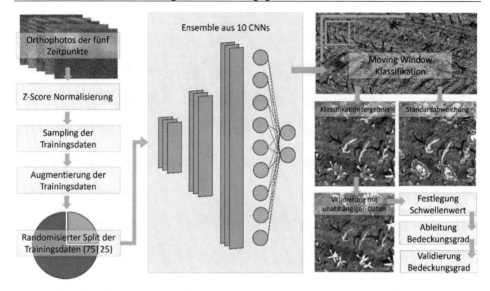

Abb. 2: Ablauf des vorgestellten Ansatzes mit einer schematischen Abbildung der Architektur des CNNs

3 Ergebnisse

Mithilfe des vorgestellten Ensembles aus CNNs wurden die fünf Testdatensätze klassifiziert, durch manuell extrahierte Validierungsdaten unabhängig validiert und für die Ableitung des Bedeckungsgrads verwendet. In Abbildugn 3 sind die Klassifikationsergebnisse in einem Teilausschnitt des Testgebietes abgebildet. Es ist erkennbar, dass mit der fortschreitenden phänologischen Entwicklung und dem Wachstum der Pflanzen die als *C. arvense* klassifizierten Bereiche zunehmen. Auch ist zu erkennen, dass die Klassifikationswahrscheinlichkeit in den mittleren Bereichen um die Distelpflanze herum nahe 100 % liegt, während sie zu den Randbereichen abnimmt. Hier sind weiterhin Fehlklassifikationen zu erkennen: Die äußeren Bereiche der Blätter werden nicht erkannt, während der Boden nahe dem Zentrum der Distel mit klassifiziert wird. Ebenfalls sind Fehlklassifikationen punktuell in Bereichen einzelner Maispflanzen zu erkennen. Aufwachsendes Beikraut, erkennbar beispielsweise im Teilausschnitt des 18.05., wird nicht als Distel klassifiziert. In Abbildung 4 lässt sich anhand der Standardabweichung das Verhalten des CNN-Ensembles in den Randbereichen der Disteln erkennen. Im Gegensatz zu Bodenflächen und den Bereichen im Zentrum der Disteln weisen die Randbereiche eine hohe Standardabweichung auf, unabhängig der Größe der Distelpflanze. Durch die Verwendung des Medians der Klassifikationsergebnisse im Ensemble wird diese Über- bzw. Unterschätzung des zu klassifizierenden Bereiches teilweise ausgeglichen. Es wird deutlich, dass sich die Gesamtgenauigkeit je nach Zeitpunkt der Aufnahme unterscheidet und zu den späteren Terminen kontinuierlich geringer wird.

Abb. 3: Klassifikationsergebnisse von Teilausschnitten des Testgebiets an den fünf Aufnahmeterminen mit einer Klassifikationswahrscheinlichkeit von 50-100 %

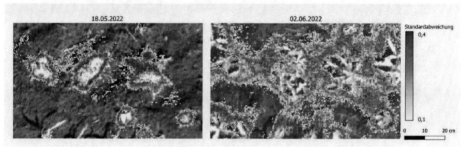

Abb. 4: Standardabweichung der Klassifikationsergebnisse innerhalb des CNN-Ensembles an zwei exemplarischen Teilausschnitten des Testgebiets. Bereiche mit einer Standardabweichung < 0,1 sind transparent dargestellt

Besonders auffällig ist die Gesamtgenauigkeit der Klassifikation am 13.06.2022, bei einem Schwellwert von 50 % liegt diese lediglich bei 48,53 %. Ebenfalls ist zu erkennen, dass mit einem steigenden Schwellenwert die Gesamtgenauigkeit an den ersten beiden Aufnahmeterminen nahezu konstant bis leicht verringert ist, während sie an den drei späteren Aufnahmeterminen in Folge eines steigenden Schwellwerts steigt. Bei einem Schwellwert von 99 % liegt die Gesamtgenauigkeit aller Klassifikationen bei über 80 %. Die Güte der Klassifikation der Klasse Distel nimmt jedoch bei einem steigenden Schwellwert ab, besonders deutlich im Bereich zwischen 95 % und 100 %. Der Anteil der falsch als Distel klassifizierten Pixel der Klassen Boden, Mais und Beikraut ist in Tabelle 2 bei einem Schwellenwert von 50 % und 99 % dargestellt. Es ist zu erkennen, dass der Anteil der falsch klassifizierten Pixel bei einem höheren Schwellwert abnimmt. Der Anteil der falsch klassifizierten Beikraut Pixel liegt sowohl bei einem Schwellenwert von 50 % als auch von 99 % nahe Null bzw. bei Null. Die Ergebnisse der Schätzung des Bedeckungsgrads sind in Abbildung 6 A abgebildet. Es wird jeweils der aus dem Klassifikationsergebnis bei einem Schwellwert von 95 % berechnete Bedeckungsgrad pro 0,25 m² dem aus unabhängigen Validierungsdaten berechneten Bedeckungsgrad gegenübergestellt. Anhand der eingezeichneten 1:1-Linie lässt sich erkennen, dass die Werte bei sehr geringen Bedeckungsgraden unterschätzt, und bei höheren Bedeckungsgraden, insbesondere am 13.06., überschätzt werden. Dieses Verhalten zeigt sich auch in der Gegenüberstellung des tatsächlichen und abgeleiteten durchschnittlichen Bedeckungsgrads (s. Abb. 6 B). An den ersten vier Befliegungsterminen wird der Bedeckungsgrad um

Kartierung des Bedeckungsgrads von *Cirsium arvense* im Mais

3-5 % unterschätzt, am 13.06. jedoch um 15 % überschätzt. Der Korrelationskoeffizient nach *Pearson* ergibt für den Bedeckungsgrad des 12.05. *0,84*, für den 18.05. *0,85*, für den 02.06. *0,95*, für den 07.06. *0,91* und für den 13.06. *0,84*. Für die gesamte Datenreihe ergibt sich ein Korrelationskoeffizient von *0,91*.

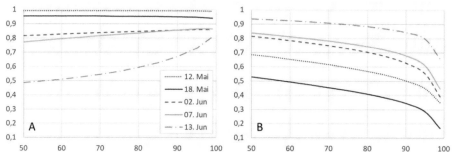

Abb. 5: A: Gesamtgenauigkeit der Klassifikationen der fünf Aufnahmetermine bei steigendem Schwellwert. B: Präzision für die Klasse Distel bei steigendem Schwellwert

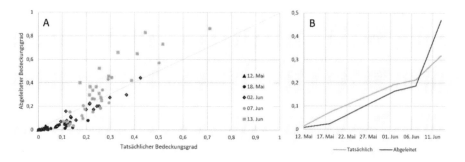

Abb. 6: A: Verhältnis von tatsächlichem zu abgeleitetem Bedeckungsgrad pro 0,25 m² der Testfläche sowie eingezeichnete 1:1-Linie. B: Tatsächlicher und abgeleiteter durchschnittlicher Bedeckungsgrad der Testfläche an den fünf Aufnahmeterminen.

	Schwellwert = 50 %					Schwellwert = 99 %				
	Gesamt (A)	*Distel* (B)	*Boden*	*Mais*	*Beikraut*	*Gesamt* (A)	*Distel* (B)	*Boden*	*Mais*	*Beikraut*
12.05.2022	99,05	68,52	34,34	1,41	0	98,99	34,85	20,98	0	0
18.05.2022	96,63	52,28	18,24	4,69	0,03	93,95	16,9	7,75	1,19	0
02.06.2022	81,67	81,40	27,01	22,58	0,01	86,08	39,31	8,62	1,79	0
07.06.2022	77,29	83,75	43,87	9,05	0,03	86,54	44,79	14,56	4,03	0
13.06.2022	48,53	93,51	48,31	14,96	0	80,98	65,67	20,55	9,04	0

Tab. 2: Validierung der Klassifikation bei Schwellwerten von 50 % und 99 %. Dargestellt sind Gesamtgenauigkeit der Klassifikation (*Gesamt*), Präzision für Distel (*Distel*), Anteil der fälschlicherweise als Distel klassifizierten Pixel der Klassen *Boden*, *Mais*, und *Beikraut*

4 Diskussion

4.1 Klassifikation von *C. arvense* durch ein CNN-Ensemble

Wie die Ergebnisse zeigen, ist eine Klassifikation von *C. arvense* in verschiedenen Wachstumsstadien und bei unterschiedlichen Belichtungsverhältnissen durch ein Ensemble von CNNs möglich. Anhand der dargestellten Standardabweichung (s. Abb. 4) und der Validierungsergebnisse (s. Tab. 2) wird jedoch deutlich, dass es insbesondere in den Randbereichen der Distelpflanzen zu Fehlklassifikationen kommt. Eine pixelweise Klassifikation von *C. arvense* ist daher mit der vorgestellten Methodik so nicht möglich. Mit einer erweiterten Menge an Trainingsdaten und einer veränderten Architektur könnte jedoch auch eine pixelweise Klassifikation umgesetzt werden. Betrachtet man die Distelpflanzen als Objekt, werden diese zuverlässig klassifiziert, unabhängig von ihrem Wachstumsstadium. Neben den Fehlklassifikationen in den Randbereichen werden auch einzelne Maispflanzen als *C. arvense* klassifiziert. Dies lässt sich durch ein Erhöhen des Schwellwerts der Klassifikationswahrscheinlichkeit in vielen Bereichen größtenteils beheben. Weiterhin lässt sich beobachten, dass der Anteil an fälschlicherweise klassifizierten Maispflanzen mit Fortschreiten des Pflanzenwachstums und sich stärker überlappenden Pflanzenteilen zunimmt. Beikräuter werden hingegen kaum als Distel erkannt und können über einen hohen Schwellenwert erfolgreich ausgeschlossen werden. Eine artspezifische Klassifikation von *C. arvense* in den betrachteten Bereichen ist somit möglich.

Durch das Ensemble wird der Einfluss einzelner Netze, die Disteln in ihrer Größe über- oder unterschätzen, gemindert, und somit eine genauere und einheitlichere Klassifikation ermöglicht. Durch die 10-fache Klassifikation eines jeden Pixels ist dieser Ansatz jedoch sehr zeitintensiv. Gerade in Bereichen, in denen keine Disteln aufwachsen, ist eine wiederholte Klassifikation nicht notwendig. Durch den hohen Zeitaufwand ist eine großflächige Anwendung der vorgestellten Methodik ohne weitere Anpassung nicht möglich. Ein erster Ansatz für effizientere Algorithmen könnte hier eine dynamische Anpassung der Klassifikationsauflösung sein. Gestartet mit einer niedrigen Auflösung könnte so in der Umgebung von gefundenen Disteln die Auflösung erhöht werden, um die Pflanzen pixelgenau abzubilden, ohne viel Rechenzeit in Anspruch zu nehmen.

4.2 Schätzung des Bedeckungsgrads

Wie in Abbildung 6 A erkennbar ist, wird der Bedeckungsgrad pro 0,25 m² zu den ersten vier Terminen überwiegend unterschätzt, am 13.06 jedoch deutlich überschätzt. Der durchschnittliche Bedeckungsgrad der gesamten 9 m² großen Testfläche wird an den ersten vier Terminen konstant um 3-5 % unterschätzt (s. Abb. 6 B). Es lässt sich daher vermuten, dass der Bedeckungsgrad der ersten vier Termine mit einem konstanten Faktor korrigiert werden könnte. Die deutliche Überschätzung des Bedeckungsgrads am 13.06. lässt sich mit der schlechten Klassifikationsgenauigkeit an diesem Termin erklären (s. Tab. 2). Bei dem verwendeten Schwellwert von 95 % für die Ableitung des Bedeckungsgrades

Kartierung des Bedeckungsgrads von *Cirsium arvense* im Mais 203

liegt diese bei 73,03 % (s. Abb. 5) und damit mehr als 10 % geringer als die Klassifikationsgenauigkeit vom 07.06. (86,65 %). Im Gegensatz zu den vorherigen Terminen gibt es am 13.06. sich deutlich überlappende Pflanzenbereiche, sodass einzelne *C. arvense*-Pflanzen nicht mehr gut voneinander oder von Maispflanzen abgrenzbar sind. Wie in Abbildung 3 erkennbar, werden so größere zusammenhängende Bereiche von Boden oder hereinragenden Pflanzenteilen mit klassifiziert. Der ausgleichend wirkende Effekt von Fehklassifikationen an den äußeren Blättern der Distelpflanzen kommt so vermutlich nicht mehr zur Geltung, woraus die Überschätzung des Bedeckungsgrads resultiert. In der Arbeit von Mink et al. [Mi18] wurde der Bedeckungsgrad von *C. arvense*, bei einer Mindesthöhe von 6 cm, mithilfe eines indexbasierten Ansatzes auf 9 × 9 m großen Testflächen sowohl aus spektralen Informationen als auch Informationen über die Pflanzenhöhe geschätzt. Auch hier wurde der tatsächliche Bedeckungsgrad um 1-10 % unterschätzt. Der in dieser Arbeit vorgestellte Ansatz auf Basis von Neuronalen Netzen ist somit mit einem indexbasierten Ansatz vergleichbar. Für eine präzise Schätzung des Bedeckungsgrads von *C. arvense* eignet sich der vorgestellte Ansatz durch die auftretende Unterschätzung jedoch nur bedingt. Mit einer pixelbasierten, segmentierenden Klassifikation anstelle des vorgestellten patchbasierten Ansatzes könnten bessere Ergebnisse in Bezug auf die Schätzung des Bedeckungsgrads erzielt werden und auch genauere Aussagen in Bezug auf die Pflanzengröße getroffen werden. Mithilfe dieser Informationen könnten weiterhin einzelpflanzenspezifische Aussagen über den idealen Behandlungszeitpunkt abgeleitet werden.

5 Fazit und Ausblick

Durch den schnellen Wiederaustrieb des perennierenden Beikrauts ist eine frühzeitige Erkennung und Abpassung des optimalen Behandlungszeitpunktes für einen hohen Regulierungserfolg mit geringem Herbizidaufwand unerlässlich. Eine frühzeitige Erkennung ist mit dem in dieser Arbeit vorgestellten System möglich und kann damit zu einem resilienten Umgang mit dem Auftreten von *C. arvense* in Ackerkulturen beitragen. Durch das Ensemble aus CNNs kann *C. arvense* zuverlässig auch in frühen Wachstumsstadien detektiert und von anderen aufwachsenden Beikräutern differenziert werden. Diese Klassifikation kann genutzt werden, um den Bedeckungsgrad mit einem Toleranzbereich von etwa 5 % zu detektieren. Mit fortschreitendem Wachstum und sich überlappenden Pflanzenteilen wird die Klassifikation von *C. arvense* jedoch erschwert und der Bedeckungsgrad deutlich überschätzt. Es ist zu vermuten, dass die Klassifikationsgenauigkeit und auch die Schätzung des Bedeckungsgrads durch einen segmentierenden, pixelbasierten Ansatz verbessert werden kann. Diese Segmente könnten zusätzlich genutzt werden, um die Größe einzelner *C. arvense*-Pflanzen abzuleiten und den optimalen Behandlungszeitpunkt zu bestimmen. Ein regelmäßiges Monitoring ausgewählter Distelnester könnte so realisiert werden. Die Effizienz der in dieser Arbeit behandelten Methodik könnte durch die Konzipierung spezialisierter Algorithmen deutlich verbessert werden. Speziell die Nutzung der räumlichen Kohärenz der Pflanzen bietet hier Potential. Um den vorgestellten Ansatz auf andere Kulturen und Beikrautarten zu übertragen, müsste eine entsprechende Menge an Trainingsdaten bereitgestellt werden. Die Ergebnisse zeigen, dass mit einer entsprechenden Normalisierung Daten mehrerer Aufnahmetermine zu unterschiedlichen phänologischen Phasen und wechselnder Wetterbedingungen in einer gemeinsamen Klassifikation verwendet werden können, wodurch die Erstellung einer solchen Datenbasis für Trainingsdaten erleichtert wird.

Anmerkung

Der verwendete UAV-Datensatz sowie die Parametrisierung des verwendeten CNN-Ensembles können auf begründete Anfrage zur Verfügung gestellt werden.

Förderhinweis und Danksagung: Das Projekt CognitiveWeeding wird durch die Mittel des Bundesministeriums für Umwelt, Naturschutz, nukleare Sicherheit und Verbraucherschutz (BMUV) aufgrund eines Beschlusses des Deutschen Bundestages gefördert. Ein besonderer Dank geht an den Studenten Lukas Grund, der durch die Erstellung von Polygonen auf der Testfläche wichtige Vorarbeiten für die Validierung der Klassifikationsergebnisse geleistet hat.

Literaturverzeichnis

[Ba22] Bayrische Landesanstalt für Landwirtschaft: Acker-Katzdistel: Unkrautsteckbrief, 2022, url: https://www.lfl.bayern.de/ips/unkraut/u_steckbriefe/053954/index.php

[CH21] Christensen, S.; Dyrmann, M.; Laursen, M.; Jørgensen, R.; Rasmussen, J.: Sensing for Weed Detection. In: Sensing Approaches for Precision Agriculture. Springer, S. 275-300, 2021.

[DGK04] Dicke, D.; Gerhards, R.; Kühbauch, W.: Überprüfung bestehender Schadschwellen auf ihre Eignung für die teilschlagspezifische Unkrautkontrolle in Braugerste unter Verwendung eines Geoinformationssystems. Integration und Datensicherheit–Anforderungen, Konflikte und Perspektiven, Referate der 25. GIL Jahrestagung/, 2004, url:https://dl.gi.de/bitstream/handle/20.500.12116/29083/GI.Proceedings.4982.pdf?sequence=1&isAllowed=y, Stand: 19. 01. 2022.

[EU20] The European Commission: Communication from the Commission to the European Parliament, the Council, the European economic and social committee and the Committee of the regions, A Farm to Fork Strategy for a fair, healthy and environmentally-friendly food system, 20. Mai 2020, url: https://eur-lex.europa.eu/resource.html?uri=cellar:ea0f9f73-9ab2-11ea-9d2d01aa75ed71a1.0001.02/DOC_1&format=PDF.

[Ka21] Kattenborn, T.; Leitloff, J.; Schiefer, F.; Hinz, S.: Review on Convolutional Neural Networks (CNN) in vegetation remote sensing. ISPRS Journal of Photogrammetry and Remote Sensing 173/, S. 24-49, 2021.

[Ha21]	Hasan, A. M.; Sohel, F.; Diepeveen, D.; Laga, H.; Jones, M. G.: A survey of deep learning techniques for weed detection from images. Computers and Electronics in Agriculture 184/, S. 106067, 2021.
[NS11]	Nkurunziza, L.; Streibig, J. C.: Carbohydrate dynamics in roots and rhizomes of Cirsium arvense and Tussilago farfara. Weed Research 51/5, S. 461-468, 2011.
[Pa17]	Pawara, P.; Okafor, E.; Schomaker, L.; Wiering, M.: Data augmentation for plant classification. In: International conference on advanced concepts for intelligent vision systems. Springer, S. 615-626, 2017.
[RAN21]	Rasmussen, J.; Azim, S.; Nielsen, J.: Pre-harvest weed mapping of Cirsium arvense L. based on free satellite imagery – The importance of weed aggregation and image resolution. European Journal of Agronomy 130/, S. 126373, 2021.
[RN20]	Rasmussen, J.; Nielsen, J.: A novel approach to estimating the competitive ability of Cirsium arvense in cereals using unmanned aerial vehicle imagery. Weed research 60/2, S. 150-160, 2020.
[Ry21]	Rydahl, P.; Bøjer, O.; Jensen, N. - P.; Nielsen, M.; Paz, L. -C.; Pedersen, K.; Jensen, K.; Rasmus, J.; Scovill, A.; Laursen, M.; Teimouri, N.; Hartmann, B.: Analysis of potential herbicide savings using experience and data from the RoboWeedMaPS project: Report prepared as a result of participation in project 2020-68795, under the Danish Environmental Protection Agency. "Precision Spraying Partnership". 2021
[SL09]	Sokolova, M.; Lapalme, G.: A systematic analysis of performance measures for classification tasks. Information processing & management 45/4, S. 427-437, 2009.
[Sö10]	Sökefeld, M.: Variable rate technology for herbicide application. In: Precision crop protection-the challenge and use of heterogeneity. Springer, S. 335-347, 2010.
[TVL19]	Tavaziva, V. J.; Verwijst, T.; Lundkvist, A.: Growth and development of Cirsium arvense in relation to herbicide dose, timing of herbicide application and crop presence. Acta Agriculturae Scandinavica, Section B—Soil & Plant Science 69/3, S. 189-198, 2019.

Towards model-based automation of plant-specific weed regulation

Marian Renz[1], Mark Niemeyer[1] and Joachim Hertzberg[1,2]

Abstract: Weeds are commonly known as a major factor for yield losses in agriculture, competing with crops for resources like nutrients, water, and light. However, keeping specific weeds could benefit agricultural sites for example by nitrogen fixation, erosion protection, or increasing biodiversity. This comes with technological challenges like plant detection and classification, damage estimation, and selective removal. This paper presents a model-based approach to the problem of damage estimation of perceived plants. The system uses contextual and background knowledge in the form of rules about the plant count per square meter and the distance to the nearest crop together with thresholds for each weed species. The functionality is demonstrated using an artificial dataset and exemplary thresholds, showing the potential of using knowledge about plant-crop interactions for more sophisticated weed control systems.

Keywords: selective weeding, biodiversity, rule-based reasoning

1 Introduction

Within the yield-reducing factors in agriculture, weeds have the biggest damage potential when not mitigated [Oe06]. However, the extensive use of herbicides brings further problems. Selective herbicides can increase the occurrence of resistant weeds [No12], while a decline in biodiversity is observable. Furthermore, herbicide accumulation in soil and water bodies negatively impacts the ecosystem and increases health risks in humans [Al21].

In Germany, however, only 20 of the 350 species of spontaneously growing plants on fields are considered harmful [Le13]. Keeping specific weeds may have beneficial effects like nitrogen fixation, reduction of erosion, or serving as a host and food source for birds and beneficial insects [We14]. Of course, the benefit and the damage from specific weeds are circumstantial, depending for example on species and inter-species relations, degree of coverage, or periods, where the crop is more vulnerable to weeds [Ma21].

Taking the benefits and damage potential into consideration for automated weed regulation is challenging. Besides automated weed detection, classification, and removal

---

[1] German Research Center for Artificial Intelligence, Plan-Based Robot Control Group, Berghoffstr. 11, 49090 Osnabrück, firstname.lastname@dfki.de
[2] Osnabrück University, Knowledge-Based Systems Group, Wachsbleiche 27, 49090 Osnabrück, joachim.hertzberg@uos.de

a model for estimating the potential damage is needed. The applied principle of weed-specific damage thresholds falls short when it comes to inter-species interactions and is only available for a limited number of crops and weeds [Ma21].

Progress has been made in selective weed control due to the use of artificial neural networks for weed detection, some systems already combine deep learning-based detection and selective regulation using smart sprayers [PCA19; LAN21; Hu20; Ab20]. In contrast, the approaches for plant-specific damage estimation are scarce. While a learning-based approach might be possible, collecting, and labeling datasets in the required size for damage estimation for individual weeds is impractical. A model-based approach using context and background knowledge has the advantage of not depending on high amounts of data. Already existing knowledge about the agricultural domain can be used to formulate rules from which plant-specific decisions can be made.

Furthermore, the importance of transparency and trust in AI is increasing in Europe [Eu20]. Rule-based systems have some advantages when it comes to explainability since all results are inferred deterministically from explicitly formulated rules [va21].

A model-based approach to the challenge of plant-specific weed removal is presented by using context- and background knowledge in the form of rules to make plant-specific decisions about the potential benefit of a weed. The resulting rule-based system generates an application map, which contains the position of harmful weeds on the field. The presented system can be seen as a general pipeline, which leaves the possibility for more sophisticated knowledge to be integrated. The functionality is demonstrated on a synthetic dataset containing RGB images of maize plants and 5 different weed species.

2 Related work

Integrated smart spraying systems with deep learning-based weed detection technology already exist. These systems usually aim to reduce the applied amount of spraying liquid. Patel et al. [PCA19] present a low-cost smart sprayer system utilizing deep convolutional neural networks for the distinction between artificial targets and non-targets. Similarly, Hussain et al. [Hu20] present a smart sprayer detecting weed-infected potato plants, reducing the sprayed amount of liquid by up to 42% in a laboratory setting. Comparable systems are developed for crop-specific applications like strawberry fields [LAN21] or citrus trees [PCA21].

While all these approaches successfully integrate deep learning-based weed- or target detection with variable spraying systems, none of them consider including domain knowledge for a more integrated approach to weed control. They limit their scope to the discrimination between targets and non-targets. The same situation can be found in non-AI-based smart spraying solutions [Ab20].

An extensive model for integrated weed management is FLORSYS, a biophysical simulation environment for cropping systems [Co21]. FLORSYS enables predictions for weed development based on inputs like crop succession, weed management techniques, soil characteristics, and weather data. Based on FLORSYS, a decision support system for integrated weed management has been developed [Co20]. The decision support system utilizes the FLORSYS simulation and a learned meta-model to communicate the effects of different cropping systems on weed development.

Extensive background knowledge is integrated into the biophysical models of FLORSYS. This can provide high-quality decision support for the design of integrated weed management but cannot be integrated into an automated weed regulation system working on sensor data due to missing interfaces. This paper presents an approach using a knowledge model based on rules as well as the necessary interfaces, which can be used in a smart spraying system.

In general, there are plenty of applied model- and rule-based systems for agricultural applications. Different systems have been developed for crop, pest, and disease management [Gh18; MRS11] but rule-based systems for weed management or even integrated weed management are scarce.

Typically, weed related approaches only consider the negative effects of weeds and are targeted at reducing effort and resources for weed management. This approach considers a system that not only detects and removes weeds but rather integrates background and domain knowledge. The system can be integrated into a smart weed regulation system with interfaces for deep learning-based plant detection and classification as well as selective actuators. In contrast to other model-based systems in agriculture, the knowledge is modeled for actuator control and not for decision support.

3 System architecture

The overall system for weed damage estimation consists of four major parts (Fig. 1): the semantic environment representation (SEEREP) [NPH22] for storing labeled sensor data, a grid map for spatial representation and attribute calculation, a rule engine including a knowledge base of rules for inference and the generation of an application map as the interface to the weeding system. In this section, each part is described in more detail. The plant detection and classification are considered as an external module and are summarized with other potential sources of information as "Input Data".

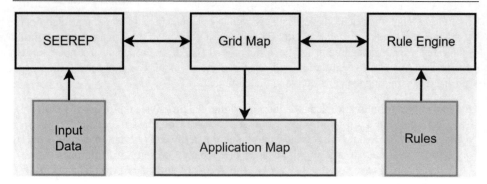

Fig. 1: Architecture diagram and data flow of the model-based weed regulation system

3.1 Spatio-temporal-SEmantic Environment REPresentation – SEEREP

The weed damage estimation cannot be performed on a sensor data stream directly. The sensor data must be stored and processed so that the model-based system can access the data in an efficient and unified way. To achieve this, the spatio-temporal-semantic environment representation (called SEEREP) is used [NPH22]. SEEREP stores the sensor data and creates indices to enable queries in the modalities of space, time, and semantics.

For the spatial modality, the geo-location, and the spatial extent of each sensor reading are indexed so that data queries regarding a specific position can be executed. Additionally, the point in time of the sensor reading is indexed in the temporal domain so that it is possible to store and access historical data. The temporal index is not used in the use-case of this paper but may be used in the future. The last modality, the semantics, is important for the model-based system because it enables symbolic reasoning. The semantic annotations in the data (for example bounding boxes in images with the semantic label of the plant shown) are also indexed, which enables queries for specific labels.

The usage of the three described modalities enables the analysis of the environment and the efficient data query in all three modalities. The model-based system cannot handle the annotated sensor data directly. It requires the position and the semantic label of specific plant instances. Thus, SEEREP can link the semantic annotations of the same object in multiple datasets to a common instance. This instance is not only linked to the sensor data but the position of the instance, which may be calculated based on the sensor data, can also be stored in SEEREP and be linked to the instance. This enables the query of an instance based on its position. Additionally, triple-based attributes can be stored alongside the instance enabling the storage of reasoning results.

Based on these capabilities of SEEREP, the following data handling steps are needed. (1) The raw sensor data is stored in SEEREP and the indices for the spatial and temporal modality are created. (2) The raw sensor data is processed, for example by convolutional neural networks, so that semantic annotations can be added to the data. For those annotations, a common vocabulary, which the model-based system understands, defined by an ontology must be used. (3) In addition to the general semantic annotations, the annotations of the same real-world object (plant) must be linked to an instance. For this anchoring problem, the assumption can be used that the plants do not move. (4) When all the annotations of the same plant are linked to the same instance the number of the instances is known. For the rule-based system also the position of each instance must be known and linked to the instance. For this, the sensor data must be processed to get the position. This may be done via a projection of image data to the ground plane or via 3D information from point clouds or depth images. (5) The instances with their semantic annotations and their positions are obtained via the spatio-temporal-semantic query interface. This enables queries for plants of a specific type in a specific region. The obtained instances with semantic annotation and with their position can be handled by the rule-based system for decision generation. (6) Finally, the triple-based attribute store of the instances can be used to store the decision results.

3.2 Grid map value calculation

For the convenient representation of the agricultural field and value calculation, a grid map is used. Plant instances are inserted into the grid map based on their global position in the field. A plant instance has the following attributes: a unique identifier (UUID), a species name, a global 2D position, a category as result of the rule inference, and numeric values for the rule inference, being the count of the species per square meter and the distance to the nearest crop. The global position can be determined using high-precision GNSS during recording.

The grid map has three internal representations:

- a 2D grid map of plant instances,
- a 3D tensor with the same size for the first 2 dimensions as the 2D map and a third dimension with the number of known species as size, used for counting plant instances,
- a key-value map with the instance identifier as the key and the plant instance as the value.

When inserting a plant into the grid map, the plant instance and all attributes known beforehand are inserted into the 2D grid map based on the plant's global position. Accordingly, the respective counter in the 3D tensor is increased by one and the instance is added to the key-value map.

After retrieving all available plant instances from SEEREP, the numeric attributes are calculated for each plant. The count per square meter is calculated using a sliding window with the size of 1m x 1m. For each grid cell, the plants within the window are summed up per species, using the plant counts from the 3D tensor. The accumulated sum per species is then assigned to all plant instances in the grid cell under consideration. The distance to the nearest crop is calculated by searching for the closest cell with crops for each cell with weeds. The distance is then calculated by using the L2 norm on the plant's global position.

After calculating and assigning the numeric values for each plant instance they are sent into the rule-based system's working memory for inference about the plant's categories.

3.3 Rule-based system

For rule-based inference Drools is used as the backend, an open-source Business Rules Management System [Re22]. The modeled rules categorize whether a plant is considered a crop, a harmful weed, a harmless weed, or an endangered species.

A total of five rules are currently implemented as a working example:

- If the plant's name is listed as a crop, it is categorized as crop.
- If a plant's name is listed as endangered species, it is categorized as endangered species.
- If a plant's count per m² exceeds a species-specific threshold, it is categorized as harmful weed.
- If a plant's distance to the nearest crop falls below a species-specific threshold, it is categorized as harmful weed.
- If a plant is not categorized by any of the rules above, it is considered a harmless weed.

Even though these rules are rudimentary, they already allow for a more plant-specific weed regulation strategy, considering species-specific background knowledge. The specific thresholds as well as more sophisticated rules need to be estimated by more extensive research for weed management. An Excel file is used as an interface to input the crop, the species-specific thresholds, and the list of endangered species.

The declarative nature of rule-based systems allows for easy extensibility. Rules and data sources can be added and modified without modifying the program flow. More sophisticated sources of knowledge like weather forecasts, geometric attributes about the plants, or geographical information can be included.

3.4 Output

To utilize the system together with a selective sprayer, an application map is generated from the grid map. Weeds categorized as harmful are stored as points in shapefiles. To estimate the area for the sprayer to cover, the bounding box from the plant detection is converted into an area estimate in cm and added as an attribute to each point. The shapefile therefore contains a list of coordinates and areas to which chemicals are to be applied.

4 Example with synthetic data

The system is tested using a synthetic dataset consisting of RGB images of maize plants and 5 different weed species (Tab. 1) with ground truth labeling. The images are created using Blender [B.o.J.]. The simulated scene consists of a field of maize plant models placed in rows and the randomly distributed weed models.

The images are rendered from a virtual camera (1280*960 px), which is placed approximately 2 m above the ground facing down orthogonally. For each image, the camera's position is changed by 0.5 m along the maize row, rendering 40 images over 20 m. 2 rows of images are rendered next to each other, resulting in 80 images covering 3 adjacent maize rows and 485 plants in total.

Species name	Plant count per m^2	Crop distance	Total count	% categorized as weed
Maize	-	-	200	0 %
Autumn Hawkbit	-	-	7	0 %
Common Daisy	6	0.04 m	157	48 %
Curly Duck	1	0.2 m	7	100 %
Ground Elder	2	0.2 m	34	79 %
Plantain Ribwort	5	0.15 m	80	65 %

Tab. 1: Simulated plant species with thresholds for plant count per m^2, distance to the nearest crop, total count within the simulation, and percentage of plants categorized as weed

Using synthetic data enables pixel-correct classification results for the input data, delivering ground truth quality bounding boxes for each plant. In a real-world use case, this would be substituted by a plant perception pipeline. However, for demonstrating the functionality of the model-based system, the simulated data is sufficient.

The images and bounding boxes are stored in SEEREP and retrieved using a query, obtaining all 485 detected plants with species names and global positions. Then, the plant instances are inserted into the grid map for the attribute calculation. The used grid cell size is 10 * 10 cm. The plant count per m^2 and the distance to the nearest crop are calculated for each plant, which are then submitted into the rule-based system's working memory.

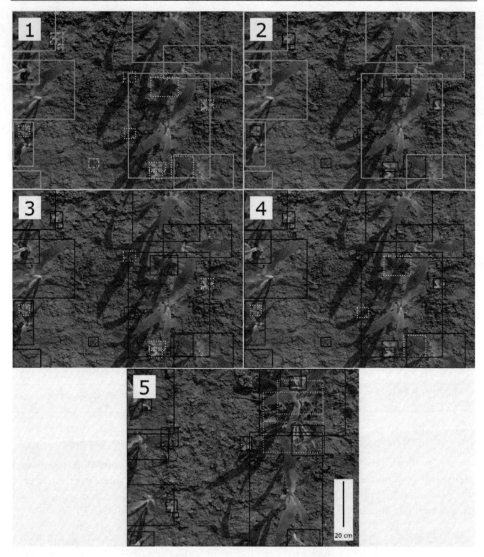

Fig. 2: Result of the rule-based system marking plants as crop (green, solid line), harmless weed (yellow, dashed line), harmful weed (white, dotted line), endangered species (green, dotted line) or as not categorized (black, solid line). Image 1 shows the total result. Image 2 displays the result of the effect of the crop rule, all maize plants are marked with a green bounding box. In Image 3, weeds categorized as harmful by the plants per m² rule are marked white. Image 4 shows weeds marked as harmful by the distance rule. Image 5 displays a different section of the field, showing the Autumn Hawkbit categorized as endangered species.

Based on the plant's species and the respective thresholds (Tab. 1), the rule-based system infers whether a plant is to be categorized as crop, harmful or harmless weed, or endangered species. Plants exceeding the plant count threshold as well as plants falling below the distance threshold are considered harmful weeds, otherwise, they are considered harmless weeds. Maize and Autumn Hawkbit have no threshold values since Maize is listed as a crop and Autumn Hawkbit as an endangered species. The threshold values and the listing as endangered species are exemplary due to the limited availability of other plant models.

After inference, the result is written back into the grid map. Based on this, the application map can be generated, which is not necessary for the example with synthetic data.

For transparency purposes, the resulting category of each rule can be displayed in the original images (Fig. 2).

5 Discussion

The percentages of each plant species categorized as a weed (Tab. 1) give an impression of the functionality of the model-based system.

Maize and Autumn Hawkbit are never categorized as weed at all, as they should not. The other plants, however, are categorized as weeds to different proportions. It is worth mentioning, that stricter thresholds lead to a higher number of weeds within a species. The Common Daisy for example has the least strict thresholds and therefore only 48 % of all Daisies are categorized as harmful weeds. The Curly Duck on the other hand shows the strictest rule with 1 plant per m^2 as threshold, thus all Curly Ducks are categorized as harmful weeds.

This was expected, but it confirms the effect the rules have on the categorization and therefore the overall functionality of the system to mark some weeds as worthy of maintaining.

The rules and thresholds must be evaluated carefully though. While keeping individual weeds is beneficial for biodiversity, this must not result in significant crop losses.

The quality and design of the plant detection and classification model also limit the effectiveness of the system. The design of the rules is dependent on the types of plants the classification model can identify. Nevertheless, the presented system works with any kind of plant perception if the detections are stored in SEEREP in the presented manner. A further constraint for this would be precise plant localization, so plants appearing in multiple images can be fused to a single instance.

The current implementation can be used by any precision weeding system that works on in advance generated application maps but not in an online fashion, where plant detection, categorization, and removal are done simultaneously.

The visualization of each rule effect (Fig. 2) provides an intuitive way to make the internal processes of the system more transparent. It must be mentioned though, that the presented images were ground truth data and that a deep learning-based plant perception system adds a non-transparent black box to the system.

6 Conclusion

A model-based system for plant-specific automated weed regulation is presented which formulates background knowledge about the damage potential of weeds as rules. The system infers plant-specific information about weeds and crops, categorizing plants as crops, harmful or harmless weeds, and endangered species.

The presented rule set does not integrate much background or domain knowledge, but the rule base and the system architecture can easily be extended. Thus, additional rules and information sources such as weather, data about the agricultural site, soil analysis results, or geographical data can be added, depending on the recommendations in integrated weed management. This work is providing a pipeline, which enables the integration of sensor data as well as symbolic knowledge for integrated weed management.

Further steps include integration and testing into a working perception and weed regulation pipeline, expanding the rule set and the utilized background knowledge, and extending the explanatory potential of the rule-based system.

Acknowledgements: The DFKI Niedersachsen (DFKI NI) is sponsored by the Ministry of Science and Culture of Lower Saxony and the VolkswagenStiftung. This work is supported by the Federal Ministry for the Environment, Nature Conservation, Nuclear Safety and Consumer Protection (BMUV) within the CognitiveWeeding project (grant number: 67KI21001B).

Bibliography

[Ab20]   Abbas, I. et al.: Different sensor based intelligent spraying systems in Agriculture. Sensors and Actuators A: Physical 316, p. 112265, 2020.

[Al21]   Alengebawy, A. et al.: Heavy Metals and Pesticides Toxicity in Agricultural Soil and Plants: Ecological Risks and Human Health Implications. Toxics 3/9, 2021.

[B.o.J.]   B. Foundation: blender.org. Home of the Blender project - Free and Open 3D Creation Software. https://blender.org/, accessed 20 Oct 2022.

[Co20]   Colas, F. et al.: Co-development of a decision support system for integrated weed management: Contribution from future users. European Journal of Agronomy 114, p. 126010, 2020.

[Co21]	Colbach, N. et al.: The FLORSYS crop-weed canopy model, a tool to investigate and promote agroecological weed management. Field Crops Research 261, p. 108006, 2021.
[Eu20]	White Paper on Artificial Intelligence. A European approach to excellence and trust, Brussels, 2020.
[Gh18]	Ghosh, I. et al.: Artificial Intelligence in Agriculture: A Literature Survey. International Journal of Scientific Research in Computer Science Applications and Management Studies IJSRCSAMS 3/7, pp. 1-6, 2018.
[Hu20]	Hussain, N. et al.: Design and Development of a Smart Variable Rate Sprayer Using Deep Learning. Remote Sensing 24/12, p. 4091, 2020.
[LAN21]	Liu, J.; Abbas, I.; Noor, R. S.: Development of Deep Learning-Based Variable Rate Agrochemical Spraying System for Targeted Weeds Control in Strawberry Crop. Agronomy 8/11, p. 1480, 2021.
[Le13]	Leuschner, C.: Vorwort. In (Meyer, S., Hilbig, W, Steffen, K., Schuch, S. Ed.): Ackerwildkrautschutz – eine Bibliographie. Ergebnisse aus dem F+E-Vorhaben (FKZ 3512 86 0300). BfN Bundesamt für Naturschutz, Bonn, 2013.
[Ma21]	Masson, S. et al.: Neue Entscheidungshilfen für eine nachhaltige Unkrautbekämpfung. Agrarforschung Schweiz 12, pp. 78-89, 2021.
[MRS11]	Mercy Nesa Rani, P.; Rajesh, T.; Saravanan, R.: Expert Systems in Agriculture: A Review. Journal of Computer Science and Applications 1/3, pp. 59-71, 2011.
[No12]	Norsworthy, J. K. et al.: Reducing the Risks of Herbicide Resistance: Best Management Practices and Recommendations. Weed Science SP1/60, pp. 31-62, 2012.
[NPH22]	Niemeyer, M.; Putz, S.; Hertzberg, J.: A Spatio-Temporal-Semantic Environment Representation for Autonomous Mobile Robots equipped with various Sensor Systems: 2022 IEEE International Conference on Multisensor Fusion and Integration for Intelligent Systems (MFI). IEEE, pp. 1-6, 2022.
[Oe06]	Oerke, E.-C.: Crop losses to pests. The Journal of Agricultural Science 1/144, pp. 31-43, 2006.
[PCA19]	Partel, V.; Charan Kakarla, S.; Ampatzidis, Y.: Development and evaluation of a low-cost and smart technology for precision weed management utilizing artificial intelligence. Computers and Electronics in Agriculture 157, pp. 339-350, 2019.
[Re22]	Red Hat: Drools. https://www.drools.org, accessed 20 Oct 2022.

[va21] van der Waa, J. et al.: Evaluating XAI: A comparison of rule-based and example-based explanations. Artificial Intelligence 291, p. 103404, 2021.

[We14] Weiss, M., Weiss, K., Krebs, S.: Ackerwildkräuter am Württembergischen Riesrand. In (Naturschutz und Landschaftspflege Baden-Württemberg Band 76. Systemedia GmbH Ed.): Landesanstalt für Umwelt; Messungen und Naturschutz Baden-Württemberg (LUBW), pp. 112-151, 2014.

KI-basiertes Computer-Vision-System zur Qualitäts- und Größenbestimmung von Kartoffeln

Andreas Schliebitz[1], Henri Graf[1], Tobias Wamhof[1], Heiko Tapken[1] und Andreas Gertzen[2]

Abstract: Diese Arbeit untersucht die Weiterentwicklung einer stichprobenbasierten zu einer kontinuierlichen Qualitätsmessung von Kartoffellieferungen. Das dafür entwickelte KI-basierte Computer-Vision-System lokalisiert mithilfe eines YOLOv5-Detektors Kartoffeln auf einem Förderband mit einer Genauigkeit von 0,96 mAP@[.5:.95]. Eine anschließende Qualitätsbestimmung der detektierten Kartoffeln erfolgt mit einem EfficientNetV2-Klassifkator, der zur Familie der Convolutional Neural Networks zählt. Dieser zeigt auf einem qualitativ hochwertigen Referenzdatensatz eine Genauigkeit von 96 % auf acht Mängelklassen, welche auf dem zu erweiternden Förderband-Datensatz bei zwei Klassen auf 81 % und bei drei Klassen auf 72 % abfällt. Das Quadratmaß, Volumen und Gewicht einer Kartoffel werden über Segmentierungsmasken und Tiefenbilder approximiert. Zur echtzeitfähigen Annäherung der Geometrie wird anhand dieser Daten für jede erkannte Kartoffel ein triaxialer Ellipsoid berechnet. Weiterhin wird ein Ansatz zur Verbesserung der mit einem optimalen Schwellenwertalgorithmus berechneten Segmentierungsmasken auf Basis eines Mask R-CNN Segmentierungsmodells erarbeitet.

Keywords: Computer Vision, Kartoffel, Qualitätsmanagement, Künstliche Intelligenz, Agri-Food

1 Einleitung

Im Rahmen des Forschungsprojekts Agri-Gaia wird in Zusammenarbeit mit der Wernsing Feinkost GmbH untersucht, ob eine echtzeitfähige Qualitäts- und Größenbestimmung von Kartoffeln mit einem KI-basierten Computer-Vision-System umgesetzt werden kann. Ein solches Systems ist notwendig, da sowohl die Qualitäts- als auch Größenverteilung einer Kartoffellieferung aktuell an einer häufig nicht repräsentativen Stichprobe abgeschätzt wird. Der in dieser Näherung enthaltene Schätzfehler erlaubt in den meisten Fällen keine präzise Steuerung nachgelagerter Produktionsschritte, die aus wirtschaftlichen Gründen eine maximale Verwertung der Kartoffel anstreben. Durch eine genauere Erfassung der Qualitäten und Größen kann der Warenausschuss während der Produktion verringert und es können mehr Lebensmittel aus derselben Menge an Kartoffeln hergestellt werden.

Der Einsatzort des in dieser Arbeit vorgestellten Computer-Vision-Systems befindet sich unmittelbar nach einer Waschstraße, welche die angelieferten Kartoffeln von Verschmutzungen befreit. Die zu diesem Zeitpunkt sichtbar gewordenen Mängel auf der Kartoffeloberfläche werden von einem planparallel zum Vereinzelungsband

---

[1] HS Osnabrück, Fakultät IuI, Albrechtstr. 30, 49076 Osnabrück, a.schliebitz@hs-osnabrueck.de, h.graf@hs-osnabrueck.de, t.wamhof@hs-osnabrueck.de, h.tapken@hs-osnabrueck.de
[2] Wernsing Feinkost GmbH, Kartoffelweg 1, 49632 Addrup-Essen/Oldb. andreas.gertzen@wernsing.de

ausgerichteten Kamera-Array erfasst und für die Erstellung eines gelabelten Bilddatensatzes gespeichert. Während des manuellen Labeling-Prozesses werden jeder aufgenommenen Kartoffel mindestens eine von elf Qualitätsklassen und genau eine Bounding-Box zur Lokalisierung zugewiesen. Auf Grundlage dieses annotierten Datensatzes werden im Laufe dieser Arbeit verschiedene KI-Modelle trainiert, welche sowohl die Erweiterung des Bilddatensatzes erleichtern als auch letztendlich zwischen Qualitäts- und Größenklassen unterscheiden können. Die vorliegende Arbeit umfasst im Anschluss an diese Einleitung einen Überblick über den aktuellen Stand der Forschung, gefolgt von den verwendeten Methoden, einer Quantifizierung der erzielten Ergebnisse sowie ihrer Diskussion und einem abschließenden thematischen Ausblick.

2 Stand der Forschung

In der Fachliteratur existieren aufgrund der weltweiten Funktion der Kartoffel als Grundnahrungsmittel eine Vielzahl von Veröffentlichungen, die sich sowohl mit der Qualitäts- als auch Geometriebestimmung dieser Feldfrucht beschäftigen. So entwickeln beispielsweise Su et al. [Su20] ein automatisches Kartoffelsortiersystem, das in einem nicht industriellen Kontext primär mit Tiefenbildern aus einer aktiven Tiefenkamera arbeitet. Die aufgezeichneten Kartoffeln werden mithilfe eines Softmax-Regressionsmodells und eines Convolutional Neural Networks (CNN) in sechs Qualitätsklassen unterteilt. Dieselbe Autorengruppe untersucht in einer vorangegangenen Veröffentlichung [Su18] die Möglichkeit der Gewichtsbestimmung unterschiedlich geformter Kartoffeln anhand von Tiefendaten und den daraus errechneten Volumina. Die aufgezeichneten Tiefenbilder von 110 Kartoffeln werden außerdem genutzt, um ein Virtual-Reality-System zu konzipieren, welches die händische Untersuchung von Kartoffeln in einem 3D-Raum simuliert.

Im Gegensatz dazu fokussieren sich Oppenheim et al. [Op19] auf die Klassifizierung von Mängeln auf der Kartoffeloberfläche. Der 400 verschiedene Kartoffeln umfassende Datensatz besteht aus Farbbildern, die während des Labelings über Bounding-Boxen auf die mängelbehafteten Areale der Kartoffelschale zugeschnitten werden. Als Klassifikator kommt erneut ein CNN zum Einsatz, das auf diesem Datensatz eine Genauigkeit von über 92 % erzielt. Die reine Klassifikation äußerer Mängel wird sowohl von Hasan et al. [Ha21] als auch Wang et al. [WX21] mithilfe verschiedener CNN-Architekturen durchgeführt. Als Datengrundlage kommen Farbbilder ganzer Kartoffeln zum Einsatz. Wang et al. verwenden in ihrem Deep-Transfer-Learning-Ansatz ein Region-based Fully Convolutional Network (R-FCN) basierend auf der ResNet101-Architektur. Sie erzielen damit eine maximale Klassifikationsgenauigkeit von 98,7 % auf drei Mängelklassen. Beide Veröffentlichungen nutzen pro Mängelklasse einige hundert bis wenige tausend gelabelte Exemplare, wobei Hasan et al. die Größe ihres Datensatzes durch Augmentierung verfünffachen.

Eine dieser Arbeit ähnelnde Veröffentlichung stammt von Pandey et al. [PKP18], in der auf Basis eines U-Net Segmentierungsmodells und verschiedenen Bildverarbeitungsalgorithmen einzelne Kartoffeln auf einem Förderband lokalisiert werden. Die Geometriebestimmung wird ausschließlich auf Grundlage der erzeugten Segmentierungsmasken in der 2D-Ebene des Förderbands durchgeführt. Für die Geometriebestimmung werden keine Tiefendaten erhoben. Die Klassifikation von sichtbaren Mängeln wird über ein Transfer-Learning-Ansatz realisiert. Abgrenzend zu diesen Veröffentlichungen wird in der vorliegenden Arbeit ein Prototyp eines echtzeitfähigen Systems zur Qualitäts- und Größenbestimmung von Kartoffeln auf einem Förderband vorgestellt. Die Größen-, Volumen- und Gewichtsbestimmung wird im Gegensatz zu Pandey et al. über Tiefenkameras um eine dritte Dimension erweitert. Eine Umsetzung erfolgt zusammen mit der Mängelklassifikation echtzeitfähig in Hard- und Software.

3 Methoden

Die Planung und Umsetzung des Computer-Vision-Systems umfasst im Wesentlichen die beiden Bereiche der Hard- und Software. Während mit der Kamerahardware Bilddaten sowohl für das Training als auch für die Inferenz von KI-Modellen aufgenommen werden, übernimmt die Software die Automatisierung zahlreicher Prozesse. Dazu gehört z. B. die Aktualisierung der Lokalisierungs-, Klassifikations- und Segmentierungsdatensätze mit neu gelabelten Kartoffeln sowie das Training-, Testing und Deployment von KI-Modellen. Der Lokalisierungsdatensatz wird für das Training eines Objektdetektors genutzt, der in einem ersten Schritt Kartoffeln auf einem Vereinzelungsband über Bounding-Boxen lokalisiert. Nach der Lokalisierung werden in einem händischen Labeling-Prozess die Bounding-Boxen mit Qualitätsklassen versehen. Der so gebildete Klassifikationsdatensatz besteht aus einer Menge von Qualitätsklassen mit einer jeweils variablen Anzahl an Bildern von Kartoffeln dieser Qualität. Das Ziel des mit diesem Datensatz trainierten Klassifikators ist die Unterscheidung zwischen Kartoffeln unterschiedlicher Qualitätsklassen. Basierend auf dem Lokalisierungsdatensatz wird ein Segmentierungsdatensatz erstellt, der für das Training eines Segmentierungsmodells genutzt wird. Dieses soll die Genauigkeit der mittels optimalem Schwellenwertalgorithmus erstellten Binärmasken verbessern und somit die Genauigkeit der Geometriebestimmung erhöhen. Eine Zusammenfassung dieses Ablaufs ist in Abbildung 1 dargestellt.

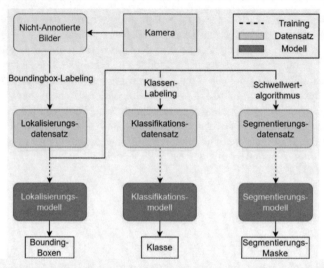

Abb. 1: Ablauf der KI-basierten Qualitäts- und Geometriebestimmung von Kartoffel

3.1 Kameraaufbau

Der Kameraaufbau wird über einem zwei Meter breiten Vereinzelungsband in einer Höhe von 550 mm installiert. Im Gegensatz zu herkömmlichen Förderbändern ermöglicht ein Vereinzelungsband die räumliche Trennung einzelner Kartoffeln. Als Kameras kommen drei OAK-D PoE der Firma Luxonis zum Einsatz, welche in einer Aluminiumkonstruktion mit Streulichtblende eingefasst sind. Die Kameras blicken orthogonal von oben auf das Vereinzelungsband und weisen zueinander einen Abstand von 650 mm auf (s. Abb. 2).

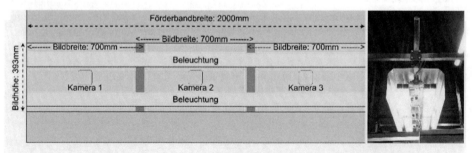

Abb. 2: Kameraaufbau über Vereinzelungsband bestehend aus drei RGBD-Kameras

Jede dieser Kameras nimmt zeitgleich Farb- und Tiefenbilder auf. Die Auflösung der Farbbilder (RGB) beträgt 1920 × 1080 Pixel, wohingegen die Tiefenbilder für eine passgenaue Überlagerung mit den Farbbildern von ihrer nativen Auflösung (1280 × 720 Pixel) auf 1920 × 1080 Pixel hochskaliert werden. Der Datenaustausch und die Stromversorgung der Kameras wird über einen Gigabit-Ethernet-Switch mit PoE-

KI-basiertes Computer-Vision-System zur Qualitäts- und Größenbestimmung

Funktionalität (IEEE 802.3) abgewickelt. Die drei Kameras sind in einem lokalen Netzwerk über Cat6-Ethernet-Kabel mit einem Edge-Rechner verbunden. Dieser Computer besitzt neben einem Intel i7-6700 Vierkernprozessor, 500 GB NVMe Fest- und 32 GB Arbeitsspeicher eine NVIDIA Quadro P6000 Grafikkarte zur hardwarebeschleunigten Ausführung von KI-Modellen.

Die Beleuchtung besteht aus insgesamt acht LED-Leuchtstoffröhren, die in zwei Gruppen zu jeweils einer Balkenbeleuchtung zusammengeschaltet werden. Durch eine gute Ausleuchtung des Förderbands können die RGB-Kameras mit einer kurzen Verschlusszeit von 450 µs und einer Lichtempfindlichkeit (ISO) von 650 betrieben werden. Die resultierenden Aufnahmen sind, wie in Abbildung 3 zu sehen, kontrastreich und scharf.

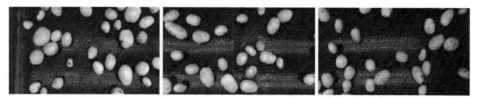

Abb. 3: Aufnahmen der drei Kameras vom Vereinzelungsband mit Kartoffeln

Damit während der Inferenz alle Kartoffeln von den Kameras erfasst werden können, darf das System eine minimale Bildrate (FPS_{min}) von ungefähr $3{,}18\,s^{-1}$ nicht unterschreiten. Diese berechnet sich als der Quotient aus der maximalen Förderbandgeschwindigkeit $v_{max} \approx 1{,}25$ m/s und der realen Bildhöhe $h_{Welt} \approx 0{,}393$ m.

3.2 Lokalisierung

Für die Lokalisierung einzelner Kartoffeln wird in einem Transfer-Learning-Ansatz ein auf dem COCO-Datensatz [Li14] vortrainierter YOLOv5-Objektdetektor des Größentyps X6 verwendet. Dieser wird zunächst mit semi-synthetischen Trainingsdaten trainiert, um das spätere Labeling eines echten Kartoffeldatensatzes durch automatisches Einzeichnen von Bounding-Boxen zu erleichtern. Das rechts in Abbildung 4 dargestellte Beispiel einer solchen Trainingseingabe wird mithilfe eines Referenzdatensatzes und Aufnahmen des leeren Förderbands zufällig generiert. Diese semi-synthetischen Bilddaten ermöglichen das Training eines ersten einsatzfähigen Kartoffel-Detektors, indem sie die in Abbildung 3 gezeigten Aufnahmen des realen Förderbands imitieren.

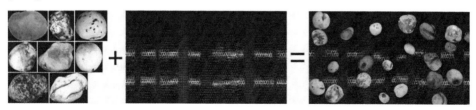

Abb. 4: Generierung semi-synthetischer Trainingsdaten zur Lokalisierung von Kartoffeln

Aufgrund der computergestützten Generierung dieser Bilddaten können die für das Training eines ersten Kartoffeldetektors benötigten Label in Form von Bounding-Boxen pixelgenau erzeugt werden. Das auf den synthetischen Daten trainierte KI-Modell zeigt auf den realen Bilddaten eine gute Generalisierungsfähigkeit mit vereinzelt ungenauen Bounding-Boxen und nicht detektierten Kartoffeln. Die nachfolgende Abbildung 5 zeigt die Verbesserung der Lokalisierungsgenauigkeit eines zweiten YOLOv5-Detektors, der mit den durch Menschen korrigierten Bounding-Boxen des ersten Detektors trainiert wird.

Abb. 5: Präzise Lokalisierung von Kartoffeln (rechts) nach Ausbesserung der synthetisch erzeugten Bounding-Boxen (links) und erneutem Training eines YOLOv5-Detektors

3.3 Geometriebestimmung

Für die echtzeitfähige Durchführung einer Geometriebestimmung wird das trainierte YOLOv5-Modell auf die Farbbilder des Förderbands angewendet. Die erzeugten Bounding-Boxen (rot) sind achsenorientiert und trennen einzelne Kartoffeln voneinander. Unabhängig von diesen Detektionen wird das Farbbild in einem nächsten Schritt in den HSV-Farbraum überführt, um mithilfe eines Hochpassfilters auf dem Sättigungskanal (S) störende Lichtreflexionen zu entfernen (s. Abb. 6). Eine Segmentierung der Kartoffeln erfolgt über eine optimale Schwellenwertbinarisierung des Wert-Kanals (V) nach dem Verfahren von Otsu [Ot79].

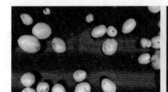 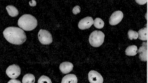 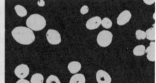

Abb. 6: Binarisierung mit dem Otsu-Verfahren nach Entfernung störender Reflexionen

Typischerweise verschmelzen bei einer Binarisierung manche Kartoffeln im Binärbild zu einem Objekt, welche mit herkömmlichen Methoden der Bildverarbeitung nur schwer wieder zu trennen wären. Die YOLOv5-Detektionen vermeiden dieses Problem im Binärbild, da die erzeugten Bounding-Boxen stets einzelne Objekte und somit auch ihre Vordergrundkomponenten voneinander separieren. Jede dieser Komponenten wird für die Längen- und Breitenbestimmung einer Kartoffel in ein Polygon umgewandelt (s. Abb. 7).

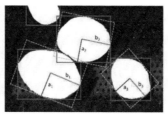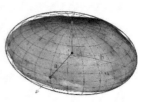

Abb. 7: Approximation der Kartoffelgeometrie mithilfe eines triaxialen Ellipsoids

Da einzelne Kartoffeln quer in ihrer axial ausgerichteten Bounding-Box liegen können, wird für eine genauere 2D-Geometriebestimmung ihr Minimum Rotated Rectangle (MRR, grau) berechnet. Ein Ansatz zur Annäherung des MRR bei Kartoffeln ist aufgrund ihrer Exzentrizität die Hauptkomponentenanalyse mit einer Rotation um den zwischen erster Hauptkomponente und x-Achse eingeschlossenen Winkel. Mit dem Rotating Calipers Algorithmus von Shamos [Sh78] existiert ein auf konvexen Polygonen schneller arbeitendes Verfahren, das in dieser Arbeit genutzt wird. Die Länge und Breite einer Kartoffel entspricht dann der Länge der kürzeren ($2a$) und längeren Seite ($2b$) des MRR in Millimetern.

Unter Miteinbeziehung des zeitgleich zum Farbbild aufgenommenen Tiefenbilds können anhand der beiden Halbachsen a, b sowie der halben Kartoffelhöhe c eine Volumen- und Gewichtsapproximation durchgeführt werden. Die Einträge eines Tiefenbilds D speichern die Entfernungen von der Kamera zu jedem Oberflächenpunkt in Millimetern. Das für die halbe Kartoffelhöhe c benötigte Höhenbild H berechnet sich über die Differenz eines Tiefenbilds des leeren Förderbands D_r (Referenz) und D über $H = D_r - D$.

Aufgrund der angestrebten Echtzeitfähigkeit des Systems wird das Volumen einer Kartoffel nicht über rechenintensive Punktwolken oder Dreiecksgitter, sondern über einen triaxialen Ellipsoid mit den drei Halbachsen a, b, c angenähert. Nach einer Abschätzung des Volumens über $V_{\text{Kartoffel}} \approx \frac{4}{3}\pi abc$ mm^3 kann unter Annahme einer Kartoffeldichte[3] von $\rho \approx 1{,}0851$ mg/mm^3 ihr Gewicht über $m_{\text{Kartoffel}} \approx V_{\text{Kartoffel}} \cdot \rho$ mg angenähert werden.

Die in diesem Abschnitt durchgeführte Binarisierung der Farbbilder funktioniert bei hellen Kartoffeln aufgrund des hohen Kontrasts zum dunklen Förderband besonders gut. Da dieser Kontrast bei dunkleren Kartoffeln abnimmt, können ihre Konturen durch die erzeugten Binärmasken nur weniger genau abgebildet werden. In diesen Fällen kann für eine genauere Konturdetektion ein KI-basiertes Segmentierungsverfahren eingesetzt werden. Aufgrund der Generalisierungsfähigkeit solcher Modelle besteht die Möglichkeit, dass ein auf den nicht einwandfreien Binärbildern trainiertes Segmentierungsmodell die Genauigkeit der Geometriebestimmung durch präzisere Freistellung der Kartoffeln verbessern kann.

---

[3] Durchschnittliche Dichte einer Kartoffel aus: https://blogs.imperial.ac.uk/physics-of-cooking/2011/03/09/potato-density-changes-with-age-karim-bahsoon (Stand: 09.12.2022)

3.4 Klassifikation

Zur Durchführung einer Mängelklassifikation werden mit dem in Abschnitt 3.1 beschriebenen Kameraaufbau Farbbilder von Kartoffeln aufgenommen und für ein händisches Labeling gespeichert. Der aus elf Mängelklassen bestehende Bilddatensatz wird mithilfe des Annotationsprogramms CVAT[4] (Computer Vision Annotation Tool) erstellt. Der Labeling-Prozess in CVAT besteht aus einer Korrektur fehlender oder ungenauer Bounding-Boxen sowie der Zuweisung mindestens einer der folgenden elf Qualitätsklassen: Wachstumsrisse (growth crack), mängelfrei (no defect), Trockenfäule (dryrot), Nassfäule (wet rot), Schorf (scab), mechanische Beschädigung (mechanical damage), grün (green), welk (withered), Wurmfraß (worm damage), Rüsselkäferbefall (weevilled) und Schwarzfleckigkeit (black spot).

Aufgrund des natürlichen Ursprungs von Kartoffeln entsteht nach dem Labeling-Prozess ein großes Ungleichgewicht zwischen den einzelnen Mängelklassen. Eine solche Unausgewogenheit kann während der Evaluierung eines Klassifikators die Leistungsmetriken Precision (P), Recall (R) und $F_{\beta=1}$ verfälschen. Aus diesem Grund wird vor dem Training eine Angleichung der Klassen durchgeführt, indem aus allen Klassen so viele Bilder ausgewählt werden, wie in der jeweils kleinsten Klasse enthalten sind.

Die in CVAT annotierten Bilddaten werden für das Training eines Convolutional Neural Networks verwendet. Die Kartoffeln werden anhand ihrer Bounding-Boxen aus den Förderbandbildern ausgeschnitten und über ihre erste Annotation in gleichnamige Verzeichnisse einsortiert. Für eine binäre Klassifikation werden alle mängelbehafteten Exemplare zu einer Klasse „defective" zusammengefasst. Ein im Ergebniskapitel aufgeführtes Experiment umfasst die Klassifikation des Wernsing-Datensatzes, der in Abschnitt 3.2 für die Erzeugung der semi-synthetischen Förderbandbilder genutzt wird.

Als Klassifikator wird die von Torchvision (PyTorch Vision) bereitgestellte und auf dem ImageNet-1K Datensatz [Ru15] vortrainierte EfficientNetV2S-Architektur verwendet. Mit 21,5 Millionen Parametern ist diese CNN-Architektur kleiner, moderner und auf dem ImageNet-1K Datensatz um 8 % leistungsstärker als ein herkömmliches ResNet50. Das Training und die Auswertung des Klassifikators wird auf einzelnen Kartoffeln durchgeführt. Die Fähigkeit des YOLOv5-Detektors zwischen mehreren Klassen unterscheiden zu können, wird aufgrund des noch vergleichsweise kleinen Datensatzes nicht genutzt. Zur Verbesserung der Genauigkeit wird eine dedizierte Klassifikator-Architektur in einem zweistufigen System aus Lokalisierung (YOLOv5) und Klassifikation (EfficientNetV2S) eingesetzt.

3.5 Verwertung

Die anhand der Bounding-Boxen und Segmentierungsmasken bestimmten Geometrien, Klassen und Volumina werden zum Zeitpunkt der Detektion mit einem Zeitstempel

---

[4] Quelloffene Anwendung zur Annotation von Bild- und Videodaten: https://cvat.ai (Stand: 09.12.2022)

versehen. Die gesammelten Daten werden im JSON-Format über einen Publish-Subscribe-Mechanismus kontinuierlich bereitgestellt. Es werden keine Nachrichten gepublisht, wenn keine Kartoffeln erkannt werden. An das System per MQTT angebundene Applikationen (Datensenken) können die Detektionen empfangen und beliebig weiterverarbeiten. Die Speicherung der Daten erfolgt in einer relationalen PostgreSQL-Datenbank, welche die eintreffenden Detektionen in Blöcken von 1000 Nachrichten empfängt. Auf diese Weise wird eine echtzeitfähige Persistierung aller Detektionen gewährleistet.

Aus den gesammelten Daten können verschiedene Berichte generiert werden. Die Ergebnisse dieser Auswertungen werden in einem Fünfsekundentakt auf einem Grafana-Dashboard[5] visualisiert. Durch diese kontinuierliche Darstellung wird eine frühzeitige Reaktion auf unerwartete Qualitätsschwankungen im Warenstrom ermöglicht. Beispielhaft umgesetzte Auswertungen umfassen sowohl die Größen- und Massenverteilung sowie die absolute Anzahl an Kartoffeln einer Mängelklasse.

Durch Eingrenzen der Zeitstempel ist es zudem möglich, nur die Detektionen eines bestimmten Zeitraums auszuwerten. Mit dieser Funktion können rückwirkend Statistiken für die Zusammensetzung beliebiger Lieferungen erstellt und analysiert werden. Das System verarbeitet im normalen Betrieb etwa 200.000 Kartoffeln pro Stunde. Ein Datensatz hat in persistierter Form eine Größe von etwa 60 Bytes, sodass an einem Tag mit durchschnittlich 280-300 MB an Daten zu rechnen ist.

4 Ergebnisse

Die in diesem Kapitel vorgestellten Ergebnisse basieren auf einem Trainings- zu Testdatensatzverhältnis von 8:2. Trainings- und Testdatensätze werden stets derselben Grundgesamtheit entnommen und nicht mit andersartig erzeugten Datensätzen vermischt. Sämtliche Metriken, die in diesem Kapitel tabellarisch aufgelistet werden, beziehen sich auf den Testdatensatz. Das Training der KI-Modelle findet parallel auf vier Tesla V100 Grafikkarten einer NVIDIA DGX Station statt.

4.1 Lokalisierung

Die beiden Lokalisierungsdatensätze, die für das Training der in Tabelle 1 aufgelisteten YOLOv5-Detektoren verwendet werden, weisen zum einen generierte und zum anderen händisch ausgebesserte Bounding-Boxen auf. Der generierte Datensatz umfasst 10.000 Bilder mit einer Auflösung von 1920 × 1080 Pixeln und jeweils 18-24 Kartoffeln pro Bild. Die Gesamtsumme an Kartoffeln beläuft sich auf 230.484. Der gelabelte Förderband-Datensatz ist mit einer Größe von 22.331 Kartoffeln etwa zehnmal so klein.

---

[5] Quelloffene Anwendung zur visuellen Aufbereitung von Daten: https://grafana.com/ (Stand: 09.12.2022)

Label	Epochen	Batch	Eingabegröße	Box Loss	mAP@[.5:.95]
generiert	50	48	(720, 1280, 3)	0,0018	0,97
gelabelt	100	48	(720, 1280, 3)	0,0057	0,96

Tab. 1: Lokalisierungsgenauigkeiten des YOLOv5-Detektors auf generierten und echten Daten

Die beiden YOLOv5-Detektoren werden jeweils mit einer Batchgröße von 48 trainiert, wobei das zweite Modell mit dem gelabelten Datensatz doppelt so lange trainiert wird. Beide Modelle zeigen auf ihren jeweiligen Testdatensätzen unabhängig von der Kartoffelgröße sehr gute Lokalisierungsgenauigkeiten von über 0,95 mAP@[.5:.95] bei einem Box Loss nahe null. Der auf den gelabelten Daten trainierte Detektor wird für die Erweiterung des Klassifikations- und Segmentierungsdatensatzes verwendet.

4.2 Klassifikation

Die Untersuchung der Klassifizierbarkeit von Kartoffelmängeln wird mithilfe von zwei verschiedenen RGB-Datensätzen durchgeführt. Der erste dieser beiden Bilddatensätze wird von der Firma Wernsing bereitgestellt und umfasst acht Mängelklassen mit jeweils besonders repräsentativen Mängelausprägungen. Der zweite Datensatz beinhaltet die in elf Mängelklassen unterteilten Kartoffelbilder, welche mit dem Kamerasystem über dem Vereinzelungsband aufgenommen werden. Die Größen der jeweiligen Datensätze werden in der nachfolgenden Aufzählung durch Semikolons getrennt: 1. No defect (79; 13619), 2. Weevilled (1282; 10420), 3. Dryrot (1183; 2255), 4. Withered (0; 1725), 5. Mechanical damage (1210; 1527), 6. Scab (352; 1260), 7. Growth crack (0; 375), 8. Wet rot (124; 259), 9. Worm damage (0; 223), 10. Green (1250; 135), 11. Black spot (0; 108).

Eine Angleichung der Klassengrößen auf die jeweils kleinste ausgewählte Klasse findet nur bei den Klassifikationsdurchläufen des Förderband-Datensatzes statt. Alle EfficientNetV2S-Modelle werden in 50 Epochen mit dem AdamW-Optimierungsverfahren [LH18] und einer Verringerung der Lernrate um den Faktor zehn nach jeweils zehn Epochen trainiert. Der auf dem Wernsing-Datensatz trainierte Klassifikator liefert aufgrund der visuell eindeutigen Mängelausprägungen eine sehr gute Testgenauigkeit von über 96 % auf acht Qualitätsklassen (s. Tab. 3). Eine binäre Klassifikation des Förderband-Datensatzes zeigt eine Genauigkeit von etwa 81 %, die durch ein Hinzufügen der jeweils nächst größeren Mängelklasse aktuell noch auf bis zu 59 % bei vier Klassen abfällt.

Datensatz	Klassen	Batch	Acc@1	Acc@2	P	R	$F_{\beta=1}$
Wernsing	Alle	32	96,06%	99,94%	1,00	0,96	0,96
Förderband	1, Rest	32	80,55%	100,0%	0,99	0,81	0,89
Förderband	1, 2, 3	8	71,83%	91,37%	0,98	0,72	0,82
Förderband	2, 3, 4	8	71,13%	90,67%	0,99	0,71	0,81
Förderband	1, 2, 3, 4	8	59,08%	82,89%	0,96	0,59	0,70

Tab. 2: Erzielte Klassifikationsgenauigkeiten auf dem Wernsing- und Förderband-Datensatz

4.3 Segmentierung

Für eine Untersuchung, ob die mit dem Otsu-Verfahren erstellten Segmentierungsmasken durch ein KI-basiertes Segmentierungsmodell verbessert werden können, wird der aus 1980 Förderbandbildern bestehende Lokalisierungsdatensatz binarisiert. Die Binärmasken werden zusammen mit den Bounding-Boxen für das Training eines Mask R-CNN Modells genutzt. Dieses wird in 50 Epochen auf einer Klasse unter Verwendung des AdamW-Optimierers und einer Batchgröße von zwei trainiert. Das trainierte Modell zeigt auf den Testdaten sowohl eine hohe Segmentierungs- als auch Bounding-Box-Genauigkeit von 0,94 bzw. 0,93.

5 Diskussion und Ausblick

Das in dieser Arbeit präsentierte System zur Bestimmung von Kartoffelqualitäten und Größen ist in der Lage, sehr gute Genauigkeiten in der Lokalisierung und erste gute Ergebnisse in der Segmentierung einzelner Kartoffeln zu erreichen. Letzteres hat direkten Einfluss auf die Geometriebestimmung, weshalb ein KI-basierter Segmentierungsansatz in Zukunft noch genauer zu untersuchen ist. Eine echtzeitfähige Umsetzung der Detektion und Klassifikation ist in Abhängigkeit der verwendeten Edge-Hardware und Netzgröße möglich. Die Inferenzrate kann dabei über eine Abstimmung der KI-Modelle auf die zur Verfügung stehende Edge-Hardware gesteuert werden. Für eine Verbesserung der Klassifikationsergebnisse wird ein größerer Datensatz mit aussagekräftigeren Exemplaren pro Mängelklasse benötigt. Der Klassifikator tendiert bei mehr als zwei bis drei Klassen dazu, diese mit anderen ähnlichen Klassen zu verwechseln (bspw. „no defect" mit „weevilled"). Grund hierfür ist wahrscheinlich die zum Teil noch unzureichende Mängelausprägung in den jeweiligen Bilddatensätzen, gepaart mit einer vergleichsweise kleinen Grundgesamtheit. Eine Erweiterung des Förderband-Datensatzes wird durch den sehr genau arbeitenden Detektor erleichtert. Der bisherige Datensatz könnte im Rahmen eines Self-Supervised-Learning-Ansatzes zur Feinabstimmung eines selbstlernenden Klassifikators genutzt werden. KI-Modelle dieser Art benötigen während des Trainings keine Label, sind aber extrem groß und daher langsam zu trainieren.

Die mit dem System aufgezeichneten Kartoffelgrößen und Massen erscheinen, gemessen an ihren Absolutwerten und Normalverteilungen, plausibel. Eine genauere Annäherung der Kartoffelgeometrie ist vermutlich mit aktiven Tiefenkameras und Punktwolken möglich. Die Echtzeitfähigkeit eines solchen Systems wird jedoch durch den erhöhten Rechenaufwand wahrscheinlich reduziert. Durch eine Einbettung dieses KI-Systems in bestehende Prozesse der Firma Wernsing wird zukünftig mit einer verbesserten Rohstoffverwertung gerechnet. Das entstandene Computer-Vision-System birgt aufgrund seiner Modularität und Übertragbarkeit auf andere landwirtschaftliche Erzeugnisse ein großes Wertschöpfungspotenzial.

Förderhinweis: Wir danken dem Bundesministerium für Wirtschaft und Klimaschutz für die Förderung des Projektes Agri-Gaia unter dem Förderkennzeichen 01MK21004G.

Literaturverzeichnis

[Ha21] Hasan, Md; Zahan, Nusrat; Zeba, Nahid; Khatun, Amina; Haque, Mohammad Reduanul et al.: A Deep Learning-Based Approach for Potato Disease Classification. In: Computer Vision and Machine Learning in Agriculture, S. 113-126. Springer, 2021.

[LH18] Loshchilov, Ilya; Hutter, Frank: Decoupled Weight Decay Regularization. In: International Conference on Learning Representations. 2018.

[Li14] Lin, Tsung-Yi; Maire, Michael; Belongie, Serge; Hays, James; Perona, Pietro; Ramanan, Deva; Dollár, Piotr; Zitnick, C Lawrence: Microsoft coco: Common objects in context. In: European conference on computer vision. Springer, S. 740-755, 2014.

[Op19] Oppenheim, Dor; Shani, Guy; Erlich, Orly; Tsror, Leah: Using deep learning for image-based potato tuber disease detection. Phytopathology, 109(6):1083-1087, 2019.

[Ot79] Otsu, Nobuyuki: A threshold selection method from gray-level histograms. IEEE transactions on systems, man, and cybernetics, 9(1):62-66, 1979.

[PKP18] Pandey, Nikhil; Kumar, Suraj; Pandey, Raksha: Grading and defect detection in potatoes using deep learning. In: International conference on communication, networks and computing. Springer, S. 329-339, 2018.

[Ru15] Russakovsky, Olga; Deng, Jia; Su, Hao; Krause, Jonathan; Satheesh, Sanjeev; Ma, Sean; Huang, Zhiheng; Karpathy, Andrej; Khosla, Aditya; Bernstein, Michael et al.: Imagenet largescale visual recognition challenge. International journal of computer vision, 115(3):211-252, 2015.

[Sh78] Shamos, Michael Ian: Computational geometry. Yale University, 1978.

[Su18] Su, Qinghua; Kondo, Naoshi; Li, Minzan; Sun, Hong; Al Riza, Dimas Firmanda; Habaragamuwa, Harshana: Potato quality grading based on machine vision and 3D shape analysis. Computers and electronics in agriculture, 152:261-268, 2018.

[Su20] Su, Qinghua; Kondo, Naoshi; Al Riza, Dimas Firmanda; Habaragamuwa, Harshana: Potato quality grading based on depth imaging and convolutional neural network. Journal of Food Quality, 2020, 2020.

[WX21] Wang, Chenglong; Xiao, Zhifeng: Potato Surface Defect Detection Based on Deep Transfer Learning. Agriculture, 11(9):863, 2021.

An overview of visual servoing for robotic manipulators in digital agriculture

Redmond R. Shamshiri [1,2], Volker Dworak[1], Mostafa Shokrian Zeini[1], Eduardo Navas[3], Jana Käthner[1], Nora Höfner[1] and Cornelia Weltzien[1,2]

Abstract: Innovations in terms of robotic manipulator control in digital agriculture have advanced considerably in the last decade with the aim of reducing costs and increasing efficiencies. The availability of compact imaging sensors such as digital cameras that can perceive depth information besides the flexibility of open-source image processing software that can be trained for different applications has played significant roles in accelerating this sector. Preliminary studies have shown that the majority of available robot manipulators in agriculture are using Image-Based Visual Servo (IBVS) control to reach a target position. The presented study provides an overview of different redundant manipulators that are controlled by means of visual servoing for automating various field tasks in digital agriculture including (i) pruning, thinning, and trimming, (ii) harvesting, and (iii) inspection and target spraying. The reviewed works suggest that developing optimal tree shapes and planting techniques is necessary to improve the performance of visual servo control and automate farming operations with robots. In addition, selection of the right imaging sensors, graphics processing units, and training of the computer vision algorithms with more fruits and plants datasets have been highlighted as the three main elements for improving the functionality of IBVS in manipulator control for agricultural applications.

Keywords: robot arms, RGB-D camera, Visual Servo, agricultural robotics, image processing

1 Introduction

Agricultural robotics have contributed to producing more yields with higher quality at lower expenses in a sustainable way via a mechanization approach that is less dependent on the manual workforce. The use of compact robot manipulators that benefits from Distributed Control Systems (DCS) and modular components is growing rapidly and becoming an active field of research, drawing designers' attention to affordable components that can be easily replaced upon failure. Various published works have reviewed the latest achievements in the use of non-mobile robots for agricultural applications, including those that are used for autonomous weed control, field scouting, mowing, and harvesting [Sh18a]. Some of the active fields toward developing a robust and flexible robotic platform for farming applications include object identification, task

---

[1] Leibniz Institute for Agricultural Engineering and Bioeconomy, Max-Eyth-Allee 100, 14469 Potsdam-Bornim, Germany, rshamshiri@atb-potsdam.de, https://orcid.org/0000-0002-5775-9654
[2] Technische Universität Berlin, Fachgebiet Agromechatronik, Straße des 17. Juni 135, 10623 Berlin, Germany
[3] Centre for Automation and Robotics, UPM-CSIC, Carretera CAMPO-REAL Km 0.2, Arganda del Rey, 28500 Ma-drid, Spain, eduardo.navas@csic.es

planning algorithms, digitalization and optimization of sensors, synchronization of multi-robots, human-robot collaboration, environment reconstruction from aerial images (or ground-based sensors) for the creation of virtual farms. More recently, trending research in robot manipulators control is towards building multi-robot arms that operate separately using distributed visual servo control systems and are installed on a mobile platform for optimizing a task such as fruit harvesting (Fig. 1). An example includes a dual-arm robotic prototype system shown in Figure 1a that was designed for harvesting pears and apples on joint V-shaped trellis and is claimed to be capable of picking fruits at the same speed as a human [YKF22]. The robot uses an Intel Realsense D435 RGB-D (red, green, blue, and depth) camera, an infrared projector, and an adapted version of Mask R-CNN [He20] that runs on a Jetson AGX Xavier processor for fruit detection [YKF22]. Figure 2a shows the FFRobotics solution with multiple linear robot arms that combines accurate yet simple controls and rapid image processing with advanced algorithms for harvesting ripe apple fruits. These kinds of machines can be modified for harvesting different types of fresh fruits. Figure 3c shows the RB-VOGUI mobile robot platform that has been integrated with two Universal robot arms for active inspection and picking grapes in vineyards.

Fig. 1: Multi-robot arms used for increasing efficiency, (a) dual-robot arm for pears and apples harvesting (Image: NARO), (b) apple harvesting machine with multi-robotic arms, (Image: FFRobotics), and (c) integration of a mobile robot with dual-robot arms for grapes harvesting (Image: Robotnik)

2 Visual servo control

Visual servoing is a method to control the motion of a robot with the feedback extracted from a vision sensor. It is classified into two main classes, image-based visual servoing (IBVS), and position-based visual servoing (PBVS). The information to control the end effector of a robotic system is collected by one or more cameras observing the operation range. The biggest advantage of this technique is the increased flexibility for robots of all kinds in a changing environment and unstructured orchards. The two configurations for positioning the camera in VS are eye-to-hand, and eye-in-hand. The first method has the advantage to have a panoramic sight of the workspace, whereas with eye-in-hand the sight is limited, but with more accuracy, because the camera is closer to the target (usually fixed on the gripper) and has the possibility to explore the workspace. Figure 2 shows IBVS technique which is based on the error between the current and the desired visual features. In order to reach the desired feature set, the error to the current feature set has to be minimized. Therefore, this method uses 2D image data in contrast to the PBVS technique, which is a model-based approach. There are several research works that studied the possibility of cooperation among multiple cameras [Zh16],[MMB16]. For example, systems consisting of a fixed eye-to-hand camera and an eye-in-hand camera. The control of both cameras is completely independent in this case and the global camera controls the translating degrees of freedom with a landmark at the end of the translating joins.

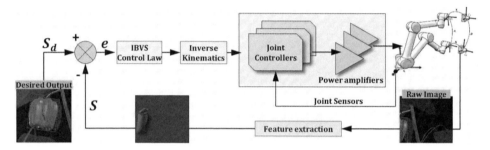

Fig. 2: Image-based visual servoing with eye-in hand configuration for robotic harvesting [Sh18b]

It is a common practice to use the RGB camera sensor in visual servoing in combination with distance detection sensors, especially when the robot is subjected to work in environments such as an agricultural field, in which the target can be occluded by the leaves. In this case, the feedback is provided by both the camera and the other sensors (i.e., infrared sensor), known as RGB-D cameras. This architectural choice is due to the difficulty to calculate the distance between the arm and the desired object only by a 2D image with a single in-hand camera. Furthermore, the visual servoing software routine is implemented on the low-performance application processor. RGB-D sensors have computer vision blocks that estimate the position of the desired object in the image as a pixel coordinate. Instead, the distance estimation block of an RGB-D camera calculates the distance in the z-direction between the hand and the object. The visual servoing block of the robot is the main system controller and drives the arm using a set of motors. Figure 3 shows three of the most popular RGB-D cameras that are used with robot arm manipulators in agriculture.

Microsoft Xbox 360 Kinect Sensor   Intel RealSense D435i   FRAMOS D435e CAMERA

Fig. 3: Common RGB-D cameras used in visual servoing of agricultural robot manipulators

Simulation environments such as Robot operating system (ROS), MATLAB (The MathWorks Inc, Natick, MA, USA), and CoppeliaSim provide designers with a flexible approach for experimenting and implementing IBVS algorithms in order to optimize plant/fruit localization, improvement of plant/fruit scanning, and developing strategies for finding collision-free paths [Sh18c]. There are published studies that demonstrate a completely simulated workspace environment, including an exact replica of the robot manipulator in Inverse Kinematic mode, object tracking, and the orchard or the field with bushes and plants [Sh18b],[Sh18c]. It should be noted that any visual servo system must be capable of tracking image features in a sequence of images. A simulation demo is presented in Figure 4 for sweet pepper harvesting based on the image moment method [LLB22]. In an actual experiment with one or more RGB-D cameras, feature-based and correlation-based methods (as well as artificial intelligence and deep learning training methods) are used to improve the robot's image classification for tracking. These studies use image data taken from the robot camera as the input to the IBVS control algorithm in MATLAB. The extracted information is then fed back to the simulated workspace for IK calculation and for determining the trajectory path to the fruit. In most cases, ROS is used for bi-directional communication between the simulated environment and the robot via its publish and subscribe architecture. The proposed approach allows researchers to review, approve, and execute different trajectories for placing the sensor in the most desired positions, as well as providing a flexible framework for evaluating different sense-think-act scenarios to verify the functional performance of future manipulators with zero risk to the robots and operators.

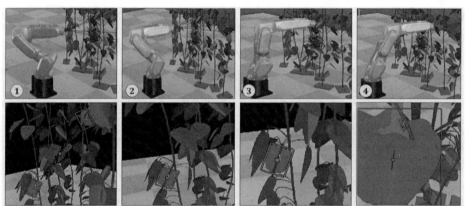

Fig. 4: Simulation of visual servo control experiment with the eye-in-hand configuration and PID Control law on joint angles with feedbacks from image moments. Stability was achieved in 2.5 seconds [Sh18b]

3 Pruning, thinning, and trimming robots

Pruning refers to the selective removal of branches prior to the spring growing season. Thinning is when small or undeveloped fruits, known as fruitlets, are removed from trees to allow for bigger and better fruits to grow. Trimming is carried out to cut the dead and damaged leaves and branches of bushes and in some cases for giving a better-looking shape to the bushes. Figure 5 shows three different robotic manipulators with vision-based control systems for the automation of pruning, thinning, and trimming. These robots are expected to significantly contribute to cost saving by reducing the demand for the human workforce.

Fig. 5: Vision-based control of robotic manipulators for automation of (a) pruning [Za21] (photo courtesy of Penn State University), (b) thinning [Ve21] (photo courtesy of Ai-Ping Hu, Georgia Tech Research Institute), (c) trimming [St18],[Va22]

Reports indicated that pruning of apple trees comprises about 20% of total pre-harvest production costs [Sh18a]. Between 30 and 35 working hours of skilled labor are required per acre for the manual pruning of apple trees. Determining branch diameter is one of the most important and challenging parts of robotic pruning. Figure 5a shows a robotic pruner developed by Penn State University that combines a three-rotation wrist end-effector for cutting the branches, and a three-directional linear manipulator that houses and moves the end-effector to targeted pruning locations. The robot uses light detection and ranging (LiDAR) sensor for the 3D reconstruction of apple trees, and an RGB-Depth camera vision system to accurately measure the branch diameter to automatically make the pruning decisions. Figure 5b shows an intelligent thinning robot to take over the manually-intensive tasks of thinning and pruning peach trees. This robot also uses a LiDAR sensing system and RTK-GPS for autonomous navigation within the orchards while avoiding collision with random obstacles. The detection of peaches is realized using an embedded 3D camera and a claw end-effector. Figure 5c shows the Trimbot robot that can navigate over different terrains, approaches boxwood plants, and trims them to the desired shape. The robot platform is based on a modified Bosch robot lawn mower, which navigates autonomously using 3D-based vision scene analysis. During trimming, a robotic arm is controlled by visual servo in order to trim the bush. A novel end-effector had to be designed to guarantee the flexibility of the manipulator, precision of trimming, and smoothness of the trimmed bush surface. It should be highlighted that the outdoor light conditions (i.e., sunny or cloudy) can affect the performance of these robots. In an orchard, no two bushes or trees are ever the same, hence the technology is not yet mature to perform these tasks as well as a human.

4 Harvesting robots

In general, a robot has to perform five main tasks for harvesting, including fruit detection, fruit localization, image processing and extracting information from cameras, inverse kinematics, and path planning. The main challenges in robotic harvesting have been defined as detection, and localization of fruits under high-density leaves and under the changing outdoor light intensity [Sh18a],[Yo22]. Recently, RGB images have been used in combination with deep learning algorithms to overcome the issues with shadowing and occlusion [Yo22],[Le20]. To avoid collision between the robot arm and the tree branches or the plant supporting system, path planning is performed while the robot manipulator is being controlled in inverse kinematic mode. A review of the published literature reveals that most of the studies on robotic harvesting have used commercially available UR3 or UR5 robot manipulators from Universal Robots due to their compact size, light weight, accuracy, and easy control. Virtual replicas of these arms are available in various robot simulators and can be used for experimenting with different harvesting scenarios. For the vision-based control of the robot, RGB-D cameras that can simultaneously obtain RGB and depth information are used to detect and locate the fruits in the images. Figure 6 shows four robotic harvesting manipulators that benefit from RGB-D cameras in their sensing and control. Multiple studies have reported that the position of the point cloud that RGB-D cameras acquire under unsteady outdoor light conditions is inaccurate [YKF22],[Zh16],[Zh21a]. In addition, fruits need to be judged for ripeness and harvesting, which can be extremely challenging solely from color information.

Fig. 6: Imaged-based visual servo control with eye-in-hand configuration using RGB-D camera for (a) dual-arm fruit harvesting [Yo22], (b) 6 DOF UR5 robot arm for sweet pepper harvesting [Le20], (c) 3 DOF custom-built manipulator for apple harvesting [Zh21a], and (d) 6 DOF UR5 robot arm for apple harvesting [KZC20]

Figure 6a shows a dual-arm fruit harvesting robot [Yo22] that consists of four Real sense D435 RGB-D cameras for detection and localization of the fruits, and two robot arms (UR3 and UR5) to increase work efficiency by harvesting the upper side and lower side of the trees simultaneously. The robot has a central computer that performs all the computation and control tasks. Two of the robot cameras are adjusted to look up at the fruit tree from directly below, one to look diagonally upward, and one to look directly to the side. This configuration allows viewing the fruit tree from different directions and minimizes the number of fruits in the blind spots hidden behind leaves and branches. Deep learning is performed on the RGB image acquired from the RGB-D camera to detect the position of fruits in the image. Next, the 3D positions of the fruits are identified by combining the positions of the fruits in the RGB image and the depth image. To this aim, the RGB images are acquired from the RGB-D cameras mounted on the robot and the fruits in the images are detected. It is necessary to combine information such as color and texture in order to achieve sufficient accuracy. Single Shot Multibox Detector (SSD), which is one of the object detection algorithms, is applied to detect fruits in images. SSD is a method for detecting objects in images using a single neural network. The reason for using SSD was due to the speed and accuracy of the method. All the information about the detected bounding box D is obtained from the results of the detection of the fruit in the image by SSD.

Figure 6b shows the Harvey sweet pepper harvesting robot [Le20] that has achieved a 76.5% success rate on 68 fruit within a modified scenario. Harvey benefits from a 6 DOF UR5 for manipulation, and an RGB-D camera as input for the perception system (segmentation of sweet peppers and peduncles). During the fruit segmentation stage, the robot captures a 3D color image of the whole scene using an eye-in-hand RGB-D camera. A target sweet pepper is localized at the long-range perspective and used to move the camera to a close-range perspective of the targeted fruit to improve the performance of the peduncle segmentation. The next stage localizes the peduncle of the target sweet pepper using a Deep Convolutional Neural Network and a 3D filtering method to estimate the centroid of the peduncle. A grasp selection is then performed on the segmented 3D points of the targeted sweet pepper. The grasp selection uses a heuristic to rank possible grasp poses on the target sweet pepper using surface and position metrics. Figure 6c and Figure 6d show two robotic platforms for apple harvesting that also benefit from RGB-D cameras and IBVS [Zh21a],[KZC20]. These two studies suggest that the development of an affordable and efficient harvesting robot requires modification of the cultivation systems for overcoming the problems of fruit visibility and accessibility. Robotic harvesting must be economically viable which means it must sense fast, calculate fast, and move fast to pick a large number of fruits every hour that are bruise-free.

5   Weeding and target spraying robots

Robotic weeding and target spraying contribute significantly to overall crop production and are the two main viable solutions for efficient weed removal and reduction of chemicals used in the fields. However, the development of these robots is challenging due to several specific complexities including (i) correct identification between weeds and healthy plants which can be extremely difficult due to the variation in plant physiology and genetics differences in size, shape, and color, (ii) non-uniform locations of weeds that can be deteriorated more due to rains and wet muddy soil, (iii) shading and occlusions, and (iv) control of the robot arm under strong winds and volatile climate conditions. The two main approaches toward automated weeding and target spraying are the offline method (using georeferenced prescription maps), and on-the-go method (also referred to as the real-time or online method which uses weed detection sensors on the robot). Similar to the studies on robotic harvesting, RGB-D cameras are also used in robotic weeding, target spraying, and phenotyping, but other optical sensors are usually involved too. For example, Figure 7 shows four different robot arms, each with a different sensing solution, that has been mounted on commercial autonomous mobile platforms such as Husky A200 or Jackal for performing real-time weeding, spraying, and phenotyping. Lidar solutions such as the Velodyne's Puck VLP-16 shown in Figure 7a are used for constructing a real-time 2D or 3D navigation map of the field at close range and for providing real-time 3D point cloud information for precise navigation [Zh21b]. In general, these robots require higher-performance onboard computers, such as the workstation PC shown in Figure 7a that can carry out rapid computation to simultaneously detect the weed and control the robot arm. As a result, the operating speeds of most of the available prototypes are still below the threshold level to be deployed in large-scale farms. For the case of spraying robots, the small size of the robot platform and the spraying tanks is also a limitation, suggesting that these robots should be mounted on autonomous tractors with large chemical tanks.

Fig. 7: Examples of robot manipulators with different sensing systems used in weeding, target spraying, and phenotyping, (a) a 6 DoF UR5 robot arm mounted on Husky A200 mobile robot for automated weeding in cornfields [Zh21b], (b) 7-DoF Kinova Gen3 robot arm for target spraying of vineyard [VVK22], and (c) CROPS manipulator for target spraying of grapevines [Ob16]

The weeding robot shown in Figure 7a uses the RealSense D435i depth camera for multi-target depth ranging and a quadratic traversal algorithm for shortest path planning [Zh21b]. To recognize weeds and corn, a fast R-CNN neural network is implemented for real-time recognition. The experimental results with this robot have shown a success rate of 90.0%. Figure 7b shows the Kinova Gen3 7 DoF robot arm that has been integrated for target spraying [VVK22] and uses Optitrack cameras to measure the position of the spray frame on-the-go. Optitrack markers are attached to the end-effector of the robot arm. The robot is still under development and is planned to be based on a combination of deep learning and depth information captured by an RGB-D camera. The robot arm uses an Ethernet connection to communicate with ROS drivers running on the PC. Low-level control of the arm is then achieved via joint velocity commands, while encoder measurements from arms are used as feedback. Figure 7c shows a custom-built robotic system with eye-to-hand visual servoing configuration for selective targeting of pesticide applications that deposit chemical spray only where and when they are needed and at the correct dose. The sensing instruments for this robot are installed on a frame beside the manipulator with a 700 mm longitudinal offset between the camera and the robot arm base. The robot benefits from disease sensing sensors by means of multispectral imaging of a grapevine canopy under diffuse illumination. Multispectral images of the canopy are acquired by a 3-CCD, R-G-NIR camera model MS4100 (DuncanTech, Auburn, CA, USA) which captures 1912 by 1076-pixel, 8-bit images in three distinct spectral channels: green (540 nm), red (660 nm) and NIR (800 nm). The multispectral camera and a regular RGB camera are mounted on a sliding holder that allows positioning adjustments from 800 mm to 2500 m in height. A computer is also mounted on the robot perform and is dedicated for to real-time image processing of multispectral images for disease detection, target position computation, and transmission to the manipulator control computer.

6 Human-robot collaboration

Major factors that are limiting the widespread use of robotics arm in agriculture are related to effectiveness, costs, and issues with electrical power consumption (battery) in actual field conditions. Most of the published studies in this area conclude that to this date, the best existing visual servoing algorithms, regardless of the manipulator, are unable to continuously and efficiently perform tasks such as pruning, harvesting, weeding, or target spraying in order to completely replace human workforces and meet the farmers' requirements. Therefore, teleoperation or human-robot collaboration might be necessary to solve the challenges in robotic arm control for enhancing their functionalities. For example, in collaborative harvesting with a human-robot interface, occluded fruits that are missed by the robot vision system are identified by an operator on a screen using input devices such as a mouse or Sony PS3 Gamepad as shown in Figure 8, or the robot actuation can be controlled entirely in a virtual environment. The main limitation of these solutions is the communication between the human and the robot for exchanging live streaming images and control messages which is currently realized via WiFi [Ad17]. Additional studies for the possibility of using 5G and LoRaWAN are underway to remotely control the robotic arm more stably. Some studies suggest applying a framework for switching the levels of autonomy in human-robot collaboration research that determines whether the current robot operation is fully autonomous, semi-autonomous, or teleoperated (manually controlled).

Fig. 8: Human-robot collaboration for increasing the efficiency of robot control in agriculture, (a) teleoperation via simulation environment (Image: Adaptive AgroTech),

(b) selecting targets grape clusters using a mouse, (c) digital pen on a smart interactive touchscreen whiteboard, and (c) Nintendo Wii remote [Ad17]

7 Conclusion

This paper provided an overview of robotic manipulators that are used for three categories in crop production, including pruning, harvesting, and target spraying. Despite the intensive studies on the use and control of robotic manipulators in agriculture there are still no fully functional systems in the market that can replace the human workforce. Other than the safety regulations and costs, one of the most limiting factors for the widespread use of robots in agriculture lies in the existing sensing solutions that are not mature enough to generate precise information when facing different trees and plants shape and sizes, unstructured environments, varying outdoor weather and light conditions, and navigating on uneven terrains. Some studies have investigated the possibility of cooperation among multiple visual servoing methods, such as systems that consist of two or more independent fixed eye-to-hand and eye-in-hand cameras. Other studies have discussed the feasibility of human-robot collaboration in which one or more human operators perform the sensing task of plants/fruit identification based on the live images and the robots carry out the actuation tasks in the field. It can be concluded that the development of an affordable and efficient robotic system requires collaboration in areas of horticultural engineering, machine vision, sensing, robotics, control, intelligent systems, software architecture, system integration, and crop management. In addition, practicing other cultivation systems in the open-field and closed field, such as single row planting might be necessary for overcoming the problems of plant/fruit visibility and accessibility.

Bibliography

[Sh18]   Shamshiri, R.R.; Weltzien, C.; Hameed, I.A.; Yule, I.J.; Grift, T.E.; Balasundram, S.K.; Pitonakova, L.; Ahmad, D.; Chowdhary, G. Research and development in agricultural robotics: A perspective of digital farming. Int. J. Agric. Biol. Eng. 2018, 11(4): 1–14

[YKF22] Yoshida, T.; Kawahara, T.; Fukao, T. Fruit recognition method for a harvesting robot with RGB-D cameras. ROBOMECH J. 2022, 9, 15.

[He20]   He, K.; Gkioxari, G.; Dollár, P.; Girshick, R. Mask R-CNN. IEEE Trans. Pattern Anal. Mach. Intell. 2020, 42, 386–397.

[Zh16]   Zhao, Y.; Gong, L.; Huang, Y.; Liu, C. A review of key techniques of vision-based control for harvesting robot. Comput. Electron. Agric. 2016, 127, 311–323.

[MMB16] Mehta, S.S.; MacKunis, W.; Burks, T.F. Robust visual servo control in the presence of fruit motion for robotic citrus harvesting. Comput. Electron. Agric. 2016, 123, 362–375.

[Sh18a] Shamshiri, R.R.; Hameed, I.A.; Karkee, M.; Weltzien, C. Robotic Harvesting of Fruiting Vegetables: A Simulation Approach in V-REP, ROS and MATLAB. In Automation in Agriculture-Securing Food Supplies for Future Generations; InTech, 2018.

[Sh18b] Shamshiri, R.R.; Hameed, I.A.; Pitonakova, L.; Weltzien, C.; Balasundram, S.K.; Yule, I.J.; Grift, T.E.; Chowdhary, G. Simulation software and virtual environments for acceleration of agricultural robotics: Features highlights and performance comparison. Int. J. Agric. Biol. Eng. 2018, 11.

[LLB22] Le Hanh, D.; Luat, N. Van; Bich, L.N. Combining 3D matching and image moment based visual servoing for bin picking application. Int. J. Interact. Des. Manuf. 2022, 1–9.

[Za21] Zahid, A.; Mahmud, M.S.; He, L.; Heinemann, P.; Choi, D.; Schupp, J. Technological advancements towards developing a robotic pruner for apple trees: A review. Comput. Electron. Agric. 2021, 189, 106383.

[Ve21] Verbiest, R.; Ruysen, K.; Vanwalleghem, T.; Demeester, E.; Kellens, K. Automation and robotics in the cultivation of pome fruit: Where do we stand today? J. F. Robot. 2021, 38, 513–531.

[St18] Strisciuglio, N.; Tylecek, R.; Blaich, M.; Petkov, N.; Biber, P.; Hemming, J.; Henten, E. v.; Sattler, T.; Pollefeys, M.; Gevers, T.; et al. TrimBot2020: an outdoor robot for automatic gardening. In Proceedings of the ISR 2018; 50th International Symposium on Robotics; 2018; pp. 1–6.

[Va22] Van Marrewijk, B.M.; Vroegindeweij, B.A.; Gené-Mola, J.; Mencarelli, A.; Hemming, J.; Mayer, N.; Wenger, M.; Kootstra, G. Evaluation of a boxwood topiary trimming robot. Biosyst. Eng. 2022, 214, 11–27.

[Yo22] Yoshida, T.; Onishi, Y.; Kawahara, T.; Fukao, T. Automated harvesting by a dual-arm fruit harvesting robot. ROBOMECH J. 2022, 9, 19.

[Le20] Lehnert, C.; McCool, C.; Sa, I.; Perez, T. Performance improvements of a sweet pepper harvesting robot in protected cropping environments. J. F. Robot. 2020, 37, 1197–1223.

[Zh21a] Zhang, K.; Lammers, K.; Chu, P.; Li, Z.; Lu, R. System design and control of an apple harvesting robot. Mechatronics 2021, 79, 102644.

[KZC20] Kang, H.; Zhou, H.; Chen, C. Visual perception and modeling for autonomous apple harvesting. IEEE Access 2020, 8, 62151–62163.

[Zh21b] Zhang, L.; Li, R.; Li, Z.; Meng, Y.; Liang, J.; Fu, L.; Jin, X.; Li, S. A Quadratic Traversal Algorithm of Shortest Weeding Path Planning for Agricultural Mobile Robots in Cornfield. J. Robot. 2021, 2021, 6633139.

[VVK22] Vatavuk, I.; Vasiljević, G.; Kovačić, Z. Task Space Model Predictive Control for Vineyard Spraying with a Mobile Manipulator. Agriculture 2022, 12.

[Ob16] Oberti, R.; Marchi, M.; Tirelli, P.; Calcante, A.; Iriti, M.; Tona, E.; Hočevar, M.; Baur, J.; Pfaff, J.; Schütz, C.; et al. Selective spraying of grapevines for disease control using a modular agricultural robot. Biosyst. Eng. 2016, 146, 203–215.

[Ad17] Adamides, G.; Katsanos, C.; Constantinou, I.; Christou, G.; Xenos, M.; Hadzilacos, T.; Edan, Y. Design and development of a semi-autonomous agricultural vineyard sprayer: Human–robot interaction aspects. J. F. Robot. 2017, 34, 1407–1426.

Erste Praxiserfahrung mit einem Feldroboter – Ergebnisse einer Fokusgruppendiskussion mit *early adopters*

Olivia Spykman [1], Stefan Kopfinger [2], Andreas Gabriel [3] und Markus Gandorfer [4]

Abstract: Aufgrund der erst kurzen Marktverfügbarkeit von Feldrobotern gibt es nur wenige wissenschaftliche Erkenntnisse zur Anwendererfahrung. Eine Fokusgruppendiskussion mit sieben Teilnehmenden von bayerischen Betrieben, die den Sä- und Hackroboter Farmdroid FD20 seit zwei Anbausaisons im Einsatz haben, gibt wichtige Hinweise auf Art und Umfang des Betreuungsaufwandes und die notwendigen Veränderungen in der betrieblichen Arbeitsorganisation, die sich durch den Einsatz von Feldrobotik ergeben. Die Erkenntnisse aus der Diskussion der Anwender zeigen, dass sich die „early adopters" bei Feldrobotern auf einen zusätzlichen Zeitaufwand zur Überwachung, zur Logistik und zur technischen Optimierung einstellen müssen. Dennoch sind Einsparungen bei repetitiven Arbeitsabläufen auf dem Feld erkennbar – ein Vorteil, der zukünftig noch an Bedeutung gewinnen wird.

Keywords: Robotik, mechanische Unkrautregulierung, Investitionsförderung, Arbeitswirtschaft

1 Einleitung

Marktverfügbare Feldroboter sind erst seit Kurzem auf deutschen Feldern im Einsatz. Aufgrund der noch jungen Historie stützten sich Untersuchungen zur Einstellung von Landwirten zu deren Einsatz anfänglich vor allem auf Erkenntnisse zu verwandten, jedoch etablierteren Technologien. Beispielsweise sind Melkroboter bereits seit den 1990er Jahren marktverfügbar und wurden vor allem aufgrund der physischen Arbeitserleichterung und zeitlichen Flexibilisierung gut angenommen [He22]. Obwohl schon viele Jahre verfügbar, sind hingegen Precision-Farming-Technologien aus dem Bereich der Teilflächenbewirtschaftung, die Vorteile durch Betriebsmitteleinsparung und Umweltschutz versprechen, weniger im Praxiseinsatz als erhofft. Dies deutet darauf hin, dass Technologien, die die Arbeit erleichtern, in der Praxis häufiger zum Einsatz kommen [Ga22]. Ob und inwieweit eine Technologie dem Anwender die Arbeit erleichtert, hängt von weiteren Effekten auf die Arbeitswirtschaft ab, wie beispielsweise die Unterstützung

---

[1] Bayerische Landesanstalt für Landwirtschaft, Institut für Landtechnik und Tierhaltung, Kleeberg 14, 94044 Ruhstorf a.d. Rott, olivia.spykman@lfl.bayern.de, https://orcid.org/0000-0002-8650-9283;
stefan.kopfinger@lfl.bayern.de, https://orcid.org/0000-0002-0624-153X;
andreas.gabriel@lfl.bayern.de, https://orcid.org/0000-0001-5736-1593;
markus.gandorfer@lfl.bayern.de, https://orcid.org/0000-0002-0624-153X

bei gesetzlichen Dokumentationspflichten durch Farm-Management-Informationssysteme [Fo15].

Der Aspekt der Arbeitserleichterung kommt auch bei der Feldrobotik zum Tragen, die Produktions- und Arbeitsabläufe automatisieren und somit zeitliche Freiräume schaffen soll. Die wirtschaftlichen Effekte dieser Arbeitszeiteinsparung wurden bereits in ersten Modellbetrachtungen analysiert, die zu der Schlussfolgerung kommen, dass mit steigender Betriebsgröße mehrere kleine autonome Traktoren einem großen Traktor mit Fahrer wirtschaftlich überlegen sein können [Lo21a]. Dabei ist zu beachten, dass Annahmen zu Flächenstruktur und Betreuungsaufwand die praktische Relevanz solcher Modellergebnisse limitieren. Des Weiteren konnten negative Einflüsse restriktiver Gesetzgebung für den Betrieb autonomer Feldroboter [Lo21b] und erhöhter Fehleranfälligkeit der Systeme [Ma22a] auf die Wirtschaftlichkeit dargestellt werden. Jedoch zeigt die Erfahrung mit anderen digitalen Technologien in der Landwirtschaft, wie bereits beschrieben, dass ökonomische Effizienz nicht der einzige ausschlaggebende Faktor für deren Akzeptanz bei potenziellen Nutzern ist.

Um Akzeptanzhemmnisse neuer Technologien frühzeitig im Entwicklungsprozess zu berücksichtigen, wurde u. a. das *Responsible Research and Innovation* Konzept entwickelt, welches jedoch im landwirtschaftlichen Bereich bisher wenig Anwendung findet [Ro21]. Dieses Konzept umfasst eine Vorausabschätzung der Auswirkungen, Reflexivität und gegebenenfalls Anpassung der Arbeit, Einbindung verschiedener Interessensgruppen und Berücksichtigung ihrer Anmerkungen und Einwände [Ro21]. Die Relevanz des Ansatzes für die Feldrobotik wird durch Ergebnisse einer Befragung US-amerikanischer landwirtschaftlicher Akteure unterstrichen, welche ergab, dass der mangelnde Austausch zwischen Maschinenherstellern und Landwirten als mögliches Hindernis für die Akzeptanz von Robotern gesehen wird [Ri18].

Bisherige Befragungen von Landwirten zu Feldrobotern fanden *ex ante* statt, um die Erwartungen an die bis dato kaum marktverfügbaren Technologien zu erfassen. Drei in Deutschland durchgeführte Studien zeigen, dass Anwendungsmöglichkeiten im Ökolandbau sowie Arbeitserleichterung als Treiber für erhöhte Investitionsbereitschaft in Feldrobotik identifiziert werden können [RH21; RTH21; Sp21]. Gleichzeitig wurden unklare rechtliche Rahmenbedingungen sowie mögliche negative Reaktionen der Gesellschaft als hemmende Faktoren identifiziert [RH21; Sp21]. Diese Erkenntnisse decken sich mit Befragungen von Landwirten in Australien, welche zusätzlich die Verlässlichkeit der Roboter beim autonomen Arbeiten, Kostenreduktion beim Pflanzenschutzmitteleinsatz sowie die sichere Datenspeicherung als wichtige Eigenschaften hervorheben [Re15]. Weitere Akteure aus dem landwirtschaftlichen Sektor (z. B. Maschinenhersteller, Wissenschaftler, Berater) sahen eine mangelnde Verfügbarkeit sowie Kosten von Handarbeitskräften als treibende Kraft für das Interesse in Feldrobotik zu investieren [Ri18; RCH21]. Als zusätzliche Akzeptanzfaktoren wurden unter anderem noch Datensicherheit und -hoheit, Betreuungsaufwand, Verbleib der Entscheidungsgewalt beim Nutzer und Kompatibilität mit bestehender Technologie genannt [Ri18; RCH20; RH20].

Somit wurden bisher zwar viele Erwartungen an den Einsatz von Robotik in der Landwirtschaft formuliert, jedoch gab es bis dato wenig Gelegenheit, diese auf Basis von Anwendererfahrung zu evaluieren. Denn aktuell verfügbare Feldroboter sind erst seit wenigen Jahren auf dem Markt, so dass nur wenige Anwender für Befragungen zur Verfügung stehen. Einer dieser marktverfügbaren Roboter ist der Farmdroid FD20, welcher Feinsämereien (z. B. Zuckerrübe, Raps) autonom sät und anschließend zur Beikrautregulierung hackt. Dieser Roboter ist im Rahmen des Bayerischen Sonderprogramms Landwirtschaft (BaySL) Digital förderfähig, welches eine Investitionsförderung von 40 % bis zu einer Investitionssumme von 100.000 € netto für automatische Beikrautregulierung, u. a. mittels Feldroboter vorsieht. Seit der Einführung der Förderkomponente Digitale Hack- und Pflanzenschutztechnik in BaySL Digital (Teil C) wurden insgesamt 74 Förderanträge für den Farmdroid FD20 gestellt (Stand Oktober 2022); Feldrobotik anderer Hersteller wurde in deutlich geringerem Umfang beantragt. Die Antragsteller erklärten sich bereit, für Umfragen und Interviews zur Verfügung zu stehen. Im Rahmen dieser *ex post* Befragung bietet sich nun die Gelegenheit, die tatsächlichen Motivationsgründe für die Investition in Feldrobotik sowie die Relevanz der möglichen Akzeptanzhemmnisse zu eruieren. In einer Fokusgruppendiskussion wurden im Speziellen die Beweggründe für die Investition, Anmerkungen zum Förderprozess sowie Erfahrungen aus dem Einsatz des FD20 adressiert. Diese erstmalige Diskussion unter Anwendern des FD20 erlaubt die Erfassung von Praxiserfahrungen aus den ersten beiden Jahren der Anwendung. Das Format der Fokusgruppendiskussion ermöglicht auch differenzierte Perspektiven aus der Praxis und bietet Maschinenherstellern, Wissenschaftlern und Fördermittelgebern wichtige Hinweise für technische Optimierung, zukünftige Forschungsfragen und zielgruppengenaue Bildungs- und Förderangebote.

2 Material und Methode

Aus der Liste der FD20-Förderungen wurden sechs Betriebe selektiert, die die Bewilligung für den FD20 bereits vor Saisonbeginn 2020 erhalten haben und somit schon über zwei Anbausaisons Erfahrungen mit der Technologie sammeln konnten. Die Liste wurde um weitere neun Betriebe ergänzt, die den FD20 nach Saisonbeginn 2020 jedoch noch vor Saisonbeginn 2021 erhielten. Diese 15 Erstnutzerbetriebe wurden telefonisch kontaktiert und zu einer Online-Fokusgruppendiskussion eingeladen, um Erfahrungen und Herausforderungen in den jeweiligen Einsatzbereichen in unterschiedlichen bayerischen Regionen zu erörtern.

Fokusgruppendiskussionen ermöglichen es, im Gegensatz zu Einzelinterviews, trotz eines begrenzten Zeitrahmens, eine Vielzahl an zwischenmenschlichen Interaktionen zu provozieren, um mehr Details und Hintergrundinformationen zu erfahren [Ma16]. Typisch für diese Erhebungsmethode ist ein grober Rahmen inhaltlicher Themenfelder, der durch vorgegebene Fragestellungen vorbereitet wird [Sc09]. Die Teilnehmer der Fokusgruppen können innerhalb der vorbereiteten Themen (Erwartungen, Förderprozess, Erfahrungen, Probleme und Herausforderungen, Verbesserungsvorschläge) frei diskutieren, wobei der

Moderator eingreift, sobald Themenfelder verlassen werden oder sich Inhalte in der Diskussion wiederholen.

Schließlich nahmen sieben der 15 kontaktierten Betriebsleiterinnen und Betriebsleiter an der Online-Diskussionsrunde teil und gaben eingangs Informationen zu ihrer Person, zum Betrieb und zu den Einsatzfeldern des FD20 preis (Tabelle 1). In den aufgenommenen Merkmalen zu dem teilnehmenden Betriebsleiter, Betriebsformen, Standorten und relevanten Kulturen konnte eine breite Variabilität in der Gruppe festgestellt werden. Dies ist vorteilhaft für eine Fokusgruppendiskussion, da homogene Gruppen einen Erkenntnisgewinn über die Gesamtpopulation eher einschränken [Mo88].

TN	Geschlecht	Regierungsbezirk	Boden, Standort	Betriebsform	Relevante Kulturen FD20
1	männlich	Niederbayern	Löss-Lehm	Ackerbau, konventionell, Nebenerwerb	Zuckerrübe (säen und hacken)
2	männlich	Unterfranken	Löss; HN: 0-15%	Ackerbau, konventionell, Haupterwerb	20-25 ha Zuckerrübe
3	männlich	Oberbayern	Sandiger Lehm; BP: 50-60; höherer Niederschlag	Ackerbau, biologisch, Haupterwerb	Vertragsanbau Südzucker, 18 ha Zuckerrübe
4	männlich	Unterfranken	Löss, teils steinige Flächen; HN: 15%	Bio-Junghennenaufzucht und 170ha Ackerbau	10-15 ha Zuckerrübe (säen und hacken)
5	weiblich	Schwaben	nicht genannt	Naturlandbetrieb, Nebenerwerb	10 ha Zuckerrübe; kommendes Jahr: 3 ha Grünkohl
6	männlich	Oberbayern	Löss-Lehm-Kies; BP: 75	Ackerbau, Forst, Obst; seit 2018 Bioanbau	8-10 ha Zuckerrüben (Testanbau Südzucker); 1,5 ha Raps (säen und hacken)
7	männlich	Schwaben	Löss-Lehm-Kies; Seiten-HN: z.T. >15%	Ackerbau, biologisch	10 ha Winterraps, 13 ha Zuckerrübe

Tab. 1: Übersicht und Charakteristika der Teilnehmer (TN) der Fokusgruppendiskussion; HN=Hangneigung; BP=Bodenpunkte

Die Tonspur der 90-minütigen Diskussionsrunde wurde aufgenommen, um sie im Anschluss für die Inhaltsanalyse zu transkribieren. Im Transkript wurden einzelne Aussagen der Teilnehmer kodiert und den ursprünglich untersuchten Themenfeldern der Fokusgruppendiskussion zugeordnet. Dabei wurden die ursprünglichen Themenfelder auf deren Relevanz in der Diskussionsrunde geprüft, abgeändert oder ergänzt. Das

Themenfeld „Förderprozess" wurde beispielsweise nicht weiter behandelt, da sich alle Teilnehmer als sehr zufrieden mit dem Ablauf der Förderung im Rahmen von BaySL Digital äußerten. Am Ende der Analyse konnten fünf Themenfelder hervorgehoben werden. Die Diskussionsbeiträge je Themenfeld werden im Folgenden zusammengefasst dargestellt und teilweise durch Ankerzitate der FD20 Erstnutzer aus dem Transkript unter Angabe der Teilnehmernummer (TN) aus Tabelle 1 unterlegt.

3 Ergebnisse

3.1 Motive für die Investitionsentscheidung

Die Gründe für die Investitionsentscheidung für den FD20 waren bei allen Landwirten ähnlich gelagert. Zum einen war die Sorge vorhanden, durch die Folgen von Covid-19 keine oder nur eingeschränkt Saisonarbeitskräfte anwerben zu können, die überwiegend aus dem EU-Ausland für diese Arbeiten anreisen. Auch deren Unterbringung in den Betrieben war aufgrund der Hygienebestimmungen mit Unsicherheiten verbunden. Der FD20 war zum Zeitpunkt des Pandemiebeginns in Deutschland marktverfügbar. BaySL Digital ermöglichte eine deutliche Minderung des Investitionsrisikos in diese neue Technologie. Die Erwartungen an den FD20 waren vor allem die Reduktion der benötigten Handarbeitsstunden und somit eine Resilienz der Produktion (Nichtverfügbarkeit von Saisonarbeitskräften für die manuelle Beikrautregulierung) sowie eine spürbare Kosteneinsparung.

3.2 Robotereinsatz und Standortbedingungen

Bei den Diskussionsteilnehmern wird der FD20 hauptsächlich zum Anbau von Zuckerrüben, aber auch für die Aussaat von Raps sowie das nachfolgende Hacken zwischen den Reihen eingesetzt. Ein Betriebsleiter plant im kommenden Jahr zusätzlich den Robotereinsatz im Grünkohlanbau. Bezüglich der vom FD20 bearbeiteten Fläche zeigte sich bei den Diskussionsteilnehmern eine bemerkenswerte Spannweite zwischen 8 ha und 25 ha. Der Hersteller nennt hingegen einen maximalen Einsatz von 20 ha pro Saison [Fa22a].

Die Erwartungen an den Roboter wurden bei den meisten Betriebsleitern erfüllt. Der Roboter reduzierte die benötigten Handarbeitsstunden, aber ersetzte sie nicht vollständig. Wie zuverlässig der FD20 seine Arbeit erledigte, variierte stark in Abhängigkeit der betrieblichen und standörtlichen Rahmenbedingungen. Vor allem die Beschaffenheit der Bodenoberfläche (möglichst feines Bodengefüge, möglichst frei von Steinen, möglichst eben) zeigte sich als zentrale Voraussetzung für den technisch erfolgreichen Einsatz des Roboters.

Während die vorherrschenden Standortbedingungen schon vor dem Kauf des Roboters bekannt sind, bleibt die Stochastik des Witterungsverlaufs, welcher für die Befahrbarkeit des Ackers von sehr hoher Bedeutung ist, eine Herausforderung. Hiervon hängt auch die Anzahl der benötigten Resthandhackstunden ab. Bei einer erfolgreichen Beikrautregulierung mit dem Roboter kann der Aufwand des manuellen Nachhackens stark reduziert werden. Im Gegensatz dazu sinkt bei einer schlechten Befahrbarkeit und daraus verminderten Beikrautregulierung durch den Roboter auch die Einsparung bei den Handhackstunden.

„Ich glaube, dass wir uns im besten Fall 50-60 % Handhackarbeitsstunden eingespart haben. Komplett ohne Handhacken funktioniert es auf keinen Fall. Durch den Roboter hat man einen lockeren Boden und weniger Unkraut, sodass das Handhacken zügig abgeschlossen werden kann." (TN 2)

Der Erfolg der Beikrautregulierung schwankte bei den meisten Teilnehmern der Diskussionsrunde zwischen den bisherigen Einsatzjahren. Dies wird vor allem mit unterschiedlichen Wetterbedingungen begründet. Der Roboter sollte bei Zuckerrüben zwischen Aussaat und Reihenschluss idealerweise einmal pro Woche über das zu bearbeitende Feld fahren und Beikräuter hacken. Ist das Feld aufgrund längerer Nässeperioden nicht befahrbar, können sich die Beikräuter zu stark etablieren, um mit den eher filigranen Hackwerkzeugen des FD20 noch wirksam entfernt werden zu können. Hier ist vor allem die geringe Geschwindigkeit des FD20 von < 1 km/h ein limitierender Faktor. Als Vorteil wird dagegen gesehen, dass der FD20 aufgrund seines relativ geringen Gewichts früher als konventionelle Technik auf einen nach Niederschlägen abtrocknenden Boden fahren kann. Im Vergleich zur Variante mit einer traktorgebundenen Hacke wurden in der Diskussion sowohl arbeitsorganisatorische Vorteile als auch Vorteile bei der Bodenschonung genannt. Bei sehr nassen Wetterbedingungen, in denen das Feld über lange Perioden nur mit dem deutlich leichteren Roboter befahrbar ist, kann also sogar ein strategischer Vorteil entstehen.

„Dieses Jahr sind wir mit dem konventionellen Hackgerät durchgefahren, da die Wetterbedingungen dafür optimal waren. Letztes Jahr war dies nicht der Fall, somit konnte nur der Roboter hacken. Hierbei sieht man, dass der Roboter nicht so wetterabhängig ist wie die klassische Hacktechnik." (TN 3)

„Letztes Jahr konnten wir die Rüben ernten, während viele andere Bio-Bauern ohne FD ihre Rüben umreißen mussten." (TN 3)

Eine eventuell stärkere Spätverunkrautung wird von den Landwirten als weitestgehend unproblematisch angesehen. Sie störe nicht bei der Ernte und führe bislang nach Meinung einiger Diskussionsteilnehmer auch zu keinen Einbußen im Ertrag der jeweiligen Kultur. Auch ein eventuell vermehrtes Aussamen von Beikräutern wurde von einem Teilnehmer als unproblematisch betrachtet, da die Böden ohnehin mit Beikrautsamen gesättigt seien.

„Das Aussamen von der Spätverunkrautung sehe ich nicht als problematisch. Gerade bei den konventionellen Kollegen, die immer saubere Bestände haben, kommt jedes Jahr aufs neue Unkraut. Die Samenbank des Bodens ist immer prall gefüllt und wird wachsen." (TN 2)

3.3 Erfahrungen zum Betreuungsaufwand und zur Systemzuverlässigkeit

Es zeigte sich eine große Übereinstimmung unter den Diskussionsteilnehmern im Hinblick auf den hohen Betreuungsaufwands der Roboter im Einsatz. Während des Betriebs des Roboters brauche es durchgehend eine Person in Bereitschaft, um eventuelle Standzeiten durch Fehler und Defekte zu vermeiden. In diesem Kontext wurde von den Diskussionsteilnehmern die mangelnde Zuverlässigkeit und Stabilität des Systems im Jahr 2020 hervorgehoben. Hier traten gehäuft Probleme und Defekte bei Hardwarekomponenten (Antriebsmotoren, Getrieben, Saatgutvereinzelung) auf. Ein Großteil dieser anfälligen Bestandteile wurden allerdings vor der Saison 2021 vom Hersteller gegen stabilere Ersatzteile ausgetauscht. Somit konnte für die folgenden Saisons bei einem Großteil der fehlerbehafteten Komponenten die Zuverlässigkeit erhöht werden. Weiterhin bemängelte einer der Diskussionsteilnehmer neben dem hohen Betreuungsaufwand die fehlende Möglichkeit, direkt in die Pfadplanung der Maschine eingreifen zu können:

„Der Betreuungsaufwand ist der gleiche wie beim Melkroboter: Man muss immer erreichbar sein. Je intensiver man sich mit dem FD und der Bearbeitungsweise beschäftigt, desto genauer arbeitet er. Als Betreuungsperson muss man den Roboter ständig per App und Kamera überwachen und ggf. eingreifen. Sie muss immer erreichbar und einsatzfähig sein." (TN 4)

Der Betreuungsaufwand für den Landwirt steigt weiterhin durch ein aufwändiges Umsetzen zwischen Feldern. Der FD20 darf nicht autonom auf öffentlichen Straßen fahren und ist auch auf Feldwegen durch die geringe Geschwindigkeit (< 1 km/h) und eine Breite von 3,6 m in seiner Manövrierfähigkeit eingeschränkt. Zwar ist ein Adapter für den Dreipunkt-Kraftheber des Traktors marktverfügbar, jedoch ist auch damit aufgrund der genannten Breite ein Transport nur auf Feld und Feldwegen, nicht aber auf öffentlichen Straßen möglich. Für den Transport auf öffentlichen Straßen muss der Roboter auf einen Tiefladeanhänger verladen werden. Vor allem bei mehreren kleineren und weiter verstreuten Feldern wird dies von den FD20-Nutzern in der Diskussion als spürbarer Mehraufwand hervorgehoben.

3.4 Erfahrungen zu den zusätzlichen Anforderungen beim Einsatz des Roboters

Die Landwirte in der Fokusgruppendiskussion sehen in der Filigranität der Maschine eine zusätzliche Herausforderung und zusätzliche Ansprüche an die Rahmenbedingungen am Feld. Zum einen wird ein Mehraufwand in der Bodenbearbeitung beobachtet, um die Felder möglichst fein herzurichten. So können vor allem größere Steine auf dem Acker schnell zu einem Problem für die Funktionalität des Systems werden.

„Die Bodenbearbeitung muss präziser, ebener und gleichmäßiger sein als vor dem Robotereinsatz. Der FD verzeiht weniger als die klassischen Sägeräte am Schlepper" (TN 6)

Einen weiteren Nachteil stellen auch die im Vergleich zu traktorgebunden Hacken mit weniger Kraft einwirkenden Hackwerkzeuge dar. Somit können etablierte Beikräuter nur eingeschränkt ausgehackt werden. Die dadurch notwendigen frühzeitigeren und regelmäßigeren Hackdurchgänge mit dem FD20 stellen eine Veränderung der Arbeitsweise und teilweise auch eine Mehrbelastung dar.

„Wenn der Roboter – vom Wetter aus – fahren kann, dann muss man ihn auch unbedingt fahren lassen. Das Unkraut darf nicht zu groß werden" (TN 6)

Teilnehmer von Betrieben, die eine größere Fläche (> 18 ha) mit dem Roboter bewirtschaften, beklagen zudem den ungenügenden Energiespeicher, um den FD20 24 Stunden am Stück einsetzen zu können. Mit häufig auftretenden Standzeiten sinkt die Flächenleistung. Hier wusste sich einer der Betriebsleiter zur Ladung des FD20 mit einem Dieselaggregat zu helfen und übertraf damit sogar mehr als die vom Hersteller empfohlene Fläche von 20 ha. Der Hersteller bietet nun auch Akkus mit einer höheren Kapazität an [Fa22b].

„Wenn ich Anfang März bzw. Ende April mit dem FD fahren will, dann reichen die Sonnenstunden nicht aus, damit das Gerät fahren kann. Somit bleibt er die ganze Nacht stehen. Meine Lösung war ein Stromaggregat, dass ich eingebaut habe, damit er die ganze Nacht durchfahren kann, aufgrund des schlechten bevorstehenden Wetters. Wenn man die volle Schlagkraft des FDs braucht, dann fehlt sie." (TN 2)

Die Diskussionsrunde verdeutlichte insgesamt, dass die Landwirte, die den FD20 im Einsatz haben, sich bei vielen technischen Problemen selbst zu helfen wussten. Als Beispiel wurde genannt, dass aufgrund der Modularität des Roboters Probleme wie das Einklemmen von Steinen durch kleinere konstruktive Veränderungen zu lösen waren. So nahmen beispielsweise mehrere Diskussionsteilnehmer Modifikationen an den werksseitigen Hackwerkzeugen vor. Ein betroffener Betriebsleiter veränderte die Konstruktion, indem er den Klutenräumer verbreiterte, um Steine aus dem Weg zu schieben, die ansonsten die Andruckrollen des Säaggregats verklemmt hätten. Durch die langsame Fahrgeschwindigkeit des FD20 kann der Landwirt neben dem Roboter herlaufen, um die Arbeitsqualität zu beurteilen und iterative Verbesserungseinstellungen oder eigene Umbauten zu testen. Die Möglichkeit, selbst Umbauarbeiten vorzunehmen, wurde positiv bewertet.

„Es ist gut, dass die Gerätschaft nicht sehr schwer ist und ich ihn selbstständig umbauen kann." (TN 5)

Die Fokusgruppendiskussion zeigte generell, dass bei den „early adopters" des Feldroboters ein gewisses Maß an technischem und agronomischem Verständnis vorhanden sein sollte, um die Implementierung des FD20 im eigenen Betrieb möglichst effektiv umzusetzen.

3.5 Fazit der Nutzer nach den ersten beiden Einsatzjahren

Die finale Frage in der Diskussionsrunde „Würden Sie den Roboter mit den Erfahrungen, die sie jetzt haben, nochmal kaufen?" wurde von den Teilnehmern differenziert beantwortet. Ein Teil der Betriebsleiter ist grundsätzlich zufrieden mit dem FD20, würde aber den Roboter aufgrund des deutlich gestiegenen Listenpreises bei Wegfall der Förderung (BaySL Digital) aktuell nicht mehr kaufen. Eine zweite Gruppe schätzt die neu gewonnene Sicherheit bzw. Resilienz der Produktion in Bezug auf die geminderte Abhängigkeit und Unsicherheit bei der Verfügbarkeit von Saisonarbeitskräften für Hackarbeiten und würde zu ähnlichen Konditionen wieder investieren. Eine dritte Gruppe empfand den FD20 als Arbeitserleichterung, würde aber mit heutigem Erfahrungswissen zuerst weitere technologische Entwicklungen abwarten und sich gegebenenfalls ein anderes autonomes System zur Beikrautregulierung kaufen, das „*mit der Technik weiter*" ist (TN 3). Der Roboter wurde von den Diskussionsteilnehmern grundsätzlich als geeignete Technologie für ihre Pflanzenproduktion eingeschätzt, da damit manuelle Pflegearbeiten ersetzt werden können. Er wird vor allem geschätzt, weil er als zweite Säule zur Handhacke Kosteneinsparung und Sicherheit für die Produktion bietet. Jedoch hängt die Kaufentscheidung stark von der Investitionssumme und damit von der Förderung ab. Ebenso wird auf die Verfügbarkeit von Alternativprodukten gehofft.

4 Diskussion und Ausblick

Die bayerischen „early adopters" des Farmdroid FD20 zeigten in der Fokusgruppendiskussion eine grundsätzliche Zufriedenheit mit dem Einsatz des FD20 in den ersten beiden Anbaujahren, kommunizierten jedoch auch mehrere Ansatzpunkte für technische Verbesserungen an dem Feldroboter. Da der FD20 werksseitig mit filigranen Hackwerkzeugen ausgestattet ist, müssen Hackdurchgänge in einer höheren Regelmäßigkeit erfolgen als beispielsweise mit einer traktorgeführten Hacke. Während des Roboterbetriebs sind die Landwirte zudem in ständiger Bereitschaft, um Standzeiten zu vermindern und den Transport zwischen den Feldern zu organisieren. Somit müssen die Nutzer des FD20 einen hohen zeitlichen Aufwand für die Betreuung, aber auch für notwendige eigene Modifikationen an Antriebskomponenten oder Hack- und Säwerkzeugen betreiben, um die Einsatzfähigkeit des Feldroboters im eigenen Betrieb zu verbessern und das System an die spezifischen Standortbedingungen anzupassen.

Der Einsatz eines Feldroboters unterscheidet sich stark von der Feldbearbeitung mit dem Traktor, nicht nur in Bezug auf die Arbeitsgänge selbst, sondern auch in Bezug auf die technische Zuverlässigkeit. „Early adopters" müssen daher bereit sein, das Risiko von erhöhten Einarbeitungskosten und Anfangsschwierigkeiten in Kauf zu nehmen. Die Relevanz eines direkten Austausches zwischen Hersteller und Anwender für die Weiterentwicklung von Feldrobotik [vgl. Ri18; Ro21] wird auch von den Teilnehmern der Fokusgruppendiskussion bestätigt. In diesem Kontext ist hervorzuheben, dass die Teilnehmer die Kommunikation mit dem Hersteller des FD20 und die Bereitschaft, auf Änderungsvorschläge einzugehen, durchaus positiv bewerten.

Die Diskussionsteilnehmer erwarteten sich von dem Feldroboter eine deutliche Reduktion der Handhackstunden, vor allem vor dem Hintergrund der Covid19-Pandemie und der damit verbundenen Unsicherheit der Verfügbarkeit der Handarbeitskräfte. Die

Einschränkungen der Pandemie verstärkten das bereits bestehende Problem sinkender Verfügbarkeit von Handarbeitskräften, welche bereits vor dem Jahr 2020 als möglicher Faktor für die Adoption von Feldrobotern genannt wurde [Ri18]. Jedoch verdeutlichte die Diskussion auch die Unsicherheit bei der Arbeitsersparnis durch Feldroboter [vgl. Ri18; RCH21]. So lässt sich durch den Roboter die Handarbeit in der Beikrautregulierung unter günstigen Rahmenbedingungen (Boden, Witterung) zwar reduzieren, aber nicht vollständig ersetzen. Dies und die zusätzliche Mehrarbeit für den Anwender relativieren die erwartete Arbeitszeitreduktion [RH21; RTH21; Sp21]. Vielmehr lässt sich sagen, dass die Einsparung repetitiver Arbeitsabläufe, wie das manuelle Hacken, einer Erhöhung von zeitlichem Aufwand durch Logistik, Betreuung und technische Tätigkeiten am Roboter gegenüberzustellen ist.

Diese Beobachtungen verweisen auf Parallelen zu Veränderung der Arbeitsorganisation durch den Einsatz von Melkrobotern. Erfahrungen mit automatischen Melksystemen in der Milchviehhaltung zeigen, dass sich die Art der Arbeit verändert, aber nicht zwangsläufig reduziert [Ma22b; He22]. Gleichwohl sollte bedacht werden, dass die Feldrobotik im Gegensatz zur Melkrobotik erst seit Kurzem marktverfügbar ist und somit Rückmeldungen von Anwendern in den kommenden Jahren erheblich zum technischen Fortschritt beitragen können. Aktuelle Projekte aus Forschung und Wirtschaft [bspw. DR22; Fr22a; Fr22b] deuten an, dass in den kommenden Jahren Effizienzgewinne in bestimmten, aktuell noch arbeitsintensiven Schritten, z. B. dem Einmessen der Felder, zu erwarten sind. Jedoch unterliegen bestimmte Arbeiten wie Aufsichtspflichten [Lo21b] oder der Transport auf öffentlichen Straßen rechtlichen Restriktionen, so dass dieser Mehraufwand durch Feldrobotik längerfristig bestehen bleiben wird.

Literaturverzeichnis

[DR22] Dahlia Robotics, Our Solution, https://dahliarobotics.com/, Stand: 10.10.2022.

[Fa22a] Farmdroid ApS, FAQ, https://farmdroid.dk/de/faq-deutsch/, Stand: 28.09.2022.

[Fa22b] Farmdroid ApS, Upgrade from AGM to Lithium batteries, https://knowledge.farmdroid.io/upgrade-to-lithium-batteries-on-2020-robots, Stand: 28.09.2022.

[Fo15] Fountas, S. et al.: Farm management information systems: Current situation and future perspectives. Computers and Electronics in Agriculture, 115, S. 40-50, 2015.

[Fr22a] Fraunhofer-Institut für Angewandte Informationstechnik, CERES Kooperative Cloud-Plattform für die Landwirtschaft, https://www.fit.fraunhofer.de/de/geschaeftsfelder/digitale-gesundheit/fraunhofer-anwendungszentrum-symila/projekt-highlights/ceres.html, Stand: 10.10.2022.

[Fr22b] Fraunhofer-Institut für Verkehrs- und Infrastruktursysteme, helyOS® Control Tower Softwareframework für mobile Maschinen, https://www.ivi.fraunhofer.de/de/forschungsfelder/automatisierte-systeme/helyos-control-tower-softwareframework-fuer-mobile-maschinen.html, Stand: 10.10.2022.

[Ga22] Gandorfer, M. et al.: Adoption and Acceptance of Digital Farming Technologies in Germany. In (Dörr, J.; Nachtmann, M. Hrsg.): Handbook Digital Farming. Springer Berlin, Heidelberg, S. 30-34, 2022.

[He22] Henchion, M.M. et al.: Developing 'Smart' Dairy Farming Responsive to Farmers and Consumer-Citizens: A Review. Animals 12, 360, 2022.

[Lo21a] Lowenberg-DeBoer, J. et al.: Economics of autonomous equipment for arable farms. Precision Agriculture, 22, S. 1996-2006, 2021.

[Lo21b] Lowenberg-DeBoer, J. et al. Lessons to be learned in adoption of autonomous equipment for field crops. Applied Economic Perspectives and Policy, 44, 2, S. 848-864, 2021.

[Ma16] Mayring, P.: Einführung in die qualitative Sozialforschung. Beltz, Weinheim, Basel, 2016.

[Ma22a] Maritan, E. et al.: Economically optimal farmer supervision of crop robots. Smart Agricultural Technology, 3, 100110, 2022.

[Ma22b] Martin, T. et al.: Robots and transformations of work in farm: a systematic review of the literature and a research agenda. Agronomy for Sustainable Development, 42, 66, 2022.

[Mo88] Morgan, D.L.: Focus Groups as Qualitative Research. Sage, Newbury Park, CA, 1988.

[RCH21] Rübcke von Veltheim, R.; Clausen, F.; Heise, H.: Autonomous Field Robots in Agriculture: A Qualitative Analysis of User Acceptance According to Different Agricultural Machinery Companies. In (Gotter, C. et al. Hrsg.): Vorträge der 60. Jahrestagung der GEWISOLA, Halle (Saale) 2020. Landwirtschaftsverlag, Münster, S. 49-61, 2021.

[Re15] Redhead, F. et al.: Bringing the Farmer Perspective to Agricultural Robots. In (ACM Hrsg.): CHI'15 EA: Proceedings of the 33rd Annual ACM Conference Extended Abstracts on Human Factors in Computing Systems, 18.-23. April 2015, Seoul, Republik Korea, S. 1067-1072, 2015.

[RH20] Rübcke von Veltheim, F.; Heise, H.: The AgTech Startup Perspective to Farmers Ex Ante Acceptance Process of Autonomous Field Robots. Sustainability, 12, 10570, 2020.

[RH21] Rübcke von Veltheim, F.; Heise, H.: German Farmers' Attitudes on Adopting Autonomous Field Robots: an Empirical Survey. Agriculture, 11, 216, 2021.

[Ri18]	Rial-Lovera, K.: Agricultural Robots: drivers, barriers and opportunities for adoption. In (ISPA Hrsg.): Proceedings of the 14th International Conference on Precision Agriculture, 24.-27. Juni 2018, Montreal, Quebec, Canada, 2018.
[Ro21]	Rose, D.C. et al.: Responsible development of autonomous robotics in agriculture. Nature Food, 2, S. 306-309, 2021.
[RTH21]	Rübcke von Veltheim, F.; Theuvsen, L.; Heise, H.: German farmers' intention to use autonomous field robots: a PLS-analysis. Precision Agriculture, 2021.
[Sc09]	Schirmer, D. et al.: Empirische Methoden der Sozialforschung: Grundlagen und Techniken. Basiswissen Soziologie, 3175. UTB, Stuttgart, 2009.
[Sp21]	Spykman, O. et al.: Farmers' perspectives on field crop robots – Evidence from Bavaria, Germany. Computers and Electronics in Agriculture, 186, 106176, 2021.

Wirtschaftlichkeitsbewertung eines Feldroboters auf Basis erster Erfahrungen im Praxiseinsatz

Olivia Spykman [1], Andreas Roßmadl[2], Johanna Pfeiffer [3], Stefan Kopfinger [4] und Axel Busboom [5]

Abstract: Bisherige ökonomische Bewertungen von Feldrobotern basieren vorrangig auf Prototypen oder theoretischen Modellbetrachtungen. In diesem Beitrag wird ein Modell zur Bewertung der Wirtschaftlichkeit von Feldrobotern dargestellt, das auf Basis von Feldversuchen mit dem Hackroboter Farmdroid FD20, dem aktuell in Bayern am weitesten verbreiteten Roboter, parametrisiert wurde. Die Ergebnisse zeigen, dass der FD20 in bestimmten betrieblichen Szenarien zur Produktion von Ökozuckerrüben wirtschaftlich eingesetzt werden kann. In einer Sensitivitätsanalyse wurden unter anderem der Einfluss der Kosten für Saisonarbeit und notwendiger Nacharbeit mittels Handhacke betrachtet. Die Ergebnisse zeigen dabei, dass mit steigendem Mindestlohn auch der Gewinnbeitrag des FD20 steigt. Unter Annahme des aktuellen Mindestlohns erzeugt der FD20 in dem betrachteten Szenario auch dann einen positiven Gewinnbeitrag, wenn nur 42 % der Handhacke zum Reihenschluss durch Robotik ersetzt werden können. Die Analyse liefert wichtige Anhaltspunkte für weitere ökonomische Bewertungen von Feldrobotern unter besonderer Berücksichtigung arbeitswirtschaftlicher Aspekte.

Keywords: Hackroboter, Saisonarbeit, Zuckerrübe, mechanische Unkrautregulierung

1 Einleitung

Feldroboter versprechen die autonome Durchführung einzelner oder mehrerer Arbeitsschritte im Pflanzenbau. Vor allem handarbeitsintensive Tätigkeiten wie die mechanische Unkrautregulierung stehen dabei im Fokus. Die Anzahl der marktverfügbaren Systeme nahm in den letzten Jahren dynamisch zu, wobei die Roboter in Form, Funktion, Größe und Energiekonzept variieren. Es gibt sowohl Multifunktionsplattformen, die als Zugfahrzeug für landtechnische Maschinen dienen, als

---

[1] Bayerische Landesanstalt für Landwirtschaft, Institut für Landtechnik und Tierhaltung, Kleeberg 14, 94044 Ruhstorf a.d. Rott, olivia.spykman@lfl.bayern.de https://orcid.org/0000-0002-8650-9283
[2] Hochschule München, Fakultät für Wirtschaftsingenieurwesen, Lothstr. 64, 80335 München, andreas.rossmadl@hm.edu
[3] Bayerische Landesanstalt für Landwirtschaft, Institut für Landtechnik und Tierhaltung, Kleeberg 14, 94044 Ruhstorf a.d. Rott, johanna.pfeiffer@lfl.bayern.de https://orcid.org/0000-0002-6045-4878
[4] Bayerische Landesanstalt für Landwirtschaft, Institut für Landtechnik und Tierhaltung, Kleeberg 14, 94044 Ruhstorf a.d. Rott, stefan.kopfinger@lfl.bayern.de https://orcid.org/0000-0002-8455-3707
[5] Hochschule München, Fakultät für Wirtschaftsingenieurwesen, Lothstr. 64, 80335 München, axel.busboom@hm.edu https://orcid.org/0000-0003-1032-5872.

auch Spezialroboter, bei denen das Werkzeug und das Fahrzeug eine Einheit bilden und für einen speziellen Anwendungszweck eingesetzt werden. Eines dieser Spezialsysteme ist der Farmdroid FD20, welcher der momentan in Bayern verbreitetste Feldroboter ist.

Der Farmdroid FD20 übernimmt sowohl Aussaat als auch Unkrautregulierung von Feinsämereien, darunter überwiegend der Zuckerrübe. Aufgrund der erst kurzen Marktverfügbarkeit bestehen nur wenig Kenntnisse über dessen Wirtschaftlichkeit. Erste Modellstudien legen nahe, dass Feldrobotik die Wettbewerbsfähigkeit kleiner Betriebe stärken kann [Lo21a] und daher für diese eine zukunftsweisende Investition darstellen könnte. In diesem Kontext soll im folgenden Beitrag die Wirtschaftlichkeit des FD20 am Beispiel der bayerischen Agrarstruktur untersucht werden.

2 Literaturüberblick

In Befragungen von Landwirten zur Feldrobotik spielen die Aspekte Arbeitserleichterung und Gewinnsteigerung eine maßgebliche Rolle [RH21; RTH21; Sp21]. Von weiteren Akteuren im Landwirtschaftssektor (z. B. Maschinenherstellern) wird unter anderem die schwindende Verfügbarkeit von Arbeitskräften als Treiber für die Feldrobotik gesehen [Ri18], gleichwohl deren Beitrag für die Gesamtwirtschaftlichkeit der Technologie nicht eindeutig zugeordnet wird [RCH21]. Somit bleibt zu eruieren, ob Feldroboter die an sie gestellten Erwartungen hinsichtlich Wirtschaftlichkeit durch Arbeitszeitreduktion erfüllen können.

In einem Review zur Wirtschaftlichkeit von Feldrobotern fassen Lowenberg et al. [Lo20] zusammen, dass die analysierten Studien vor allem auf Simulationsmodellen und an Universitäten entwickelten Prototypen basieren und überwiegend den Einsatz autonomer Maschinen im Obst- und Gemüsebau betrachten. Unter den bisher analysierten ackerbaulichen Kulturen befinden sich Zuckerrübe, Getreide, Mais und Soja, wobei die jeweils zugrunde gelegten Annahmen nicht auf Feldversuchen basieren [Lo20]. Jedoch unterliegen die betrachteten Publikationen einigen Einschränkungen hinsichtlich ihrer Aussagekraft. So stellen Sørensen et al. [SMJ05] zwar arbeitsintensive Verfahren im ökologischen Anbau von Zuckerrüben in den Fokus, basieren ihr Ergebnis zur Arbeitszeitreduktion durch Robotik allerdings auf damalige Prototypen, welche nicht mit heute marktverfügbaren Modellen zu vergleichen sind. Pedersen et al. [Pe06] betrachten Robotik zur Unkrautregulierung und zur Bonitur in Getreide auf Basis einer Gegenüberstellung von eingesparten Lohn- sowie Betriebsmittelkosten und zusätzlichen Investitionskosten. Die Autoren kommen, je nach Annahmen in den Sensitivitätsanalysen, zu unterschiedlichen Ergebnissen hinsichtlich der Wirtschaftlichkeit von Robotik gegenüber herkömmlichen Verfahren. Gaus et al. [Ga18] untersuchen die Wirtschaftlichkeit von mechanischer Unkrautregulierung in Getreide mittels kleiner Schwarmrobotik im Rahmen einer Konzeptstudie mit der Schlussfolgerung, dass dieser Ansatz vor dem Hintergrund hoher Herbizidkosten eine Alternative darstellen könnte. Zuletzt wenden Shockley et al. [SDS19] zwar ein gesamtbetriebliches Modell mit Berücksichtigung der Lohnkosten an, berechnen damit jedoch die Gewinnschwelle für die Nachrüstung herkömmlicher Maschinen mittels hypothetischer intelligenter, autonomer Kontrolleinheiten. Zusammenfassend über alle betrachteten Studien schlussfolgern Lowenberg-DeBoer et al. [Lo20], dass die bisherigen ökonomischen Analysen zu autonomen landwirtschaftlichen Maschinen vor allem durch mangelnde Daten aufgrund der bis dato geringen Erfahrung mit Feldrobotik limitiert sind.

Als erste gesamtbetriebliche Wirtschaftlichkeitsbetrachtung von autonomen Maschinen legt eine Folgepublikation von Lowenberg-DeBoer et al. [Lo21a] nahe, dass autonome Bewirtschaftung sowohl für kleine als auch für große Betriebe wirtschaftliche Vorteile gegenüber konventioneller Technik haben kann [Lo21a]. Diese Erkenntnis basiert jedoch auf Erfahrungen mit nachgerüsteten Traktoren und nicht mit marktverfügbaren Robotern. Zudem ist in Bezug auf das verwendete Modell anzumerken, dass dieses die betrachtete Betriebsgröße zu 90 % als arrondiert bewirtschaftbare Fläche betrachtet [Lo21a]. Weiterhin wird in dem Modell die notwendige Arbeitszeit als pauschal 10 % der Maschinenzeit betrachtet [Lo21a], so dass trotz der gesamtbetrieblichen Analyse wesentliche Zusammenhänge zwischen Betriebsstruktur und wirtschaftlichem Einsatz von Robotik nur eingeschränkt erkenntlich werden.

Ein wesentlicher Diskussionspunkt bezüglich Feldrobotik ist die Einsparung von Arbeitskraft. Zwar können rechnerisch die Lohnkosten des Traktorfahrers eingespart werden [Ga17], gleichwohl zeigen weiterführende Untersuchungen, dass potenzielle Beaufsichtigungspflichten [Lo21b], die Häufigkeit der Fehlerbehebung durch den Menschen [Ma22b] oder auch die Effizienz des Verladevorgangs des Roboters [HB19] die Höhe dieser Einsparungen schmälern können. Da befragte Landwirte insbesondere Potenzial für kleine Robotik im Bereich der Unkrautregulierung sehen [vgl. Sp21], gilt es auch den Effekt auf die in diesem Bereich eingesetzten Saisonarbeitskräfte zu betrachten. Wie die COVID19-Pandemie verdeutlichte, ist die Saisonarbeit ein unabdingbarer Bestandteil der Landwirtschaft. Bereits vor der Pandemie sahen sich die von Saisonarbeitern abhängigen landwirtschaftlichen Betriebe mit einem schwindenden Angebot an Aushilfskräften konfrontiert, da diese aufgrund alternativer Einkommensquellen [BL22] seltener für die körperlich fordernden Tätigkeiten auf dem Feld zur Verfügung stehen. Somit bestehen im Bereich des Unkrautmanagements reelle Treiber für die Adoption von Robotik [vgl. MR20], welche die theoretischen Berechnungen untermauern.

3 Modell und Datenbasis

Für die Wirtschaftlichkeitsbewertung wurde ein Microsoft Excel-basiertes Modell erstellt, welches eine Farmdroid FD20-Variante einer ortsüblichen, nicht-autonomen Vergleichsvariante beim Anbau von Öko-Zuckerrüben gegenüberstellt (siehe Tabelle 1). Dieses Modell wurde auf Basis von Arbeitszeitdokumentation beim Einsatz des FD20 im Jahr 2021 sowie von Daten des KTBL-Feldrechners [Ku21] parametrisiert. Als Zielgröße wird der Gewinnbeitrag je Hektar und Jahr betrachtet. Dabei wird im Rahmen dynamischer Investitionsrechnungen eine Nutzungsdauer von 10 Jahren sowie ein Kalkulationszinssatz von 3 % zugrunde gelegt.

FD20-Variante	Vergleichsvariante
1x Blindsäen[6]	
1x Säen	1x Säen
1x Blindhacken[7]	
3x Hacken zwischen den Reihen	1x Handhacke (1. Hacke)
3x Hacken in den Reihen	3x Maschinenhacke
0,3x Handhacke (Reihenschluss)	1x Handhacke (Reihenschluss)

Tab. 1: Berücksichtigte Arbeitsdurchgänge in den zwei betrachteten Varianten

Die Annahme eines anteiligen Durchgangs Handhacke zum Reihenschluss in der FD20-Variante basiert auf Erfahrungen aus Feldversuchen, nach denen der FD20 einen Sicherheitsabstand um die Rüben nicht bearbeitet. Zudem muss aufgrund der bauartbedingten niedrigen Durchgangshöhe des FD20 im Vergleich zu einer traktorgebundenen Hacke mit verstärkter Blattverletzung der Rüben bei Durchfahrten zu beginnendem Reihenschluss gerechnet werden. Somit können Hackdurchgänge mit dem FD20 nicht so spät wie in der Vergleichsvariante durchgeführt werden. Daraus resultierten in Feldversuchen in den Jahren 2020 und 2021 zwar vergleichbare Zuckererträge, jedoch auch eine höhere Spätverunkrautung in der FD20-Variante [u. a. KV21]. Auf Basis dieser ersten Erkenntnisse wird angenommen, dass der FD20 die menschliche Arbeitskraft nicht vollständig ersetzen kann. Diesen Beobachtungen wird in der Kalkulation des Ausgangsszenarios Rechnung getragen durch die Annahme, dass der Roboter unter den örtlichen Gegebenheiten 70 % der notwendigen Handhacke ersetzen kann und somit jedes Jahr das Äquivalent von 30 % eines Handhackdurchgangs zum Reihenschluss notwendig wird.

Ausgehend von den regionalen Gegebenheiten, in denen die Feldversuche durchgeführt wurden, sowie der Preissituation im Herbst 2022 wurde das Ausgangsszenario definiert. Die Versuchsflächen am Standort Ruhstorf a. d. Rott bestehen aus Lösslehm (Schluff,

---

[6] Während des Blindsäens fährt der FD20 in Säkonfiguration seine Fahrspur entlang, ohne tatsächlich Saatgut abzulegen. Dies dient der Saatbettbereitung, der Verfestigung des Bodens und dem Räumen der Saatgutablagestellen von Steinen und Kluten.
[7] Das Blindhacken ist ein Hackgang, der vor dem Auflaufen der Zuckerrüben durchgeführt wird. Dies dient der frühzeitigen Unkrautregulierung und ist möglich, da der Roboter mit RTK GNSS navigiert und so keine visuellen Anhaltspunkte benötigt.

tonig, feinsandig) und sind frei von Steinen, die für den Roboter problematisch werden könnten. Klimatisch befinden sich die Flächen in Klimazone 6 mit im Mittel 59 verfügbaren Feldarbeitstagen von Anfang März bis Anfang Juli [Ac20]. Die verfügbaren Feldarbeitstage wurden in Sä- und Hackzeiträume unterteilt und mit den in Feldversuchen erhobenen Daten zur Arbeitsgeschwindigkeit des FD20 bei den jeweiligen Tätigkeiten verrechnet. Für das Ausgangsszenario am Versuchsstandort ergibt sich somit eine maximal mögliche jährliche Auslastung von 18 ha, welche aufgrund der durchschnittlichen Schlaggröße in Bayern von 1,74 ha [BL14] auf zehn Schläge verteilt wird. Als Kaufpreis wurden 90.000 € netto veranschlagt [Mi22], die Lohnkosten wurden mit 21 €/Akh für Facharbeitskräfte [Ac20] und 16 €/Akh für Saisonarbeitskräfte (12 €/h Mindestlohn [DB22] zzgl. 31,2 % Sozialabgaben [Ac20], gerundet) angesetzt. Als Agrardieselpreis wurde 1,40 €/l angenommen [Of22]. Der Wiederverkaufswert von 20 % bei einem Nutzungspotential von zehn Jahren orientiert sich an den Angaben des KTBL für landwirtschaftliche Maschinen [Ac20]. Das Ausgangsszenario wurde sowohl mit als auch ohne die aktuell in Bayern verfügbare staatliche Förderung (Bayerisches Sonderprogramm Landwirtschaft Digital) von 40 % des Nettokaufpreises untersucht.

3.1 Sensitivitätsanalyse

Die in Tabelle 1 beschriebenen Arbeitsschritte beeinflussen die Modellergebnisse über die Positionen „Lohnkosten" und „Maschinenkosten". Jedoch besteht in beiden Fällen aufgrund der bisher nur begrenzt verfügbaren Daten keine Sicherheit. Aus diesem Grund wurde eine Sensitivitätsanalyse durchgeführt, wobei die Variablen notwendige Handhacke bzw. Spätverunkrautungsgrad, Mindestlohn, bewirtschaftete Fläche, Restwert des FD20 nach zehn Jahren, Dieselpreis sowie staatliche Investitionsförderung betrachtet wurden. Im Folgenden liegt der Fokus auf den Einflussgrößen Spätverunkrautungsgrad, Mindestlohn und bewirtschaftete Fläche.

Der Variation der Handhacke in der FD20-Variante liegt die Annahme zugrunde, dass dem Betrieb Saisonarbeitskräfte zur Verfügung stehen, welche je nach Bedarf auf dem Zuckerrübenfeld oder für andere Tätigkeiten eingesetzt werden können. Somit entstehen keine über die eigentlichen Lohnkosten hinausgehenden Transaktionskosten für eine kurzfristige Suche nach Arbeitskräften bei sich abzeichnender Notwendigkeit der Handhacke in der FD20-Variante. Ebenso müssen diese Transaktionskosten nicht berücksichtigt werden, sollte die Handhacke nicht notwendig werden. Um der jährlichen und regionalen Variabilität des Handhackumfangs nach dem FD20-Einsatz Rechnung zu tragen, wurde im Modell der Einfluss der notwendigen Handhacke in der FD20-Variante in 10%-Schritten zwischen keiner Handhacke (0 %) und einem vollständigen Durchgang Handhacke (100 %) betrachtet.

Die Saisonarbeitskräfte werden mit dem deutschen Mindestlohn entlohnt, welcher im Zeitraum von Januar 2021 bis Oktober 2022 von 9,50 €/h auf 12 €/h angehoben wurde [DB22]. Nach der Addierung der Sozialabgaben [Ac20] werden aktuell Lohnkosten von rund 16 €/Akh als Ausgangswert erreicht. In der Sensitivitätsanalyse wurde dieser Wert in 0,50 €/Akh-Schritten bis zu einem Höchstwert von 20 €/Akh gesteigert. Sinkende Lohnkosten wurde aufgrund mangelnder Plausibilität nicht betrachtet.

Die maximal pro Saison durch den FD20 bewirtschaftbare Fläche variiert mit der Klimazone. Nach Abgleich der Zuckerrübenanbaugebiete in Deutschland [WV22] mit den Klimagebieten [Ac20] wurden analog zum Ausgangsszenario die maximal zu bewirtschaftenden Flächen je Klimazone errechnet. Dies ergab eine Spanne von 8 ha bis rund 21 ha und ist somit vergleichbar mit der Herstellerangabe von maximal 20 ha pro Saison [Fa22]. Der Effekt des Gesamtflächeneinsatzes von 8 bis 20 ha auf die Wirtschaftlichkeit wurde für zwei Schlaggrößen, 2 ha und 4 ha, in den entsprechenden Divisionsschritten betrachtet.

Ein weiterer flächenbezogener Einflussfaktor ist die Schlagstruktur. Da der FD20 nicht autonom auf öffentlichen Straßen fahren darf, ist dessen Einsatz auf mehreren Feldern mit Arbeitsaufwand beim Umsetzen verbunden. Um diesen Effekt auf die Wirtschaftlichkeit zu untersuchen, wurden daher ausgehend von der Gesamteinsatzfläche von 18 ha des Ausgangsszenarios die Anzahl Schläge zwischen einem und 15 mit entsprechenden Veränderungen in der Durchschnittsfeldgröße variiert. Die Variation dieser Einflussgröße wird sowohl über die Diesel- als auch die Lohnkosten, die aufgrund der zusätzlichen Rüstarbeiten sowie Fahrten zwischen den Feldern anfallen, im Modell berücksichtigt.

4 Ergebnisse

Das Ausgangsszenario (Einsatzfläche 18 ha, 10 Schläge) resultiert in einem Gewinnbeitrag von 304 €/ha*a bei 0 % Förderung und in einem Gewinnbeitrag von 794 €/ha*a bei einer 40 %-Förderung des Feldroboters FD20. Bei einem Gesamtflächeneinsatz von 18 ha pro Saison zeigt sich, dass der Gewinnbeitrag für die betrachtete Schlagverteilung (1 Schlag à 18 ha; 15 Schläge à 1,2 ha) positiv ist – sowohl bei 0 % als auch bei 40 % Förderung. Bei einer Investitionsförderung von 40 % ist der Gewinnbeitrag auch bei dem niedrigsten betrachteten Gesamtflächeneinsatz von 8 ha pro Saison noch positiv (betrachtete durchschnittliche Schlaggrößen: 2 ha und 4 ha). Ohne Investitionsförderung wird der Gewinnbeitrag jedoch erst ab einem höheren Gesamtflächeneinsatz positiv. Der hierfür notwendige Gesamtflächeneinsatz unterscheidet sich nach durchschnittlicher Schlaggröße: so wird der Break-Even unter Annahme einer durchschnittlichen Schlaggröße von 4 ha bei ca. 11,5 ha und unter Annahme einer durchschnittlichen Schlaggröße von 2 ha bei ca. 13,7 ha erreicht.

Die Relevanz des Ersatzes von Handarbeit durch den FD20 wird durch den Effekt des Mindestlohns auf den Gewinnbeitrag unterstrichen. Der Gewinnbeitrag ist im Ausgangsszenario sowohl mit als auch ohne Förderung bei den niedrigsten betrachteten Lohnkosten von 16,00 €/Akh positiv. Die in Zukunft zu erwartende weitere Steigerung des Mindestlohns und somit der Lohnkosten für Saisonarbeitskräfte würden den Gewinnbeitrag entsprechend erhöhen (Abbildung 1).

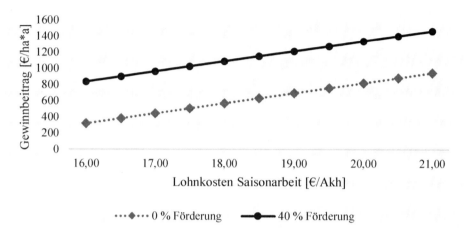

Abb. 1: Effekt der Lohnkosten auf den Gewinnbeitrag des FD20 (Gesamtflächeneinsatz: 18 ha)

Der starke Einfluss der Saisonarbeit auf die Wirtschaftlichkeit des FD20 wird durch die Untersuchung der potenziell notwendigen Nacharbeit per Handhacke verdeutlicht. Hierbei wurde im Ausgangsszenario unterstellt, dass der FD20 im Durchschnitt etwa 70 % der Handhacke zum Reihenschluss ersetzt und somit etwa 30 % eines regulären Durchgangs notwendig sind (vgl. Tabelle 1). Abbildung 2 illustriert, welche Auswirkungen im Gewinnbeitrag Veränderungen dieser Annahme mit sich bringen. Der Gewinnbeitrag nimmt mit zunehmender Notwendigkeit der Nacharbeit in Form von Handhacke bei Reihenschluss in der FD20-Variante ab. Ohne Förderung liefert die Investition in den FD20 bis zu einer Nacharbeit von 58 % eines regulären Arbeitsgangs zum Reihenschluss einen positiven Gewinnbeitrag. Mit Förderung (40 %) bleibt der Gewinnbeitrag hingegen positiv, selbst wenn stets ein voller Handhackdurchgang zum Reihenschluss benötigt wird.

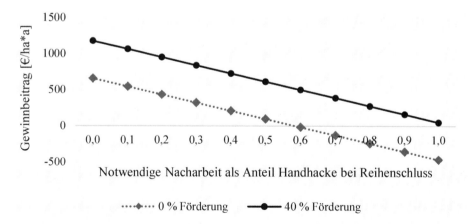

Abb. 2: Effekt der notwendigen Nacharbeit mittels Handhacke bei Reihenschluss als Anteil eines vollwertigen Arbeitsdurchgangs auf den Gewinnbeitrag des FD20 (Gesamtflächeneinsatz: 18 ha)

5 Diskussion

Die vorliegende Wirtschaftlichkeitsbetrachtung des Feldroboters FD20 verdeutlicht, dass dieser auch unter Berücksichtigung kleiner Schlagstrukturen innerhalb der vom Hersteller angegebenen maximalen Schlagkraft von 20 ha pro Saison [Fa22] in der Nische der Ökozuckerrübenproduktion rentabel eingesetzt werden kann. Gleichwohl sollte dabei berücksichtigt werden, dass durch die Anzahl der nutzbaren Feldarbeitstage [Ac20] teilweise geringere Obergrenzen in den verschiedenen Klimazonen [Ac20] gelten, so dass sich die Wirtschaftlichkeit regional unterscheiden kann. Dieser standortbezogene Nachteil sowie auch durch kleine Agrarstrukturen bedingte wirtschaftliche Nachteile können jedoch durch eine Investitionsförderung adressiert werden, welche somit den *digital divide* zwischen kleineren und größeren Betrieben [vgl. Ma22a] abschwächen kann.

In Bezug auf die Saisonarbeit gilt es, auch die Perspektive der temporär Beschäftigten zu betrachten. Die Handarbeit auf dem Feld, ob Handhacke im Zuckerrübenanbau oder andere Tätigkeiten, stellt eine körperlich belastende Arbeit dar. Es ist daher nicht überraschend, dass die Zahl der Saisonarbeitskräfte, die in der deutschen Landwirtschaft arbeiten, stetig sinkt, da den Personen mittlerweile alternative Einkommensquellen zur Verfügung stehen [BL22]. Somit können Feldroboter zukünftig eine zunehmend größer werdende Lücke während landwirtschaftlicher Arbeitsspitzen füllen, welche zuvor mithilfe von Saisonarbeitskräften bewältigt wurden. Dieser Aspekt der Bewertung von Feldrobotern bedarf weiterer Untersuchung.

Ein zweiter Aspekt im Kontext der Automatisierung von Arbeit in der Landwirtschaft ist die Verfügbarkeit von entsprechend ausgebildeten Fachkräften. Immer komplexere Maschinen führen zu immer komplexeren Arbeitsabläufen für den Betreuer der Maschine, in kleinstrukturierten Regionen häufig der Betriebsleiter selbst. In Bezug auf digitale Technologien im Allgemeinen werden jedoch in Deutschland mangelnde IT-Kenntnisse als Hindernis für die Adoption genannt [GGS21], was allerdings nicht zwangsläufig auf Robotik übertragbar ist [RH21]. Gleichwohl deuten auch internationale Ergebnisse auf die Notwendigkeit der Berücksichtigung von digitalen und autonomen Technologien in der Ausbildung landwirtschaftlicher Fachkräfte hin [Ro19], welche vor allem auf größeren Betrieben angestellt sind. Marinoudi et al. [Ma19] sprechen in diesem Zusammenhang von einer Job Polarisation, wonach gerade Arbeitsplätze der mittleren Qualifikationsebene aufgrund wachsender technischer Anforderungen schwinden. Insgesamt könnte ein Großteil der standardisierten landwirtschaftlichen Arbeit durch Robotik ersetzt werden [Ma21]. Der Ersatz von händischer Unkrautregulierung durch einen Roboter wie den FD20 würde somit nicht zwangsläufig ohne eine entsprechende Steigerung des Facharbeiterlohns möglich sein. Zukünftige Robotisierung weiterer Arbeitsabläufe sollte unter Berücksichtigung der sozialen Auswirkungen sowie von Angeboten für angepasste Weiterbildungsmaßnahmen stattfinden [vgl. Ma21].

Die dargestellten Modellergebnisse sind mit verschiedenen Limitationen versehen, die in zukünftigen Analysen zu adressieren sind. So wird modellbedingt beim Umsetzen des Roboters zwischen zwei Schlägen aktuell angenommen, dass die Fahrt zuerst zurück zur

Hofstelle und erst von dort zum nächsten Schlag führt, was das ökonomische Potential der FD20-Variante schmälern könnte. Dahingegen wurde das einmalig notwendige Einmessen eines Feldes mit dem FD20 nicht in der Berechnung berücksichtigt und somit der entsprechende Arbeitsaufwand außer Acht gelassen. In der Summe ist jedoch davon auszugehen, dass der aktuelle Modellansatz die Wirtschaftlichkeit des FD20 eher konservativ bewertet.

Schließlich ist anzumerken, dass es sich bei der vorliegenden Betrachtung um ein spezielles Szenario, sowohl in Bezug auf die Technologie als auch auf den Einsatzbereich, handelt. Der Farmdroid FD20 fordert spezielle Einsatzbedingungen hinsichtlich der Topografie, eine flächendeckende Mobilfunkabdeckung und eine möglichst feine Bodenbeschaffenheit ohne größere Steine. Nur so kann der Roboter als Präzisionswerkzeug die intendierten Arbeiten verrichten. Des Weiteren stellen sich Fragen der Übertragbarkeit auf andere Feldfrüchte, andere Arbeitsgänge und andere Roboterfabrikate. Die vorliegende Analyse kann nur einen ersten Hinweis auf mögliche Zusammenhänge liefern, welche es zur Verbesserung der Erkenntnisse auch unter anderen Annahmen zu testen gilt.

6 Schlussfolgerungen

Das vorgestellte Modell zur Bewertung der Wirtschaftlichkeit des Feldroboters Farmdroid FD20 zeigt dessen ökonomisches Potential in Abhängigkeit von u. a. der Anzahl benötigter Resthandhackstunden und den Lohnkosten für Saisonarbeitskräfte, welche der FD20 ersetzt. Obwohl die Studie nur einen ersten Ansatz einer Wirtschaftlichkeitsbewertung darstellt und somit vor allem als Anhaltspunkt für weitere Untersuchungen verwendet werden sollte, verdeutlicht sie das Potenzial der Robotik für arbeits- und somit kostenintensive Verfahren. Insbesondere in Situationen mit aus Bewirtschaftungssicht ungünstiger Flächenstruktur oder begrenzter betrieblicher Flächenausstattung kann eine Investitionsförderung wichtige Impulse zur Verbreitung der Feldrobotik leisten.

Literaturverzeichnis

[Ac20] Achilles, W. et al.: Betriebsplanung Landwirtschaft 2020/21. KTBL e.V., Darmstadt, 2020.

[BL14] Bayerische Landesanstalt für Landwirtschaft (LfL): Agrarstrukturentwicklung in Bayern – IBA-Agrarstrukturbericht 2014, https://www.lfl.bayern.de/mam/cms07/publikationen/daten/informationen/agrarsturkturentwicklung-bayern_lfl-information.pdf, Stand: 04.10.2022.

[BL22] Bundesinformationszentrum Landwirtschaft: Warum benötigt die Landwirtschaft so viele ausländische Saisonarbeitskräfte?, https://www.landwirtschaft.de/landwirtschaft-verstehen/haetten-siesgewusst/pflanzenbau/warum-benoetigt-die-landwirtschaft-so-viele-auslaendische-saisonarbeitskraefte, Stand: 27.10.2022

[DB22] Die Bundesregierung, Anpassung des gesetzlichen Mindestlohns, https://www.bundesregierung.de/breg-de/aktuelles/mindestlohn-gestiegen-1804568, Stand: 28.09.2022.

[Fa22] Farmdroid ApS, FAQ, https://farmdroid.dk/de/faq-deutsch/, Stand: 28.09.2022.

[Ga17] Gaus, C.-C. et al.: Mit autonomen Landmaschinen zu neuen Pflanzenbausystemen. Johann Heinrich von Thünen-Institut, Braunschweig, 2017.

[Ga18] Gaus, C.-C. et al.: Economics of Mechanical Weeding by a Swarm of Small Field Robots. In (Sauer, J. et al. Hrsg.): Vorträge der 57. Jahrestagung der GEWISOLA, München 2017. Landwirtschaftsverlag, Münster, S. 321-322, 2018.

[GGS21] Gabriel, A.; Gandorfer, M.; Spykman, O.: Nutzung und Hemmnisse digitaler Technologien in der Landwirtschaft – Sichtweisen aus der Praxis und in den Fachmedien. Berichte über Landwirtschaft, 99(1), 2021.

[HB19] Handler, F.; Blumauer, E.: Nebenzeiten und ablaufbedingte Wartezeiten beim Einsatz von Feldrobotern. In (Agroscope): 22. Arbeitswissenschaftliches Kolloquium, Agroscope Science Nr. 94/2020, S. 19-27, 2019.

[Ku21] Kuratorium für Technik und Bauwesen in der Landwirtschaft: KTBL-Feldarbeitsrechner, https://daten.ktbl.de/feldarbeit/home.html, Stand: 02.12.2021

[KV21] Kopfinger, S.; Vinzent, B.: Erprobung und Bewertung eines autonomen Feldroboters. In (Meyer-Aurich, A. et al.): Referate der 41. GIL-Jahrestagung, Gesellschaft für Informatik, Bonn, S. 175-180, 2021.

[Lo20] Lowenberg-DeBoer, J. et al.: Economics of robots and automation in field crop production. Precision Agriculture, 21, 278-299, 2020.

[Lo21a] Lowenberg-DeBoer, J. et al.: Economics of autonomous equipment for arable farms. Precision Agriculture, 22, S. 1996-2006, 2021.

[Lo21b] Lowenberg-DeBoer, J. et al. Lessons to be learned in adoption of autonomous equipment for field crops. Applied Economic Perspectives and Policy, 44, 2, S. 848-864.

[Ma19] Marinoudi V. et al.: Robotics and labour in agriculture. A context consideration. Biosystems Engineering, 184, S. 111-121, 2019.

[Ma21] Marinoudi V. et al.: The Future of Agricultural Jobs in View of Robotization. Sustainability, 13, 12109, 2021.

[Ma22a] Martin, T. et al.: Robots and transformations of work in farm: a systematic review of the literature and a research agenda. Agronomy for Sustainable Development, 42, 66, 2022.

[Ma22b] Maritan, E. et al.: Economically optimal farmer supervision of crop robots. Smart Agricultural Technology, 3, 100110, 2022.

[Mi22] Miller, C.: persönliche Mitteilung, Farmdroid-Händler Süddeutschland, 12.09.2022

[MR20] Mitaritonna, C.; Ragot, L.: After Covid-19, will seasonal migrant agricultural workers in Europe be replaced by robots?. CEPII Policy Brief No. 33 – June 2020. Centre d'études prospectives et d'informations internationales, Paris, 2020.

[Of22] Offermann, F. et al.: Umsetzung der EU Krisenmaßnahme nach Art. 219 GMO – Auswirkung des Preisanstiegs in Folge des Ukrainekriegs auf die verschiedenen Agrarsektoren – Stellungname für das BMEL. Thünen-Institut, Braunschweig, 2022.

[Pe06] Pedersen, S.M. et al.: Agricultural robots – system analysis and economic feasibitlity. Precision Agriculture, 7, S. 295-308, 2006.

[RCH21] Rübcke von Veltheim, R.; Clausen, F.; Heise, H.: Autonomous Field Robots in Agriculture: A Qualitative Analysis of User Acceptance According to Different Agricultural Machinery Companies. In (Gotter, C. et al. Hrsg.): Vorträge der 60. Jahrestagung der GEWISOLA, Halle (Saale) 2020. Landwirtschaftsverlag, Münster, S. 49-61, 2021.

[RH21] Rübcke von Veltheim, F.; Heise, H.: German Farmers' Attitudes on Adopting Autonomous Field Robots: an Empirical Survey. Agriculture, 11, 216, 2021.

[Ri18] Rial-Lovera, K.: Agricultural Robots: drivers, barriers and opportunities for adoption. In (ISPA Hrsg.): Proceedings of the 14th International Conference on Precision Agriculture, 24.-27. Juni 2018, Montreal, Quebec, Canada. 2018.

[Ro19] Rotz, S. et al.: Automated pastures and the digital divide: How agricultural technologies are shaping labour and rural communities. Journal of Rural Studies, 68, S. 112-122, 2019.

[RTH21] Rübcke von Veltheim, F.; Theuvsen, L.; Heise, H.: German farmers' intention to use autonomous field robots: a PLS-analysis. Precision Agriculture, 2021.

[SDS19] Shockley, J.M.; Dillon, C.R.; Shearer, S.A.: An economic feasibility assessment of autonomous field machinery in grain crop production. Precision Agriculture, 20, S. 1068-1085, 2019.

[SMJ05] Sørensen, C.G.; Madsen, N.A.; Jacobsen, B.H.: Organic Farming Scenarios: Operational Analysis and Costs of implementing Innovative Technologies. Biosystems Engineering, 91(2), S. 127-137, 2005.

[Sp21] Spykman, O. et al.: Farmers' perspectives on field crop robots – Evidence from Bavaria, Germany. Computers and Electronics in Agriculture, 186, 106176, 2021.

[WV22] Wirtschaftliche Vereinigung Zucker e. V.; Verein der Zuckerindustrie e. V.: Jahresbericht 2021/2022, https://www.zuckerverbaende.de/wp-content/uploads/2022/06/WVZ_VdZ_Jahresbericht_2021-2022.pdf, Stand: 05.10.2022

Instance-level augmentation for synthetic agricultural data using depth maps

Applying deep image compositing inspired techniques for augmentation

Henning Wübben[1], Raphaela Butz[2], Kai von Szadkowski[3] and Marco Barenkamp[4]

Abstract: Image augmentation is a key component in computer vision pipelines. Its techniques utilize different levels of data annotation. A lack of methods can be observed when it comes to data that supplies depth maps, in particular synthetic data. We propose a novel augmentation method named DepthAug that utilizes depth annotations in image data and examine its performance in the context of object detection tasks. Results show a boost in MAP score performance compared to previous related methods.

Keywords: image augmentation, synthetic data, deep image compositing, object detection, domain gap

1 Introduction

Generating synthetic data (SD) for machine learning applications is a promising method to overcome the lack of annotated data in computer vision. SD reduces human workload compared to the standard method of recording real world data and manually labeling it. Additionally, SD allows to create data for use cases where it is difficult to record real world data. In agriculture, such a use case could be the detection of a rare case of plant disease.

The drawbacks of this approach, however, are twofold. Firstly, computer-generated and specifically photo-realistically rendered images have a high demand in energy usage and rendering-time [Gr22]. Secondly, SD is never a perfect portrayal of the real world, an issue that is known as the reality gap in the machine learning community [Tr18].

Closing this gap is one of the purposes of Image Augmentation (IA), which is therefore of interest when working with SD. IA is the umbrella term of creating new training images from existing ones. IA is used to increase the performance of subsequent machine learning models. IA is an integral part of most computer vision machine learning pipelines and can be used during training, where it is an easy and in terms of computational effort cheap

---

[1] LMIS AG, Neumarkt 1, 49074 Osnabrück, hew@lmis.de
[2] LMIS AG, Neumarkt 1, 49074 Osnabrück, rbu@lmis.de
[3] DFKI GmbH, Berghoffstraße 11, 49090 Osnabrück, kai.von_szadkowski@dfki.de
[4] LMIS AG, Neumarkt 1, 49074 Osnabrück, mab@lmis.de

possibility to increase the performance of resulting models. In addition, IA allows for an increase in prediction quality in the inference stage [Ya22].

However, state of the art IA techniques are not designed to specifically work with SD. This is a waste of potential since SD can provide additional data such as depth maps that could be beneficial for augmentation techniques. [Gr22] recently underlined the need for such specialized techniques with emphasis on a more energy efficient data generation, stating that "As such, the design of surrogate synthesis models capable of augmenting synthetic datasets in a more energy-efficient fashion, […] is an important line of future research.". In the domain of agricultural image data, further characteristics can be identified, since images often contain a high degree of occlusion and order of only few instance classes, e.g., rows of maize plants on a field. Utilizing this domain-specific knowledge could also be a resource for better DA.

2 Related work

The related work differentiates between augmentation techniques which refer to basic operations and augmentation methods which bundle together different augmentation techniques. Generally, augmentations can be applied on whole images (image level), on the bounding boxes of instances (box level) or the actual pixels of an instance (instance level). Since SD allows annotations on the pixel level, instance level augmentations are of particular interest in this context.

2.1 Augmentation Techniques

Augmentation techniques include geometric transformations, color space augmentations and image compositing. Geometric transformations cover rescaling, rotating, flipping, and shearing operations. Their benefits for training and testing have been verified in several works [Le21; Sh21]. Color space augmentations exist in many different variants. They encompass techniques such as color jitter, change of contrast or brightness as well as blurring. Image compositing is the technique of combining visual elements from two or more images into a new one. This has been used for augmentation in techniques such as CutMix [Yu19] or AugMix [He19].

2.2 Augmentation Methods

Several methods exist that apply a mixture of the aforementioned augmentation techniques, few of which are concerned with instance level augmentation. *Cut, Paste and Learn* [Dw17] creates new datapoints for object detection tasks by randomly adding object instances to background images and applying further augmentation techniques like rotation to them. *InstaBoost* [Fa19] requires instance segmentations to move, scale and rotate instances within an image. It calculates appearance consistency maps to estimate appropriate positions for an object to appear in an image. *ObjectAug* [Zh21a] operates in a similar fashion while focusing on a category aware strategy that allows to effectively treat underrepresented classes in a dataset. *Copy-Paste* [Gh20] copies object instances of a dataset between images and argues against applying geometric transformations or blurring.

All these methods perform image compositing, but only Copy-Paste operates on a dataset rather than an image level and only InstaBoost tries to preserve realism by regarding object positions. None of the methods are designed to utilize depth information.

2.3 Deep image compositing

Image compositing is a technique that is frequently used in the realm of photography and raster graphic editors but is usually performed manually. Augmentation methods that combine elements of various images can be thought of as an imperfect but quick and autonomous image compositing technique.

Adding depth to this process enters the realm of deep image compositing which is an active field of research with the aim of creating image compositions of higher quality by utilizing depth information. It is especially interesting when working with synthetic data since the required amount of depth information is hard to obtain with real life data sets. Deep image compositing is used in semi-automatic manner [Eg15], but some researchers try to automate this process with the use of GANs [Zh21b].

Generally, compositing two images A and B to create a new image C can be broken down into 3 key problems:

1. Which parts of A and B to choose for composition
2. Where to place them in C
3. How to deal with artefacts in C

The first two points are highly dependent on the domain and the use case. Dealing with artefacts can be done by blending [Zh20] or inpainting [Te04].

2.4 Synthetic data

In terms of synthetic data, various software tools with differing focuses have been created in recent years. Many of which build upon the popular software Blender [Bl18] e.g., BlenSor [Gs11], Kubric [Gr22] and Syclops. BlenSor provides a collection of light detection, ranging (LIDAR/LADAR) and Kinect sensors. Kubric aims to provide a generic and scalable dataset generator. Syclops is designed to provide datasets specifically for the agricultural domain and is currently being developed within Agri-Gaia[5], the same context as this contribution.

---

[5] https://www.agri-gaia.de/

3 Method

The following method assumes input from Syclops or a similar synthetic data pipeline that can provide images with pixel-perfect instance segmentations as well as depth maps. The described algorithm is henceforth referred to as DepthAug.

The main idea of DepthAug is to improve upon the first two points of the key problems enumerated in 2.4 by utilizing the provided depth maps from Syclops. This is achieved by identifying object instances that can be considered as prototypes for their class. These prototypes are then subjected to color space and geometric augmentations. The manipulated prototypes are used to replace instances of the same class over the whole dataset.

In the initial setup DepthAug creates two collections from the dataset: the prototype collection (PC) and the background collection (BC).

3.1 Generating collections

The PC is comprised of all segmented objects that are fully visible. An object is fully visible if it is within the field of view of the image and is not occluded by another object. Hence, the PC consists exclusively of complete instances and stores them by class. One prototype is created by scanning the dataset and analyzing each object's instance segmentation mask. An object is complete if its segmentation mask does not touch the border of the image and its dilated segmentation mask does not overlap with any other objects segmentation mask that is closer to the camera according to the depth map. The PC stores each object together with its class, its depth value, and the position of its centroid relative to the camera in 3d space. After creation, the PC is enriched by applying the left-right flip operation on each of its members and adding it to the PC with its centroid position mirrored along the central vertical axis of the image.

The BC consists of all the images backgrounds. To create these backgrounds, each image is stripped of all objects leaving behind blank spaces in the image. These blank spaces are filled using the Telea inpainting algorithm [Te04] and are henceforth referred to as slots.

3.2 Generating new data

Generating new datapoints is achieved by iterating over the slots of all backgrounds in the BC and adding elements from the PC to them. This is done in a 3-step approach:

1. Selection
2. Augmentation
3. Positioning

The selection of appropriate objects from the PC for a given slot and its associated original object o is class and position sensitive. The position is regarded by drawing from the PC in a weighted manner. The weight $w(o,c)$ (Equation 1) applied to a candidate object c is the inverse L2 norm of the vector $v(o,c)$, which is the difference vector of the objects' centroids p_o and p_c.

$$w(o,c) = \frac{1}{||v(o,c)||}; \ v(o,c) = p_o - p_c$$

Equation 1: Priority weight of a candidate object c from the PC to be chosen for slot of original object o.

The augmentations applied to the selected object include rotation, scaling, color jitter, shearing. The strength of these augmentations is controllable via appropriate parameters.

The positioning of the selected object c within the slot is done in such a way that the centroids of o and c align. This approach serves as an easy heuristic to minimize the visible area of inpainted pixels.

Furthermore, the insertion enforces the depth value of o onto c and therefore ensures that the objects of the augmented image are placed in the same order as the ones in the original image.

4 Experiments

Two sets of experiments are performed. A synthetic dataset consisting of 110 images generated by Syclops will be subjected to augmentation and used to fine-tune a YOLOv5s model for object detection. The resulting models will be tested against different test data to retrieve MAP scores (MAP0.5 and MAP0.5-0.95) as the metric of comparison. The methods that are being compared with DepthAug are InstaBoost [Fa19] and Copy-Paste [Gh20]. Additionally, the unaugmented dataset will be used as a baseline for the experiment's results. For training, all YOLOv5 internal augmentations are turned off, otherwise all hyper parameters are kept at their default values. The number of epochs is set to 500.

The datasets contain a single class of objects, namely maize plants. Example images of the synthetic data set with their corresponding depth maps can be seen in Fig. 1.

Fig. 1: Example images from the Syclops dataset with depth maps

For the first set of experiments, the synthetic dataset is split into training, test and evaluation data with a 60:20:20 ratio. It is aimed at evaluating the performance boost of solely the image compositing mechanic of the three mentioned methods. Therefore, all other augmentation techniques are deactivated for each method by an appropriate choice of parameters. The respective augmentation methods are then applied to the training and validation data.

The second set of experiments aims to evaluate the capability of the methods to generalize onto real life datasets. Therefore, all augmentation techniques are activated and only 10 images of the synthetic dataset are used for training and evaluation. The 10 images are inflated by augmentation to a dataset of 110 images by creating 10 augmentations per image. The test dataset will be a small hand labeled real life dataset of maize plants. An example image of this dataset can be seen in Fig. 2.

Fig. 2: Example image from the real-life test data set

5 Results

Results show the visual differences of the regarded augmentation methods for only the image compositing technique of the first set of experiments in Fig. 3. For the second set of experiments, the full range of augmentations including compositing, geometric transformations and color augmentations can be seen in Fig. 4.

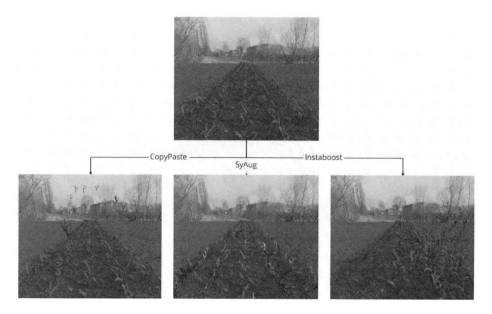

Fig. 3: Example results of the used augmentation methods for the first set of experiments. Showcasing only their image compositing capabilities

Fig. 4: Example results of the used augmentation methods for the second set of experiments. Showcasing compositing, geometric transformations and color augmentations

Tab. 1 shows the accuracy in terms of MAP0.5 and MAP0.5-0.95 for the object detection task as defined for the first set of experiments. Compared to the unaugmented baseline, results show an absolute increase of both MAP scores for the methods Copy-Paste and InstaBoost of 0.07 and 0.08 for MAP0.5 as well as 0.001 and 0.002 for MAP0.5-0.95 respectively. DepthAug shows an absolute increase of both MAP scores of 0.213 for MAP0.5 and 0.126 for MAP0.5-0.95.

Tab. 2 shows the accuracy in terms of MAP0.5 and MAP0.5-0.95 for the object detection task as defined for the second set of experiments. Compared to the unaugmented baseline, results show an absolute decrease of both MAP scores for the methods Copy-Paste and InstaBoost of 0.112 and 0.07 for MAP0.5 as well as 0.0392 and 0.0349 for MAP0.5-0.95 respectively. DepthAug shows an absolute increase of both MAP scores of 0.019 for MAP0.5 and 0.051 for MAP0.5-0.95.

Method	MAP0.5	MAP0.5-0.95
no augmentations / baseline	0.49	0.164
Copy-Paste	0.506	0.165
InstaBoost	0.508	0.166
DepthAug	0.703	0.29

Tab. 1: MAP0.5 and MAP0.5-0.95 scores of the methods Copy-Paste, InstaBoost and DepthAug for the object detection task from the first set of experiments

Method	MAP0.5	MAP0.5-0.95
no augmentations / baseline	0.425	0.124
Copy-Paste	0.313	0.0848
InstaBoost	0.355	0.0891
DepthAug	0.444	0.175

Tab. 2: MAP0.5 and MAP0.5-0.95 scores of the methods Copy-Paste, InstaBoost and DepthAug for the object detection task from the second set of experiments

6 Discussion

DepthAug arranges class instances in such a way that their order stays unaltered and therefore creates more realistic compositions as can be qualitatively observed in Fig. 3 and Fig. 4.

In terms of quantitative results, the first experiment shows big potential of using deep image compositing techniques for augmentation purposes. DepthAug's image compositing improves the performance on the test data set compared to the unaugmented training data. It also outperforms the image compositing of InstaBoost and Copy-Paste indicating that DepthAug's image compositing leads to a better generalization than depth agnostic approaches on agricultural data.

The results of the second experiment are less salient but DepthAug does show an improvement in performance compared to the unaugmented baseline. This is in strong contrast to Copy-Paste and InstaBoost which cause a decrease in accuracy for this use case, indicating that the augmented data created by these methods are less valuable for generalizing onto other datasets compared to the original data. A dataset consisting mainly of this kind of augmentations therefore deteriorates in quality. Augmentations created by DepthAug on the other hand seem to introduce more valuable variation into the training data and not suffer from this kind of dataset deterioration. The generally low MAP scores in this experiment may be attributed to the domain and reality gap between training and test data.

To solidify these findings, more experiments should be performed on different use cases of agricultural data as well as other domains. It is to be expected that DepthAug does perform particularly well on image data with high levels of occlusion.

7 Outlook

To further improve the augmentation on agricultural data, additional annotations and meta information from SD can be exploited. Future work could therefore focus on augmenting on the component level in addition to the instance level. In case of plants, that could entail annotating parts of the plant such as stems, leaves, or blossoms on the 3D models. This would allow the usage of domain knowledge by rearranging these components and creating more valuable augmentations that further increase model performance and decrease the demand for training data.

In addition, knowledge about the relative transform between camera frame and object during rendering could be used in the prototype selection stage to make more informed decisions and potentially even work across different datasets.

Finally, to increase the connection to the area of deep image compositing, the layer-based workflow could be replaced by a point cloud based one, which could make the applicability of DepthAug more generic and improve composition quality. This would enable advanced smoothing techniques, something that has not been considered in DepthAug yet.

Acknowledgements: We would like to thank Dr. Florian Rahe and Isabel Günther from AMAZONEN-WERKE H. Dreyer SE & Co. KG for providing the real-life data used in these experiments as well as Anton Elmiger from the DFKI for providing the synthetic data generated by Syclops.

This work was supported by the German Federal Ministry for Economic Affairs and Climate Action within the Agri-Gaia project (grant number: 01MK21004A). The DFKI Niedersachsen (DFKI NI) is sponsored by the Ministry of Science and Culture of Lower Saxony and the VolkswagenStiftung.

Bibliography

[Tr18] Tremblay, J.; Prakash, A.; Acuna, D.; Brophy, M.; Jampani, V., Anil C., To T., Cameracci, E., Boochoon, S.; Birchfield S.: „Training Deep Networks With Synthetic Data: Bridging the Reality Gap by Domain Randomization," in *Proceedings of the IEEE Conference on Computer Vision and Pattern Recognition (CVPR) Workshops*, 2018.

[Te04] Telea, A.: „An Image Inpainting Technique Based on the Fast Marching Method," *Journal of Graphics Tools*, Bd. 9, January 2004.

[Zh20] Zhang, L.; Wen, T.; Shi, J.: „Deep Image Blending," in Proceedings of the IEEE/CVF Winter Conference on Applications of Computer Vision (WACV), 2020.

[Zh21a] Zhang, J.; Zhang, Y.; Xu, X.: „ObjectAug: Object-level Data Augmentation for Semantic Image Segmentation," CoRR, Bd. abs/2102.00221, 2021.

[Zh21b] Zhang, H.; Zhang, J.; Perazzi, F.; Lin, Z.; Patel, V. M.: „Deep image compositing," in Proceedings of the IEEE/CVF Winter Conference on Applications of Computer Vision, 2021.

[Yu19] Yun, S., Han, D., Oh, S. J., Chun, S., Choe, J., Yoo, Y.: „CutMix: Regularization Strategy to Train Strong Classifiers with Localizable Features," CoRR, Bd. abs/1905.04899, 2019.

[Ya22] Yang, S., Xiao, W., Zhang, M., Guo, S., Zhao, J., Shen, F.: *Image Data Augmentation for Deep Learning: A Survey*, arXiv, 2022.

[Le21] Lewy, D.; J. Mandziuk: „An overview of mixing augmentation methods and augmentation strategies," *CoRR*, Bd. abs/2107.09887, 2021.

[He19] Hendrycks, D., Mu, N., Cubuk, E. D., Zoph, B., Gilmer, J., Lakshminarayanan, B.: *AugMix: A Simple Data Processing Method to Improve Robustness and Uncertainty*, arXiv, 2019.

[Gs11] Gschwandtner, M., Kwitt, R., Uhl, A., Pree, W.: „BlenSor: Blender Sensor Simulation Toolbox," in *Advances in Visual Computing*, Berlin, 2011.

[Gr22] Greff, K., Belletti, F., Beyer, L., Doersch, C., Du, Y., Duckworth, D., Fleet, D. J., Gnanapragasam, D., Golemo, F., Herrmann, C., Kipf, T., Kundu, A., Lagun, D., Laradji I., Liu Hsueh-Ti, Meyer H., Miao, Y., Nowrouzezahrai, D., Oztireli, C., Pot, E., Radwan N., Rebain, D., Sabour, S., Sajjadi, M. S. M., Sela, M., Sitzmann, V., Stone, A., Sun ,D., Vora, S., Wang, Z., Wu, T., Yi, K. M., Zhong, F., Tagliasacchi A.: *Kubric: A scalable dataset generator*, arXiv, 2022.

[Gh20] Ghiasi, G., Cui, Y., Srinivas, A., Qian, R., Lin, T.-Y., Cubuk, E. D., Le, Q. V., Zoph B.: „Simple Copy-Paste is a Strong Data Augmentation Method for Instance Segmentation," *CoRR*, Bd. abs/2012.07177, 2020.

[Fa19] Fang, H., Sun, J., Wang, R., Gou, M., Li, Y., Lu, C.: „InstaBoost: Boosting Instance Segmentation via Probability Map Guided Copy-Pasting," *CoRR*, Bd. abs/1908.07801, 2019.

[Eg15] Egstad, J., Davis, M. Lacewell, D.: „Improved deep image compositing using subpixel masks," in *Proceedings of the 2015 Symposium on Digital Production*, 2015.

[Dw17] Dwibedi, D., Misra, I., M. Hebert: „Cut, Paste and Learn: Surprisingly Easy Synthesis for Instance Detection," *CoRR,* Bd. abs/1708.01642, 2017.

[Bl18] Community, B. O., „Blender - a 3D modelling and rendering package," Stichting Blender Foundation, Amsterdam, 2018. [Online]. Available: http://www.blender.org.

Vom RESTful Webservice für Pflanzenschutzmittelregistrierungsdaten zur anwendungsunabhängigen Ontologie

Öffentliche Daten auf die nächste Stufe heben

Katharina Albrecht [1], Kristoffer Janis Schneider[1] und Daniel Martini[1]

Abstract: Bei der Ausbringung von Pflanzenschutzmitteln müssen Abstandsauflagen eingehalten werden. Allerdings müssen diese händisch ermittelt und berücksichtigt werden. Um den Landwirt dabei zu unterstützen, wurde im PAM-Projekt ein Entscheidungshilfesystem entwickelt. Ein Teil dieses Systems ist der Abstandsauflagendienst, den das KTBL bereitstellt. Für diesen Dienst wurde ein Prozess entwickelt, welcher die Pflanzenschutzmittelregistrierungsdaten aus einer REST-Schnittstelle ausliest, die ausgelesenen Informationen mit Hilfe eines RML-Mappings in eine Ontologie überführt und diese über einen SPARQL-Endpoint anwendungsunabhängig abrufbar macht.

Keywords: Linked Open Data, Ontologie, Semantic Web, RML, SPARQL

1 Einleitung

Die maschinelle Ausbringung von Pflanzenschutzmitteln (PSM) ist Stand der Technik; Schläge werden GPS-geführt befahren, mit Applikationskarten können Abstände zu Saumstrukturen, Oberflächengewässern oder urbanen Strukturen definiert werden und über die Teilbreitenabschaltung können die PSM gezielt appliziert werden. Dies geschieht jedoch nicht automatisch. Noch immer obliegt es dem Landwirt, diese einzuhaltenden Abstände manuell aus den Auflagentexten in der vom Bundesamt für Verbraucherschutz und Lebensmittelsicherheit (BVL) bereitgestellten Zulassungsdatenbank, im Folgenden PSM-DB genannt, zu ermitteln und sie entweder in die Applikationskarte einzupflegen oder während der Ausbringung einzuhalten. Des Weiteren müssen Aktualisierungen regelmäßig überprüft und vorgenommen werden. Dieses Vorgehen ist nicht nur zeitintensiv, sondern auch fehleranfällig.

Um den Landwirt dabei zu unterstützen, wurde in den PAM-Projekten ein Entscheidungshilfesystem [Sc16] entwickelt. Während der Projektlaufzeiten ist am KTBL ein Prozess entstanden, welcher die Auflagendaten mit Hilfe von Linked Open Data

---

[1] Kuratorium für Technik und Bauwesen in der Landwirtschaft e.V., Digitale Technologien, Bartningstraße 49, 64289 Darmstadt, k.albrecht@ktbl.de, https://orcid.org/0000-0002-3400-8102, k.schneider@ktbl.de, d.martini@ktbl.de

(LOD) maschinenlesbar und anwendungsunabhängig bereitstellt. Dabei werden die Zulassungsdaten mit Hilfe eines deklarativen Mappings aus der vorhandenen Datenbank in als Resource Description Framework (RDF) [BG04] triples repräsentierte Aussagen überführt. Die triples wiederum werden in einem Triplestore bereitgestellt und mit Hilfe von SPARQL Queries abgefragt. Das BVL hat im Jahr 2020 an der Initiative tech4germany[2] teilgenommen und stellt seitdem die PSM-DB über eine RESTful Schnittstelle bereit. So ist es möglich, mit geeigneten technischen Werkzeugen auf die verschiedenen Tabellen zuzugreifen. Dies ist ein bedeutender Schritt hinsichtlich der Maschinenlesbarkeit der Zulassungsdaten.

2 Stand des Wissens

In den vergangenen PAM-Projekten wurde der Abstandsauflagendienst entwickelt und fortwährend an neue Entwicklungen angepasst und verbessert. [Ma15] stellt die initiale Entwicklung eines Mappingprozesses dar und [Ma18] beschreibt den PSM Mappingprozess, der während des ersten PAM-Projektes entstanden ist. Im Folgeprojekt PAMrobust wurde besonderer Wert auf die Nutzung von Standards und auf die Reduktion der Medienbrüche gelegt. Dieser Mappingprozess ist in [AMS19] zusammengefasst. Die Datenstruktur und inhaltliche Darstellung wurden in PAM3D verfeinert und bilden somit die Basis für die nachfolgend beschriebenen Arbeiten, welche während der Laufzeit von PAM-M durchgeführt wurden.

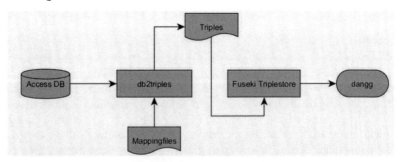

Abb. 1: PSM-Daten liegen in einer Access DB vor, werden mit db2triples gemappt und über den Fuseki Triplestore via Webdienst dangg bereitgestellt

In Abb. 1**Fehler! Verweisquelle konnte nicht gefunden werden.** ist der bisherige Mappingprozess dargestellt. Zunächst bildete eine relationale Datenbank die Datengrundlage. Mit Hilfe des Mapping-Tools db2triples, welches R2RML [DSC12] implementiert, wurden die relationalen Daten in RDF triples übersetzt. Diese triples wurden über den Apache Jena Fuseki[3] Triplestore publiziert, sodass über SPARQL-

---
[2] https://tech.4germany.org/project/psm/
[3] https://jena.apache.org/documentation/fuseki2/

Abfragen [HS13] auf die Daten zugegriffen werden konnte. Zusätzlich wurden die Informationen über einen Webdienst des KTBL veröffentlicht.

Bisher bestand hinsichtlich der Aktualität der bereitgestellten Ontologie eine starke Abhängigkeit gegenüber der Access DB, welche manuell bereitgestellt, gespeichert und verarbeitet wurde. Dank der Bereitstellung der PSM-DB als REST-Service ist diese Abhängigkeit nicht mehr gegeben. Die RESTful-Bereitstellung ermöglicht zukünftig ein vollständig automatisiertes Auslesen der Daten. Für den PAM-Prozess bedeutete dies zunächst eine Überarbeitung des bestehenden Vorgehens. Es musste ein neuer Prozess zur Abfrage der REST API implementiert werden, und das darauf aufbauende Mapping sowie die Bereitstellung der Daten mussten den neuen Ansprüchen genügen. Zudem wurde das Quellcode-Repositorium für db2triples auf GitHub geschlossen und das Werkzeug offenbar nicht mehr weiterentwickelt oder aktualisiert. Daher musste für das Mapping eine Alternative gefunden und eingesetzt werden.

3 Der PAM-Prozess

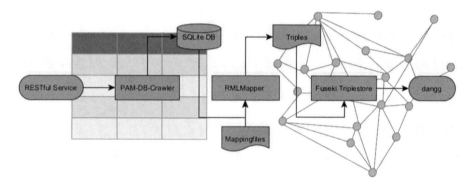

Abb. 2: PSM-Daten werden als RESTful-Service bereitgestellt, mit dem PAM-DB-Crawler abgefragt und in einer SQLite DB gespeichert. Das Mapping wird mit dem RMLMapper prozessiert und die Bereitstellung erfolgt über einen Fuseki Triplestore und via Webservice dangg

Abb. 2 zeigt den weiterentwickelten PAM-Prozess. Die PSM-DB, welche über den RESTful Webservice bereitgestellt wird, wird vom PAM-DB-Crawler[4] abgerufen und in eine SQLite-Datenbank gespeichert. Dies wird in Abschnitt 3.1 erläutert. Im nachfolgenden Abschnitt 3.2 wird das Mapping erläutert. Dabei werden die Informationen aus der SQLite-DB mit Hilfe von Mapping-Dateien und des Mapping tools RMLMapper[5] von rml.io in RDF triples übertragen. In Abschnitt 3.3 folgt dann die Erläuterung der Bereitstellung per Fuseki Triplestore.

---

[4] https://github.com/KTBL/PAM-DB-Crawler
[5] https://github.com/RMLio/rmlmapper-java

3.1 PAM-DB-Crawler

Die Inhalte der PSM-DB werden vom BVL bereitgestellt und können dort via REST-API abgefragt werden. Der REST-Service[6] liefert die Daten im JSON-Datenformat zurück. Jede Tabelle aus der PSM-DB wird als eigene Schnittstelle bereitgestellt und kann per HTTP-GET abgefragt werden. Da die meisten Schnittstellen sehr große Datenmengen zurückliefern (deutlich über 100 Datenelemente), wird ein Paging-Mechanismus genutzt. Um weitere Elemente abzufragen, kann der „offset" Parameter URL-kodiert mitgegeben werden. Bei Bedarf kann die Page-Größe via des „limit" Parameter verändert werden.

Um das bereits entwickelte Mapping weiter nutzen zu können, werden die PSM-Daten in einer relationalen Datenbank benötigt. Mithilfe des REST-Service bietet sich die Möglichkeit, alle Daten abzufragen und in einer lokalen Datenbank zu speichern. Ein Weg, dies umzusetzen, wäre die Datenmodelldefinitionen zu nutzen, um händisch passende Datenstrukturen zu erstellen, diese mittels API-Abfragen zu befüllen und die abgefragten Daten in einer SQLite-Datenbank zu speichern. Bei diesem Vorgehen ist jedoch viel Boilerplate-Code notwendig. Zur Reduktion des Boilerplate-Codes bietet es sich an, einen Generator im Sinne der Meta-Programmierung zu verwenden. Ein solcher Generator erzeugt auf Basis von Definitionsinformationen den Code automatisch.

Ein großer Vorteil dieses Vorgehens ist, dass Änderungen am Datenmodell oder an der Adresse der Schnittstellen schnell eingepflegt und auf verschiedenen Wegen angepasst werden können.

3.2 PSM-Mapping

Die nun in einer SQLite-DB vorliegenden PSM-Daten müssen mit Hilfe eines Mappingverfahrens aus der relationalen Darstellung in RDF triples überführt werden. Dabei reicht es nicht, nur die einzelne Tabelle zu mappen, sondern es müssen auch Beziehungen zwischen Tabellen berücksichtigt werden, wie in nachfolgendem Beispiel zu sehen ist.

AWG_ID	...
034028-60/07-004	...
...	...

AWG_ID	KULTUR	...
034028-60/07-004	RUBID	...
...	...	...

Abb. 3: links: ein Auszug aus Tabelle AWG, rechts: ein Auszug aus Tabelle AWG_KULTUR

Abb. 3 zeigt Auszüge aus zwei Tabellen der PSM-DB. Die Tabelle AWG beinhaltet übergreifende Informationen zu den jeweiligen Indikationen. Dabei ist die AWG_ID die ID der Indikation und verbindet somit die jeweiligen Informationen miteinander. Die zweite Tabelle zeigt einen Auszug aus AWG_KULTUR, also jene Kultur, auf die das Pflanzenschutzmittel mit der jeweiligen Indikation angewandt wird. Um aus diesen zwei

---

[6] https://psm-api.bvl.bund.de

Tabellen eine Aussage, also ein RDF triple zu erstellen, müssen diese gemeinsam gemappt werden. Dafür werden in der Mappingdatei mit Hilfe von Triples Maps die Aussagen definiert. Diese bestehen immer aus einem Subjekt und ein oder mehreren Prädikaten und Objekten. Triples Maps werden dann über sogenannte Join-Conditions verknüpft. Abbildung 4 zeigt die Umsetzung des oben genannten Beispiels.

```
psmr:ind_034028-60-07-004
        rdf:type          psm:Indication ;
        psm:appliedOnCrop psmr:crop_RUBID .
```

Abb. 4: Mapping-Ergebnis für die Beispielindikation 034028-60/07-004

3.3 Triplestore und Bereitstellung

Um die generierte Ontologie abrufbar zu machen, müssen die Triple in einen Triplestore geladen werden. Dieser Triplestore wird über einen SPARQL-Endpoint verfügbar gemacht und kann dann mittels der standardisierten Abfragesprache SPARQL abgefragt werden. Zur Publikation der Daten wird der Fuseki-Server genutzt. SPARQL Queries können entweder direkt in der Benutzeroberfläche des Fuseki oder per HTTP-POST abgesetzt werden. Über eine DESCRIBE Query können alle Informationen abgerufen werden, die mit der gewählten Indikation verknüpft sind. Weiterhin können SELECT Queries, welche einfache Abfragen mit tabellarischer Ausgabe ähnlich SQL ermöglichen, oder CONSTRUCT Queries, mit deren Hilfe selektiv Untergraphen erstellt werden, definiert werden. Sofern bei der Implementierung des Endpoints vorgesehen, sind auch UPDATE Queries möglich. Als Rückgabeformat stehen eine Reihe von Formaten zur Verfügung, darunter Turtle, JSON-LD, N-Triples oder XML.

4 Ergebnisse und Diskussion

Der am KTBL entwickelte Abstandsauflagendienst gibt alle Abstandsauflagen, welche für eine bestimmte Indikation berücksichtigt werden müssen, im JSON-LD[7] Format zurück. Die Bereitstellung der PSM-DB über eine RESTful-Schnittstelle vereinfacht den PAM-Prozess deutlich. Durch die Nutzung des PAM-DB-Crawlers können die Daten flexibel in die SQLite-DB gespeichert und gemappt werden. Der RML-Mapper ist ein adäquater Ersatz für db2triples und bietet Raum für weitere Verbesserungen, z.B. das Einbeziehen weiterer Datenquellen in anderen Datenformaten wie JSON oder CSV. Die Nutzung von Fuseki hat sich ebenfalls bewährt. Insgesamt bietet der PAM-Prozess nun einen zuverlässigen Weg, um insbesondere die Abstandsauflagen der PSM-DB anwendungsunabhängig und maschinenlesbar bereitzustellen.

---

[7] https://json-ld.org/

5 Ausblick

Die BVL REST-API ermöglicht die vollständige Automatisierung des PAM-Prozesses. Die Entwicklung des PAM-DB-Crawlers ist dabei ein essenzieller Schritt hinsichtlich dieser Automatisierung. Um Redundanzen und Fehlinformationen bei Aktualisierungen zu vermeiden, muss hier jedoch noch ein geeignetes Vorgehen entwickelt werden. Des Weiteren ist es mit dem RML-Mapper möglich, das erstellte Mapping automatisch auf einen SPARQL Endpoint via SPARQL-Update zu publizieren. Hierfür sind noch Überlegungen zum Aufbau einer stabilen Infrastruktur notwendig, um sowohl eine stabile Bereitstellung als auch einen sicheren Betrieb gewährleisten zu können.

Förderhinweis: Die Förderung des Vorhabens FKZ 321-06.01-28-RZ-5-105 erfolgt aus Mitteln der Landwirtschaftlichen Rentenbank. Die Projektträgerschaft erfolgt über die Landwirtschaftliche Rentenbank im Förderprogramm Innovationsförderung.

Literaturverzeichnis

[AMS19] Albrecht, K.; Martini, D.; Schmitz, M.: Linked Open Data im Pflanzenschutz – Maschinenlesbare Bereitstellung der notwendigen Informationen zu Indikationen und Abstandsauflagen. In: Meyer-Aurich, A.; Gandorfer, M.; Barta, N.; Gronauer, A.; Kantelhardt, J.; Floto, H. (Hrsg.): 39. GIL-Jahrestagung, Digitalisierung für landwirtschaftliche Betriebe in kleinstrukturierten Regionen – ein Widerspruch in sich? Bonn: Gesellschaft für Informatik e.V. S. 19-24, 2019.

[DSC12] Das, S.; Sundara S.; Cyganiak, R.: R2RML: RDB to RDF Mapping Language, https://www.w3.org/TR/r2rml/, Stand: 12.10.2022.

[HS13] Harris, S.; Seaborne, A.: SPARQL 1.1 Query Language. World Wide Web Consortium, 2013. http://www.w3.org/TR/sparql11-query/, Stand: 12.10.2022.

[Ma15] Martini, D. et al.: KTBL-Planungsdaten auf dem Weg in die Zukunft – Bereitstellung über Linked Open Data. In: Ruckelshausen, A.; Schwarz, H.-P.; Theuvsen, B. (Hrsg.), Informatik in der Land-, Forst- und Ernährungswirtschaft 2015, Geisenheim. GI-Edition Lecture Notes in Informatics, Bd. 238, Bonn, S. 105-108, 2015.

[Ma18] Martini, D.: Webservices auf heterogenen Datenbeständen – Methoden der Umsetzung am Beispiel der KTBL-Planungsdaten. In: Ruckelshausen, A.; Meyer-Aurich, A.; Borchard, K.; Hofacker, C.; Loy, J.-P.; Schwerdtfeger, R.; Sundermeier, H.-H. F.; Theuvsen, B. (Hrsg.): 38. GIL-Jahrestagung, Digitale Marktplätze und Plattformen. Bonn: Gesellschaft für Informatik e.V. S. 155-158, 2018.

[PC13] Prud'hommeaux, E.; Carothers, G.: Turtle – Terse RDF Triple Language. World Wide Web Consortium, 25 February 2014. http://www.w3.org/TR/turtle/, Stand: 12.10.2022.

[Sc16] Scheiber, M. et al.: Pflanzenschutz-Anwendungs-Manager (PAM): Automatisierte Berücksichtigung von Abstandsauflagen. Praktische Vorführung und Feldtestergebnisse. In: Ruckelshausen, A.; Meyer-Aurich, A.; Rath, T.; Recke, G.; Theuvsen, B. (Hrsg.): Informatik in der Land-, Forst- und Ernährungswirtschaft 2016. Bonn: Gesellschaft für Informatik e.V. S. 177-180, 2016.

A systematic approach to the development of long-term autonomous robotic systems for agriculture

Tim Bohne[1], Gurunatraj Parthasarathy[1] and Benjamin Kisliuk[1]

Abstract: For robots to compete with conventional machinery in agriculture, improving their long-term autonomy seems necessary. In this article, we provide concepts and intermediate results of our work aimed at a long-term autonomous robotic system performing a plant monitoring task. Based on notions from literature, we introduce a structured approach to defining long-term autonomy and report on the system we develop that meets this definition in practical experiments. Finally, we present intermediate results from simulation and discuss further avenues of research.

Acknowledgements: The DFKI Niedersachsen (DFKI NI) is sponsored by the Ministry of Science and Culture of Lower Saxony and the Volkswagenstiftung. The paper describes work carried out in the context of the funded projects PORTAL (BMEL, FKZ: 28DK111B20) and ZLA (NiMWK, Volkswagenstiftung, ZDIN 11-76251-14-3/19).

Keywords: long-term autonomy, agricultural robotics

1 Introduction

The agricultural domain poses distinctive challenges for robotic systems to act independently of human supervision over prolonged periods of time due to the typical farm environment being neither under full control nor fully known to the system at any point in time. This might be the reason why most available products and prototypes deployed over long durations fulfill only very basic tasks and often require a controlled environment. However, as long-term autonomy (LTA) promises to be a cornerstone for robots competing with conventional machinery in more complex tasks in the future, it remains a challenge to develop flexible robotic systems for LTA deployment. To enable systematic improvement and evaluation of LTA capabilities, a sound definition of the concepts of *long-term* and *autonomy* in this context is essential. We reuse the AROX platform from [Ho20], seen in Figure 1a. Figure 1b shows the test site created in 2022 to facilitate long-term autonomy experiments by providing agricultural test beds in an enclosed area. The goal of the system is to accomplish the plant monitoring application described in [Ti22], i.e., to continuously acquire canola plant data.

---

[1] Deutsches Forschungszentrum für Künstliche Intelligenz (DFKI) GmbH, Plan-Based Robot Control, Berghoffstraße 11, 49090 Osnabrueck, Germany, <firstname.lastname>@dfki.de

Fig. 1: (a) AROX platform and base station [Ho20] (b) Test plot for canola monitoring

2 Relevant work and definitions

Although work regarding robotic LTA reaches back at least a decade [BKS13], the special case of LTA in agriculture as an application domain with very specific requirements [BV16] is gaining traction with many publications in recent years. Kunze et al. describe technological building blocks for addressing LTA in robotic systems, with work concerning agriculture focusing on navigation and mapping in changing environments [Ku18]. The following sections rely on the work described in [Pa22; Bo22].

2.1 What is autonomy?

In practice, robots are not expected to operate in complete isolation, but to act and self-preserve within the scope of their task without external supervision. Moreover, some functions of a robot may operate autonomously while others do not, rendering the integrated robot "partially autonomous". Figure 2 shows concepts of different degrees of autonomy, derived from [He15]. For this work, the AROX should be able to operate fully autonomously for what we call an *LTA episode,* i.e., a period of time that is plausible in the context of plant monitoring.

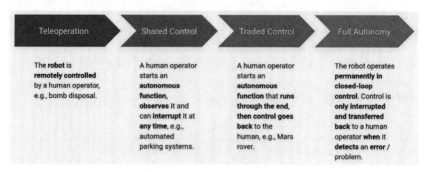

Fig. 2: Spectrum of autonomy

2.2 How long is long-term?

Likewise, LTA is usually not expected to persist indefinitely, and other authors have defined varying time spans for their respective applications [Ha17; Ku18; Br18]. While the hardware and process can be considered static for the scope of our work, the environment introduces dynamics that occur on various time scales such as hours (day-night), days (predictable weather changes), weeks (plant growth), seasons (snow, leaf discoloration), and years (tree growth / removal) posing requirements for the implemented system. Moreover, robotic hardware constraints introduce a "temporal action radius" by enforcing interruptions for refueling, data storage clearing, or maintenance. A typical agricultural process might consist of multiple refueling cycles for single events such as harvesting, where a robot must return to a power supply station or unload harvested crops several times. For continuous applications, e.g., weeding or monitoring, such multi-cycle missions may be repeated and spread over a certain growth period spanning weeks. If other factors lead to multiple upper bounds, the lowest one defines the limit for an LTA episode. In our case, we found that the hardware maintenance interval sets a plausible upper bound of one week for LTA episodes.

2.3 Simplified LTA plant monitoring scenario

To approach the complex problem of LTA in a structured way, the core idea of our research is to start from a simplified practical scenario that allows to conduct experiments with a likewise simplified system that nevertheless satisfies the previously given definition. In earlier work, we described a monitoring application for plant breeding [Ti20], which is outlined in Figure 3. With a time frame of one week per LTA episode and a few hours per multi-cycle mission derived from practical experience, we can initially assume unexpected changes in energy consumption as the only dynamic to consider, which occurs frequently in practice.

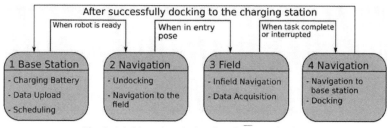

Fig. 3: Multi-cycle mission for plant monitoring [Ti20]

3 Implementation of the system

In literature, there are overviews of robotic capabilities related to LTA that have been the subject of extensive research [Ku18; BV16], focusing on motion control, navigation, mapping, and localization for agricultural scenarios, for which a plethora of established software modules are available in the ROS ecosystem. For top-level control and plan execution, a simple state machine was implemented that can handle external interruptions from modular health monitoring solutions such as the battery watchdog (cf. sec. 3.2). Since robustness and verifiability of robotic systems is mentioned in many publications as a focus of future research, we anticipate this already in the design of the control architecture. Initially, we consider only energy consumption as an uncontrolled dynamic, so we concentrate on autonomous energy supply (cf. sec. 3.1) and a battery monitoring system (cf. sec. 3.2) as a substitute for other monitoring systems to be included in the future.

3.1 Autonomous energy supply

The ability to recharge is crucial for multi-cycle missions. Arvin et al. divide it into three subproblems: observing the charge level, localization and navigation to the charging station, and docking [ASR09]. The latter is implemented by a *Hough transform* based shape detection of the base station in a continuously updated laser scan (cf. fig. 4), upon which we compute a goal pose inside that can be adopted using the navigation module. As a prerequisite, the robot must be in the vicinity of the base station and roughly oriented towards it.

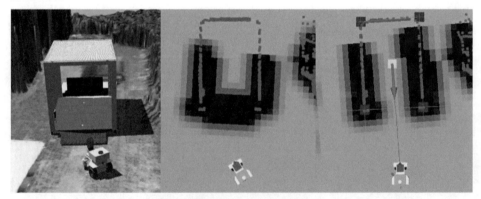

Fig. 4: (a) Robot facing base station (b) Base station perception based on lidar data (c) Successful detection of base station shape

3.2 Battery watchdog system

In practice, even with good planning, there is a risk of the robot not reaching the base station due to battery depletion because of unexpectedly high energy consumption. In this work, this is ensured by a real-time battery watchdog system that interrupts current actions and drives to the base station for recharging when the battery level drops below a safety threshold, which is the sum of a pre-set value and a dynamically calculated prediction of how much energy the return to base will consume. This prediction is continuously updated using the navigation module, which means that improving the navigation planner will also improve battery management. If the remaining energy is determined to be insufficient to return to base safely, human assistance is called for by the robot. Naturally, the parameters for these calculations were optimized for a tradeoff between safety and not having to return to recharge too frequently.

4 Experiments and evaluation

At the time of writing this article, first successes have been realized in running the described components on the physical AROX platform, but no integrated runs have yet been conducted. Therefore, we report on experiments performed using the *Gazebo* simulator for ROS systems. When an LTA episode in a physical experiment were to span a week, this would roughly correspond to *2* to *4* missions repeated on non-consecutive days, with the time in between waiting in the base station. In simulation, this number of missions can be reasonably completed in about *5* hours of runtime by skipping idle time. A single multi-cycle mission is represented as a plan incorporating all the steps of the simplified scenario, including several planned returns to base for recharging and all the actions described. Moreover, it covers a variety of situations by navigating to different locations.

To evaluate the experiments, two metrics were used, namely *mission failures* and *autonomy percentage* based on [Ha17]. The autonomy percentage is the ratio of time spent performing autonomous tasks to the total runtime; this is expected to be higher than in real applications, though, as we omit the main waiting times. We define a mission as failed when a timeout $t = 900\ s$ is exceeded without action completion. Also, any occurrence of a failure signal in the state machine is considered a failed mission, e.g., in case of a completely discharged battery. The experiment was performed three times with no failures, at an average of *5.09* hours, *3.67* completed missions, and *106.67* tasks. It required an average of *9.67* charge cycles, and the average total distance traveled was *1102.68 m*. The autonomy percentage was *97.15 %* on average. Although three runs do not guarantee flawless usage of the system, they demonstrate that the expected basic functionality is achieved in a setup meeting the definition of long-term autonomy.

5 Discussion and future avenues

The experiments show that the introduced definitions can be used for the development and evaluation of an LTA system. We argue that the choice of a particular time frame for an LTA episode depends on the combination of robot, application, and domain. In turn, the challenges that must be solved for successful integration of such a system depend on the application and episode length. To narrow down the initial tests, we only considered energy supply and consumption. However, it can be argued that longer LTA episodes are of interest for actual productive use, leading to additional dynamics that need to be addressed in the future, especially along seasonal cycles. These include weather extremes, harsh ground conditions, lighting changes, obstacles (static / dynamic) blocking the robot's path, but also less tangible aspects such as perceptual aliasing, which involves recognizing certain objects or places under altered circumstances, which is far from trivial. In addition, system dynamics such as connectivity issues that do not necessarily affect the environment but the robot itself, must be managed adequately to achieve true long-term autonomy. We plan to integrate the described system into the physical AROX and extend it to enhance its LTA capabilities. This includes a more general framework for monitoring various relevant aspects of system health and the ability to deal with broader environmental dynamics. Additionally, the navigation and mapping modules will be improved to enable intelligent adaptation of the used planners.

Bibliography

[ASR09] Arvin, F. et al.: Swarm robots long term autonomy using moveable charger. International Conference on Future Computer and Communication. IEEE, 2009.

[BKS13] Barfoot, T.; Kelly J.; Sibley, G.: Special issue on long-term autonomy. IJRR, 2013.

[Bo22]   Bohne, T.: Execution Monitoring for Long-Term Autonomous Plant Observation with a Mobile Robot, Osnabrück University, 2022.

[Br18]   Brommer, C. et al.: Long-Duration Autonomy for Small Rotorcraft UAS Including Recharging. IEEE International Conference on Intelligent Robots and Systems, 2018.

[BV16]   Bechar, A.; Vigneault, C.: Agricultural robots for field operations: Concepts and components. Bio. Eng., 2016.

[Ha17]   Hawes, N. et al.: The STRANDS Project. IEEE Robotics & Automation Magazine, 2017.

[He15]   Hertzberg, J.: Technische Gestaltungsoptionen für autonom agierende Komponenten und Systeme. In: Das Recht vor den Herausforderungen der modernen Technik, 2015.

[Ho20]   Hoellmann, M. et al.: Towards Context-Aware Navigation for Long-Term Autonomy in Agricultural Environments. IEEE/RSJ International Conference on Intelligent Robots and Systems, 2020.

[Ku18]   Kunze, L. et al.: Artificial Intelligence for Long-Term Robot Autonomy: A Survey. IEEE Robotics and Automation Letters, 2018.

[Pa22]   Parthasarathy, G.: Towards Long-Term Autonomous Survivability in Agriculture: A real-time safety watchdog to ensure the survivability of an outdoor plant monitoring robot., KTH Royal Institute of Technology, 2022.

[Ti22]   Tieben, C. et al.: Erste Schritte zu einem virtuellen Zuchtgarten. 42. GIL-Jahrestagung. Bonn: Gesellschaft für Informatik e.V. (S. 295-300), 2022.

Data sovereignty needs in agricultural use cases

Fredrik Boye[1], Raghad Matar[2] and Philipp Neuschwander[2]

Abstract: With today's shift towards digital farming, data transfer and processing are becoming increasingly essential for optimizing farm operations. In the complex arable farming sector, there exist numerous use cases involving a variety of actors and processes. Designing new digital ecosystems, such as agricultural data spaces that support existing workflows while enabling new opportunities for data-driven services, requires a good understanding of existing processes and data sovereignty needs. In this paper, we categorize data exchange use cases in arable farming and analyze the respective data sovereignty needs for each category. The results of our contribution can be used as a basis for further analysis and evaluation of data-sharing approaches in terms of their suitability for meeting different data sovereignty needs in agriculture, as well as in the process of requirements analysis when designing such systems.

Keywords: digital agriculture, data sovereignty, agricultural data space, data sharing

1 Introduction

With the technological advancement and the emergence of big data applications, legal questions related to data collection and usage are being discussed. Within the European Union, the General Data Protection Regulation [Eu18] is the most prominent legal act related to personal data. However, for non-personal data, the legal situation is more complicated. This issue has been discussed in the agricultural domain [Sy16; Vo20], where the situation is still rather unsatisfactory from the farmer's viewpoint.

Nowadays, agricultural data is collected from multiple sources. This data must be shared between different entities to realize its full potential. However, due to the absence of data privacy regulations and the lack of trust in agricultural service providers, farmers have concerns about misuse and loss of control over their data [Ja19; Wi19]. These concerns should be considered when designing and implementing smart farming applications [Ja19]. According to [Ma22], introducing appropriate data sovereignty models would address these concerns and thus increase farmers' willingness to share farm data. In the context of the Fraunhofer lighthouse project COGNAC (Cognitive Agriculture), we motivate the need for an agricultural data space (ADS) that takes farmers' considerations into account by its design [Ka22]. Data sovereignty was one of the key domain challenges we identified while analyzing the requirements of such a data space. In COGNAC, we

---

[1] Fraunhofer IVI, Fraunhofer Institute for Transportation and Infrastructure Systems, 01069 Dresden, fredrik.boye@ivi.fraunhofer.de
[2] Fraunhofer IESE, Fraunhofer Institute for Experimental Software Engineering, 67663 Kaiserslautern, raghad.matar@iese.fraunhofer.de, philipp.neuschwander@iese.fraunhofer.de

define data sovereignty in the agricultural domain as "the ability to make self-determined decisions about the use of data collected in the context of one's own farm, to understand the impact of these decisions, and to change these decisions at any time" [Fh19].

To build sound and holistic concepts for agricultural data spaces, it is necessary to identify possible data exchange use cases in the agricultural domain. Although such classes of use cases are well known in practice, to the best of our knowledge no study in literature provides a clear classification of agricultural data exchange use cases. During the process of designing a concept of an ADS in COGNAC, we investigated agricultural data exchange use cases and developed a general classification based on our analysis of the domain. Then we extracted the farmer's data sovereignty needs for each category. In Chapter 2, we present our results for the categories and derived needs, and in Chapter 3, we discuss the findings and provide an outlook on future work.

2 Data sovereignty in agriculture

In this chapter, we will first introduce a categorization for data exchange use cases in agriculture and then take a closer look at an exemplary agricultural process consisting of multiple use cases that fall under different categories. Finally, we will derive the respective data sovereignty needs from the farmer's point of view. Our analysis is based on discussions with domain experts from academia and on structured expert interviews we conducted with 18 farmers and six representatives from the agricultural industry (e.g., machine manufacturers) in the context of the COGNAC project.

2.1 Agricultural data exchange categories

We propose a categorization of agricultural data exchange use cases based on the relationship of the involved participants and the purpose of the data exchange.

1. **Data commercialization**: The data provider (in our case the farmer) offers farm data to an interested data consumer and defines usage conditions. The data consumer is allowed to use the data provided they comply with the agreed conditions and provide an economic benefit to the farmer in return. The benefit can either be realized by direct payment or through a discount or free access to a service offered by the consumer.

2. **Data reporting to fulfill regulations**: The farmer must fulfill regulations that apply to their farming operations and provide evidence to the data consumer (e.g., the authorities). Thus, the farmer shares data with the data consumer as proof of fulfillment. The shared data is limited to the minimal content needed for validation (e.g., a summary of performed farm work). The data consumer must prove that they represent the authority.

3. **Data sharing with external partners**: The farmer shares farm data with an external data consumer (e.g., an agricultural service provider). The shared data is needed by the data consumer to perform a service for the farmer. A legal contract between the two actors exists, and the data consumer is paid by the farmer for executing the service. Additional agreements for data usage can be included in the contract. The work performed by the service provider can be purely digital (e.g., fertilizer application optimization) or include a physical task executed on the farm (e.g., weed regulation).

4. **Data donation**: The farmer shares data with a data consumer that is interested in the data (e.g., a research institute). The farmer allows the consumer to use the data for free under certain conditions; for example, that the data can be used for research purposes only and the consumer is only allowed to publish anonymized results of the analysis.

5. **Data transparency with end-customers (public data)**: The farmer acts as a producer of an ingredient. The customer who buys the end-product is interested in getting the product's details. The farmer wants to prove that certain quality criteria are fulfilled and thus shares data for free with interested parties, like the mill that processes the wheat, or makes it publicly available (e.g., by using blockchain technology).

2.2 Example agricultural data exchange use cases

To demonstrate how the data exchange categories discussed in section 2.1 would be applicable in agricultural use cases, we investigated use cases derived from the process for growing winter wheat, starting after sowing (based on [Lf22]).

Our example process is as follows: The farmer buys and applies an optimized amount of mineral fertilizer in October. The farmer agrees to share data related to fertilizer usage with the company providing the fertilizer. In return, they get a discount on purchasing the fertilizer (data exchange category 1). The farmer documents this process in their internal system and provides the local authorities with access to a subset of the data that is required to ensure their fulfillment of certain legal obligations[3] (category 2). When the crops start to grow, the farmer orders a weed detection and removal service from a sub-contractor. To perform the service, the sub-contractor requests related field data (e.g., weed status from previous seasons and geographical field data). Thus, the farmer provides the sub-contractor with the requested data (category 3). Finally, when harvesting is done and the farmer has the information about the yield and the quality of the wheat, the farmer decides to donate the data related to the whole process for research purposes (category 4). If there is a company that is willing to pay for such data, the farmer could also choose to share the data under other conditions (category 1). Moreover, the farmer shares the wheat quality

---

[3] According to current national regulations, e.g., *Düngeverordnung* in Germany

data on a platform dedicated to tracking the ingredients from farm to fork, so that customers who consume the food can track the ingredients (category 5).

2.3 Derived data sovereignty needs

Although concerns related to digitalization in agriculture have been discussed in literature (see Chapter 1), to the best of our knowledge, no clear categorization of resulting data sovereignty needs in the agricultural domain exists. We therefore analyzed the needs introduced in other domains and found those introduced in the TrUSD[4] project to be applicable to the agricultural domain. Using these, we can differentiate several top-level data sovereignty needs (see Table 1).

Use Case / Need	Data Transparency	Self-Determination	Protection	Understanding & Empowerment	Legal ability & Entitlement
Sell fertilizer data	+	+	+	+	+
Fulfill regulations	+	-	+	+	+
Share data with contractor for weed control	+	+	+	+	+
Research donation	+	+	+	+	+
End-customer	-	-	-	+	+

Tab. 1: Relevancy of data sovereignty needs for different data exchange categories in the agricultural domain (+ important, - less important)

In the following, we will explain our analysis of the example weed control use case (see section 2.2) where the service provider needs field data to provide a service to the farmer. We derived questions based on the TrUSD framework to evaluate the importance of each need. We then rated the needs as "important" or "less important" based on our evaluation.

Regarding transparency, the farmer needs to know what data the contractor requires, why, and where the data will be stored and processed. Concerning self-determination, the farmer wants to have the ability to choose the company offering the best service and the most convenient conditions. Regarding protection, the farmer might want to be assured that the weed control contractor will not use the data for any other purposes than providing the agreed service nor share sensitive data (protection needs are higher for historical weed data than for geographical information) with other parties. Furthermore, the farmer might

---

[4] In the TrUSD project, research was conducted to develop an approach to technology-based employee data protection. One of the goals was to provide employees with means regarding transparency and self-determination related to the usage of their data in the context of their company (https://www.trusd-projekt.de)

want to be assured that the contractor will delete all related data from their storage after the job is done. It is a prerequisite that the farmer is in control of the data needed for fulfilling the service. Concerning understanding and empowerment, the farmer wants to understand their options and the respective consequences regarding their data in order to be able to make informed decisions. Finally, the farmer must have the legal ability to use their data in the way they choose and the assurance that the involved parties will respect the agreed usage conditions.

2.2 We conducted a similar analysis for the remainder of the agricultural data exchange use cases from section 2.2. The summarized findings are shown in Table 1, as presenting the detailed analysis for all use cases would exceed the space of this publication.

3 Discussion and outlook

Our proposed workflow of first categorizing the data exchanges in the analyzed process and then deriving the data sovereignty needs based on the categories can be helpful for gathering requirements when designing data exchange frameworks (e.g., ADS). Looking at the derived needs, one can conclude that several data exchange categories (e.g., *Data Donation* and *Commercialization*) show similar needs, which might be due to the similar nature of the exchanged data in those categories. Looking at the needs across the categories, we can see that fundamental needs like *Understanding* and *Transparency* about what happens with the shared data are important in many categories. *Self-determination* needs, on the other hand, are of less importance for the "*Data Transparency to Fulfill Regulations*" data exchange category as one can assume that both the scope of the data and the receiving authority will be defined precisely.

This first draft of the order of precedence for data sovereignty needs must be validated with further research and more examples and the involvement of the affected stakeholders.

Currently, the willingness of farmers to share data differs depending on the party with whom the data is shared [Wi19]. To establish trust, it is essential to lay the legal foundation for data sharing (e.g., the European Data Act[5] currently under discussion), and to design agricultural data spaces that provide the technical realization for these regulations and enable the supervision of data usage terms. One promising European initiative for developing a trusted digital infrastructure is Gaia-X, which can, in combination with the reference architecture from IDSA – International Data Spaces Association, lay the ground for a sound implementation of data spaces in different domains [Br21].

As future work, we will further analyze the concepts of Gaia-X and IDS and evaluate whether they are suitable for the data exchange categories we introduced and whether their technologies can guarantee the fulfillment of the farmers' data sovereignty needs.

---

[5] https://digital-strategy.ec.europa.eu/en/policies/data-act

Acknowledgments: The work presented in this paper was performed as part of the Fraunhofer lighthouse project Cognitive Agriculture (COGNAC).

Bibliography

[Br21] Braud, A.; Fromentoux, G.; Radier, B.; Le Grand, O.: The Road to European Digital Sovereignty with Gaia-X and IDSA. IEEE Network, 35(2), p. 4-5, 2021.

[Eu18] EU directive for GDPR, https://eur-lex.europa.eu/eli/reg/2016/679/oj, 2016, visited 01.10.2022.

[Fh19] Fraunhofer Whitepaper "Agricultural Data Space" https://www.iese.fraunhofer.de/content/dam/iese/dokumente/media/studien/cognac_ads_whitepaper-en-fraunhofer_iese.pdf, visited: 17.10.2022.

[Ja19] Jakku, E.; Taylor, B.; Fleming, A.; Mason, C.; Fielke, S.; Sounness, C.; & Thorburn, P.: "If they don't tell us what they do with it, why would we trust them?" Trust, transparency and benefit-sharing in Smart Farming. NJAS-Wageningen Journal of Life Sciences, 90, 100285, 2019.

[Ka22] Kalmar, R.; Rauch, B.; Dörr, J.; Liggesmeyer, P.: Agricultural Data Space. In: Otto, B.; ten Hompel, M.; Wrobel, S. (eds): Designing Data Spaces. Springer, Cham. https://doi.org/10.1007/978-3-030-93975-5_17, 2022.

[Lf22] Complementary data 2.3.4 from the Machbarkeitsstudie Betriebliches Datenmanagement und FMIS, Schriftenreihe des LfULG, Heft 4/2022 https://www.landwirtschaft.sachsen.de/download/LfULG-Machbarkeitsstudie-PV-Uebersicht-WW_mit_Vorfrucht_SM.pdf, 2022, visited 05.10.2022.

[Ma22] Martens, K.; Zscheischler, J.: The Digital Transformation of the Agricultural Value Chain: Discourses on Opportunities, Challenges and Controversial Perspectives on Governance Approaches. Sustainability, 14(7), 3905, 2022.

[Sy16] Sykuta, M. E.: Big data in agriculture: Property rights, privacy and competition in ag data services. International Food and Agribusiness Management Review, 19, p. 57–74, 2016.

[Vo20] Vogel, P.: Datenhoheit in der Landwirtschaft 4.0. In: Gandorfer, M., Meyer-Aurich, A., Bernhardt, H., Maidl, F. X., Fröhlich, G. & Floto, H. (Hg.), 40. GIL-Jahrestagung, Digitalisierung für Mensch, Umwelt und Tier. Bonn: Gesellschaft für Informatik e.V., p. 331-336, 2020.

[Wi19] Wiseman, L.; Sanderson, J.; Zhang, A.; & Jakku, E.: Farmers and their data: An examination of farmers' reluctance to share their data through the lens of the laws impacting smart farming. NJAS-Wageningen Journal of Life Sciences, 90, 100301, 2019.

Digital weed reduction

Sebastian Burkhart [1] and Patrick Noack [1]

Abstract: In an effort to reduce the usage of herbicides in herb cultivation, we discuss strategies to detect and eliminate toxic weeds, exemplified by Senecio vulgaris. This paper presents a method to classify plants based on their spectral characteristics utilizing hyperspectral imagery in the range between 400 nm and 1100 nm. We are able to remove background material by masking it automatically using the well-established NDVI and Otsu's thresholding prior to classification. Based on a neural network, we correctly classify 93% of the leaf area from Senecio vulgaris even with a relatively low spectral resolution of 50 nm. Apart from data collection, all steps were implemented in open source software and the Python language using open source libraries.

Keywords: weed reduction, hyperspectral imaging, spectroscopy, machine learning

1 Introduction

In the food industry, there are high requirements for consistent quality, particularly where food safety is concerned. In herb cultivation (in context of this work, parsley cultivation), contamination with pyrrolizidine alkaloids (PA) originating from Senecio vulgaris is causing issues, as even a few plants can result in relevant contamination. Strict regulations and limits on this contaminant have been established [Eu20] to ensure the required quality, but these regulations also lead to risks for both farmers and manufacturers, as even low contamination can cause considerable financial damage. Furthermore, prickly thistles are undesirable because they are inedible. Since sorting out problematic weeds in already harvested material is difficult to implement, the aim is to minimize weed manifestation in the production area. However, due to declining public acceptance and growing legal restrictions, the use of herbicides for weed control permanently needs to be reduced.

Weeds between visible rows (post-emergence stage) can be removed with conventional, tractor mounted cultivation hoes. For weeds in the rows, special equipment is needed. There is an autonomous field robot [Fa22a] which works between appropriately spaced crops based on their stored, absolute coordinates, making weeding possible even in the pre-emergence state. For spaced, transplanted crops there is a tractor mounted in-row weeder [Ga18], which works with video analysis techniques. Similarly, another autonomous robot [Fa22b] detects plants and weeds based on an annotated plant image

---

[1] Hochschule Weihenstephan-Triesdorf, Fakultät Landwirtschaft, Lebensmittel und Ernährung, Markgrafenstraße 16, 91746 Weidenbach, sebastian.burkhart@hswt.de, https://orcid.org/0000-0003-3844-4208; patrick.noack@hswt.de, https://orcid.org/0000-0002-0226-6609

database. Multispectral cameras mounted to unmanned aerial vehicles (UAVs), e.g. [Dj22], are used to monitor plant health by computing vegetative indexes such as the normalized difference vegetation index (NDVI) [Ro73]. High resolutions in the sub-centimeter domain achieved by low altitudes might allow the detection of undesirable weeds and bare spots prone to weeds shortly before harvest for targeted, manual removal. Hyperspectral imaging (HSI) cameras mounted on top of conveyor belts could work to detect remaining weeds in harvested material during preparation for dehydration / freezing. Both multispectral and HSI cameras, however, require known and ideally constant lighting conditions.

An optical plant detection system therefore can be based on (1) spectrometers (one pixel, multiple spectral bands), (2) RGB cameras (three visible spectral bands: red, green and blue), (3) RGB/NIR cameras (RGB with additional channel for the NIR band), (4) multispectral cameras (few, typically named spectral bands), and (5) HSI cameras (multiple spectral bands). While spectrometers record only one pixel and are limited to the spectrum, imagery captured by the various camera types also contains information on texture and shape of the sample. In this paper, we investigate the spectral characteristics of parsley and relevant weeds based on hyperspectral imagery for classification.

2 Classification with hyperspectral imagery

Hyperspectral imaging cameras record three-dimensional data structures called hypercubes. These structures contain layered images, where each layer corresponds to a spectral band. Therefore, multiple spectral bands are stored for each individual pixel. In our project, we used inno-spec's GreenEye [In22], a HSI camera operating in the spectral range between 400 nm and 1100 nm. The sensor resolves a line with 1312 pixels and the associated spectra with 1082 pixels (1070 after Smile correction) each. A halogen light bar equipped with eight lamps (20 W each, type OSRAM DECOSTAR) from the same manufacturer was used for illumination. Since the camera is a line scanner, ideally constant relative motion between the camera and the sample is required to capture a second spatial dimension. Changes in velocity lead to distorted imagery and changing exposure time. In applications prone to velocity changes (e.g. tractor-mounted implements), therefore the current speed has to be recorded for compensation.

2.1 Data collection

Two sets of plant samples grown (1) indoors under artificial lighting and (2) outdoors on a parsley field were collected. The respective measurements took place on different days. Both sample groups, shown as a concatenated image in Fig. 1, were taped to cardboard. It should be noted that both images were taken with a phone camera for demonstration purposes. The lighting conditions, especially regarding the shadows, therefore do not correspond to the actual measurement. Apart from stretching due to movement speed and exposure time, the photo is congruent with the data shown in Fig. 2. After setting up illumination and calibrating the camera (i.e. collecting white and black references, focusing and setting exposure time), the hypercubes were captured by using inno-spec's capturing software SICap-GB in "Transmission/Reflectance" mode. During the measurement, the samples were manually moved past the camera lens at a distance of 20 cm with constant speed. The resulting files contain the reflectance and are in ENVI format.

Fig. 1: Two plant sample groups taped to cardboard: Left (lighter background, grown indoors): Senecio vulgaris (2x), parsley (flat leaf), and parsley (curly). Right (darker background, grown outdoors): Senecio vulgaris, parsley (flat leaf) and thistle

2.2 Data preparation

We used the Python language for this task. Importing the ENVI files containing the hypercubes was achieved by using the library Spectral Python (SPy) [Bo02], which provides the data as numpy arrays [Ha20]. As the original ENVI files are large (5.2 GB for the samples used in this paper), we reduced the number of spectral bands by binning: in the range between 400 nm and 1100 nm, the spectra were separated in intervals of 50 nm width. Then the mean reflectance for each bin was calculated, reducing the number of features (i.e. spectral bands) from 1070 to 14. This decreased the size (68.3 MB), reducing processing time for the further steps. This binning also serves to abstract the data so that it can be directly compared with results of other sensors (e.g. spectrometers) in future works. Again using SPy, the binned data then was exported to new hypercubes in ENVI format. To obtain a data set with all relevant herbs and weeds, we combined the two sets shown in Fig. 1 into one hypercube by concatenation.

In order to prevent the results from being influenced by changing backgrounds and to be able to create labels for later training, a mask for the plants was created by first calculating the NDVI, and then applying automatic thresholding with Otsu's method [Ot79]. The latter step was achieved by utilizing methods available in OpenCV [Br00]. This masking step was fully automated and should, according to the NDVI definition, be applicable to properly illuminated soil, too. Other background materials, particularly conveyor belts, were not tested so far. The resulting binary mask, which distinguishes between plant and background on pixel level, was then exported to an image.

For training, we labelled the data set manually. An easy method to achieve this is to import the binary mask from the previous step in a graphics editor such as the GNU Image Manipulation Program (GIMP) and mark each variety on a separate layer. The actual labels result from the logical conjunction (AND operator) of the new layers (exported as images and loaded back to Python) and the original binary mask.

2.3 Evaluation

For data analysis and visualization, the Python-based software Orange3 [Ja13] was used. While there is an add-on specifically for spectroscopy that is compatible with ENVI-files, the authors chose to create a custom Python module to import the data and apply masks for labelling. All pixels of interest (i.e. plants without background) were selected based on the previously calculated mask, eliminating the cardboard background. The manually drawn variety-masks were used to assign the true classes to each pixel. The actual evaluation was conducted by using the component "Test and Score" with 20-fold, stratified cross validation. A neural network configured according to the rules listed in [He05] was chosen as the model to train: the network consisted of one hidden layer where the contained neurons amounted to 2/3 of the sum of input and output neurons. That is 12 neurons for the dataset with 14 binned spectral bands as input and 4 varieties as output.

2.4 Results

For our purposes, we consider both Senecio vulgaris and thistle as harmful (positives), whereas both varieties of parsley are harmless (negatives). The most critical metric for our classifier therefore has to be the number of false negatives (i.e. actual Senecio vulgaris classified as parsley). The overall performance of the classifier is illustrated in Tab. 1 as a confusion matrix. Six percent of Senecio vulgaris are critical false negatives. Similarly, 6.2% of the thistles are wrongly classified as parsley. Weeds, incorrectly classified as each other, can be considered unproblematic as they are detected as positives anyway. False positives (i.e. actual parsley classified as either Senecio vulgaris or thistle) total to 4% of the actual parsley, while even the two varieties of parsley could be correctly predicted in most cases. While the number of incorrectly classified weeds appears to be high, it needs to be noted that the results are on pixel basis in the sub millimeter domain, i.e. each instance corresponds to one pixel of a larger leaf area. This is illustrated in Fig. 2: here, the classes predicted by the classifier are displayed. As can be seen, only a fraction of the leaf area, particularly around the edges and leaf veins, is classified wrong. The classification result thus has to be interpreted as a proportion of the respective leaf area and not in terms of individual plants. As long as the plant parts do not get too small, a reliable classification should be possible despite the false negative rate. However, this hypothesis needs to be further tested with more complex setups and more plant material.

		Predicted class				
		Senecio vulgaris	parsley (flat leaf)	parsley (curly)	thistle	Σ
Actual class	Senecio vulgaris	93.3 %	3.9 %	2.1 %	0.7 %	53911
	parsley (flat leaf)	1.7 %	95.3 %	1.9 %	1.0 %	90494
	parsley (curly)	1.3 %	2.6 %	96.1 %	0.0 %	53710
	thistle	2.1 %	4.1 %	0.0 %	93.8 %	33534
	Σ	53259	91095	54522	32773	231649

Tab. 1: Confusion matrix for the neural network (showing proportion of actual)

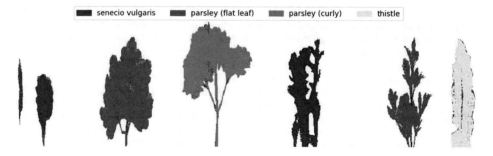

Fig. 2: Classification result. The majority of the leaf area was assigned to the correct classes

3 Conclusion

We showed that even with a relatively low spectral resolution of 50 nm, herbs are distinguishable from dangerous weeds in hyperspectral imagery. This reduced number of bands corresponds almost to multispectral imagery. The approach, including an automated masking step based on the NDVI and Otsu's thresholding during preprocessing, should be robust against changing backgrounds. Given appropriate lighting, the masking approach should also work outdoors on soil, making it feasible to preprocess multispectral imagery captured by UAVs or tractor-mounted sensors this way. It needs to be noted, though, that our experiments were conducted under lab conditions with artificial lighting. Outdoor applications do not take place under lab conditions, so special attention must be paid to lighting. Sorting of harvested material on conveyor belts could also be a use case for the method presented. However, whether other artificial background materials (e.g. conveyor belt) can be removed based on the NDVI has to be further tested. While some of the leaf area is classified incorrectly, simple image processing based on morphology could further improve the result. As the classification on pixel level works in images, it is plausible that cheaper spectrometers with similar spectral range and resolution are useable, too. This could allow for cost-effective in-row monitoring on a tractor-mounted implement (e.g. cultivation hoes) to detect missed weeds. A spectral index that can distinguish herbs from weeds also appears feasible considering the low number of spectral bands after binning and is currently under investigation.

Bibliography

[Bo02] Boggs, T.: Spectral Python. https://www.spectralpython.net/, accessed 31 Oct 2022.

[Br00] Bradski, G.: The OpenCV Library. Dr. Dobb's Journal of Software Tools, 2000.

[Dj22] DJI Official: P4 Multispectral - DJI. https://www.dji.com/de/p4-multispectral, accessed 31 Oct 2022.

[Eu20] The European Commission: Commission Regulation (EU) 2020/2040 of 11 December 2020 amending Regulation (EC) No 1881/2006 as regards maximum levels of pyrrolizidine alkaloids in certain foodstuffs. Official Journal of the European Union, 2020.

[Fa22a] FarmDroid ApS: FarmDroid ApS - Økologisk og CO_2 neutral autonom markrobot. https://farmdroid.dk/, accessed 31 Oct 2022.

[Fa22b] Farming revolution GmbH: farming revolution GmbH. https://farming-revolution.com/, accessed 31 Oct 2022.

[Ga18] Garford Farm Machinery: Robocrop InRow Weeder | Remove Inter Row Weeds | Garford Farm Machinery. https://garford.com/products/robocrop-inrow-weeder/, accessed 31 Oct 2022.

[Ha20] Harris, C. R. et al.: Array programming with NumPy. Nature 7825/585, pp. 357–362, 2020.

[He05] Heaton, J.: Introduction to neural networks with Java. Heaton Research, Chesterfield, MO, 2005.

[In22] inno-spec GmbH: GreenEye en - INNO-SPEC. https://inno-spec.de/en/greeneye-en/, accessed 31 Oct 2022.

[Ja13] Janez Demšar et al.: Orange: Data Mining Toolbox in Python. Journal of Machine Learning Research 14, pp. 2349–2353, 2013.

[Ot79] Otsu, N.: A threshold selection method from gray-level histograms. IEEE transactions on systems, man, and cybernetics 1/9, pp. 62–66, 1979.

[Ro73] Rouse Jr, J. W. et al.: Monitoring the vernal advancement and retrogradation (green wave effect) of natural vegetation, 1973.

Analyse und Klassifizierung von Digitalisierungsinitiativen in der Landwirtschaft

Vorschlag eines Klassifizierungsmodells und Ergebnisse einer Landwirtebefragung

Michael Clasen [1], Jasmin Westermann[2]

Abstract: In diesem Beitrag wird zunächst ein Reifegradmodell zur Messung des Digitalisierungsgrades von landwirtschaftlichen Betrieben vorgeschlagen. Es basiert auf bestehenden Reifegradmodellen, welche an die landwirtschaftlichen Besonderheiten angepasst wurden. Im zweiten Teil werden die Ergebnisse einer Befragung von 151 Landwirten in Deutschland geschildert, in der sich Landwirte mit den Stufen des Reifegradmodells identifizieren sollten. Zusätzlich wurde gefragt, warum sich Landwirte in einen bestimmten Reifegrad eingruppiert haben und was sie daran hindert, einen höheren Reifegrad zu erreichen.

Keywords: Reifegradmodell, Digitalisierungsgrad, Landwirtschaft

1 Einleitung

Reifegradmodelle dienen der Bewertung von Prozessqualität und ihrer kontinuierlichen Verbesserung. Dies gelingt, indem bewährte Prozesse und Praktiken auf unterschiedlichen Entwicklungsstufen zunächst einmal beschrieben werden. Anhand dieser Entwicklungsstufen kann dann die Reife eines konkreten Unternehmens bzgl. des betrachteten Untersuchungsgegenstandes bewertet werden. Reifegrade helfen dabei, die Fähigkeit einer Organisation beziehungsweise eines Unternehmens in Bezug auf Anwendungsmethoden oder -modelle zu bestimmen. Anhand eines solchen Reifegrades kann mit Hilfe einer mehrstufigen Skala eingeschätzt werden, auf welcher Entwicklungsstufe sich ein Unternehmen derzeit befindet und wie es sich für die nächste Stufe qualifizieren kann. Die meisten Reifegradmodelle verfügen über fünf verschiedene Reifegrad-Stufen. Neben den bekannten Reifegradmodellen für Prozesse wird auch der Digitalisierungsgrad von Unternehmen über Reifegradmodelle gemessen.

---

[1] Hochschule Hannover, Abteilung Wirtschaftsinformatik, Ricklinger Stadtweg 120, 30459 Hannover, michael.clasen@hs-hannover.de, https://orcid.org/0000-0002-2453-8484
[2] Hochschule Hannover, Abteilung Betriebswirtschaft, Ricklinger Stadtweg 120, 30459 Hannover, jasmin09@gmx.net

2 Digitales Landwirtschaftliches Reifegradmodell

Zunächst wurden folgende Reifegradmodelle gesichtet:

- Capability Maturity Model Integration (CMMI) und Software Process Improvement and Capability Determination (SPICE) [Gr11, S. 113-116]
- Reifegradmodell der Windindustrie nach Wildemann [Wi21]
- Reifegradmodell Mittelstand Industrie 4.0 nach Fiedler, Krieger, Sackmann und Wenzel-Schinzer [FKWS18]
- IT-Reifegradmodell nach Sames [Sa19, S. 503]
- Reifegradmodell für Nachhaltigkeitsmanagement nach Glanze, Nüttgens und Ritzrau [GNR20]
- Reifegradmodell zur organisationalen Anpassung (DigiOrg) nach Schnitzler [Sc19, S. 92]
- Stufen der Digitalisierung in der Landwirtschaft nach dem BMEL [BM22, S. 16]

Für eine nähere Beschreibung der einzelnen Modelle siehe Westermann [We22, S. 14ff.]. Zur Messung des digitalen Reifegrades in der Landwirtschaft waren die beiden letztgenannten Ansätze am erfolgsversprechendsten. Es wurde das Grundkonzept von DigiOrg nach Schnitzler [Sc19, S. 92] mit den agrarspezifischen Klasseneinteilungen des BMEL [BM22, S. 16] kombiniert. DigiOrg entstammt aus dem Bereich der Organisation industrieller Großunternehmen und definiert eine Digitalisierungsinitiative als „[...] Teil einer Digitalisierungsstrategie [...]", die als Ableitung aus der Unternehmensstrategie entstanden ist [Sc19, S. 92]. Obwohl vermutlich nur die wenigsten landwirtschaftlichen Betriebe eine explizite Digitalisierungsstrategie haben, ist vor allem die Zweiteilung in effizienzorientierte (Stufen I-III) und innovationsorientierte Organisationsgestaltung (Stufen IV-V) auch für die Agrarbranche interessant (siehe Abb. 1). Die effizienzorientierten Digitalisierungsszenarien I-III haben das Ziel, durch Automatisierung Kosten einzusparen oder die Produktivität zu steigern; Ziele die einem Agrarinformatiker nicht fremd sind. Dabei nimmt sowohl der potentielle Nutzen, aber auch die Komplexität der Digitalisierungsinitiativen mit den Stufen I bis III zu. Klassische Precision-Farming-Anwendungen würde man, je nach Intensität des Einsatzes, den Stufen I oder II zuordnen. Ansätze des E-Commerce, des E-Business oder auch der Einsatz cloudbasierter Farm-Management-Information-Systems würden in die dritte Stufe fallen. Auffällig ist jedoch, dass sich die bisherigen Anstrengungen der Agrarinformatik stark auf die Effizienzverbesserung von Produktionsprozessen konzentriert haben und weit weniger auf die Steigerung der Innovationskraft landwirtschaftlicher Betriebe ausgerichtet sind. Zumindest scheint es lohnend, die Digitalisierung stärker als bisher für die Schaffung neuer Produkte oder Services innerhalb des bisherigen Geschäftsmodells zu nutzen (Szenario IV) oder sogar für völlig neue Geschäftsmodelle, die jedoch eine „[...] Bereitschaft zu einem radikalen Umbau des Unternehmens (Disruption)" [Sc19, S. 93] voraussetzen.

Analyse und Klassifizierung von Digitalisierungsinitiativen 305

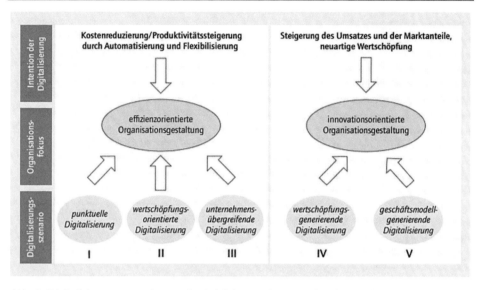

Abb. 1: Digitalisierungsszenarien zur Produktivitäts- oder Wertschöpfungssteigerung [Sc19, S. 92]

Aufbauend auf dem DigiOrg Reifegradmodell und der Einteilung der Stufen der Digitalisierung in der Landwirtschaft des BMEL wird das V-förmige **Digitale Landwirtschaftliche Reifegradmodell** vorgeschlagen. Digitale Technologien können sowohl für effizienzorientierte Innovationen (grüner rechter Ast) oder innovationsorientierte Innovationen (blauer linker Ast) genutzt werden. Dabei wurden die Stufen S1 bis S5 der effizienzorientierten Innovationen wie vom BMEL definiert. „In der ersten Stufe kommt nur ein einzelnes ‚digitales' Produkt zum Einsatz. Die nächste Stufe ist ein intelligenteres Produkt – beispielsweise ein Schlepper mit verschiedenen digitalen Steuerungen. Stufe 3 beschreibt ein intelligent vernetztes Produkt. Hierbei wird der Schlepper mithilfe von Managementprogrammen vernetzt, die verschiedene Daten empfangen und verarbeiten können. Stufe 4 der Digitalisierung beschreibt ein digital vernetztes Produktionssystem. Hier ist nicht nur der einzelne Schlepper angebunden, sondern auch die je nach Produktionssystem oder Arbeitsschritt benötigten Geräte. Die höchste Stufe der Digitalisierung beschreibt ein System von Systemen, in dem die unterschiedlichen Systeme miteinander kommunizieren". Damit auch viehhaltende Betriebe eingestuft werden konnten, wurden die oben genannten Beispiele erweitert. So kann z. B. an die Stelle eines modernen Schleppers auch ein Melkroboter treten. Da das Reifegradmodell nicht einfach zu verstehen ist, wurde es in einem auf YouTube verfügbaren Video erläutert, welches über einen Link aus dem Fragebogen aufgerufen werden konnte.

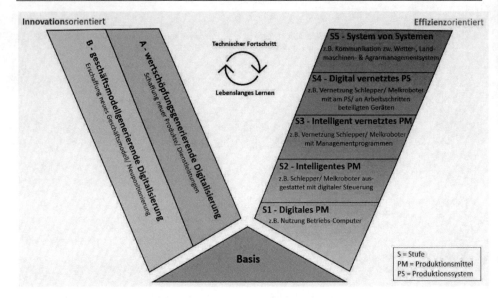

Abb. 2: Digitales Landwirtschaftliches Reifegradmodell
(angelehnt an [BM22, S.16] und [Sc19, S. 92]

3 Digitaler Reifegrad deutscher Landwirtschaftsbetriebe

Die Befragung wurde online im Zeitraum vom 13. Juni bis zum 3. Juli 2022 durchgeführt. Der Fragebogen sowie weitere Details können Westermann [We22] entnommen werden. Es haben 151 Landwirte teilgenommen, von denen 26 % weiblich waren. Die Teilnehmer waren überdurchschnittlich jung. 81 % der Teilnehmer wurden zwischen 1986 und 2005 geboren. Die meisten Landwirte hatten ihre Betriebe in Niedersachsen (55), gefolgt von Bayern (24), Schleswig-Holstein (14) und Baden-Württemberg (12) und waren ca. zu je einem Drittel im Pflanzenbau, in der Tierhaltung oder in beiden Geschäftsfeldern tätig. 71 % der Betriebe bewirtschafteten Flächen zwischen 50 und 500 Hektar und von den viehhaltenden Betrieben wiesen 72 % zwischen 50 und 500 Großvieheinheiten auf. Knapp die Hälfte der Befragungsteilnehmer war gut ausgebildet. Als höchsten Bildungsabschluss gaben 18 Befragungsteilnehmer „Agrarbetriebswirt", 16 „Meister" und 37 ein Hochschulstudium an. Da einige Teilnehmer noch keine 20 Jahre alt waren, wird der Anteil der Studienabschlüsse vermutlich noch steigen.

3.1 Effizienzorientierte Digitalisierung

Wie Tabelle 1 zu entnehmen ist, sind nur 29 der befragten Landwirte der Meinung, bereits auf einer Stufe angekommen zu sein, auf der man von einem (weitgehend) vernetzten Produktionssystem (S4 + S5) sprechen kann. Als Hindernisse wurden mit 63 % der

Nennungen „hohe Kosten" genannt; es folgten „Desinteresse" mit 18 %, „ein zu hoher Zeitaufwand" mit 11 %, „eine geringe Bereitschaft der Mitarbeiter" mit 9 % und „eine zu hohe Komplexität der Systeme" mit 8 %. Weit überwiegend wurden also Kostenargumente genannt. Konkret wurde bemängelt, dass der monetäre Nutzen kaum messbar sei, das ständige Erneuern zu immer wiederkehrenden Kosten führe, Betriebe zu klein seien und die Zuverlässigkeit der Schnittstellen aufgrund fehlender herstellerübergreifender Funktionen schlecht sei.

Stufe	S1	S2	S3	S4	S5	Summe
Anzahl Nennungen	37	41	38	20	9	145

Tab. 1: Selbsteinstufung der Landwirte in Reifegradstufen

Die Unterschiede zwischen den Gruppen sind schwer zu interpretieren. So finden sich auf allen fünf Stufen der Melkroboter und der moderne Schlepper als Grund für die gewählte Eingruppierung wieder. Dies kann daran liegen, dass diese Systeme in unterschiedlichen Ausbaustufen verwendet wurden, aber auch an einem fehlenden Verständnis für die Unterschiede zwischen den einzelnen Gruppen. Vielleicht ist die vom BMEL vorgeschlagene Unterscheidung zu uneindeutig.

Interessanter sind die Antworten auf die Frage, ob die digitalen Innovationen halten, was sie versprechen. Hier sind die Antworten durchgängig sehr positiv, wie Tabelle 2 zu entnehmen ist. Fast niemand ist mit den eingesetzten Technologien wirklich unzufrieden.

	S1	S2	S3	S4	S5
zufrieden	18	25	31	10	6
bedingt	4	3	1	3	0
nicht zufrieden	0	0	0	2	0

Tab. 2: Zufriedenheit mit digitalen Innovationen nach Reifegradstufen

3.2 Innovationsorientierte Digitalisierung

Bisher wurde die Digitalisierung bei den befragten Landwirten kaum dazu genutzt, neuartige Produkte oder Dienstleistungen anzubieten. So antworteten 79 % der Befragten mit „Nein" und nur 19 % mit „Ja" oder „in Planung" (9 %). Wie bei Innovationen nicht anders zu erwarten, ist die Variationsbreite der genannten digitalen Innovationen sehr groß. Häufig genannt wurden Möglichkeiten zur Direktvermarktung wie Online-Shops (7), 24-Stunden-Automaten (5), Hofläden (3) und Online-Buchungen von

Ferienwohnungen (1). Insgesamt ist der Umsatzanteil dieser innovativen Geschäftsmodelle aber sehr gering. Bei 9 von 44 Nennungen liegt er unter 5 % des Gesamtumsatzes und nur 3 Landwirte gaben an, einen Umsatz von mehr als 40 % mit den innovativen Geschäftszweigen zu verzeichnen.

4 Ergebnis

Insgesamt kann festgehalten werden, dass die Zuordnung einer digitalen Investition zu einer Reifegradstufe je nach Nutzung nicht eindeutig und somit schwierig ist. Die Befragung ergab, dass die allermeisten digitalen Investitionen derzeit aus Gründen der Effizienzsteigerung vorgenommen werden und nur selten, um neue innovative Produkte oder Dienstleistungen anzubieten. Vielleicht sollte künftig der Fokus stärker auf den innovativen Geschäftsmodellen liegen?

Literaturverzeichnis

[BM22] Bundesministerium für Ernährung und Landwirtschaft: Digitalisierung in der Landwirtschaft – Chancen nutzen – Risiken minimieren.

[FKSW18] Fiedler, A.; Krieger, C.; Sackmann, D.; Wenzel-Schinzer, H.: RMI 4.0: Ein Reifegradmodell für den Mittelstand. Industrie 4.0 Management, Nr. 2, 2018, S. 48-52.

[GNR21] Glanze, E.; Nüttgens, M.; Ritzrau, W.: Unternehmenserfolg durch Nachhaltigkeit – Reifegrad- und Vorgehensmodell zum Aufbau eines datenbasierten Nachhaltigkeitsmanagements. HMD (2021) 58: 155-166 https://link.springer.com/article/10.1365/s40702-020-00694-9.

[Gr11] Grande, M.: 100 Minuten für Anforderungsmanagement. Reifegradmodelle. S. 113-116. Vieweg+Teubner Verlag, Wiesbaden. Verfügbar unter: 10.1007/978-3-8348-8135-9_15.pdf (springer.com).

[Sa19] Sames, G.: IT-Reifegradmodell für Fabriken. IT-Legacy-Strukturen für Industrie 4.0 harmonisieren. Zeitschrift für wirtschaftlichen Fabrikbetrieb, Heft 7-8/ 2019, S. 501-503. WISO.

[Sc19] Schnitzler, C.: Digitalisierungsinitiativen umsetzen. Ein Reifegradmodell zur organisationalen Anpassung. ZFO – Zeitschrift Führung und Organisation – 02/2019, S. 91.

[We22] Westermann, J.: Analyse und Klassifikation von Digitalisierungsinitiativen in der Landwirtschaft, Bachelorarbeit. https://doi.org/10.25968/opus-2328.

[Wi21] Wildemann, H.: Digitalisierung in der Windindustrie – Teil 1 Reifegradmodell zur Bewertung des Digitalisierungsfortschritts. Fabriksoftware.info - GITO mbH Verlag für Industrielle Informationstechnik und Organisation. Verfügbar unter: https://fabriksoftware.info/node/1034.

Prototypische Entwicklungen zur Umsetzung des Resilient Smart Farming (RSF) mittels Edge Computing

Daniel Eberz-Eder [1], Franz Kuntke [2], Gerwin Brill[3], Ansgar Bernardi[4], Christian Wied[5], Philippe Nuderscher[3], Christian Reuter [2]

Abstract: Landwirtschaft als essenzieller Teil der Nahrungsmittelproduktion gehört zu den kritischen Infrastrukturen (KRITIS). Dementsprechend müssen die eingesetzten Systeme für einen widerstandsfähigen Betrieb ausgelegt sein. Dies gilt auch für die auf landwirtschaftlichen Betrieben eingesetzte Software, die Sicherheits- und Resilienzkriterien genügen muss. Jedoch ist die Zunahme an Software zu beobachten, welche eine permanente Internetkonnektivität erfordert, d. h. eine stabile Verbindung zu Servern oder Cloud-Applikationen ist für deren Funktionsweise erforderlich. Dies stellt eine erhebliche Schwachstelle hinsichtlich der Resilienz dar und kann bei Ausfällen der Telekommunikationsinfrastruktur zu großen Problemen führen. Mit Entwicklungen aus dem Bereich Resilient Smart Farming (RSF) zeigen wir, wie Datenhaltung nach dem Offline-First-Prinzip gestaltet werden kann. Ein zentraler Bestandteil hierbei ist das Resilient Edge Computing (REC) und die entwickelte HofBox: ein Mini-Server, der das Datenmanagement im Betrieb übernimmt und mittels innovativer Open-Source basierender Container-Technologie (Open Horizon) umsetzt. Dadurch werden in Zukunft weitere Anwendungsfälle innerhalb der landwirtschaftlichen Produktions- und Wertschöpfungskette durch Public-Private-Partnership-Modelle realistisch und realisierbar.

Keywords: Resilient Smart Farming, Resilienz, Digital Farming, HofBox, Resilient Edge Computing

1 Motivation

Der Prozess der landwirtschaftlichen Produktion erfährt insbesondere in Industrieländern eine fortwährende Digitalisierung, die als Digital Farming oder Smart Farming bezeichnet wird [DLG19], d. h. der Anteil Software-gestützter Werkzeuge und reiner Software-

---

[1] Dienstleistungszentrum Ländlicher Raum (DLR) Rheinhessen-Nahe-Hunsrück, Rüdesheimer Str. 60-68, 55545 Bad Kreuznach, daniel.eberz@dlr.rlp.de, https://orcid.org/0000-0002-6539-5221
[2] Technische Universität Darmstadt, PEASEC, Pankratiusstraße 2, 64298 Darmstadt, kuntke@peasec.tu-darmstadt.de, https://orcid.org/0000-0002-7656-5919 und reuter@peasec.tu-darmstadt.de, https://orcid.org/0000-0003-1920-038X
[3] expeer GmbH, Wachsbleiche 10-12, 53111 Bonn, brill@expeer.de und nuderscher@expeer.de
[4] Deutsches Forschungszentrum für Künstliche Intelligenz (DFKI) Trippstadterstr. 122, 67633 Kaiserslautern, bernardi@dfki.de
[5] IBM, Mies-van-der-Rohe-Straße 6, 80807 München, christian.wied@de.ibm.com

basierter Prozesse wie Planungsaufgaben nimmt nachweislich stetig zu [DN22; BI22; Ba20]. In Zeiten diverser Krisen wie dem Ukrainekrieg, der COVID-19-Pandemie, Cyberattacken und der Klimaveränderung zeigt sich mehr als je zuvor, dass die Landwirtschaft multiplen Risiken ausgesetzt ist und sich in Zukunft stärker mit der Krisen- und Katastrophenvorsorge beschäftigen muss.

Im Innovationsprojekt GeoBox sind die experimentelle Entwicklung und Erprobung eines praxistauglichen Prototyps einer dezentralen Datenhaltung nach dem Offline-First-Prinzip im Fokus. Dabei soll das Konzept einer standardisierten und resilienten GeoBox-Infrastruktur umgesetzt werden. Die zentrale Frage ist hierbei: (Wie) Kann eine dezentrale Datenhaltung mit hybrider IT-Infrastruktur umgesetzt werden und dabei den ökonomischen und ökologischen Nutzen von Anwendungen im Smart Farming unterstützen und die Resilienz steigern. Dafür wurde ein Konzept entwickelt und durch agile Methodik umgesetzt, so dass nun mit Hilfe eines Software-Prototyps die Praxistauglichkeit sowie Vor- und Nachteile von dezentraler Datenhaltung in der Landwirtschaft ermittelt werden. Wir erwarten von der Lösung, dass diese weniger anfällig gegenüber Angriffen auf zentrale Infrastruktur sowie Blackout-Szenarien ist.

Resilient Smart Farming (RSF) ist ein Konzept zur Nutzung digitaler Technologien und Anwendungen mit dem Fokus auf die Steigerung der Resilienz in der digitalen Landwirtschaft. Zentraler Begriff ist hierbei die Resilienz als wünschenswerter Zustand einer widerstandsfähigen digitalen Infrastruktur in der KRITIS Landwirtschaft [BI16; BLE20]. Resilienz wird im Zusammenhang mit technischen Systemen oft durch drei Kapazitäten definiert: Absorption, Erholung und Wandel. Um diesen Kapazitäten gerecht zu werden, haben sich für das Vorhaben einer Datenverwaltung im landwirtschaftlichen Kontext folgende technische Anforderungen ergeben: (1) Offline-Fähigkeit, (2) Datensicherheit und (3) Integration und Kompatibilität zu (offenen) Datenstandards.

Offline-Fähigkeit beschreibt hierbei die Möglichkeit, wesentliche Dienste auch ohne aktive Verbindung zu anderen Computern (Servern) nutzen zu können. Auch wenn eine Internetverbindung für längere Zeit nicht zur Verfügung steht, soll das Gesamtsystem weiterhin funktional sein. Somit ergibt sich eine Absorption gegenüber Störungen in der Internet-Infrastruktur. Diese Anforderung kann durch unterschiedliche Strategien umgesetzt werden. Eine Software-Hardware-Kombination, die keine Netzwerktechnik voraussetzt, wie dies bei klassischen Desktopanwendungen der Fall ist, erfüllt hier oftmals die Anforderung. Aber auch Cloud-Anwendungen können durch geschickte Caching- und Synchronisations-Mechanismen einen längerfristigen Netzwerkausfall ohne Datenverlust erlauben. Diese sind allerdings mit höheren Anforderungen seitens der Software-Architektur verbunden.

Datensicherheit bezeichnet die Eigenschaft, dass gespeicherte Daten nicht verloren gehen. Klassische Methoden dafür sind das Erzeugen von gewollten Daten-Redundanzen, wie durch RAID-Systeme und Backups. Aber auch dezentrale Datenverteilungen haben oft die positive Eigenschaft, durch die Nutzung selbst bereits die Daten auf mehrere Datenträger zu verteilen. Wichtig ist hierbei, dass redundante Datenhaltung auch für eine Datenrettung genutzt werden kann. So sollte im Fall von (gewollter) Datenduplizierung auf mobilen Endgeräten auch die Möglichkeit bestehen, diese wieder auf andere Systeme (zurück) zu spiegeln. Dies fördert die Möglichkeit, sich nach Krisenereignissen zu erholen, indem beispielsweise defekte Geräte ersetzt und zügig mit dem alten Datenbestand in einen nutzbaren Zustand überführt werden können.

Integration und Kompatibilität zu (offenen) Datenstandards erlauben eine hohe Flexibilität im Umgang mit größeren Software-Ökosystemen und somit die Möglichkeit, auf sich ändernde – gegebenenfalls unvorhergesehene – Umstände zu reagieren. Dies ermöglicht auch das komplette System nach einem Krisenereignis anzupassen – zu *wandeln* – beispielsweise, wenn nach den Erkenntnissen durch das Krisenereignis andere Software-Hardware-Systeme geeigneter erscheinen.

2 Konzept des Resilient Edge Computing im GeoBox-Kontext

Der Begriff Resilient Edge Computing (REC) ist das Kompositum aus den Begriffen Resilienz (im Sinne von Widerstands-/Anpassungsfähigkeit) und Edge Computing als Systemarchitektur-Ansatz [EKR22]. Edge Computing beschreibt dabei eine Systemarchitektur, bei der grundlegende Datenverarbeitungsleistung (vorrangig CPU- und Speicherkapazität) nicht durch zentrale Cloud-Systeme erbracht wird, sondern stattdessen direkt am Entstehungsort der Daten. Im Rahmen der GeoBox-Projekte wurde das REC auf zwei Ebenen geplant: auf der Ebene der Infrastruktur (1) und der Ebene der Anwendungen (2).

Auf der Intrastrukturebene bildet redundante lokale Rechenkapazität – die sogenannte HofBox – das Herzstück. Als zentraler Baustein unserer resilienten Infrastruktur stehen HofBoxen auf den landwirtschaftlichen Betrieben zur Verfügung und stellen im Krisenfall – stellvertretend für zentrale Cloud-Systeme – den missionskritischen Datenbestand sowie lokale Sensornetzwerke inkl. zugehöriger Tools und Anwendungen bereit. Die HofBoxen werden mittels der Open-Source Edge-Computing-Plattform „Open Horizon" ohne Nutzerinteraktion (sog. Zero Touch) initialisiert, installiert und mit Updates versorgt. Für die Applikationen der Anwendungsebene gilt, dass diese „containerisierbar" sein müssen und somit sowohl im Rechenzentrum, cloudbasiert oder eben lokal auf der HofBox lauffähig sind. Die Anwendungen sollen dabei mittels eines Standard-Internetbrowsers, also ohne zusätzliche Software, nutzbar, über eine spezielle Startseite auf der HofBox zugänglich und grundsätzlich ohne Verbindung zum Internet funktionsfähig sein. Über die Integration eines App-Stores können zudem weitere Anwendungen auf Nutzerwunsch installiert werden. Zur Unterstützung der täglichen Arbeit wird eine (erweiterbare) Basis-Software (GeoBox-App) standardmäßig ausgeliefert.

3 Stand der GeoBox-App, HofBox und Backend-Infrastruktur

Die bislang umgesetzte Architektur der GeoBox-Infrastruktur besteht sowohl aus serverseitigen Komponenten und Anwendungen, die auf zentralen Systemen (Cloud-Servern) betrieben werden, als auch aus lokalen Komponenten zur resilienten dezentralen Anwendung auf der Seite des Edge Computings (hier: sog. HofBoxen). Insgesamt besteht die Architektur dabei aus den folgenden drei Ebenen: Ebene 1 (Hybrid- und Multicloud-Management) stellt die zentralen Services und Anwendungen der GeoBox-Infrastruktur für Anwender (derzeit z. B. GeoBox-Viewer) sowie die Backend-Infrastruktur als zentrale Dienste zur Verfügung. In der darunterliegenden Ebene 2 (Netzwerkserver) befindet sich die Netzwerkinfrastruktur in Form z. B. des öffentlichen Internets oder öffentlich zugänglicher LoRaWAN-Installationen (z. B. via TheThingsNetwork). Es besteht hier auch die Möglichkeit, eigene lokale Netzwerke (privates 5G oder LoRaWAN) aufzubauen. Dies ist im Krisenfall für eine funktionstüchtige Kommunikation von entscheidender Bedeutung. Die unterste Ebene 3 (Resilient Edge Computing) beinhaltet zurzeit ein regionales Edge-Gateway, eine regionale Serverinstanz auf der Open Data Farm Neumühle und die HofBoxen als Edge Devices mit der GeoBox-App.

Die GeoBox-Applikation (GeoBox-App) [Ku20] ist eine modulare Basis-Software, die mittels eines SDK um Teil-Apps erweitert werden kann. So konnten Anwendungen wie z. B. prototypische KI-basierte Beratungstools für Pflanzenschutz im Wein- und Ackerbau auf Basis des IBM Watson leichtgewichtig implementiert werden. Die GeoBox-App bietet durch das Dashboard einen Überblick über verfügbare Anwendungen und dient als mobile Interaktionskomponente, die auf den üblichen Smartphone- (bzw. Tablet-) Betriebssystemen eingesetzt werden kann. Aktuell umfasst die GeoBox-App unter anderem Anwendungen zur Kommunikation (Geobox-Messenger), für die Verwaltung der Schläge des landwirtschaftlichen Betriebs (GeoBox Feldatlas) und zur Dokumentation von Beobachtungen und Maßnahmen im Feld (GeoBox Buchungsjournal). Der GeoBox-Watson-Chatbot nutzt die lokal erhobenen Daten, um in einem Beratungsdialog Hilfe bei der Anwendung von Pflanzenschutzmitteln im Wein- oder Ackerbau zu geben.

Die Architektur der GeoBox-App hält die notwendigen Daten zunächst lokal auf dem jeweiligen Mobilgerät und synchronisiert diese dann gegen die betriebliche HofBox (Offline-First-Prinzip). Die konzeptuelle Offenheit manifestiert sich auch in der verwendeten Datenmodellierung: Das GeoBox Buchungsjournal repräsentiert Beobachtungen und durchgeführte Maßnahmen als Instanzen einer formalen Aktivitäts-Ontologie und überführt die Dokumentationseinträge in einen umfassenden betrieblichen Wissensgraph auf RDF-Basis. Die jeweiligen Inhalte werden durch Verwendung von Begriffen aus dem AGROVOC Thesaurus der Food and Agricultural Organisation (FAO) eindeutig und maschinenlesbar formalisiert. So kann die Integration und Kompatibilität zu (offenen) Datenstandards in der GeoBox umgesetzt werden. Der Ortsbezug der jeweiligen Einträge wird über die Verknüpfung zum GeoBox Feldatlas ermittelt; dieser ermöglicht die Modellierung, Auswahl, Teilung und Verknüpfung von Schlagumrissen und Schlageigenschaften und verwendet dazu auch die replizierten Geo-Basisdaten der bereitgestellten öffentlichen Quellen. Der damit entstehende betriebliche Wissensgraph steht für vielfältige Abfragen bereit, wobei die ermittelten Ergebnisse in der jeweiligen Anwendung (wie etwa dem Watson Chatbot) erst nach menschlicher Kontrolle und Freigabe übertragen werden. Als Interaktionsparadigma hat sich das Füllen und explizite Versenden von „Formularen" bis hin zum umfassenden „Feldpass" bewährt.

In den letzten Monaten wurde unterschiedliche Hardware zur Entwicklung der HofBox getestet. Die erste HofBox-Generation basierte dabei auf einem Raspberry Pi 4 Modell B mit 4GB. Tests der GeoBox-App sowie des REC konnten darauf erfolgreich ausgeführt werden. Eine gleichzeitige Funktion als lokales LoRaWAN-Gateway wurde aufgrund der unzureichenden Reichweite des eingesetzten LoRa-Erweiterungsboards für den landwirtschaftlichen Praxisbetrieb jedoch als ungeeignet eingeschätzt. Um den zukünftigen Auslieferungsprozess möglichst einfach und gleichzeitig sicher zu gestalten, unterstützt die zweite Iteration der HofBox-Hardware das sogenannte Secure-Device-Onboarding-Protokoll (SDO). Hierfür verfügt der x86-kompatible Mini-Rechner über eine spezielle Initialisierungs-Software sowie eine in Hardware hinterlege ID (sog. Ownership Voucher). Mittels eines im begleitenden Projekt AgriRegio entstandenen Dialogs zur Aktivierung einer HofBox, der diese nicht-initialisierte und nicht-installierte Hardware-Box mit einem konkreten Benutzer verknüpft, führt die Box beim ersten Einschalten und der ersten Online-Verbindung den SDO-Prozess folgendermaßen aus:

1. Das Device kontaktiert einen SDO-Rendezvous-Service. Dieser Service kann auf Basis des im Device hinterlegten Ownership Voucher die technische Adresse des zugehörigen Plattform-Service feststellen.
2. Das Device wird vom SDO-Rendezvous-Service an den Plattform-Service weitergeleitet.
3. Das Device registriert sich am Plattform-Service – in diesem Fall mit dem Open-Source Framework Open Horizon / IEAM Management Hub – und wird mit der intendierten Node Policy und den Benutzer-Informationen versehen.
4. Auf Basis der Node Policy bezieht und installiert der auf der HofBox laufende Open-Horizon-Agent die für diesen Knoten vorgesehenen Software-Container.

Sobald die Basis-Softwares auf der HofBox einen lauffähigen Zustand erreicht haben, also die lokale Setup-Prozedur der Docker-Container abgeschlossen ist, verschickt die HofBox über einen jimverse-Service eine E-Mail sowie eine SMS mit der lokalen URL der HofBox-Startseite (jimBox) an den registrierten Benutzer. Die Initialisierung und Erst-Installation der HofBox ist damit abgeschlossen.

4 Fazit und Ausblick

Digitale Landwirtschaft muss nicht zwangsläufig zu einer internetabhängigen und damit anfälligen Architektur führen. Dies konnten wir anhand des entwickelten Konzepts und der anschließenden Entwicklung einer prototypischen technischen Umsetzung des Resilient Smart Farming mittels Edge Computing aufzeigen. Eine IT-Architektur im landwirtschaftlichen Kontext ist somit mit technischen Resilienz-Prinzipien vereinbar.

Die bisherigen Ergebnisse zeigen die Chancen des Edge Computing in Verbindung mit einem hybriden Cloud-Management in der Landwirtschaft. Die entstandenen Prototypen und Softwareartefakte bieten nun die Möglichkeit, weitergehende praktische Tests durchzuführen und gemeinsam mit der Wirtschaft im Rahmen von Public-Private-Partnership (PPP) sinnvolle Implementierungen zu initiieren und eine resiliente digitale Infrastruktur aufzubauen. Ziel ist es, die vorgestellte IT-Architektur im Rahmen des begleitenden AgriRegio-Projekts [Re22] des BMEL durch unterschiedliche Anwendungsfälle der Landwirtschaft in den nächsten Monaten in einen praxisnahen Probebetrieb zu überführen und zu evaluieren.

Förderhinweis: Das Innovationsprojekt GeoBox-II wird gefördert durch das Bundesministerium für Ernährung und Landwirtschaft (BMEL) aus Mitteln des Zweckvermögens des Bundes bei der Landwirtschaftlichen Rentenbank.

Literaturverzeichnis

[Ba20] Bartels N. et al.: Machbarkeitsstudie zu staatlichen digitalen Datenplattformen für die Landwirtschaft, IESE-Report Nr. 022.20/ D Version 1.1 - final 21. Dezember 2020.

[Bl22] Bitkom-Research, Studie: Die Digitalisierung der Landwirtschaft, Bitkom e.V., Berlin, 12. Mai 2022.

[Bl16] Bundesministerium des Innern (BMI): Verordnung zur Bestimmung Kritischer Infrastrukturen nach dem BSI-Gesetz (BSI-Kritisverordnung–BSI-KritisV), Bundesgesetzblatt Jahrgang 2016 Teil I Nr. 20, 2016.

[BLE20] Bundesanstalt für Landwirtschaft und Ernährung (BLE): Ernährung — eine Kritische Infrastruktur; Ernährungssicherstellungs- und Vorsorgegesetz, https://www.gesetze-im-internet.de/esvg/, zuletzt abgerufen am: 01.12.2022.

[DLG19] DLG-Merkblatt 447: Digitalisierung in der Landwirtschaft – Wichtige Zusammenhänge kurz erklärt, DLG e.V. Fachzentrum Landwirtschaft Eschborner Landstraße 122, 60489 Frankfurt am Main, 2019.

[DN22] Dörr, J.; Nachtmann, M.: Summary. In: Dörr, J., Nachtmann, M. (eds) Handbook Digital Farming. Springer, Berlin, Heidelberg. 2022. https://doi.org/10.1007/978-3-662-64378-5_7.

[EKR22] Eberz-Eder D.; Kuntke F.; Reuter C.: Sensibilität für Resilient Smart Farming (RSF) und seine Bedeutung in Krisenzeiten, RSF für eine nachhaltige, umweltgerechte und resiliente digitale Landwirtschaft. 42.GIL-Jahrestagung: Informatik in der Land-, Forst- und Ernährungswirtschaft, 2022.

[Ku20] Kuntke, F. et al.: Die GeoBox-Vision: Resiliente Interaktion und Kooperation in der Landwirtschaft durch dezentrale Systeme. In: *Mensch und Computer 2020 - Workshopband* (2020), S. 1-6.

[Re22] Reuter C. et al.: AgriRegio: Infrastruktur zur Förderung von digitaler Resilienz und Klimaresilienz im ländlichen Raum am Beispiel der Pilotregion Nahe-Donnersberg. 52. Jahrestagung der Gesellschaft für Informatik,2022. https://doi.org/10.18420/inf2022_81

Route-planning in output-material-flow operations using side-headlands

Santiago Focke Martinez[1] and Joachim Hertzberg[1,2]

Abstract: This paper presents an extension to a previously presented planning tool which was developed to generate routes for the machines participating in output-material-flow operations. The extension refers to the support of a headland region consisting of a set of partial side-headlands, comprised by main headlands, located in the sides of the field where inner-field tracks end; and connecting headlands, which border the field boundary and connect the main headlands. Eleven fields were used to test the corresponding tool updates in the planning process, including the geometric representation of the field with the new headland type, and the route planning for a harvesting test-scenario with one non-capacitated harvester and two transport vehicles.

Keywords: route planning, Precision Farming, Smart Farming

1 Introduction

In-field route planning for arable farming operations has been a focus of research in recent years aiming to improve the efficiency of the process in terms of operational costs, energy consumption, in-field transit, and soil compaction, among others [Nø22; Mo20; NZ20]. Current research deals with input-, output-, and neutral-flow operations, where both capacitated and non-capacitated machines are involved. A planning tool was previously presented [Fo21; FH22], which was developed to generate routes for the machines participating in output-material-flow operations (e.g., harvesting) following different optimization criteria. However, the tool was limited to the generation and usage of a headland that surrounds the main field region (referred here as inner-field) with a set of closed surrounding headland tracks (passes) determined by the desired headland width and the working-width of the machine working the field. This tool was further developed to generate and use a new type of headland region, which comprises a set of main headlands that are located at ends of the inner-field tracks, and a set of single-track-headlands bordering the field boundary connecting the main headlands. Thanks to the latter headlands, it is possible to cover the headland region continuously without leaving the field. Compared to the complete surrounding headland, using the presented headland type will result in a lower overall headland area, and consequently, a higher inner-field area.

This paper presents a brief overview of the route planning tool focusing on the updates to adopt the new headland type in the planning process. The updates were tested by planning

---
[1] German Research Centre for Artificial Intelligence (DFKI), PBR, Berghoffstraße 11, 49090 Osnabrück, santiago.focke@dfki.de
[2] University of Osnabrück, Berghoffstraße 11, 49090 Osnabrück, joachim.hertzberg@uos.de

the routes of an output-material-flow case scenario on 11 real field geometries with different shapes and sizes, involving one non-capacitated primary machine (*PM*) performing the work in the field and two service units (*SU*) for the overload of material from the PM and its transportation to an unloading location. Exemplary results of the planning process are presented, followed by limitations, discussion, and future work.

2 Methods

The overall route planning process of the presented tool is divided into three main steps: 1) the generation of the field geometries, including the headland and inner-field boundaries and tracks; 2) the generation of the so-called 'base' route of the primary machine (*PM*) working in the field; and 3) the final planning of the routes for all machines participating in the operation, including extraction of material, overloading, and transit to and from the unloading locations. This section is focused on the updates developed to adopt the new headland type; further details on the planning process can be found in [Fo21; FH22].

To generate the field geometric representation in step 1), a reference line for the inner-field (*IF*) tracks is given as an input. The IF tracks are generated by extending said reference line and recursively translating it into a distance equal to the working width of the primary machine (*PMww*) until the IF region is completely covered. An initial set of IF tracks is generated to determine the sides of the field where the main headlands (*MHLs*) will be located. Next, the boundaries of the main headlands are generated based on the desired headland width, followed by the generation of the corresponding tracks with a track width equal to the PMww (the resulting headland width will be a multiple of PMww). These tracks are generated so that the distance between the track-ends and the headland boundary is equal to PMww. Next, the connecting headlands (*CHLs*) are generated, which are located in the remaining sides of field boundary and comprise only one track. The CHL tracks also have a width equal to the PMww, but the track-ends intersect the corresponding headland boundary. Finally, the boundary of the IF region is obtained by subtracting the headland areas from the field boundary, and the IF tracks are regenerated to cover this new boundary. Depending on the shape and area of the field boundary and desired headland width, three cases of geometric representation result from step 1). If the boundaries of the two MHLs do not intersect, the set of headlands will comprise two MHLs connected by two CHLs (type M2C2). If the boundaries of the two initially generated MHLs intersect in one side, these headlands will be merged into a single MHL, and one CHL will connect both sides of the MHL (type M1C1). A third case arises when both sides of the initially generated MHLs intersect; in this case, a complete surrounding headland is generated, and the planning processes presented in [Fo21] will be followed.

In step 2), the base route of the PM is generated, which represents the route that the PM will follow to cover the field area without considering the capacity constraints or unloading activities. As on [Fo21], the base route will cover the headland region first, followed by the IF region. The PM will start from one of the two ends of the outermost track of the first headland to be worked. The first headland will be automatically selected based on the locations of the PM and the field access points, and can be either a MHL or a CHL. At least one access point must be located near an outer-most headland track-end. The PM will work the headland from the outermost track to the innermost track and then continue with the non-worked adjacent headland which is closest to the last worked track point. This process will be repeated until all headlands are covered. Thanks to the CHLs, it is possible to work all headlands continuously; however, if a MHL is neither the first nor the last headland to be worked, and its number of tracks is even, the PM will have to transit over one already-worked track to reach the next CHL, which should be avoided not to introduce undesired non-working transit. In the connections from a CHL to an MHL, the PM will work a segment of the MHL before starting to work on the MHL outermost track. This segment is built by connecting the track-ends of the MHL that are closest to the CHL end point, from the innermost- to the outermost- track. Once all headlands are worked, the PM will cover the IF following the IF tracks from one side of the field to the other, starting with the track closest to the last worked headland point (as done in [Fo21]). The transit between IF tracks is done over the headland region either by direct connections using Dubins paths or via connected headland tracks.

Step 3) follows the same procedure as presented in [Fo21; FH22] for the two supported case scenarios, namely a) one capacitated PM that works the field and transports the material; and b) one non-capacitated PM that works the field in coordination with one or more capacitated service units (SU). First, the search graph that is used for in-field path planning is built based on the generated geometries and the base route. Next the working windows for each capacitated machine are computed based on the container capacity and the amount of material in the field. The working windows divide the process into a set of sub-processes (tours), each of them involving transit to the field, working of the field and overloading of material (if applicable), and transit to an unloading location (e.g., a clamp next to the field or a silo). The routes generated in each tour are finally combined to obtain the machine routes, which are smoothened based on the corresponding turning radii.

3 Results

The new updates were tested by planning a harvesting operation on 11 fields with varying shapes, belonging to cases M2C2 and M1C1. The operation consisted of one non-capacitated harvester (PM) with a working width of 6m, and two transport vehicles (SU) with a container capacity of 10t. A headland width of 24m was selected, resulting in five tracks per MHL. Tab. 1 contains the geometric properties of the test fields, including the total field areas, the areas of the resulting MHL-, CHL-, and IF- regions, and the number of generated side-headlands. Fig. 1 shows the resulting geometries for six of the test fields.

For the route planning, an average yield mass of 50t/ha was selected. The routes were planned aiming to optimize the overall duration of the harvesting operation [FH22], and the switch between overloading windows from one SU to the other was not restricted to the IF track-ends. Results for the planning process in field F9 are presented next. Fig. 2

shows the resulting geometric representation and the generated graph for this field. The harvester route and the route of one of the transport vehicles are depicted in Fig. 3.

Id	FA[m^2]	P/A [m^{-1}]	IFA[m^2] (% FA)	MHLA[m^2] (% FA)	CHLA[m^2] (% FA)	HL type
F1	117120	0.013	97342 (83.1%)	14402 (12.3%)	5376 (4.6%)	M2C2
F2	14688	0.038	4914 (33.5%)	8958 (61.0%)	816 (5.6%)	M1C1
F3	27630	0.028	13600 (49.2%)	12704 (46.0%)	1326 (4.8%)	M1C1
F4	108840	0.014	85894 (78.9%)	18566 (17.1%)	4380 (4.0%)	M2C2
F5	23117	0.031	9549 (41.3%)	12768 (55.2%)	800 (3.5%)	M1C1
F6	32072	0.035	21279 (66.3%)	6097 (19.0%)	4696 (14.6%)	M2C2
F7	9061	0.047	4172 (46.0%)	3858 (42.6%)	1032 (11.4%)	M2C2
F8	146962	0.011	118801 (80.8%)	23974 (16.3%)	4186 (2.8%)	M2C2
F9	15609	0.033	7908 (50.7%)	6661 (42.7%)	1041 (6.7%)	M2C2
F10	55231	0.018	38547 (69.8%)	14716 (26.6%)	1968 (3.6%)	M2C2
F11	49633	0.021	37815 (76.2%)	8015 (16.1%)	3803 (7.7%)	M2C2

Tab. 1: Test fields. FA: Field Area; P/A; Perimeter/Area; IFA: *IF* Area, MHLA: Area of *MHLs*; CHLA: Area of *CHLs*; %FA: % of field area; HL type: headland type

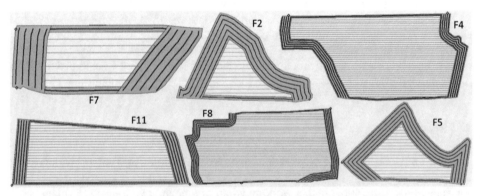

Fig. 1: Field geometries: Headlands (grey background) and Inner-field (white background) with corresponding tracks. Note: the field images are not in the same scale (see Tab. 1)

Because the planner does not support complex manoeuvres involving reverse driving, some limitations arise during the base-route planning. As can be seen in Fig. 3 (left), the connection between headland tracks is done by a simple connecting path between track-ends (with reduced speed). In practice, however, it is expected that the driver needs to perform more complex manoeuvres to harvests these small segments whilst remaining inside the field boundary. This also applies for other headland track segments with steep turns. Another current limitation arises when the field boundary segments adjacent to the CHLs are not fairly parallel to the reference line, causing some IF tracks-ends to be

Route-planning in output-material-flow operations 319

adjacent to a CHL and not to an MHL. Such case can be seen, for instance, in field F11. Depending on the geometries of the adjacent CHL and the working direction of the IF track, complex manoeuvres and/or longer transit segments over the headland tracks might be needed to connect to the IF track. As a result, the planned connection paths might significantly differ to the paths driven in practice. This drawback can be resolved by removing the conflicting CHL and combining the two MHLs to ensure that all IF track-ends are adjacent to an MHL.

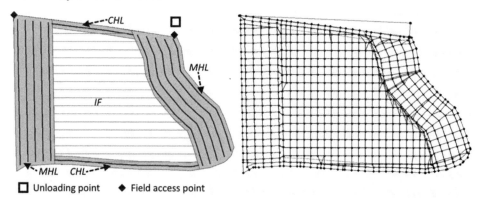

Fig. 2: Field F9 geometries (left) and graph (right)

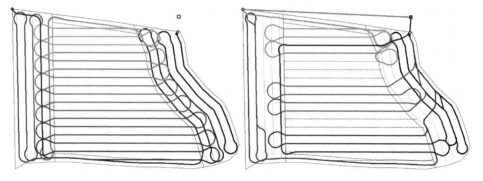

Fig. 3: Harvester route (left); transport vehicle route (right)

4 Conclusions

This paper presented an extension to the planning tool from [Fo21; FH22] to support in-field route planning with a new type of headland region. This region consists of a set of partial headlands, comprised by main headlands (located at the inner-field track-ends) and connecting headlands (bordering the field boundary and connecting the main headlands). This headland type results in a reduced overall headland region focused on the areas where the primary machine performs the turns to transit between IF tracks.

The tool updates were tested by planning a harvesting campaign in 11 test fields with one non-capacitated harvester and two transport vehicles. The results show that the generated field geometric representation is highly dependent on the headland width and the field shape and size. The limitations of the planning component related to complex manoeuvres involving reverse driving translated into the generation of route segments that are expected to differ from real driving on the field. However, the tool is currently meant to be used as a reference global planner, hence it is expected that the driver will perform the appropriate manoeuvres to satisfy the field and operation constraints. Aside from the presented limitations, the tool satisfyingly planned the routes for all participating machines in all test fields. The preliminary results suggest that the usage of the presented headland type should depend on the field base geometries (shape, access points, etc.) to avoid the introduction of complex manoeuvring for the drivers and long non-working travel distances. Future work includes improvements on the headlands generation to ensure that all IF track-ends are adjacent to an MHL, as well as the further testing of the planning tool in different output-material-flow operations and traffic analysis comparing the two supported headland types.

Acknowledgements: The SOILAssist project is funded by the Federal Ministry of Education and Research (BMBF) within the framework of the BonaRes-initiative (grant no. 031B1065B). The DFKI Niedersachsen (DFKI NI) is sponsored by the Ministry of Science and Culture of Lower Saxony and the VolkswagenStiftung.

Bibliography

[FH22]   Focke Martinez, S.; Hertzberg, J.: Route-planning in output-material-flow arable farming operations aiming for soil protection, in 42. GIL-Jahrestagung, Künstliche Intelligenz in der Agrar- und Ernährungswirtschaft, Bonn, 2022.

[Fo21]   Focke Martinez, S. et.al: Overview of a route-planning tool for capacitated field processes in arable farming, in 41. GIL-Jahrestagung, Informations- und Kommunikationstechnologie in kritischen Zeiten, Bonn, 2021.

[Mo20] Moysiadis, V. et.al: Mobile Robotics in Agricultural Operations: A Narrative Review on Planning Aspects. Applied Sciences 10/10, p. 3453, 2020.

[No22]   Nørremark, M. et.al: In-Field Route Planning Optimisation and Performance Indicators of Grain Harvest Operations. Agronomy 12/5, p. 1151, 2022.

[NZ20] Nilsson, R.S.; Zhou, K. Decision Support Tool for Operational Planning of Field Operations. Agronomy 10/2, p. 229, 2020.

/ „CognitiveWeeding": Entwicklung von Entscheidungsregeln für ein kontextbezogenes KI-Expertensystem auf Einzelpflanzenbasis – pflanzenbauliche Aspekte

David Hagemann [1], Tim Zurheide[1] und Dieter Trautz[1]

Abstract: Beikräuter stehen in Konkurrenz zur Ertragsbildung der Kulturpflanze. Die Konkurrenzkraft einzelner Arten und das heterogene Auftreten ermöglichen das gezielte Regulieren einzelner Teilflächen. Kriterien zur Ableitung der kontextbezogenen Regulierungswürdigkeit werden aus Feldversuchen und Literaturrecherchen abgeleitet. Als Basis dient ein Schadschwellenkonzept, welches anhand der Häufigkeit ein akzeptables Maß an Beikrautbesatz bemisst. Aufbauend darauf sollen die Parameter Lichtkonkurrenz, Standraum, Biodiversität, Erosion, Wirteignung für Schaderreger und Samenpotential einbezogen werden. Ziel ist es, für jede Einzelpflanze im Expertensystem eine Regulierungsentscheidung abzuleiten, die es ermöglicht, nur wirklich schädliche Pflanzen der Ackerbegleitflora zu regulieren und damit eine höhere Biodiversität auf der Ackerfläche zu erhalten.

Keywords: Beikrautregulierung, Schadschwelle, selektiv, teilflächenspezifisch, Entscheidungsunterstützung

1 Einleitung

Biotische Schadorganismen verursachen weltweit zwischen 50 % und 80 % Ertragsverluste. Beikräuter sind mit 34 % der größte Verursacher [Oe06]. Jedoch sind nicht alle Arten der Ackerbegleitflora dabei gleichermaßen ertragsmindernd. Zudem bieten sie durch Blüten und Samen Lebensgrundlage für zahlreiche Organismen. Durch ihr räumlich aggregiertes Auftreten ist eine ganzflächige Regulierung nicht immer nötig. Nachteile wie die Störung des Bodenlebens, erhöhte Erosionsgefahr, eine erhöhte Verdunstung sowie Einträge von Pflanzenschutzmitteln in die Umwelt und Lebensmittelkette können so vermindert werden [BC90]. Ziel des Projektes „CognitiveWeeding" ist es daher, standortspezifisch für jede sensorisch erkannte Pflanze eine kontextbezogene Entscheidung über die Regulierungswürdigkeit abzuleiten, um dann kleinräumig selektiv mit Hack- oder Spritztechnik zu agieren.

---

[1] Hochschule Osnabrück, Fakultät Agrarwissenschaften und Landschaftsarchitektur, Am Krümpel 31, 49090 Osnabrück, david.hagemann@hs-osnabrueck.de, https://orcid.org/0000-0003-3896-2064; t.zurheide@hs-osnabrueck.de; d.trautz@hs-osnabrueck.de

2 Material und Methoden

Zur Ableitung einzelpflanzenspezifischer Regulierungswürdigkeiten wird im Projekt ein Expertensystem verwendet. Dieses benötigt im Vergleich zu Neuronalen Netzwerken keine Trainingsdaten, die in Bezug auf solche komplexen Entscheidungsfindungen nur schwer zu generieren sind. Wissensbasierte Systeme wie ein Expertensystem können hier vorhandenes Fachwissen in Form von Wenn-Dann Regeln abbilden. Das Expertensystem stuft anhand zugrundeliegender Kriterien die Regulierungswürdigkeit jeder einzelnen Ackerbegleitpflanze ein [Al22]. Diese Kriterien sind damit, neben technischen Limitierungen, entscheidend dafür, wie viele Beikräuter nach der Regulierung auf der Fläche verbleiben und einen Beitrag zur Steigerung der Biodiversität leisten können. Aufgrund der automatisierten Anwendung der Regeln kann von Gesamt- oder größeren Teilflächen auf die Einzelpflanze heruntergeskaliert werden. Eine solch kleinräumige Differenzierung wäre von einem Landwirt in der Praxis nicht möglich. Es besteht das Potential, Beikräuter sehr kleinräumig mit erheblicher Verringerung der zu behandelnden Fläche zu regulieren. Infolgedessen ist eine große Einsparung von Pflanzenschutzmitteln im Bereich der Herbizide zu erwarten.

Grundlage bildet das bekannte Schadschwellenprinzip [BH81]. Jedoch sind für die im Projekt betrachteten Kulturen Mais (*Zea mays* L.) und Rüben (*Beta vulgaris subsps.* L.) keine Schwellenwerte für einzelne Beikrautarten vorhanden. Zudem darf nicht außer Acht gelassen werden, dass die Beikräuter nicht nur in Konkurrenz zu der Kulturpflanze stehen, sondern auch unterschiedliche Arten der Ackerbegleitflora untereinander interagieren. Ergebnis ist eine geringere Ertragsauswirkung von Mischverunkrautungen gegenüber einer durch eine dominante Art bestimmte Begleitflora [Ad19; PMM09]. Dies wird durch die vorhandenen Schadschwellensysteme nicht berücksichtigt.

Nach eingehender Literaturrecherche wurden einige potentielle Parameter mit dazugehörigen Indikatoren für ein KI-Expertensystem ausgewählt. Diese Parameter sollen sensorisch oder von externen Quellen akquiriert werden und dann zur Fällung der Regulierungsentscheidung jeder einzelnen Begleitpflanze herangezogen werden.

3 Zwischenergebnisse und Diskussion

Ergebnisse der Literaturrecherche zu möglichen Entscheidungsregeln sind in untenstehender Tabelle nach Entscheidungsparameter und zugehörigem Indikator aufgelistet und werden im Folgenden im Detail erläutert (Tab. 1). Wie bei dem zugrundeliegenden Schadschwellenprinzip wird zunächst die Pflanzenanzahl mit entsprechendem Schwellenwert in die Entscheidungsfindung einbezogen. Um das zeitlich versetzte Auflaufen und die dadurch verminderte Konkurrenzwirkung mit verspäteter Keimung eines Beikrauts zu berücksichtigen [KS91], sollen die Parameter Wuchshöhe und Deckungsgrad der Pflanze in Zukunft implementiert werden. Insbesondere der relative Deckungsgrad der Begleitpflanze im Verhältnis zur Kulturpflanze kann hier das zeitlich versetzte Auftreten der Konkurrenz adäquat abbilden [NLL99; LVV03].

Hinzu kommt der Konkurrenzfaktor Standraum, bei welchem die Entfernung der Begleitpflanze zur Kulturpflanze als Indikator verwendet werden soll. Mit zunehmender Entfernung wird die Konkurrenz in Bezug auf Wasser, Nährstoffe und Licht abnehmen und der Schwellenwert zur Regulierung kann höher gewählt werden [KNM19, MSW79 nach Al87]. Damit sind die beiden Parameter der Licht- und Nährstoffkonkurrenz weitestgehend abgedeckt.

Weitere Parameter, die abseits der Konkurrenzbeziehung zur Wahrung der Biodiversität und zum Schutz von Boden und für ein langfristiges Ertragspotential mit eingehen können, sind zum einen die Besuchshäufigkeit durch Arthropoden in Abhängigkeit der Attraktivität der Blüte, der Zugänglichkeit und der Nektar- und Pollenqualität und -quantität [BG15; Ga17]. Entscheidende Faktoren für die Attrakivität sind der Geruch, die Farbe und Reflektionen im UV-Spektrum. Die Zugänglichkeit ergibt sich aus der Morphologie der Blüte in Zusammenspiel mit dem jeweiligen Blütenbesucher. Außerdem bestimmen Blühdauer und -beginn über die Eignung für Blütenbesucher in Abhängigkeit der Synchronität mit deren Aktivität.

Zum anderen können durch Einbringung einer Regel zu seltenen Arten diese gezielt geschützt werden. Durch den breitflächigen Einsatz von Herbiziden und Stickstoffdüngern ist die Vielfalt der Ackerwildkräuter zurückgegangen [Mo04; An20]. Um diese Artenvielfalt nicht weiter zu gefährden, müssen Ackerstandorte, auf denen sie vorkommen, in ihrer Bewirtschaftungsform bewahrt werden. Der pflanzenspezifische Verzicht auf Herbizide ermöglicht den Schutz dieser Arten [Ge22; Al22].

In Bezug auf Erosion kann die Hangneigung und Wettervorhersage verwendet werden, um auf gefährdeten Teilflächen gezielt die flächige Durchwurzelung auch durch Beikräuter zu tolerieren [Bl18; Ga17; Ja22; Mo20]. Für folgende Jahre ist des Weiteren wichtig, ob die potentiell auf der Fläche tolerierbaren Beikräuter Wirtspflanzen für relevante Schaderreger in der Fruchtfolge vorkommender Kulturen sind [NK00; Bu02; Ga17]. Die Beikräuter können dem Schaderreger als Zwischenwirt, zur Vermehrung oder auch als Nahrungsquelle dienen. Andererseits können Beikräuter auch von der Kulturpflanze ablenken oder natürlichen Antagonisten Lebensraum bieten.

Parameter	Indikator
Lichtkonkurrenz	Wuchshöhe
Standraum	Entfernung des Beikrauts zur Kulturpflanze
Nährstoffe	Anzahl, Deckungsgrad
Biodiversität	Insektenbeflug, seltene Arten, Bodenbrüter
Erosion	Hangneigung
Wirteignung	Wirt für relevante Schaderreger, Wirt für Antagonisten
Samenpotential	Samenanzahl je Pflanze * Pflanzenanzahl * Persistenz * Reifezeit

Tab. 1: Mögliche Parameter und dazugehörige Indikatoren für das KI-Expertensystem zur Fällung der Regulierungsentscheidung

Weitere Parameter, die in Zukunft auf ihre Eignung zur Entscheidungsfindung geprüft werden, sind z. B. die Vermehrungseigenschaften sowie die Ernteauswirkungen der Beikräuter. Das Samenpotential besonders kritischer Pflanzen sowie die Etablierung schwer zu regulierender Wurzelunkräuter dürfen nicht außer Acht gelassen werden [Ma21]. Dies kann über eine Herabsetzung der Schadschwelle oder auch durch die Berücksichtigung von Parametern wie Samenanzahl je Pflanze [Si09], die Persistenz der Samen im Boden [Ge22] sowie den Zeitpunkt der Abreife der Samen erfolgen [RO13]. Reifen die Beikrautsamen erst nach der Ernte der Kulturpflanzen ab, ist das Beikraut bezüglich des Samenpotentials als unkritisch einzustufen. In Bezug auf die Beerntung können Faktoren wie erhöhte Feuchtigkeit durch Beikräuter, erhöhter Besatz und Ernteerschwernis durch zum Beispiel rankende Pflanzen Berücksichtigung finden.

Neben dem Schutz seltener Pflanzenarten und der Habitatförderung für Arthropoden könnten auch Gelege bodenbrütender Vögel erkannt und gezielt geschützt werden [St15].

4 Schlussfolgerung

Das bekannte Schadschwellenprinzip bietet eine gute Grundlage, um weitere Parameter, die aufgrund veränderter Anforderungen an den Pflanzenschutz auftreten, einzubinden und kontextbezogen Regulierungsentscheidungen für einzelne Pflanzenarten der Ackerbegleitflora zu treffen. Die Verwendung eines Expertensystems ist für die Ableitung dieser Entscheidungen aus Regeln das System der Wahl. Genannte Regeln werden in dem Projekt durch das DFKI in ein Expertensystem implementiert. In Feldversuchen werden in den folgenden Jahren die Umsetzbarkeit und Ertragswirkung in der Anwendung der Regeln überprüft. Die Regeln können dann bei Erkenntnisgewinn verändert oder ergänzt werden. Weitere Parameter, die in Zukunft interessant werden können, sind Regulierungserfolg, Wasserhaushaltsdaten, Ernteerschwernis und Qualitätsminderung.

Es wäre also sinnvoll, das System modular aufzubauen, um die Erweiterung des Expertensystems um weitere Regeln angepasst an standortspezifische Begebenheiten einfach zu ermöglich. Weiterhin sollte auch die Nutzung eines standardisierten Inputs von Sensordaten und Outputs in Form von Applikationskarten eine Implementierung in die Prozesskette der Beikrautregulierung herstellerübergreifend ermöglichen. [Al22].

Förderhinweis: Gefördert vom Bundesministerium für Umwelt, Naturschutz, nukleare Sicherheit und Verbraucherschutz (BMUV) aufgrund eines Beschlusses des Deutschen Bundestages (FKZ 67KI21001C).

Literaturverzeichnis

[Ad19] Adeux, G. et al.: Mitigating crop yield losses through weed diversity. Nature Sustainability 11/2, S. 1018-1026, 2019.

[Al22] Allmendinger, A. et al.: Precision Chemical Weed Management Strategies: A Review and a Design of a New CNN-Based Modular Spot Sprayer. Agronomy 7/12, S. 1620, 2022.

[Al87] Aldrich, R. J.: Predicting Crop Yield Reductions from Weeds. Weed Technology 3/1, S. 199-206, 1987.

[An20] Anton, C. et al.: Biodiversität und Management von Agrarlandschaften. Umfassendes Handeln ist jetzt wichtig. Stellungnahme. Deutsche Akademie der Naturforscher Leopoldina e. V. - Nationale Akademie der Wissenschaften; acatech - Deutsche Akademie der Technikwissenschaften e. V; Union der deutschen Akademien der Wissenschaften e. V, Halle (Saale), 2020.

[BC90] Brain, P.; Cousens, R.: The Effect of Weed Distribution on Predictions of Yield Loss. The Journal of Applied Ecology 2/27, S. 735, 1990.

[BG15] Bretagnolle, V.; Gaba, S.: Weeds for bees? A review. Agronomy for Sustainable Development 3/35, S. 891-909, 2015.

[BH81] Beer, E.; Heitefuss, R.: Ermittlung von Bekämpfungsschwellen und wirtschaftlichen Schadensschwellen für monokotyle und dikotyle Unkräuter in Winterweizen und -gerste II. Bekämpfungsschwellen und wirtschaftliche Schadensschwellen in Abhängigkeit von verschiedenen Bekämpfungskosten, Produktpreisen und Ertragsniveau. Zeitschrift für Pflanzenkrankheiten und Pflanzenschutz / Journal of Plant Diseases and Protection 6/88, S. 321–336, 1981.

[Bl18] Blaix, C. et al.: Quantification of regulating ecosystem services provided by weeds in annual cropping systems using a systematic map approach. Weed Research 3/58, S. 151-164, 2018.

[Bu02] Buhler, D. D.: 50th Anniversary – Invited Article: Challenges and opportunities for integrated weed management. Weed Science 3/50, S. 273-280, 2002.

[Ga17] Gaba, S. et al.: Response and effect traits of arable weeds in agro-ecosystems: a review of current knowledge. Weed Research 3/57, S. 123-147, 2017.

[Ge22] Gerhards, R. et al.: Advances in site-specific weed management in agriculture – A review. Weed Research, 2022.

[Ja22] Jafari, M. et al.: Slope Stabilization Methods Using Biological and Biomechanical Measures. In (Jafari, M. et al. Hrsg.): Soil Erosion Control in Drylands. Springer International Publishing; Imprint Springer, Cham, S. 445-647, 2022.

[KNM19] Korres, N. E.; Norsworthy, J. K.; Mauromoustakos, A.: Effects of Palmer Amaranth (Amaranthus palmeri) Establishment Time and Distance from the Crop Row on Biological and Phenological Characteristics of the Weed: Implications on Soybean Yield. Weed Science 1/67, S. 126-135, 2019.

[KS91]   Kropff, M. J.; Spitters, C. J. T.: A simple model of crop loss by weed competition from early observations on relative leaf area of the weeds. Weed Research 2/31, S. 97-105, 1991.

[LVV03] Lemieux, C.; Vallée, L.; Vanasse, A.: Predicting yield loss in maize fields and developing decision support for post-emergence herbicide applications. Weed Research 5/43, S. 323-332, 2003.

[Ma21]   Masson, S. et al.: Neue Entscheidungshilfen für eine nachhaltige Unkrautbekämpfung. Agrarforschung Schweiz 12, S. 79-89, 2021.

[Mo04]   Moss, S. R. et al.: The Broadbalk long-term experiment at Rothamsted: what has it told us about weeds? Weed Science 5/52, S. 864-873, 2004.

[Mo20]   Moreau, D. et al.: In which cropping systems can residual weeds reduce nitrate leaching and soil erosion? European Journal of Agronomy 119, S. 126015, 2020.

[MSW79] Miller, P. C.; Stoner; W. A.: Canopy structure and environmental interactions. In (Johnson, G. B. et al. Hrsg.): Topics in Plant Population Biology. Columbia University Press, New York, S. 428-460, 1979.

[NK00]   Norris, R. F.; Kogan, M.: Interactions between weeds, arthropod pests, and their natural enemies in managed ecosystems. Weed Science 1/48, S. 94-158, 2000.

[NLL99] Ngouajio, M.; Lemieux, C.; Leroux, G. D.: Prediction of corn (Zea mays) yield loss from early observations of the relative leaf area and the relative leaf cover of weeds. Weed Science 3/47, S. 297-304, 1999.

[Oe06]   Oerke, E.-C.: Crop losses to pests. The Journal of Agricultural Science 1/144, S. 31-43, 2006.

[PMM09] Pollnac, F. W.; Maxwell, B. D.; Menalled, F. D.: Weed community characteristics and crop performance: a neighbourhood approach. Weed Research 3/49, S. 242-250, 2009.

[Ro13]   Gerhards, R.: Precision weed management. In (Oliver, M.; Bishop, T.; Marchant, B. Eds.): Precision Agriculture for Sustainability and Environmental Protection. Routledge, 2013.

[Si09]   Simard, M.-J. et al.: Validation of a Management Program Based on A Weed Cover Threshold Model: Effects on Herbicide Use and Weed Populations. Weed Science 2/57, S. 187-193, 2009.

[St15]   Steen, K. A. et al.: Detection of bird nests during mechanical weeding by incremental background modeling and visual saliency. Sensors (Basel, Switzerland) 3/15, S. 5096-5111, 2015.

Satellitengestützte Analyse der räumlichen Variabilität für die Ableitung von Ertragszonen und deren Ursachen

Ludwig Hagn[1], Johannes Schuster[1], Martin Mittermayer[1] und Kurt-Jürgen Hülsbergen[1]

Abstract: Die Kenntnis der räumlichen Variabilität und deren Ursachen bietet zahlreiche Ansatzpunkte für Managementmaßnahmen. Dennoch ist das Interesse an räumlich variablen Erträgen (z. B. Biomassekarten) und teilschlagspezifischer Düngung in der landwirtschaftlichen Praxis noch sehr begrenzt. Satellitendaten sind eine kostengünstige und praktische Möglichkeit, Flächenheterogenität zu erfassen. In der vorliegenden Untersuchung wurde die räumliche Variabilität auf einem Praxisschlag in Südostbayern anhand von mehrjährigen Satellitendaten erfasst und validiert. Indirekt erfasste Biomassekarten auf Basis des NDVI wurden in Beziehung zu räumlich variablen Bodendaten (C_{org}, N_t, pH-Wert) und multispektralen Sensormessungen gesetzt. Die Ergebnisse zeigten enge Zusammenhänge zwischen den Satellitendaten und den Sensormessungen (EC 32, r = 0,64; EC 43, r = 0,70). Die Satellitendaten wiesen enge Beziehungen mit den Bodenparametern auf (C_{org}, r = 0,60; N_t, r = 0,60). Auf Basis von hochauflösenden Biomassekarten können Teilflächen mit geringen Ertragspotenzialen identifiziert und Maßnahmen eingeleitet werden.

Keywords: Bodenheterogenität, Satellitendaten, Remote Sensing, Sensorsysteme

1 Einleitung

Aufgrund heterogener Bodeneigenschaften auf Ackerflächen (Textur, nutzbare Feldkapazität, Topographie etc.) kommt es zu räumlichen Unterschieden des Kornertrags und des N-Entzugs der Kulturpflanzen [Go03]. Räumlich variable Erträge können bei schlageinheitlicher N-Düngung zur N-Überversorgung in Niederertragszonen führen [Mi21], verbunden mit negativen ökologischen Folgen durch Stickstoffverluste [Mi22]. Dennoch ist das Interesse an räumlich variablen Erträgen (z. B. Biomassekarten) und teilschlagspezifischer Düngung in der landwirtschaftlichen Praxis noch sehr begrenzt. In den meisten landwirtschaftlichen Betrieben in Bayern wird die schlageinheitliche Bewirtschaftung praktiziert [Ga20]. Die Kenntnis der räumlichen Variabilität und deren Ursachen bietet zahlreiche Ansatzpunkte für Managementmaßnahmen, nicht nur im Bereich der Düngung. Satellitendaten sind eine kostengünstige und praktische Möglichkeit, Flächenheterogenität zu erfassen. Im Gegensatz zu traktormontierten Sensormessungen, Messungen von elektrischer Leitfähigkeit und georeferenzierten Bodenproben können Satellitendaten auch für mehrere Jahre rückwirkend ausgewertet

---

[1] Technische Universität München, Lehrstuhl für Ökologischen Landbau und Pflanzenbausysteme, Liesel-Beckmann-Straße 2, 85354 Freising, ludwig.hagn@tum.de; johannes.schuster@tum.de; martin.mittermayer@tum.de; huelsbergen@wzw.tum.de

werden. Es gibt bereits mehrere Ansätze und Verfahren, um die räumliche Variabilität von landwirtschaftlichen Nutzflächen anhand von Satellitendaten zu erfassen und auf deren Basis landwirtschaftliche Flächen in Ertrags- bzw. Managementzonen zu unterteilen. Jedoch fehlen oft Validierungen [Ge17; Ch21] (z. B. über Bodenparameter, Sensormessungen), ausreichende Transparenz des Vorgehens [Ba16] oder es werden wichtige agronomische Parameter (Kulturart, Entwicklungsstadium, klimatisch bedingte Jahreseffekte) umgangen bzw. vernachlässigt [Li07]. Mähdrescherdaten sind für die Definition und Validierung von räumlicher Variabilität auf landwirtschaftlichen Nutzflächen eher kritisch zu sehen. Es gibt klimatisch bedingte Jahreseffekte beim Ertrag, welche besonders bei der Verwendung von einjährigen Datensätzen bedenklich sind. Zum anderen gibt es erhebliche Fehlerquellen (Bedienungsfehler, Fehler aufgrund von Betriebsbedingungen, fehlende Kalibration, verschiedene Messsysteme bedingt durch die Hersteller, Schwankungen im Erntefluss und Variabilität der Erntekörner) [St22].

Der C_{org}- bzw. Humusgehalt zeigte in vorangegangen Studien den höchsten Erklärungsansatz für Kornertrag und Korn N-Entzug auf teilflächenspezifischer Ebene [Mi21; Mi22]. Der Humusgehalt hat positive Effekte auf die nutzbare Feldkapazität, Bodenstruktur und Nährstoffverfügbarkeit im Boden und somit einen direkten Einfluss auf das Ertragsniveau [Ko15]. Als langjährig konstanter Parameter kann der Humusgehalt demnach als geeigneter Parameter für die Validierung angesehen werden.

In der vorliegenden Untersuchung wird die räumliche Variabilität auf einem Praxisschlag in Südostbayern im 10 x 10 m Raster anhand von mehrjährigen Satellitendaten erfasst und validiert. Die Ursache der räumlichen Variabilität steht dabei im besonderen Fokus. Indirekt erfasste Biomassekarten auf Basis des NDVI werden in Beziehung zu räumlich variablen Bodendaten (C_{org}, N_t, pH-Wert) und multispektralen Sensormessungen gesetzt.

2 Material und Methoden

Die Untersuchungen fanden in einem Trinkwassereinzugsgebiet der Modellregion Burghausen/Burgkirchen in Südostbayern im Rahmen des vom Bayerischen Staatsministerium für Ernährung, Landwirtschaft und Forsten (StMELF) geförderten FE-Projekts „Minderung von Nitrataustragen durch digitales Stickstoffmanagement und sensorgestützte Düngung (digisens)" statt. Der Untersuchungsschlag wurde aufgrund seiner ausreichenden Größe (7,5 ha), Heterogenität und langjährig einheitlichen Bewirtschaftung ausgewählt.

2.1 Datenerfassung und Datenverabeitung

Die Datenerhebung erfolgte im Jahr 2022. Die verwendeten Satellitendaten entstammen aus dem Datensatz des Deutschen Zentrums für Luft- und Raumfahrt (DLR), welcher auf den Daten der European Space Agency (ESA) basiert. Es wurden Satellitendaten der Sentinel-2 Satelliten der Jahre 2016 bis 2021 ausgewertet. Die verschiedenen

Satellitenbilder wurden zu charakteristischen Entwicklungsstadien der Kulturpflanzen Winterweizen (April bis Mitte Juni), Wintergerste (März bis Ende Mai) und Mais (Mitte Juli bis Mitte August) mit vier bis sechs Terminen je Kultur ausgewählt. Auf Basis des Vegetationsindex NDVI wurde die Variabilität des relativen Biomassebildungspotenzials der einzelnen Schläge zu jedem Untersuchungstermin analysiert. Für jedes Untersuchungsjahr wurde eine relative Biomassepotenzialkarte erstellt, welche durch Übereinanderlegen zu einer mehrjährigen, (mind. 5 Jahre) relativen Biomassepotenzialkarte (relative BMP-Karte) berechnet wurde. Die relative BMP-Karte stellt das mehrjährige, konstante Biomassebildungspotenzial der Fläche dar. Die Datenverarbeitung erfolge mit QGIS und R Studio.

Die Bodenparameter (C_{org}, N_t, pH-Wert) wurden über eine flächendeckende georeferenzierte Bodenbeprobung erhoben. Acht Bodenproben wurden in einem Radius von maximal 50 cm um einen georeferenzierten Beprobungspunkt entnommen und zu einer Mischprobe zusammengefügt. Die Verteilung der Beprobungspunkte war auf Basis von geostatistischen Verfahren systematisch zufällig.

Mit einem traktorgetragenen multispektralen Sensor (TEC 5 2010) wurden zusätzlich Sensormessungen bei Winterweizen zu EC 32 und EC 43 durchgeführt und der REIP-Index als Parameter für die räumliche Variabilität berechnet.

2.2 Statistische Datenauswertung

Die Überprüfung der Plausibilität und Nutzbarkeit der mehrjährigen relativen BMP-Karte erfolgte anhand von Korrelationsanalysen nach Pearson. Die Bodenparameter und Ergebnisse der Sensormessungen wurden in dasselbe Raster, wie das der mehrjährigen relativen BMP-Karte gebracht, Ausreißer wurden bereinigt und die Daten wurden interpoliert. Anschließend erfolgte eine geostatistische Korrelationsanalyse. Die Korrelationskoeffizienten (r) wurden als sehr stark ($r > 0,9$), stark ($0,9 > r > 0,7$), mäßig ($0,7 > r > 0,5$), schwach ($0,5 > r > 0,3$) oder sehr schwach ($r < 0,3$) eingestuft [Sc22]. Die Daten der Reichsbodenschätzung wurden zur Interpretation hinzugezogen. Die Auswertung erfolgte in R Studio.

3 Ergebnisse

Die Ergebnisse zeigten, dass die Erfassung der räumlichen Variabilität durch die digitalen Methoden (Satellitendaten und Sensormessungen) bei der Zonierung der Fläche sehr ähnlich war. Die relative BMP-Karte wies ähnliche Bereiche der Fläche als Hochertragszone (grün), Mittelertragszone (gelb) und Niederertragszone (rot) aus wie die Erfassung über den traktormontierten Sensor. Nach der Reichsbodenschätzung wurde die Fläche als homogen mit Ackerzahlen von 57 bis 62 eingestuft. Die digitalen Methoden zeigten allerdings, dass die Fläche für die Region stark heterogen ist. Auffällig war auch, dass sowohl die relative BMP-Karte als auch der Sensor den Bereich mit ehemaligem

Dauergrünland als Hochertragszone definierten. Das Dauergrünland wurde an dieser Stelle bereits 1980 umgebrochen, die Wirkungen im Boden sind aber wohl immer noch ertragsbestimmend. Nach der relativen BMP-Karte ist das relative Biomassebildungspotenzial im Bereich des ehemaligen Dauergrünlands tendenziell höher. Der Vergleich mit den Bodenparametern mittels geostatistischer Auswertung von C_{org}- und N_t-Gehalten bestätigt, dass im Bereich der deklarierten Hochertragszone über die relative BMP-Karte, die C_{org}- und N_t-Gehalte innerhalb der Fläche höher sind. Außerdem wurde die erfasste räumliche Heterogenität über die relative BMP-Karte und den Sensor anhand der Bodenparameter bestätigt (Abb. 1). Die räumliche Verteilung der Bodenparameter C_{org} und N_t war nahezu identisch. Der pH-Wert ist in der Hochertragszone höher als in der Niederertragszone.

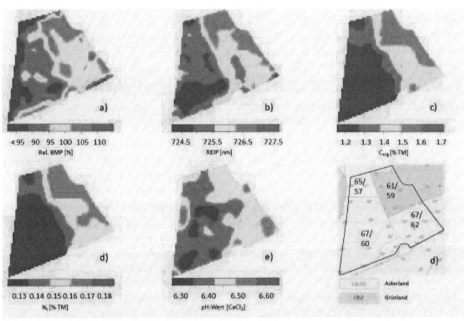

Abb. 1: Analyse der räumlichen Variabilität, Beispielschlag, Burghausen/Burgkirchen: a) mehrjähriges rel. BMP, b) Sensormessung EC 32, c) C_{org}-Gehalte, d) N_t-Gehalte, e) pH-Wert, d) Reichsbodenschätzung mit Acker- und Grünlandzahl

Die Korrelationsanaylse ergab einen mäßigen Zusammenhang zwischen der relativen BMP-Karte und der Sensormessung zu EC 32 (r = 0,64) und einen starken Zusammenhang zur Sensormessung zu EC 43 (r = 0,70). Die Zusammenhänge zwischen der relativen BMP-Karte und den Bodenparametern waren mäßig (C_{org}, r = 0,60; N_t, r = 0,60), bzw. sehr schwach (pH-Wert, r = 0,19). Die Sensormessungen korrelierten stark mit den N_t- und C_{org}-Gehalten und mäßig mit dem pH-Wert. Die Bodenparameter N_t- und C_{org}-Gehalte korrelierten sehr stark (Tab. 1).

r	rel BMP (%)	Sensor (EC 32)	Sensor (EC 43)	C_{org}-Gehalte (%TM)	N_t-Gehalte (%TM)	pH-Wert ($CaCl_2$)
rel BMP (%)	1,00	0,64	0,70	0,60	0,60	0,19
Sensor (EC 32)		1,00	0,93	0,81	0,79	0,58
Sensor (EC 43)			1,00	0,82	0,82	0,52
C_{org}-Gehalte (%TM)				1,00	0,99	0,67
N_t-Gehalte (%TM)					1,00	0,65
pH-Wert ($CaCl_2$)						1,00

Tab. 1: Korrelationsanalyse (nach Pearson), Beispielschlag, Burghausen/Burgkirchen

4 Diskussion und Ausblick

In den Ergebnissen hat sich gezeigt, dass die relative BMP-Karte eine geeignete Methode ist, um räumliche Variabilität in heterogenen Flächen zu erfassen. Es hat sich auch gezeigt, dass es enge Zusammenhänge mit den Bodenparametern gibt (C_{org} und N_t, r = 0,60). Bei der Datenverarbeitung wurden charakteristische EC-Stadien der Kulturen Winterweizen, Wintergerste und Mais gewählt. Die exakte Fruchtfolge wurde jedoch bei der Datenverarbeitung nicht eingehalten, dennoch zeigten sich positive Ergebnisse. Es stellte sich heraus, dass die Sensormessungen zu EC 32 (r = 0,81) und EC 43 (r = 0,82) bei Winterweizen noch engere Zusammenhänge mit den Bodenparametern C_{org} und N_t aufwiesen, jedoch sind sie mit hohem Arbeitsaufwand und Kosten verbunden. Außerdem ist es nicht möglich, rückwirkend Daten zu erfassen. Satellitenbilder sind diesbezüglich aufgrund der Datenverfügbarkeit klar im Vorteil. Des Weiteren können anhand von relativen BMP-Karten mehrere Flächen oder gar ein ganzes Areal erfasst und ausgewertet werden.

Durch den Einsatz von hochauflösenden Biomassekarten auf Basis des NDVI können Teilflächen mit geringen Ertragspotenzialen bedingt durch geringe Humusversorgung bzw. Teilflächen mit hoher Ertragsvariabilität identifiziert und z.B. bei Düngemaßnahmen berücksichtigt werden. Maßnahmen zum Humusaufbau auf humusverarmten Teilschlägen, zur Verbesserung der Bodenfruchtbarkeit sowie optimierte Fruchtfolgen mit ständiger Bodenbedeckung, reduzierte Bodenbearbeitung, aber auch Extensivierung (Umstellung auf Grünlandnutzung) auf besonders auswaschungsgefährdeten Teilflächen können eingeleitet werden.

In diesem Beitrag wurde das Prinzip der satellitengestützten Erfassung von räumlicher Variabilität und deren Ursachen vorgestellt. In weitergehenden Untersuchungen wird analysiert ob, a) die in dieser Arbeit verwendeten Datenquellen und Methoden auch auf anderen Flächen und Standorten ähnliche Ergebnisse erzielen, b) welche Ergebnisse erzielt werden, wenn die exakte Fruchtfolge und die dazugehörenden kulturspezifischen EC-Stadien bei der Auswahl der Termine der Satellitenbilder berücksichtigt werden.

Literaturverzeichnis

[Ba16] Bach, Heike; Migdall, Silke; Brohmeyer, Franziska; Brüggemann, Lena; Buddeberg, Marion; VISTA GmbH (2016): LfULG-Schriftenreihe, Heft 21/2016 „Satellitengestützte Ertragserhebung" (21).

[Ch21] Charvát, Karel; Lukas, Vojtěch; Horáková, Šárka (2021): Delineation of Management Zones Using Satellite Imageries. In: Big Data in Bioeconomy: Springer, Cham, S. 235-245. Online verfügbar unter https://link.springer.com/chapter/10.1007/978-3-030-71069-9_18-

[Ga20] Gabriel, A.; Gandorfer, M. (2020): Landwirte-Befragung 2020 Digitale Landwirtschaft Bayern. In: Landesanstalt für Landwirtschaft. Online verfügbar unter https://www.lfl.bayern.de/mam/cms07/ilt/dateien/ilt6_praesentation_by_2390_270820 20.pdf, zuletzt geprüft am 12.09.2022.

[Ge17] Georgi, Claudia; Spengler, Daniel; Itzerott, Sibylle; Kleinschmit, Birgit (2018): Automatic delineation algorithm for site-specific management zones based on satellite remote sensing data. In: Precision Agric 19 (4), S. 684-707. DOI: 10.1007/s11119-017-9549-y.

[Go03] Godwin, R. J.; Wood, G. A.; Taylor, J. C.; Knight, S. M.; Welsh, J. P. (2003): Precision Farming of Cereal Crops: a Review of a Six Year Experiment to develop Management Guidelines. In: Biosystems Engineering 84 (4), S. 375-391. DOI: 10.1016/S1537-5110(03)00031-X.

[Ko15] Kolbe, Hartmut (2016): Leitfaden zur Humusversorgung. Informationen für Praxis, Beratung und Schulung. Online verfügbar unter http://www.tll.de/www/daten/publikationen/schriftenreihe/2016_bh1_humus_ges.pdf, zuletzt geprüft am 05.11.2020.

[Li07] Li, Yan; Shi, Zhou; Li, Feng; Li, Hong-Yi (2007): Delineation of site-specific management zones using fuzzy clustering analysis in a coastal saline land. In: Computers and Electronics in Agriculture 56 (2), S. 174-186. DOI: 10.1016/j.compag.2007.01.013.

[Mi21] Mittermayer, Martin; Gilg, August; Maidl, Franz-Xaver; Nätscher, Ludwig; Hülsbergen, Kurt-Jürgen (2021): Site-specific nitrogen balances based on spatially variable soil and plant properties. In: Precision Agric 22 (5), S. 1416-1436. DOI: 10.1007/s11119-021-09789-9.

[Mi22] Mittermayer, Martin; Maidl, Franz-Xaver; Nätscher, Ludwig; Hülsbergen, Kurt-Jürgen (2022): Analysis of site-specific N balances in heterogeneous croplands using digital methods. In: European Journal of Agronomy 133 (5-6), S. 126442. DOI: 10.1016/j.eja.2021.126442.

[St22] Stettmer, Matthias; Mittermayer, Martin; Maidl, Franz-Xaver; Schwarzensteiner, Jürgen; Hülsbergen, Kurt-Jürgen; Bernhardt, Heinz (2022): Three Methods of Site-Specific Yield Mapping as a Data Source for the Delineation of Management Zones in Winter Wheat. In: Agriculture 12 (8), S. 1128. DOI: 10.3390/agriculture12081128.

Erhöhung der Biodiversität von Graslandbeständen mittels p-Wert-korrigierter Assoziationsregeln

Jens Harbers [1]

Abstract: In dieser Ausarbeitung wird gezeigt, wie Pflanzenarten zur Erhöhung der Biodiversität mithilfe der Assoziationsanalyse identifiziert werden. Basierend auf einem frei zugänglichen Datensatz einer Vegetationserhebung wurden eine Assoziationsanalyse durchgeführt und die mit dem Apriorialgorithmus erstellten Regeln mittels dem Chi-Quadrat-Test auf Signifikanz ($p < 0{,}05$) überprüft. Anschließend wurden die p-Werte nach verschiedenen Methoden adjustiert, um insignifikante Regeln aus der Regelsatztabelle auszuschließen. Je nach Korrekturmethode konnte untermauert werden, dass der Datenumfang der Simulationsstudie zur Erstellung von signifikanten Mustern nicht ausreicht. Somit muss eine Simulationsstudie mit mehr Parzellen angefertigt werden, wie die p-Wert-Korrektur zeigte. Bei unterbleibender Korrektur der p-Werte waren etwa 18 % aller Regeln nach der Filterung relevant, während bei einer p-Wert-Korrektur hingegen keine der erkannten 11 768 312 Regeln statistisch signifikant waren.

Keywords: R, Patternmining, p-Wert-Korrektur, Grasland, Assoziationsregeln

1 Einleitung

Der fortschreitende Verlust an artenreichem Grasland stellt die Landwirtschaft sowie den Naturschutz vor Herausforderungen. Auf artenarmen Flächen muss daher die Biodiversität wieder erhöht werden, um einerseits die Stabilität eines Bestandes zu fördern und andererseits Lebensraum für Insekten und Vögel zu schaffen. Dies setzt resiliente Grünlandbestände voraus, sollen die Bestände langfristig erhalten bleiben. Zudem soll die Landwirtschaft selbst nicht zu stark beeinträchtigt werden, damit keine Betriebe in existenzbedrohende Situationen gelangen, deren Flächen nach Betriebsaufgabe ggf. nicht weiter als Grünland bewirtschaftet werden. Daher muss eine Möglichkeit gefunden werden, passende Arten zu identifizieren, die auf einem Standort ausgebracht werden können, und diese möglichst sicher im Bestand zu etablieren. Eine Methodik stellt hier die Assoziationsanalyse dar, die seit langem in der Mustererkennung eingesetzt wird. Das Ziel ist es, aus einer Transaktionsliste von Items passende Muster (Regeln) zu finden, um relevante Informationen aufzudecken. Die Regeln können in der Ausgangsmenge nur Spezies enthalten, die auf einer Parzelle gefunden wurden, und müssen auf neue, nicht auf der Parzelle befindliche Spezies hinweisen. In der Landwirtschaft stellt dabei die Validierung passender Spezies ein Problem dar, da das Austesten der Saatgutmischungen aus den Regeln erheblichen Aufwand darstellt. Der Stand der Literatur ist es, die Regeln

---

[1] Landwirtschaftsverlag Münster, Data Analyst, Hülsebrockstraße 2-8, 48165 Münster, jens.harbers@lv.de
 https://orcid.org/0000-0001-6634-623X

nach Support, Konfidenz und dem Lift absteigend zu sortieren und auszugeben. Hingegen wird in diesem Beitrag eine andere Vorgehensweise genutzt, da hier stochastische Elemente berücksichtigt werden. Die Forschungsfrage besteht darin, aus der Vielzahl an Assoziationsregeln die geeignetsten zur Biodiversitätserhöhung ausfindig zu machen und so mit den vielversprechendsten Regeln zu arbeiten.

2 Material und Methoden

Dieser Abschnitt beschreibt die Datenverarbeitung und den Ablauf der Berechnungen. Es wird zudem folgendes Szenario angenommen: Eine Parzelle wird aufgrund einer Begehung als ökologisch verbesserungswürdig befunden. Anschließend wurden in direkter Umgebung weitere Parzellen in Hinblick auf vorkommende Pflanzenarten untersucht, um daraus Assoziationen abzuleiten. Im Folgenden wird die Parzelle A10_16, deren Biodiversität mit neuen Pflanzenspezies verbessert werden soll, aus dem ‚schedenveg'-Datensatz herangezogen, der im R-Paket ‚goeveg' [FJ21] liegt. Alle Daten wurden in R 3.4.3 [R 21] verarbeitet. Die Vorverarbeitung wurde mit den Grundfunktionen in R vorgenommen, während die Assoziationsregeln im ‚arules'-Paket mittels der Apriori-Funktion [MBK05] erstellt wurden.

2.1 Definition relevanter Begriffe und Maße

Nachfolgend werden relevante Maße der Assoziationsregeln definiert.

Das Itemset bezeichnet die Menge aller Spezies auf einer Parzelle.

Die Hypothese (X) einer Assoziationsregel wird Vorläufer bzw. Antecedent genannt.

Der Konsequent (Y) beschreibt das Itemset des Folgegliedes einer Assoziationsregel.

Der Support kennzeichnet die relative Häufigkeit, wie oft eine Regel zutrifft.

Die bedingte Wahrscheinlichkeit, die angibt, wie oft Y zutrifft, wenn X eingetreten ist, wird als Konfidenz bezeichnet.

Der in R ausgegebene p-Wert beschreibt die Grenzwahrscheinlichkeit, an der die Nullhypothese des Chi-Quadrat-Tests auf Unabhängigkeit von X und Y verworfen wird und dient als Ausgangswert für die p-Wert-Korrekturmethoden.

2.2 Datenverarbeitung

Der verwendete Datensatz ‚schedenveg' zeigt 28 verschiedene Parzellen an zwei Standorten, auf denen insgesamt 155 verschiedene Pflanzenspezies aufgenommen wurden. Zuerst wurde der Datensatz in ein Transaktionsdatenformat gebracht, in dem jede Parzelle eine Zeile darstellt und jede Spezies eine Spalte. Der Mindestsupport betrug 0,12.

Um Regeln auszuschließen, die kein hohes Vertrauensmaß enthalten, wurde vor der Berechnung außerdem eine Mindestkonfidenz von 0,05 gewählt. Der p-Wert wurde im Vorhinein auf 0,05 festgelegt.

Es wurden folgende Datenverarbeitungsschritte ausgeführt:

1. Umformen der Daten in ein Transaktionsformat, sodass die Parzellen und Spezies in zwei Spalten vorliegen.
2. Bestimmung der Itemsets der Vorläufer und Nachfolger.
3. Filterung von Regeln, damit nur Regeln, deren Vorläufer nur auf existierende Spezies im Bestand verweisen, enthalten sind.
4. Reduktion des Regeldatensatzes auf Nachfolger, deren Items ausschließlich auf neue, nicht im Feld vorhandene, Spezies hinweisen.
5. Ausführen des Chi-Quadrat-Tests und Ausgabe des p-Wertes.
6. Anwendung der p-Wert-Korrekturmethoden von Holm [Ho79], Benjamini-Yekutieli [BY01] und der Falscherkennungsrate (FDR) nach Benjamini-Hochberg [BH95]. Diese ist notwendig, um die Alphafehlerkumulierung zu adjustieren, die bei der mehrfachen Anwendung des Chi-Quadrat-Tests auf denselben Datenbestand entsteht.
7. Entfernung von insignifikanten Regeln ($p \geq 0{,}05$) nach p-Wertadjustierung und Regeln ohne p-Wert.
8. Sortieren der Liste nach Signifikanz (aufsteigend), Konfidenz (absteigend) und Support (absteigend).
9. Entnahme der ersten Regel je Nachfolger und Speicherung in einem neuen Objekt.
10. Sortieren des neuen Objektes nach Konfidenz (absteigend) und Support (absteigend) sowie Ausgabe einer Tabelle mit den zehn passendsten Spezies (siehe Tab. 1).

3 Ergebnisse

3.1 p-Wert-adjustierte Regeln

Abhängig von der Methodik einer p-Wert-Korrektur zeigte sich, dass je nach Stärke der Korrektur viele Regeln als insignifikant gelten. Insbesondere bei der Korrektur nach Holm ist erkennbar, dass alle p-Werte nach einer Korrektur als nichtsignifikant gelten und somit die Datengrundlage für das Pattern-Mining unzureichend ist. Diese zeigen durchwegs den Wert 1 in Abbildung 1. Bei der unterbliebenen p-Wert-Korrektur zeigten sich 80 % aller Regeln in Abbildung 1 als insignifikant. Je nach der Entscheidungsschwelle (dem kritischen p-Wert) sinkt die Anzahl signifikanter Regeln beim Anstieg des globalen

Signifikanzniveaus. Zudem ist erkennbar, dass alle Regeln je nach Korrekturmethode als insignifikant zu allen betrachteten Signifikanzniveaus (0,05;0,01;0,001) ausfielen. Damit stellen sich bei Anwendung einer der gewählten Korrekturmethoden keine vom Zufall unterscheidbaren Regeln dar. Abbildung 1 zeigt, dass bei Anwendung einer Korrekturmethode keine signifikanten Regeln bei einem Niveau von p = 0,05 mehr verbleiben. Ohne p-Wert-Korrektur blieben 8 855 signifikante Regeln übrig (p < 0,05). Gemessen am Ausgangsregeldatensatz von 11 768 312 Regeln wurden 99,924 % aller Regeln entfernt.

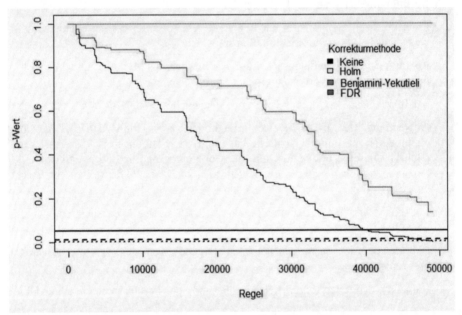

Abb. 1: p-Werte von 49 138 Regeln, die nach verschiedenen p-Wert-Korrekturmethoden adjustiert wurden. Es wurden nur Regeln berücksichtigt, deren Vorläufer auf einer Parzelle vorkommen und deren Nachfolger nicht in der Ausgangsmenge enthalten sind. Waagerechte Linien kennzeichnen Signifikanzschwellen von 0,05 (durchgezogen) sowie 0,01 (gestrichelt) und 0,001 (punktiert). Die FDR kennzeichnet die Falscherkennungsrate. Die Linie der Benjamini-Yekutieli-Korrektur überdeckt die p-Werte der Korrekturmethode nach Holm. Sie zeigen für alle Regeln einen korrigierten p-Wert von 1.

3.2 Die Top 10 der Spezies zur Bestandsverbesserung

In Tabelle 1 wurden Assoziationsregeln für zehn Spezies ausgegeben, die nach den Sortierkriterien oben standen und sich für die Ansaat auf dem Plot A10_16 eignen. Es zeigte sich, dass die Regeln in Tabelle 1 einen signifikanten p-Wert (p < 0,05) aufwiesen, wobei der Support eine Bandbreite zwischen 0,179 und 0,750 hatte.

Erhöhung der Biodiversität von Graslandbeständen 337

Vorläufer	Nachfolger	Support	Konfidenz	p-Wert
{DacGlom}	{ArrElat}	0,750	0,875	0,000183
{GalAlbu,LeuIrcu, TarRude,TriPrat}	{ConArve}	0,179	0,833	0,000197
{GalAlbu,HolLana, LolPere,TarRude}	{RhiMino}	0,179	0,833	0,00245
{HolLana}	{FesRubr}	0,500	0,824	0,000805
{DacGlom,LeuIrcu}	{TriDubi}	0,321	0,818	0,00021
{MedLupu}	{PriVeri}	0,429	0,800	0,0248
{HolLana,TriPrat}	{AntOdor}	0,286	0,800	0,000267
{HolLana,TriPrat}	{HelPube}	0,286	0,800	0,00101
{DacGlom,PlaLanc}	{RumAcet}	0,643	0,783	0,000933
{GalAlbu,LeuIrcu}	{VicAngu}	0,321	0,750	0,000805

Tab. 1: Top-10-Regelsätze für die Ansaat neuer Spezies auf dem Plot A10_16, geordnet nach Konfidenz (absteigend) und Support (absteigend). ArrElat: Arrhenatheretalia elatioris; AntOdor: Anthoxanthum odoratum; ConArve: Convolvulus arvensis; DacGlom: Dactylis glomerata; FesRubr: Festuca rubra; GalAlbu: Galium album; HelPube: Helictotrichon pubescens; HolLana: Holcus lanatus; LeuIrcu: Leucanthemum ircutianum; LolPere: Lolium perenne; MedLupu: Medicago lupulina; PriVeri: Primula veris; RhiMino: Rhinanthus minor; RumAcet: Rumex acetosa; TarRude: Taraxacum sect. Ruderali; TriDubi: Trifolium dubium; TriPrat: Trifolium pratensis; VicAngu: Vicia angustifolia

4 Diskussion und Ausblick

Dieses Vorgehen zeigt, wie einzelne Spezies als neue Etablierungskandidaten identifiziert werden können, allerdings hat die Methodik Anpassungspotential. In der Ökologie ist bei der Aufwertung der Flächen mittels Saatgutmischungen gängig, jedoch bietet das R-Paket ‚arules' keine Möglichkeit für Saatgutmischungen, daher sei auf das Python-Modul ‚mlxtend' [Se18] verwiesen, womit Nachfolger mit mehreren Items ausgeben werden. Zudem ist zu beachten, dass es für das Ranking der Regeln auch nullinvariante Maße gibt, die entgegen dem Chi-Quadrat-Test nicht auf Nulltransaktionen reagieren und in Betracht gezogen werden sollen. Nullinvariante Maße kennzeichnen solche, die sich nicht ändern, wenn die Anzahl der Regeln, die weder den betrachteten Vorläufer noch den betrachteten Nachfolger beinhalten, sich ändert. Beispiele für Maße sind Cosine, Kulczynski und Max Confidence, wie in [WCH10] dargestellt. Diese sind die am besten geeigneten Maße, um Regeln auch aus nichtbalancierten Datensätzen zu sortieren [KBH11].

Ferner kommen biotische und abiotische Faktoren hinzu, die für die Bestimmung der optimalen Spezies als Etablierungskandidat relevant sind. Die Trieb- und Konkurrenzkraft einer Spezies stellt eine essentielle Kenngröße zur Etablierungswahrscheinlichkeit dar und ist wiederum von vielen Umweltfaktoren abhängig [AYQ20]. Auch abiotische Faktoren wie die Frosthärte und Sonneneinstrahlung werden durch die Assoziations-analyse nur unzureichend gewürdigt, da hier keine Vorgruppierung der Standorte erfolgte und zudem eine Analyse mit Assoziationsregeln konstant bleibende Umweltfaktoren annimmt, was beim Klimawandel nicht haltbar ist. In einer Folgeuntersuchung sollen die Standorte vor der Assoziationsanalyse vorgruppiert werden und Assoziationsregeln je Standort berechnet werden.

Danksagung: Ich bedanke mich herzlich bei der Landwirtschaftsverlag GmbH für die Bereitstellung der notwendigen Ressourcen für das Projekt.

Literaturverzeichnis

[AYQ20]   Ahmed, H. A.; Yu-Xin, T.; Qi-Chang, Y.: Optimal control of environmental conditions affecting lettuce plant growth in a controlled environment with artificial lighting: A review. South African Journal of Botany 2/130, S. 75-89, 2020.

[BH95]   Benjamini, Y.; Hochberg, Y.: Controlling the False Discovery Rate: A Practical and Powerful Approach to Multiple Testing. Journal of the Royal Statistical Society: Series B (Methodological) 1/57, S. 289–300, 1995.

[BY01]   Benjamini, Y.; Yekutieli, D.: The control of the false discovery rate in multiple testing under dependency. The Annals of Statistics 4/29, S. 1165–1188, 2001.

[FJ21]   Friedemann Goral; Jenny Schellenberg: goeveg: Functions for Community Data and Ordinations, 2021.

[Ho79]   Holm, S.: A Simple Sequentially Rejective Multiple Test Procedure. Scandinavian Journal of Statistics 2/6, S. 65–70, 1979.

[KBH11]   Kim, S.; Barsky, M.; Han, J.: Efficient Mining of Top Correlated Patterns Based on Null-Invariant Measures. In (Gunopulos, D. et al. Hrsg.): Machine Learning and Knowledge Discovery in Databases. Springer Berlin Heidelberg, Berlin, Heidelberg, S. 177-192, 2011.

[MBK05]   Michael Hahsler; Bettina Gruen; Kurt Hornik: arules - A Computational Environment for Mining Association Rules and Frequent Item Sets. Journal of Statistical Software 15/14, S. 1-25, 2005.

[R 21]   R Core Team: R: A Language and Environment for Statistical Computing. R Foundation for Statistical Computing, Vienna, Austria, 2021.

[Se18]   Sebastian Raschka: MLxtend: Providing machine learning and data science utilities and extensions to Python's scientific computing stack. The Journal of Open Source Software 24/3, 2018.

[WCH10]   Wu, T.; Chen, Y.; Han, J.: Re-examination of interestingness measures in pattern mining: a unified framework. Data Mining and Knowledge Discovery 3/21, S. 371-397, 2010.

Nutzerzentrierte Entscheidungstools und dynamische Steuerungsalgorithmen für eine differenzierte mehrparametrische N-Düngung

Andreas Heiß [1, 2], Dimitrios S. Paraforos [1, 2], Galibjon M. Sharipov [1] und Hans W. Griepentrog [1]

Abstract: Gängige Verfahren für die teilflächenspezifische Stickstoff (N)-Düngung berücksichtigen oft nur den aktuellen N-Status der Pflanzen, können auf die Komplexität hinsichtlich zeitlicher und räumlicher Dynamiken nicht ausreichend eingehen und lassen zugleich das Expertenwissen von Landwirten unberücksichtigt. Gleichzeitig besteht bei der präzisen technischen Realisierung der variablen Applikation weiteres Optimierungspotenzial. Im Forschungsprojekt FuzzyFarmer wurde ein ganzheitlicher Ansatz für eine verbesserte N-Düngung entwickelt, bei der ein agronomischer Experte für jede Gabe flexibel die Wirkzusammenhänge in Abhängigkeit mehrerer räumlich variierender Parameter über ein web-basiertes Managementsystem festlegen kann. Mithilfe dynamischer Algorithmen in einer Echtzeitsteuerung wurde eine räumliche Synchronisation von Dosiermengenvorgabe und -applikation erreicht. Durch die generischen Eigenschaften ist der Ansatz mit unterschiedlichen Parametern, Datenquellen sowie Sensor- und Applikationstechnologien realisierbar. Auch eine Hybridisierung mit etablierten modellbasierten Ansätzen für künftig noch robustere Entscheidungen ist direkt möglich.

Keywords: teilflächenspezifische N-Düngung, Fuzzy Systeme, Echtzeit-Datenfusion, Applikationsgenauigkeit, User-Interfaces

1 Einleitung

Gängige Ansätze zur teilflächenspezifischen Stickstoff (N)-Düngung nutzen vorwiegend den aktuellen N-Status der Pflanze, welcher über spektrale Messungen ermittelt wird. Zugrundeliegende Algorithmen zur Ableitung der N-Dosiermenge handeln jedoch oft deterministisch und berücksichtigen nicht die genauen Ursachen der räumlichen Variabilität, die durch mehrere biotische und abiotische Parameter verursacht wird und von zeitlichen Dynamiken überlagert ist [Co21]. Das sorgt wiederum für spezifische Bedingungen bei jeder einzelnen Gabe. Auf diese Komplexität können auch modellbasierte oder sogar Machine-Learning-Algorithmen nur begrenzt eingehen.

Obwohl Landwirte oder Pflanzenbauberater oftmals über spezifische Standortkenntnisse und Erfahrung verfügen und dieses Wissen mit Fuzzy-Systemen in maschinenlesbarer Form erfasst werden kann, findet es allgemein nur wenig Beachtung in der differenzierten

---

[1] Universität Hohenheim, Institut für Agrartechnik 440d, Garbenstr. 9, 70599 Stuttgart, Korrespondenz: andreas.heiss@uni-hohenheim.de,
[2] Hochschule Geisenheim University, Institut für Technik, Von-Lade-Straße 1, 65366 Geisenheim

N-Düngung [Le18]. Neben der Eignung für Prozesse, denen Unsicherheiten und Nicht-Linearitäten inhärent sind, eignen sich diese Systeme sehr gut für die Echtzeit-Fusion von mehreren Parametern, was vor allem bei den weit verbreiteten Echtzeit-Sensorsystemen von Bedeutung ist. Bei der Applikation bestehen außerdem bis heute Limitierungen in der Präzision, zumal ein dynamisches Modell für die Kompensation von technischen Latenzen und Längsversätzen im Sensor-Streuer-System, wie von Griepentrog und Persson [Gr01] beschrieben, bisher nicht als Steuerungsalgorithmus implementiert ist.

Das Forschungsprojekt FuzzyFarmer hat sich mit der Entwicklung eines ganzheitlichen, nutzerzentrierten Ansatzes für eine optimierte teilflächenspezifische N-Düngung befasst. Dabei wurden konkret folgende Ziele verfolgt:

- Entwurf eines Fuzzy-Expertensystems für die Fusion von mehreren Parametern unter variierenden natürlichen Bedingungen und Produktionszielen,
- Entwicklung und Verifizierung von dynamischen Steuerungsalgorithmen für die Echtzeit-Datenfusion und räumliche Synchronisation von Messung und Applikation sowie
- Integration eines web-basierten Managementsystems für die Vereinfachung von Systemkonfiguration und Datenmanagement, der Echtzeitsteuerung sowie von Schnittstellen für automatisierten Datenaustausch in ein Gesamtsystem.

2 Material und Methoden

2.1 Aufbau des Gesamtsystems

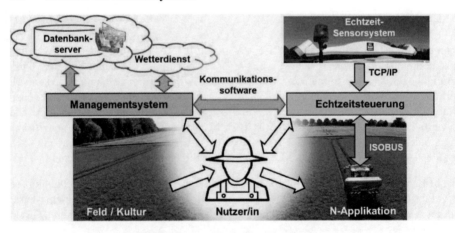

Abb. 1: Architektur des Gesamtsystems

Fehler! Verweisquelle konnte nicht gefunden werden. zeigt die Architektur des Gesamtsystems. Methodischer Kern ist dabei das von Heiß et al. [He21] beschriebene

Fuzzy-Expertensystem, bei dem die Echtzeit-Information über die N-Aufnahme des Bestandes (SN-Wert) aus dem Sensorsystem Yara N-Sensor ALS2 mit kartierter Information über die scheinbare elektrische Leitfähigkeit des Bodens (ECa-Wert) verknüpft wird. Dieser Ansatz wurde in einem vollständig integrierten System für die teilflächenspezifische N-Dünung implementiert. Im Zentrum steht dabei der Nutzer, welcher zunächst als agronomischer Experte das Systemverhalten anhand einer aktuellen Beurteilung für einen bestimmten Schlag und eine bestimmte Gabe über das Managementsystem festlegt. Über die Echtzeitsteuerung erfolgt dann die anschließende Steuerung und Überwachung der variablen N-Applikation.

2.2 Web-basiertes Managementsystem und Kommunikationssoftware

Für das Managementsystem wurde eine grundsätzlich Internet-basierte Lösung forciert, um vor allem einen ortsunabhängigen Zugriff durch unterschiedliche Personen zu ermöglichen. Die Implementierung erfolgte durch Containervisualisierung mit Docker (Docker Inc., Palo Alto, CA, USA). Zur Datenspeicherung und -verwaltung wurde ein Datenbankserver eingerichtet. Das Managementsystem selbst wurde mit Shiny for R (RStudio PBC, Boston, MA, USA) entwickelt und ebenfalls auf einem Server installiert.

Um das Expertenwissen ohne Notwendigkeit eines Wissensingenieurs abgreifen zu können, wurde unter Berücksichtigung der Arbeit von Zhai et al. [Zh20] ein User-Interface entwickelt. Die Konfiguration des Expertensystems wurde dabei als schrittweiser Prozess umgesetzt. Neben dem Anlegen der Aufgabe beinhaltete dies die optionale Anwendung eines Fuzzy-Logic-basierten Modells der agronomischen Algorithmen des N-Sensors nach Heiß et al. [He21]. Die Konfiguration des Fuzzy-Systems bezüglich der einzelnen Parameter SN und ECa, deren Verknüpfung über mehrparametrische Regeln sowie die Ausführung und kartierte Darstellung einer Simulation der teilflächenspezifisch variierenden Dosiermengen wurde in Tabs umgesetzt. Als wichtige Information wurden lokale Wetterdienste (LTZ Augustenberg) in die Oberfläche eingebunden. Zur Durchführung der Simulation wurde in Matlab (The Mathworks Inc., Natick, MA, USA) eine Stand-Alone Anwendung entwickelt und auf dem Server ausgelagert. Ein weiterer Tab wurde zur Darstellung der As-Applied Daten aus der Echtzeitsteuerung eingerichtet.

Zum automatisierten Datenaustausch zwischen Managementsystem und Echtzeitsteuerung wurde eine Kommunikationssoftware in Python entwickelt und auf einem Laptop installiert, welcher auch als Controller-Plattform für die Echtzeitsteuerung fungierte. Über den Windows Task Scheduler wurde dabei zyklisch ein Austausch der aktuellsten Daten versucht, sobald eine Netzwerkverbindung vorhanden war. Dies waren die Auftragsdateien und ECa-Karten aus dem Managementsystem sowie N-Sensor-Aufzeichnungen und As-Applied-Daten aus der Echtzeitsteuerung.

2.3 Echtzeitsteuerung

Die Echtzeitsteuerung wurde in Matlab als Anwendung mit User-Interface entwickelt, wobei eine Untergliederung in zwei Tabs für die Konfiguration bzw. die Überwachung der Applikation erfolgte. Bedienfelder dienten zum optionalen manuellen Datenaustausch. Außerdem wurden Schaltflächen für die Auswahl des gewünschten Auftrags und die Neu-Kalibrierung in Bezug auf den Parameter SN erstellt. Dies war erforderlich aufgrund der hohen zeitlichen Dynamik der SN-Werte und des anzunehmenden zeitlichen Abstands zwischen Systemkonfiguration im Managementsystem und eigentlicher N-Applikation.

Dem Softwareteil für die Ansteuerung des Applikationssystems lag die von Heiß et al. [He22] präsentierte Methode zugrunde. Dabei wurde aus den Auftragsdaten ein Fuzzy-Inferenzsystem erstellt, mit dessen Hilfe die SN-Werte aus einem Yara N-Sensor ALS2 in Echtzeit mit kartierten ECa-Werten fusioniert wurden, um separate Dosiermengen für zwei Teilbreiten eines RAUCH AXIS-H 30.2 EMC+W Zweischeiben-Schleuderstreuers zu definieren. Ein dynamischer Steuerungsalgorithmus plante das Senden der Dosiermengenbefehle über ISOBUS unter Berücksichtigung der Fahrgeschwindigkeit sowie vorhandener technischer Latenzen und Längsversätze, um eine größtmögliche räumliche Übereinstimmung von Dosiermengenvorgabe und -realisierung zu erreichen. Dabei wurden mit RTK-GNSS die generierten Dosiermengenvorgaben und Referenzpunkte im Streubild georeferenziert, die Distanzen zwischen ihnen berechnet und ihre Übereinstimmung kontinuierlich über die zurückgelegte Fahrstrecke ermittelt.

3 Ergebnisse und Diskussion

3.1 System-Setup im Managementsystem

Anhand der Konfiguration des Nutzers über das User-Interface wurde im Backend des Managementsystems ein Fuzzy-System konstruiert. Neben der Eingabe grundlegender Informationen über die Aufgabenverwaltung konnte der Nutzer optional die notwendigen Parameter eingeben, die bei der agronomischen Kalibrierung des N-Sensors erforderlich wären. Darauf basierend wurde automatisch eine Konfiguration für den SN-Wert vorgeschlagen. Diese konnte im einparametrischen Setup angepasst werden, welches in Abb. 2 schematisch veranschaulicht ist. Das Setup wurde separat für den SN und die ECa durchgeführt, wobei über Schieberegler, die mit einer aktuellen Karte des Parameters interagierten, die Input-Werte klassifiziert wurden. Im Backend wurde dies in Zugehörigkeitsfunktionen für das Fuzzy-System übersetzt. Die Dosiermenge als Output wurde mit Singletons klassifiziert. Anschließend konnten einparametrische Regeln definiert und gewichtet werden, welche letztlich das Systemverhalten wesentlich bestimmten. Im Setup von mehrparametrischen Regeln konnten die Input-Parameter zusätzlich mit ‚AND' verknüpft werden. Ebenso war es möglich, durch Weglassen betreffender Regeln einen Parameter gänzlich auszulassen. Unter Nutzung von vorhandenen ECa- und vorab aufgezeichneten SN-Karten, sowie des Fuzzy-System-

Setups konnten die Dosiermengen simuliert und als Karte dargestellt werden, wodurch eine iterative Anpassung der Entscheidung ermöglicht wurde.

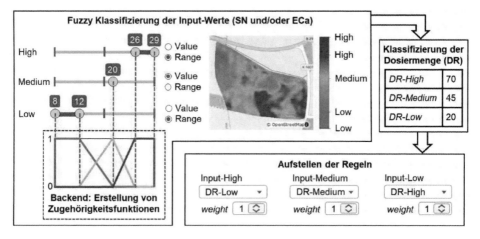

Abb. 2: Schematischer Ablauf des einparametrischen Fuzzy-System-Setups im Managementsystem

3.2 Validierung

Das Managementsystem wurde unter Nutzung von Daten aus realen Feldversuchen sowie unter Einbezug agronomischer Experten evaluiert. Dabei wurde deutlich, dass die starke Nutzerzentrierung mit einem gewissen Risiko für eine falsche Düngestrategie behaftet ist, sofern nicht ausreichend Erfahrung und Expertise vorhanden ist. Vor allem die Systemkonfiguration erfordert zusätzliche Zeit in der ohnehin arbeitsintensiven Düngesaison, was aber durch den Einbezug von Pflanzenbauberatern abgemildert werden kann. Außerdem wurden neben einer hohen Automatisierung beim Datenmanagement besonders im User-Interface technische Lösungen implementiert, welche die Konfiguration vereinfachen. Kernaspekte sind hier die Möglichkeit einer kartenbasierten Klassifizierung der Input-Parameter mit unmittelbarer visueller Rückkopplung sowie ein Herunterbrechen des Fuzzy-System-Setups im Frontend auf die essenziellsten Aspekte. Insgesamt wurde deutlich, dass das Managementsystem eine hohe Flexibilität hinsichtlich der Adressierung spezifischer Begebenheiten bei jeder einzelnen Gabe aufweist. Über einen relativ einfachen Weg können mehrere Parameter verknüpft und so auch komplexe Systemcharakteristiken direkt durch den Nutzer definiert werden.

In der Arbeit von Heiß et al. [He22] wurde die Tauglichkeit der Echtzeitsteuerung in umfassenden Feldversuchen verifiziert. Dabei wurde bei mehreren Messfahrten die theoretische räumliche Synchronisation von Dosiermengenvorgabe und -realisierung in sehr unterschiedlichen Fahrgeschwindigkeitsszenarien, die teils deutlich über die üblichen Betriebsbedingungen hinausgingen, überprüft. Für die vom Hersteller des Streuers empfohlene Geschwindigkeit von 12 km h^{-1} lagen die Mediane der Abweichung zwischen den entsprechenden georeferenzierten Spots im Bereich von 0,25 m, was angesichts der Bedeutung von externen Störeinflüssen auf das Streubild als ausreichend bewertet wurde.

4 Schlussfolgerungen und Ausblick

Der vorgestellte Ansatz ist eine neuartige Herangehensweise, um die Wirkzusammenhänge mehrerer für die N-Düngung relevanter Parameter zu definieren. Gleichzeitig kann dabei auf die zum Teil hohe zeitliche und räumliche Dynamik sowie variierende Produktionsziele eingegangen werden. Das System hat generische und flexible Eigenschaften zur Einbindung weiterer Parameter und Anwendung mit beispielsweise Satelliten-basierten Datenquellen bzw. anderen Sensor- und Applikationstechnologien. Als performante Schnittstelle zur Erfassung von Expertenwissen eignet es sich für eine Hybridisierung mit gängigen Ansätzen, wobei jeweils von einer Minimierung der Schwächen und einer insgesamt größeren Robustheit auszugehen ist. Die Validierung der agronomischen Vorteilhaftigkeit erfordert umfassende, mehrjährige Feldversuche.

Förderhinweis: Die Förderung des Vorhabens erfolgte aus Mitteln des Bundesministeriums für Ernährung und Landwirtschaft (BMEL) aufgrund eines Beschlusses des deutschen Bundestages. Die Projektträgerschaft erfolgte über die Bundesanstalt für Landwirtschaft. Projektdauer vom 01.09.2018 bis 31.10.2021. Beteiligte Projektpartner: Universität Hohenheim (Gesamtkoordination), TU Chemnitz, Hanse Agro GmbH, DISY Informationssysteme GmbH, YARA GmbH & Co. KG, RAUCH Landmaschinenfabrik GmbH.

Literaturverzeichnis

[Co21] Colaço, A.F.; Richetti, J.; Bramley, R.G.V.; Lawes, R.A.: How will the next-generation of sensor-based decision systems look in the context of intelligent agriculture? A case-study. Field Crops Research 270, 108205, 2021.

[Le18] Leroux, C.; Jones, H.; Pichon, L.; Guillaume, S.; Lamour, J.; Taylor, J.; Naud, O.; Crestey, T.; Lablee, J.L.; Tisseyre, B.: GeoFIS: An open source, decision-support tool for precision agriculture data. Agriculture 8, 73, 2018.

[Gr01] Griepentrog, H.W.; Persson, K.: A model to determine the positional lag for fertiliser spreaders. In: Proceedings of the 3rd European Conference on Precision Agriculture, Montpellier, France, June 18-20, 2001.

[He21] Heiß, A.; Paraforos, D.S.; Sharipov, G.M.; Griepentrog, H.W.: Modeling and simulation of a multi-parametric fuzzy expert system for variable rate nitrogen application. Computers and Electronics in Agriculture 182, 106008, 2021.

[Zh20] Zhai, Z.; Martínez, J.F.; Beltran, V.; Martínez, N.L.: Decision support systems for agriculture 4.0: Survey and challenges. Computers and Electronics in Agriculture 170, 105256, 2020.

[He22] Heiß, A.; Paraforos, D.S.; Sharipov, G.M.; Griepentrog, H.W.: Real-time control for multi-parametric data fusion and dynamic offset optimization in sensor-based variable rate nitrogen application. Computers and Electronics in Agriculture 196, 106893, 2022.

Digitales Assistenzsystem zur Applikation von Pflanzenschutzmitteln

Daniel Herrmann [1], Jan-Philip Pohl[1], Steffi Rentsch[2], Daniel Jahncke[3], Nina Lefeldt[3] und Dieter von Hörsten[1]

Abstract: Es gibt zahlreiche digitale Tools und Anwendungen, die den Landwirt dabei unterstützen sollen, den Pflanzenschutz nach guter fachlicher Praxis umzusetzen. Dazu kommen diverse Anwendungsbestimmungen, die beim Einsatz von Pflanzenschutzmitteln zu berücksichtigen sind. Für den Landwirt fehlt eine Plattform, die all diese Informationen bündelt und praxisgerecht aufarbeitet. Das digitale Assistenzsystem, umgesetzt in der Web-Anwendung OPAL, ist eine digitale Infrastruktur, das die verschiedenen Tools und Anwendungen bündelt und aufarbeitet. Das Ergebnis ist eine maschinenlesbare Applikationskarte, mit der im Feld vollautomatisch appliziert werden kann. So wird auch die komplexe teilflächenspezifische Bewirtschaftung in der Umsetzung wesentlich erleichtert.

Keywords: digitales Assistenzsystem, teilflächenspezifische Bewirtschaftung, Applikationskarten, Anwendungsbestimmungen, Pflanzenschutz

1 Einleitung

Der Anwender ist beim sachgerechten Pflanzenschutz einer Vielzahl von gesetzlichen Reglementierungen und den Prinzipien der guten fachlichen Praxis ausgesetzt. Diese vollumfänglich zu berücksichtigen und die Anwendung rechtssicher zu dokumentieren, ist eine Herausforderung für jeden Praktiker. Das digitale Assistenzsystem zur Applikation von Pflanzenschutzmitteln setzt an dieser Stelle an, indem es dem Anwender eine Handlungsempfehlung gibt. Darüber hinaus unterstützt es den Anwender, die Handlungsempfehlungen in der Praxis umzusetzen und abschließend zu dokumentieren. Die anwenderfreundliche Bedienoberfläche leitet den Anwender durch eine Eingabemaske. Als Ergebnis entsteht eine fertige Applikationskarte, die die Anwendungsbestimmungen und Abstandsauflagen berücksichtigt. Das Assistenzsystem ist dabei in drei Funktionalitäten untergliedert:

---

[1] Julius Kühn-Institut, Institut für Anwendungstechnik im Pflanzenschutz, Messeweg 11/12, 38104 Braunschweig, daniel.herrmann@julius-kuehn.de; jan-philip.pohl@julius-kuehn.de; dieter.von-hoersten@julius-kuehn.de
[2] Bayer CropScience Deutschland GmbH, Alfred-Nobel-Str. 50, 40789 Monheim; steffi.rentsch@bayer.com
[3] GID GeoInformationsDienst GmbH, Götzenbreite 10, 37124 Rosdorf; jahncke@geoinformationsdienst.de; lefeldt@geoinformationsdienst.de

1. Auflagen und Risiken: Analyse der Landschaftsstruktur und Berücksichtigung der spezifischen Abstandsauflagen inklusive eines Risikoservice;

2. Teilflächenspezifische Applikation: gezielter Einsatz von Pflanzenschutzmitteln mit Hilfe von Satellitenbildern oder Zonenmanagementkarten;

3. Benchmarking und Dokumentation: betriebswirtschaftlicher Vergleich der Applikation sowie Cross Compliance-konforme Dokumentation.

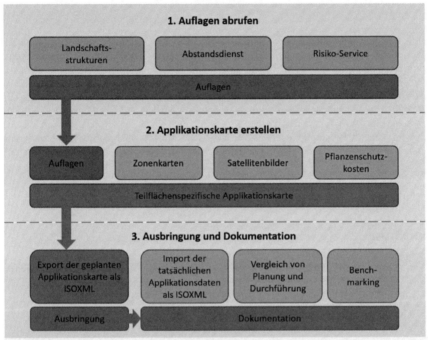

Abb. 1: Schematischer Aufbau Assistenzsystem OPAL

Für eine praxistaugliche Entwicklung des digitalen Assistenzsystems sind umfangreiche Informationen über den zukünftigen Einsatz der Anwendung und die Arbeitsweisen der Nutzer erforderlich. Eine dreistufige Marktanalyse dient als Grundlage zur wissenschaftlichen Aufarbeitung der Anforderungen an das digitale Assistenzsystem:

1. Qualitative Analyse: Bestimmung der notwendigen Funktionalitäten des digitalen Assistenzsystems (Stichprobenumfang 9 Landwirte);

2. Quantitative Analyse: Evaluierung der Ergebnisse der qualitativen Analyse (Stichprobenumfang 706 Landwirte);

3. Praktischer Produkttest zur Optimierung der Webanwendung.

2 Qualitative Analyse

Um eine praxistaugliche Webanwendung zu erstellen, sind die Anforderungen der zukünftigen Nutzer und deren Arbeitsweise zu ermitteln. Dazu wurden neun Landwirte ausgesucht, die hinsichtlich ihrer Region, Betriebsgröße und -ausrichtung sowie Arbeitsweise eine große Bandbreite der deutschen Landwirtschaft darstellen. Die Betriebe zeichnen sich durch eine Flächenausstattung von unter 50 bis über 2000 Hektar aus, befinden sich in sieben Bundesländern und haben unterschiedliche Kulturen im Anbau. Die erste Funktionalitätsstufe der automatischen Abfrage und Berücksichtigung der Anwendungsbestimmungen ist dabei von übergeordneter Bedeutung. Die Landwirte würden dies im täglichen Arbeitsablauf nutzen, insbesondere um einen besseren Überblick zu haben und sich sicherer beim Einsatz chemischer Pflanzenschutzmittel zu fühlen. Besonders wichtig sind dabei jedoch die Aktualität und Qualität der ausgegebenen Daten [BA22-6].

Die teilflächenspezifische Bewirtschaftung bietet ein großes Potential, Betriebsmittel einzusparen, den Eintrag von Dünge- und Pflanzenschutzmitteln in den Naturhaushalt zu verringern und das betriebswirtschaftliche Ergebnis zu optimieren. Die teilflächenspezifische Applikation wird durch die zweite Funktion des digitalen Assistenzsystems abgedeckt (Abb. 1. Teilflächenspezifische Applikationskarte mit

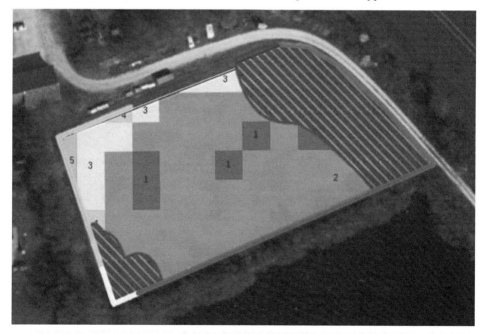

Abb. 2: Applikationskarte zur teilflächenspezifischen Bewirtschaftung mit Sperrzonen (grau gestreift), die Anwendungsbestimmungen berücksichtigt. Erstellt in Web-Anwendung OPAL

Sperrzonen). Bei Aussaat und Düngung gibt es Parameter, anhand derer sich die teilflächenspezifische Bewirtschaftung planen und umsetzen lässt. Der teilflächenspezifische Pflanzenschutz ist dagegen wesentlich komplexer. Das Auftreten von Schaderregern ist zeitlich variabel und wird von verschiedenen Parametern beeinflusst. Dementsprechend hoch ist das Interesse an einer unterstützenden und beratenden Planung des teilflächenspezifischen Pflanzenschutzes durch das digitale Assistenzsystem. Das Vorliegen einer manuell erstellten Zonenmanagementkarte und die Umwandlung in eine maschinenlesbare Applikationskarte geht den Anwendern dabei nicht weit genug. Vielmehr sollte die Zonenmanagementkarte direkt im digitalen Assistenzsystem erstellt werden. Als Datengrundlage dienen beispielsweise Satellitendaten wie die NDVI-Karten des Sentinel-2-Satelliten oder eigene Daten, die durch Sensorik an Traktor oder Drohne erfasst werden können. Unter Berücksichtigung von Prognosemodellen ist so die automatisierte Erstellung von Zonenmanagementkarten gewünscht [BA22-06].

Die pflanzenbaulichen Auswirkungen eines teilflächenspezifischen Pflanzenschutzes sind dabei verglichen mit einer teilflächenspezifischen Düngung deutlich komplexer. Bei einer variablen Düngung ändert sich das Nährstoffniveau einer Teilfläche. Die Auswirkungen daraus sind bekannt und für den Landwirt nachvollziehbar. Wird die Aufwandmenge eines Pflanzenschutzmittels reduziert, kann dies auch negative Auswirkungen, wie eine verringerte Wirksamkeit der Maßnahme oder Resistenzbildungen, haben. Diese negativen Auswirkungen sind für den Landwirt nicht sofort ersichtlich und zeigen sich oft erst zu einem späteren Zeitpunkt. Dementsprechend ist von den Landwirten eine pflanzenbauliche Unterstützung gefordert, um den teilflächenspezifischen Einsatz auszubauen. Dazu zählen auch technische Hinweise, wie die geeignete Düsenwahl oder Ähnliches [BA22-06].

Die dritte Funktionalität, die Dokumentation und das betriebswirtschaftliche Benchmarking, gliedert sich im betrieblichen Alltag in zwei wesentliche Schritte:

- Dokumentation der Maßnahmen zur Erfüllung der Cross Compliance Vorgaben;

- teilweise zusätzliche Dokumentation zur betriebsinternen Optimierung.

Insbesondere die digitalisierte Dokumentation ist ein erheblicher Mehrwert für den Landwirt. So lassen sich die Cross-Compliance-Vorgaben ohne Mehraufwand erfüllen und Technik und Maßnahmen kontrollieren und auch optimieren. Von großer Bedeutung wäre darüber hinaus die Integration von Witterungsdaten in die Planung und Dokumentation der Maßnahme [BA22-06].

3 Quantitative Analyse

Zur statistischen Bewertung der Ergebnisse aus der qualitativen Analyse ist ein wesentlich größerer Stichprobenumfang notwendig. Der Stichprobenumfang beträgt 706 Landwirte und somit potenzielle Anwender des digitalen Assistenzsystems. Diese Zahl steht den aktuell rund 256.000 landwirtschaftlichen Betrieben in Deutschland gegenüber. Für eine vollständige Repräsentativität der quantitativen Umfragen ist ca. der doppelte Stichprobenumfang nötig. Bei der Teilnahme an der Umfrage kommt es ebenfalls zu einer gewissen Selbstselektion der Teilnehmer. So ist es denkbar, dass insbesondere besonders technikaffine Landwirte oder Ackerbaubetriebe, die von der Thematik hauptsächlich betroffen sind, bevorzugt an der Umfrage teilnehmen könnten. Dies bestätigen die Umfrageergebnisse, die eine Überrepräsentanz großer Betriebe und von Betrieben aus Ostdeutschland ergaben [BA22-10].

Zur Veranschaulichung der Anwendung wurden kurze Videosequenzen gezeigt, um einen Eindruck für die Bedienbarkeit und Funktionalität zu übermitteln. Abschließend wurden noch allgemeine Fragen zur Anwendung sowie dem betrieblichen Hintergrund erhoben.

Das grundsätzliche Interesse an einer teilflächenspezifischen Bewirtschaftung ist sehr hoch. Über 90 % der befragten Betriebe bewirtschaften ihre Flächen bereits teilflächenspezifisch oder wollen dies zukünftig tun. Die technischen Voraussetzungen sind dabei jedoch nur eingeschränkt erfüllt. Auf ca. 50 % der Betriebe sind Spritzgeräte mit GPS-gesteuerter Teilbreitenschaltung vorhanden. Dies ist eine Voraussetzung zur automatischen Abschaltung an Randbereichen, sofern Abstandauflagen berücksichtigt werden müssen. Durch Anpassung der applizierten Menge ist auf 25 % der befragten Betriebe eine variable Ausbringmenge möglich. Dabei kann jedoch nur ein Pflanzenschutzmittel appliziert werden oder eine Tankmischung verschiedener Mittel appliziert werden. Lediglich 2 % der Betrieb verfügen über eine Technik, mit der sowohl die Aufwandmenge als auch Zusammensetzung variabel verändert werden kann. Dies erfolgt über Mehrtanksysteme oder eine Pflanzenschutzmitteldirekteinspeisung [BA22-10].

Grundsätzlich ist die eingesetzte Technik sehr vielfältig. Daraus ergibt sich eine weitere Anforderung an das digitale Assistenzsystem, dass Applikationskarten in unterschiedlichen Dateiformaten bereitstellen muss. Von besonderer Wichtigkeit ist für 62 % der befragten Betriebe das Abrufen der aktuellen Informationen und die Dokumentation der Maßnahme, lediglich 40 % würden die Pflanzenschutzmaßnahmen gezielt in der Webanwendung OPAL planen oder die Applikationskarten exportieren. 80 % der befragten Betriebe können sich vorstellen, zukünftig mit dem digitalen Assistenzsystem zu arbeiten. Wichtig ist dabei insbesondere die Rechtssicherheit, sodass keine zusätzliche Überprüfung der im digitalen Assistenzsystem vorgeschlagenen Maßnahmen notwendig ist [BA22-10].

4 Praktischer Produkttest

Parallel zur quantitativen Analyse wurde ein praktischer Produkttest mit einer Vorversion der Web-Anwendung durchgeführt. Dabei konnte insbesondere die Handhabung der Anwendung und Datenübertragung mit der eingesetzten Pflanzenschutztechnik analysiert werden. Die Erfahrungen des Produkttests zeigen die Anwendung als klar strukturiert und von den meisten Anwendern leicht bedienbar. Entgegen der quantitativen Analyse ergab sich bei jedem der besuchten Betriebe der Wunsch, dass das digitale Assistenzsystem in ein bestehendes Farmmanagementsystem eingebunden ist (lediglich 20 % der befragten Betriebe forderten dies in der quantitativen Befragung). Der betriebsübliche Arbeitsablauf soll somit nicht um ein weiteres Tool ergänzt, sondern die bestehenden Anwendungen in ihrer Funktionalität erweitert werden [JKI22].

Die Vielzahl der eingesetzten Pflanzenschutzgeräte verschiedener Baujahre und Funktionsumfänge stellt hohe Herausforderungen an eine Anwendung, die maschinenlesbare Applikationskarten erstellt, sowie an deren Nutzer. Neben den hardwaremäßigen Anforderungen zeigt sich immer wieder die Software als Herausforderung. So müssen die notwendigen Softwarefreischaltungen beispielsweise für eine automatische Teilbreitenschaltung auf dem Spritzgerät vorhanden sein. Nur so kann der Landwirt sämtliche Funktionen nutzen, die die Anwendung OPAL bietet.

5 Zusammenfassung

Das digitale Assistenzsystem bündelt verschiedene Informationen und bereitet diese praxisgerecht auf. Der Landwirt kann von der Kompaktheit der bereitgestellten Daten profitieren und seinen Betriebsablauf vereinfachen und sicherer machen. Die Anwendung wird in mehreren Schritten getestet und die Anforderungen aus der Praxis werden definiert.

Förderhinweis: Das Projekt OPAL wird von der Bundesanstalt für Landwirtschaft und Ernährung (BLE) und der Deutschen Innovationspartnerschaft Agrar (DIP) gefördert.

Literaturverzeichnis

[BA22-06] BayerCropScience Deutschland GmbH; Qualitative Umfrage zur Markteinführung des digitalen Assistenzsystems, unveröffentlichte Daten, Monheim Juli 2022.

[BA22-10] BayerCropScience Deutschland GmbH; Quanitative Umfrage zur Markteinführung des digitalen Assistenzsystems, unveröffentlichte Daten, Monheim Oktober 2022.

[JKI22] Herrmann, D.; Lefeldt. N.; Praxistest BLE-Verbundprojekt OPAL, unveröffentlichte Daten, Braunschweig 2022.

Metaanalyse zum aktuellen Stand der Digitalisierung in der Landwirtschaft

Niklas Hilbert[1], Jens-Peter Loy[1] und Karsten Borchard[2]

Abstract: Die Primärproduktion von Lebensmitteln hat sich in den letzten Jahrzehnten rasant verändert. So rücken beispielsweise Themen wie eine teilflächenspezifische Bewirtschaftung oder auch die digitale Überwachung des Tierbestandes in den Vordergrund. Die Forschung entwickelt immer neue Ansätze für die Nutzung digitaler Technologien in der Landwirtschaft. Daher stellt sich die Frage, inwieweit diese digitalen Technologien bereits heute in der landwirtschaftlichen Praxis genutzt werden. Des Weiteren ist von Interesse, welche hemmenden und fördernden Faktoren es bei der Nutzung digitaler Technologien in der Praxis gibt. Um diesen Fragestellungen nachzugehen, werden im Rahmen einer Literaturrecherche die derzeit verfügbaren Studien zu dem Thema zusammengetragen und analysiert.

Keywords: Digitalisierung, Landwirtschaft, Deutschland

1 Einleitung

Seit einigen Jahren verändert die Digitalisierung große Teile des Arbeitslebens. Auch in der Agrarbranche ist von einem neuen Abschnitt der Entwicklung die Rede. In der Landwirtschaft 4.0 sollen vor allem die intelligente Arbeitserledigung und die Verknüpfung der einzelnen Geräte miteinander mit Hilfe von Digitalisierung im Vordergrund stehen [Kr18]. Diese neuen Technologien, ihr Einsatz in der landwirtschaftlichen Praxis und mögliche Chancen und Hemmnisse, die im Zusammenhang mit ihnen stehen, sind Bestandteil verschiedener Studien der letzten Jahre. Im Rahmen der folgenden Literaturanalyse werden diese Studien zusammengefasst und diskutiert.

2 Material und Methoden

In Tabelle 1 werden die wesentlichen Ergebnisse der Literaturrecherche zusammengefasst. Die in den Studien durchgeführten Befragungen erfolgten von 2016 bis 2022. Die Anzahl befragter LandwirtInnen reicht von 92 [Vb17] bis 2390 [Lf21]. Im Rahmen dieser Metastudie sind ausschließlich Studien verwendet worden, in denen LandwirtInnen aus Deutschland bzw. bestimmten Regionen Deutschlands befragt wurden. Zwei Studien befragen ausschließlich LandwirtInnen aus Bayern [Vb17; Lf21]. Außer in einer Studie, in

---

[1] Christian-Albrechts-Universität zu Kiel, Marktlehre, Olshausenstraße 40, 24118 Kiel, nhilbert@ae.uni-kiel.de; jploy@ae.uni-kiel.de,
[2] Christian-Albrechts-Universität zu Kiel, MultiMediaLabor und Marktlehre, Olshausenstraße 40, 24118 Kiel, kbo@mml.uni-kiel.de

der die LandwirtInnen persönlich interviewt wurden, handelt es sich um Online-Befragungen.

Studie	Region	Art der Befragung	Anzahl Betriebe (n)	Größe der Betriebe in ha	Anzahl der Rinder
[Pw16]	D	persönlich	100	k.A.	k.A.
[Re19]	D	k.A.	401	k.A.	k.A.
[Bu20)	D	k.A.	500	k.A.	k.A.
[GMD22]	D	Online	329	470	358 Rinder
[Vb17]	BY	k.A.	92	k.A.	k.A.
[Lf21]	BY	Online	2390	k.A.	k.A.
[PGG21] (Gr. kl. Betriebe)	D	Online	415	77 Futterbau	80 Milchkühe
[PGG21] (Gr. gr. Betriebe)	D	Online	46	530 Futterbau	564 Milchkühe
[Ag22]	D	Online	155	k.A.	k.A.
[So22]	D	Online	267	k.A.	k.A.
[St22a; St22b]	D	k.A.	k.A.	64,1 (2022)	72 (2022)

Tab. 1: Regionen, Art der Befragung, Anzahl der Befragten, durchschnittliche Betriebsgröße und Tierzahlen der berücksichtigten Studien

3 Ergebnisse

Zusammenfassend haben die Autoren der verschiedenen Studien schwerpunktmäßig den aktuellen Stand der Nutzung digitaler Technologien und die Chancen bzw. Hemmnisse dieser betrachtet.

3.1 Aktueller Stand über die Nutzung digitaler Technologien

Aus Tabelle1 geht hervor, dass der Einsatz verschiedener Technologien in der landwirtschaftlichen Praxis deutlich unterschiedlich beurteilt wird. Somit sind pauschale Aussagen über den konkreten Stand der Digitalisierung in der Landwirtschaft schwer möglich. Es ist auffällig, dass die vier Technologien mit dem höchsten Ergebnis der Verbreitung ausschließlich im Ackerbau eingesetzt werden (Ertragskartierung, Karten aus Satellitendaten, GPS-Teilbreitenschaltung und automatische Lenkhilfen). Außerdem ist zu berücksichtigen, dass die Ergebnisse der Tierproduktion sich in Abhängigkeit der Tierart noch deutlich unterscheiden können. So sind automatische Fütterungen in der Schweinehaltung zu 94 %

verbreitet, in der Rinderhaltung nur zu 22 % [GMD22]. Sensortechnik ist im Ackerbau wie auch in der Tierproduktion am wenigsten verbreitet.

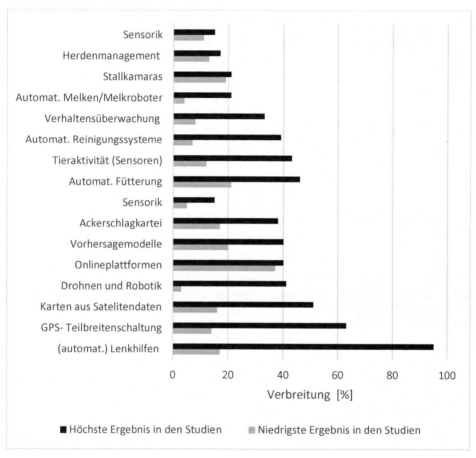

Abb. 1: Höchste und niedrigste Ergebnisse zur Verbreitung verschiedener Technologien in den berücksichtigten Studien

3.2 Hemmnisse der Digitalisierung

Die Hemmnisse der LandwirtInnen hinsichtlich des Einsatzes digitaler Technologien lassen sich in die folgenden Hauptaspekte untergliedern:

Wirtschaft: Für 92 % bzw. 76 % der LandwirtInnen stellen die hohen Anschaffungskosten ein Hemmnis bei einer Investition in digitale Technologien dar [Bu20; Pw16]. Außerdem ist mehr als die Hälfte der befragten LandwirtInnen nicht davon überzeugt, dass sich eine Investition überhaupt auszahlt [Pw16].

Technik: Die meisten LandwirtInnen sehen in der Inkompatibilität digitaler Technologien ein Hemmnis, diese auf dem eigenen Betrieb anzuwenden [So22; Pw16]. Eine andere Studie kommt zu dem Ergebnis, dass nur jeder zehnte Landwirt hierin ein Problem sieht [Re19]. Außerdem sieht knapp die Hälfte der befragten LandwirtInnen ein Problem in der fehlenden Infrastruktur in Form eines fehlenden Breitbandausbaus [Pw16].

Bildung: Drei Viertel der befragten LandwirtInnen verbinden mit dem Einsatz digitaler Technologien Anwendungsprobleme auf Grund einer hohen Komplexität der Systeme [Bu20].

Daten: Rund 84 % der befragten LandwirtInnen teilen die Einschätzung einer gefährdeten IT-Sicherheit [Bu20]. Besonders eine höhere staatliche Kontrollmöglichkeit wird bei einer steigenden Digitalisierung thematisiert. So beurteilen etwa 9 von 10 befragten LandwirtInnen die Situation [Bu20].

3.3 Chancen und Motive

Die Chancen und Motive, die die LandwirtInnen in digitalen Technologien sehen, lassen sich in die folgenden Gruppen einteilen:

Wirtschaft: Grundsätzlich kann die Steigerung der Wirtschaftlichkeit eine Chance digitaler Technologien sein. So sehen beispielsweise 81 % der befragten LandwirtInnen die Chance einer steigenden Produktionseffizienz [Bu20]. Aber auch die Steigerung der Produktqualität wird als große Chance betrachtet [Vb17; So22].

Arbeitsalltag: Ein Großteil der befragten LandwirtInnen sieht durch digitale Technologien in erster Linie eine grundsätzliche Arbeitserleichterung [Vb17; So22]. Knapp vier von fünf LandwirtInnen erwarten eine körperliche Entlastung [Bu20]. Ein großes Thema spielen auch Veränderungen im Pflanzen- und Tiergesundheitsmanagement [Vb17].

Umwelt: Durch die Digitalisierung besteht für 79 % bzw. 67 % der befragten LandwirtInnen eine Chance zur Reduktion von Umwelteinflüssen [Bu20; Re19]. Auch die Ergebnisse weiterer Studien kommen zu einem ähnlichen Ergebnis [So22].

3.4 Mögliche Gründe für unterschiedliche Digitalisierungsgrade

Ein möglicher Grund liegt in der positiven Korrelation zwischen dem Digitalisierungsgrad und der Betriebsgröße [So22; Pw16]. Gegensätzlich hierzu gibt es auch durch die Grenzen heutiger digitaler Systeme einen Vorteil für die Digitalisierung in kleinstrukturierten Regionen [Vb17]. Der Betriebsschwerpunkt gilt als weitere Ursache unterschiedlicher Digitalisierung [Ag22]. So sind automatische Fütterungen in der Schweinehaltung deutlich weiter verbreitet als in der Rinderhaltung [GMD22]. Der Anteil von Nutzern digitaler Technologien korreliert negativ zum Alter und dem Bildungsabschluss. [So22]

4 Limitierungen der Befragungen

Alle betrachteten Studien befassen sich mit digitalen Technologien im Pflanzenbau. Beim Blick auf digitale Technologien in der Tierhaltung ist die Datengrundlage für eine Auswertung deutlich geringer. Des Weiteren handelt es sich bei den meisten Studien, mit Ausnahme von PwC (2016), um Online-Befragungen. Somit ist davon auszugehen, dass diese eher digital-affine LandwirtInnen beantwortet haben und die Ergebnisse der Studien zum Einsatz digitaler Technologien über den tatsächlichen Nutzungshäufigkeiten der digitalen Technologien liegen. Es ist ebenfalls festzustellen, dass die abgefragten Technologien sich im Detail unterscheiden oder zu allgemein abgefragt werden, um belastbare Ergebnisse zu erhalten. So ergibt die Frage nach dem Einsatz von Herdenmanagementsystemen einen Nutzeranteil von höchstens 17 % [Re19]. Wird die Frage nach Farm- und Herdenmanagementanwendungen gestellt, wird ein Nutzeranteil von 40 % erreicht [Bu20]. Außerdem erschweren fehlende Angaben in den Studien die Interpretation der Ergebnisse.

5 Fazit

Aus den Ergebnissen der verschiedenen Studien können einzelne Tendenzen hinsichtlich der Nutzung bestimmter Technologien abgeleitet werden, dennoch bestehen große Unterschiede zwischen den Studien. Laut der analysierten Studien werden die Gründe für den unterschiedlichen Grad der Digitalisierung in der Betriebsgröße, wobei diese kontrovers diskutiert wird, dem Ausbildungsniveau des Betriebsleiters, und dessen Alter sowie im Betriebsschwerpunkt gesehen. Gerade im Bereich der Tierhaltung ist eine differenzierte Betrachtung notwendig, da sich der Digitalisierungsgrad in verschiedenen Arbeitsbereichen der Tierhaltung deutlich unterscheidet. Gegen den Einsatz digitaler Technologien stehen die Zweifel an der aktuellen Technik, der Wirtschaftlichkeit, die Datensicherheit sowie mangelndes Wissen über die Technologien im Vordergrund. Die LandwirtInnen sehen die größten Chancen in einer möglichen Arbeitserleichterung, einer steigenden Wirtschaftlichkeit und einer Reduzierung von Umwelteinflüssen. Somit besteht ein Forschungsbedarf, bei welchem die heterogene Agrarlandschaft sowie Chancen und Hemmnisse der LandwirtInnen berücksichtigt werden.

Förderhinweis: Dieses Projekt wird gefördert durch die H.-Wilhelm-Schaumann-Stiftung. Die Autoren danken der H.-Wilhelm-Schaumann-Stiftung für die finanzielle Unterstützung.

Literaturverzeichnis

[Ag22] Agrarzeitung (2022): Trendstudie. Autonomie, Robotik, Vernetzung.

[Bu20] Bundesverband Informationswirtschaft, Telekommunikation und Neue Medien e.V. (Bitkom); Deutscher Bauernverband (DBV) (2020): Digitalisierung in der Landwirtschaft 2020.

[GMD22] Gscheidle; M.; Munz, J.; Doluschitz, R. (2022): Strukturwirkung der Digitalisierung in der Landwirtschaft (100). In: *Berichte über Landwirtschaft* (1).

[Kr18] Krombholz, K.: Gedanken zur Vorgeschichte von Landwirtschaft 4.0. In: Jahrbuch Agrartechnik 2018, Bd. 30, S. 234-254. Online verfügbar unter https://publikationsserver.tu-braunschweig.de/receive/dbbs_mods_00066169, zuletzt geprüft am 05.08.2022.

[Lf21] LfL, Bayerische Landesanstalt für Landwirtschaft (2021): Landwirte Befragung. Digitale Landwirtschaft Bayern. Ergebnisübersicht. Unter Mitarbeit von A. Gabriel und M. Gandorfer.

[PGG21] Pfeiffer, J.; Gabriel, A.; Gandorfer, M. (2021): Klein gegen Groß- Vergleich von klein- und großstrukturierten Agrarregionen beim Einsatz digitaler Technologien. In: *Referate der 41. GIL-Jahrestagung*, S. 247–252. Online verfügbar unter https://gil-net.de/Publikationen/GIL2021_Gesamt_finalb.pdf, zuletzt geprüft am 11.07.2022.

[Pw16] PwC, PricewaterhouseCoopers AG Wirtschaftsprüfungsgesellschaft (2016): Quo vadis, agricola? Smart Farming: Nachhaltigkeit und Effizienz durch den Einsatz digitaler Technologien. Unter Mitarbeit von G. Bovensiepen, R. Hombach und S. Raimund.

[Re19] Rentenbank (2019): "Digital Farming" - Die Landwirtschaft im technologischen Wandel, S. 11-26. Online verfügbar unter https://cms.rentenbank.de/export/sites/rentenbank/dokumente/Geschaeftsbericht-2018-Deutsch.pdf, zuletzt geprüft am 11.07.2022.

[So22] Sonntag; W. I.; Wienrich, N.; Severin, M.; Schulze Schwering, D. (2022): Precision Farming - Nullnummer oder Nutzbringer? Eine empirische Studie unter Landwirten (100). In: *Berichte über Landwirtschaft* (2).

[St22a] Statistisches Bundesamt (2022a): Betriebsgrößenstruktur landwirtschaftlicher Betriebe nach Bundesländern. Online verfügbar unter https://www.destatis.de/DE/Themen/Branchen-Unternehmen/Landwirtschaft-Forstwirtschaft-Fischerei/Landwirtschaftliche-Betriebe/Tabellen/betriebsgroessenstruktur-landwirtschaftliche-betriebe.html, zuletzt geprüft am 05.12.2022.

[St22b] Statistisches Bundesamt (2022b): Viehhaltung im letzten Jahrzehnt: Weniger, aber größere Betriebe Online verfügbar unter https://www.destatis.de/DE/Presse/Pressemitteilungen/2021/07/PD21_N043_41.html., zuletzt geprüft am 05.12.2022

[Vb17] vbw, Vereinigung der bayrischen Wirtschaft e.V. (2017): Digitalisierung in der Land- und Ernährungswirtschaft. Unter Mitarbeit von J. Roosen.

Automatisierte Verarbeitung von heterogen aufgelösten Datenquellen zur Berechnung einer teilflächenspezifischen Flüssigmistapplikationskarte

Stefan Hinck[1] und Daniel Kümper[2]

Abstract: Bei der Ermittlung des Stickstoffdüngebedarfes (N-Düngebedarf) ist die Düngeverordnung maßgeblich zu befolgen. Die Berechnung des N-Düngebedarfes erfolgt pro Feld und ist zu dokumentieren. Weiter ist zu beachten, dass die Berechnung vor der Ausbringung zu erfolgen hat. Verschiedene Daten sind bei der Ermittlung zu berücksichtigen. Insbesondere bei der teilflächenspezifischen N-Düngebedarfsermittlung können die notwendigen Daten mit einem unterschiedlichen räumlichen Bezug vorliegen. Beispielsweise liegen die Ertragsdaten vom Mähdrescher in der Regel als Punktdaten vor und sind zur Nutzung bei der teilflächenspezifischen Düngebedarfsermittlung auf einen flächenbasierten räumlichen Bezug zu interpolieren. Ebenfalls können zwei oder mehrere Polygondatensätze flächenbasierte Daten beinhalten aber einen unterschiedlichen räumlichen Bezug haben, z. B. Ertragspotenzialkarten auf Teilflächenbasis und die letztjährige Ausbringmenge organischen Stickstoffs aus Gülle für den gesamten Ackerschlag. In diesem Fall sind die Ebenen mit unterschiedlichen räumlichen Bezügen durch Verschneidung auf denselben räumlichen Bezug zu bringen. Für diese Zwecke ist das OPeRAte-NPK-Düngemodul entwickelt und umgesetzt worden. Die Arbeiten erfolgten im OPeRAtePlus-Forschungsprojekt am Beispiel der kooperativen Flüssigmistausbringung.

Keywords: OPeRAte NPK-Düngemodul, Flüssigmistausbringung, Digitalisierung Düngeberechnung, automatisch generierte Dokumentation, Teilfläche

1 Einleitung

Der sich aus der Düngeverordnung (DüV22) ergebende Berechnungsablauf des Stickstoffdüngebedarfes (N-Düngebedarf) ist in Abbildung 1 skizziert. Der Berechnungsablauf kann in folgende Prozessschritte unterteilt werden:

1. Ermittlung des 5-jährigen Ertragsdurchschnitts;
2. Vergleich des 5-jährigen Ertragsdurchschnitts mit dem vorgegebenen kulturspezifischen Tabellenertragswert (s. DüV22, Anlage 4, Tab. 2);
3. Entspricht der 5-jährige Ertragsdurchschnitt dem Tabellenertragswert, so ist der vorgegebene Stickstoffbedarfswert zu übernehmen. Bei bestehenden Abweichungen zwischen 5-jährigem Ertragsdurchschnitt und Tabellenertragswert sind nach

---

[1] FARMsystem Hinck, c/o Hochschule Osnabrück, Nelson-Mandela Str. 1, 49076 Osnabrück, hinck@farmsystem.de,
[2] Field-Expert GmbH, Albert-Einstein-Str. 30, 49076 Osnabrück, gis@daniel-kuemper.de

weiteren Tabellenangaben Abschläge vom Stickstoffbedarfswert vorzunehmen bzw. können Zuschläge zum Stickstoffbedarfswert bis zu einer maximalen Höhe vorgenommen werden (s. DüV22, Anlage 4, Tab. 3);

4. Es sind folgende Kriterien zu ermitteln und deren Abzugswerte zu bestimmen:
   - Nmin-Wert
   - Humuswert (N-Nachlieferung aus dem Boden)
   - Organische Düngung (Kompost: letzte 3 Jahre; Gülle u.ä.: Vorjahr)
   - Vorfrucht
   - Zwischenfrucht

5. Subtraktion der ermittelten Abzugswerte vom zuvor ermittelten Stickstoffbedarfswert, somit ergibt sich der Stickstoff-Düngebedarfswert.

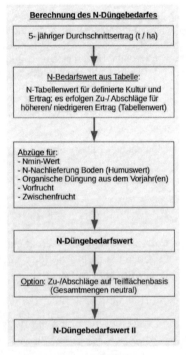

Abb. 1: Prozessablauf der Ermittlung des N-Düngebedarfs; zusätzlich ist bereits in den Prozessablauf die Option der mengenneutralen Zu- und Abschläge integriert

Nach DüV22 hat die Berechnung pro Acker zu erfolgen und Unterschiede innerhalb der Fläche können unberücksichtigt bleiben. Abbildung 1 beinhaltet bereits eine zusätzliche Option. Innerhalb eines Ackers können für Bereiche / Teilflächen Zuschläge bzw.

Abschläge definiert werden. Dabei wird berücksichtigt, dass die Zuschläge zu keiner Erhöhung des zuvor korrekt ermittelten Stickstoff-Düngebedarfswerts führen.

Ziel ist die einfache, transparente und schnelle Erstellung von Flüssigmistapplikationskarten auf Teilflächenbasis bzw. für den Ackerschlag [HNK19]. Mit der Berechnung wird die dazugehörige Dokumentation generiert. Für diese Zwecke ist das OPeRAte-NPK-Düngemodul entwickelt und umgesetzt worden. Die Arbeiten erfolgten im OPeRAtePlus-Forschungsprojekt am Beispiel der kooperativen Flüssigmistausbringung.

2 Material und Methode

Für die Nutzung von Datensätzen mit unterschiedlichen Geometrietypen (Punkt- oder Polygondaten) und unterschiedlichem räumlichem Bezug für die N-Düngebedarfsermittlung zur Generierung von teilflächenspezifischen Flüssigmistapplikationskarten bedarf es verschiedener, kombinierter Softwareroutinen, welche georeferenzierte Daten verarbeiten. In der Regel werden georeferenzierte Daten mit Geographische Informationssysteme (GIS) verarbeitet. Für die Nutzung im OPeRAte-NPK-Düngemodul sind spezialisierte GIS-Werkzeuge zu entwickeln, welche die Praktikabilität, eine einfache Bedienung und die Anwenderorientierung mit der eigentlichen speziellen Funktionalität (z. B. geostatistischem Kriging) des jeweiligen Werkzeugs kombinieren [HMK18]. Die GIS-Werkzeuge sind in die Software-Routine zur N-Düngebedarfsermittlung zu integrieren. Die Software-Routinen sind an die genauen Aufgabenstellungen anzupassen und lassen keine fehlerhaften Arbeitsschritte (z. B. die Generierung von Teilflächen aus den Maishäckslerertragsdaten) zu, welche bei der Kombination mehrerer Werkzeuge in einem GIS-System auftreten können. Hierfür sind für den Anwendungsfall spezialisierte Lösungen zu entwickeln, welche verschiedene Software-Module, z. B. die automatisierte Verarbeitung der – vorverarbeiteten – Ertragsdaten und deren Visualisierung, die Verifizierung der Topologie und Geometrien, die Analyse der Eingangsdaten, Berechnung der Ausgangsdaten durch eine Prozessmodellierung miteinander kombinieren. Die Ergebnisse und notwendigen Eingaben bzw. Schnittstellen werden an die jeweiligen nachfolgenden Prozessschritte bereitgestellt.

3 Ergebnisse und Diskussion

Es ist im Rahmen des Forschungsprojektes OPeRAtePlus ein anwenderorientiertes, webbasiertes und GIS-unterstützendes Berechnungswerkzeug „OPeRAte-NPK-Düngemodul" für die teilflächenspezifische N-Düngebedarfsermittlung entwickelt und umgesetzt worden. Der Berechnungsablauf ist um die notwendigen GIS-Werkzeuge ergänzt und kombiniert worden (s. Abb. 2). Es können Datensätze mit unterschiedlichen Geometrietypen – Punktdaten und Flächendaten – geladen und verarbeitet werden. Beispielhaft wird an der Verarbeitung der Ertragsdaten vom Maishäcksler die Vorgehensweise gezeigt, wie die punktbasierten Ertragsdaten geostatistisch aufbereitet und zu flächenbasierten Daten transformiert werden. Die Transformation von punktbasierten Ertragsdaten zu flächenbasierten Daten ist notwendig, da eine Düngeberechnung für eine Fläche oder Teilfläche erfolgt und nicht für einen Punkt bzw. mehrere Punkte innerhalb einer Fläche. Nach dem Laden der Ertragsdaten erfolgt die Abfrage der entsprechenden Attributspalte mit den Ertragsdaten und nach dem 5-jährigen Ertragsdurchschnitt. Die zeitlich geordneten Messpunkte der vorliegenden Ertragsdaten werden mit Hilfe der Kriging-Methode gleichmäßig auf die Fläche interpoliert. Hierbei erfolgt die Parameter-Einstellung des Variogrammes automatisiert, sodass AnwenderInnen keine komplexen Einstellungen vornehmen müssen (s. Abb. 3)

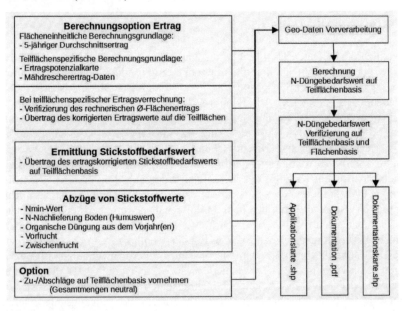

Abb. 2: Erweiterter Prozessablauf zur Ermittlung des teilflächenspezifischen N-Düngebedarfs, der Prozessablauf ist um die notwendigen GIS-Werkzeuge erweitert worden

Eine Zuordnung der Erträge zu Ertragsklassen erfolgt mit der K-Means-Methode (s. Abb. 4). In Kombination mit der Erstellung eines Voronoi-Diagrammes werden die Flächen der abgegrenzten Ertragsklassen in flächenbasierte Daten gewandelt. Hierzu ist lediglich die Anzahl der zu erzeugenden Clusterklassen von den AnwenderInnen einzugeben. Die Clusterklassenanzahl gibt die Anzahl der zu bildenden Teilflächen an. Es besteht die Möglichkeit, eine Minimumgröße für die Teilflächen zu definieren. Teilflächen, welche jene Minimumgröße unterschreiten, werden den angrenzenden Teilflächen in einem weiteren Prozessschritt zugeordnet. Auf zu kleinen Teilflächen, z. B. mit wenigen Quadratmetern, kann aus technischen Gründen, z. B. aufgrund einer größeren Arbeitsbreite, nicht die vorgegebene Düngemenge korrekt ausgebracht werden. In diesem Fall empfiehlt es sich, die zu kleinen Teilflächen zu eliminieren bzw. den benachbarten Teilflächen zuzuordnen. Auf den generierten Teilflächen-Polygonen wird der durchschnittliche Teilflächenertrag jener Ertragsklasse übertragen. Der sich ergebende durchschnittliche geometrische Flächenertrag aller Teilflächen wird mit dem eingegebenen 5-jährigen Ertragsdurchschnitt verifiziert und ggf. angeglichen.

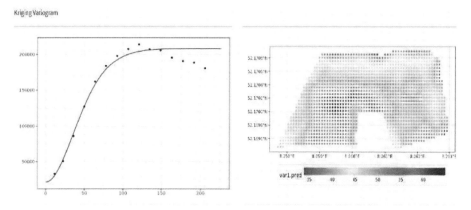

Abb. 3: Automatisierte Kriging Variogramm-Parametrisierung, um die linienhaften Ertragsdaten gleichmäßig auf die Fläche zu übertragen

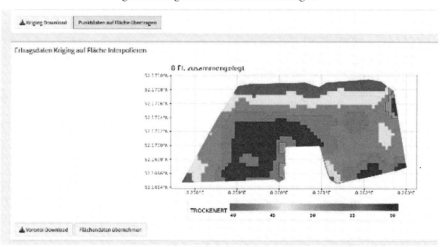

Abb. 4: Wandeln der Punktdaten in Teilflächen (zu Polygonen) mit Hilfe eines Voronoi-Diagrammes; Eingabewert: Anzahl der Clusterklassen und Minimumgröße der Teilflächen; rot-markiert sind die Teilflächen, welche aufgrund der Minimumgröße eliminiert werden

Im weiteren Prozessverlauf erfolgt die Abfrage aller weiteren Faktoren für die Düngebedarfsermittlung. Dabei können alle Faktoren als georeferenzierter Teilflächenwert oder als Standardwert für die gesamte Fläche geladen und verarbeitet werden. Die räumlichen Bezüge eines jedes Datensatz werden geprüft. Bei räumlicher Abweichung werden die Ebenen verschnitten und die dazugehörigen Daten entsprechend übertragen. Bei Vorhandensein eines Standardwerts wird dieser auf die einzelnen Teilflächen übertragen.

Nach Beendigung der Berechnung erfolgt die Generierung einer Applikationskarte im Shape-Format, welche genutzt werden kann oder mit Hilfe der OPeRAte-Plattform in eine isoxml-fähige Applikationskarte gewandelt wird. Mit der Generierung der Applikationskarte erfolgt eine Dokumentation der N-Düngebedarfsermittlung. Diese wird im PDF-Format zur Verfügung gestellt.

4 Zusammenfassung

Mit Hilfe des OPeRAte-NPK Düngemoduls kann eine teilflächenspezifsche Applikationskarte für die Flüssigmistausbringung erstellt werden. Es können Datensätze mit unterschiedlichen Geometrietypen und räumlich unterschiedlichen Bezügen verarbeitet werden. Es besteht unter anderem die Möglichkeit, Ertragsdaten vom Maishäcksler für die Generierung von Teilflächen zu nutzen. Unter anderem wurden einzelne Prozessschritte, z. B. die Konfiguration des Variogrammes für das Kriging der Ertragsdaten, automatisiert, damit AnwenderInnen keine komplexen Einstellungen vornehmen müssen. Damit wird der Komfort bei der Anwendung erhöht und gleichzeitig wird die Fehleranfälligkeit gesenkt. Die Vorgaben zur Ermittlung des Düngebedarfs nach der DüV22 werden beachtet. Mit der Generierung der Applikationskarte wird eine Dokumentation der Berechnung als PDF-Dokument bereitgestellt.

Förderhinweis: Das Projekt OPeRAtePlus wurde von der Bundesanstalt für Landwirtschaft und Ernährung (BLE) und der Deutschen Innovationspartnerschaft Agrar (DIP) der Landwirtschaftlichen Rentenbank gefördert.

Literaturverzeichnis

[HMK18] Hinck, S., Mentrup, D., Kerssen, S., Kümper, D.: Anwendungsorientierte, webbasierte GIS-Lösung. In Proc. 38. Jahrestagung der GIL, Kiel, S. 103-106, 2018.

[HNK19] Hinck, S., Nordemann, F., Kraatz, F., Iggena, T., Tönjes, R., Tapken, H., Kümper, D.: User-oriented, Web-based GIS Application for Liquid Manure Fertilisation. In Proc. 12th European Conference on Precision Agriculture, Book of Posters, S. 96-97, 2019.

[DüV22] Düngeverordnung, https://www.gesetze-im-internet.de/d_v_2017/, letzter Aufruf 25.10.2022.

Configurations of human-AI work in agriculture

Adoption and use of intelligent systems by agricultural workers

Joschka Andreas Hüllmann[1], Hauke Precht[2] and Carolin Wübbe[3]

Abstract: Agriculture is making leaps in digitalization and the development of artificial intelligence (AI) systems, e.g., decision support systems, sensors, or autonomous vehicles. However, adoption and widespread use of these technologies remains below expectations with negative consequences for digitally advancing the agricultural industry. Therefore, this study investigates the configurations of human-AI work, in particular, human-AI decision-making. Configurations describe the interactions between workers and intelligent systems, emphasizing the adoption and use of technologies *in-situ*. This study targets agricultural farms in Germany, collecting qualitative data at small and medium-sized businesses. From this data, the paper examines how configurations of human-AI work emerge and how explanations influence these configurations in the context of agricultural work. Theoretical contributions include a new understanding of how agricultural workers adopt and work with AI to make decisions. Practical contributions include more accessible AI systems, easing transfer into practice, and improving agricultural workers' interactions with AI.

Keywords: explainability, adoption and use, decision-making, human-AI interaction, work, farming

1 Introduction

Agriculture is making leaps in digitalization and artificial intelligence (AI) systems with autonomous machines, sensor data, and decision support systems. However, despite technological advances and high spending on developing novel AI-based systems, the adoption and use of these technologies remains below expectations in agricultural practice [We18]. The lacking adoption and use results in little value being captured. Especially small and medium-sized agricultural companies fall behind in innovation and economic performance [KJL19].

The lagging adoption and use of new technologies such as AI impedes the digitalization in agriculture with severe impacts on reaching sustainability and climate goals. Adoption at scale and effective use of these novel technologies would enable precision farming and

---

[1] University of Twente, Department of High-tech Business and Entrepreneurship, Hallenweg 17, 7522 NH Enschede, The Netherlands, j.huellmann@utwente.nl
[2] Universität Oldenburg, Department für Informatik, Ammerländer Heerstr. 114-118, 26129 Oldenburg, Germany, hauke.precht@uni-oldenburg.de
[3] Ascora GmbH, Birkenallee 43, 27777 Ganderkesee, Germany, wuebbe@ascora.de

sustainable intensification, with a profound impact on climate change, sustainable soil, and groundwater quality due to reductions in fertilization.

The novel characteristics of AI-based technologies and the idiosyncrasies of farmwork render it unclear if established theories on technology acceptance can sufficiently explain the scant adoption and use of AI in farming [GBS22; Wa22]. Jobs, tasks, and norms in farming follow a different paradigm, and the boundary conditions of existing theories may be violated [KJL19; We18].

Therefore, this short paper asks: *"Why do agricultural workers not adopt and use novel intelligent (AI-based) systems?"* The question is addressed by conducting qualitative interviews with agricultural workers and manufacturers. The theoretical lens of *configurations* is used for analysis. Drawing from Suchman [Su07], configurations are defined as the individual interactions with technology *in-situ*, emphasizing humans' choice for adoption and use practices. As this text is a short paper, the preliminary results focus on the adoption aspect of such configurations.

2 Methodology

Empirically, we address the research question by conducting informal, unstructured interviews about the adoption and use of machine-learning-based technologies. These unstructured interviews allow for a rich qualitative analysis of how choices about adoption are made [BGM87; Fi04]. It follows guidelines by Myers and Newman [MN07]. Open coding was performed by the first author alone, following the steps by Saldana [Sa09]. The qualitative data was broken down into discrete parts and then compared "for similarities and differences" [Sa09, p.81].

Fig. 1: Left: Predict vegetation levels from satellite images and optimize fertilizer using machine learning. Right: Transfer fertilizer estimations to tractor for precise distribution

As configurations are contingent on the application domain's boundary conditions, the research question must be inquired in context [MHS17]. This study focuses on the empirical context of North Rhine-Westphalia and Lower Saxony, which is characterized by family-owned farm businesses (SMEs) that are resource-constrained with up to five workers. Data collection focuses on arable farms that produce crops under recurring observations by scientists. Intelligent systems under study include crop yield and disease prediction systems [In20]. Figure 1 shows an example of machine learning-based functionality that was discussed with the interviewees[4].

Four unstructured expert interviews with farmers and one with a farm advisor, as well as two expert focus groups (five people each) with agricultural manufacturers took place in 2021. In total, eleven hours of interviews were conducted (cf. Table 1).

#	Occupation	Agricultural workers	Duration
1	Farmer	1	1 hr
2	Farmer	2	2 hrs
3	Farmer	4	1 hr
4	Farmer	2	2 hrs
5	Farm Advisor	n/a	1 hr
6	Agricultural Manufacturer	n/a	2 hrs
7	Agricultural Manufacturer	n/a	2 hrs

Tab. 1: Interviews and expert groups

3 Preliminary results

According to the interviewees, the farmers' lifelong experience matters over technological innovations, with one interviewee reciting an old proverb in their statement: "I have worked on this field for more than 25 years. The farmer's eye fattens the cattle, not a faulty tool." Farmers appreciate innovations in engineering, which they understand due to their expertise. However, they are skeptical about innovations in information technology. They question the systems' validity "If it's cloudy, the satellite tool is giving wrong results," and criticize the opacity of the back-box algorithms.

Furthermore, they understand their farm as a business. Although the interviewees can appreciate the value propositions of the technologies, they doubt the AI systems' profitability. They are unsure how these systems would integrate with their farm infrastructure: "Ultimately, my farm is a business, and these systems are expensive with diminishing returns and high maintenance costs. I cannot repair it myself."

Information technology affinity and age seem relevant, as a younger interviewee mentioned their excitement for AI-based systems. Young farmers enroll in higher education and study agriculture at universities, which might change agricultural workers' perspectives toward new technologies in the future.

The interviewees from agricultural manufacturing describe being unable to provide an outlook on the financial benefits to the agricultural workers: "We cannot guarantee productivity gains, as the technology is new". The interviewed companies mostly sell new systems to large enterprises in Eastern Europe instead of small family-owned businesses

---

[4] https://www.claas.de/produkte/digitale-loesungen/farm-management/365farmnet (accessed 2022-10-20).

because the technologies are oversized for small farms. The interviewed organization struggles with the digital transformation and selling digital services: "We build a lot of engineering technology and sensors but are unsure what we can do with the collected data."

4 Discussion and implications

Comprehensibility of the algorithmic mechanisms is the key barrier that prevents agricultural workers from working with AI systems. Whereas previous research suggests that a lacking explainability leads to ineffective use [AMN21; Hü21], our findings highlight that lacking explainability impedes adoption altogether and agricultural workers are hesitant to procure AI-based precision farming technologies.

While research has focused on the users' lacking skills for effective human-AI work [KJL19], our findings show that statistical skills are lacking both on the agricultural workers and manufacturing sides. Agricultural companies are still figuring out what they can do with the data they are collecting and analyzing [KH18]. Comprehension may also help to estimate the financial returns of AI systems.

Lastly, the farmer's identity as the sole decision-maker affects the use of AI for decision-making. This is in line with existing research from other domains, which found changes in professional role identity, for example, in finance [SMF21]. However, agricultural workers' identity is not just about a professional role but rather a life identity, a calling [KJL19]. Hence, the identity shift from manual laborer towards manual laborer plus knowledge worker is more fundamental – as our research shows. Therefore, the deployment of AI explanations should account for the experience, authority, and identity of the agricultural worker. 'Identity-aware' user interfaces should be developed and evaluated [LWH03; Sc19].

Comprehension can increase the agricultural worker's trust in AI systems and make them more effective [Wa22]. Explanations should build on top of the agricultural workers' engineering expertise. The trend towards higher education in agriculture may accelerate future innovations in AI for farming. Public policy can support higher education programs for farmers and manufacturers. Manufacturers should build the capability to quantify and explain the benefits of novel AI systems.

This study extends the understanding of configurations of human-AI work with implications for designing AI-based systems and deploying AI-based systems with explanations in organizational settings. Thereby, it contributes to recent research on end-user-centered AI by looking at the context of agriculture [Ab18; Ch19]. This novel understanding contributes to the transfer of AI systems into practice.

5 Conclusion and next steps

Based on unstructured interviews, we develop an understanding of configurations of human-AI work. This study's insights support the statement from Ågerfalk [Åg20], showing that the comprehensibility of intelligent systems is crucial for adoption and use. Consequently, explanations and potentially the effects of higher education in agriculture may offer a remedy to the lagging adoption. Furthermore, the findings show that the idiosyncrasies of agricultural work, including the agricultural workers' identities and the quantifiability of financial benefits are relevant.

This preliminary study has some limitations. Only the first author coded a small sample of qualitative data. All interviewed farmers were from small farms. Hence, generalizability to other farm businesses and agricultural workers may be impeded. Our next steps are to derive ideas for technological and organizational interventions, prototypically test and experimentally evaluate them with agricultural workers – following established RCT protocols [SAM10]. Specifically, interventions that improve the explainability of these technologies are in focus because they affect trustworthiness, transparency, and comprehensibility as the necessary conditions for widespread adoption and use of intelligent systems by agricultural workers. Advancing the effectiveness of such AI explanations is crucial for making AI systems accessible to the agricultural industry and reaching climate and sustainability goals.

Bibliography

[Ab18]   Abdul, A. et.al.: Trends and Trajectories for Explainable, Accountable and Intelligible Systems. In: Proceedings of the Conference on Human Factors in Computing Systems, New York, S. 1-18, 2018.

[Åg20]   Ågerfalk, P.J.: Artificial intelligence as digital agency. European Journal of Information Systems 01/20, S. 1-8, 2020.

[AMN21] Asatiani, A.; Malo, P.; Nagbøl, P.R.: Sociotechnical Envelopment of Artificial Intelligence: An Approach to Organizational Deployment of Inscrutable Artificial Intelligence Systems. Journal of the Association for Information Systems 02/21, S. 325-352, 2021.

[BGM87] Benbasat, I.; Goldstein, D.; Mead, M.: The Case Research Strategy in Studies of Information Systems. MIS Quarterly, 03/87, S. 369-386, 1987.

[Ch19]   Cheng, H.-F. et.al.: Explaining Decision-Making Algorithms through UI. In: Proceedings of the Conference on Human Factors in Computing Systems, New York, S. 1-12, 2019.

[Fi04]   Fiske, S.T.: Mind the Gap: In Praise of Informal Sources of Formal Theory. Personality and Social Psychology Review 02/04, S. 132-137, 2004.

[GBS22]   van Giffen, B.; Barth, N.; Sagodi, A.: Characteristics of Contemporary AI Technologies and Implications for IS Research. In: Proceedings of the International Conference on Information Systems, Copenhagen, S. 1-9, 2022.

[Hü21]   Hüllmann, J.A.: Smarter Work? Promises and Perils of Algorithmic Management in the Workplace Using Digital Traces, University of Münster, Münster, 2021.

[In20]   Inoue, Y.: Satellite- and drone-based remote sensing of crops and soils for smart farming – a review. Soil Science and Plant Nutrition 06/20, S. 798-810, 2022.

[KH18]   Klein, S.; Hüllmann, J.A.: Datenkapitalismus akademischer Wissenschaftsverlage. Wirtschaftsdienst 07/18, S. 477-480, 2018.

[KJL19]   Klerkx, L.; Jakku, E.; Labarthe, P.: A review of social science on digital agriculture, smart farming and agriculture 4.0: New contributions and a future research agenda. NJAS: Wageningen Journal of Life Sciences 01/19, S. 1-16, 2019.

[LWH03]   Liu, J.; Wong, C.K.; Hui, K.K.: An adaptive user interface based on personalized learning. IEEE Intelligent Systems 02/03, S. 52-57, 2003.

[MHS17]   Miller, T.; Howe, P.; Sonenberg, L.: Explainable AI: Beware of Inmates Running the Asylum Or: How I Learnt to Stop Worrying and Love the Social and Behavioural Sciences. arXiv, https://arxiv.org/abs/1712.00547, Stand: 01.08.2023.

[MN07]   Myers, M.D.; Newman, M.: The qualitative interview in IS research: Examining the craft. Information and Organization 01/07, S. 2-26, 2007.

[Sa09]   Saldana, J.: The coding manual for qualitative reseachers. 1. Aufl., SAGE Publications Ltd, London, 2009.

[SAM10]   Schulz, K.F.; Altman, D.G.; Moher, D.: CONSORT 2010 Statement: updated guidelines for reporting parallel group randomised trials. the BMJ 03/10, S. 698-702, 2010.

[Sc19]   Schaffer, J. et.al.: I can do better than your AI. In: Proceedings of the International Conference on Intelligent User Interfaces. New York, S. 240-251, 2019.

[SMF21]   Strich, F.; Mayer, A.-S.; Fiedler, M.: What Do I Do in a World of Artificial Intelligence? Investigating the Impact of Substitutive Decision-Making AI Systems on Employees' Professional Role Identity. Journal of the Association for Information Systems 02/21, S. 304-324, 2021.

[Su07]   Suchman, L.: Human-Machine Reconfigurations: Plans and Situated Actions. Cambridge University Press, Cambridge, 2007.

[Wa22]   Wanner, J. et.al.: The effect of transparency and trust on intelligent system acceptance: Evidence from a user-based study. Electronic Markets 04/22, S. 1-24, 2022.

[We18]   Weersink, A. et.al.: Opportunities and Challenges for Big Data in Agricultural and Environmental Analysis. Annual Review of Resource Economics 01/18, S. 19-37, 2018.

Ökonomische Bewertung zum Spot-Spraying durch Drohnentechnik

Tobias Jorissen [1], Silke Becker[1], Konstantin Nahrstedt[2], Maren Pöttker [2], Guido Recke[1] und Thomas Jarmer[2]

Abstract: Mittels hochaufgelöster drohnenbasierter Bilddaten können Durchwuchskartoffeln in Maisbeständen erkannt und räumlich verortet werden. Eine Überführung dieser Verortung in eine maschinenlesbare Applikationskarte ermöglicht durch Einsatz von Spot-Spraying mit einer Feldspritze eine bedarfsorientierte Applikation von Pflanzenschutzmitteln (PSM). Zur ökonomischen Bewertung wurden Kalkulationen auf Basis von praxisnahen Feldversuchen und Experteninterviews durchgeführt. In Abhängigkeit der Flächenauslastung der Drohne, der gewählten Pflanzenschutzstrategie und möglichen PSM-Einsparpotentialen von 50-80 % reichen die Mehrkosten des Spot-Spraying-Verfahrens von -32 € ha^{-1} bis 60 € ha^{-1}. Ein Haupteinflussfaktor für die Wirtschaftlichkeit des Verfahrens sind die Kosten des einzusparenden PSM.

Keywords: Spot-Spraying, Drohnentechnik, Pflanzenschutz, Ökonomie, Durchwuchskartoffeln

1 Einleitung

Mit dem Green Deal soll der Einsatz von Pflanzenschutzmitteln (PSM) bis 2030 um 50 % reduziert werden, was die Landwirtschaft vor eine schwierige ökonomische Aufgabe stellt. [Mi21]. Eine Möglichkeit der Reduktion ist der Einsatz der Spot-Spraying-Technik. Hierbei wird nicht die gesamte Anbaufläche, sondern nur der mit Beikräutern dominierte Bereich mit PSM behandelt. Ein Anwendungsfall ist die Behandlung von Durchwuchskartoffeln im Mais. Durch Ernteverluste und zunehmend milde Winter sind Durchwuchskartoffeln ein Problem und aus phytosanitären Gründen zu vermeiden. Vor dem Reihenschluss im Mais können durch Drohnenüberflüge Durchwuchskartoffeln detektiert, Applikationskarten erstellt und Spot-Spraying-Maßnahmen durchgeführt werden. Unter Einsatz von Bildauswert-Algorithmen werden Nutzpflanze und Beikraut in Drohnenbilddaten räumlich erfasst. Anschließend erfolgt die Spritzung spotspezifisch in Abhängigkeit vom Standort der Kartoffeln. Zur Bewertung der Machbarkeit und frühen

---

[1] Hochschule Osnabrück, Fachgebiet Landwirtschaftliche Betriebswirtschaftslehre, Am Krümpel 31, 49090 Osnabrück, t.jorissen@hs-osnabrueck.de, https://orcid.org/0000-0001-8290-6284; s.becker.1@hs-osnabrueck.de; g.recke@hs-osnabrueck.de

[2] Universität Osnabrück, Arbeitsgruppe Fernerkundung und Digitale Bildverarbeitung, Wachsbleiche 27, 49090 Osnabrück, konstantin.nahrstedt@uni-osnabrueck.de; maren.poettker@uni-osnabrueck.de, https://orcid.org/0000-0002-0711-732X; thomas.jarmer@uni-osnabrueck.de

Erkennung möglicher sensitiver Parameter sind ökonomische Begleitforschungen wegweisend.

2 Material und Methoden

Die ökonomische Bewertung von Spot-Spraying durch Drohnentechnik erfolgt auf Basis von Praxisversuchen in den Jahren 2021 und 2022, die im Rahmen des Forschungsprojektes Experimentierfeld Agro-Nordwest, in Kooperation mit zwei landwirtschaftlichen Betrieben in Nordwestdeutschland und dem Landtechnikunternehmen Amazone durchgeführt wurden. Zur Bewertung der Umsetzbarkeit erfolgte die Befliegung von zwei Versuchsflächen mit einer DJI Phantom Multispectral mit RTK Mobile Station. In einer Flughöhe von 25 m wurden Bilddaten mit einer Auflösung von 1,2 cm aufgezeichnet und anschließend zu einem Orthophoto mosaikiert. Zur Differenzierung der Bestandsstruktur zwischen Mais und Durchwuchskartoffel wurde ein Bildklassifikationsalgorithmus implementiert und trainiert [Ch21]. Das resultierende Klassifikationsergebnis wurde anschließend in eine maschinenlesbare Applikationskarte übersetzt und auf das Terminal eines Fendt 724 Vario mit einer Amazone Anbaufeldspritze UF 2002 überführt [AM22; BLS22]. Auf Basis des in der Applikationskarte ablesbaren Standortes der Durchwuchskartoffeln erfolgte anschließend die spotspezifische Spritzung.

Neben den Praxisversuchen stützen sich die ökonomischen Analysen auf Daten von Experteninterviews aus der Landwirtschaft sowie der Drohnen- und Landtechnik [AM22; BLS22; SS22]. Dies sind im Wesentlichen Kostendaten zur Spot-Spraying- und Drohnentechnik. Kalkuliert wurden ein 200-ha und ein 500-ha-Marktfruchtbetrieb mit jeweils einem Anteil von 20 % Mais in der Fruchtfolge (Tab. 1). Die Anzahl an Überfahrten beim Pflanzenschutz und die PSM-Kosten sind pauschalisiert aus Web-Anwendungen zur landwirtschaftlichen Deckungsbeitragsrechnung [LFL22]. Die pauschalisierten PSM-Kosten zwischen 100-300 € ha^{-1} der drei Ackerfrüchte sind Bestandteil für die Berücksichtigung der Einsparung von PSM-Kosten durch Teilbreitenschaltung, die durch die Spot-Spraying-Technik ebenfalls möglich ist, und in die ökonomische Analyse mit einfließt.

Ackerfrüchte	Anteile Fruchtfolge	Anzahl Überfahrten	PSM-Kosten
Getreide / Raps	60 %	5	150 € ha^{-1}
Kartoffeln	20 %	8	300 € ha^{-1}
Mais	20 %	2	100 € ha^{-1}

Tab. 1: Modellierte Fruchtfolge und PSM-Aufwand [BLS]

Für den 500-ha-Betrieb ist ein leistungsstärkerer Traktor angenommen als für den 200-ha-Betrieb. Beim 200-ha-Betrieb wurde eine angehängte Pflanzenschutzspritze mit einer Arbeitsbreite von 24 m kalkuliert, beim 500-ha-Betrieb eine gezogene Pflanzenschutzspritze mit einer Arbeitsbreite von 30 m [AM22; BLS22]. Durch die notwendige Aufrüstung für Spot-Spraying ist eine Teilbreitenabschaltung und PSM-Einsparung möglich [BLS22]. Beim 200-ha-Betrieb werden kleinere Flächendimensionen unterstellt als beim 500-ha-Betrieb (Tab. 2).

Parameter	Betrieb 1	Betrieb 2
Betriebsfläche (ha)	200	500
Traktorleistung (kW)	102	132
Applikationstechnik (Firma Amazone)	UF 2002	UX 6200
Mitteleinsparung durch Teilbreitenabschaltung	4,5 %	3,8 %

Tab. 2: Parameter der zwei Modellbetriebe bei der Feldtechnik [BLS]

Die Investitionskosten in Drohnentechnik beinhalteten den Aufwand für Drohne, Kamera und RTK-Basisstation (Tab. 3) [GF22]. Im Vergleich zur Instandhaltungsquote für landwirtschaftliche Technik ist für Drohnentechnik mit 10 % ein vergleichsweise hoher Wert angenommen worden. Dieser beinhaltet vor allem den Aufwand bei der Anschaffung von Ersatzakkus. Die angenommene Flächenleistung von 8 ha h^{-1} und eine maximal mögliche Flugzeit von 5 h d^{-1} ergeben sich für die eingesetzte Drohne aus den Erfahrungen der zwei Versuchsjahre.

Parameter	Wert
Investitionskosten Drohnentechnik (€)	11.000
Instandhaltungskosten (% Investitionskosten)	10
Lohnkosten (€ h^{-1})	30
Kosten Transportfahrzeug für Drohne (€ ha^{-1})	2
Vor- und Nachbereitung Drohneneinsatz (€ ha^{-1})	5
Flächenleistung (ha h^{-1})	8
Maximal mögliche Flugzeit (h d^{-1})	5

Tab. 3: Parameter beim Drohneneinsatz

Bei den Analysen wird ein PSM-Maßnahmensplitting angenommen [Kl22]. Die Bekämpfung von Durchwuchskartoffeln mittels Spot-Spraying-Technik erfolgt bei der 2. Überfahrt. Analysiert werden eine hochpreisige Variante 1 und eine niedrigpreisige Variante 2 (Tab. 4) [VS22]. Kalkuliert werden die zwei PSM-Varianten für eine betriebsübliche Bewirtschaftung sowie den Einsatz mit Drohnen- und Spotspraying-Technik.

Variante (Überfahrt)	PSM	Kosten in € ha^{-1}
1 (1.)	Elumis und Spectrum Gold	41,65
1 (2.)	Callisto, Onyx und Effigo	78,32
2 (1.)	Gardo Gold, Temsa, Primero und Peak	41,33
2 (2.)	Temsa	9,69

Tab. 4: Varianten bei der Bekämpfung von Durchwuchskartoffeln [BLS]

Die Kostenvergleichsrechnung erfolgt auf Basis der approximativen Durchschnittskosten. Kalkuliert werden Abschreibungskosten, Zinskosten auf das durchschnittlich gebundene Kapital, Lohnkosten, Instandhaltungskosten und Betriebsmittelkosten. Anschließend werden die Mehrkosten der Spot-Spraying-Variante gegenüber der betriebsüblichen Variante kalkuliert, jeweils für die PSM-Variante 1 und 2.

3 Ergebnisse

Im Kontext der drohnendatenbasierten Differenzierung von Mais und Durchwuchskartoffeln wurden in den Praxisversuchen versuchsübergreifend Klassifikationsgenauigkeiten von mindestens 88 % erzielt. Aus der hieraus generierten Applikationskarte ergaben sich in den Feldversuchen Einsparpotentiale für das PSM von 50-80 %. Zur Befliegung der Maisflächen beim 200-ha-Betrieb wird ein Flugtag benötigt, beim 500-ha-Betrieb 2,5 Flugtage. In Abhängigkeit vom Modellbetrieb, der angenommenen Traktorleistungen und Pflanzenschutztechniken schwanken die PSM-Applikationskosten zwischen 28,26 € ha^{-1} und 35,44 € ha^{-1} (Tab. 5).

Parameter	Betrieb 1	Betrieb 2
Kosten Drohneneinsatz (€ ha^{-1})	64,19	29,13
PSM Applikationskosten betriebsübliche Variante (€ ha^{-1})	32,34	28,26
PSM Applikationskosten Spot-Spraying Variante (€ ha^{-1})	35,44	31,02
PSM-Einsparung durch Teilbreitenschaltung (€ ha^{-1})	7,62	6,46

Tab. 5 Ausgewählte Parameter der Kostenvergleichsrechnung

Die Mehrkosten für die Ausstattung in Spot-Spraying-Technik betragen für den 200-ha-Betrieb 3,10 € ha^{-1} und für den 500-ha-Betrieb 2,76 € ha^{-1}. Durch Mitteleinsparungen aufgrund von Teilbreitenschaltung können die Mehrkosten auf -4,52 € ha^{-1} für den 200-ha-Betrieb und auf -3,70 € ha^{-1} für 500-ha-Betrieb gesenkt werden. Die Kosten für den Drohneneinsatz (inkl. Vor- und Nachbereitung) betragen für den 200-ha-Betrieb 69,19 € ha^{-1}, für den 500-ha-Betrieb 34,13 € ha^{-1}. Einen wesentlichen Anteil an den Kosten für den Drohneneinsatz haben Abschreibungen, Zinsansatz und Instandhaltung, die beim 200-ha-Betrieb bei 87 % und beim 500-ha-Betrieb bei 74 % liegen. In Abhängigkeit der Betriebsgröße, des gewählten PSM und der nicht zu behandelnden Spot-Spraying-Fläche (≈ Durchwuchsrate der Kartoffeln) schwanken die Mehrkosten für den drohnenbasierten Pflanzenschutz zwischen -48 € ha^{-1} und 65 € ha^{-1} (Abb. 1). Einen wesentlichen Effekt auf die Mehrkosten der Spot-Spraying-Varianten hat die Wahl der PSM-Variante und die Betriebsgröße. Bei der hochpreisigen PSM-Variante 1 beträgt in Abhängigkeit von der nicht zu behandelnden Spot-Spraying-Fläche der Break-Even-Point beim 200-ha-Betrieb 83 % und beim 500-ha-Betrieb 39 %. Bei der niedrigpreisigen PSM-Variante 2 wird unabhängig vom Modellbetriebs kein Break-Even-Point erreicht. Bei der PSM-Variante 1 sind beim 200-ha-Betrieb die Kosten der Pflanzenschutzbekämpfung mittels Spot-

Spraying um 34 € ha^{-1} höher als beim 500-ha-Betrieb. Bei der PSM-Variante 2 beträgt der Kostenunterschied 38 € ha^{-1}.

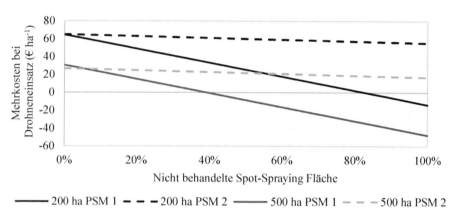

Abb. 1: Mehrkosten beim Pflanzenschutzeinsatz unterstützt durch Drohnentechnik

4 Diskussion

Ein Großteil der Kosten der PSM-Applikation durch Spot-Spraying sind auf die Kapital- und Betriebskosten der Drohne zurückzuführen. Hierbei wirken Betriebsgröße und Flächenauslastung kostensenkend. Ferner kann sich der Investitionsaufwand für die Anschaffung einer Drohne durch den zusätzlichen Einsatz in alternativen Anwendungsgebieten abseits der spotorientierten Spritzung schneller amortisieren. Eine noch höhere Auslastung ist gegeben, wenn ein externer Drohnendienstleister überbetrieblich arbeitet. Die Auslastung der Drohne ist allerding durch potentielle Flugtage begrenzt. Im kalkulierten Beispiel mit Maßnahmensplitting erfolgte die Durchwuchskartoffelbekämpfung bei der 2. Pflanzenschutzmaßnahme. Drohneneinsatz und anschließende 2. PSM-Applikation sollten nicht direkt nach der 1. PSM-Applikation erfolgen, aber vor dem Reihenschluss des Mais. Hierbei sind ein gutes Flächenmanagement und eine geeignete Wetterlage entscheidend. Weiterhin könnte der technische Fortschritt kostensenkend wirken. Zum einen ist für das gleiche Drohnenprodukt eine Kostenreduktion in den nächsten Jahren zu erwarten, zum anderen wird die Flächenleistung der Drohnentechnik durch effizientere Kamerasysteme und Akkuleistungen steigen. Eine Kostenersparnis lässt sich unter Berücksichtigung der Datenskalierbarkeit im Zuge dessen auch durch eine gesteigerte Flughöhe mit bestehenden Kamerasystemen erreichen. Durch eine verbesserte Algorithmik in der Beikrautdetektion sollte es weiterhin möglich sein, auch bei einer gesteigerten Flughöhe gleichbleibende Klassifikationsergebnisse zu erzielen. Bei den zwei Modellbetrieben ist der Drohneneinsatz nur bei hochpreisigen PSM wirtschaftlich. In dem Zusammenhang ist die Durchwuchsrate der Kartoffeln und infolgedessen die nicht zu behandelnde Spot-Spraying-Fläche ein notwendiges Kriterium. Der Break-Even-Point in Abhängigkeit der nicht zu behandelnden Spot-Spraying-Fläche hin zu einer Wirtschaftlichkeit des Drohneneinsatzes ist bei hohen Flächenleistungen der Drohne niedriger und bei niedrigen Flächenleistungen höher. In weiteren Analysen sind mögliche Ertragseffekte auf den Mais zu quantifizieren, die einen wesentlichen Effekt haben dürften.

Förderhinweis und Danksagung: Das Projekt Agro-Nordwest wird durch Mittel des Bundesministeriums für Ernährung und Landwirtschaft und des Projektträgers Bundesanstalt für Landwirtschaft und Ernährung gefördert. Ein besonderer Dank geht an die Studierenden Carina Breckling, Christian-Alexander Langner und Hagen Henning Schulze für die wichtigen ökonomischen Vorarbeiten. Ein weiterer Dank geht an die Landwirte Michael Seelmeyer und Stephan Künne sowie Gregor Bensmann von den AMAZONEN-Werke für ihre großartige Unterstützung bei den Praxisversuchen.

Literaturverzeichnis

[AM22] AMAZONEN-WERKE H. DREYER SE & Co. KG: Anleitung zum absetzigen Spot-Spraying mit Hilfe von Applikationskarten. Interview mit Gregor Bensmann, Produktmanager Smart Farming/Elektronik, Stand: 23.03.2022.

[BLS22] Breckling, C. M.; Langner, C.-A.; Schulze, H. H.: Reduktion von Pflanzenschutzmitteln unter Einbeziehung von Drohnentechnik im Mais. Projekbericht. Hochschule Osnabrück, 2022.

[Ch21] Christensen, S. et al.: Sensing for Weed Detection. In (Kerry, R. und Escolà, A., Hrsg.): Sensing Approaches for Precision Agriculture. Springer Cham, S. 275-300, 2021.

[GF22] GF, Globe Flight GmbH, www.globeflight.de, Stand: 20.10.2022.

[Kl22] Klingenhagen, G.: Unkrautbekämpfung im Mais. In (Landwirtschaftskammer Nordrhein Westphalen, Hrsg.): Ratgeber Pflanzenbau und Pflanzenschutz, Rheinbreitbach, S. 368-375, 2022.

[LFL22] LFL, Bayerische Landesanstalt für Landwirtschaft, www.stmelf.bayern.de, Stand: 16.06.2022.

[Mi21] Michel, J.: Neue Studien: Green Deal trifft Ackerbauern härter als Tierhalter. agrarheute, www.agrarheute.com, Stand: 14.10.2021.

[SS22] Schmid Solution: Zum Stand der Drohnentechnik für die landwirtschaftliche Nutzung. Interview mit Jan Schmidt, Stand: 07.06.2022.

[VS22] Vereinigte Saatzuchten eG: Pflanzenschutzpreisliste 2022. Excel-Tabelle, Stand 01.04.2022

Horticulture Semantic (HortiSem)

Eine Service-Infrastruktur für automatisierte Annotation, Named Entity Linking, Suche und Abfrage von Informationsressourcen für den Gartenbau

Jascha Daniló Jung[1] und Daniel Martini[1]

Abstract: Im Projekt HortiSem wird ein semantisches Netzwerk entwickelt, das speziell für den Bereich Landwirtschaft gedacht ist. Das Projekt hat inzwischen wichtige Fortschritte gemacht. Zum einen wurde die API „destreak" entwickelt, die es ermöglicht, vorgefertigte Abfragen mithilfe von http-Requests auszuführen. Dadurch können einfache Abfragen leicht in Suchmasken integriert werden, ohne dass eine SPARQL-Query formuliert werden muss. Zudem wurde ein Crawler implementiert, der neue Warndienstmeldungen von hortigate.de automatisch herunterlädt, annotiert, ins RDF-Format umwandelt und abschließend auf den Triplestore hochlädt. Dies zeigt, wie der Knowledge Graph von HortiSem kontinuierlich wachsen kann und neue Informationen automatisch hinzugefügt werden können. Darüber hinaus ist es möglich, einen eigenen Triplestore aufzusetzen und ihn mit den Daten von HortiSem zu verknüpfen. Dadurch können auch Daten integriert werden, die nicht öffentlich zugänglich sein sollen.

Keywords: Datenmanagement, Smart und Big Data, künstliche Intelligenz, Machine Learning, Natural Language Processing, Linked Open Data, semantisches Netzwerk

1 Einleitung

Im Horticulture Semantic (HortiSem) Projekt wird ein semantisches Netzwerk speziell für den Bereich der Landwirtschaft entwickelt [Ju22]. Dieses Netzwerk verbindet Informationen und stellt sie in Beziehung zueinander. Der Fokus liegt auf Begriffen aus den Kategorien „Kultur", „Schädlinge", „Nützlinge" und „Pflanzenschutzmittel". Der Schwerpunkt dieses Beitrags liegt auf Zugriffs- und Nutzungsmöglichkeiten, insbesondere der parallel entwickelten API „destreak", die es ermöglicht, vorgegebene Abfragen an den Knowledge Graphen zu stellen, indem komplizierte SPARQL-Queries im Backend musterhaft implementiert und als vorgefertigte Vorlagen über einfachere HTTP-Requests gestellt werden können. Diese lassen sich auch leicht in bereits vorhandene Suchmasken implementieren. Ein Crawler wurde ebenfalls entwickelt, der neue Daten von hortigate[2] automatisch erkennen und verarbeiten kann. Im Folgenden soll diskutiert werden, welche Vorteile die Verwendung der „destreak" API im Vergleich zu

---

1 Kuratorium für Technik und Bauwesen in der Landwirtschaft, Datenbanken und Wissenstechnologien, Bartningstraße 49, 64289 Darmstadt, j.jung@ktbl.de
2 https://www.hortigate.de/

konventionellen SPARQL-Queries im Zusammenhang mit der Nutzung des Knowledge Graphen von HortiSem im Bereich der Landwirtschaft bietet.

2 Bedeutung semantischer Netzwerke für die Landwirtschaft

Semantische Netzwerke sind ein Bereich der Künstlichen Intelligenz, der sich mit der Verarbeitung und Interpretation natürlicher Sprache befasst. Sie werden häufig verwendet, um Bedeutungen von Wörtern und Sätzen in einem bestimmten Kontext zu verstehen und zu analysieren. Die Forschung an und mit semantischen Netzwerken hat in den letzten Jahren deutliche Fortschritte gemacht. Eine der Herausforderungen in diesem Bereich ist es, das Verständnis von semantischen Netzwerken für die Verarbeitung natürlicher Sprache zu verbessern, insbesondere im Hinblick auf die sogenannte „kontextuelle Bedeutung" von Wörtern und Sätzen. Diese kontextuelle Bedeutung ist wichtig, um die Bedeutung von Wörtern und Sätzen in einem bestimmten Kontext zu verstehen und zu analysieren.

In der Landwirtschaft könnten semantische Netzwerke beispielsweise zur Analyse von Wetterdaten benutzt werden, oder um Anweisungen für landwirtschaftliche Maschinen zu verstehen und umzusetzen, wodurch die Arbeit effizienter automatisiert werden könnte.

Insgesamt bieten semantische Netzwerke vielversprechende Möglichkeiten für die Landwirtschaft und könnten dazu beitragen, die Effizienz und Präzision landwirtschaftlicher Prozesse zu verbessern. Die andauernde Forschung in diesem Bereich wird dazu beitragen, die Anwendungsmöglichkeiten von semantischen Netzwerken weiter zu erweitern und zu verbessern.

3 HortiSem Workflow: Daten, Methoden und Infrastruktur

3.1 Übersicht

Der Workflow von HortiSem wird in Abbildung 1 gezeigt (s. unten).

Kurz zusammengefasst werden Daten aus dem Web gecrawlt und mit einem NER-Model annotiert. Die annotierten Daten werden in ein RDF-Format gemappt und in einem Triplestore gespeichert. Dort stehen sie durch einen öffentlichen SPARQL-Endpoint zur Verfügung. Zusätzlich ermöglicht die API „destreak" einen vereinfachten Abruf der Daten per http-Requests. Die Daten im Triplestore verweisen wiederum auf die Datenquelle.

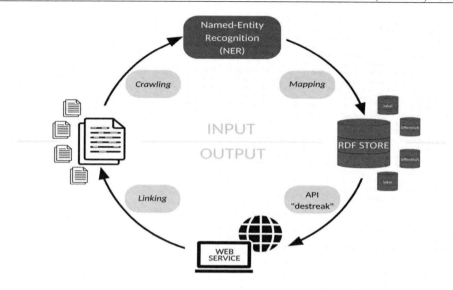

Abb. 1: Der HortiSem Workflow

Die einzelnen Schritte werden in den folgenden Unterkapiteln kurz beschrieben.

3.2 Knowledge Graphen: die Grundlage des semantischen Netzwerks

Ein semantisches Netzwerk ist ein Netzwerk aus Informationen, das Beziehungen und Bedeutungen zwischen Daten veranschaulicht. Im Falle des HortiSem-Projekts bilden bekannte Datenquellen über Kulturen, Schädlinge, Nützlinge und weitere Begriffe aus der Landwirtschaft die Basis (etwa aus dem AGROVOC Thesaurus[3] und von PS Info[4]). Diese Datenquellen werden in das RDF-Format gemappt und bilden das „Grundgerüst" des Knowledge Graphen. Um den Knowledge Graphen zu erweitern, werden Beziehungen von neuen Daten zu bereits vorhandenen Daten beschrieben und das Netzwerk aus Informationen so erweitert.

3.3 Erweiterung des semantischen Netzwerks: neue Daten

Im Projekt HortiSem wurde ein automatisiertes Verfahren entwickelt, das neue Daten im RDF-Format in den Triplestore hochladen kann. Dabei werden die neusten PDF-Dateien von hortigate.de automatisch heruntergeladen, in Text-Format umgewandelt und bereinigt. Anschließend werden sie mit einem NER-Model annotiert, um Entitäten zu identifizieren. Gefundene Entitäten werden dann mit vorhandenen Daten im Knowledge

---

3 https://agrovoc.fao.org/browse/agrovoc/en/
4 https://www.pflanzenschutz-information.de/

Graphen abgeglichen und bei einem Treffer eine Verlinkung erstellt. Die PDF-Dateien werden dann in eine RDF-Repräsentation umgewandelt, die Metadaten zum Text sowie gefundene und verifizierte Entitäten mit entsprechenden Verlinkungen zum Knowledge Graphen enthält. Die RDF-Dateien werden schließlich in den Triplestore hochgeladen, während die PDF-Dateien gelöscht werden, da sie oft kostenpflichtige Informationen enthalten und daher nicht im Knowledge Graphen gespeichert werden. Stattdessen wird im Knowledge Graphen per URL auf die Quelle der Publikation verwiesen.

3.4 Vereinfachte Abfragen: die „destreak" API

Triplestores wie Fuseki[5] ermöglichen die Abfrage von Daten mithilfe von SPARQL-Queries. Im Rahmen des Projekts HortiSem soll es einen frei verfügbaren SPARQL-Endpoint geben. SPARQL-Abfragen können für Laien allerdings sehr kompliziert sein, da sie eine spezielle Syntax und Kenntnisse in der Semantik der verwendeten Daten erfordern. Daher wird die API „destreak" entwickelt.

Bei „destreak" handelt es sich um eine API, die http-Requests verwendet. Sie kann eine einfachere Alternative zu SPARQL-Abfragen sein, da sie es Benutzern ermöglicht, Anfragen in einer intuitiver zu verwendenden Syntax zu stellen. Diese API ist nicht nur für Laien einfacher zu verwenden, sondern auch einfacher in bereits vorhandene Systeme zu integrieren. Im Gegensatz zu SPARQL-Abfragen, die spezielle Kenntnisse und Fähigkeiten erfordern, können http-Requests von vielen verschiedenen Systemen und Programmiersprachen verwendet werden. Dadurch wird der Zugang zu den Daten vereinfacht und ihre Verwendung benutzerfreundlicher.

Die Implementation von „destreak" erfolgt mit FastAPI[6].

3.5 Vollständige Automatisierung

Der Prozess zum Einpflegen neuer Daten kann vollständig automatisiert werden. Der Crawler für hortigate.de beispielsweise ruft die neuste im Knowledge Graphen vorhandene Publikationsnummer ab und prüft dann die Webseite auf neuere Publikationen. Dieser Prozess kann regelmäßig automatisch durchgeführt werden. Neue Warndienstmeldungen können dann automatisch heruntergeladen, ihre wichtigen Inhalte und Metadaten in das RDF-Format umgewandelt und dem Triplestore hinzugefügt werden. Damit ist auch die Abfrage tagesaktueller Informationen möglich.

---

5 https://jena.apache.org/documentation/fuseki2/
6 https://fastapi.tiangolo.com/

3.6 Die Infrastruktur von HortiSem

Der Code, der dem gezeigten HortiSem Workflow zugrunde liegt, ist derzeit nicht öffentlich zugänglich. Nur der SPARQL-Endpoint ist testweise verfügbar. Zusätzlich ist geplant, eine Version von „destreak" öffentlich zu machen. Es wird daran gearbeitet, die Setup-Informationen für lauffähige Docker-Container zur Verfügung zu stellen. Es ist auch möglich, einen eigenen Triplestore neben dem für das Projekt am KTBL aufgesetzten Triplestore zu hosten (siehe Abb. 2). Auf diesem lokalen Server könnten Unternehmen auch sensible Daten speichern. Auch können eigene Crawler und RDF-Mappings erstellt werden, um den lokalen Server damit zu erweitern. Die Daten von HortiSem können dann als Referenzpunkt und Teil des eigenen Knowledge Graphen verwendet werden. Das Ziel des Projekts ist es, eine große Zahl relevanter Daten in den Knowledge Graphen aufzunehmen und miteinander zu verknüpfen. Hierzu sollen neben Referenzen zu bereits vorhandenen Datenbeständen auch neue Knowledge Graphen hinzugefügt werden.

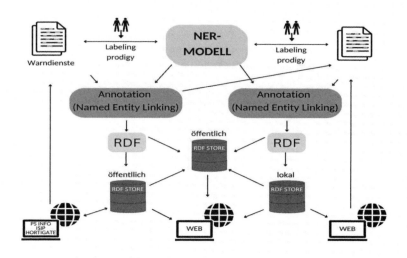

Abb. 2: Workflow und HortiSem-Infrastruktur

3.7 GUI

Für die vereinfachte Nutzung wurde für den Crawler, das automatische Mapping und den Upload der Daten auf den Triplestore ein einfaches GUI (Graphical User Interface) entwickelt. Dieses ermöglicht es, die neuesten Daten von hortigate.de automatisch herunterzuladen, zu annotieren und anschließend entweder auf einen lokalen Server oder direkt auf den KTBL-Server hochzuladen. Neben der Verwendung des Crawlers können auch eigene PDF-Dateien für die Annotation und das Mapping oder RDF-Dateien für den Upload auf den Triplestore von der Festplatte ausgewählt werden. Das GUI wird hauptsächlich für Testzwecke verwendet, um die automatisierten Schritte kontrolliert starten und die Ergebnisse überprüfen zu können. Es dient aber auch zu Demonstrationszwecken, da ein solches Interface deutlich einfacher zu verstehen ist als die Verwendung von Shell- oder Command-line-Interfaces.

4 Fazit

Im Projekt HortiSem wurden Mappings für Daten aus verschiedenen Quellen erstellt und in den Knowledge Graphen eingefügt. Die Automatisierung des Prozesses der Umwandlung von PDF-Dateien in RDF-Dateien mit Bezug zum Knowledge Graphen wurde mit hortigate-Warndienstmeldungen demonstriert. Durch die Verwendung der „destreak" API können Abfragen vereinfacht in Suchmasken integriert werden, sodass für häufige Abfragen keine komplizierten SPARQL-Abfragen erforderlich sind. Neue Daten können automatisch durch einen Crawler in den Knowledge Graphen hinzugefügt werden, wobei es möglich ist, eigene Daten auf einem eigenen Server zu hosten und mit den Daten von HortiSem zu verknüpfen. Die aktuelle Entwicklung konzentriert sich auf die Erweiterung des Knowledge Graphen und das Containerisieren von Triplestore und destreak, um das Hosten in „abgeschlossenen" Umgebungen zu ermöglichen. Schließlich wird noch mit der automatischen Erweiterung des Netzwerks experimentiert, um HortiSem aktuell zu halten.

Literaturverzeichnis

[Ju22] Jung, J. D.; He, X.; Martini, D.; Golla, B.: Horticulture Semantic (HortiSem) – Natural Language Processing bei Entwicklung und Interaktion mit einem semantischen Netzwerk für die Landwirtschaft. In: Gandorfer, M., Hoffmann, C., El Benni, N., Cockburn, M., Anken, T. & Floto, H. (Hrsg.), 42. GIL-Jahrestagung, Künstliche Intelligenz in der Agrar- und Ernährungswirtschaft. Bonn: Gesellschaft für Informatik e.V.. (S. 141-146). 2022.

Konzeption und Realisierung einer feldbasierten landwirtschaftlichen Versuchsumgebung zur dynamischen Umgebungswahrnehmung

Jan Christoph Krause[1], Jaron Martinez[2], Henry Gennet[2], Martin Urban[3], Jens Herbers[4], Stefan Menke[4], Sebastian Röttgermann[5], Joachim Hertzberg[1,6] und Arno Ruckelshausen[2]

Abstract: Für die Automatisierung von landwirtschaftlichen Prozessen werden autonome Maschinen entwickelt, die zuverlässig und sicher in ihren Arbeitsgebieten navigieren müssen. Die insbesondere beim Pflanzenbau typischerweise harschen und wechselnden Umgebungsbedingungen erschweren die hierfür notwendige sensorbasierte Erfassung und Interpretation des Umfelds. Für die funktionale Sicherheit ist die robuste Erkennung des Menschen im Umfeld der Maschine in allen definierten, zulässigen Betriebsbereichen essenziell. In diesem Beitrag wird eine Versuchsumgebung vorgestellt, mit der die Einflüsse von unterschiedlichen Umgebungsbedingungen, wie beispielsweise das Wetter und die Vegetation, auf die Zuverlässigkeit von Sensorsystemen zur semantischen Umfeldwahrnehmung untersucht werden. Mit einem schienenbasierten Trägersystem werden Sensoren verschiedener Messprinzipien reproduzierbar durch eine landwirtschaftliche Umgebung bewegt. Hierbei werden die Rohdaten der Sensoren als Evaluationsdaten aufgezeichnet. Durch eine wiederkehrende und wiederholbare Aufnahme bei unterschiedlichen Umgebungsbedingungen wird die Erzeugung von Evaluationsdatensätzen, die sich zum Vergleich der Erkennungsgüte eignen, ermöglicht.

Keywords: agricultural automation; field robots; human detection and tracking

1 Einleitung

Hochautomatisierte Maschinen mit sensorbasierten Assistenzsystemen bieten auch in der Landwirtschaft das Potenzial, die Leistung und Effizienz zu steigern und gleichzeitig die Umweltbelastung zu reduzieren. Die Verfügbarkeit von räumlich und zeitlich hochauflösenden Sensoren ist dabei ein wichtiger Innovationstreiber. Für den sicheren Betrieb von automatisierten und autonomen Maschinen ist eine robuste Umfeldwahrnehmung essenziell.

---

[1] DFKI GmbH Niedersachsen, Planbasierte Robotersteuerung, Berghoffstraße 11, 49090 Osnabrück, jan_christoph.krause@dfki.de, joachim.hertzberg@dfki.de
[2] Hochschule Osnabrück, Labor für Mikro- und Optoelektronik, Sedanstraße 26, 49076 Osnabrück, j.martinez@hs-osnabrueck.de, henry.gennet@hs-osnabrueck.de, a.ruckelshausen@hs-osnabrueck.de
[3] UR Automation GmbH, Hanauerstraße 6, 66976 Rodalben, Martin.Urban@URautomation.de
[4] Maschinenfabrik Bernard KRONE GmbH & Co. KG, Vorentwicklung, Heinrich-Krone-Straße 10, 48480 Spelle, jens.herbers@krone.de stefan.menke@krone.de
[5] LEMKEN GmbH & Co. KG, Vorentwicklung, Weseler Straße 5, 46519 Alpen, s.roettgermann@lemken.com
[6] Universität Osnabrück, Institut für Informatik, Berghoffstraße 11, 49090 Osnabrück

Die Maschinenumfelder müssen bei oft harschen und wechselnden Umgebungsbedingungen stetig sicher überwacht werden. Neben der Vegetation und den Wetterbedingungen haben auch weitere Störgrößen wie Staub und Vibrationen Einfluss auf die Überwachung.

Die für die Validierung von Umfeldwahrnehmungssystemen frei verfügbaren Benchmark-Datensätze enthalten in der Regel urbane Szenarien. Um die Funktion derartiger Sensorsysteme zur Erkennung von Hindernissen, wie z. B. dem Menschen, im landwirtschaftlichen Kontext zu validieren, werden allerdings domänenspezifische Testdaten benötigt.

2 Stand der Technik und Zielsetzung

Es existieren vielfältige Ansätze mit unterschiedlichen Sensorsystemen zur Umfeldwahrnehmung [Re16]. Durch die zuvor beschriebenen, harschen und wechselnden Umgebungsbedingungen entstehen im Kontext der Agrarrobotik besondere Anforderungen an die verwendeten Sensorsysteme. Im Gegensatz zum urbanen Umfeld treten unerwartete Hindernisse im Fahrkorridor deutlich seltener auf, müssen aber genauso zuverlässig erkannt werden. Für den meist urbanen Anwendungsbereich existieren eine Reihe von frei verfügbaren Datensätzen zur Objekterkennung. Während der CoCo Datensatz [Li15] typische Alltagsszenen enthält, liegt beim KITTI Datensatz der Fokus auf Szenen im Straßenverkehr [GLU12]. Es gibt aber auch Datensätze, die sich auf landwirtschaftliche Umgebungen fokussieren. In [Pe17] wird ein Datensatz zur Erkennung von Personen auf Obstplantagen vorgestellt, in [Kr17] ein Datensatz von einem Graserntszenario.

In den beschriebenen Datensätzen werden jedoch die in der Landwirtschaft typischerweise harschen und wechselnden Umgebungsbedingungen nicht explizit betrachtet. Damit die Funktion von Sensorsystemen bei unterschiedlichen Umgebungsbedingungen bewertet werden kann, ist die Durchführung von reproduzierbaren Versuchsszenarien essenziell. Diese Thematik wird durch den in [Me21] beschriebenen Versuchsstand aufgegriffen, bei dem Sensoren und Prüfkörper relativ zueinander bewegt werden. Hier liegt der Fokus bei den wetterbedingten Einflüssen auf ganzheitlichen Sensorsystemen, die bereits eine interne Interpretation der Rohdaten durchführen. Durch begrenzte Bewegungsradien ist die Variabilität des Umfelds begrenzt.

In dem vorliegenden Beitrag wird ein Outdoor-Teststand für die reproduzierbare Aufnahme von Sensorrohdaten wie Bilder und Punktwolken vorgestellt. Um den Einfluss von Umgebungsbedingungen auf die Zuverlässigkeit von Sensorsystemen zu bewerten, ist eine wiederkehrende Aufnahme in unterschiedlichen Situationen (diverse Wetterbedingungen und unterschiedliche Vegetationsperioden) notwendig. Die Anforderungen an die Gestaltung des Teststands orientieren sich an den allgemeinen Prozessparametern aus der Landwirtschaft. Konkretisiert werden diese Parameter anhand der Konzeptstudie „Combined Powers" [Ko22]. Diese autonome „Verfahrenstechnische Einheit" (VTE) ist eine Gemeinschaftsentwicklung der Projektpartner Maschinenfabrik Bernard KRONE GmbH & Co. KG und LEMKEN GmbH & Co. KG. In die Entwicklung fließen, basierend auf dem Austausch mit dem TÜV NORD Mobilität GmbH & Co. KG, sicherheitsbezogene

Aspekte ein. Das hier beschriebene Testfeld ist eine von drei Testebenen, welche zusammen mit separaten Einzelversuchen und einem Transfer auf reale Landmaschinen eine Grundlage für die Erarbeitung von Zertifizierungsprozessen bildet. Das unter [Kr22] vorgestellte Konzept bildet eine Grundlage für das im Folgenden beschriebene Versuchsfeld.

3 Beschreibung des Versuchsfelds

Das Versuchsfeld gliedert sich in drei Feldbereiche, die unterschiedlich bestellt werden. Abbildung 1 stellt die Abgrenzung der drei Feldbereiche Brachland, Grünland und die Reihenkultur Mais dar. Senkrecht zu den Schienen beträgt die Breite des Feldes auf der einen Seite 40 m und auf der anderen Seite 20 m. Für den als relevant festgelegten Erkennungsbereich von 30 m endet das Feld auf der einen Seite mit einem freien Horizont. Auf der anderen Seite mündet der Feldbereich in natürliche Feldgrenzen, wie Bäume und Sträucher, sowie einen Strommast. Auf dem Testfeld stehen zwei Masten, an denen WiFi-Zugangspunkte sowie Kameras zur Überwachung des Testfelds montiert sind. Darüber hinaus befindet sich auf Mast 1 eine RTK-Referenzstation sowie eine Wetterstation und ein Sichtweitenmessgerät. Mit diesen Messgeräten wird die Sichtweite, die Windgeschwindigkeit sowie die Helligkeit, Temperatur und relative Luftfeuchtigkeit zur Einordnung der Umgebungsbedingungen aufgezeichnet.

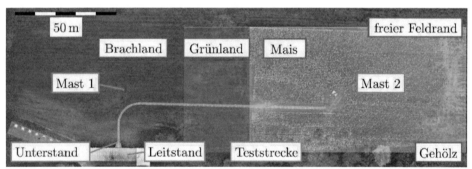

Abb. 1: Der Schienenparcours verläuft durch die drei Bereiche Brachland (braun), Grünland (grün) und Mais (gelb). Auf dem Testfeld stehen zwei Masten zur Befestigung der Infrastruktur und weiterer Sensorik. (Foto: Edgar Walter, Hochschule Osnabrück)

Hinsichtlich der Beurteilung der funktionalen Sicherheit von landwirtschaftlichen Maschinen ist der Mensch das entscheidende Objekt. Aus diesem Grund werden zwei realistische humanoide Prüfkörper verwendet, die einer durchschnittlichen erwachsenen männlichen Person bzw. einem siebenjährigen Kind entsprechen[7]. Der Körperbau sowie die Reflektionseigenschaften bei Radar-, Ultraschall-, Kamera- und Infrarotsystemen sind denen eines echten Menschen nachempfunden. Die Prüfkörper werden auf Bodenhülsen mit Magneten befestigt, sodass diese reproduzierbar, aber auch flexibel an verschiedenen Positionen auf

---

[7] https://www.4activesystems.at/4activeps

dem Testfeld aufstellbar sind. Zur exakten Positionsbestimmung, die insbesondere zur Generierung von Grundwahrheiten notwendig ist, werden die Positionen der Prüfkörper mit einem RTK-Messstab vermessen.

4 Beschreibung des Sensorträgers

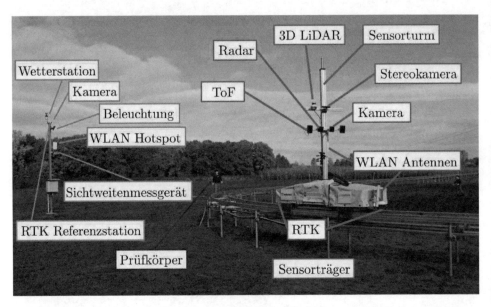

Abb. 2: Die zu evaluierende Sensorik wird auf dem drehbaren Sensorturm befestigt. Auf dem Testfeld steht ein Mast, an dem die Hardware zur Überwachung und Kommunikation mit dem Dolly befestigt ist.

Zur reproduzierbaren Bewegung der Sensoren durch das Testfeld wurde ein schienenbasiertes Trägersystem auf der Grundlage von Gerüstbaukomponenten und Aluminiumprofilen aufgebaut. Der Sensorträger hat eine Breite von 0,7 m und eine Länge von 1,80 m. Zur Positionierung wird der Träger von einem Seilantrieb über einen 100 m langen L-förmigen Parcours mit einer Kurve, die einen Radius von 10 m aufweist, gezogen. Das Trägersystem erreicht dabei eine Geschwindigkeit von 5,5 m s^{-1} bei einer Beschleunigung von 1,6 m s^{-2}. Auf dem Trägerschlitten ist ein auch im Messbetrieb um 350° drehbarer Sensorturm montiert, auf dem mehrere Sensoren frei und flexibel in einer Höhe von 1,5 m bis 4 m montierbar sind. Zur Evaluierung werden Sensoren verschiedener Technologien wie beispielsweise RGB-Kameras, Tiefenkameras (Stereo, Time-of-Flight), LiDAR, Radar und Ultraschall herangezogen. Neben den Sensoren ist der Trägerschlitten mit Akkus, Industriecomputern, Peripherie und einer Lokalisierungseinheit (RTK-GNSS)

Abb. 3: Exemplarische Sensordaten einer Messfahrt mit dem dargestellten Sensorträgersystem. Oben: Bild einer RGB-Kamera, unten: Punktewolken eines 3D LiDAR

zur exakten Positions- und Orientierungsbestimmung ausgestattet. Das zulässige Gesamtgewicht beträgt 300 kg, von denen für die Experimente eine Zuladung von 110 kg frei ist.

Durch ein automatisches Ladesystem und die verwendeten robusten Industriekomponenten ist ein 24/7-Betrieb auch bei harschen Umgebungsbedingungen möglich. Die Aufzeichnung der Messdaten erfolgt direkt auf dem Trägersystem, sodass Datenverluste und Einschränkungen bei der Zeitsynchronisierung durch die Datenübertragung per WLAN vermieden werden. Zur Durchführung kontinuierlicher Messungen wird die Bewegung des Sensorträgers und Aufzeichnung der Sensordaten durch Wetterereignisse oder Benutzereingaben gestartet. Im Anschluss erfolgt ein automatischer Transfer der aufgenommenen Messdaten zu einer zentralen Datenbank.

5 Zusammenfassung und Ausblick

Der Aufbau des Outdoor-Teststandes in einer Nachbildung von landwirtschaftlichen Nutzflächen ermöglicht es, im Rahmen des Projekts (und darüber hinaus) verschiedene Typen von Sensoren reproduzierbaren Testszenarien zu unterziehen. Hierdurch wird es ermöglicht, die unterschiedlichsten Sensormodalitäten mit Bezug zu den Anforderungen im landtechnischen Umfeld zu untersuchen, um eine geeignete Auswahl für den jeweiligen Einsatzzweck treffen zu können.

Mit diesem Versuchsaufbau ist es nun möglich, Rohdaten von verschiedenen Sensorsystemen im Verlauf einer gesamten Feldsaison mit unterschiedlichen Umgebungsbedingungen aufzuzeichnen. Es wird eine Datenbank mit Sensorrohdaten erzeugt, aus der Evaluationsdatensätze mit realen Testdaten für verschiedene Algorithmen generiert werden können. Hierzu wird eine semantische Umgebungsrepräsentation [NPH22] integriert. Ein Anwendungsfall ist beispielsweise die Eignungsprüfung von Sensorik für landwirtschaftliche Arbeitsgeräte.

Förderhinweis: Die Förderung des Vorhabens erfolgt aus Mitteln des Bundesministeriums für Ernährung und Landwirtschaft (BMEL) aufgrund eines Beschlusses des deutschen Bundestages. Die Projektträgerschaft erfolgt über die Bundesanstalt für Landwirtschaft und Ernährung (BLE) im Rahmen des Programms zur Innovationsförderung. Das DFKI Niedersachsen (DFKI NI) wird gefördert im Niedersächsischen Vorab durch das Niedersächsische Ministerium für Wissenschaft und Kultur und die Volkswagen Stiftung.

Literaturverzeichnis

[GLU12] Geiger, A.; Lenz, P.; Urtasun, R.: Are we ready for Autonomous Driving? The KITTI Vision Benchmark Suite. In: 2012 IEEE Conference on Computer Vision and Pattern Recognition, S. 3354-3361, 2012.

[Ko22] Kooperationsprojekt Combined Powers: Maschinenfabrik Bernard KRONE GmbH & Co. KG und LEMKEN GmbH & Co. KG, www.combined-powers.com, Stand: 31.10.2022.

[Kr17] Kragh, M. F. et.al.: FieldSAFE: Dataset for Obstacle Detection in Agriculture. In: Sensors 2017, Bd. 17(11), 2579, 2017.

[Kr22] Krause, J. C. et al.: Concept of a Test Environment for the Automated Evaluation of Algorithms for Robust and Reliable Environment Perception. In (VDI Wissensforum GmbH (Hrsg.)): LAND.TECHNIK 2022: The Forum for Agricultural Engineering Innovations, VDI-Berichte Bd. 2395, VDI Verlag, Düsseldorf, S. 177-184, 2022.

[LI15] Lin, TY. et al.: Common Objects in Context. In (Fleet, D., Pajdla, T., Schiele, B., Tuytelaars, T., Hrsg.): Computer Vision – ECCV 2014, Lecture Notes in Computer Science, Bd. 8693. Springer, Cham, S. 740-755, 2014.

[Me21] Meltebrink, C. et al.: Concept and Realization of a Novel Test Method Using a Dynamic Test Stand for Detecting Persons by Sensor Systems on Autonomous Agricultural Robotics. In: Sensors 2021, Bd. 21(7), 2315, 2021.

[NPH22] Niemeyer, M.; Pütz, S.; Hertzberg, J.: A Spatio-Temporal-Semantic Environment Representation for Autonomous Mobile Robots equipped with various Sensor Systems. In: 2022 IEEE International Conference on Multisensor Fusion and Integration for Intelligent Systems, S. 1-6, 2022.

[Pe17] Pezzementi, Z. et.al: Comparing apples and oranges: Off-road pedestrian detection on the National Robotics Engineering Center agricultural person-detection dataset. Journal of Field Robotics Bd. 25(4), S. 545-563, 2018.

[Re16] Reina, G. et.al: Ambient awareness for agricultural robotic vehicles. In: Biosystems Engineering, Bd. 146, S. 114-132, 2016.

Different methods of yield recordings in grassland – how accurate are they in practice?

Comparison and use of digital tools for measuring and estimating yields in grassland in standing crop and after cutting

Priska Krug[1], Adriana Förschner[1], Tobias Wiggenhauser[1], Hansjörg Nußbaum[1] and Jonas Weber[1]

Abstract: The aim of the study is to determine the yields in grassland using various methods. Yield recording in grassland has not been common practice so far. Yields can be recorded using various methods as height measurement, for example by using a rising-plate-meter (Grasshopper), measuring the weight of sample cut or by capturing the weight of harvested biomass. A yield estimation with the Grasshopper is carried out on three plots and is validated via sample cuts. The harvest chain is recorded digitally and the harvest quantity (weight) is measured with the load cells in the loader wagon, a validation is carried out via a wagon scales. The results presents underestimated yields when using the Grasshopper. The recording of harvest weights via the loader wagon's load cells was confirmed by the wagon scales. This method can be easily used in practice, if available. However, a determination of the dry matter content remains key. The correct determination of dry matter is crucial for accurate yield recording, but this is where very great challenges lie, especially for practice. Further investigations have to be carried out.

Keywords: yield estimation, Grasshopper, grassland, annual yield, digital yield recording

1 Introduction

Measuring or estimating yields in grassland is laborious and rarely done in practice. Yields can be measured before harvesting or after harvesting, taking field losses into account. So far, grassland yields have not been measured at the research station in Aulendorf. In the following study, various methods will therefore be used. Among other things, an estimation is to be made in the standing crop by measuring the compressed sward height with a rising-plate meter called Grasshopper. Especially for intensive grass swards such as ryegrass-white clover meadows, this estimate can already predict an accurate yield for the farmer via an appropriately stored regression curve [Mc19]. In addition, the yields will be measured using the load cells on a short-cut loader wagon and validated via a wagon

---

[1] Agricultural Centre for cattle production, grassland management, dairy food, wildlife and fisheries Baden-Wuerttemberg (LAZBW), Atzenberger Weg 99, 88326 Aulendorf, Germany; priska.krug@lazbw.bwl.de; adriana.foerschner@lazbw.bwl.de; Tobias.Wiggenhauser@lazbw.bwl.de; Hansjoerg.Nussbaum@lazbw.bwl.de; jonas.weber@lazbw.bwl.de

scales. The aim of this study is to collect the yields in grassland using practical and also digital methods specifically at the research station Aulendorf and to check the accuracy in the process.

2 Materials and methods

Yields were recorded on three plots with five cuts in Aulendorf. The measurements were carried out on 09 May 2022 for the first cut (silage), on 10 June 2022 for the second cut (silage), on 11 July 2022 for the third cut (hay), on 31 August 2022 for the fourth cut (silage) and on 17 October 2022 for the fifth cut (silage). For this purpose, three plots were selected, which were as homogeneous as possible. The areas Hillacker, Bohnerwiese and Lenzenbreite are located around Aulendorf. Their altitude is approx. 570 m above sea level with an average temperature of 7.6 °C and an annual precipitation of approx. 902 mm. The average daily hours of sunshine are 4.5 hours.

Before cutting in the standing crop, sward measurements were carried out within a trial frame (TF). For this purpose, three TF with a frame size of 1 m² were randomly distributed on the field, the compressed sward height was measured in advance with the Grasshopper (GH) within the trial frame at 9 points with a preset cutting height of 50 mm and a dry matter content of 18 %. The GH measured the compressed sward height in mm and estimated yields by means of a deposited, unpublished equation. The area was cut manually with battery shears to a cutting height of approximately 50 mm, the fresh mass was measured. For the determination of the dry matter content, sample cuts were dried at 105 °C for more than 24 hours in the drying cabinet until the weight was constant. The sward was assessed within the TF for the composition of grass, herbs and legumes, and the gap percentage was determined. Grasshopper measurements were also taken on the total area in a specific pattern (EGH).

After cutting, the yields were recorded via the loader wagon with load cells (manufacturer Maschinenfabrik Bernard Krone GmbH & Co. KG, designation short-cut loader wagon ZX 450 GD with integrated weighing device via weighing measuring bolts on drawbar and axle unit) and via wagon scales. A composite sample was formed from each loader wagon and taken from the silo in order to be able to determine the dry matter content.

The measured yields within the TF are compared with the GH yield estimation within the TF before cutting. For the first cut, the weight measurement of the loader wagon was additionally validated. The yield of the loader wagon was measured once via load cells on the field (EL) and on a flat surface in front of the silo (ELS) and validated with a wagon scales (EF). An overview of the different measurement treatments and their abbreviations is given in Table 1.

The statistical evaluation was carried out with the programme Microsoft Excel 2016 and R (version 1.4.1717).

Treatment	Abbreviations
Trial frames	TL
Grasshopper within the trial frames	GH
Grasshopper total area	EGH
Loader wagon with the load cells in the field	EL
Loader wagon with the load cells on flat surface	ELS
Loader wagon on wagon scales	EF

Tab. 1: Description of the treatments and addreviations used in the study

3 Results and discussion

3.1 Dry matter content

The dry matter content before cutting is about 15 to 19 % and increases differently depending on the area, in the case of silage use to 26 to 40 % and in the case of use as hay to about 84 to 88 %. For the measurement of yield, the dry matter content is essential. The differences in dry matter are particularly striking. If this is estimated but not measured, this already results in large estimation errors.

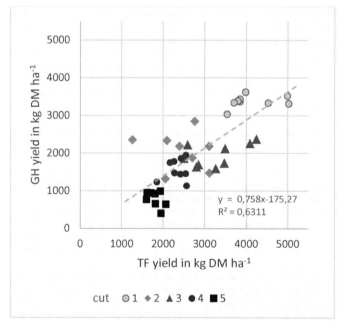

Fig. 1: Comparison of the measurement results of the sample cuts within the trial frames (TF) to the yield estimate of Grasshopper (GH) within the trial frames for each cut (1-5)

3.2 Accuracy of yield estimates with the Grasshopper

The measurements of TF in comparison to GH are shown in Figure 1. It is striking here that the Grasshopper underestimates the yield on all plots in almost every cut. Therefore, a statement of the yields in the cutting use with the Grasshopper was not perfect in this experiment. To improve the grasshopper estimation by Stumpe et al. the estimation is adapted to other factors such as location, time of season and stock [St22].

3.3 Accuracy of the weight measurement on the loader wagon

The weights of the harvested quantity in fresh mass were also measured with the loader wagon and the wagon scales (Fig. 2). The EL, EF and ELS measurements correspond very well for practice, the differences lie at +/- 400 kg fresh mass (FM). The yield measurements via the load cells of the loader wagon are therefore a very good method for getting an overview, if available. However, for the estimation of grassland yields on a farm the dry matter content is absolutely essential.

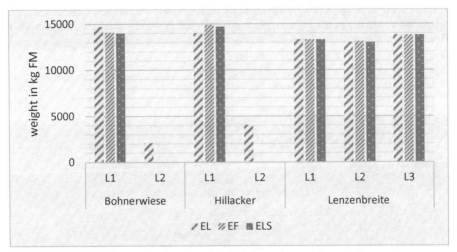

Fig. 2: Recording the harvest weight on the Bohnerwiese, Hillacker and Lenzenbreite areas via different methods, the weight is measured via the load cells on the loader wagon directly in the field (EL), via the load cells on the loader wagon in front of the silo plate on a flat surface (ELS) and the weight is measured with the wagon scales (EF) for L1, L2 and L3 (loader wagon 1-3)

3.4 Annual yield

Recording yields in agriculture, especially in grassland, is key to record annual yields. For this purpose, it is important that the yields are available for each cut. In grassland, different harvesting methods are used throughout the year, from forage harvesters to loader wagons to baling. Intermittent grazing can also be problematic for recording the annual yield. The aim is therefore to estimate an annual yield and also to be able to take various methods into account.

The yields differ depending on the area and method (Fig. 3). Overall, the yields are in the average range of the last few years for the Aulendorf site and a 5-cut meadow, the first cut in particular was above average. Yields cannot be directly compared because TF and EGH were measured in the standing crop and EL, on the other hand, were measured after harvest with field losses of approxomatily 10 % [Ko13]. Due to the implementation of various procedures, values are missing for EL in the fourth and fifth cut. Hence, these missing values for EL (Bohnerwiese, Hillacker and Lenzenbreite) fourth cut and EL (Hillacker) fifth cut were estimated.

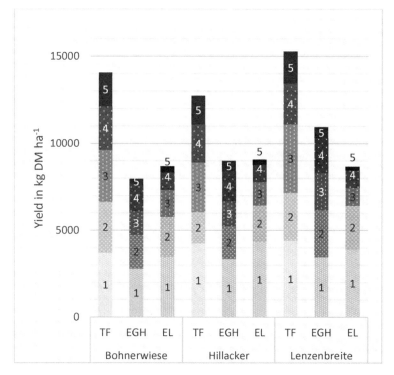

Fig. 3: Annual yield divided into individual cuts (1-5) for all three plots (Bohnerwiese, Hillacker and Lenzenbreite) with different measuring methods such as sample cuts within the trial frames (TF), the Grasshopper measurements taken on the total area (EGH) and via the load cells on the loader wagon directly in the field (EL)

In 2022, an average annual yield of approx. 90 dt DM ha^{-1} was achieved on these three areas in Aulendorf when measured with the loader wagon (Tab. 2). This yield was actually removed from the field and, accordingly, this proportion of nutrients left the field. Under the fertilizer ordinance, yields for a 5-cut meadow in Baden Württemberg are given as

110 dt DM ha^{-1} [Me22]. For grassland stands, it is already progress that measurements have been taken and the values are already going in the right direction.

	TF	GH	EGH	EL
Bohnerwiese	14074	8763	7978	8700
Hillacker	12742	9756	9013	9088
Lenzenbreite	15284	10651	10953	8683

Tab. 2: Annual yield in kg DM ha^{-1} with different measuring methods such as sample cuts within the trial frames (TF), the Grasshopper measurements taken within the trial frames (GH) and on the total area (EGH) and via the weighing cells on the loader wagon directly in the field (EL)

4 Conclusion

It is very difficult to determine the yield reliably with methods available in practice. Even a digital tool such as Grasshopper could not simplify the determination of yield. However, the use of a loader wagon with load cells is recommended for individual cuts. There is a lack of further research on how different measuring methods can be meaningfully combined into an annual yield. An automated recording of the yield measurements and a corresponding transfer to farm management information systems are also important for the future. It will be important for farmers to get a value for each cut and for classification. And then there is the fact that it has to be even more precise.

Acknowledgements: This project was carried out with the funds of the Ministry of Food, Rural Affairs and Consumer Protection of Baden-Wuerttemberg (MLR) and was developed by the Agricultural Centre for cattle production, grassland management, dairy food, wildlife and fisheries Baden-Wuerttemberg (LAZBW).

Bibliography

[Ko13] Koehler B., Diepolder, M., Thurner, S. und Spiekers, H.: Effiziente Futterwirtschaft auf Betriebsebene. In: Tagungsband Agrarforschung hat Zukunft - Wissenschaftstagung der LfL, Schriftenreihe 04/2013, S. 203-212. 2013.

[Mc19] McSweeney D., Coughlan N.E., Cuthbert R.N., Halton P. and Ivanov S.: Micro-sonic sensor technology enables enhanced grass height measurement by rising plate meter. Information Processing in Agriculture 6, 279-284, 2019.

[Me22] Messner, J.: Merkblatt zur Ermittlung des Stickstoff-Düngebedarfs für Grünland und mehrschnittigen Feldfutterbau (§ 4 DüV), www.duengung-bw.de/landwirtschaft/views/informationen.xhtml, 20.10.2022.

[St22] Stumpe C., Mundt M. and Böttinger S.: Exemplary on-farm research of region-, period- and swardspecific grassland yield prediction using geoprocessing methods. In Grassland at the heart of circular and sustainable food systems. Grassland Science in Europe 22, 853-855. 2022.

Automatisierte Erkennung von Gruppenaktivitätsverhalten von Schweinen in der Aufzucht mithilfe von KI-Kamerasystemen

Alexander Kühnemund[1] und Guido Recke[1]

Abstract: Kameras zur Überwachung von Tieren und Tierverhalten sind schon häufig Thema bisheriger Untersuchungen gewesen und werden in Zukunft stetig wachsende Bedeutung haben. Ein Nachteil von Liegeverhaltensbeobachtungen war die Notwendigkeit menschlicher Arbeit bei der Identifikation liegender Tiere. Diese Untersuchung zeigt, dass eine automatische Erkennung von Bewegungen durch ein System künstlicher Intelligenz eine Lösung für dieses Problem sein kann. Mit einer Erfolgsrate von über 90 % konnten liegende und aktive Tiere als solche identifiziert werden. Im Rahmen des Projektes „5G-Agrar – Nachhaltige Landwirtschaft" wurde dieser Fall untersucht und liefert für zukünftige Automatisierungen wichtige Erkenntnisse.

Keywords: Precision Agriculture, künstliche Intelligenz, Stallüberwachung, Schwein

1 Einleitung

In Deutschland befanden sich im Mai dieses Jahres über 10,6 Millionen Ferkel und Jungtiere in der Aufzucht [SB22]. Die Temperatur der Ställe, in denen die Schweine heranwachsen, ist hierbei ein kritischer Faktor. Einerseits beeinflusst die Stalltemperatur die Gesundheit und das Wohlbefinden der Tiere, da zu niedrige Temperaturen zu Unterkühlung und zu hohe Temperaturen zu Überhitzung führen können. Anderseits steht die Stalltemperatur im Zusammenhang mit produktionsökonomischen Größen sowie der Leistung der Schweine [BR13; PT20]. Dies ist vor dem Hintergrund der zunehmenden Bedeutung des Tierwohls [PT20] zu sehen, worunter die Berücksichtigung von Temperaturansprüchen der Tiere zu zählen ist. Dem entgegen stehen Heizkosten und weitere Kosten für die Klimasteuerung im Stall, die es notwendig machen, in der Aufzucht von Schweinen nach Lösungen zur Optimierung zu suchen. Eine optimale Temperatursteuerung im Stall ist aufgrund der sich verändernden Ansprüche im Wachstumsverlauf der Schweine komplex.

Ein Ansatz zur Temperaturbestimmung ist, neben der Temperaturmessung im Stall, die bildbasierte Analyse des Liegeverhaltens von Schweinen in Gruppen. Dieses Vorgehen wurde bereits in Großbritannien im Rahmen einer Studie mit Schweinen untersucht und validiert [Na15]. Allerdings wurden die Untersuchungszeiträume der Bildanalyse durch manuelle Sichtung der Videodaten vorgenommen, was an personelle wie zeitliche

---

[1] Hochschule Osnabrück, Fachgebiet Landwirtschaftliche Betriebswirtschaftslehre, Am Krümpel 31, 49090 Osnabrück, alexander.kuehnemund@hs-osnabrueck.de

Ressourcen geknüpft ist [Ch22]. Des Weiteren fokussierte sich diese Untersuchung zunächst auf Schweine in der Mast. Jedoch sind im Stadium der Aufzucht die Temperaturempfindlichkeit sowie die veränderten Temperaturbedürfnisse bedeutend [MB89].

Die optimale Lufttemperatur in Bezug auf die Masse des Einzeltieres wird nach DIN 18-910-1 in Sollwert-Intervallen angegeben [Gr06]. Da diese Werte in unterschiedlichen Ställen mit unterschiedlicher Technik [Ch20] bei unterschiedlicher Genetik der Schweine hinsichtlich ihres Optimums variieren [Br19], nutzt auch diese Arbeit das Tier als Sensor für Wohlbefinden. Jedoch fehlt bisher ein automatisiertes System, das die Landwirte bei der Erkennung der Tiere im ruhenden Zustand im Schweinestall unterstützt und so automatisch aus dem Liegeverhalten das Wohlbefinden der Tiere im jeweiligen Stall ableitet.

Deshalb soll in diesem Forschungsvorhaben mit Hilfe eines KI-gestützten Kamerasystems, das die Bewegung von Schweinen analysiert, die Positionierung von Schweinen als Gruppe ausgewertet werden. Entgegen den bisherigen Forschungsarbeiten erfolgt in dieser Untersuchung die Auswahl der zu bewertenden Bilder durch das automatische Erkennen der Bewegungsrate. Ziel dieser Untersuchung ist es, die Genauigkeit des Bewegungsparameters und die Qualität der ausgewählten Bilddaten zu bestimmen, um eine zuverlässige automatisierbare Methode zum Erkennen von Gruppenliegeverhalten zu generieren. Weiterhin verfolgt diese Arbeit das Ziel, zu überprüfen, ob der Bewegungsparameter geeignet ist, um Gruppenliegeverhalten zu erkennen, um in weiteren Untersuchungen Grenzwerte zur Echtzeitanalyse zu validieren und die Implantation in ein automatisiertes System zu gewährleisten.

2 Material und Methoden

2.1 Untersuchte Tiere und Lokalisation

Die Untersuchung fand im Rahmen einer Tierbeobachtung für das Projekt „5G – Agrar: Nachhaltige Landwirtschaft" statt. Das Stallklima der im Untersuchungszeitraum betrachteten Tiere wurde nicht durch die Forschenden beeinflusst, sondern folgte den in der Praxis verwendeten Parametern des Untersuchungsstalls. Für die Untersuchung wurden Bildaufnahmen von sechs Buchten aus zwei Abteilen analysiert. Die Buchten waren jeweils mit 16 Tieren belegt und wurden im Rahmen der Untersuchung für 13 Tage zu je 24 Stunden gefilmt, um eine ganzheitliche Analyse der betrachteten Buchten zu gewährleisten.

2.2 Bilddatenuntersuchung

Die Kameras (zwei MP AcuSense Fixed Dome Network Camera) wurden in 3,5 Metern Höhe direkt über den untersuchten Buchten positioniert, sodass eine Ansicht der vollständigen Bucht in der Vogelperspektive ermöglicht wurde. Die Bilddaten wurden mit

Hilfe von „PigBrother", einer KI-basierten Verhaltensbewertungstechnologie, analysiert. Das Programm erhebt einen Geschwindigkeitsparameter anhand der durchschnittlichen Summe von Positionsveränderungen von einem Bildframe zum anderen im Verhältnis zur Zeit in Sekunden. Dieser Parameter ergibt eine numerische Variable, die Aufschluss über die Bewegung in den einzelnen Buchten gibt. Für diese Untersuchung haben die Wissenschaftler*innen im System liegend definiert, wenn der Bewegungsparameter zwischen 0 und 0,001 m/s beträgt. Im Gegensatz zu früheren Untersuchungen erfolgt somit die Auswahl der Bilddaten durch die Bewegungsrate der Tiere. Diese Form der Datenauswahl ist unabhängig von ausgewählten Zeiträumen, an denen die Tiere Aktivität zeigen. Außerdem liefert das Bildmaterial Daten zu tatsächlicher Inaktivität, also zum Liegeverhalten der Schweine, an allen als nicht aktiv erkannten Zeiten und Bewegungsverhalten an allen als aktiv bewerteten Datenpunkten. Aus den von der KI gelieferten Bilddaten wird im nächsten Schritt eine zufällige Stichprobe gezogen. Diese Stichprobe wird von zwei Wissenschaftler*innen visuell bewertet. Die Bewertung erfasste eine binäre Zuordnung der Tiere als „aktiv", mindestens ein Tier wird von den Wissenschaftler*innen als nicht liegend identifiziert (=1) oder „liegend", um die visuelle Bewertung mit der Bewertung durch die Bewegungsparameter vergleichen und interpretieren zu können. Bei der der Kodierung „liegend" (=0) werden alle Tiere visuell als liegende Tiere identifiziert. Anschließend werden divergierende Interpretationen genauer untersucht.

3 Ergebnisse

Im Untersuchungszeitraum 19.08.2022 bis 31.08.2022 wurden 3.745 Bewegungsdatenpunkte von der KI-basierten Kamera erhoben. Abbildung 1 zeigt die ermittelten Datenpunkte des Bewegungsverhaltens der Schweine.

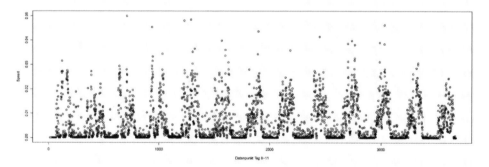

Abb. 1: Bewegungsdaten innerhalb der Bucht im zeitlichen Verlauf

Die Grafik stellt die durchschnittliche Bewegungsrate der Tiere in einem Abstand von fünf Minuten dar. Die Bewegungsrate des Tieres wird in Metern/Sekunde (m/s) angegeben und ist unabhängig von der Anzahl der Tiere. Eine Nullstelle der Bewegungsrate deutet auf ein liegendes Verhalten der beobachteten Tiere hin. Da die Bewegungsrate aus der durchschnittlichen Bewegung aus fünf Minuten errechnet wird, wurde die tatsächliche Aktivität der Tiere durch die Bewegungsrate „liegend als Gruppe" definiert mit 0 bis <=0,001 Meter/Sekunde. Im Folgenden konnten die nicht-aktiven und aktiven Datenpunkte als liegend und aktiv bewertet werden.

Anhand der vorliegenden Bewegungsdaten wurden Bilddaten von einer zufälligen Stichprobe (n=287) von 13 Tagen generiert, die durch die zwei Wissenschaftler*innen bewertet wurden. Die Bewertung des Systems erkennt bei 265 von 287 zu bewertenden Datenpunkten die liegenden beziehungsweise aktiven Tiere. Abbildung 2 zeigt die ausgewerteten Daten und stellt graphisch das Vorgehen des Vergleichs zwischen visueller und systemischer Bewertung dar.

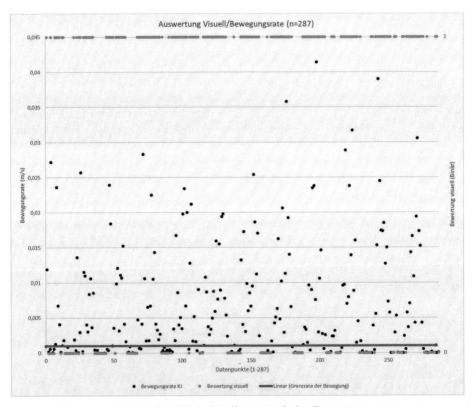

Abb. 2: Vergleich visueller/systemischer Bewertung

Abbildung 2 zeigt auf der primären Ordinate die von „PigBrother" ermittelten Bewegungsraten in m/s sowie die für die ruhende Position bestimmte Grenzrate der Bewegung (rote Horizontale). Unterhalb dieser Grenzrate wurden alle Schweine als liegend definiert. Die sekundäre Ordinate zeigt die binäre Bewertung der Wissenschaftler*innen, definiert als 0 = liegende Gesamtheit der Gruppe und 1 = Tiere in Bewegung. Buchten, in denen mindestens ein Tier nicht in liegender Position war, wurden als aktiv bewertet. Die Grafik veranschaulicht, dass von der KI erkanntes Liegeverhalten auch zu großer Übereinstimmung auf der Sekundärachse mit dem Wert null kodiert wurde. Schwarze Punkte, die durch das System unter 0,001 m/s kodiert wurden, stimmten also mit den in grau als null kodierten Punkten überein. Ähnlich verhält es sich mit dem Bewegungsverhalten innerhalb der Gruppe oder durch einzelne Tiere. Die Übereinstimmung der Bewertung ist kontinuierlich im Zeitverlauf.

Tabelle 1 führt die einzelnen Bewertungen von Tag 1 bis 13 auf sowie die Rate an korrekt bewerteten Daten zur Aktivität beziehungsweise der Bewertung der Gruppe als liegend.

Tag	Anzahl der bewerteten Bilder	Korrekte systemische Bewertung (%)
1	17	100,00%
2	24	100,00%
3	24	91,67%
4	24	87,50%
5	24	87,50%
6	24	95,83%
7	24	100,00%
8	24	87,50%
9	24	91,67%
10	24	95,83%
11	24	91,67%
12	24	87,50%
13	6	66,67%
Summe	287	

Tab. 1: Übereinstimmungsrate im Zeitverlauf

Die detaillierte Gegenüberstellung der Daten zeigt eine durchschnittliche Genauigkeit von 92,33 % der durch das System bewerteten Bewegungsdaten.

4 Diskussion

Die Stichprobe zeigt, dass eine KI-gesteuerte Identifikation des Liegeverhaltens in über neun von zehn Fällen gelingt. Allerdings ist die Qualität der Ergebnisse an den jeweils beobachteten Tagen unterschiedlich. Eine zweite Sichtung der Bilder zeigte, dass insbesondere Tiere, die die Nahrungsaufnahme in der Ruhephase der anderen Tiere vornahmen, ein Störfaktor für die Identifikation sind. Diese Tiere sind zwar aktiv, bewegen sich aber unter der Grenzrate der Bewegung von 0,001 Meter/Sekunde im Durchschnitt der erfassten Periode und werden so als inaktive Tiere erkannt. Ein Lösungsansatz besteht darin, die Erfassungsperiode der Bewegung von fünf Minuten auf einen geringeren Zeitraum zu verkürzen. Ein solches Vorgehen würde zu einer sensibleren Erfassung der Tierbewegung führen. Allerdings resultiert diese Anpassung in einer geringeren Anzahl an Bildern und zu einer geringeren Bewertungsdichte im Falle einer KI-basierten Auswertung der Bilder.

Auf dieser Untersuchung aufbauend wird das hier beschriebene Verfahren praktisch angewendet und die Bilddatenbewertung durch ein System automatisiert. Es benötigt allerdings weitere Forschung mit einer größeren Stichprobe, um die Ergebnisse dieser Arbeit zu validieren. Weiterhin wird in folgenden Untersuchungen der Wert des Bewegungsparameters weiter untersucht, um eine genauere Erfassung über den gesamten Lebenszyklus zu gewährleisten. Weitere Untersuchungen zu verschiedenen Jahreszeiten könnten genutzt werden, um Analysen zu saisonalen Effekten bei der Erkennung durchzuführen. Darüber hinaus wäre es sinnvoll, einen größeren Zeitraum zu betrachten, da die Qualität der Aufnahmen im Zeitverlauf, unter anderem durch Verschmutzung der Kameras, abnehmen kann.

Gegenüber bisherigen Studien, die unter personellen und zeitlichen Ressourcen händisch Bilddaten generierten [Na15], kann mit dieser Art der Detektion liegender Tiere die genaue Betrachtung zu verschiedenen Zeitpunkten bei sich schnell ändernden Anforderungen des Tieres an das Stallklima erfolgen. Diese Methode ermöglicht eine Anpassung in Echtzeit.

Schlussendlich zeigt die vorliegende Analyse, dass eine KI-gestützte Erfassung liegender Schweinegruppen sehr zuverlässig und damit eine Automatisierung möglich ist.

Literaturverzeichnis

[SB22]   Statistisches Bundesamt. Schweinebestand 2022 im Vergleich zum Vorjahr gesunken. https://www.destatis.de/DE/Themen/Branchen-Unternehmen/Landwirtschaft-Forstwirtschaft-Fischerei/Tiere-Tierische-Erzeugung/schweine.html, Stand 26.10.2022.

[BR13]   Baumgard, L. H.; Rhoads, R. P.: Effects of heat stress on postabsorptive metabolism and energetics. Annu Rev Anim Biosci 1, S. 311-337, 2013.

[PT20]   Pietrosemoli, S.; Tang, C.: Animal Welfare and Production Challenges Associated with Pasture Pig Systems: A Review. Agriculture 10/6, S. 223, 2020.

[Na15]   Nasirahmadi, A. et al.: Using machine vision for investigation of changes in pig group lying patterns. Computers and Electronics in Agriculture 119, S. 184-190, 2015.

[Ch22]   Chen, C.-P. J. et al.: VTag: a semi-supervised pipeline for tracking pig activity with a single top-view camera. Journal of Animal Science 100/6, 2022.

[MB89]   Marx, D.; Buchholz, M. (1989). Verbesserungsmöglichkeiten der Haltung junger Schweine im Sinne der Tiergerechtheit anhand der Untersuchungen von Einflussfaktoren auf das Verhalten. In (Boehncke, E. Hrsg.): Artgemässe Nutztierhaltung und ökologisch orientierte Landwirtschaft, Birkhäuser Basel, Basel, S. 55-69, 1989.

[Gr06]   Grote, D. et al.: Stallklimaprüfung in der Tierhaltung - Empfehlungen der Länderarbeitsgruppe Stallklima, 2006.

[Ch20]   Chantziaras, I. et al.: Environment-, health-, performance- and welfare-related parameters in pig barns with natural and mechanical ventilation. Preventive Veterinary Medicine, S. 183, 2020.

[Br19]   Brumm, M. C.: Effect of Environment on Health. In Diseases of Swine, S. 50-58, 2019.

Beurteilung von Use Cases zur Tierortung nach dem Grad des Informationsgehalts

Marie Lamoth[1], Heiko Neeland[1] und Christina Umstätter[1]

Abstract: In der Nutztierhaltung ist das rechtzeitige Erkennen von kranken Tieren von großer Bedeutung. Um dies zu unterstützen, werden automatisierte Assistenzsysteme entwickelt. Die Tierortung kann eine Technik sein, um Verhaltensabweichungen zu detektieren. Für ein solches Erkennungssystem ist es wichtig zu definieren, worüber es Auskunft geben soll. Stachowicz und Umstätter [SU21] unterscheiden drei Nachweisebenen nach dem Grad ihres Informationsgehalts. Die ersten beiden Ebenen beinhalten umwelt- oder tierbezogene Aspekte und die dritte Ebene spezifische krankheitsbezogene Indikatoren. In dieser Studie wurden auf Tierortung beruhende Use Cases für Assistenzsysteme hinsichtlich der Nachweisebene bewertet. Dafür wurde der jeweilige Indikator betrachtet und in dem Entscheidungsbaum der passenden Stufe verortet. Bei allen untersuchten Use Cases fallen die Indikatoren in die Ebene 1. Das heißt, die unspezifischen Daten der Tierortung können genutzt werden, um generelle Probleme des Wohlbefindens automatisch zu identifizieren. Eine Erkennung oder Vorhersage von spezifischen Erkrankungen ist hingegen mit diesen technischen Systemen nicht möglich.

Keywords: Milchvieh, Tierwohl, Früherkennung, Assistenzsystem, Nachweisebene

1 Einleitung

Automatisierte Assistenzsysteme sollen die Landwirtinnen und Landwirte bei den Arbeitsprozessen unterstützen und diese vereinfachen. Aufgrund der steigenden Tierzahlen auf den Milchviehbetrieben steht dabei auch die Erkennung von Erkrankungen bei den Kühen im Fokus. Viele Forschungsvorhaben in der landwirtschaftlichen Tierhaltung beschäftigen sich mit der Anwendung und dem Nutzen dieser Systeme.

Eine mögliche Komponente von Assistenzsystemen können Ortungssysteme sein, deren Aufgaben im Milchviehbereich vom schnelleren Auffinden der Kühe [Ra17] über die kontinuierliche Beobachtung verschiedener Grundverhaltensweisen, wie Bewegung, Fressen, Saufen und Liegen [Me18; Be20] bis hin zur automatischen Erkennung von Brunst [Be20; Ar16] oder Krankheiten [Wa20; VMS17] reichen.

Für die Entwicklung und den Einsatz von Assistenzsystemen in der Praxis ist es wichtig, deren Aufgaben und Ziele zu definieren. Die Bedeutung dessen haben auch Stachowicz und Umstätter [SU21] in ihrem Framework herausgearbeitet.

---

[1] Thünen-Institut für Agrartechnologie, Bundesallee 47, 38116 Braunschweig, marie.lamoth@thuenen.de, heiko.neeland@thuenen.de, christina.umstaetter@thuenen.de, https://www.thuenen.de/de/

Die vorliegende Studie hat zwei Ziele verfolgt. Zum einen wurden Use Cases für die Nutzung der Tierortung und kontinuierlichen Positionsbestimmung im Milchviehstall identifiziert. Zum anderen erfolgte eine Einordnung der Use Cases basierend auf dem Framework von Stachowicz und Umstätter [SU21] nach ihrem Informationsgehalt.

2 Material und Methoden

Im Rahmen des Projektes „CattleHub" wurden 25 Use Cases identifiziert und zusammengestellt, die auf der Ortung oder dem Tracking von Kühen im Innenbereich beruhen.

Als Tierortung oder Lokalisierung wird dabei die Bestimmung des aktuellen Aufenthaltsortes der Kuh bezeichnet und Tracking ist die kontinuierliche Positionsbestimmung und die Rückverfolgbarkeit der gegangenen Wege.

Für die Tierortung gibt es verschiedene Technologien, die in den Ställen Einsatz finden. Dabei haben alle Indoor-Systeme miteinander gemein, dass sie für die Ortung eine Infrastruktur, beispielsweise in Form von Ankern und individuellen Tags für die Tiere, benötigen. Bildgebende Ortungsverfahren wurden hingegen für die Milchviehhaltung bisher eher selten entwickelt.

Zur Bewertung der Aufgaben und Ziele der Use Cases wurde das Framework von Stachowicz und Umstätter [SU21] herangezogen. Es besteht aus drei Entscheidungsbäumen, mit deren Hilfe sich die Use Cases nach dem Grad ihrer Information einordnen lassen. Jeder Entscheidungsbaum gehört zu einer der Ebenen „generelle Tierwohlprobleme" (1), „Gesundheits- oder disstressbezogene Probleme" (2) oder „definierte krankheitsbezogene Probleme" (3). Anhand unterschiedlicher tier- oder umweltbezogener Indikatoren, Merkmalen wie Frequenz oder Dauer eines Indikators und verschiedener beeinflussender Faktoren erfolgt die Einordnung in die ersten beiden Stufen. Dabei werden bei der zweiten Ebene die Indikatoren etwas genauer abgefragt als in der ersten. Die Einordnung in die dritte Ebene erfordert spezifische Informationen, wie beispielsweise die Krankheitsursache und einen möglichen chronischen oder klinisch manifesten Verlauf.

Um die Use Cases in die Ebenen einzuordnen, wurde zunächst der jeweilige Indikator identifiziert. Dieser wurde mit seinen Merkmalen betrachtet und seinem Informationsgehalt entsprechend in einen Entscheidungsbaum eingeordnet. Daraus ergibt sich die dazugehörige Ebene, auf der mit diesem Indikator Nachweise erbracht werden können.

3 Ergebnisse und Diskussion

Bei der Betrachtung der Use Cases fiel auf, dass sich bestimmte Indikatoren nicht direkt durch die Tierortung erfassen lassen, sondern sich über den Tierstandort ableiten. Dazu zählen die Use Cases Fressen [VMS17], Saufen [Me18] und Nutzung des Minerallecksteins sowie der Putzbürste [Me18]. Für die Unterscheidung zwischen Liegen und Stehen über die Tierortung wird die zuverlässige Erfassung der Z-Koordinate benötigt. Diese Zuverlässigkeit wird in den kommerziellen Ortungssystemen bisher nicht hinreichend sichergestellt [Hi20]. In der Literatur wurde daher oftmals die zusätzliche Verwendung von Beschleunigungssensoren oder visuellen Kontrollen beschrieben.

Die Use Cases Bewegung, Liegen und Fressen werden als Indikatoren für eine Reihe von Anwendungen herangezogen. Veränderungen in diesen Grundverhaltensweisen können zum Beispiel auf eine Brunst [Be20; VMS17], Mastitis [Ma22; VMS17], Lahmheit [VMS17; Va18] oder Hitzestress [HA18] hindeuten (Tab. 1).

Bewegung (Anzahl der Schritte, zurückgelegte Wegstrecke und Laufgeschwindigkeit) und Stehen bzw. Liegen wird in vielen Studien in der Aktivität zusammengefasst. Eine erhöhte Aktivität wird dabei meistens mit einer Brunst in Verbindung gebracht. So betrachteten Benaissa et al. [Be20] die Aktivität im Zeitraum von zwei Wochen vor bis zwei Wochen nach der Brunst und stellten fest, dass die Anzahl der Schritte und die zurückgelegte Strecke anstieg, während die Liegezeiten sanken, wenn die Kuh brünstig war. Arcidiacono et al. [Ar18] beobachteten einen signifikanten Anstieg in der Laufgeschwindigkeit am Tag der Brunst. Auch Veissier et al. [VMS17] stellten eine Steigerung im Aktivitätslevel, bei dem neben Ruhen und Aufenthalt in den Laufgängen auch Fressen mit einbezogen wurde, fest. Sofern die Kuh kurz vor dem errechneten Abkalbetermin steht, kann eine erhöhte Aktivität zusammen mit einem Rückgang in den Liegezeiten auch auf den Beginn der Geburt hindeuten [Be20]. Verkürzte Liegezeiten und ein erhöhtes Aktivitätslevel [VMS17] bzw. gesteigerte Schrittzahl [Ma22] können aber ebenso im Zusammenhang mit einer Mastitis stehen. Diese Veränderung wird meistens mit Schmerzen wegen des geschwollenen Euters beim Liegen erklärt [Si11]. Ein weiteres viel untersuchtes Problem in der Milchviehhaltung sind Lahmheiten bei Kühen. Von einem Rückgang der Aktivität bzw. einer Erhöhung der Liegezeiten berichten verschiedene Studien [VMS17; Va18; Tu21].

Werden mehrere Tiere parallel betrachtet, lassen sich über die Anzahl und Dauer der Kuhkontakte soziale Interaktionen und Entwicklungen nach Umgruppierungen [Ro19] sowie synchrones Gruppenverhalten [SPS12] untersuchen. Sofern die Z-Koordinate erfasst werden könnte, ist auch der Nachweis von Aufspringen und Duldung in der Brunst [Ho13] sowie die Berechnung von verschiedenen Indices denkbar. Diese Indices könnten der Stall Standing Index (SSI: Anteil stehender Kühe in Liegeboxen an allen Kühen, die sich in Liegeboxen befinden), der Stall Use Index (SUI: Anteil der liegenden Kühe in Liegeboxen an der Gesamtzahl der Kühe im Stall, die nicht fressen) oder der Cow Comfort Index (CCI: Anteil liegender Kühe in Liegeboxen an der Gesamtzahl Kühe, die sich in

Liegeboxen befinden) sein [CBN05]. Diese Indices können Änderungen im generellen Wohlbefinden anzeigen [CBN05].

Alle genannten Use Cases basieren auf Verhaltensweisen von Tieren, meist sogar auf Grundverhaltensweisen wie Fressen, Liegen oder Bewegung. Diese können auf ein Individuum oder auch auf die Gruppe bezogen sein. Die Ortungsdaten liefern unspezifische Indikatoren, die eine Vielzahl von Interpretationen zulassen und somit nur einen Hinweis auf das generelle Wohlbefinden der Tiere geben können. Eine genaue Aussage, ob es sich um Disstress oder ein Gesundheitsproblem handelt oder gar um eine spezifische Erkrankung, kann mit der Tierortung allein nicht erfolgen. Um die Ursache für eine Verhaltensveränderung herauszufinden, ist beispielsweise der Einsatz von spezifischen Sensoren oder visuellen Kontrollen nötig.

Use Cases mit Nachweis von Verhaltensweisen	Use Cases mit Veränderungen in Verhaltensweisen
Bewegung [Me18; Be20]	Brunst [Be20; VMS17], Abkalbung [Be20], Lahmheit [VMS17; Va18; Tu21], Hitzestress [HA18], Mastitis [Ma22; VMS17], Ketose [He22], Subakute Pansenazidose [Wa20]
Zurückgelegte Wegstrecke [Be20; Va18]	Brunst [Be20], Lahmheit [Va18]
Laufgeschwindigkeit [Ar18]	Brunst [Ar18]
Stehen [Wa20]	Subakute Pansenazidose [Wa20]
Liegen [VMS17; Wa20]	Brunst [Be20; VMS17], Lahmheit [VMS17; Va18; Tu21], Hitzestress [HA18], Mastitis [VMS17], Metritis [Ba18], Ketose [He22], Subakute Pansenazidose [Wa20]
Fressen [VMS17; Go08]	Brunst [VMS17], Lahmheit [Va18], Mastitis [VMS17], Ketose [Go08], Subakute Pansenazidose [Wa20]
Raumnutzungsverhalten [Me18; Va18]	Lahmheit [Va18]

Tab. 1: Die wichtigsten identifizierten Use Cases für die Tierortung

4 Schlussfolgerung

Das Framework von Stachowicz und Umstätter [SU21] wurde erfolgreich für die tierortungsbasierten Use Cases angewandt. Bei der Einordnung der Ortungsdaten ohne eine Verknüpfung mit weiteren Variablen lassen sich Aussagen treffen, die in der Nachweisebene der „generellen Tierwohlprobleme" anzusiedeln sind, da Veränderungen im Grundverhalten nachgewiesen werden können. Tiefere Aussagen zu den Nachweisebenen „Disstress- oder Gesundheitsproblemen" oder sogar zu „speziellen Krankheiten" sind aufgrund des fehlenden Informationsgehalts nicht möglich.

Das Prinzip des Frameworks lässt sich auch auf andere Technologien und deren Use Cases übertragen. Es bietet mit den Entscheidungspfaden einen praktikablen Weg, um herauszufinden, was für Informationen ein Sensor- oder Assistenzsystem liefern kann. Das Framework kann auch für die Planung weiterer Forschung angewandt werden, da Potentiale von neuen Systemen frühzeitig bewertet werden können.

Förderhinweis: Die Förderung des Vorhabens erfolgt aus Mitteln des Bundesministeriums für Ernährung und Landwirtschaft (BMEL) aufgrund eines Beschlusses des deutschen Bundestages. Die Projektträgerschaft erfolgt über die Bundesanstalt für Landwirtschaft und Ernährung (BLE) im Rahmen der Förderung der Digitalisierung in der Landwirtschaft mit dem Förderkennzeichen 28DE108A18 (Experimentierfeld CattleHub).

Literaturverzeichnis

[Ar18] Arcidiacono, C., et al.: A software tool for the automatic and real-time analysis of cow velocity data in free-stall barns: The case study of oestrus detection from Ultra-Wide-Band data. Biosystems Engineering, S. 157-165, 2018.

[Ba18] Barragan, A. A., et al.: Assessment of daily activity patterns and biomarkers of pain, inflammation, and stress in lactating dairy cows diagnosed with clinical metritis. Journal of dairy science 9, S. 8248-8258, 2018.

[Be20] Benaissa, S., et al.: Calving and estrus detection in dairy cattle using a combination of indoor localization and accelerometer sensors. Computers and Electronics in Agriculture, Art.-Nr. 105153, 2020.

[CBN05] Cook, N. B.; Bennett, T. B.; Nordlund, K. V.: Monitoring Indices of Cow Comfort in Free-Stall-Housed Dairy Herds. Journal of dairy science 11, S. 3876-3885, 2005.

[Go08] González, L. A., et al.: Changes in feeding behavior as possible indicators for the automatic monitoring of health disorders in dairy cows. Journal of dairy science 3, S. 1017-1028, 2008.

[He22] Hendriks, S. J., et al.: Associations between peripartum lying and activity behaviour and blood non-esterified fatty acids and β-hydroxybutyrate in grazing dairy cows. Animal: an international journal of animal bioscience 3, Art.-Nr. 100470, 2022.

[HA18]	Herbut, P.; Angrecka, S.: Relationship between THI level and dairy cows' behaviour during summer period. Italian Journal of Animal Science 1, S. 226-233, 2018.
[Hi20]	Hindermann, P., et al.: High precision real-time location estimates in a real-life barn environment using a commercial ultra wideband chip. Computers and Electronics in Agriculture, Art.-Nr. 105250, 2020.
[Ho13]	Homer, E. M., et al.: Technical note: a novel approach to the detection of estrus in dairy cows using ultra-wideband technology. Journal of dairy science 10, S. 6529-6534, 2013.
[Ma22]	Mainau, E., et al.: Alteration in Activity Patterns of Cows as a Result of Pain Due to Health Conditions. Animals: an open access journal from MDPI 2, 2022.
[Me18]	Meunier, B., et al.: Image analysis to refine measurements of dairy cow behaviour from a real-time location system. Biosystems Engineering, S. 32-44, 2018.
[Ra17]	Rackwitz, R.: CowView. Lokalisierungs,- Gesundheits- und Fruchtbarkeitsmanagement., https://www.tlllr.de/www/daten/veranstaltungen/materialien/melksysteme/300517_rackwitz.pdf, 04.10.2022.
[Ro19]	Rocha, L.E.C., et al.: Real-Time Locating System to study the persistence of sociality in large-mammal group dynamics. In (O'Brien, B.; Hennessy, D.; Shalloo, L., Hrsg.): Precision Livestock Farming '19. Fermoy Print & Design, Cork S. 894-898, 2019.
[Si11]	Siivonen, J., et al.: Impact of acute clinical mastitis on cow behaviour. Applied Animal Behaviour Science 3-4, S. 101-106, 2011.
[SPS12]	Stoye, S.; Porter, M. A.; Stamp Dawkins, M.: Synchronized lying in cattle in relation to time of day. Livestock Science 1-2, S. 70-73, 2012.
[SU21]	Stachowicz, J.; Umstätter, C.: Do we automatically detect health- or general welfare-related issues? A framework. Proceedings. Biological sciences 1950, Art.-Nr. 20210190, 2021.
[Tu21]	Tucker, C. B., et al.: Invited review: Lying time and the welfare of dairy cows. Journal of dairy science 1, S. 20-46, 2021.
[Va18]	Vázquez Diosdado, J. A., et al.: Space-use patterns highlight behavioural differences linked to lameness, parity, and days in milk in barn-housed dairy cows. PloS one 12, Art.-Nr. e0208424, 2018.
[VMS17]	Veissier, I.; Mialon, M.-M.; Sloth, K. H.: Short communication: Early modification of the circadian organization of cow activity in relation to disease or estrus. Journal of dairy science 5, S. 3969-3974, 2017.
[Wa20]	Wagner, N., et al.: Machine learning to detect behavioural anomalies in dairy cows under subacute ruminal acidosis. Computers and Electronics in Agriculture, Art.-Nr. 105233, 2020.

IoT in der Milchviehhaltung am Beispiel von Gesundheitssensoren – Akzeptanzbarrieren im Adoptionsprozess

Greta Langer [1], Sarah Kühl[1] und Sirkka Schukat[2]

Abstract: Der Einsatz von „Internet of Things" (IoT)-Sensoren kann zu einer nachhaltigeren und tierwohlgerechteren Milcherzeugung beitragen. IoT-Sensoren werden vermehrt für die Gesundheitsüberwachung von Milchkühen entwickelt. Die Verbreitung von IoT-Technologien erfolgt, trotz vieler Vorteile für die Praxis, aber nur langsam. Hinsichtlich der Nutzungsintention und möglichen Akzeptanzbarrieren ist konkret für den Bereich der IoT-gestützten Gesundheitsüberwachung in der Milchviehhaltung nur wenig bekannt. Eine Online-Umfrage aus dem Jahr 2022 zeigt, dass die Nutzungsintention mehrheitlich vorhanden ist, die tatsächliche Nutzung solcher Sensoren aber nur auf einem geringen Niveau liegt. Vor allem hohe Investitionskosten, eine mangelnde Kompatibilität mit anderen Geräten und ein langsamer Breitbandausbau konnten als die wichtigsten Akzeptanzbarrieren im Adoptionsprozess unter Milchviehhaltern identifiziert werden. Die Ergebnisse implizieren, dass politische Entscheidungsträger und Technologiehersteller gefragt sind, den Adoptionsprozess zu unterstützen und auf die Bedürfnisse der Landwirte in Bezug auf die jeweilige Technologie einzugehen, damit das Potenzial von IoT-Sensoren nicht an Akzeptanzbarrieren scheitert.

Keywords: Internet of Things-Sensoren, Gesundheitsüberwachung, Akzeptanz, Barrieren, Milchviehhaltung

1 Einleitung

Die Digitalisierung in der Landwirtschaft bietet Betrieben die Möglichkeit, effizienter zu wirtschaften und den Tier-, Umwelt- und Klimaschutz zu verbessern [TFG19]. IoT-Sensoren (z. B. Halsband- und Pansensensoren) ermöglichen mehr Tierwohl und eine verbesserte Tiergesundheit durch eine digitale Überwachung der Tiere [LBG20]. Mit der Implementierung von IoT-Sensoren kann entsprechend auf gesellschaftliche Forderungen nach Tier- und Ressourcenschutz reagiert werden und sie stellt damit einen wichtigen Erfolgsfaktor für das nachhaltige Bestehen von Milchviehbetrieben dar [So21; LBG20]. Vor diesem Hintergrund gewinnt die Frage nach der Akzeptanz von IoT-Sensoren für die Gesundheitsüberwachung von Milchkühen und die Identifizierung von potenziellen Akzep-

---

[1] Department für Agrarökonomie und Rurale Entwicklung, Universität Göttingen, Marketing für Lebensmittel und Agrarprodukte, Platz der Göttinger Sieben 5, 37073 Göttingen, greta.langer@uni.goettingen.de https://orcid.org/0000-0002-6786-1343, skuehl@gwdg.de

[2] Department für Agrarökonomie und Rurale Entwicklung, Universität Göttingen, Betriebswirtschaftslehre des Agribusiness, Platz der Göttinger Sieben 5, 37073 Göttingen, sirkka.schukat@uni-goettingen.de

tanzbarrieren an Bedeutung; eine erfolgreiche Verbreitung von IoT-Sensoren setzt die Zustimmung potenzieller Nutzer voraus [Su18]. Barrieren können durch Technologieanpassung an die Bedürfnisse der Landwirte und die Betriebe überwunden werden. Dies erfordert jedoch konkrete Erkenntnisse über die Akzeptanzbarrieren der jeweiligen Zielgruppen in der Landwirtschaft (Ackerbau, Nutztierhaltung) [Kn15]. Der Blick in die Literatur zeigt, dass die Akzeptanz von IoT in der Tierhaltung nur lückenhaft erforscht ist. Die Verbreitung digitaler Technologien erfolgte bisher vor allem im Bereich des Precision Agriculture Farmings und weniger im Smart Livestock Farming [BB15; Ru18], sodass diesbezüglich Forschungsbedarf besteht.

Das Ziel des vorliegenden Beitrags liegt darin, den Status Quo der Nutzungsintention (Akzeptanz) und die Nutzungshäufigkeit am Beispiel von Halsband- und Pansensoren von Milchviehhaltern zu erfassen. Beide Sensoren ermöglichen die Erfassung von Abweichungen vom Gesundheitszustand der Kühe und werden seit nicht allzu langer Zeit kommerziell vertrieben. Zudem werden Akzeptanzbarrieren im Adoptionsprozess unter Milchviehhaltern aufgezeigt sowie Übereinstimmungen mit und Abweichungen vom Forschungsstand sichtbar gemacht. Durch die gewonnenen Ergebnisse können Handlungsempfehlungen formuliert werden, wie die Akzeptanzbarrieren überwunden und die Akzeptanz von IoT-Sensoren zielgruppengenau verbessert werden könnten.

2 Material und Methoden

Grundlage der Studie bildet eine Online-Befragung mit 212 Milchviehhaltern aus dem Frühjahr 2022. Die Milchviehhalter wurden über verschiedene Kanäle akquiriert (z. B. landwirtschaftliche Fachzeitschriften, Molkereien, Mitglieder der Landesvereinigung Milch). Der standardisierte Fragebogen gliederte sich in verschiedene Bereiche und enthielt sowohl Fragen zu betrieblichen und soziodemografischen Merkmalen als auch zu potenziellen Akzeptanzbarrieren und zur grundsätzlichen Wahrnehmung der Digitalisierung in der Landwirtschaft. Dem Fragebogen wurde ein Informationstext zu den IoT-Beispielsensoren (Halsband- und Pansensensoren) vorangestellt, um ein einheitliches Verständnis unter den Landwirten sicherzustellen. Die Aussagen mussten überwiegend auf fünfstufigen Likert-Skalen beantwortet werden[3]. Zudem wurde eine Kontrollfrage in den Fragebogen integriert, um die Qualität der Datensätze zu gewährleisten. Die Akzeptanzbarrieren wurden auf Grundlage einer intensiven Literaturrecherche formuliert. Die deskriptive Analyse erfolgte mit dem Statistikprogramm IBM SPSS 27.

---

[3] 1 = „stimme voll und ganz zu/sehr kritisch/mehrmals täglich" bis 5 = „stimme überhaupt nicht zu/sehr unkritisch/nie"

3 Ergebnisse

3.1 Stichprobe

Die Stichprobe (n=212) setzt sich aus 73,1 % Männern und 26,9 % Frauen zusammen. Das Durchschnittsalter liegt bei 40 Jahren. Der Frauenanteil, der in der Landwirtschaft tätig ist, liegt bei etwa 36 %; somit sind Frauen in der Umfrage leicht unterrepräsentiert [Db21]. 47,6 % der Landwirte haben einen Fachschulabschluss oder sind Landwirtschaftsmeister. Mit 28,7 % der befragten Landwirte, die einen universitären Abschluss haben, zeigt die Stichprobe ein überdurchschnittlich hohes Bildungsniveau: Im bundesweiten Durchschnitt haben nur ca. 14 % einen Universitätsabschluss [Db21]. Die Mehrheit der Befragten (70,3 %) arbeitet als Betriebsleiter. Fast alle Befragten sind im Haupterwerb tätig (99,1 %), wobei 17,0 % nach ökologischen Richtlinien und 80,2 % konventionell wirtschaften, die weiteren Betriebe befinden sich in der Umstellung. Die Mehrheit der Befragten (29,7 %) hält zwischen 100 und 199 Milchkühen, wobei 27,4 % angeben, zwischen 50 und 99 Milchkühe zu halten. Im Bundesdurchschnitt werden derzeit 70 Kühe pro Betrieb gehalten und ungefähr 6 % aller Milchviehbetriebe in Deutschland sind ökologisch [Db21]. Damit weist die Stichprobe eine vom Durchschnitt abweichende Verteilung hinsichtlich der Herdengröße und der Anzahl der Biobetriebe auf. Die Mehrheit der befragten Milchviehhalter (25,9 %) kommen aus Bayern, gefolgt von Niedersachsen (25,5 %) und Baden-Württemberg (11,8 %). Diese Verteilung hingegen entspricht der des bundesweiten Durchschnitts [Db21].

3.2 Akzeptanzbarrieren im Adoptionsprozess

Von den befragten Milchviehhaltern beabsichtigt etwa die Hälfte (49,1 %) in den kommenden Jahren grundsätzlich IoT-Sensoren einzusetzen. Etwas weniger Milchviehhalter (43,0 %) haben bereits konkrete Pläne für den zukünftigen Einsatz von IoT-Sensoren [4]. Die Nutzungsintention (Akzeptanz) ist somit mehrheitlich gegeben – auch wenn fast ein Drittel der Landwirte angeben, den Einsatz solcher Sensoren für die Zukunft nicht zu planen. Die tatsächliche Nutzung der genannten Sensorhalsbänder zeigt Unterschiede zwischen den einzelnen Sensoren[5]: Sensorhalsbänder werden bereits von 53,8 % und Pansensensoren von 21,8 % der Milchviehhalter regelmäßig (täglich und mehrmals täglich) genutzt. Es scheinen Akzeptanzbarrieren vorzuliegen, die den Implementierungsprozess bremsen (siehe Abb. 1). Die größte Barriere im Adoptionsprozess für die Milchviehhalter sind die hohen Investitionskosten für IoT-Sensoren. Insgesamt bewerten 63,7 % der Land-

---

[4] Fragestellung: Was planen Sie in Hinblick auf die Nutzung von IoT-Sensoren? (ohne Spezifizierung auf die Beispielsensoren) Item eins: Ich plane in den kommenden Jahren IoT-Sensoren auf meinem Betrieb zu nutzen, Item zwei: Es gibt bereits konkrete Pläne, für meinen Betrieb IoT-Sensoren in Zukunft zu nutzen.
[5] Fragestellung: Bitte geben Sie die Nutzungshäufigkeit der folgenden Produkte an (jeweils für Halsband- und Pansensensor abgefragt)

wirte dies als sehr kritisch oder kritisch (μ=2,21; σ=0,916). Eine mangelnde Kompatibilität wird als zweitgrößte Barriere angesehen; mehr als die Hälfte der Milchviehhalter (52,4 %) schätzt dies als sehr kritisch oder kritisch ein (μ=; σ=2,54; σ=1,072).

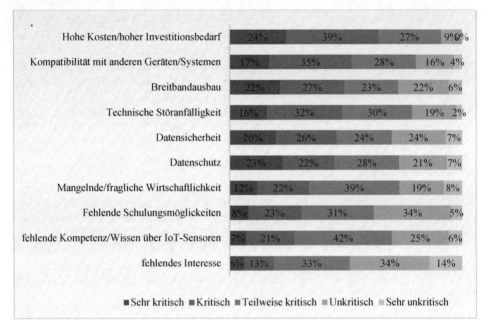

Abb. 1: Akzeptanzbarrieren im Adoptionsprozess von IoT-Sensoren im Allgemeinen [6]

An dritter Stelle steht der langsame Breitbandausbau, der von 49,1 % als sehr kritisch oder kritisch eingeschätzt wird (μ=2,63; σ=1,207). Hinsichtlich technischer Störanfälligkeit sind 48,1 % der Milchviehhalter sehr kritisch bis kritisch eingestellt (μ=2,60; σ=1,046). Bedenken hinsichtlich der Datensicherheit und -hoheit werden von 45,7 % bzw. 44,8% geäußert. Deutlich unkritischer sind die Milchviehhalter mit Blick auf eine mangelnde/fragliche Wirtschaftlichkeit von IoT-Sensoren: 66,0 % geben an, dass sie nur teilweise kritisch, unkritisch bzw. sehr unkritisch sind (μ=2,90; σ=1,097). Auch fehlende Schulungsmöglichkeiten, konkret für den Bereich der digitalen Gesundheitsüberwachung, werden unkritisch beurteilt, denn insgesamt 69,3 % geben an, nur teilweise kritisch, unkritisch bzw. sehr unkritisch zu sein (μ=3,04; σ=1,036). Das für die korrekte Nutzung von IoT-Sensoren notwendige Wissen wird von nur wenigen Milchviehhaltern als Barriere wahrgenommen; insgesamt 72,2 % schätzen es als teilweise kritisch, unkritisch bzw. sehr unkritisch ein (μ=3,01; σ= 0,986). Am unkritischsten sind die Milchviehhalter hinsichtlich eines fehlenden Interesses an IoT-Sensoren im Gesundheitsmonitoring: 81,1 % sind teilweise kritisch, unkritisch bzw. sehr unkritisch (μ= 3,38; σ=1,071).

---

[6] Fragestellung: Wie bewerten Sie folgende Punkte zum Einsatz von IoT-Sensoren für die Gesundheitsüberwachung? Bitte kreuzen Sie nach Ihrer kritischen Beurteilung an.

4 Diskussion und Fazit

Ziel des vorliegenden Beitrags ist es, neben der Messung der Akzeptanz und der Nutzungshäufigkeit, die Akzeptanzbarrieren im Adoptionsprozess von IoT-Sensoren unter Milchviehhaltern zu identifizieren. Die hohen Investitionskosten stellen die größte Barriere im Adoptionsprozess von IoT-Sensoren im Allgemeinen dar. Dieses Ergebnis bestätigt andere Studien, die ebenfalls zeigen, dass hohe Kosten, die mit der Digitalisierung in der Landwirtschaft einhergehen, den Implementierungsprozess in der Praxis bremsen [BI16; MK21]. Zum einen sind es Anfangsinvestitionen und zum anderen Wartungskosten, die Landwirte als Nutzungsbarriere beurteilen [MK21]. Die fehlende Wirtschaftlichkeit von IoT-Sensoren wird von nur einem Drittel der Landwirte als Barriere beurteilt, es mangelt also nicht an der Überzeugung bezüglich der Wirtschaftlichkeit der Sensoren. Zur Überwindung der hohen Anfangsinvestitionen, die für einige IoT-Sensoren erforderlich sind, könnten somit Investitionszuschüsse die Akzeptanz und schlussendliche Adoption deutlich erhöhen. Ein zweites wichtiges Ergebnis der vorliegenden Studie ist, dass Landwirte die Kompatibilität mit anderen IoT-Technologien und Systemen äußerst kritisch beurteilen. Eine Studie von [SG18] konnte zeigen, dass dies bereits im Jahr 2009 eine erhebliche Akzeptanzbarriere im digitalen landwirtschaftlichen Transformationsprozess darstellte. Konkret für den IoT-Bereich hat sich diese Barriere weiter erhöht, da sie von den Milchviehhaltern sogar als zweitgrößtes Hemmnis wahrgenommen wird. Derzeit bieten IoT-Systeme nicht die notwendige Kompatibilität und Flexibilität, die Landwirte fordern [GSE18]. Zudem müssen die Rahmenbedingungen auf den Betrieben, die unter anderem darüber entscheiden, ob Landwirte in digitale Tools investieren, verbessert werden. Hier sind politische Entscheidungsträger gefragt, den Breitbandausbau in den ländlichen Regionen zu beschleunigen, denn dieser stellt die drittgrößte Barriere im Adoptionsprozess dar. Auch im Bereich Datensicherheit und -schutz sollten von politischer aber auch Anbieterseite Maßnahmen getroffen werden, da dies für knapp die Hälfte ein kritisches Thema ist. Die Implementierung von IoT auf den Betrieben konfrontiert Landwirte mit neuen Managementaufgaben, die eine gewisse Digitalkompetenz (korrekte Bedienung, Dateninterpretation) voraussetzt [BI16]. Die Milchviehhalter unserer Befragung zeigen sich jedoch unkritisch hinsichtlich fehlender Schulungsmöglichkeiten und mangelnden Vorkenntnissen. Das Ergebnis bestätigt, dass Landwirte in den letzten Jahren dazugelernt haben, denn in älteren Studien zählten fehlendes Know-how und Berührungsängste gegenüber digitalen Technologien noch zu den größten Barrieren [Bi16; GSE18].

Insgesamt zeigt die vorliegende Studie, dass die Nutzungsintention auf einem hohen Niveau liegt, die tatsächliche Nutzung der abgefragten Sensoren unter Milchviehhaltern aber noch nicht weit verbreitet ist. Diesbezüglich ist zu erwähnen, dass größere Milchviehbetriebe in der vorliegenden Stichprobe überrepräsentiert sind, was das Ergebnis möglicherweise beeinflusst hat. Andere Studienergebnisse deuten allerdings darauf hin, dass digitale Technologien von Milchviehhaltern aller Größenordnungen als nützlich empfunden werden [MBO19]. Diese Erkenntnis gilt es für den Bereich der IoT-Sensoren zu konkretisieren. Nichtsdestotrotz sind politische Entscheidungsträger und Hersteller gefragt, um die aufgezeigten Barrieren abzubauen und den Adoptionsprozess von IoT-Sensoren zu beschleunigen. Dies ist insbesondere vor dem Hintergrund des hohen Nutzens von IoT-Sensoren für die Nachhaltigkeit der Milchviehhaltung von großer Bedeutung.

Literaturverzeichnis

[Bi16] Bitkom - Digitalisierung in der Landwirtschaft, https://www.bitkom.org/sites/default/files/file/import/Bitkom-Pressekonferenz-Digitalisierung-in-der-Landwirtschaft-02-11-2016-Praesentation.pdf, 12.10.2022.

[BB15] Borchers, M.R.; Bewley, J.M.: An assessment of producer precision dairy farming technology use, prepurchase considerations, and usefulness. Journal of Dairy Science 98(6), S. 4198-4205, 2015.

[Db21] Situationsbericht 2021/22 des Deutschen Bauernverbands, https://www.bauernverband.de/fileadmin/berichte/2021/index.html#96, 12.10.2022.

[GSE18] Gandorfer, M.; Schleicher, S.; Erdle, K.: Barriers to Adoption of Smart Farming Technologies in Germany. In 14th International Conference on Precision Agriculture, Montreal, Quebec, Canada, S. 1-8, 2018.

[Kn15] Knierim, A.; Boenning, K.; Caggiano, M.; Cristóvão, A.; Dirimanova, V.; Koehnen, T.; Labarthe, P.; Prage, K.: The AKIS concept and its relevance in selected EU member states. Outlook on Agriculture. 44/1, S. 29-36, 2015.

[LBG20] Lovarelli, D.; Bacenetti, J.; Guarino, M.: A review on dairy cattle farming: Is precision Livestock farming the compromise for an environmental, economic and social sustainable production? Journal of Cleaner Production 262/2, S. 121409, 2020.

[MK21] Mohr, S.; Kühl, R.: Acceptance of artificial intelligence in German agriculture: an application of the technology acceptance model and the theory of planned behavior. Precision Agriculture 22, S.1816-1844, 2021.

[MBO19] Michels, M.; Bonke, V.; Musshoff, O.: Understanding the adoption of smartphone apps in dairy herd management. Journal of Dairy Science 102, S. 9422-9434, 2019.

[Ru18] Rutten, C.J.; Steeneveld, W.; Lansink, A.; Hogeveen, H.: Delaying investments in sensor technology: The rationality of dairy farmers' investment decisions illustrated within the framework of real options theory. Journal of Dairy Science 101/8, S. 7650-7660, 2018.

[SG18] Schleicher, S.; Gandorfer, M.: Digitalisierung in der Landwirtschaft: Eine Analyse der Akzeptanzhemmnisse. In (A. Ruckelshausen et al. Hrsg.): Digitale Marktplätze und Plattformen, Lecture Notes in Informatics (LNI), Gesellschaft für Informatik, Bonn, S. 203-206, 2018.

[Su18] Sundrum, A.: Big Data – Mittel zu welchen Zwecken? In: 7. Wilhelm-Stahl-Symposium Big Data im Stall –Zukunftsmodell oder Sackgasse? Dummerstorf, S. 15-19, 2018.

[TFG19] Tullo, E.; Finzi, A; Guarino, M.: Review: Environmental impact of livestock farming and Precision Livestock Farming as a mitigation strategy. Science of the Total Environment 650, S. 2751-2760, 2019.

For5G: Systematic approach for creating digital twins of cherry orchards

Lukas Meyer[1], Andreas Gilson[2], Franz Uhrmann[2], Mareike Weule[2], Fabian Keil[2], Bernhard Haunschild[3], Joachim Oschek[2], Marco Steglich[2], Jonathan Hansen[2], Marc Stamminger[1] and Oliver Scholz[2]

Abstract: We present a systematic approach for creating digital twins of cherry trees in orchards as part of the project "For5G: Digital Twin". We aim to develop a basic concept for 5G applications in orchards using a mobile campus network. Digital twins monitor the status of individual trees in every aspect and are a crucial step for the digitalization of processes in horticulture. Our framework incorporates a transformation of photometric data to a 3D reconstruction, which is subsequently segmented and modeled using learning-based approaches. Collecting objective phenotypic features from individual trees over time and storing them in a knowledge graph offers a convenient foundation for gaining new insights. Our approach shows promising results at this point for creating a detailed digital twin of a cherry tree and ultimately the entire orchard.

Keywords: 5G, cherry tree, deep learning, digital horticulture, digital twin, knowledge graph, orchard, phenotyping, photogrammetry, precision farming, UAV

1 Introduction

Smart farming and precision agriculture rely on accurate data as a foundation for decisions to counteract current problems such as climate change and to meet the ever-growing food needs of the world's population. Using digital twins in agriculture can help growth optimization, early pest detection, yield forecasting and conserve resources in cultivation. The digital twin can inform the farmer about crop conditions or anomalies and thus assist in decision-making processes or provide information to agricultural robots. Ultimately, the goal is to relieve the farmer of having to be on-site and allow them to assess the condition of their crops solely through the digital twin.

In recent years, the creation of digital twins in agriculture has become an increasingly important topic in research [PN22]. The main task is to capture and model the complexity

---

[1] Friedrich-Alexander-Universität Erlangen-Nürnberg, Chair of Visual Computing, Cauerstraße 11, 91058 Erlangen, lukas.meyer@fau.de, https://orcid.org/0000-0003-3849-7094, marc.stamminger@fau.de, https://orcid.org/0000-0001-8699-3442
[2] Fraunhofer Institut für Integrierte Schaltungen (IIS/EZRT), Am Wolfsmantel 33, 91058 Erlangen, {andreas.gilson, franz.uhrmann, mareike.weule, fabian.keil, joachim.oschek, marco.steglich, jonathan.hansen, oliver.scholz}@iis.fraunhofer.de
[3] Hochschule Weihenstephan-Triesdorf, Neueser Straße 1, 91732 Merkendorf, bernhard.haunschild@hswt.de

of a living entity and its dynamic reaction to the environment [PCA21]. Several approaches exist in related work acquiring digital twins, from plant modeling to real-time monitoring with feedback mechanisms [PN22].

In this paper, as part of the project "For5G: Digital Twin", we present a concept for creating a digital twin using an unmanned aerial vehicle (UAV) with a 5G network for cloud access. Figure 1 shows an overview of the approach. The core idea is to acquire photometric data of a cherry tree using the UAV. The obtained 2D image data is sent through the 5G network to a cloud server for real-time analysis. 3D point clouds are generated using the images and subsequently segmented into separate plant organs such as leaves, trunks, branches, etc. Each organ instance is then separately modeled using a geometric model, resulting in a set of parameters describing the phenotypic traits. Combining the data of all tree organs into a knowledge graph provides a snapshot of the tree in time. Repeating the scans makes it possible to track the trees' development over time, intra- and inter-seasonal. Making this data accessible to the farmer can be a valuable aid in his decision-making process.

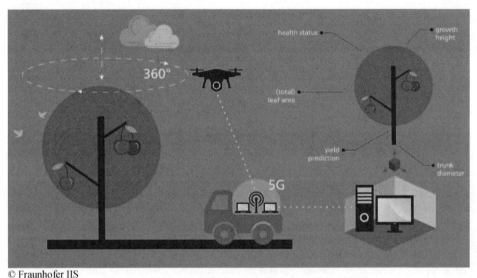

© Fraunhofer IIS

Fig. 1: Workflow of the presented pipeline. The mobile 5G campus network enables the system to operate at different locations

2 Methodology

For the development and testing of our setup, we cooperate with a local cherry orchard research facility, the Obstinformationszentrum Fränkische Schweiz (OIZ). The project is divided into five sub-projects, which will be presented in detail in the following sections.

2.1 Data acquisition and campus network

We use a DJI M300 UAV equipped with a photogrammetric camera to record high-resolution videos. The UAV autonomously flies around the cherry trees on a pre-programmed flight path covering as many views as possible. Through this approach, our solution is very flexible regarding application environments, as data can be acquired very efficiently and independently of the local topography. Since a 5G network is not yet available everywhere, a mobile campus network is used to provide high-speed connectivity between UAV and server. The server provides the resources to evaluate the data immediately after acquisition without needing locally available public data networks.

2.2 3D reconstruction

We use state-of-the-art open-source software to reconstruct the cherry trees from the recorded image stream. The reconstruction is based on Structure from Motion (SfM) [SF16] and Multi-View Stereo (MVS) [Sc16] algorithms. SfM attempts to capture the scene's structure using a moving sensor. It determines camera and scene geometries by matching image features across corresponding images. The camera geometry contains information about the camera's poses and the scene geometry is composed of triangulated points representing the scene as a sparse map. With the retrieved geometry, MVS searches for stereo correspondences in the image stream and computes the depth map for every image individually. Afterwards, the depth images are fused to obtain a dense point cloud. Since monocular reconstructions suffer from scale factor ambiguity, calibration targets are placed in the scene to obtain metrically scaled reconstructions. A result of a cherry tree in vegetation dormancy is depicted in Figure 2 on the left.

2.3 Segmentation

The generated point clouds form the basis for further analysis. In order to do meaningful feature extraction, a semantic understanding of the data (e.g. differentiation between different tree organs and background noise) is required. Our goal is to develop an automated solution for this semantic segmentation based on an artificial neural network (ANN). Manually annotated data is used to train an ANN to map each individual point of the 3D tree reconstruction to a corresponding target class, e.g. cherry, stem, leaf, etc. Prior experiments revealed that relying on network architectures that interpret the data points in the form of graph representations [Wa19] outperforms approaches based on raw point clouds like PointNet++ [Qi17]. To train and infer this learning-based model on large point clouds, we experiment with different data preprocessing steps like subsampling [SGS23] to develop a streamlined pipeline for efficient semantic segmentation of trees. The segmentation results in a separate point cloud for each instance of each organ (e.g. each individual cherry).

2.4 Model and feature extraction

The following processing step automatically extracts relevant and interpretable features from each segmented point cloud. To ensure robust feature extraction, we use a model-based approach incorporating prior knowledge of a cherry tree's morphology. For each tree organ with a corresponding segmentation class, we have developed/will develop a specific geometric model that represents relevant features as numeric parameters. Therefore, the feature extraction step is actually an optimization problem fitting a model to the segmented point cloud by varying the model's parameters.

The cherry tree's leaves are modeled using an existing leaf model adapted to cherry tree leaves. Currently, geometric models for trunks and cherries are being developed. The trunk is modeled using a sequence of cylinders with different radii. The cherries are currently modeled as simple spheres. Other plant organs like blossoms and buds will be considered in the future.

2.5 Knowledge graph

Finally, a cherry tree-specific knowledge graph is constructed to store collected data and phenotypic characteristics. Observing the graph over time can assess a cherry tree's current state and temporal development.

The knowledge graph is based on a Prov-Ontology [PR22], which organizes the results of the feature analysis in a straightforward graph structure. We have developed an appropriate ontology based on the characteristics of a cherry tree. It contains types like tree, branch, trunk diameter, cherry size, etc. Thus, using a semantic query language such as SPARQL, the knowledge graph can be queried to obtain specific information about the tree's features and provides the basis for assessing each tree's performance over time.

3 Results

As interim results, we present the workflow and our pipeline exemplary for one characteristic tree organ – the trunk. Based on already acquired images, multiple cherry trees have been reconstructed as 3D point clouds and annotated, as displayed in Figure 2 on the left. In a subsequent step, an ANN was trained on subsampled parts of these point clouds with the goal of creating a model to perform semantic segmentation, exemplarily shown in Figure 2, by differentiating trunk data points, highlighted in orange, from non-trunk data points.

Fig. 2: Exemplary picture of a 3D cherry tree reconstruction with original colorization (left) and hand-labeled visualization with colored target classes (right). Orange indicates the class tree trunk.

Once a sufficient fraction of the trunk data points has been segmented, they are fitted into the geometric trunk model based on meshes (see Fig. 3). The metric point cloud reconstructions allow us to precisely measure core features like the trunk diameter at arbitrary heights with high precision. In the first tests, the deviation between the measured diameter of the real trunk and our modeled trunk was below 6 mm. We expect the segmentation results to further improve once more training data is available.

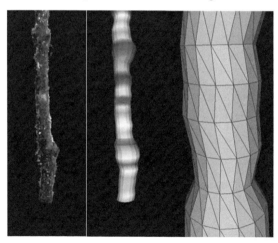

Fig. 3: The segmented point cloud of the trunk (left) and the trunk model was automatically fitted to the data in the feature extraction step (middle). The red mark indicates the detected position where manual measurements of the trunk diameter are taken for validation. At the right, a close-up view of the stem model is shown to illustrate the geometry of cylindrical pieces with different radii.

4 Conclusion and future work

The proposed framework for digital twins of cherry trees opens a wide range of opportunities in research as well as in the operation of orchards. At pomiculture research stations, digital twins could help replace labor-intensive manual assessments of individual trees like counting buds, flowers and fruits with a highly automated data acquisition and evaluation process. Thereby, this technology not only reduces labor expenses but also facilitates an accurate and objective means of monitoring tree conditions. For example, the effect of the environment on the plant can be assessed more accurately. Researchers and farmers could benefit from digital cherry tree twins as collecting objective features over time enables precise monitoring of the seasonal development of trees and thus potentially improves yield predictions and the optimal harvest time estimation. Furthermore, the data can support the farmer in recognizing critical conditions of individual trees, such as drought stress, nutrient deficiency or pest infestation, allowing him to take countermeasures early. This could lead to a more efficient and more sustainable operation of orchards.

Acknowledgment: The For5G project is funded by the 5G innovation program of the German federal ministry for digital and transport under the funding code 165GU103B.

Bibliography

[PCA21]   Pylianidis, C.; Osinga, S.; Athanasiadis, I.: Introducing digital twins to agriculture. In: Computers and Electronics in Agriculture 184/2021, 2021.

[PN22]   Purcell, W.; Neubauer, T.: Digital Twins in Agriculture: A State-of-the-art review, In: Smart Agricultural Technology 3/2023, 2022.

[PR22]   PROV-O: The PROV Ontology, https://www.w3.org/TR/prov-o/, 24.10.2022.

[Sc16]   Schönberger, J. et al.: Pixelwise View Selection for Unstructured Multi-View Stereo, In: European Conference on Computer Vision (ECCV), 2016.

[SF16]   Schönberger, J.; Frahm, J.: Structure-from-Motion Revisited, In: Conference on Computer Vision and Pattern Recognition (CVPR), 2016.

[SGS23]   Scholz, O.; Gilson, A.; Schmid, U.: Spherical Subsampling as a new Approach for Augmentation of 3D Point Cloud Data of biological Scans, In: North American Plant Phenotyping Network, 2023.

[Qi17]   Qi, C. et al.: PointNet++: Deep Hierarchical Feature Learning on Point Sets in a Metric Space, In: Computer Vision and Pattern Recognition, 2017.

[Wa19]   Wang, Y. et al.: Dynamic Graph CNN for Learning on Point Clouds, In: ACM Transactions on Graphics 38/2019, 2019.

Understanding German foresters' intention to use drones

Marius Michels [1], Hendrik Wever[2] and Oliver Mußhoff[3]

Abstract: As unmanned aerial vehicles or drones are a cost-effective tool for several forest management purposes, this is the first study investigating the use of drones for forestry purposes and identifies factors influencing foresters' intention to use drones. By using partial least square structural equation modelling (PLS-SEM), an extended Technology Acceptance Model (TAM) was estimated to investigate factors influencing German foresters' intention to use drones based on a sample with 215 foresters collected in 2022. The TAM explains 42% of the variation in the intention to use a drone of which perceived usefulness for forest management is the strongest predictor. The results are of interest to policy makers, extension services as well as practitioners.

Keywords: drone; digitalization; Technology Acceptance Model; Partial Least Squares Structural Equation Modelling; Unmanned Aerial Vehicle; forestry

1 Introduction

Sustainable forest management and planning requires foresters' understanding of the forest dynamics for which the collection of field data is necessary, which can be time consuming and expensive. Unmanned aerial vehicles or drones can improve the efficiency of traditional acquisition since data collected by satellites or airplanes do not meet the needed spatial and temporal resolutions for regional or local forestry objectives. Drones can overcome these shortcomings as they can be equipped with GIS as well as infrared/thermal and multispectral cameras, which are suitable for real-time applications as they combine high spatial resolution, quick turnaround times and low operational costs. As a result, drones can be used for (precision) forestry inventory, 3D mapping, disease detection and management, forest stockpiles measurement as well as forest fire management and documentation [Da21]. Despite the promised benefits of this instrument for (sustainable) forest management, no study has yet focused on the usage of drones in forestry from the users' point of view. In specific, foresters' perceived barriers and benefits of drone usage have so far not yet been captured in the literature. Furthermore, as drones are not yet widespread, it is worthwhile to focus on foresters' first perceptions and attitudes

---

[1] Georg-August-Universität Göttingen, Department für Agrarökonomie und Rurale Entwicklung, Arbeitsbereich Landwirtschaftliche Betriebslehre, Platz der Göttinger Sieben 5, 37073 Göttingen, marius.michels@agr.uni-goettingen.de, https://orcid.org/0000-0002-4391-4457

[2] Georg-August-Universität Göttingen, Department für Agrarökonomie und Rurale Entwicklung, Arbeitsbereich Landwirtschaftliche Betriebslehre, Platz der Göttinger Sieben 5, 37073 Göttingen, hendrik.wever@stud.uni-goettingen.de

[3] Georg-August-Universität Göttingen, Department für Agrarökonomie und Rurale Entwicklung, Arbeitsbereich Landwirtschaftliche Betriebslehre, Platz der Göttinger Sieben 5, 37073 Göttingen, oliver.musshoff@agr.uni-goettingen.de

towards drones. Hence, this study aims to investigate the factors, which influence the foresters' intention of using drones. For this purpose, an online survey using a standardized questionnaire was conducted from December 2021 to February 2022 resulting in a sample of 215 German foresters. Perceived barriers and benefits in drone use are assessed. The Technology Acceptance Model (TAM) framework [Da89] is adapted in the context of drone usage in forestry and influencing latent factors for foresters' intention to use drones are estimated and evaluated by applying partial least squares structural equation modelling (PLS-SEM) [Ha16].

2 Material, methods and hypothesis generation

Before the survey started, foresters were informed that they could stop the survey at any point. The questionnaire was divided into four parts and was evaluated by practitioners before it was sent to forest managers via e-mails from forestry professional associations in Germany. In the first part, the foresters were asked to provide socio-demographic and forest business-related information. In the second part, foresters were asked if they use a satellite, smartphone and/or tablet for forestry purposes. Foresters who use a smartphone and/or tablet for forestry purposes were asked if they use apps for forestry purposes. The third part of the survey focused on the use of drones. Users of drones were asked what benefits they see in their use. Non-users were asked what potential benefits and what reasons they see against the use of drones. In the last and fourth part, foresters were asked to evaluate 13 statements to estimate a TAM (Fig. 1) on a 5-point Likert scale (1 = high disagreement; 5 = high agreement). The TAM was estimated using PLS-SEM in SmartPLS3 [RWB15] and is explained in the following.

The TAM is the most applied framework to study an individuals' intention to adopt a technology. In the TAM, perceived usefulness is defined as an individuals' belief it enhances their job performance. Perceived ease of use refers to an individuals' belief that using a technology is effortless. The TAM proposes a positive relationship between perceived usefulness and an individuals' intention to use a technology. Hence, the more useful a technology is perceived, the higher the intention is to use a technology (ITU). Likewise, the easier the use of the technology is perceived, the higher the intention is to use the technology. Furthermore, the model assumes that the easier it is perceived to use the technology, the higher the perceived usefulness of the technology [Da89] is. Figure 1 shows the adapted model for the context of drones in forestry and associated hypotheses. Since drones can be useful for the forest management in general (e.g. forest inventory), but also for forest health management in specific (e.g. detection of diseases), the original construct perceived usefulness in the TAM was adapted to the construct perceived usefulness for forest management (PUFM) and supplemented by the upstream construct perceived health management benefits (PHMB). The original construct perceived ease of use is divided in two sub-constructs for the perceived ease of use in controlling the drone for take-off, landing and flying (PEOU – Handling) as well as for the perceived ease of use in the use of data and knowledge of data formats (PEOU – Data).

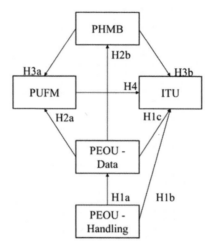

Fig. 1: Proposed TAM for the intention to use drones for forestry purposes. PEOU - Data = Perceived Ease of Use - Data, PEOU - Handling = Perceived Ease of Use - Handling, ITU = Intention to Use Drones, PHMB = Perceived Health Management Benefits, PUFM = Perceived Usefulness for Forest Management, H = Hypothesis

3 Results, discussion and concluding remarks

3.1 Descriptive results

215 usable records remained for the analysis after data cleaning. The average participant is 49 years old and 12% of the participants are female. Out of all participants, 20% completed an apprenticeship in forestry and 47% hold a technical college or university degree in forest science. Based on the self-reported risk attitude, the participants are on average risk-averse. Most participants were the owner (37%) or manager (34%) of the forest enterprise. The larger share of managers might also explain partly the high share of highly educated participants. More than half of the participants work in private forest enterprises (61%) followed by communal forest enterprises (14%) and state-owned forest enterprises (13%). The average size of the forest area managed amounts to 10,594 ha. With respect to digital instruments, 10% of the participants currently use a drone, while 6% have used a drone in the past, but are no longer using one. 27% of the participants use satellites. 69% of the foresters use a smartphone for forestry purposes, of which 62% also use apps related to forestry. A tablet is used by 43% of the foresters for forestry purposes, of which 72% use apps related to forestry. The most stated reasons against the use of drones are that the technical equipment as well as technical knowledge are not yet sufficiently developed to use the data provided by drones. Furthermore, costs are another reason stated against the use of drones (Fig. 2). Drone users and non-users perceive a

timelier response to calamities, a quick help in decision making as well as faster and more accurate data collection as the benefits when using a drone (Fig. 3).

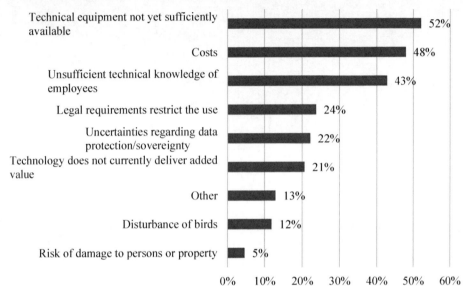

Fig. 2: Reasons against drone usage by non-users (N=194). Multiple answers possible

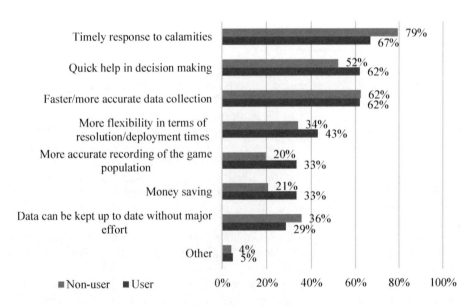

Fig. 3: Benefits of user's drone usage (N=21) and expected benefits for non-user's drone usage (N=194). Multiple answers possible

3.2 Model results, discussion and concluding remarks

All quality criteria given for models in PLS-SEM are met. Indicator reliability (lowest factor loading 0.795, cut-off level > 0.7), internal consistency (lowest composite reliability 0.848, cut-off level > 0.7), convergent validity (lowest average variance extracted 0.658, cut-off level > 0.5) and discriminant validity (highest Heterotrait-Monotrait ratio 0.866, cut-off level 0.9) are given [Ha16]. Explained variance (R^2) of the target construct *Intention to Use Drones* amounts to 42.8 %.

Table 1 shows the estimation results for the PLS-SEM model. All hypotheses are supported by the model except for H1b and H3b. Hence, just being able to control a drone does not statistically significantly positively influence a foresters' intention to use a drone. Likewise, perceived health management benefits do not trigger foresters' intention to use a drone. H1a (PEOU – Handling → PEOU – Data) is given support by the model since the path coefficient is statistically significant with the expected positive sign. If the control of a drone is perceived as easy, then also the use of the data is perceived more easily. Hence, a forester who is informed about the control of a drone, might also be more inclined to become familiar with the data formats and information provided by a drone to use them effectively. H2a (PEOU – Data → PUFM), H2b (PEOU – Data → PHMB) and H1c (PEOU – Data → ITU) are also given support by the model, as all path coefficients are statistically significant with the expected positive sign. The combined results imply that especially knowledge and familiarity about data formats are important to increase the perceived usefulness for forest management, perceived health management benefits and intention to use drones. H3a (PHMB → PUFM) can be given support by the model as the path coefficient is statistically significant with the expected positive sign. Hence, gaining information about the health of the stock via drones increases the perceived usefulness of drones for the forest management. Lastly, H4 (PUFM → ITU) is also supported by the model which implies that if the usage of drones is perceived useful for the forest management, it also increases a foresters' intention to use drones.

The results imply that foresters need more information on how a drone can be used in their forestry enterprise. In detail, it could be helpful for foresters to be educated in the areas in which drones can not only assist them but also the associated cost and time savings as well as potential decision support and improvement. For this purpose, future research should focus in depth on one or two areas of drone application, e.g. forest monitory, and investigate foresters' associated barriers, motives and expectations. This could be helpful to specifically help professionals to assist foresters in understanding the benefits of using a drone. In this context, policy makers should provide (financial) support for consultation and support. With respect to the construct PEOU - Data, the results are also underlined by the descriptive results of barriers stated by the non-user (Fig. 2) that technical knowledge and equipment is not sufficiently developed yet to use the information provided by a drone effectively. Hence, providers of drones should strive for clarification which equipment is needed and in which data formats the information is provided. Furthermore, recurring in-person visits by professionals to assist forest managers in performing certain analysis. Likewise, developers should focus in providing user-friendly software environments to handle data that is also robust to individual tasks. For further research, it could also be of interest to investigate the familiarity of foresters with several aspects of digitalization (e.g. data formats, data security). This could be fruitful for developers to make the software more user-friendly. Furthermore, it could help professionals to assist foresters as they can precisely tackle knowledge gaps. As a result, (perceived) costs for foresters could be reduced (Fig. 2). Costs might not only include the costs of purchasing the software but also time costs for designing and programming flight routes as well as performing technical analysis of the collected data.

H [a]		β [b]	Support H?
PEOU – Handling → PEOU – Data	H1a	0.613***	Yes
PEOU – Handling → ITU	H1b	0.086	No
PEOU – Data → ITU	H1c	0.186*	Yes
PEOU – Data → PUFM	H2a	0.463***	Yes
PEOU – Data → PHMB	H2b	0.149*	Yes
PHMB → PUFM	H3a	0.397***	Yes
PHMB → ITU	H3b	0.030	No
PUFM → ITU	H4	0.473***	Yes

[a] H = Hypothesis, PEOU - Data = Perceived Ease of Use - Data, PEOU - Handling = Perceived Ease of Use – Handling, ITU = Intention to Use Drones, PHMB = Perceived Health Management Benefits, PUFM = Perceived Usefulness for Forest Management, β = Path coefficient
[b] Bootstrapping results with 10,000 subsamples.
R^2(ITU) = 0.429; R^2(PHMB) = 0.022; R^2(PUFM) = 0.426; R^2(PEOU – Data) = 0.376
$p < 0.001$ ($p < 0.01$; $p < 0.05$) is indicated by *** (**; *)

Tab. 1: Estimation results (N=215)

Bibliography

[Da21] Dainelli, R. et al.: Recent advances in unmanned aerial vehicle forest remote sensing – A systematic review. part I: A general framework. Forests 12 (3). 2021.

[Da89] Davis, F.: Perceived Usefulness, Perceived Ease of Use, and User Acceptance of Information Technology. MIS Quarterly 13 (3). 1989.

[Ha16] Hair, J.F. et al.: A primer on partial least squares structural equation modeling (PLS-SEM). Sage publications, Thousand Oaks, California, USA. 2016.

[RWB15] Ringle, C.M.; Wende, S.; Becker, J.-M.: SmartPLS3: Boenningsted, SmartPLS GmbH. https://www.smartpls.com/. Accessed 02 October 2022. 2015.

Chancen der Remote-Zertifizierung im Agrar- und Ernährungssektor am Beispiel ausgewählter IFA-Zertifizierungsaudits von GLOBALG.A.P

Ariane Moser-Beutel[1], Luisa Kiesecker[2], Andreas Meyer-Aurich [3] und Kristian Möller[4]

Abstract: Unternehmen des Agrar- und Ernährungssektors bestreiten zunehmend nicht nur einen Qualitäts- und Nachhaltigkeitswettbewerb, sondern auch einen Wettbewerb um das Vertrauen der Verbraucher*innen. In diesem Zusammenhang stehen Verbraucherschutz und Lebensmittelsicherheit ebenso im Fokus wie Transparenz in der Produktherkunft, sozialverträgliche Arbeitsbedingungen sowie nachhaltiger Ressourceneinsatz und Tierschutz/-wohl. Aus diesem Grund nimmt die Seriosität von Lebensmittel-Produktkennzeichnungen und die Glaubwürdigkeit von nationalen oder internationalen Zertifizierungssystemen eine immer bedeutendere Position ein. Insbesondere Remote Audits, die nicht nur eine Antwort auf das digitale Zeitalter sind, sondern sich auch angesichts von Krisensituationen wie der COVID-19-Pandemie als zukunftsweisende Alternativen erwiesen haben, müssen in ihrer Planung und Durchführung äußerst performant sein. Dies bedingt divergente Scopes, die anhand von aufschlussreichen Daten zu identifizieren sind. Erste Ergebnisse einer Datenanalyse für das Unternehmen FoodPLUS GmbH (GLOBALG.A.P.) deuten darauf hin, dass ein Remote-System unter bestimmten Voraussetzungen durchaus eine Alternative zu bisherigen Vor-Ort-Zertifizierungen sein kann.

Keywords: GLOBALG.A.P., Remote Audits, Zertifizierung, Lebensmittelsicherheit

1 Einleitung

Bis 2050 wird die Weltbevölkerung auf über neun Milliarden Menschen wachsen [UN22]. Insbesondere mit Blick auf die Energieversorgung, die Verfügbarkeit nachwachsender Rohstoffe und die Folgen des Klimawandels wird die Produktion ausreichender, aber auch sicherer und gesunder Nahrungsmittel zu einer globalen Herausforderung. Zur Gewährleistung von Qualität und Sicherheit landwirtschaftlicher Produkte, Dienstleistungen und Unternehmungen fordern Importländer und inländische Abnehmer von Erzeugern die Anwendung von "Good Agricultural Practices", kurz: GAP. Damit werden sowohl Kriterien im Rahmen der Lebensmittelsicherheit, des Umwelt- und

---

[1] Humboldt-Universität zu Berlin, Albrecht Daniel Thaer Institut für Agrarwissenschaften und Gartenbauwissenschaften, 10099 Berlin, moserari@hu-berlin.de,
[2] Humboldt-Universität zu Berlin, Albrecht Daniel Thaer Institut für Agrarwissenschaften und Gartenbauwissenschaften, 10099 Berlin, kieseckl@hu-berlin.de
[3] Leibniz-Institut für Agrartechnik und Bioökonomie, 14469 Potsdam, ameyer@atb-potsdam.de, https://orcid.org/0000-0002-8235-0703
[4] GlobalG.A.P., 50672 Köln, moeller@globalgap.org

Tierschutzes als auch hinsichtlich der Gesundheit und Sicherheit der Angestellten sowie grundlegende Sozialstandards sichergestellt [FA22]. Elementare Vorkehrungen, die ein unterschiedlich hohes Gefahrenpotential bieten und die Lebensmittelsicherheit gefährden, beginnen bereits auf landwirtschaftlicher Betriebsebene, innerhalb der verschiedenen Stufen der Produktionskette. Zur Eindämmung der Risikofaktoren und aufgrund der hohen Nachfrage sowie dem wachsenden Wunsch nach mehr Sicherheit haben sich Zertifizierungssysteme entwickelt, die Standards für „Gute fachliche Praxis" entwickelten und über Anforderungen der staatlichen Regulierung hinausgehen [HBB05; Al09]. Ausgewählte Beispiele hierfür sind die Standards von GLOBALG.A.P., QS Qualität und Sicherheit oder der Red Tractor (UK) [Hu22]. Im Zuge der COVID-19-Pandemie und der damit gekoppelten Reise- und Kontaktbeschränkung, die eine Umsetzung von Vor-Ort-Audits teilweise unmöglich machten, entwickelte die FoodPLUS GmbH, die Eigentümerin der GLOBALG.A.P.-Standards, ein äquivalentes Remote-Verfahren. Die Umstellung auf ein digitales, wirksames und effizientes Zertifizierungsverfahren verlangt andersartige, sowohl unternehmensinterne als auch externe Anforderungen und bringt neue Herausforderungen mit sich. Hierzu zählen die technischen Voraussetzungen und die elektronische Dokumentation ebenso wie die Daten- und Informationssicherheit. Darüber hinaus stellt sich die Frage, inwieweit die Wahl der Prüfmethodik die Integrität und Qualität der Zertifizierung beeinflusst. Der vorliegende Beitrag führt in die Evaluation der erhobenen Daten ein und diskutiert das Potential von Remote Audits im Rahmen von GLOBALG.A.P.-Zertifizierungen

2 Methodisches Vorgehen

Die vorgestellten Analysen basieren auf anonymisierten Daten, die das Unternehmen FoodPLUS mittels GLOBALG.A.P. IFA Audits erhoben und für diese Untersuchung zur Verfügung gestellt hat. Ziel der quantitativen Auswertung ist es, Differenzen zwischen den etablierten Vor-Ort-Audits und der Fernzertifizierung herauszuarbeiten und in einem nächsten Schritt Verbesserungsmöglichkeiten abzuleiten. Insgesamt setzen sich die Datensätze aus den Kategorien Remote Assessed, Audit ID, Standardversion, Certification Option, Status, Producer ID, DOCD (Date of Certificate Decision), Cert Committee Decision, Level, CPNo (= Module des Standards für die kontrollierte landwirtschaftliche Unternehmensführung, kurz: IFA-Standard), CP Description, Answer und Justification zusammen. Für die Auswertung wurden die Einheiten Remote Assessed, Level, CPNo und Answer mit ihren Untereinheiten herangezogen (Abb. 1).

Anhand der Filterfunktion lässt sich dokumentieren, dass 358 Betriebe im Not Remote-Verfahren und 103 Betriebe im Remote-Verfahren geprüft wurden. Daraus ergibt sich folgend eine ungleiche Anzahl an Einträgen: 78.838 für das Not Remote-Verfahren und 23.143 für das Remote-Verfahren. Um eine Aussage darüber treffen zu können, inwieweit die Häufigkeiten der No-Antworten innerhalb der Verfahren variieren, wird eine statistische Auswertung mittels des Statistikprogramms SAS und unter Anwendung des Chi²-Tests, explizit des Homogenitätstests, durchgeführt. Demzufolge werden die Antwortmöglichkeiten (Yes und No), die als nominalskalierte Variablen vorliegen, entsprechend aufsummiert, um schließlich Zahlenwerte für die Berechnung zu erhalten. Grundsätzlich ist zu berücksichtigen, dass immer 2x2-Tabellen vorliegen und sich Yes % und No % zu 100 % aufsummieren. Folgende Null- und Alternativhypothese (H_0, H_A) werden für alle Abfragen, bei einem Signifikanzniveau von $\alpha=0{,}05$, gleich definiert:

H_0: Wahrscheinlichkeit, die Häufigkeiten der No-Antworten innerhalb der Verfahren stimmen überein.

H_A: Wahrscheinlichkeit, die Häufigkeiten der No-Antworten innerhalb der Verfahren stimmen nicht überein.

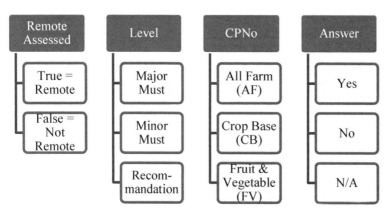

Abb. 1: Ausgewählte Kategorien zur Datenanalyse

3 Ergebnisse

Um ein möglichst umfassendes Ergebnis zu erhalten, sind alle Kontrollfragen der Module AF, CB und FV des IFA-Standards anhand der o.g. Methode ausgewertet worden. Der Übersicht halber werden ausschließlich die Kontrollkategorien mit statistisch signifikanten Unterschieden bei den Antworten abgebildet und erläutert. Tabelle 1 zeigt die Kontrollkategorien der einzelnen Module und ihre Schwerpunktthemen sowie die Levels und die Gesamtzahl der statistisch signifikanten Ergebnisse (innerhalb der beiden Zertifizierungsmethoden).

Es wird ersichtlich, dass im Modul AF die Anzahl der statistisch signifikanten Ergebnissen zwischen den beiden Zertifizierungsmethoden am höchsten ist. Dagegen am geringsten, mit nur zwei Ergebnissen unter dem festgelegten Niveau, im Modul FV. Zudem ist hervorzuheben, dass ausschließlich im Modul AF das Level Major Must (das essentielle Level um eine Zertifizierung zu erhalten) statistisch signifikant auftritt. Hier explizit im sensiblen Bereich der Kategorie 4 „Gesundheit, Sicherheit und Wohlergehen der Arbeitnehmer". Im Vergleich dazu wird in den Modulen CB und FV kein Effekt in Bezug auf das genannte Level beobachtet. Hinsichtlich aller Module ist auffällig, dass das Level Recommendation die höchste Anzahl an Signifikanzen verzeichnet.

Modul	Kontrollkategorie	Level	Anzahl signifikanter Ergebnisse
AF	4. Gesundheit, Sicherheit und Wohlergehen der Arbeitnehmer	Major Must	3
	6. Abfall- und Umweltmanagement, Recycling und Wiederverwendung	Recom.	2
	7. Auswirkungen auf Umwelt und Biodiversität, Energieeffizienz	Minor Must/ Recom.	1/ 5
FV	5. Räumlichkeiten für Arbeitnehmer/ sachgemäße Durchführung von Wasseranalysen	Minor Must/ Recom.	1/ 1
CB	3. Bodenkartierung	Recom.	1
	4. Dokumentation der Düngemittelanwendung	Recom.	1
	5. Optimierte Bedarfsbewässerung und Instandhaltung der Wasserspeicher	Minor Must/ Recom.	1/ 1
	7. Dokumentation der Pflanzenschutzmaßnahmen, Maßnahmen zur Vermeidung von Abdrift der Pflanzenschutzmittel, sachgemäße Rückstandsanalysen	Minor Must/ Recom.	2/ 1
	8. Kalibrierung der Ausrüstung	Recom	1

Tab. 1: Übersicht der Signifikanzen nach Kontrollpunkten

Des Weiteren ist im allgemeinen Vergleich zu erkennen, dass sich die Irrtumswahrscheinlichkeit im Modul CB auf fünf verschiedene Kontrollkategorien verteilt. Wohingegen das Modul FV nur in der Kategorie 5 „Räumlichkeiten für Arbeitnehmer, sachgemäße Durchführung von Wasseranalysen" Effekte zu verzeichnen hat.

Abschließend ist festzuhalten, dass diese Auswertung zunächst nur eine allgemeine Aussage über die Wahrscheinlichkeiten der unterschiedlichen Prüfergebnisse ist. Trotz der signifikanten Ungleichheiten ist zu beachten, dass der Chi^2-Test keine Aussage über die Effektstärke trifft. Bereits kleine Differenzen können zu einem signifikanten Ergebnis führen. Zudem ist festzuhalten, dass alle Erzeuger die Zertifizierung erlangt haben. Dort, wo Kontrollpunkte zunächst nicht erfüllt werden konnten, wurden Korrekturen durchgeführt, sodass die Vorgaben schließlich als zufriedenstellend bewertet wurden.

4 Diskussion und Schlussfolgerung

Insgesamt zeigt der Vergleich der beiden Zertifizierungsverfahren, dass das Remote Verfahren mit leichten Abstrichen zu ähnlichen Ergebnissen führt, wie das Vorort-Verfahren. Damit ist gezeigt, dass ein remote-Verfahren bei der Zertifizierung ersetzen oder komplementieren kann, ohne gravierende Auswirkungen auf die Zertifizierungsergebnisse zu erzeugen.

Die Analyse verfolgt nicht das Ziel, einem der beiden Verfahren – Remote Audits oder Vor-Ort-Audits – eine Präferenz (für die Zukunft) zuzusprechen. Vielmehr liegt der Fokus auf der Identifizierung zentraler Differenzen und der Darstellung gegenwärtiger Herausforderungen, die durch Anpassung interner Prozesse systematisch gesteuert werden können. Hierin sind die Nachhaltigkeitsziele der Vereinten Nationen, die Sustainable Development Goals (SDGs), ebenso einzubeziehen wie der monetäre Aufwand für die Zertifizierung und Audits. Zur Gewährleistung der Wettbewerbsfähigkeit aller Beteiligten sind die aufkommenden Kosten grundsätzlich fair zu gestalten – ohne dabei die Lebensmittelsicherheit oder die sozialen Mindeststandards der Arbeitnehmenden zu belasten.

Die Auswertung der Ergebnisse zeigt mit Blick auf die Kontrollpunkte in der Kategorie 4 „Gesundheit, Sicherheit und Wohlergehen der Arbeitnehmer", dass mitarbeiterfokussierte Kriterien im Rahmen der beiden derzeitigen Auditierungsverfahren eher über ein klassisches Audit vor Ort abgewickelt werden sollten, da hier noch deutliche Unterschiede sichtbar sind. Bei genauerer Betrachtung fällt außerdem auf, dass die signifikanten Unterschiede im Modul CB im Vergleich zu AF und FV in deutlich mehr Kontrollkategorien auftreten. Dies könnte ein Anzeichen dafür sein, dass dieses Modul komplex zu prüfen ist und das Remote-Verfahren noch Optimierungsbedarf aufweist. Darüber hinaus ist zu erkennen, dass im Modul FV kaum signifikante Unterschiede auftreten. Dies könnte darauf hindeuten, dass das zurzeit bestehende Remote-Verfahren bereits gut in diesem Bereich funktioniert. In den Modulen FV und CB sind keine signifikanten Unterschiede des Levels Major Must zu verzeichnen. Ein weiteres, mögliches Indiz für die Eignung eines Remote-Verfahrens. Zudem ist zu erwähnen, dass zu jedem geprüften Kontrollpunkt eine Bewertung, sog. Justification, durch den/die Auditor*in angefertigt wird. Für eine vertiefende Auswertung hinsichtlich des Verbesserungspotentials der beiden Prüfverfahren sollten diese unbedingt einbezogen werden, da sie explizit auf spezifische Problemstellungen hinweisen können. Bei der

Auswertung der Recommendations innerhalb der Kategorie AF und CB ist aufgefallen, dass erheblich mehr Verneinungen bei den Remote Audits als bei den Vor-Ort-Audits aufgetreten sind (in Tab. 1 nicht sichtbar). Diese Verteilung könnte darauf zurückzuführen sein, dass die Kontrollpunkte des Levels Recommendations für das Zertifizierungsergebnis nicht ausschlaggebend sind und deshalb häufiger aus Zeitersparnis einfach mit Nicht erfüllt beantwortet wurden. Auch hier kann eine Analyse der Justifications ggf. zu weiteren Erkenntnissen führen. Schließlich beabsichtigt GLOBALG.A.P. aus den Antworten Erkenntnisse zu sammeln, um daraus in Zukunft neue Kontrollpunkte der Level Minor Must und Major Must zu entwickeln.

Grundsätzlich zeigt die Auswertung, dass sich ein wesentlicher Teil der Kontrollpunkte per Remote Audits überprüfen lassen, ohne dabei Indikatoren für einen möglichen Integritäts- und Qualitätsverlust zu aufzuzeigen. Mehr Auditierung remote durchzuführen bietet einen außerordentlichen Vorteil hinsichtlich der Reduzierung von Transaktionskosten, die in Form von Flug-, Transfer- und Übernachtungskosten entstehen oder Auslagen, die der Einreisegenehmigung dienen. Zugleich können bei geringerer Reisetätigkeit Umweltbelastungen minimiert werden, indem CO_2 eingespart wird. Auch kann die persönliche Sicherheit für Auditor*innen dadurch gewährleistet werden, indem Aufenthalte in politisch unsteten Gebieten vermieden werden. Infolgedessen verringert sich der organisatorische und zeitliche Aufwand erheblich. Diese neu geschaffene Kapazität kann in anderen Bereichen, zum Beispiel staatlichen Überwachungsmaßnahmen, nutzbringend eingesetzt werden.

Literaturverzeichnis

[Al09]   Albersmeier, F.; Schulze, H.; Jahn, G.; Spiller, A. The reliability of third-party certification in the food chain: From checklists to risk-oriented auditing. Food Control 20, S. 927-935, 2009.

[FA22]   Food and Agriculture Organization of the United Nations (FAO): A Scheme and Training Manual on Good Agricultural Practice (GAP) for Fruit and Vegetables, www.fao.org/3/i5739e/i5739e.pdf, Abrufdatum: 26.10.2022.

[HBB05] Hatanaka, M.; Bain, C.; Busch, L.: Third-party certification in the global agrifood system. Food Policy 30, S. 354-369, 2005.

[Hu22]   Hu, L.; Zheng, Y.; Woods, T.A.; Kusunose, Y.; Buck, S. The market for private food safety certifications: Conceptual framework, review, and future research directions. Applied Economic Perspectives and Policy S.1-24, 2022.

[UN22]   United Nations Department of Economic and Social Affairs, Population Division (2022). World Population Prospects 2022: Summary of Results. UN DESA/POP/2022/TR/NO. 3.

Multilokale Modellierung der Bestandesentwicklung von Kleegrasgemengen mittels Leaf Area Index (LAI) und multispektralen Drohnendaten

Konstantin Nahrstedt [1], Tobias Reuter [2], Maria Vergara Hernandez[2], Dieter Trautz[2] und Thomas Jarmer[1]

Abstract: Kleegrasgemenge kennzeichnen sich durch ihre ausgeprägte Heterogenität. Im Hinblick auf die Einsatzmöglichkeit als Futterpflanze sind dabei mögliche Einflüsse auf das Biomasseaufkommen zu berücksichtigen. Biomassebestimmungen sind jedoch zeit- und kostenintensiv. Mittels punktuellen Messungen des Blattflächenindex (engl. LAI) kann das Pflanzenwachstum stichprobenartig ohne größeren Aufwand bestimmt werden. Unter Einsatz von UAV-basierten Bilddaten ist folglich eine Übertragbarkeit auf den gesamten Bestand möglich. Im Zuge dessen wurden auf drei ökologisch bewirtschafteten Kleegrasflächen im Raum Osnabrück zu je zwei Terminen der LAI sowie drohnengestützte Multispektralbilder aufgenommen. Mithilfe der daraus abgeleiteten Vegetationsindizes zeichnete sich bei der Modellierung des LAI für den NDVI ein Abfall in der Modellgüte zwischen den beiden Terminen ab, während der NDRE eine verbesserte Genauigkeit aufwies. Ferner wirkten sich auch die Flächenanteile von Klee und Gras auf die Modellgüte aus.

Keywords: Grünland, Futterbau, Precision Agriculture, Remote Sensing, UAV

1 Einleitung

Kleegras wird in der Landwirtschaft hauptsächlich als Futterpflanze angebaut. In Abhängigkeit von Bodenstruktur, Relief und Nährstoffverfügbarkeit lassen sich zum Teil deutliche räumliche Unterschiede in der phänologischen Entwicklung innerhalb eines Bestandes feststellen. Verschiedene Pflanzenparameter erlauben eine punktuelle Modellierung von Bestandesstruktur und -heterogenität in Kleegrasgemengen. Darunter ist der Blattflächenindex (engl. LAI) ein geeigneter Indikator zur Abschätzung des Biomasseaufwuchses. Mittels drohnengestützter (engl. UAV) Bildaufnahmen kann dieser Parameter flächendeckend erhoben werden. Ziel der Arbeit ist daher die Ableitung des LAI aus UAV-Bilddaten unter unterschiedlichen Standortbedingungen (multilokal).

---

[1] Universität Osnabrück, Institut für Informatik, Arbeitsgruppe Fernerkundung und Digitale Bildverarbeitung, Wachsbleiche 27, 49090 Osnabrück, konstantin.nahrstedt@uni-osnabrueck.de, https://orcid.org/ 0000-0002-8116-3412; thomas.jarmer@uni-osnabrueck.de, https://orcid.org/ 0000-0002-4652-1640

[2] Hochschule Osnabrück, Fakultät Agrarwissenschaften und Landschaftsarchitektur, Am Krümpel 31, 49090 Osnabrück, tobias.reuter@hs-osnabrueck.de, https://orcid.org/0000-0002-2860-5613; m.vergara-hernandez@hs-osnabrueck.de; d.trautz@hs-osnabrueck.de

2 Methodik

Im Rahmen einer zweijährigen Studie im Zeitraum von August 2021 bis Juli 2022 wurden drei ökologisch bewirtschaftete Flächen im Raum Osnabrück zu je zwei Terminen beprobt. Jedes Versuchsfeld beinhaltete 48 in einer Rasterstruktur gleichmäßig über die Fläche angelegte Beprobungsstellen der Größe 0,25 m². Die Position der Beprobungsstellen wurde mittels Stonex GNSS-Empfänger verortet. Zur Bewertung der Bestandesstruktur und Biomasseverteilung erfolgte je Beprobungsstelle die Bestimmung des Leaf Area Index (LAI) mittels LiCOR Plant Canopy Analyzer. Der LAI ist ein dimensionsloser Index zur Bestimmung der Blattfläche je Bodenoberfläche [Br03]. Dazu wurden insgesamt fünf Messungen im Bestand und eine Referenzmessung oberhalb des Bestandes durchgeführt. Zusätzlich erfolgte eine visuelle Schätzung der Klee- und Grasbedeckungsanteile für jede Beprobungsstelle. Zur Gewährleistung einheitlicher phänologischer Stadien je Termin zwischen den Standorten orientierte sich die Wahl der Beprobungstermine an der Wuchshöhe und der Zeitspanne bis zur letzten Mahd. Begleitend zu jedem Aufnahmetermin wurden drohnengestützte Multispektralbilder mithilfe einer DJI Phantom Multispectral aufgezeichnet. Hierbei können spektrale Eigenschaften der Bodenoberfläche in den Wellenlängen Blau (450 nm), Grün (560 nm), Rot (650 nm), RedEgde (720 nm) sowie Nahinfrarot (840 nm) erfasst werden. Die Flughöhe von 12 m lieferte eine räumliche Auflösung von 6 mm pro Pixel. Die Einzelaufnahmen der Drohne wurden unter Einsatz der Bildbearbeitungssoftware AgiSoft Metashape (Version 1.7.2) radiometrisch und geometrisch korrigiert und zu einem Orthophoto mosaikiert. Über einen Lichteinstrahlsensor konnten Beleuchtungsunterschiede während der Überflüge berücksichtigt werden.

Diverse Forschungsarbeiten diskutierten unterschiedliche Vorgehensweisen zur Modellierung des LAI auf Basis von Drohnendaten in verschiedenen landwirtschaftlichen Kontexten [Tu18; Li21]. Weit verbreitet ist die indexbasierte Schätzung des LAI mittels Normalized Difference Vegetation Index (NDVI). Dieser wird zur Bewertung der Bestandesstruktur und Biomasseverteilung eingesetzt. Der NDVI berechnet sich aus den Spektralwerten im nahinfraroten (R_{NIR}) und roten (R_R) Wellenlängenbereich [RHD74]:

$$NDVI = (R_{NIR} - R_R) / (R_{NIR} + R_R) \tag{1}$$

Daneben wird auch der Normalized Difference RedEdge Index häufig zur Modellierung des LAI verwendet. Dieser berücksichtigt in Relation zum NDVI anstelle des roten Wellenlängenbereiches das Reflexionsverhalten im RedEdge (R_{Re}) [Li18]:

$$NDRE = (R_{NIR} - R_{Re}) / (R_{NIR} + R_{Re}) \tag{2}$$

Aus den aufgenommenen UAV-Bilddaten wurden für jeden Termin und Standort NDVI und NDRE bestimmt. Hierbei war das Reflexionsverhalten der Blütenstände an den Kleepflanzen durch spektrale Extremwerte auffällig. Da diese Besonderheit in dem nach Blattfläche definierten LAI nicht gleichermaßen abgebildet werden kann, wurden die Blüten mittels unüberwachter Klassifikation (Iso-Clustering) aus den Bilddaten (Indizes) ausmaskiert. Aus den bereinigten Indizes wurde je Beprobungsstelle repräsentativ der

Mittelwert berechnet und als unabhängige Variable in einem linearen Regressionsmodell zur Modellierung des feldgemessenen LAI eingesetzt. Ziel war die Bewertung der Modellierbarkeit der Biomasseverteilung in Kleegrasbeständen in unterschiedlichen Wachstumsstadien und Standortbedingungen. Darüber hinaus sollte der Einfluss der Bestandeszusammensetzung auf die Modellgüte bestimmt werden. Dazu wurden in einem folgenden Schritt die Beprobungsstellen hinsichtlich der geschätzten Gras- und Kleebedeckungsanteile unterteilt und die korrespondierenden Indexwerte zur Modellierung des LAI eingesetzt. Die Modellvalidierung erfolgte anhand einer Leave-on-out Cross-Validation (LOOCV). Zur Bilddatenverarbeitung wurde die Software Quantum GIS (3.24.1) und für die statistische Analyse der Entwicklungsumgebung R Studio (4.0.3) genutzt.

3 Ergebnisse und Diskussion

Anhand des feldgemessenen LAI ließen sich standort- und terminübergreifend deutliche räumliche Unterschiede feststellen, welche auf die für Kleegrasgemenge typische Heterogenität bedingt durch Aussaat und Bodenunterschiede zurückzuführen sind. Auf Grundlage der UAV-Bilddaten sollte die räumliche Repräsentation dieser Heterogenität mittels NDVI und NDRE über eine Regressionsanalyse abgebildet werden (Tab. 1). Der Stichprobenumfang (N) von 47 für den Standort *Belm* zum zweiten Termin ist auf eine fehlerhafte LAI-Messung zurückzuführen.

Termin	Standort	N	NDVI		NDRE	
			R^2	RMSE	R^2	RMSE
Termin 1						
11.08.2021	Kiesschacht	48	0,35	0,391	0,24	0,424
19.08.2021	Rulle	48	0,58	0,700	0,46	0,801
28.06.2022	Belm	47	0,70	0,287	0,61	0,325
Termin 2						
07.09.2021	Kiesschacht	48	0,04	0,618	0,01	0,625
06.09.2021	Rulle	48	0,57	0,786	0,52	0,824
11.07.2022	Belm	48	0,62	0,508	0,62	0,527

Tab. 1: Modellkoeffizienten der Linearen Regression

Mit Blick auf die Standortunterschiede zeigte sich der Einfluss der Bestandesstruktur auf die Modellierungsgüte. Im vergleichsweise sehr heterogen ausgeprägten Bestand am *Kiesschacht* konnte ein R^2 von lediglich 0,35 (NDVI) bzw. 0,24 (NDRE) erreicht werden. Demgegenüber stehen R^2 von mind. 0,58 (NDVI) bzw. 0,46 (NDRE) bis 0,70 (NDVI) bzw. 0,61 (NDRE) an den insgesamt homogeneren Standorten *Rulle* und *Belm*. Darüber hinaus fiel auf, dass die erklärte Varianz durch den NDVI zum zweiten Termin durchgehend sank. Dies ist auf den Aufsättigungseffekt des NDVI bei hohen LAI-Werten zurückzuführen und deckt sich mit den Beobachtungen vergleichbarer Studien [HSS99; Mu10]. Am Standort *Kiesschacht* wurden hierbei schon zum ersten Aufnahmetermin sehr hohe Messwerte in den Vegetationsindizes ermittelt. Trotz des annähernd gleichen phänologischen Stadiums war der Bestand schon zum ersten Termin dicht strukturiert. Dieser Umstand musste als zusätzlicher negativer Einflussfaktor auf die Modellgüte gewertet werden. Diese Entwicklung war in den NDRE-basierten Modellen zwischen den Terminen 1 und 2 insbesondere für die Standorte *Rulle* und *Belm* nicht zu beobachten, da der Aufsättigungseffekt bei hohen LAI-Werten weniger ausgeprägt war als beim NDVI. Ursache hierfür ist die Tatsache, dass Indizes mit benachbarten Kanälen geringere Sensitivitätsunterschiede für die Reflexion aufweisen und somit stabiler gegenüber Aufsättigung sind [Li18]. Termin 2 am Standort *Kiesschacht* soll hierbei ausgeklammert werden, da das zugehörige Modell keine hinreichende Erklärbarkeit (R^2 = 0.04) lieferte.

Eine visuelle Gegenüberstellung der Vegetationsindizes und LAI-Messungen unterstrich diesen Effekt (Abb. 1). In Korrelation mit dem LAI sättigte der NDVI bereits ab Werten >0,85 auf und reduzierte somit die Modellgenauigkeit. Mit Blick auf die geschätzten Bedeckungsanteile ließ sich dies im Besonderen an Standorten und Terminen mit hohem Kleeanteil beobachten. Ein vergleichbarer Effekt wurde für den NDRE nur am Standort *Rulle* festgestellt. Zum zweiten Aufnahmetermin konnte dort ein geringerer Gras- und damit dominierender Kleeanteil ermittelt werden. Zur Bewertung des Einflusses des Bedeckungsanteils auf die Modellierungsgenauigkeit wurden die Datensätze beider Termine folglich je Standort kombiniert, hinsichtlich Klee- und Grasanteil unterteilt und darauf aufbauend der LAI neu modelliert (Tab. 2). Ein Grasanteil < 30% korrespondiert dabei mit einem Kleeanteil ≥70 %. Diese Aufteilung resultierte aus der Verteilung der geschätzten Flächenanteile über beide Standorte und Termine. Der Standort *Kiesschacht* blieb in diesem Fall unberücksichtigt (vgl. oben).

Standort	Grasanteil	N	NDVI		NDRE	
			R^2	RMSE	R^2	RMSE
Rulle	> 30 %	24	0,78	0,504	0,67	0,612
	< 30 %	72	0,66	0,788	0,66	0,777
Belm	> 30 %	45	0,61	0,503	0,60	0,514
	< 30 %	50	0,53	0,469	0,51	0,477

Tab. 2: Modellkoeffizienten der linearen Regression nach Aufschlüsselung hinsichtlich der Bedeckungsanteile

Die Differenzierung nach Bedeckungsanteilen ermöglichte für grasdominierte Bestände eine Reduzierung des Aufsättigungseffektes in NDVI und NDRE. Dabei zeigte sich außerdem, dass der LAI mithilfe der Stichproben mit einem erhöhten Grasanteil an beiden Standorten besser zu modellieren ist. Mittels NDVI konnte ein R^2 von 0,78 bzw. 0,61 erzielt werden, während über den NDRE ein R^2 von 0,67 bzw. 0,60 erreicht wurde.

Multilokale Modellierung der Bestandesentwicklung 433

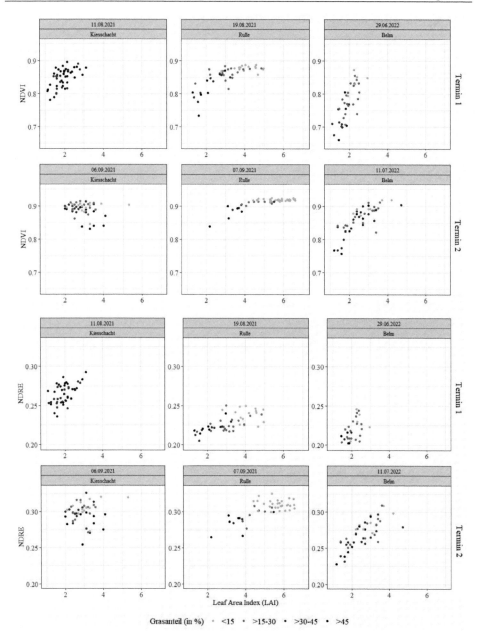

Abb. 1: Korrelationsmatrizen zwischen NDVI/NDRE und LAI

4 Schlussfolgerung

Die für Kleegrasgemenge typische Heterogenität bietet Potential für teilflächenorientierte Managementempfehlungen. Die Quantifizierung dieser Unterschiede ist durch eine räumliche Modellierung von Biomasseindikatoren wie dem LAI mittels UAV-basierter Vegetationsindizes möglich. Bei der Modellierung des LAI ist dabei der Beobachtungszeitpunkt entscheidend. Aufsättigungseffekte im LAI ließen sich standortunabhängig besonders im zweiten Aufnahmetermin beobachten. Ein linearer Zusammenhang kann hier nur eingeschränkt formuliert werden. Hierbei zeigte sich auch die Bedeutung der Bestandeszusammensetzung für die Modellierung, da diese Effekte vorwiegend an Beprobungsstellen mit hohem Kleeanteil zu beobachten waren. Zur Bewertung der Biomasseverteilung in Kleegrasbeständen eignen sich folglich vorwiegend Jungstadien. Dies gilt im Besonderen für kleedominierte Standorte. In den Folgestadien sind Informationen zur Bestandszusammensetzung von besonderer Bedeutung.

Förderhinweis: Die Förderung des Vorhabens erfolgt aus Mitteln des Bundesministeriums für Ernährung und Landwirtschaft (BMEL) aufgrund eines Beschlusses des deutschen Bundestages. Die Projektträgerschaft des Projektes Experimentierfeld Agro-Nordwest erfolgt über die Bundesanstalt für Landwirtschaft und Ernährung (BLE) im Rahmen des Programms zur Innovationsförderung.

Literaturverzeichnis

[Br03] Breda, N. J. J.: Ground-based measurements of leaf area index: a review of methods, instruments and current controversies, Journal of Experimental Botany, 54/392, S. 2403-2417, 2003.

[Li18] Li et al.: Potential of UAV-Based active Sensing for Monitoring Rice Leaf Nitrogen Status, Frontiers in Plant Science, 9/1834, 2018.

[HSS99] Hanna, M. M., Steyn-Ross, D. A., Steyn-Ross, M.: Estimating Biomass for New Zealand Pasture Using Optical Remote Sensing Techniques, Geocarto International, Vol. 14, 3: 89-94, 1999.

[Li21] Lin et al.: UAV Based Estimation of Forest Leaf Area Index (LAI) trough Oblique Photogrammetry, Remote Sensing, 13/803, 2021.

[Mu10] Munoz et al.: Nonlinear hierarchical models for predicting cover crop biomass using Normalized Difference Vegetation Index, Remote Sensing of Environment, 144, S. 2833-2840, 2010.

[RHD74] Rouse, W.; Haas, H.; Deering, W.: Monitoring Vegetation Systems in the Great Plains with ERTS. Proceedings of the Third ERTS Symposium, S. 10-14, 1974.

[Tu18] Tunca et al.: Yield and leaf area index estimations for sunflower plants using unmanned aerial vehicle images, Environ Monit Assess, 190, S. 682, 2018.

An approach to the automation of blueberry harvesting using soft robotics

Eduardo Navas[1], Volker Dworak[2], Cornelia Weltzien[2], Roemi Fernández[1], Mostafa Shokrian Zeini[2], Jana Käthner[2] and Redmond Shamshiri[2]

Abstract: Soft grippers are used to produce a significant advance in the manipulation of delicate objects. A field of application that is presented in this paper is the automation of the selective harvesting of high-value crops. This study addresses a first approach to the design of a soft gripper and its adaptation to a robotic system for blueberry harvesting. The experimental results are carried out to demonstrate the feasibility and effectiveness of the proposed prototype.

Keywords: soft robotics, soft grippers, precision agriculture, end-effectors, blueberry harvesting

1 Introduction

In the last decade, the agricultural sector has undergone a deep transformation to cope with the growing demand for food [UN15; GdPFSNE20]. Among the main tasks in agricultural processes, those that involve the manipulation of fruits and vegetables continue to be one of the most time consuming and labor intensive, resulting in low efficiency and limited competitiveness. For this reason, a great research effort is underway to automate these manual operations, as in the case of selective harvesting, combining multidisciplinary fields such as biological science, control engineering, robotics and artificial intelligence. In this regard, the gripping process in fruit harvesting is one of the most difficult tasks. Since the gripper or end effector not only needs to have the dexterity to manipulate the fruit, but also adapt to the physical properties of it to avoid bruising.

In manual harvesting, humans use their hands to move different elements of the plant, and grasp the fruits and detach them, either directly or with the help of a tool. The kinematics of human hands, the deformability of the skin and muscles, and their sense of touch give us efficient grasping abilities. Attempts to emulate human skills during harvesting have resulted in numerous mechanical end-effectors. With the emergence of soft robotics, grippers based on soft and deformable materials have recently begun to be proposed for agricultural [NFSAGdP21; NFAGdP21] and industrial applications [SFI22]. These soft grippers, which are able to continuously vary their shape without requiring complex multijoint mechanisms, have the potential to provide greater adaptability due to the intrinsic

---
[1] Centre for Automation and Robotics, UPM-CSIC, Carretera CAMPO-REAL Km 0.2, Arganda del Rey, 28500 Madrid, Spanien, eduardo.navas@csic.es, https://orcid.org/0000-0002-4314-4448
[2] Leibniz-Institut für Agrartechnik und Bioökonomie e.V. (ATB); Technik im Pflanzenbau, Max-Eyth-Allee 100; 14469 Potsdam, Deutschland, vdworak@atb-potsdam.de

properties of flexible materials while presenting lower costs and simpler structures and control algorithms than hard end-effectors [PCM17; LKK17].

One of the fields where soft robotics can offer the greatest benefits are tasks related to high-value crops. In this regard, blueberry harvesting has not yet been tackled in terms of robotic automation. Although there have been a few attempts to automate this process, all of them have been unsuccessful, since the machines had not only a lower production, but also a higher percentage of bruised and unripe fruit than manual picking [HCL83]. This work aims to present an approach in the design of a soft gripper based on a deformable structure and pneumatically actuated soft diaphragm actuators for use in automatic blueberry picking. For the design of the actuator, a detailed study for the harvesting of blueberries using finger-tracking gloves is performed, with the objective of studying the optimal movement in the harvesting of the fruit, as well as identifying the pattern of the fingers involved.

2 Materials and methods

The use of finger-tracking gloves is a novel approach to the study of fruit picking. Traditionally, the visual method has been the most common approach in the scientific literature to identify harvesting movements [DSMA15]. This method, although simple, is inaccurate to measure in detail the motion pattern made by humans in fruit harvesting. With the use of finger-tracking gloves, it is possible to monitor numerically the movement patterns performed during agricultural tasks, such as harvesting. This allows analyzing the different picking patterns in a detailed manipulation study. Harvesting experiments were conducted under real conditions at the Leibniz Institute of Agricultural Engineering and Bio-economy e.V. (ATB). The blueberries (Vaccinium corymbosum) selected for the experimental test were harvested from ATB Marquardt fields in Potsdam, Germany. The finger-tracking gloves used, shown in Figure 1, were the Manus Prime 2 gloves [MM22], which can track the angles between the different joints as well as the angle of stretch between the fingers.

Fig. 1: Blueberry harvesting with Manus Prime II finger-tracking gloves

3 Soft gripper for blueberry harvesting

To identify the soft gripper requirements to be fully operational, both fruit characteristics and manipulation patterns data have been collected. Analysis of the latter, as well as meeting other requirements such as simplicity and avoidance of bruising of the fruit, determined the limitations of the design. Finally, the soft gripper has been designed to be used as an end effector on a WLkata Mirobot robotic arm, being able to perform almost all the harvesting movements required, also known in the literature as picking patterns [NFSAGdP21]. The robotic manipulator selected is characterized by its light weight and low power consumption. It is composed of six interlinked segments providing 6 Degrees of Freedom (DoF) with a maximum payload of 0.4 kg in mid-range continuous operation, which is a suitable load capacity for blueberry harvesting.

3.1 Preliminary analysis

For the measurement of blueberry characteristics, 20 blueberry samples were randomly selected. The average diameter was 13 mm, with a maximum of 15 mm and a minimum of 10 mm. The average weight was 1 g, with a maximum and minimum weight of 1.4 g and 0.6 g, respectively. During the harvesting of 20 blueberry samples, the angles of the finger joints were tracked. As shown in Figure 2, the thumb and index finger were used in most of the manipulations. For a fast analysis to identify the fingers involved, the maximum values of the joints were used. The spread angles of the thumb, index, middle, ring and pinky were 39°, 0°, 0°, 0°, 0°, 0°, 0°, respectively. It is important to mention that those spread angles did not vary, particularly the angle of the thumb and index finger remaining completely static, which explains a greater stiffness in the grasping motion. With all of the above, it can be determined that a two-point grip is adequate for blueberry picking.

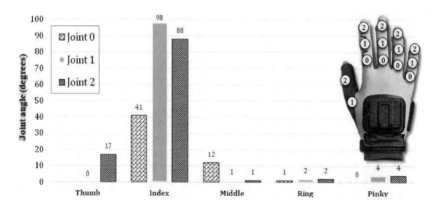

Fig. 2: Maximum angle reached by the finger joints during blueberry harvesting

3.2 Soft gripper design and control system

For the design of the soft gripper, two types of soft technologies were used, flexible structure and pneumatic actuation. The embedding of the pneumatic actuation in the flexible structure is novel, as the literature shows that although these technologies have been used together, they have always been physically independent [TGPSA19]. The integration of them gives the possibility of having a more compact and reliable gripper, as well as making them easy to manufacture by rapid prototyping printers. On this last point, it is important to highlight that the soft gripper has been designed to be manufactured on a 3D printer, as both the structure and the soft actuator have been printed in polylactic acid plastic (PLA) and AR-G1L, respectively. To drive the soft gripper, sensor and control elements are required to ensure the accuracy of the air pressure measurement and constant airflow. In Figure 3, the electronic and pneumatic systems are schematically described. Figure 3a shows that the core of the electronic system is an Arduino, particularly a Mega 2560, which controls the different elements. Furthermore, Figure 3b displays the pneumatic system, which consists of (i) an ONPIRA air pump with an airflow of 0.25 L/s; (ii) a pneumatic solenoid valve; and (iii) a Freescale Semiconductor MP2200DP air pressure sensor (measurement range: 0-200 kPa, linearity: ±0.25%).

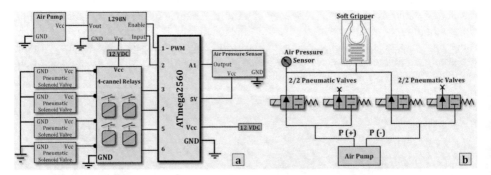

Fig. 3: Schematic presentation of the (a) electrical and (b) pneumatic circuits for controlling the soft gripper

4 Evaluation

In order to validate the feasibility of the proposed approach and evaluate its performance, several experimental tests were carried out as shown in Figure 4. To measure the gripping force a grasping force test was conducted. This study, also known in literature as a slip payload [GKK19], was performed by using a system designed to both generate a downward force and measure the slip payload. The characteristics obtained in the tests were as follows: (i) mass of the soft gripper: 38 g, (ii) max. Displacement of the soft actuator tip (50 kPa): 55 mm, (iii) operating pressure range: -60 – 50 kPa, (iv) slip payload test (-60 kPa): 350 g and (v) mean response time of around 1s. Specifically, Figure 4a shows the gripper is in its extended mode with the position that is used to adapt to the various sizes of blueberries. Figure 4b shows the gripper in its closed mode, where it can be used to move leaves or branches. In Figure 4c, another more precise type of grasping can be seen, where in addition to serving for picking, it also serves for positioning the blueberry in pick-and-place tasks as well as for putting aside branches or leaves for easier picking in a possible bimanipulation situation. Finally, Figure 4d shows the position of the gripper where it has more pulling force to pick the fruit, since the object is completely blocked.

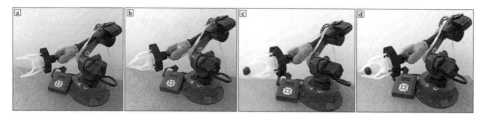

Fig. 4: WLkata Mirobot robotic arm with the custom-designed soft gripper showing (a) extended position, (b) closed position, (c) blueberry grip with the tip, and (d) blueberry grip in locked position for harvesting

5 Conclusion

The soft robotics field has been rapidly increasing, especially in sectors such as manipulation and rehabilitation. However, less attention has been given to the agricultural sector, where soft technology can have a significant impact, enabling the development of robotic harvesters with responsive, safe and adaptable grasping capabilities. This article proposes a soft gripper whose main features are its versatility, ease of manufacture and assembly, affordability and adaptability for small fruits and the capability to handle agricultural products with all the advantages offered by soft robotics technology. For this purpose, an approach to the novel concept of a flexible structure with an embedded soft diaphragm-type actuator is studied by adapting it for blueberry harvesting. As a future line, it is intended to add the gripper to ROS for its integration in the manipulator as well as in the control system.

Acknowledgements: The research leading to these results was supported in part by (i) RoboCity2030-DIH-CM, Madrid Robotics Digital Innovation Hub, S2018/NMT-4331, funded by "Programas de Actividades I+D en la Comunidad de Madrid" and cofunded by Structural Funds of the EU, (ii) MOVILIDAD DOCTORANDOS Y DOCTORANDAS UVa 2022, (iii) CSIC under Grant 202050E099, Proyecto Intramural IAMC-ROBI (Inteligencia Artificial y Mecatrónica Cognitiva para la Manipulación Robótica Bimanual, (iv) FoodChain project funded Federal Ministry for Digital and Transport (BMDV), (v) the Grant PID2020-116270RB-I00 funded by MCIN/AEI/10.13039/501100011033 and (vi) the Grant PDC2021-121578-I00 funded by MCIN/AEI/10.13039/501100011033 and by the "European Union NextGenerationEU/PRTR".

Bibliography

[UN15] UN DESA. United Nations Department of Economic and Social Affairs, Population Division. World Population Prospects: The 2015Revision, Key Findings and Advance Tables; Technical Report; Working Paper No. ESA/P/WP. 241; UN DESA: New York, NY, USA, 2015.

[GdPFSNE20] Gonzalez-de-Santos, P., Fernández, R., Sepúlveda, D., Navas, E., Emmi, L., & Armada, M. Field robots for intelligent farms – Inhering features from industry. Agronomy, 10(11), 1638, 2020.

[HCL83] Hall, I. V., Craig, D. L., & Lawrence, R. A. A comparison of hand raking and mechanical harvesting of lowbush blueberries. Canadian Journal of plant science, 63(4), 951-954, 1983.

[DSMA15] Dimeas, F., Sako, D. V., Moulianitis, V. C., & Aspragathos, N. A. Design and fuzzy control of a robotic gripper for efficient strawberry harvesting. Robotica, 33(5), 1085-1098, 2015.

[NFSAGdP21] Navas, E., Fernández, R., Sepúlveda, D., Armada, M., & Gonzalez-de-Santos, P. Soft grippers for automatic crop harvesting: A review. *Sensors, 21*(8), 2689, 2021.

[NFAGdP21] Navas, E., Fernández, R., Armada, M., & Gonzalez-de-Santos, P. Diaphragm-type pneumatic-driven soft grippers for precision harvesting. *Agronomy, 11*(9), 1727, 2021.

[MM22] Manus Meta, www.manus-meta.com, Stand: 18.10.2022.

[SFI22] Soft Robotics Inc., www.softroboticsinc.com, Stand: 18.10.2022.

[PCM17] Polygerinos, P., Correll, N., Morin, S. A., Mosadegh, B., Onal, C. D., Petersen, K. & Shepherd, R. F. Soft robotics: Review of fluid-driven intrinsically soft devices; manufacturing, sensing, control, and applications in human-robot interaction. Advanced Engineering Materials, 19(12), 1700016, 2017.

[LKK17] Lee, C., Kim, M., Kim, Y. J., Hong, N., Ryu, S., Kim, H. J., & Kim, S. Soft robot review. International Journal of Control, Automation and Systems, 15(1), 3-15, 2017.

[TGPSA19] Tawk, C., Gillett, A., in het Panhuis, M., Spinks, G. M., & Alici, G. A 3D-printed omni-purpose soft gripper. IEEE Transactions on Robotics, 35(5), 1268-1275, 2019.

[GKK19] Galley, A., Knopf, G. K., & Kashkoush, M. Pneumatic hyperelastic actuators for grasping curved organic objects. In *Actuators* (Vol. 8, No. 4, p. 76). MDPI, 2019, November.

"Ready for Autonomy (R4A)": concept and application for autonomous feeding

Burawich Pamornnak[1], Christian Scholz[1], Eduard Gode[1], Karen Sommer[1], Timo Novak[1], Steffen Hellermann[2], Benjamin Wegmann[2], and Arno Ruckelshausen[1]

Abstract: This paper presents the development of the "Ready for Autonomy (R4A)" application for evaluating the feasibility of integrating an autonomous feeding machine Strautmann Verti-Q into farmyards and evaluating the machine's performance. The proposed application consists of three main R4A checklists for telling whether the farmyard, the machine, and the farmer are ready for autonomy or not. The farmyard is the first part to be checked with the R4A application with the Verti-Q system requirements. The R4A result will be instantly generated from the application based on the Boolean function. The second part is the machine operation record which tells the overall performance of the Verti-Q machine as the R4A distribution results, e.g., excellent, good, and failure. The final part is the farmer operation training in manual and autonomous modes, in which farmers have to go through every topic to be ready to use the machine. From the experimental results, seven farmyards were observed with the R4A application. Therefore, the four farmyards are ready for autonomy with different R4A levels. The minimum working condition of the Verti-Q machine has been tested on the lowest R4A level farmyard. The distribution results from the prototype machine with 218 autonomous feeding jobs, achieving 42% in excellent distribution, 38% in good condition, and 21% in failure caused by various reasons, e.g., hardware, software, and user error, respectively. These results show the possibility of using the improved version of the autonomous feeding machine in the farmyard for sustainable farming in the future.

Keywords: feeding machine, autonomous system, feed distribution, farm-scale experiment, self-driving, mobile application

1 Introduction

A development study for the first autonomous feeding machine covering the complete feeding process on the farm ("Verti-Q") was presented at Agritechnica 2017 by Strautmann. This machine automatically picks up feed components in various silos, navigating across the yard to the barn, mixing the feedstuffs and feeding it to the cows [Ru21]. The advantage of time, feed management (Verti-Q Fütterungssystem), and the flexibility of the autonomous and person-bound operation make the system attractive to

---
[1] Hochschule Osnabrück, Competence Center of Applied Agricultural Engineering (COALA), Nelson Mandela-Str. 1, D-49076 Osnabrück, Germany,
{b.pamornnak, c.scholz, e.gode, k.sommer, timo.novak, a.ruckelshausen}@hs-osnabrueck.de
[2] B. Strautmann & Söhne GmbH u. Co. KG, D-49196 Bad Laer, Germany
{st.hellermann, b.wegmann}@strautmann.com

the market. However, due to the operation safety system with high-performance safety sensors [Me18; Me21], the system commissioning process and the specific working conditions are still needed. In the research project "Experimentierfeld Agro-Nordwest", the concept of this work focuses on integrating the Verti-Q machine into the minimum requirement farmyard and testing the prototype of the Verti-Q machine in the real farm test for the autonomous feeding mode. Various parameters from the Verti-Q system requirements, such as the driving path parameters, landmarks, and safety issues, can be confusing to process at the R4A level.

This work presents a mobile application called "R4A application", which takes three important keys to define if a farmyard, the machine, and the farmer are ready for autonomy or not. As a consequence, R4A can be a valuable tool for speeding up the transfer of sustainable technologies into practice. Based on the Google spreadsheet database, this application was developed on the Glide App platform, which is available for Android and iOS systems.

The advantage of the generated log file from the R4A mobile application is that it helps to analyze the R4A level and can easily track the experiment process. The R4A level results show the possibility of improving the prototype of the Verti-Q machine in the farmyard for sustainable farming in the future.

2 Material and methods

This section describes the R4A application implementation, and Figure 1 shows the design concept. The application consists of three main parts for R4A levels, the farmyard requirement, the machine operation record, and farmer operation training, and the additional information part, e.g., the address of the farmyard, the number of cows, the mixing ratio as well as the manual feeding process.

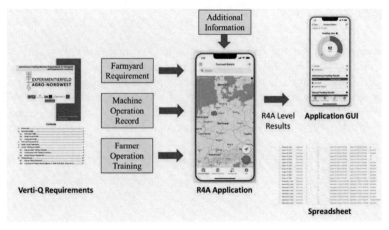

Fig. 1: R4A application structure

2.1 Ready for Autonomy of the farmyard

This experiment developed the R4A levels for farmyards based on the Boolean function. From the Verti-Q system requirements, as shown in Table 1, all required values have to be checked as "Yes", and the R4A level for the farmyard can be calculated from Eq. 1, and the R4A result will be instantly generated from the application. If not ready for autonomy, the farmer has to improve the farmyard condition if possible. If the farmyard is ready for autonomy with the R4A level, it means that it is technically ready to use the Verti-Q machine.

$$R4A_{farmyard} = tw_v + ch_v, \text{ where } tw_v \geq 3.5 \text{ and } ch_v \geq 3.5 \tag{1}.$$

Symbol	Track Parameters	Required	Scoring
p_a	Acceptable gravel and the pavement surface	Yes	
g_a	The gradient between indoor and outdoor	<5 °	
i_a	Incline path	<8 °	Yes = 1
s_a	Step between indoor and outdoor	<30 mm	No = 0
lm_a	Landmark installation area available	Yes	
sf_a	Straight feeding tables	Yes	
fm_a	Farmer confirmation that no persons in the autonomous area	Yes	
tw_v	Track width everywhere (Minimum requirement)	>3.5 m	tw_v
ch_v	Clearance height (includes cattle house gate)	>3.5 m	ch_v

Tab. 1: Verti-Q system requirements

To test the Verti-Q machine on the lowest limitation, this experiment will select the farmyard from the lowest score of $R4A_{farmyard}$. Figure 2 shows the commissioning process. Due to the Verti-Q machine navigation system using ultrasonic sensors to navigate the machine while feeding autonomously, ultrasonic landmark installation and landmark calibration with the Verti-Q machine are needed.

Landmark installation   Installed landmark   Landmark Calibration

Fig. 2: Verti-Q system commissioning process

2.2 Ready for Autonomy of the machine

This part is the machine operation record. The feeding job details from Verti-Q, e.g., date-time, distribution results, photographs, and error codes, will be recorded and reported on the R4A application. The R4A level for the machine will be categorized into three levels by the distribution level, e.g., excellent means the feed distribution is uniform, not lacking or exceeding, good means the feed distribution is uniform was slightly uneven but can also be distributed evenly for all cows, and failure means the autonomous mode cannot work or it does not finish the feeding job because of the system interruption. In case of a machine failure, these records will be investigated by the authorized technician.

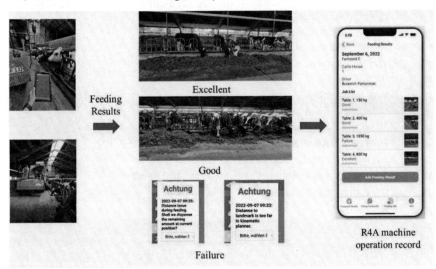

Fig. 3: R4A machine operation record

2.3 Ready for Autonomy of the farmer

This part is the farmer operation training in manual and autonomous modes. In the manual mode, farmers must learn to use the Verti-Q machine, e.g., driving, taking feedstuffs, mixing, weight monitoring, protector control, etc. The user instruction for the autonomous user interface called "Verti-Q Fütterungssystem", e.g., feeding table management and feed schedule, will be described in this part. In case of a system interruption, system failure, and emergency issue, farmers must be able to solve these problems, which can use the emergency stop system and switch back to operating in manual mode. However, the people operating the Verti-Q machine are not only the farmer. The checklist for authorized technicians is also included in this section, e.g., system commissioning, machine calibration, and machine maintenance processes. Moreover, based on the feedback of the farmers the R4A human-machine-interface can be improved.

3 Results and discussion

For the farmyard, Table 2 shows the results of the R4A level for eight farmyards, the prototype farmyard (Farmyard A), and the experimental farm (Farmyard B-H) from the site survey. From Farmyard B-H, three of them, Farmyard B, E, and F, are not ready for autonomy due to the old-style cattle house, big steepness in front of the gate, and too small entrance gate. On the other hand, four of them, Farmyard C,D,G, and H are ready for autonomy. To investigate the minimum requirement, the lowest R4A level, "Farmyard C", was chosen in this experiment with the smallest cattle house gate. For the Verti-Q machine, the distribution records are shown in Table 3. This experiment is divided into three phases, P1 for testing the Verti-Q prototype, P2 for testing the improved version of Verti-Q, and P3 for testing the Verti-Q on the new commissioning area (Farmyard C). The percent failure of P1-P3 achieves 53%, 15%, and 12%, respectively.

Track Parameters	Farmyard							
	A	B	C	D	E	F	G	H
p_a: Acceptable gravel and the pavement surface (Yes)	Y	Y	Y	Y	Y	Y	Y	Y
g_a: The gradient between indoor and outdoor (<5 °)	Y	Y	Y	Y	Y	Y	Y	Y
i_a: Incline path (<8 °)	Y	Y	Y	Y	N	Y	Y	Y
s_a: Step between indoor and outdoor (<30 mm)	Y	Y	Y	Y	N	Y	Y	Y
lm_a: Landmark installation area available (Yes)	Y	N	Y	Y	Y	Y	Y	Y
sf_a: **Straight feeding tables** (Yes)	Y	Y	Y	Y	Y	Y	Y	Y
fm_a: Farmer confirmation that no persons in the autonomous area (Yes)	Y	N	Y	Y	Y	Y	Y	Y
tw_v: Track width everywhere (>3.5 m)	Y	N	Y	Y	Y	Y	Y	Y
ch_v: Clearance height (>3.5 m)	Y	N	Y	Y	Y	N	Y	Y
$R4A_{farmyard}$	9	-	7.1	7.8	-	-	9.5	8.4

Tab. 2: R4A level for farmyard results

Phase/Farmyard	P1/A		P2/A		P3/C		Total	
	Jobs	%	Jobs	%	Jobs	%	Jobs	%
Excellent	7	18%	33	32%	51	67%	91	42%
Good	12	30%	54	53%	16	21%	82	38%
Failure	21	53%	15	15%	9	12%	45	21%
Total	40	100%	102	100%	76	100%	218	100%

Tab. 3: R4A level for Verti-Q machine results

The last checklist is the R4A level for the user/farmer. This work has classified users into three levels consisting of L1: farmers who operate the feeding machine, L2: authorized technicians who operate the commissioning process and fix some problems, and L3: Strautmann Product R&D: who can improve the performance of the machine. Table 4 shows the percentage of autonomous failure solved by the user at each level.

Problem solved by user level	Phase P1/A	Phase P2/A	Phase P3/C
L1: Farmers	13.0%	20.0%	33.3%
L2: Authorized Technician	34.0%	46.7%	56.6%
L3: Strautmann Product R&D	53.0%	33.3%	11.1%

Tab. 4: R4A machine failure solved by each user level

4 Conclusions

The "Ready for Autonomy (R4A)" application was developed for evaluating the R4A levels for the farmyard, the machine, and the farmer. In the experiment, the autonomous failure was reduced from 53% to 12% from three phases, with a 21% failure average. In the failure case, the farmers and authorized technicians can solve the problem by themselves, increasing from 13.0% to 33.3% and 34.0% to 56.6%, respectively. While the problem solved by Strautmann R&D decreased from 53% to 11.1%. These results show the possibility of using the improved version of the autonomous feeding machine in the farmyard for sustainable farming in the future.

Acknowledgement: The project "Agro-Nordwest" is supported by funds from the Federal Ministry of Food and Agriculture (BMEL) based on a decision of the Parliament of the Federal Republic of Germany via the Federal Office for Agriculture and Food (BLE) under the innovation support program. We also thank Heinz Georg Plogmann-Große Börding and Stefanie Grothmann, the farmer who gave us the experiment area.

Bibliography

[Ru21]   Ruckelshausen, A., Gode, E., Pamornnak, B., Scholz, C., Hellermann, S., Wegmann, B.: Datenfluss im Bereich Fütterungsmanagement – Praxis der Feldrobotik: Autonome Fütterung. In DigiMilch: Einblicke in die Zukunft der Milcherzeugung, Online-Vortragsveranstaltung. Grub, S.38-42, 17 Juni 2021.

[Me21]   Meltebrink, C., Komesker, M., Kelsch, C., König, D., Jenz, M., Strotdresch, M., ... & Ruckelshausen, A. (2022). REDA: A New Methodology to Validate Sensor Systems for Person Detection under Variable Environmental Conditions. Sensors, 22(15), 5745.

[Me18]   Meltebrink, C., Malewski, B., Trabhardt, A., Igelbrink, T., Hellermann, S., & Ruckelshausen, A.: Vom manuellen Selbstfahrer zum autonomen Futtermisch-wagen: Konzept, Technologie und Sicherheit. 38. GIL-Jahrestagung, Digitale Marktplätze und Plattformen, 2018.

Investitionsförderung für Agrarsoftware?

Empirische Untersuchung zum investiven Unterstützungsbedarf von Landwirten in Baden-Württemberg

Sara Anna Pfaff[1] und Michael Paulus[2]

Abstract: Die Nutzung von digitalen Technologien kann einen Beitrag zur Resilienz der Landwirtschaft leisten. Allerdings wird die Adoption bisher von finanziellen Barrieren gehemmt, daher verfolgen (öffentliche) Investitionsförderprogramme das Ziel, die Verbreitung von digitalen Technologien zu fördern. Gleichzeitig ist unbekannt, inwiefern Landwirte finanzielle Unterstützungswünsche in bestimmten Technologiebereichen äußern und ob diese von soziodemographischen Faktoren abhängig sind. Im Rahmen des DiWenkLa Projektes wurde 2021 eine quantitative Befragung von Landwirten in Baden-Württemberg durchgeführt. 290 Landwirte äußerten sich hierbei zur Investitionsförderung für Agrarsoftware. Die Ergebnisse der statistischen Tests bestätigen, dass bei den befragten Landwirten kaum signifikante Unterschiede für das Interesse an Investitionsförderung zu Agrarsoftware in Abhängigkeit von soziodemographischen und betrieblichen Merkmalen bestehen. Es wird vermutet, dass sich das auf die Skalenneutralität von Softwareanwendungen zurückführen lässt, welche diese erschwinglich für kleinstrukturierte Betriebe macht. Ferner ist anzunehmen, dass sich das bei investitionsintensiveren digitalen Technologien anders verhält, was es in weiteren Forschungsschritten zu untersuchen gilt.

Keywords: Digitalisierung, Agrarsoftware, Investitionsförderung, Economies of Scale

1 Einleitung

Grundsätzlich lassen sich digitale Technologien in softwarebasierte Informations- und Kommunikationstechnologien (IKT) und digitale Land- und Tierhaltungstechnik einteilen [BDP21]. Der vorliegende Beitrag fokussiert sich auf die Agrarsoftware (IKT). Langfristig kann die Nutzung digitaler Technologien landwirtschaftliche Betriebe im ökonomischen, ökologischen und sozialen Bereich für eine nachhaltige, resiliente Zukunft unterstützen. Größtmögliche Effekte stellen sich jedoch erst durch eine stärkere Verbreitung auf den Betrieben ein [Je12; Sh18]. Zwar nutzen Landwirte zunehmend digitale Technologien, jedoch schwanken die Verbreitungsintensitäten in Abhängigkeit von der ausgewählten Technologie [GG22]. IKT werden in Relation zu den anderen Technologien häufiger eingesetzt, allerdings ist die Verbreitung insgesamt begrenzt [GG22]. In der bisherigen Forschung zeigt sich, dass Betriebe je nach strukturellen oder

---

[1] Hochschule für Wirtschaft und Umwelt Nürtingen-Geislingen, Institut für Angewandte Agrarforschung (IAAF), Neckarsteige 6-10, 72622 Nürtingen, sara.pfaff@hfwu.de
[2] Universität Hohenheim, Fachgebiet Kommunikation und Beratung in ländlichen Räumen (430a), Schloss Hohenheim 1C, 70599 Stuttgart, m.paulus@uni-hohenheim.de

soziodemographischen Faktoren unterschiedliche Investitionsstrategien verfolgen [SS18], was sich auch auf die Adoption von digitalen Technologien übertragen lässt. Gleichzeitig ist bekannt, dass im Adoptionsprozess von Landwirten hinsichtlich digitaler Technologien finanzielle Aspekte eine wesentliche Barriere in der Innen- und Außenwirtschaft darstellen, was vor allem auf Skaleneffekte zurückzuführen ist [Sh11; HMP12] und weshalb finanzielle Unterstützungsangebote gefordert werden. Ferner besteht die Annahme, dass die Investition in eine Agrarsoftware skalenneutraler ist als bei einer komplexeren (physischen) digitalen Technologie. Denn gemäß [GGS21] sind IKT weniger kostenintensiv und einfacher in den Betriebsalltag zu integrieren. Unbekannt ist jedoch, inwiefern (i) finanzielle Unterstützungswünsche im Hinblick auf Agrarsoftware bestehen und (ii) ob es hierbei soziodemographische und betriebliche Abhängigkeitsfaktoren gibt. Daher lauten die Forschungsfragen für den folgenden Beitrag: (i) Wie äußert sich das Interesse der Landwirte in Baden-Württemberg an Investitionsförderung für Agrarsoftware? (ii) Bestehen Interessensunterschiede in Abhängigkeit von soziodemographischen und betrieblichen Faktoren?

2 Material und Methoden

Im Rahmen des DiWenkLa Projektes wurde 2021 eine quantitative Befragung von Landwirten in Baden-Württemberg durchgeführt. Zur Teilnehmerrekrutierung wurde ein Convenience Sampling Verfahren verwendet: Die Landwirte wurden mittels eines Beilegers im Gemeinsamen Antrag, (Online-) Anzeigen in Fachmedien und verschiedener Mailverteiler von landwirtschaftlichen Organisationen zur Teilnahme aufgerufen. Neben der Erfassung der soziodemographischen Merkmale, der Technologienutzung sowie Nutzungserfahrung wurden die Unterstützungswünsche der Landwirte erfragt. Aufgrund des Samplingverfahrens ist die vorliegende Erhebung nicht repräsentativ [St21], was bei der weiteren Interpretation der Ergebnisse beachtet werden sollte.

Insgesamt nahmen 749 Landwirte teil, nach der Datenbereinigung konnte eine Stichprobe von 302 in die weitere Auswertung miteinbezogen werden. 290 von 302 Landwirten äußerten sich, ob und zu welchen Technologiebereichen sie finanzielle Unterstützungsangebote wünschen. Aufgrund der Stichprobengröße und -verteilung wurde ein deskriptiver Ansatz gewählt. Die Auswertung der Daten erfolgte mit SPSS 27. Anhand von statistischen Tests (χ^2 und U-Test) wurden die Unterschiede zwischen Landwirten mit und ohne Interesse an Investitionsförderung zu Agrarsoftware analysiert. Unabhängige Variablen sind hierbei das Alter, Geschlecht, Berufserfahrung, Ausbildung, Erwerbsform, Rechtsform, Bewirtschaftungsweise, Gesamtfläche sowie Nutzung von IKT und Anzahl der insgesamt adoptierten digitalen Technologien. Anhand eines zweiseitigen U-Tests mit einem Signifikanzniveau (α) von 5 % wurde die statistische Berechnung durchgeführt. Die H_0 Hypothese verfolgt die Annahme, dass es keinen Unterschied in der zentralen Tendenz des Interesses an der agrarsoftwarespezifischen Investitionsförderung in Abhängigkeit von soziodemographischen Merkmalen gibt.

3 Ergebnisse

3.1 Deskriptive Ergebnisse

Im Sample der 290 Landwirte ist der Großteil der Landwirte zwischen 50-59 Jahre alt, 87 % sind männlich, 47 % haben eine landwirtschaftliche Aus- und Weiterbildung absolviert und verfügen durchschnittlich über 27 Jahre Berufserfahrung als Landwirt. Ferner sind die Betriebe zu 77 % Einzelunternehmen, werden zu 59 % im Haupterwerb geführt und zu 80 % konventionell bewirtschaftet. Im Durchschnitt sind die Betriebe 74 ha groß. Ein Vergleich mit der Agrarstatistik zeigt, dass der Datensatz nicht repräsentativ ist, z. B. bzgl. der Flächenausstattung (36 ha [St21]) und der Nebenerwerbsanteile (57 % [St21]). 60 % der Landwirte nutzen bereits IKT. Die Ergebnisse zeigen, dass 81 % der 290 Betriebe keine zukünftige Investitionsförderung zu Agrarsoftware wünschen, während sich 19 % für investive Fördermaßnahmen für Agrarsoftware interessieren.

3.2 Ergebnisse des χ2 und U-Test

Unabhängige Variable	Test	Interessierte (N=54)	Nichtinteressierte (N=236)
Alter	χ^2		
≤29 Jahre		7 (13 %)	21 (1 %)
30 – 39 Jahre		13 (24 %)	50 (21 %)
40 – 49 Jahre		9 (17 %)	51 (22 %)
50 – 59 Jahre		20 (37 %)	86 (36 %)
≥ 60 Jahre		5 (1 %)	28 (12 %)
Mann (Ja)	χ^2	47 (87 %)	205 (87 %)
Ausbildung	χ^2		
Hochschulabschluss		12 (22 %)	62 (23 %)
Aus- und Weiterbildung		22 (41 %)	114 (48 %)
Sonstiger Abschluss		20 (37 %)	60 (25 %)
Berufserfahrung in Jahren	U-Test	⌀ 25,7 ± SD 13,2	⌀ 27,7 ± SD 13,2

Tab.1: Ergebnisse der statistischen Tests, Teil 1; eigene Erhebung; p* ≤ 0,05, ** ≤ 0,01

Unabhängige Variable	Test	Interessierte (N=54)	Nichtinteressierte (N=236)
Einzelunternehmen (Ja)	χ^2	42 (78 %)	180 (76 %)
Haupterwerb (Ja)*	χ^2	24 (44 %)	147 (62 %)
Konventionell (Ja)**	χ^2	51 (94 %)	181 (77 %)
Gesamtfläche in ha	U-Test	⌀ 59,6 ± SD 64,5	⌀ 76,9 ± SD 77,9
Nutzung von IKT (Ja)	χ^2	38 (70 %)	136 (58 %)
Anzahl genutzter DT	U-Test	⌀ 3,3 ± SD 3,5	⌀ 2,7 ± SD 3,1

Tab. 2: Ergebnisse der statistischen Tests, Teil 2; eigene Erhebung; p* ≤ 0,05, ** ≤ 0,01

Die statistischen Tests, ob und inwiefern Zusammenhänge zwischen den persönlichen und betrieblichen Faktoren sowie der gewünschten Investitionsförderung bestehen, bestätigen überwiegend die H_0 Hypothese, dass es beim Interesse der Landwirte hinsichtlich der finanziellen Förderungen von Agrarsoftware kaum signifikante Unterschiede gibt, siehe Tabelle 1 und 2. Signifikante Zusammenhänge sind nur feststellbar in Abhängigkeit von der Erwerbsform (p=0,016) und Bewirtschaftungsweise (p=0,003). Gleichzeitig wird ersichtlich, dass die Effektstärke sowohl bei der Erwerbsform (φ=0,141) als auch bei der Bewirtschaftungsweise (φ=0,173) schwach ist [Co88]. Hinsichtlich der Erwerbsform zeigt sich, dass 147 der Haupterwerbsbetriebe kein Interesse an einer Investitionsförderung benennen, 24 Betriebe zeigen Interesse. Bei der Bewirtschaftungsweise äußert sich dies insofern, dass 181 der konventionellen Betriebe keine Investitionsförderung für Agrarsoftware wünschen, 51 Betriebe allerdings schon.

4 Diskussion

Die Ergebnisse belegen empirisch, dass bei den befragten Landwirten kaum signifikante Unterschiede im Interesse an Investitionsförderung zu Agrarsoftware in Abhängigkeit von soziodemographischen und betrieblichen Merkmalen bestehen. Das kann zu einem gewissen Maß damit begründet werden, dass Agrarsoftware, von einem Kostenstandpunkt aus, entweder verhältnismäßig günstig in der Anschaffung ist oder dass die Kosten nach Anzahl der Produktionseinheiten berechnet werden, wie z. B. Betrag je Hektar oder Tier. Gleichermaßen bekunden die Landwirte ein geringes Interesse an investiven Fördermaßnahmen für Agrarsoftware. Signifikante Zusammenhänge zeigen sich bei der Erwerbsform und der Bewirtschaftungsweise. Dies äußert sich jedoch insofern, dass konventionelle (Haupterwerbs-) Betriebe verhältnismäßig weniger Interesse an Investitionsförderung zeigen. Dies lässt sich mit der u. U. besseren (finanziellen) Ressourcenausstattung solcher Betriebstypen [St21] oder der bereits praktizierten

Nutzung von IKT erklären. Die Vermutung der Skalenneutralität und risikoärmeren Investition bei einer Agrarsoftware bieten einen (erleichterten) Einstieg in die Digitalisierung für kleinstrukturierte Agrarregionen wie z. B. Baden-Württemberg. Denn es ist bekannt, dass hier spezifische Anforderungen durch die kleine Skalierung vorliegen [Pf22]. Somit bietet sich hier die Agrarsoftware als skalenneutraler Einstieg in die Digitalisierung an, ohne dass höhere Investitionsrisiken in Kauf genommen werden müssen. Es besteht weiterhin die Annahme hinsichtlich der Investitionsförderlandschaft in Baden-Württemberg, dass sich für kostenintensivere digitale Land- und Tierhaltungstechnik [GGS21] ein unterschiedliches Profil der Unterstützungswünsche ergibt sowie dessen Abhängigkeit von soziodemographischen Merkmalen.

5 Schlussfolgerungen

Die Ergebnisse bestätigen, dass es in der vorliegenden Studie wenige signifikante Einflussfaktoren auf das Interesse an Investitionsförderung für Agrarsoftware gibt. Gleichzeitig befürwortet dies, dass IKT ein skalenneutraler Einstieg ohne höheres Investitionsrisiko v.a. für kleinstrukturierte Agrarregionen sein können. Ferner lassen die Ergebnisse vermuten, dass es verschiedene Interessensgruppen gibt. In dieser Studie liegen größtenteils Interessensgruppen vor, welche entweder keine Förderung und/oder (weitere) Digitalisierung wünschen oder bereits IKT nutzen und daher kein hohes Interesse an investiven Unterstützungen äußern. Weiterhin zeigen die Landwirte nur vereinzelt Interesse an Förderangeboten sowie der Investition in Agrarsoftware. Somit bleibt offen, inwiefern hierbei investive Fördermaßnahmen zielführend für die weitere Verbreitung von Agrarsoftware sind. Es ist zu beachten, dass die Studie nicht repräsentativ ist und die Interessensgruppen ungleich verteilt sind, jedoch sind erste Einblicke in die spezifischen Unterstützungswünsche der Landwirte möglich. Zukünftig sollten weitere Untersuchungen von Unterstützungswünschen in anderen Technologiebereichen sowie deren Zusammenhang mit soziodemographischen Faktoren durchgeführt werden, um langfristig Rückschlüsse für die bedarfsgerechte Investitionsförderung der landwirtschaftlichen Betriebe ziehen zu können.

Förderhinweis: Die Förderung des Vorhabens DiWenkLa (Digitale Wertschöpfungsketten für eine nachhaltige kleinstrukturierte Landwirtschaft) erfolgt aus Mitteln des Bundesministeriums für Ernährung und Landwirtschaft. Das Vorhaben wird ebenfalls durch das Ministerium für Ernährung, Ländlichen Raum und Verbraucherschutz Baden-Württemberg unterstützt. Die Projektträgerschaft erfolgt über die Bundesanstalt für Landwirtschaft und Ernährung im Rahmen des Programms zur Innovationsförderung unter dem Förderkennzeichen 28DE106B18. Das Vorhaben wird ebenfalls durch das Ministerium für Ernährung, Ländlichen Raum und Verbraucherschutz Baden-Württemberg unterstützt.

Literaturverzeichnis

[BDP21] Birner, Regina; Daum, Thomas; Pray, Carl: Who drives the digital revolution in agriculture? A review of supply-side trends, players and challenges. In: Applied Economic Perspectives and Policy. DOI: 10.1002/aepp.13145, 2021.

[Co88]   Cohen, J.: Statistical Power Analysis for the Behavioral Sciences. 2th ed., Hillsdale, New York u.a., 1988.

[GGS21] Gabriel, Andreas; Gandorfer, Markus; Spykman, Olivia: Nutzung und Hemmnisse digitaler Technologien in der Landwirtschaft. Sichtweisen aus der Praxis und in den Fachmedien. In: Berichte über Landwirtschaft - Zeitschrift für Agrarpolitik und Landwirtschaft 99 (1), S. 1-27. DOI: 10.12767/buel.v99i1.328, 2021.

[GG22]   Gabriel, Andreas; Gandorfer, Markus: Adoption of digital technologies in agriculture – an inventory in a European small-scale farming region. In: Precision Agric. DOI: 10.1007/s11119-022-09931-1, 2022.

[HMP12] Heikkilä, Anna-Maija; Myyrä, Sami; Pietola, Kyösti: Effects of Economic Factors on Adoption of Robotics and Consequences of Automation for Productivity Growth of Dairy Farms. In: Factor Markes Working Papers 142, 2012.

[Je12]   Jensen, Hans Grinsted; Jacobsen, Lars-Bo; Pedersen, Søren Marcus; Tavella, Elena: Socioeconomic impact of widespread adoption of precision farming and controlled traffic systems in Denmark. In: Precision Agric 13 (6), S. 661-677. DOI: 10.1007/s11119-012-9276-3, 2012.

[Pf22]   Pfaff, Sara; Paulus, Michael; Schüle, Heinrich; Thomas, Angelika; Knierim, Andrea: Besonderheiten der Implementierung digitaler Technologien in der kleinstrukturierten Landwirtschaft. Berichte über Landwirtschaft - Zeitschrift für Agrarpolitik und Landwirtschaft, Aktuelle Beiträge. DOI: 10.12767/BUEL.V100I2.404, 2022.

[Sh18]   Shepherd, Mark; Turner, James A.; Small, Bruce; Wheeler, David: Priorities for science to overcome hurdles thwarting the full promise of the 'digital agriculture' revolution. In: Journal of the science of food and agriculture 100 (14), S. 5083–5092. DOI: 10.1002/jsfa.9346, 2018.

[Sh11]   Shockley, Jordan M.; Dillon, Carl R.; Stombaugh, Timothy S.: A Whole Farm Analysis of the Influence of Auto-Steer Navigation on Net Returns, Risk, and Production Practices. In: J. Agric. Appl. Econ. 43 (1), S. 57–75. DOI: 10.1017/S1074070800004053, 2011.

[SS18]   Spengler, Bettina; Schramek, Jörg: Bedarfsanalyse für Investitionsförderungen in Grenzertragsregionen - Ergebnisse einer Befragung von Landwirtinnen und Landwirten sowie aus Expertengesprächen in Baden-Württemberg, Hessen und Rheinland-Pfalz. Berichte über Landwirtschaft - Zeitschrift für Agrarpolitik und Landwirtschaft, Band 96, Heft 1, Mai 2018. DOI: 10.12767/buel.v96i1.203, 2018.

[St21]   Statistisches Landesamt Baden-Württemberg (Stala) (2021): Landwirtschaftszählung 2020. Strukturen im Wandel. Online verfügbar unter https://www.statistik-bw.de/Service/Veroeff/Statistik_AKTUELL/803421006.pdf, zuletzt geprüft am 01.12.2022.

FarmBot-based-ISOBUS demonstrator for research and teaching

Frederick John Phillips[1], Marc-Alexandre Favier[2] and Jörg Dörr[3]

Abstract: With the rise of digitalization in today's agriculture, it is becoming increasingly important to integrate modern technology, like ISOBUS, in both research and education. That's why a certain number of products such as Hardware-in-the-Loop and physics-engine based simulators or small scale ISOBUS demonstrators have already been developed in the past [Fa20]. Still, Researchers and students have limited options to interact with this type of system. Combining ISOBUS with an open-source farming robot called FarmBot represents a unique opportunity to work and teach with a small-scale local setup. To this end, a demonstrator was created that integrates a university FarmBot with an actual tractor terminal. The demonstrator's software controls and tracks the FarmBot's movements. Written in Python, it features robust compatibility and expandability. The hardware component connects this software to the ISOBUS terminal. A simple attachment setup mimics a tractor implement and displays advanced ISOBUS functions. Section Control and Variable Rate Application are of two these functions accurately incorporated by the developed tool. This system allows for a customizable demonstrator on university grounds, enabling students and researchers to work and learn with industry-standard implements.

Keywords: sustainable farming, ISOBUS, end-to-end digitalization, FMIS, interoperability

1 Introduction

1.1 ISOBUS

ISOBUS is a protocol standard developed for farming equipment. It is used to solve compatibility problems between agricultural machinery by standardizing part communication across different manufacturers [IS19]. This type of solution is necessary for an efficient approach to modern farming. The increasing integration of digital solutions in today's agricultural space enables invaluable improvements. The deployment of technology boosting field productivity and efficiency has been made possible thanks in large part to the inter-implement communication enabled by ISOBUS equipment. Two ISOBUS features important in this paper are TC-SC (Task-Controller Section Control) and TC-GEO (Task-Controller Geo-Based) [AE22]. These allow for dynamic control of a sprayer or similar

---

[1] Technische Universität Kaiserslautern, FB Informatik, Lehrstuhl Digital Farming, Gottlieb-Daimler-Straße 47, 67663 Kaiserslautern, fphillip@rhrk.uni-kl.de
[2] Technische Universität Kaiserslautern, FB Informatik, Lehrstuhl Digital Farming, Gottlieb-Daimler-Straße 47, 67663 Kaiserslautern, favier@cs.uni-kl.de
[3] Technische Universität Kaiserslautern, FB Informatik, Lehrstuhl Digital Farming, Gottlieb-Daimler-Straße 47, 67663 Kaiserslautern, doerr@cs.uni-kl.de

implement in relation to a tractor's position. Section Control can automatically switch equipment sections on and off when overlapping with already applied areas or to avoid field boarders. TC-GEO expands location-based capabilities. In our case, this allows for variable spraying volumes based on an application map specifying exact amounts of for instance fertilizer depending on the position on a field (Variable Rate Application).

1.2 FarmBot

The FarmBot is an agriculture farming project created by Rory Aronson, Rick Carlino, and Tim Evers to aid in growing food [Fi14]. It is a CNC-style machine on top of a small vegetable patch and comes with a software package enabling automation and remote management even for non-industrial growers. Being open source allows for modifications and additions by end users. According to their website, in addition to professionals and hobbyists, more than 500 educational institutions have acquired FarmBot kits [Fa22a].

The FarmBot itself consists of several motors capable of moving a tool head in all three dimensions above a farm bed. Numerous attachments can be connected to the head, including but not limited to a watering spout connected to a water hose, a seed-planting nozzle, an LED system, and a camera [Fa22b]. This allows the FarmBot to perform most duties needed to tend to a vegetable patch autonomously. The FarmBot is controlled by a Raspberry Pi for its web server and an Arduino, which controls the motors [Fa22c]. These are easily accessible and modifiable. The web app provides extensive features and control through a browser. With its well-designed and intuitive UI, operation becomes markedly easy-to-use, which is notably advantageous in an academic setting. There is also an open-source Python and JavaScript library [Fa22d]. This allows for an even more customizable way to interact with the FarmBot and further opens it up for research purposes.

2 The FarmBot-based demonstrator tool

2.1 Concept

The demonstrator is able to scale tractor movement onto the FarmBot (see Section 2.2) and scale FarmBot movement onto a real field (see Section 2.3). This means that the FarmBot's head is considered to be a tractor, whose position is converted and sent to a real ISOBUS terminal. The terminal handles the ISOBUS functions, specifically Section Control and Variable Rate Application, and transfers instructions to a farming implement. This implement can for example be the FarmBot's watering system. This way the terminal enables Section Control on the small vegetable patch. The system knows which areas have already been watered and can automatically turn off the sprayer when moving over them again. Notably, the type of implement is heavily customizable. The demonstrator is intended to be a tool for research and education. The terminal can be attached to any number of different devices. Currently, the FarmBot's tool head only represents one section. In the future, a new multi-section sprayer attachment can be developed to further expand the demonstrator's capabilities. This open-ended implement setup allows students to experiment with a myriad of different technologies, testing ISOBUS functions with various FarmBot peripherals, simulations, or even real farming equipment. As the FarmBot's head represents a tractor, the x and y coordinates have to be converted to GPS data for the terminal to work with. Section 2.3 shows a more detailed look at the scaling process. At this point in time, this project's software has not been made publicly available. It is currently being used in University projects and is still being expanded upon. A final version might in the future be made open-source.

2.2 Software

The demonstrator requires software that connects the FarmBot and the ISOBUS terminal. The FarmBot sends positional updates once a second via the attached Raspberry Pi server. These are received by a python programme responsible for converting the data and communicating with the terminal. It consists of three major parts: the FarmBot System, which is in charge of controlling and communicating with the FarmBot server; the Terminal System, which generates the position messages and sends them over a serial bus to the ISOBUS terminal; and the Schedules System, which creates and executes automatic path schedules saved in CSV files. These schedules are an added feature of the software, moving the FarmBot along predetermined paths, allowing for precise and repeatable movements. Schedule files contain positions, speeds and timings for the FarmBot to follow. One such schedule can be seen executed in Figure 3. A specific type of schedule allows tractor movements to be scaled onto the FarmBot. Real or simulated GPS log files can be converted to demonstrator schedule files and optimized to follow the logged tractor position and timing as close as possible. The FarmBot is then able to move like the tractor had, while the system can either send the resulting FarmBot position to a terminal or have the terminal run a simulation of the same GPS data in tandem.

2.3 Farm scaling

Fig. 1: Example result field in Kaiserslautern, with MyEasyFarm field borders (right)

The FarmBot's position can be converted onto any field (see Fig. 1). In order to do this, the demonstrator tool implements a customizable result field. On setup, the user is asked to provide three field coordinates. These are requested in latitude/longitude coordinates and refer to the origin (O) and two corners of the desired real-world field. Each corner defines the direction for one of the FarmBot axes (x or y). All field points are treated as vectors. The corner positions are converted to be relative to the field's origin (C_x/C_y), seen in Figure 2. The FarmBot's position is received as relative coordinates (X_{rel}/Y_{rel}), meaning they range between 0 and 1 in relation to the FarmBot's total field size. These serve as scalars for the latitude/longitude vectors. Multiplying the corner vectors with the relative x/y coordinates and adding them to the origin coordinates forms our resulting latitude/longitude values as seen in the formula in Figure 2.

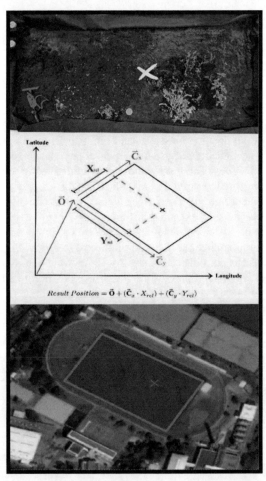

Fig. 2: Scaling of FarmBot Position onto Field Coordinates, with O as Origin Vector, C_x and C_y as Corner Vectors, and X_{rel} and Y_{rel} as relative FarmBot position

This conversion process does not consider earth curvature. The software also implements the formula for converting geocentric cartesian coordinates to GPS coordinates. This is preferable for very large field sizes. However, at parameters that do not exceed several kilometres the linear conversion process described before shows negligible error, while being more efficient to compute. The delay between sending commands and terminal reaction has to be as small as possible to ensure accurate operation. Additionally, the formula used in Figure 2 is easier for students to understand and customize.

3 Results

The developed demonstrator is able to accurately demonstrate ISOBUS functionalities. Both Section Control and Variable Rate Application are fully functional and usable with the current setup. Figure 3 shows an example of Section Control applied to evenly cover a field without surpassing the borders. The movement shown in the figure has the FarmBot pivot outside the specified result field. This mimics a real tractor which, to ensure even coverage of the entire area, will generally not spray while turning.

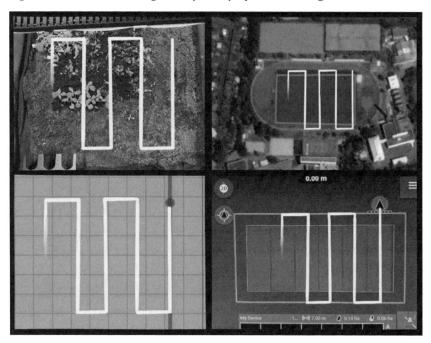

Fig. 3: FarmBot movement translated to ISOBUS Terminal, FarmBot at the University (top left), Field Boarders of Result Field (top right), FarmBot movement in the Web App (bottom left), ISOBUS Terminal movement with Section Control (bottom right)

ISOBUS represents the future of agriculture. It is important to incorporate modernized farming equipment into current education and research. The demonstrator tool represents an opportunity for the Digital Farming chair to integrate ISOBUS technology into its workflow. The FarmBot offers a more engaging scholastic environment. Combining it with ISOBUS only serves to extend the usefulness of this system and enables new academic possibilities. The proposed demonstrator tool consists of a software component and a hardware setup. The software handles the necessary front- and back-end for connecting FarmBot and ISOBUS terminal. It offers a customizable and user-friendly solution that can easily be augmented in the future. For example, further development of the user interface and schedule generation functions could extend the tool's usability and feature set. The hardware setup efficiently demonstrates ISOBUS functionality and enables work with a real terminal. Expanding the attachment represents further development opportunities. Also, integrating additional ISOBUS features is a promising prospect for future work.

Acknowledgments: We acknowledge the support of the companies making this work and the organisation of Students Workshops on ISOBUS possible, most importantly by Anedo providing the M10i ECU, by Lemken supplying the CCI 800 and by b-plus providing the ISOBUS gateway. Thanks go to the CC-ISOBUS e.V. for very helpful personal communication as well.

Bibliography

[Fa20] Favier, M. ; Le Chevanton, Y. ; Marchal, A. ; Vyndell, M. ; Xie, Y. ; Zhao, R. ; Seewig, J. ; ISOBUS simulator for small and medium-scale manufacturers and farmers Physics engine based HIL-ISOBUS-demonstrator, 2020.

[IS19] ANEDO, ISOBUS, anedo.eu/isobus/, Cited: 30.10.22.

[AE22] AEF, ISOBUS in Functionalities, www.aef-online.org/fileadmin/user_upload/Content/pdfs/AEF_handfan_EN.pdf, 11/09, Cited: 30.10.22.

[Fi14] Finley, K.; Out in the Open: This Farmbot Makes Growing Food as Easy as Playing Farmville, 2014.

[Fa22a] FarmBot Inc., FarmBot Homepage, farm.bot, Cited: 30.10.22.

[Fa22b] FarmBot Inc., FarmBot Genesis, farm.bot/pages/genesis, Cited: 30.10.22.

[Fa22c] FarmBot Inc., Electronics, genesis.farm.bot/v1.6/assembly/electronics, Cited: 30.10.22.

[Fa22d] FarmBot Inc., FarmBot Software Development, developer.farm.bot/v15/docs/farmbot-software-development, Cited: 30.10.22.

Digitalisierung im Weinbau am Beispiel der Pflanzenschutzmittelapplikation

Jan-Philip Pohl[1], Axel Dittus[2], Lorenz Berhalter[3] und Dieter von Hörsten[4]

Abstract: Das Experimentierfeld DigiVine hat zum Ziel, digitale Technologien in der Wertschöpfungskette Weinbau von der Pflanzung bis zur Traubenablieferung zu entwickeln und in der Praxis zu testen. DigiVine will die Zusammenarbeit von Forschung, Beratung und Praxis zur nachhaltigen Optimierung des Weinbaus mittels Digitalisierung fördern, passgenaue Handlungsempfehlungen für Winzer entwickeln und die Arbeits- und Ressourceneffizienz sowie die Rechtssicherheit erhöhen. Ziel ist es, die Vernetzung von heterogenen Datenquellen von Rebflächen für die Ableitung von Handlungsempfehlungen zu nutzen. Beschrieben wird im Beitrag das Einsparpotenzial durch den Einsatz von LIDAR-Sensorik mit einer intelligenten Pflanzenschutzgerätesteuerung in verschiedenen Rebanlagen.

Keywords: Weinbau, Applikationstechnik, Experimentierfeld, Digitalisierung

1 Einleitung

Im Anwendungsfall Applikationstechnik im Experimentierfeld DigiVine wird neue, über den Stand der Technik hinausgehende Applikations- und Anwendungstechnik im Pflanzenschutz entwickelt und in der Praxis überprüft. Im Weinbau treten unterschiedliche Belaubungszustände, Stockausfall und Lücken in der Laubwand auf, die durch eine anpassungsfähige Applikationstechnik berücksichtigt werden müssen. Die bisherige Applikationstechnik soll bis hin zu einer situationsangepassten, teilflächenspezifischen Ausbringung im Weinbau weiterentwickelt werden, um den Pflanzenschutzmitteleinsatz zu minimieren und Abdrift hoher biologischer Wirksamkeit zu reduzieren. Im Gegensatz zu den bisher verwendeten Ultraschallsensoren sollen stattdessen LIDAR-Sensoren zur Abtastung der Laubwand sowie zur Lückenerkennung verwendet werden. In Zukunft sollen Informationen über anzuwendende Abstandsauflagen in Form von Applikationskarten auf das Pflanzenschutzgerät übertragen werden, um die Applikation zu automatisieren. Dies beinhaltet entsprechende technische Voraussetzungen zum

---

[1] Julius Kühn-Institut, Institut für Anwendungstechnik im Pflanzenschutz, Messeweg 11/12, 38104 Braunschweig, jan-philip.pohl@julius-kuehn.de
[2] Farmunited GmbH - Gebhardstraße 7, 88046 Friedrichshafen, a.dittus@farmunited.com
[3] Farmunited GmbH - Gebhardstraße 7, 88046 Friedrichshafen, l.berhalter@farmunited.com
[4] Julius Kühn-Institut, Institut für Anwendungstechnik im Pflanzenschutz, Messeweg 11/12, 38104 Braunschweig, dieter.von-hoersten@julius-kuehn.de

Datentransfer, zu Schnittstellen, zur Steuerung und zur Positionsbestimmung, um zum Beispiel den Düseneinsatz, Druckbereich, die Luftabschaltung und die Anpassung der Gebläsedrehzahl zu automatisieren.

Der Beitrag beschreibt die konkrete Anwendung von digitalen Werkzeugen zur Optimierung von Verfahrens- und Prozessabläufen beim Pflanzenschutz im Weinbau und zeigt Ergebnisse zum Einsparpotenzial durch den Einsatz von LIDAR-Sensorik mit einer intelligenten Pflanzenschutzgerätesteuerung bei der Nutzung zur Lückenerkennung. Das System ermöglicht die Echtzeitsteuerung des Sprühgerätes für eine Anpassung der Pflanzenschutzmittelapplikation an jede Rebanlage von Neuanlage bis Altanlage. In Zukunft soll ebenfalls eine laubwandabhängige Applikation möglich sein.

2 Standard in der Praxis

Zur Reduzierung ungewollter Austräge von Pflanzenschutzmitteln (PSM) werden zurzeit unterschiedliche technische Komponenten im Weinbau eingesetzt. Ein erheblicher Beitrag zur Minimierung der Abdrift wird durch die richtige Wahl der Düsen und des dadurch erzeugten Tropfenspektrums geleistet. Seit einiger Zeit haben sich auch im Weinbau zunehmend Injektordüsen durchgesetzt. Diese erzeugen aufgrund der Anzahl an groben Tropfen deutlich weniger Abdrift. Des Weiteren sind Injektor-Hohlkegeldüsen auf dem Markt verfügbar, welche die genannten Eigenschaften beider Düsenarten kombinieren. Der Austausch der Düsen von Hohlkegel- zu Injektor- bzw. Injektor- Hohlkegeldüsen ist in der Praxis weit verbreitet, da auch bisher eingesetzte Sprühgeräte weiterhin in der Praxis eingesetzt werden können, ohne größere Investitionen zu tätigen. Die technische Ausstattung dieser Sprühgeräte ist jedoch sehr rudimentär und jegliche Assistenzsysteme bleiben unberücksichtigt [Ga14].

Tunnelsprühgeräte bieten eine Alternative, um PSM einzusparen und Abdrift zu reduzieren. Diese Gerätebauart fängt überschüssige Pflanzenschutzmitteltropfen beim Durchdringen der Rebzeile durch Kollektoren auf und führt die Spritzflüssigkeit über ein Filter- und Recyclingsystem wieder in den Gerätebehälter zurück. Diese Sprühgeräte sind aufgrund ihrer Abmessungen und des hohen Geräteschwerpunkts jedoch ungeeignet für den Einsatz im Weinanbau in Steillagen oder in Terrassenanlagen. Des Weiteren sind die Anforderungen in der Bedienung höher und die Anschaffung ist wesentlich kostenintensiver [Xi11].

Erste Ideen hinsichtlich einer luftstromangepassten Applikation in Verbindung mit einer Laubwanderkennung mittels Ultraschallsensoren wurden schon 2016 vorgestellt. Es wurden Ultraschallsensoren verwendet, um Objekte zu detektieren (binär) und in Abhängigkeit der erfassten Signalstärke wird die Luftmenge verändert. Bei diesem System gibt es jedoch keine Erfassung des Laubvolumens und dementsprechend findet keine automatische Mengenanpassung des Pflanzenschutzmittels statt [Ov15].

Generell zeigt der Einsatz einer sensorgestützten Lückenschaltung und somit Detektion von Fehlstellen im Bestand u.a. durch fehlende Reben und Lücken ein deutliches Potenzial bei der Einsparung von Pflanzenschutzmitteln. Daher soll diese Technik auf den Weinbau übertragen werden. Der Unterschied von Ultraschall- und Infrarotsystemen zu LIDAR-

Sensorik liegt darin, dass sie sich zur reinen Erkennung von Objekten (binäre Information) eignen und die Zunahme des Laubvolumens im Verlauf der Vegetation nur schwierig errechnet werden kann [Po09]. Gleichzeitig gibt es Schwächen in der Laufzeit und dem Farbspektrum. Aufgrund des zunehmenden Laubvolumens muss jedoch die Menge an applizierten Pflanzenschutzmitteln im Vegetationsverlauf angepasst werden, was durch ein lasergestütztes Applikationsverfahren ermöglicht werden soll. Vorteil des Einsatzes von zunehmend günstiger werdenden LIDAR-Sensoren ist die gute und sehr strukturierte Darstellung der Laubwand. Gleichzeitig sind diese Sensoren robuster als Kamerasysteme und somit besser für den Einsatz im Freiland unter praktischen Bedingungen geeignet [Ov15]. Um die Vorzüge der LIDAR-Sensorik vollständig zu nutzen bzw. die Ausbringmenge und Gebläsedrehzahl variabel nach dem Laubvolumen zu steuern, bedarf es noch einiger Arbeit. Aus diesem Grund wird in diesem Beitrag ausschließlich die Lückenschaltung mit Hilfe von LIDAR-Sensorik beschrieben.

3 Methodik

In der Vergangenheit wurden verschiedene technische Lösungen für die Präzisionsausbringung von PSM in Raumkulturen entwickelt, die ein hohes Einsparungspotenzial aufwiesen. Aus diesem Grund soll die Technik bei den im Einsatz befindlichen Sprühgeräten an die aktuellen Anforderungen an Sensoren und Düsen neu definiert werden, um die Praxistauglichkeit dieses Lückenerkennungssystems zu gewährleisten. Das Gesamtkonzept orientiert sich an einer geeigneten Kombination von Düsen und der erforderlichen Anzahl von Sensoren. Die technische Anforderung an die Lückenerkennung besteht darin, eine hohe Übereinstimmung zwischen dem Abtastfeld der Sensoren sowie der räumlichen Ausdehnung des Sprühbereichs einer einzelnen Düse zu erreichen. Wenn der LIDAR-Sensor ein Objekt erkennt, wird ein Signal an den Jobrechner gesendet, wo die Daten verarbeitet werden. In Kombination mit dem Geschwindigkeitssignal, welches von den Radsensoren ermittelt wird, ergeben die gesammelten Informationen ein Signal, das an die Ventile zum Öffnen oder Schließen der Düsen gesendet wird. Daher hängt die Effizienz des Lücken- und Laubwanderkennungssystems stark von einer effektiven softwaregestützten Schaltung der Düsen ab.

Die Messungen zum Einsparpotenzial durch LIDAR-Sensorik bei der Applikation von Weinreben im Freien wurden in einer Rebanlage in der Nähe von Siebeldingen, Deutschland, durchgeführt. Es wurde ein Sprühgerät mit der Geräte- und Lüftersteuerung der Firma farmunited genutzt, welches mit LIDAR-Sensorik ausgestattet ist. Das Anhängesprühgerät wurde im August 2022 zwischen Rebzeilen in zwei verschiedenen Rebanlagen (junge Rebanlage, alte Rebanlage) mit einer Anlagenlänge von 80 m gefahren, um das Einsparpotenzial in unterschiedlichen Rebanlagen darzustellen. Die Jung-Rebanlage war ca. 1,5 m hoch und hatte schlanke und einzelne Rebstöcke mit großen Abständen zwischen den Rebstöcken. Die Alt-Rebanlage war ausgewachsen. Die Rebstöcke waren ca. 2 m hoch und hatten eine dichte Laubwand mit hohem Belaubungsgrad mit üblichen Stockabständen. Die Fahrgeschwindigkeit wurde praxisüblich gewählt und in beiden Rebanlagen konstant gehalten. In beiden Anlagen wurden die Reben in einem Pflanzabstand von 1,25 m und einem Reihenabstand von 2,0 m gepflanzt. Anhand unterschiedlicher Pflanzjahre ergeben sich somit auch unterschiedliche Laubwandstrukturen, welche sich in unterschiedlichen Rebenausprägungen äußern.

4 Ergebnis und Diskussion

Die Fahrgeschwindigkeit, mit der sich das Sprühgerät fortbewegt, hat zusammen mit der Scanfrequenz einen großen Einfluss auf die Erfassung der Laubwand, da die in Fahrtrichtung zurückgelegte Distanz zwischen zwei Scanvorgängen von beiden Faktoren abhängig ist. Zur Berechnung von Tiefen- und Volumeninformationen ist jeder LIDAR in Höhensegmente mit fester Segmenthöhe eingeteilt. Diese Vorgehensweise erweist sich zur Charakterisierung bzw. Laubwandbestimmung als geeignet [HS10].

Die Ergebnisse dieser Arbeit zeigen, dass die Abbildung der Rebzeile durch räumliches Scannen ermöglicht, die Düsenschaltung besser an die räumliche Struktur der Weinreben anzupassen. Abbildung 1 zeigt, dass die Einsparung stark von der Struktur und dem Alter der Rebanlage abhängt. Die höchste Einsparung konnte in der lückigen Jung-Anlage ermittelt werden.

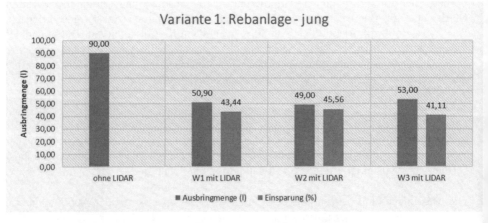

Abb. 1: Gemessene Einsparung mit 3 Wiederholungen (W1 – W3) in der Versuchsanlange für die Variante 1 (Jung-Anlage). Behandelte Gesamtfläche beträgt 0,15 ha mit einer Ausbringmenge von 600 l/ha. Die Belaubungfläche auf 0,15 ha beträgt 550 m². 90,00 Liter entsprechen 100 % Ausbringmenge auf 0,15 ha.

Zur Ermittlung der Einsparrate wurde in jeder Anlage zunächst ohne LIDAR-Sensorik appliziert und die verbrauchte Wassermenge dokumentiert und somit die Einsparung errechnet. Im Anschluss wurde mit LIDAR-Sensorik appliziert. Es wurde mit möglichst hoher Schaltpräzision ohne Vor- oder Rückverlegung der Schaltzeitpunkte gearbeitet. Die verbrauchte Wassermenge bezogen auf die applizierte Fläche beträgt 90 Liter auf 0,15 ha.

Die Ergebnisse in Abbildung 2 zeigen, dass die Einsparung von PSM von unterschiedlichen Höhen und von Stockausfällen in der Rebanlage abhängig ist. Die Einsparung war deutlich geringer als bei der jungen Rebanlage.

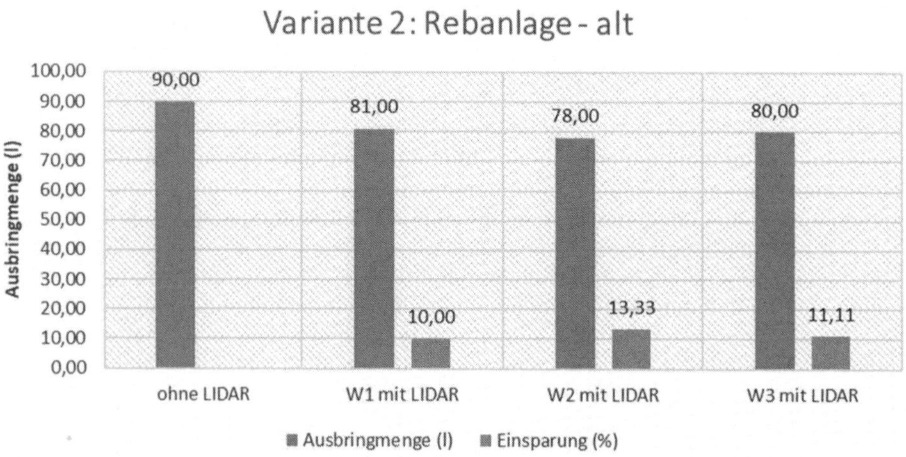

Abb. 2: Gemessene Einsparung mit 3 Wiederholungen (W1 – W3) in der Versuchsanlange für die Variante 2 (Alt-Anlage). Behandelte Gesamtfläche beträgt 0,15 ha mit einer Ausbringmenge von 600 l/ha. Die Belaubungfläche auf 0,15 ha beträgt 1460 m². 90,00 Liter entsprechen 100 % Ausbringmenge auf 0,15 ha.

5 Fazit

Die mittels des LIDAR-Sensors erfassten Daten beinhalten einen hohen Informationsgehalt über die Struktur der Rebanlage. Die Auswertung der Daten und die daraus berechneten Ergebnisse ermöglichen eine detaillierte Darstellung der Rebzeilen, welche zukünftig in eine an die Laubwand angepasste Applikation integriert werden kann. Die gewonnenen Erkenntnisse sollten dazu verwendet werden, die Technik in der Praxis umzusetzen.

Förderhinweis: Die Förderung des Vorhabens erfolgte aus Mitteln des Bundesministeriums für Ernährung und Landwirtschaft (BMEL) aufgrund eines Beschlusses des deutschen Bundestages. Die Projektträgerschaft erfolgt über die Bundesanstalt für Landwirtschaft und Ernährung (BLE) im Rahmen des Programms zur Innovationsförderung (FKZ: 28DE113S18).

Literaturverzeichnis

[Ga14] Ganzelmeier, H.: Sensorik zur Pflanzenschutzmittelreduzierung im Obstbau. Journal für Kulturpflanzen 66, S. 63-72, 2014.

[HS10] Hocevar, M.; Sirok, B.: Design and testing of an automated system for targeted spraying in orchards. Journal of Plant Diseases and Protection 2/10, S. 71-79, 2010.

[Po09] Rosell Polo, J. R. et al.: A tractor-mounted scanning LIDAR for the non-destructive measurement of vegetative volume and surface area of tree-row plantations: A comparison with conventional destructive measurements. Biosystems Engineering 102(2), S.128-134, 2009.

[Ov15] Overbeck, V. et al.: Optimized gap detection for precise application of PPP in orchards. In (JKI, Hrsg.): Young Scientists Meeting. Berichte aus dem Julius Kühn-Institut 181, S. 35, Quedlinburg, 2015.

[Xi11] Xionkui, H. et al.: Precision orchard sprayer based on automatically infrared target detecting and electrostatic spraying techniques. International Journal of Agricultural and Biological Engineering 1/11, S. 35-40, 2011.

Modellierung des organischen Kohlenstoffs in Ackerböden

Sentinel 2- und Naherkundungsdaten im Vergleich

Sandra Post[1], Ingmar Schröter[1], Eric Bönecke[2], Sebastian Vogel[3] und Eckart Kramer[1]

Abstract: Für die lückenlose Abschätzung des Gehalts organischen Kohlenstoffs in Ackerböden wurde die Eignung von kostenfrei erhältlichen Fernerkundungsdaten mit sehr kostenaufwändigen Naherkundungsdaten verglichen. Gleichzeitig wurden die Auswirkungen einer Fusion dieser Daten auf die Modellierungsergebnisse analysiert. Die auf Schlagebene durchgeführte Studie erfolgte auf sechs Schlägen im Bundesland Brandenburg. Hierfür wurden die in die Modellierungen eingegangenen Datenkombinationen in fünf Szenarien gegliedert: ausschließlich Sentinel 2-Daten (1), Sentinel 2-Daten sowie Daten des Digitalen Geländemodells (2), optische Naherkundungsdaten (3), optische, geoelektrische, radiometrische und elektrochemische Naherkundungsdaten (4) sowie eine Fusion aller Sensordaten (5). Die Kalibrierung der Modelle erfolgte unter Verwendung von vier Berechnungsmethoden: univariate lineare Regression, multiple lineare Regression, partial least squares regression sowie random forest. Die Modellgüten von Szenario (3) weisen signifikant geringe Werte auf, wobei die Ergebnisse der übrigen Szenarien statistisch miteinander vergleichbar sind. Auch der Vergleich der unterschiedlichen Algorithmen zeigt keine signifikanten Unterschiede zwischen den Ergebnissen.

Keywords: Humus, Fernerkundung, Naherkundung, Sensordatenfusion, Machine Learning

1 Einleitung

Die teilflächenspezifische Kenntnis des Humusgehalts auf Ackerböden spielt für die organische Düngung, für die Kalkung, als auch für die Quantifizierung der CO_2-Bindung eine wesentliche Rolle [GTS11]. Eine etablierte Methode für die hochaufgelöste Kartierung von Humus bzw. organischem Kohlenstoff (C_{org}) stellt Digital Soil Mapping auf Grundlage von Nah- und Fernerkundungsdaten dar. Jedoch wurde in bisherigen Untersuchungen ausschließlich eine der zwei Sensorkategorien verwendet [An19; An20]. Die vorliegende Studie hat das Ziel, die Eignung von Nah- und Fernerkundungsdaten einzeln und in Kombination für die C_{org}-Modellierung auf Schlagebene zu vergleichen.

---

[1] Hochschule für nachhaltige Entwicklung Eberswalde, Schicklerstraße 5, 16225 Eberswalde, sandra.post@hnee.de, ingmar.schroeter@hnee.de, eckart.kramer@hnee.de
[2] Leibniz-Institut für Gemüse- und Zierpflanzenbau (IGZ) e.V., Theodor-Echtermeyer-Weg1, 14979 Großbeeren, boenecke@igz.de
[3] Leibniz-Institut für Agrartechnik und Bioökonomie, Max-Eyth-Allee 100, 14469 Potsdam, svogel@atb-potsdam.de

2 Material und Methodik

2.1 Untersuchungsgebiet

Die Studie wurde auf sechs Ackerschlägen im Osten und Nordosten des Bundeslands Brandenburg durchgeführt. Fünf der sechs Schläge (GW6, GW21, KL6, PP1392, PP1401) befinden sich in einem durch die Weichseleiszeit geprägten Moränengebiet. Vorwiegend findet man dort reine bis leicht lehmige Sande. Der Schlag KL63 liegt hingegen im Oderbruch, der trockengelegten Flussaue der Oder, die sich vor allem durch eine flache, tiefliegende Landschaft mit sandigen bis schluffigen Lehmen auszeichnet [La12; La14]. Die jährliche Niederschlagsmenge beträgt in Brandenburg ca. 550 mm und die mittlere Jahrestemperatur liegt bei 9,3 °C [De20].

2.2 Verwendete Daten

Für den Zeitraum von 2015 bis 2019 wurden 50 Sentinel 2-Bilder mit einer vom Spektralbereich abhängigen räumlichen Auflösung von 10-60 m verwendet. Um temporäre Effekte (z. B. Bewirtschaftungsmaßnahmen, aufwachsende Vegetation, Wolkenschatten) zu minimieren, erfolgte die Einbeziehung mehrerer Blankbodenbilder je Schlag [Bl15]. Hierbei wurden ausschließlich Bilder genutzt, auf denen die Untersuchungsgebiete wolken- und vegetationsfrei sind. Die Szenen bestehen aus 13 Bändern, deren Spektrum den visuellen, den nah-infraroten und den kurzwelligen Infrarotbereich abdecken [Eu15]. Zusätzlich zu den Satellitenbildern wurde das Digitale Geländemodell mit einer räumlichen Auflösung von 1 m (DGM1) als weiterer Fernerkundungsdatensatz für die Modellierungen verwendet.

Die Naherkundungsdaten wurden mittels zwei mobiler Sensorplattformen akquiriert: i) Veris MSP 3, die einen pH-Sensor, einen Sensor für die Erfassung des scheinbaren elektrischen Widerstands (ECa) im Oberboden (0 bis 30 cm) und in tieferen Schichten (0 bis 60 cm) als auch zwei optischen Sensoren (Optic Mapper – OM) zur Erfassung der reflektierten Wellenlängen im Bereich des sichtbaren Rots (660 nm) sowie des Nahinfrarots (940 nm) enthält (VERIS Technologies, Salinas, KS, USA) sowie ii) das Geophilus-System, welches die Gammaaktivität und den scheinbaren elektrischen Widerstand (ERa) detektiert [LR13]. Zwischen August 2017 und September 2019 wurden die Schläge mit den Sensorplattformen kartiert, wobei je nach Plattform eine Punktdichte von 3 bis 4 m innerhalb der Spur und 10 bis 18 m zwischen den Spuren erreicht wurde. Davon ausgenommen sind die pH-Messungen, die einen Abstand von 30 m innerhalb der Spur aufweisen. Aufgrund der mangelhaften Qualität der Optic-Mapper-Daten des Schlags PP1392 auf dem Kanal des sichtbaren Rots wurden diese bei der Modellkalibrierung ausgeschlossen.

Die Referenzpunkte für die Modellkalibrierung wurden auf Grundlage der zuvor erhobenen Naherkundungsdaten festgelegt, wobei besonderes Augenmerk auf die Abdeckung des gesamten Wertebereichs, insbesondere der Extremwerte, gelegt wurde. In

Abhängigkeit der jeweiligen Heterogenität der einzelnen Schläge reicht die Probendichte von 0,7 bis 3,0 Punkte je ha. Die Probenahme erfolgte mit einem Handbohrer in einer Tiefe von 0 bis 30 cm in vier Teilproben innerhalb eines Radius von 0,5 m. Im Labor erfolgte die Trocknung der Proben bei 75 °C und im Anschluss daran die Aussiebung von Material mit einer Größe von >2 mm. Die C_{org}-Analyse wurde nach DIN ISO 10694 (1996-08) mit vorheriger Bestimmung des Kalkgehalts nach DIN ISO 10693 (1997-05) durchgeführt.

2.3 Arbeitsablauf

Die Eignung der Nah- und Fernerkundungsdaten wurde in Kombination von fünf verschiedenen Szenarien getestet: (1) Sentinel 2-Daten („Sat'), (2) Sentinel 2- und DGM1-Daten („RS'), (3) Veris Optic-Mapper-Daten („OM'), (4) sämtlichen Naherkundungsdaten („Prox') sowie (5) einer Fusion aus allen zur Verfügung stehenden Nah- und Fernerkundungsdaten („all'). Um C_{org}-Rasterkarten zu erhalten, wurden die Sensordaten mittels univariater linearer Regression (ULR), multivariater linearer Regression (MLR), partial least squares regression (PLSR) [WSE01] und random forest (RF) [Br01] kalibriert. Hierbei wurde die ULR aufgrund der Multivariabilität der übrigen Szenarien ausschließlich auf Szenario (1) angewendet.

Für die Analyse der Satellitenbilder ist ein ungestörter Blick auf den Boden notwendig, weshalb die Daten im Vorfeld der Analysen noch mittels verschiedener Verfahren vorprozessiert wurden [Bl15; Ca19]. Nach Berechnung des normalized difference vegetation index (NDVI) wurden Szenen mit erkennbarer Vegetation (NDVI >0,2) entfernt. Unregelmäßigkeiten in der Atmosphäre wurden mit dem freien Programm „Snap" und dessen Erweiterung „Sen2Cor" (Version 6.0.10.) korrigiert und die einzelnen Bänder darauffolgend auf 2 m aggregiert. Um Einflüsse von Niederschlag auf die Bodenfarbe zu minimieren [KM13], wurden Szenen mit Auftreten von Niederschlag innerhalb der letzten 24 Stunden vor Aufnahme entfernt. Szenen mit einem Pearson-Korrelationskoeffizienten (|r|) des C_{org}-Gehalts <0,4 wurden ebenfalls ausgeschlossen, um eine Integration von Bildern mit totreifem Getreide auszuschließen [Ri21]. Nach Abschluss der Szenenauswahl standen für die sechs Untersuchungsschläge insgesamt 28 Sentinel 2-Bilder für die Modellierungen zur Verfügung. Um die Dimensionen für die ULR und die MLR zu reduzieren und Interkorrelationen zu vermeiden, wurde mit den Satellitendaten eine Hauptkomponentenanalyse durchgeführt [Cr13]. Für die Kalibrierung mittels ULR wurde die Hauptkomponente mit dem höchsten |r| der Referenzwerte verwendet, während bei der MLR die zwei am höchsten korrelierenden Hauptkomponenten in die Berechnungen eingingen.

Durch Ordinary Block Kriging wurden die Naherkundungssensoren ebenfalls auf ein Raster von 2x2 m interpoliert. Zur Vermeidung von Redundanzen zwischen der ECa der Veris MSP und des ERa des Geophilus, wurde der Datensatz mit dem höheren |r| zum C_{org}-Gehalt in die Modellierung integriert.

Um Verzerrungen aufgrund unterschiedlicher Wertebereiche zu vermeiden, wurden alle Daten standardisiert [Sc06]. Durch Extraktion der Rasterdaten an den Referenzpunkten und der Verknüpfung mit den Laborergebnissen wurde die Kalibrierungsmatrix erstellt.

Die Festlegung der jeweiligen Komponenten-Anzahl der PLSR erfolgte mittels RMSE-Analyse. Auf Grundlage des mean-squared-errors wurde die Variablenanzahl für die einzelnen Splits festgelegt. Der RF wurde durchgehend mit 2000 Bäumen modelliert.

Für die Erstellung einer lückenlosen C_{org}-Rasterkarte wurden die mit den Referenzwerten kalibrierten Modelle auf die interpolierten Sensordaten angewendet. Die Modellvalidierung erfolgte mittels 5-facher Kreuzvalidierung und 100 Wiederholungen, wobei der RMSE, das R^2 sowie der Nash-Sutcliffe Modelleffizienz-Koeffizient (NSE) [Mo07] berechnet wurden. Die Ergebnisse der einzelnen Szenarien und Algorithmen wurden mittels Wilkoxon-Rangsummentest auf signifikante Abweichungen untersucht.

3 Ergebnisse und Diskussion

Die NSE-Ergebnisse der Kreuzvalidierung zeigen, dass die Modellgüten sowohl der Fern- als auch der Naherkundungsszenarien, ausgenommen des OM-Szenarios, miteinander vergleichbar sind (Abb. 1) Das OM-Szenario weist statistisch signifikant geringere Modellgüten als die übrigen Szenarien auf. Bezüglich des RMSEs unterscheiden sich die Szenarien nicht signifikant voneinander. Unterschiede zwischen den Modellierungsalgorithmen sind nicht erkennbar, was auch der Rangsummentest bestätigt. Es wird deutlich, dass die NSE-Werte der Schläge GW6 und KL6 für alle Szenarien und Algorithmen tendenziell geringer sind als auf den übrigen Schlägen.

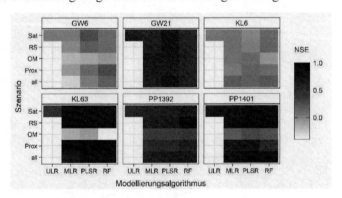

Abb. 1: Heatmap der Validierungsergebnisse für den NSE

Auch wenn der Signifikanztest keine statistisch belastbaren Ergebnisse bezüglich der Eignung der Algorithmen ergab, zeigt sich dennoch ein positiver Trend zur besseren Vorhersagegenauigkeit mittels PLSR (n=11) und zu RF (n=6) (Tab1.). Außerdem kommt es auf den Schlägen GW6 und KL6 zu hohen Vorhersagegenauigkeiten bei geringeren Bestimmtheitsmaßen.

Schlag	Szenario	Algorithmus	RMSE [%]	NSE	R²
GW6	RS	PLSR	0,10	0,14	0,31
	Prox	PLSR	0,11	0,08	0,13
	all	RF	0,11	0,15	0,17
GW21	RS	PLSR	0,14	0,70	0,71
	Prox	MLR/PLSR	0,15	0,63	0,63
	all	PLSR	0,13	0,73	0,74
KL6	RS	RF	0,13	0,13	0,14
	Prox	PLSR	0,13	0,13	0,13
	all	RF	0,12	0,19	0,19
KL63	RS	MLR	0,42	0,76	0,77
	Prox	PLSR	0,33	0,84	0,85
	all	PLSR	0,40	0,79	0,79
PP1392	RS	RF	0,26	0,80	0,80
	Prox	RF	0,36	0,61	0,61
	all	RF	0,32	0,70	0,70
PP1401	RS	PLSR	0,13	0,83	0,84
	Prox	PLSR	0,18	0,70	0,71
	all	PLSR	0,12	0,82	0,85

Tab. 1: Validierungsergebnisse mit den jeweils höchsten Modellgüten je Algorithmus für die Szenarien ‚RS', ‚Prox' und ‚all'

4 Schlussfolgerungen

Die Analysen ergaben, dass sich Nah- und Fernerkundungsdaten mit Ausnahme der reinen Optic-Mapper-Daten für die C_{org}-Modellierung gleichwohl eignen. Auch eine Fusion aller Daten führte zu keinen nennenswerten Verbesserungen der Modellgüte. Jedoch sollte neben der Eignung bzgl. der Vorhersagegenauigkeit auch der zeitliche und finanzielle Aufwand, der für die Datenakquise von Naherkundungsdaten im Vergleich zu Fernerkundungsdaten deutlich größer ist, in die Entscheidungsfindung einfließen.

Literaturverzeichnis

[An19] Angelopoulou, T. et al.: Remote Sensing Techniques for Soil Organic Carbon Estimation: A Review. Remote Sensing 11, 676, 2019.

[An20] Angelopoulou, T. et al.: From Laboratory to Proximal Sensing Spectroscopy for Soil Organic Carbon Estimation – A Review. Sustainability 12, 443, 2020.

[Bl15]　　Blasch, G. et al.: Multitemporal soil pattern analysis with multispectral remote sensing data at the field-scale. Computers and Electronics in Agriculture 113, S. 1-13, 2015.

[Br01]　　Breiman, L.: Random forests. Machine Learning, 45, S. 5-32, 2001.

[Ca19]　　Castaldi, F. et al.: Evaluating the capability of the Sentinel 2 data for soil organic carbon prediction in croplands. ISPRS Journal of Photogrammetry and Remote Sensing 147, S. 267-282, 2019.

[Cr13]　　Crawley, M. J.: The R book. 2. Edition, John Wiley & Sons, Chichester, 2013.

[De20]　　Deutscher Wetterdienst: Multi-annual station averages for the climate reference period 1981-2010, für die Stationen Angermünde, Müncheberg, Neuhardenberg, Frankfurt (Oder), Manschnow, https://opendata.dwd.de/climate_environment/CDC/observations_germany/climate/multi_annual/mean_81-10/, 30.03.2020.

[Eu15]　　European Space Agency: Sentinel-2 User Handbook, https://sentinel.esa.int/documents/247904/685211/Sentinel-2_User_Handbook, 24.07.2020.

[GTS11]　Ge, Y.; Thomasson, J.; Sui, R.: Remote Sensing of Soil Properties in Precision Agriculture: A Review. Frontiers of Earth Science 5, S. 229-238, 2011.

[KM13]　　Kuang, B.; Mouazen, A. M.: Non-biased prediction of soil organic carbon and total nitrogen with vis–NIR spectroscopy, as affected by soil moisture content and texture. Biosystems Engineering 114 (3), S. 249-258, 2013.

[La12]　　Landesvermessung und Geobasisinformation Brandenburg: Bodenübersichtskarte im Maßstab 1:300.000 – BÜK300. Potsdam, 2012.

[La14]　　Landesvermessung und Geobasisinformation Brandenburg: Geologische Übersichtskarte im Maßstab 1:100.000 – GÜK100. Potsdam, 2014.

[LR13]　　Lück, E.; Ruehlmann, J.: Resistivity mapping with GEOPHILUS ELECTRICUS – information about lateral and vertical soil heterogeneity. Geoderma 199, S. 2-11, 2013.

[Mo07]　　Moriasi, D. N. et al.: Model Evaluation Guidelines for Systematic Quantification of Accuracy in Watershed Simulations. American Society of Agricultural and Biological Engineers 50, S. 885-900, 2007.

[Ri21]　　Rivas-Tabares, D. et al.: Multiscaling NDVI Series Analysis of Rainfed Cereal in Central Spain. Remote Sensing 13, 568, 2021.

[Sc06]　　Schowengerdt, R.A.: Remote Sensing: Models and Methods for Image Processing. Third ed., Academic Press, San Diego, 2006.

[WSE01]　Wold, S.; Sjöström, M.; Eriksson, L.: PLS-regression: a basic tool of chemometrics. Chemometrics and Intelligent Laboratory Systems 58, S. 109-130, 2001.

Interactive waypoint navigation for autonomous monitoring of vegetables in complex micro-farming

Sebastian Pütz[1,2], Malte Kleine Piening[1,2] and Lars Schilling[1,2]

Abstract: We present an interactive topological waypoint navigation system for autonomous robots integrated with the open source ROS, Move Base Flex (MBF), and Mesh Navigation stack (MeshNav). In the DFKI EXIST transfer-of-research project *PlantMap*, we develop a robotic software stack towards autonomous long-term navigation in market gardens, i.e., micro-farming. To monitor vegetable plants autonomously with the developed agricultural monitoring robot Lero in a market garden, we developed an interactive flexible waypoint navigation system.

Keywords: waypoint navigation, autonomous navigation, Move Base Flex, ROS, Mesh Navigation, agricultural monitoring robot

1 Introduction

Fig. 1: Topological waypoint navigation graph and 3D AI Market Garden map from the DFKI test environment in Arenshorst, Bohmte, Germany

The path planning is performed using the underlying triangular mesh map representing the market garden environment as a surface in 3D space. In the paper, we present the whole

---
[1] Nature Robots GmbH, <first name>.<last name>@nature-robots.de
[2] German Research Center for Artificial Intelligence (DFKI), PBR, <first name>.<last name>@dfki.de

system commanding the agricultural robot Lero built within the PlantMap project to autonomously perform navigation using a mesh map which covers the market garden as shown in Figure 1. The robot is designed to record high resolution 3D data while it drives along a bed following the waypoint navigation plan. We show the novelty of this approach as it can enable long-term autonomy in a modular and well-structured way while it is fully integrated with ROS, MBF and MeshNav. Our approach is also integrated with RViz so that the developer can easily view current states, and add, remove or change waypoint positions or edges, and modify semantic meanings.

2 Related work

To get an overview of high-level execution logic architectures, Colledanchise and Ögren [Co18] list different architectures, such as subsumption architectures, teleo-reactive programs, decision trees as well as Behavior Trees (BTs), describe their advantages and disadvantages. Harel [Ha87] introduced the first hierarchical finite state machine (HFSM). The SMACH framework [BO10] implements a modern HFSM library as a task level execution engine fully integrated with ROS topics, services, and actions. We use SMACH as task level architecture as described in detail below. It allows rapid prototyping of execution strategies in ROS and python. We designed such a SMACH to execute a high-level plan defined by a topological edge sequence generated by the user or a task.

In previous work, [Pü19; Pü20; Pü21; Pü22], we developed Move Base Flex (MBF) and integrated it for the use with 2D costmaps, as well as for the use with the 2.5D Grid Map representation, and finally for the use with a 3D mesh map representation. Furthermore, we demonstrated the advantages over other frameworks like move_base which is already successfully used for long-term navigation, for example, the robot office marathon [Ma10]. Conner et al. [Co17] proposed *flexible_navigation,* a more flexible framework compatible with the planner, controller and recovery plugins used for the standard navigation middle layer framework move_base. However, with MBF, we also eliminated the shortcomings of *flexible navigation*. These days, MBF is used in several projects in academia, industry and personal projects [Pü22].

In [Pü19; Pü20], we presented the integration for mesh maps and the interaction within RViz for labeling mesh segments and selecting goal poses on the mesh surface for navigation as well as autonomous navigation in the forest using MeshNav and the Continuous Vector Field Planner (CVP). This work forms the basis for the PlantMap project where we integrated the MeshNav software stack in the AI Market Garden robotic test environment in Arenshorst as described in detail below. To allow high-level applications in such domains, such as long-term monitoring of vegetable plants, the interactive waypoint navigation framework extends these software components and forms an interactive interface used towards long-term monitoring.

3 Architecture

3.1 Waypoint navigation system

The topological waypoint graph is defined on the mesh map. Each edge can hold multiple semantic attributes used during the task level execution. This way, we can assign attributes to associate edges with a bed in the garden which can later be used by the planner to observe certain beds. Semantic information such as path-blocked, trafficability or marker readings can be added to the system in order to perform replanning to further optimize the operation outcome or even to enable a robust and smart autonomous system.

For the market garden use case, we define *free-space*, *in-row* and *inter-row* edges in order to use different navigation strategies, i.e. MBF path planners, controllers and recovery behaviors to master the given navigation tasks. Later, this will be extended with additional navigation strategies, i.e., *parking*, and *docking*. The *in-row* edges are defined over beds connecting waypoints at the beginning and end of each bed, while intermediate waypoints can be used to cover beds with curvature or to trigger certain events. In addition, each two *in-row* segments lying next to each other are connected by *inter-row* edges. Lastly, different parcels of beds, a base station with the charging station, or special places can be connected by a sequence of *free-space* edges if the robot should use a path planner suitable for free space.

The user interaction is realized using interactive markers [Go11] in RViz and ROS. It allows us to change the used planner or controller, to block the edge, to define a plant type for an edge, and to change the trafficability which is used for the planner and could also be used for the controller speed. Furthermore, it also allows you to simply add intermediate waypoints, delete an edge or node, or to save the waypoint graph. Internally, the modules use the python library networkx and communicate using ROS services, e.g. to add, update, and delete edges and nodes. Additionally, the menu allows you to select a sequence of edges for the current path which can later be executed as explained next.

3.2 Task level waypoint navigation execution

In the following, we describe the architecture and connection to MBF using a hierarchical state machine implemented using SMACH, see Figure 2.

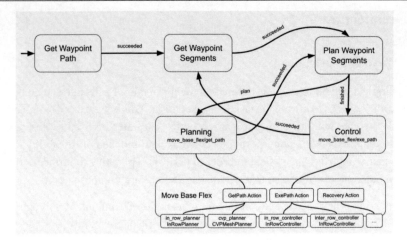

Fig. 2: Waypoint execution: performs the waypoint navigation using the MBF actions GetPath and ExePath

Figure 2 shows an implemented hierarchical state machine. The state *GetWaypointPath* waits until a topological path, i.e. a list of waypoints, is received. Next, it transitions to the State *GetWaypointSegments* which finds consecutive waypoint edges with the same controller type. Here, we combine these path segments in order to enable a continuous driving using one controller over a combined path, i.e. an array of poses which covers the sequence of topological edges. Thus, this combined list of waypoints is handed over to the *PlanWaypointSegments* state which calls the respective *in_row_planner* or *cvp_planner* in a sequence and concatenates the resulting low level plans, i.e. the lists of poses, to one plan. If the planner succeeds, the path is handed over to *PlanWaypointSegments* for the concatenation step. As soon as all paths of the waypoint segments are computed and concatenated, the concatenated path is handed over to the respective controller which computes velocity commands in order to follow the given path. Our four wheel hardware controller then translates these velocity commands to motor commands. If the robot arrives, the system transitions to *GetWaypointSegments* in order to process the next segments of the topological path.

4 Application

Our waypoint navigation system is implemented and tested in the DFKI AI Market Garden test environment in Arenshorst near Bohmte, Germany. The test environment contains several areas including 16 beds lined up, 3 heavily curved beds and free space. So far *in-row* and *inter-row* edges are being tested. The AI Market Garden mesh map is created using a Riegl VZ400i high resolution terrestrial laser scanner. Such mesh maps can also automatically be generated, see [Pü16; Pü22]. The interactive waypoints can be chosen arbitrarily as explained in Chapter 3.1. To localize the robot on the mesh map, several sensors are combined using an extended Kalman filter. We tested two localization methods, one based on RTK GPS and the other based on LiDAR, each combined with filtered IMU and wheel odometry measurements. When using GPS for localization, the mesh map must be georeferenced. We have successfully been using the navigation system in the DFKI AI Market Garden for 1.5 months now to record data of the plants twice a week. During this recording campaign, we came across no major issues with the navigation stack other than some parameters that required some tuning initially. A video of the waypoint navigation system in action can be seen here:

https://youtu.be/-HOqglSfhAc

5 Summary and future work

In this paper, we present an interactive waypoint navigation approach consisting of several software components. The *interactive waypoints* component allows the user to modify and define missions, as well as to modify the underlying graph and the strategies to execute. The *waypoint server* holds and persists the data and provides services to add, update and delete nodes and edges with its attributes. The *waypoint planner* component plans waypoint sequences using the selected edges by the user. The waypoint graph with its attributes, e.g. the used controller, plant type, and trafficability is connected to the *waypoint execution* component in order to perform navigation tasks and monitoring tasks. This modular system allows to model different use cases for autonomous robots with different kinematics navigating in complex outdoor terrains from small-scale micro-farming up to large-scale organic vegetable farms, or forest path networks with unstructured forest pathways with changing slope. We demonstrated the use in the AI Market Garden test environment in Arenshorst near Bohmte, Germany, with the developed robot Lero.

Acknowledgements: The DFKI Niedersachsen is sponsored by the Ministry of Science and Culture of Lower Saxony and the VolkswagenStiftung.

Bibliography

[Bo10]   Bohren, J.; Cousins, S.: The SMACH High-Level Executive [ROS News]. IEEE Robotics & Automation Magazine, 17(4):18-20, 2010.

[Co17]   Conner D. C., Willis, J.: Flexible Navigation: Finite State Machine-Based Integrated Navigation and Control for Ros Enabled Robots. In SoutheastCon 2017, p. 1-8, March 2017.

[Co18]   Colledanchise M., Ögren, P.: Behavior Trees in Robotics and AI: An Introduction. CRC Press, 2018.

[Go11]   Gossow, D. et al.: Interactive Markers: 3-D User Interfaces for Ros Applications [ROS Topics]. IEEE Robotics & Automation, Magazine, 18(4):14-15, December 2011.

[Ha87]   Harel, D.: Statecharts: A Visual Formalism for Complex Systems. Science of Computer Programming, 8(3):231-274, June 1987.

[Ha17]   Hawes, N. et al.: The STRANDS Project: Long-Term Autonomy in Everyday Environments. IEEE Robotics Automation Magazine, 24(3):146-156, September 2017.

[Hö20]   Höllmann, M. et al.: Towards Context-Aware Navigation for Long-Term Autonomy in Agricultural Environments. In 12th IROS Workshop on Planning, Perception, Navigation for Intelligent Vehicle (IROS PPNIV-2020), IEEE Robotics and Automation Society, October 2020.

[Ma10]   Marder-Eppstein, E. et al.: The Office Marathon: Robust Navigation in an Indoor Office Environment. In Ieee International Conference on Robotics and Automation, Icra 2010, Anchorage, Alaska, USA, 3-7 May 2010, p. 300-307. IEEE, 2010.

[Ni22]   Niemeyer, M. et al.: A Spatio-Temporal-Semantic Environment Representation for Autonomous Mobile Robots equipped with various Sensor Systems, In: International Conference on Multisensor Fusion and Integration for Intelligent Systems (MFI-2022), September 20-22, Cranfield, United Kingdom, IEEE 9/2022.

[Pü16]   Pütz, S. et al.: 3D Navigation Mesh Generation for Path Planning in Uneven Terrain. In Proceedings. IFAC Symposium on Intelligent Autonomous Vehicles (iav-2016), 9th, June 29-July 1, Leipzig, Germany. IFAC, 2016.

[Pü18]   Pütz, S. et al.: Move Base Flex: A Highly Flexible Navigation Framework for Mobile Robots. In 2018 IEEE/RSJ International Conference on Intelligent Robots and Systems (IROS), October 2018. Software available at https://github.com/magazino/move base flex tex.ids= putz 2018 movebaseflexa ISSN: 2153-0866.

[Pü19]   Pütz, S. et al.: Tools for Visualizing, Annotating and Storing Triangle Meshes in ROS and RViz. In Proceedings of the 9th European Conference on Mobile Robotics, Prague, Czech Republic, Prague, Czech Republic, September 2019. IEEE.

[Pü20]   Pütz, S. et al.: The Mesh Tools Package – Introducing Annotated 3D Triangle Maps in Ros. Robotics and Autonomous Systems (RAS), Selected papers from the 9th European Conference on Mobile Robots (ECMR 2019):1-38, November 2020.

[Pü21]   Pütz, S. et. al.: Continuous Shortest Path Vector Field Navigation on 3D Triangular Meshes for Mobile Robots. In: 2021 IEEE International Conference on Robotics and Automation (ICRA), Xi'an, China, 2021. IEEE.

[Pü22]   Pütz, S.: "Navigation Control & Path Planning for Autonomous Mobile Robots." PhD-Thesis, Osnabrueck University, Feb. 2022.

SIMLEARN – Ontologiegestützte Integration von Simulationsmodellen, Systemen für maschinelles Lernen und Planungsdaten

Nils Reinosch[1], Alexander Münzberg[2], Daniel Martini[1], Alexander Niehus[1], Liv Seuring[1], Christian Troost[3], Rajiv Kumar Srivastava[4], Thomas Berger[3], Thilo Streck[4] und Ansgar Bernardi[2]

Abstract: Maschinelle Lernverfahren bieten gerade im Agrarbereich mit kaum kontrollierbaren, natürlichen Einflüssen und entsprechender Unsicherheit eine große Chance für betriebliche Entscheidungsunterstützung. Im Projekt SIMLEARN werden die für einen solchen Ansatz benötigten großen Mengen an aufgearbeiteten Trainingsdaten durch in Simulationsmodellen kodifiziertes Wissen mit fortschreitenden Erkenntnissen erlernter Modelle iterativ ergänzt. Durch vorhandene Simulationsmodelle werden umfangreiche synthetische Trainingsdatensätze erzeugt und für das initiale Training eines lernenden Systems verwendet. Das so initiierte lernende System wird durch im landwirtschaftlichen Betrieb erhobene Daten erweitert und an die individuelle betriebliche Situation angepasst. Im Ergebnis soll das trainierte System verbesserte, für den konkreten Betrieb adaptierte Vorhersagen liefern, für die umfangreiche Datenintegration werden dabei Ontologien erprobt. Ontologien bieten hier große Vorteile in der Datenabfrage durch die mehrdimensionale Struktur und logische Verknüpfungen. Für eine bessere Handhabung wird die standardisierte Mappingsprache R2RML verwendet, um die großen Mengen tabellarischer Daten in Ontologien zu überführen. SIMLEARN betrachtet exemplarisch betriebliche Entscheidungen im Getreideanbau auf operativer und taktischer Ebene mit Vorhersagen zu Ertrags-, Einkommens- und Umwelteffekten. Expertenwissen in Form von Faustzahlen und Planungswerten füllt lückenhafte Daten. In dieser Arbeit wird die entwickelte Ontologie vorgestellt.

Keywords: Ontologie, Simulation, maschinelles Lernen, relationale Daten, Datenmanagement, Smart Data

---

[1] Kuratorium für Technik und Bauwesen in der Landwirtschaft; Team Digitale Technologien, Bartningstraße 49, 64289 Darmstadt, n.reinosch@ktbl.de, https://www.ktbl.de/
[2] Deutsches Forschungszentrum für Künstliche Intelligenz; Smart Data&Knowledge Services Dept., Trippstadter Str. 122, 67663 Kaiserslautern, Germany, www.dfki.de
[3] Universität Hohenheim, Ökonomik der Landnutzung (490d), Wollgrasweg 43, 70599 Stuttgart, landuse-economics.uni-hohenheim.de
[4] Universität Hohenheim, Biogeophysik (310d), Emil-Wolff-Str. 27, 70593 Stuttgart, biogeophysik.uni-hohenheim.de

1 Einleitung

Im 20. Jahrhundert fand die Industrialisierung der Landwirtschaft statt, heute erleben wir ihre Digitalisierung. Daten können automatisiert verarbeitet werden und so eine wichtige Basis für Entscheidungen in der Landwirtschaft bilden. Die richtigen Entscheidungen zum richtigen Zeitpunkt zu treffen ist in der Landwirtschaft essenziell und kann ökonomisch und ökologisch bedeutende Auswirkungen haben. Bislang bedienten sich Landwirte aus einer Vielzahl von Quellen, um an Informationen bezüglich Wetter, Bodenanalysen, Monitoring, Marktpreise, etc. zu gelangen, kombinierten diese mit eigenen Erfahrungswerten und zogen Schlüsse zum Anbauverfahren. In einem solch komplexen System wie der Landwirtschaft mit kaum kontrollierbaren, natürlichen Einflüssen und entsprechenden Unsicherheiten, wird es zunehmend schwerer, sich an immer schnellere Veränderungen anzupassen und die besten Entscheidungen aus ökonomischer und ökologischer Sicht zu treffen. Maschinelle Lernverfahren bietet in einem solchen komplexen System große Chancen für die betriebliche Entscheidungsunterstützung.

Maschinelle Lernverfahren können in komplexen Situationen mit vielen Variablen Muster und Abhängigkeiten erkennen und mit den erlernten Modellen Klassifikationen, Vorhersagen oder Entscheidungshilfen liefern, um die Gesamtwirtschaftlichkeit sowie umweltbewusstes Handeln zu verbessern. In der Praxis sind die für solche Ansätze notwendigen großen Mengen an aufgearbeiteten Trainingsdaten aber oft nicht verfügbar. Um hier Abhilfe zu schaffen, wird im Rahmen dieses Projektes ein innovatives Vorgehen entwickelt und erprobt: Vorhandene Daten und in Simulationsmodellen kodifiziertes Wissen werden mit fortschreitenden Erkenntnissen erlernter Modelle iterativ kombiniert. Durch vorhandene Simulationsmodelle werden umfangreiche synthetische Trainingsdatensätze erzeugt und für das initiale Training eines lernenden Systems verwendet. Exemplarisch betrachtet das Projekt SIMLEARN betriebliche Entscheidungen im Getreideanbau auf operativer und taktischer Ebene mit Vorhersagen zu Ertrags-, Einkommens- und Umwelteffekten.

Im Projekt werden ontologiegestützte Ansätze für die Datenintegration erprobt, die eine systemübergreifende Vereinheitlichung, mit eindeutigen Bezeichnern für Datenfelder und deren Beschreibung nach Datentypen, Wertebereichen und Zusammenhängen, mit anderen Datenfeldern ermöglichen. Abfragen und Inferenz auf Basis der erstellten Ontologie demonstrieren die automatische Transformation, Ableitung und Plausibilisierung von Daten. Die vorliegende Ontologie beschreibt Ein- und Ausgabeparameter einer Teilmenge der Daten. Sie annotiert Daten mit Informationen zur Verwendung im Prozess des maschinellen Lernens und strukturiert Parameter und Objekte in Eigenschafts- und Klassenhierarchien. Inferenz-Regeln zur Klassifizierung von Bodenarten und Mapping-Definitionen auf Basis des R2RML-Vokabulars zeigen die Leistungsfähigkeit. Hier soll erprobt werden, ob Ontologien eine sinnvolle Ergänzung sind, um Daten für den Einsatz in maschinellen Lernverfahren zu vervollständigen und zu vereinheitlichen sowie zusätzliches Wissen zu extrahieren und entsprechend aufzubereiten.

2 Material und Methoden

2.1 Ontologien und Vokabularien zur Datenintegration

Eine Ontologie ist eine formale Beschreibung von existierenden Konzepten und Beziehungen in einer Fachdomäne, d.h. eine Konzeptualisierung eines Wissensbereiches [Gr08]. Im Kontext des Semantic Web werden Ontologien meist als Wissensgraphen auf Basis des Resource Description Framework (RDF) und der Web Ontology Language (OWL) abgebildet [Hi12]. Solche Graphen bestehen aus sogenannten Tripeln, die Aussagen der Form Subjekt-Prädikat-Objekt darstellen. Dabei werden „Dinge" als Entitäten (Subjekt und Objekt) miteinander über Prädikate in Relation gesetzt. Auf diese Weise können Texte und Werte einzelnen Klassen und Instanzen zugeordnet werden (z. B. Name des Arbeitsgerätes und seine Arbeitsbreite), aber auch die Klassen und Instanzen untereinander in Relationen gesetzt werden, um fachlogische Zusammenhänge darzustellen. Darüber hinaus bieten Ontologien eine mehrdimensionale Datenstruktur gegenüber den zwei Dimensionen von Tabellen [Pr12].

In der Regel werden Ontologien auf Basis von RDF aus verschiedenen Vokabularien zusammengesetzt [Hi12]. Neben dem RDF-Basisvokabular und RDFS (RDF Schema [BG14]) werden dabei in diesem Projekt insbesondere XML Schema Datentypen [Pe12]), SKOS (Simple Knowledge Organisation System, [MB09]), QUDT (Quantities, Units, Dimensions, and Types Ontology [Qu11]) und OWL (Web Ontology Language, [Hi22]) verwendet.

Als syntaktisches Zielformat wird die Terse RDF Triple Language (TURTLE) genutzt [Pr12]. Da teilweise recht umfangreiche Klassenhierarchien aufzubauen waren, wurde ein spezieller Ansatz gewählt: Die initiale Sammlung abzubildender Entitäten und ihrer Eigenschaften erfolgte zunächst in MS-Excel. Anschließend wurden die dabei entstandenen Tabellenblätter über die standardisierte Mapping-Sprache R2RML [Da12] und zugehöriger Prozessierungswerkzeuge aus CSV-Dateien in die Teilontologien umgewandelt. Dieser Vorgang bietet den Vorteil, dass Änderungen sehr einfach zu handhaben sind und dass Domänenexperten ohne großes Wissen über Ontologien, unter Anleitung des Ontologieentwicklers, mit bekannten Werkzeugen wie MS-Excel an Ontologien arbeiten können [Da12]. Zur Übertragung der tabellarischen Daten nach RDF werden Regeln in R2RML formuliert und mit einer R2RML Engine (hier R2RML-F [CH01]) ausgeführt. So können aus einer CSV-Datei oder Datenbank mittels SQL-Abfrage Daten aus dem Tabellenformat in eine Ontologie umgewandelt werden. Auf diese Art können sehr große Datenmengen mit einem vergleichsweise überschaubaren R2RML Mapping in eine Ontologie übersetzt werden. Die Inhalte von Tabellenspalten werden dabei als Subjekt und Objekt mit festgelegten Prädikaten verknüpft [Da12]. Für die Abfrage der Ontologie wird ein SPARQL-Endpoint (SPARQL Protocol and RDF Query Language [HS13]) verwendet. Dabei handelt es sich um eine graphenbasierte Abfragesprache für RDF-Modelle.

3 Ergebnisse

Experimentell wird für das maschinelle Lernverfahren eine Ontologie zur Bereitstellung, gezielten Selektion, Vereinheitlichung und Zusammenführung der großen Mengen an Daten verwendet. Dabei werden verschiedene Teilbereiche abgebildet: Einerseits bezieht sich die Ontologie auf Ein- und Ausgabedaten der genutzten Simulationsmodelle, die wie oben beschrieben beispielsweise Boden- und Pflanzenparameter sowie durchgeführte Maßnahmen beinhalten. Die KTBL-Datenbank bietet weitreichende Standard- und Planungswerte, mit denen lückenhafte Datensätze vervollständigt werden können; über eingefügte Property-Hierarchien können verwandte oder ähnliche Eigenschaften unmittelbar identifiziert werden. Außerdem werden Daten vom jeweiligen landwirtschaftlichen Betrieb, auf den sich das System automatisiert anpassen lassen soll, integriert. Die Ontologie ist in mehrere Teilontologien unterteilt: Maschinen, Pflanzen, Farmaktivitäten (z. B. Maßnahmen in der Kultur), Stoffe (z. B. Betriebsmittel wie Dünger, Saatgut, Kraftstoff etc.), Böden und Realfarmdaten, wobei erstere derzeit noch am umfangreichsten ist.

Die Teilontologien Maschinen, Pflanzen, Farmaktivitäten bestehen aus einer von Fachexperten erstellten Klassenhierarchie auf bis zu fünf Ebenen mit multipler Vererbung, an den die Instanzen des entsprechenden Themengebietes angehängt wurden. In der Teilontologie Farmaktivitäten findet sich dabei die Verknüpfung zu den Pflanzen, Maschinen und Stoffen. So kann mittels SPARQL eine Abfrage gestaltet werden, die für eine festgelegte Pflanze, Maschine, Farmaktivität oder Stoff angibt, welche übrigen Maschinen, Pflanzen, Farmaktivitäten und Stoffe damit kompatibel sind.

Die Boden-Ontologie enthält 31 Klassendefinitionen, die zu unterscheidende Bodenarten gemäß der bodenkundlichen Kartieranleitung, anhand der prozentualen Anteile der Kornfraktionen, definieren. Dabei werden OWL Restrictions zur Einschränkung der gültigen Wertebereiche genutzt. Anhand allgemeiner, logischer Schlussregeln, die in der OWL-Spezifikation beschriebenen sind, können so Instanzen mit Hilfe eines sogenannten Reasoners oder Reasoning Engines automatisiert klassifiziert werden. Im konkreten Fall bedeutet dies, dass Böden (bzw. Bodenproben) mit bekannten Anteilen der Sandfraktion, Schlufffraktion und Tonfraktion durch den Reasoner automatisch den benannten Bodenarten zugeordnet werden können. Ein Vorteil der Nutzung von OWL und ihrer zugrundeliegenden logischen Grundlage zur Beschreibung von Klassifikationssystemen und -regeln wie des Systems der Bodenarten ist es, dass auf diese Art beschriebene Systeme kombinierbar sind, d.h. weitere Klassen und zugehörige Werteeinschränkungen können flexibel hinzugenommen werden. Eine Erprobung soll daher auch für weitere Betriebsdaten erfolgen. Außerdem sind solchermaßen beschriebene Klassendefinitionen mit Hilfe von SPARQL auch in „umgekehrter" Richtung abfragbar: d. h. mit einer gegebenen Klassenzuweisung zu z. B. einer Bodenart lässt sich ermitteln, welche Wertebereiche möglich sind. Auf diesem Weg können beispielsweise auch sinnvolle Variationen von Daten erstellt werden.

Einer Instanz sind mehrere Klassifizierungen zugeordnet mit rdf:type; diese Typen entsprechen allen in der Hierarchie übergeordneten Klassen. Man nennt dieses Modellierungsmuster „materialisierte Inferenz", da die sich durch logische Schlussfolgerung (Inferenz) aus der Transitivität der rdfs:subClassOf-Beziehung ergebende Aussagen explizit mit abgebildet („materialisiert") werden. Vorteile hat dies bei SPARQL-Abfragen: Es kann an einer beliebigen Stelle der Hierarchie abgebrochen werden. Mit der Abfrage „?Instanz rdf:type ktbl-plant:Weizen" werden so Instanzen vom Typ Weizen und alle untergeordneten Instanzen als Resultat zurückgegeben.

Die Farmaktivitäten-Ontologie stellt das Bindeglied zwischen Pflanzen-, Maschinen- und Stoff-Ontologie dar und ist über entsprechende Prädikate mit diesen verknüpft. Zum Beispiel für „Winterweizen – Backweizen" und die Aktivität „Säen von Weizen mit Kreiselegge und Sämaschine" ist eine der verknüpften Maschinen der „Standardtraktor, Allradantrieb, Lastschaltgetriebe, 40 km/h". Dieser ist vom rdf:type „Traktoren und Trägerfahrzeuge" mit der URI „ktbl-mash:MachinenGroup-1726". Jede Maschine besitzt eine Reihe von Eigenschaften, beispielsweise Leergewicht und zulässiges Gesamtgewicht. Des Weiteren sind noch Eigenschaften wie Maximalgeschwindigkeit, Kaufpreis, Motorleistung, usw. verfügbar. Bei Prädikaten, die physikalische Größen darstellen wie z. B. ktbl:hasEmptyWeight wird die QUDT-Ontologie sowie ein in dem Zusammenhang gängiges Modellierungsmuster zur Abbildung von Werten und Einheiten genutzt: Dabei wird ein zusätzlicher Knoten erzeugt, der typisiert ist als ktbl:EmptyWeight und mit den Properties qudt:value und qudt:unit verknüpft ist. Die zugehörigen Werte geben Zahlenwert bzw. zugehörige Einheit an. Wissen kann hierdurch flexibler modelliert werden, da auch unterschiedliche Einheiten für in diesem Beispiel Leergewicht zugelassen sind. Das Vokabular QUDT bietet eine Vielzahl von bereits definierten Einheiten, die mit hilfreichen Eigenschaften ausgestattet sind.

Mit Hilfe von R2RML können Ontologien typischerweise auf der Instanzebene, aber auch auf Ebene der Klassen- und Eigenschaftendefinitionen und der Terminologie aus Tabellen generiert werden. Für das R2RML Mapping wird pro Subjekt-Spalte in der Tabelle eine rr:TriplesMap angelegt und eine rr:subjectMap zugeordnet. Die rr:subjectMap erhält die gewünschte Präfix-URI und in geschweifter Klammer wird die Spalte mit ihrem Namen als Variable angegeben; die Daten dafür werden aus dem rr:logicalTable verwendet, das entweder Ergebnis einer SQL Abfrage sein oder eine CSV-Datei darstellen kann. Jeder rr:subjectMap können beliebig viele rr:predicateObjectMaps zugefügt werden. Die rr:predicateObjectMap legt ein Prädikat fest und eines oder mehrere Objekte, auf die das Prädikat verweist. Das Objekt als rr:objectMap kann dabei einfacher Datentyp (z. B. String, Decimal) sein oder auf mittels eines Internationalized Resource Identifier eine Beziehung zu einem weiteren Knoten etablieren. Für den Knoten selbst wird anschließend eine eigene TriplesMap erstellt.

4 Zusammenfassung und Ausblick

Für die Datenintegrationen wird die standardisierte Mapping-Sprache R2RML verwendet, um aus Datenbanken und CSV-Dateien unmittelbar Ontologien auf Basis des RDF-Basisvokabular, RDFS, XSD, SKOS, QUDT und OWL zu erstellen. Auf diese Art können alle Vorteile relationaler Datenbanken, aber auch einfacher tabellarischer Arbeitsumgebungen wie Tabellenkalkulationen für das Projekt nutzbar gemacht werden und Fachexperten unmittelbar ihr Wissen einbringen. Des Weiteren können über Restriktionen und Reasoning auch automatisierte Zuordnungen zu verschiedenen Klassen erfolgen und so eine noch bessere Handhabung der für maschinelles Lernen notwenigen Daten erreicht werden. Zum derzeitigen Punkt haben sich Ontologien als eine sinnvolle und zukunftsorientierte Ergänzung für die Datenbereitstellung zum maschinellen Lernansatz gezeigt. Die Ontologie bietet vielfältige und genaue Abfragemöglichkeiten und soll in der verbleibenden Projektlaufzeit erweitert werden, um konkrete landwirtschaftliche Betriebe noch detaillierter abzubilden und eine automatisierte Kategorisierung in weiteren Bereichen der realen Farmdaten zu ermöglichen.

Förderhinweis: Das Projekt SIMLEARN wird mit Mitteln des Bundesministeriums für Bildung und Forschung (BMBF) unter Förderkennzeichen 01|S19073 gefördert.

Literaturverzeichnis

[BG14] Brickley, G.; Guha, B.: RDF Schema 1.1. W3C Recommendation, 2014, http://www.w3.org/TR/rdf-schema/, Stand: 24.10.2022.

[CH01] Debruyne, C.: R2RML-F: an R2RML Implementation https://github.com/chrdebru/r2rml, Stand: 24.10.2022.

[Da12] Das S., Sundara S., Cyganiak R.: R2RML: RDB to RDF Mapping Language, 2012, https://www.w3.org/TR/r2rml/, Stand: 24.10.2022.

[Gr08] Gruber, T. : Ontology - to appear in the Encyclopedia of Database Systems, Ling Liu and M. Tamer Özsu (Eds.), Springer-Verlag, 2008. https://tomgruber.org/writing/ontology-in-encyclopedia-of-dbs.pdf, Stand: 24.10.2022.

[Hi22] Hitzler, P.; Krötzsch, M.; Parsia, B.; Patel-Schneider, P.; Rudolph S.: OWL 2 Web Ontology Language Primer (Second Edition), 2012, https://www.w3.org/TR/owl2-primer, Stand: 24.10.2022.

[HS13] Harris, S.; Seaborne, A.: SPARQL 1.1 Query Language, 2013, https://www.w3.org/TR/sparql11-query, Stand: 24.10.2022.

[MB09] Miles, A.; Bechhofer, S.: SKOS Simple Knowledge Organization System Reference, 2009, https://www.w3.org/TR/skos-reference, Stand: 24.10.2022.

[Pe12] Peterson, D.; Gao, S.; Malhotra, A.; Sperberg-McQueen, C. M.; Thompson, H. S.: XML Schema Definition Language (XSD) 1.1 Part 2: Datatypes. W3C Recommendation, 2012, http://www.w3.org/TR/xmlschema11-2/, Stand: 24.10.2022.

[Pr12] Prud'hommeaux, E.; Carothers, G.: Turtle: Terse RDF Triple Language, 2012, http://www.w3.org/TR/2012/WD-turtle-20120710/, Stand: 24.10.2022.

[Qu11] QUDT: Quantities, Units, Dimensions and Types, http://qudt.org, DOI: 10.25504/FAIRsharing.d3pqw7, Stand: 24.10.2022.

A coupled multitemporal UAV-based LiDAR and multispectral data approach to model dry biomass of maize

Robert Rettig [1], Marcel Storch [2], Lucas Wittstruck [3], Christabel Edena Ansah [4], Richard Janis Bald [5], David Richard [6], Dieter Trautz [7], Thomas Jarmer [8]

Abstract: The presented approach attempts to highlight the capabilities of a data fusion approach that combines UAV LiDAR (RIEGL – miniVUX-1UAV) and multispectral data (Micasense – Altum) to assess the dry above ground biomass (AGB) for maize. The combined acquisition of both LiDAR and multispectral data not only supports estimates of AGB when fusing them, but also helps to evaluate phenological stage-specific modelling differences on the individual sensor data. A multiple linear regression was applied on the multisensorial UAV data from two appointments in 2021. The resulting R^2 of 0.87 and RMSE of 14.35 g/plant for AGB was then transferred to AGB in dt/ha.

Keywords: LiDAR, multispectral, multisensorial, maize, biomass, MLR

1 Introduction

Due to the technological development and advantages of UAV-based remote sensing solutions, new possibilities arise for monitoring agricultural crops while efficiently sensing crop biophysical parameters (CBP) in a close-range scenario [Wa21]. The approach presented here attempts to highlight the capabilities of a data fusion approach that combines UAV LiDAR (RIEGL – miniVUX-1UAV) and multispectral data (Micasense – Altum) to assess the dry above ground biomass (AGB) for maize, which is

---

[1] Osnabrück University, Inst. of Computer Sc., Wachsbleiche 27, 49090 Osnabrück, rrettig@uos.de, https://orcid.org/0000-0002-4632-1286

[2] Osnabrück University, Inst. of Computer Sc., Wachsbleiche 27, 49090 Osnabrück, marcel.storch@uos.de, https://orcid.org/0000-0001-5726-6297

[3] Osnabrück University, Inst. of Computer Sc., Wachsbleiche 27, 49090 Osnabrück, lwittstruck@uos.de

[4] Osnabrück University, Inst. of Computer Sc., Wachsbleiche 27, 49090 Osnabrück, cansah@uos.de, https://orcid.org/0000-0002-7194-4944

[5] University of Applied Science Osnabrück, Fac. of Agric. Sc. and Landscape Architecture, Am Krümpel 31, 49090 Osnabrück, janis.bald@hs-osnabrueck.de, https://orcid.org/0000-0002-0512-7735

[6] University of Applied Science Osnabrück, Fac. of Agric. Sc. and Landscape Architecture, Am Krümpel 31, 49090 Osnabrück, d.richard-guionneau@hs-osnabrueck.de, https://orcid.org/0000-0002-9072-7363

[7] University of Applied Science Osnabrück, Fac. of Agric. Sc. and Landscape Architecture, Am Krümpel 31, 49090 Osnabrück, d.trautz@hs-osnabrueck.de

[8] Osnabrück University, Inst. of Computer Sc., Wachsbleiche 27, 49090 Osnabrück, tjarmer@uos.de, https://orcid.org/0000-0002-4652-1640

one of the worldwide most cultivated crops [OF 22]. Due to its canopy structure, it is relatively challenging to assess maize plant parameters, especially at later phenological stages where the crop canopy is almost closed and usable parts such as cobs are hidden, when focussing on non-destructive estimations [Ji20]. The comparison of the individual data to the combination of UAV-based LiDAR- [HBK20] and UAV-multispectral [Ni19] data not only supports estimating AGB, but also helps to evaluate or potentially neglect phenological stage-specific differences [Wa17]. This could help farmers either directly via close-range monitoring or indirectly via Earth Observation missions, powered with close-range UAV-based ground truth models, to improve plant management or crop growth models [ACH21].

2 Study site

The study site was a 0.7 ha maize field near Osnabrück in Lower Saxony (DE). It was managed in close collaboration with a local farmer and agricultural experts of the University of Applied Sciences Osnabrück. Various treatment strategies were pursued to create heterogeneous properties: with or without application of chemical herbicides, different sowing densities (7 or 9 plants/m²) and two varying degrees of fertilizer use. This results in eight different possible combinations, so that the study area was divided into a total of eight different management zones (see Fig. 1).

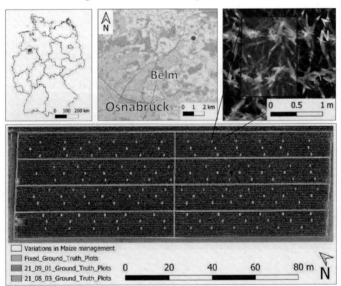

Fig. 1: Maize field with management zones and plots, season 2021

3 Materials and methods

The flight with the LiDAR system took place at an altitude of 20 m above ground, resulting in an average point spacing of approx. 0.05 m. A flight altitude of 25 m above ground was chosen for the multispectral system which resulted in a ground sample distance of approx. 0.01 m. The UAV data were acquired either at the day of ground truth data collection or a few days before (see Tab. 1). The data were taken in plots of approx. 1.5 m² and georeferenced by RTK-GPS. The plants for each plot were counted and the dry weight was harmonized by plant, summing up to a total of 95 samples of AGB in g/plant (Min = 91.1 g, Max = 236.4 g, SD = 39.4 g, Mean = 155.0 g).

Date of Ground Truth	BBCH	Date of flight	System	n
03.08.2021	67	03.08.2021	LiDAR + MS	47
01.09.2021	85	20.08.2021	LiDAR	48
		30.08.2021	MS	

Tab. 1: Data acquired

The multispectral data was processed with Agisoft Metashape (Vers. 1.7.2.) whereas the RIEGL RiPROCESS software was used for the LiDAR data captured. The LiDAR derived information were the mean range corrected single return intensity, mean return ratio (the number of first returns divided by the number of all returns), and the mean height. An additional correction processing chain, which considered cleaning overlapping LiDAR data, was developed for the LiDAR data. This reduction of overlapping areas was necessary due to the ratio concept: the percentage of first returns in the total number of returns decreases as the number of leaf layers increases. Canopy height was calculated as the median based on the raster data created with PDAL (Point Data Abstraction Library). Subsequently, they were combined with the multispectral bands (B-G-R-RE-NIR-LWIR), vegetation indices (NDVI and EVI [Al20]), and textural parameters (see Fig. 2). Multiple linear regression was then applied onto the individual and combined independent data sources, employing the train function of the caret package (Caret Vers. 6.0-93, R Vers. 4.2.1, RStudio Vers. 2022.07.2), to predict AGB in g/plant and validating it with the Leave-One-Out-Cross-Validation (LOOCV).

4 Results

The highest R² of 0.87 and RMSE of 14.35 for predicting the AGB of maize was achieved when both data sources were combined (see Fig. 2). However, the sole use of the LiDAR data resulted in an R² of 0.79 and an RMSE of 18.07 while the multispectral data alone reached an R² of 0.86 and an RMSE of 14.84. The prediction fit shows a good correlation to the ideal 1:1 line resulting in rather low RMSE of 14.4 g/plant, which indicates strong

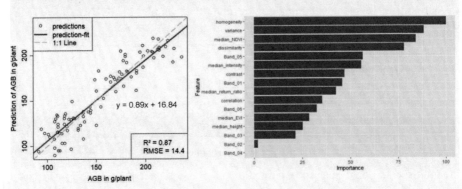

Fig. 2: Prediction of the MLR model and importance of variables

model performance. The model slightly overestimated lower AGB, while it underestimated highest AGB. Most important variables for the multitemporal prediction were textural parameters, including homogeneity, variance and dissimilarity, followed by NDVI, the NIR band and the intensity of the LiDAR derived data. Lowest explanation power was achieved by single bands (G, R, RE), the height and the EVI.

In the next step, the prediction of AGB per plant was transferred to the spatial domain by deriving AGB on the raster stack. To convert the data into comparable agronomic units, the results were multiplied by the assumed number of plants per m² resulting from the predefined sowing density (see Fig. 3).

Prediction of AGB per plant - 30.08.2021

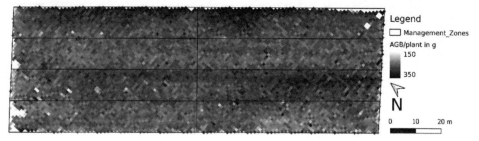

Prediction of AGB in dt/ha - 30.08.2021

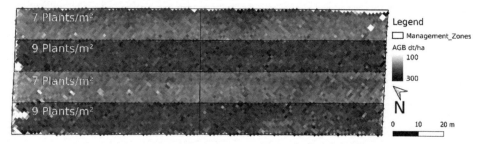

Fig. 3: Spatial prediction of AGB per plant (upper map), the results are multiplied with the sowing density for the spatial prediction of AGB in dt/ha (lower map)

5 Discussion and conclusion

Combining multiple data sources and merging multitemporal ground truth data increased the prediction capability comparable to other related research, see e.g. [Wa17]. LOOCV was used for validation of the model predictions due to the small sampling amount. We gathered ground truth data from two field campaigns with different growth stages and respectively, different reflectance patterns. This has to be considered for comparing the results of both, multisensorial derived data and the sole use of LiDAR information. The explanatory power while adding the LiDAR derived information did not increase the prediction accuracy significantly. However, testing the LiDAR data alone proves the spectral independence of growth stage-dependent reflection differences. This makes the prediction model potentially more robust for later growth stages when biomass is accumulated and the plants reach senescence. Ground truth data collected more frequently through the entire phenological cycle while matching with multisensorial data, may lead to more reliable predictions on a wider range of growth stages. Including the plant density (plants/m^2) as information for extrapolating the AGB prediction to the field is prone to errors since the field emergence is not always optimal or other effects cause differences in the initially planned plant density. This is taken into account and can be improved by detecting field emergence with UAV-based LiDAR [Ga22] and/or RGB neural network approaches [Pa20]. This research is intended to the serve as a basis for more detailed observation.

Acknowledgement: Data acquisition was done within the framework of the project "Agri-Gaia", a project funded by the Federal Ministry for Economic Affairs and Climate Action (01MK21004K).

Bibliography

[ACH21]   Alvarez-Vanhard, E.; Corpetti, T.; Houet, T.: UAV & satellite synergies for optical remote sensing applications: A literature review. Science of Remote Sensing 3, 2021.

[Al20]   Alvino, F. C. G. et al.: Vegetation Indices for Irrigated Corn Monitoring. Engenharia Agrícola 3/40, pp. 322-333, 2020.

[Ga22]   Gao, M. et al.: Individual Maize Location and Height Estimation in Field from UAV-Borne LiDAR and RGB Images. Remote Sensing 10/14, 2022.

[HBK20]   Harkel, J. ten; Bartholomeus, H.; Kooistra, L.: Biomass and Crop Height Estimation of Different Crops Using UAV-Based Lidar. Remote Sensing 1/12, 2020.

[Ji20]   Jin, S. et al.: Non-destructive estimation of field maize biomass using terrestrial lidar: an evaluation from plot level to individual leaf level. Plant methods 16, p. 69, 2020.

[Ni19]   Niu, Y. et al.: Estimating Above-Ground Biomass of Maize Using Features Derived from UAV-Based RGB Imagery. Remote Sensing 11/11, p. 1261, 2019.

[OF 22]   OECD-FAO Agricultural Outlook 2022-2031. Table C.1 - World cereal projections. https://doi.org/10.1787/d3e50944-en.

[Pa20]   Pang, Y. et al.: Improved crop row detection with deep neural network for early-season maize stand count in UAV imagery. Computers and Electronics in Agriculture 178, 2020.

[Wa17]   Wang, C. et al.: Estimating the Biomass of Maize with Hyperspectral and LiDAR Data. Remote Sensing 1/9, 2017.

[Wa21]   Wang, T. et al.: Applications of UAS in Crop Biomass Monitoring: A Review. Frontiers in plant science 12, 2021.

Evaluation of a decision support system for the recommendation of pasture harvest date and form

Tobias Reuter [1], Juan Carlos Saborío Morales[2], Christoph Tieben[2], Konstantin Nahrstedt[3], Franz Kraatz[4], Hendrik Meemken[2], Gerrit Hünker[1], Kai Lingemann[2], Gabriele Broll[5], Thomas Jarmer[3], Joachim Hertzberg[2] and Dieter Trautz[1]

Abstract: The task of generating automatic recommendations of pasture harvest date and form was previously addressed through a knowledge-based decision support system (DSS). The system follows expert rules and exploits data such as the weather history and forecast, the growth stage of grass and legumes, plant height and crude fibre content. In this paper, we present the results of our evaluation of this DSS on 26 fields in West and Northwest Germany. We compared the suggestions made by the DSS with the decisions of expert farmers and obtained an accuracy of $R^2=0.746$ and RMSE=7.83 days. The best results occurred for intensively managed fields for dairy cows, with an R^2 of 0.891 and RMSE of 3.20 days. We conclude our DSS and its underlying methodology have the potential to support farmers and secure high-quality fodder.

Keywords: expert system, grassland harvesting, forage, knowledge representation, decision-support

1 Introduction

The tasks of farmers have become more complex in the last decades with increasing farm size and complex legal framework conditions. Monitoring pastures includes challenges such as widely distributed fields and the uncertainty of weather forecast, which makes the decision for the right harvest date difficult. An optimised management of grassland is crucial for an economic dairy farm [In19], but currently, at many farms, a single person manages animals, crops and pasture at the same time which creates a need for widespread competence [Ro18]. One way to address this issue is through the application of artificial intelligence (AI) principles, such as a decision support system (DSS), which can make

---

[1] Hochschule Osnabrück Fakultät Agrarwissenschaften und Landschaftsarchitektur, tobias.reuter@hs-osnabrueck.de https://orcid.org/0000-0002-2860-5613, gerrit.huenker@hs-osnabrueck.de, d.trautz@hs-osnabrueck.de
[2] Deutsches Forschungszentrum für Künstliche Intelligenz (DFKI) GmbH, Berghoffsttr. 11, 49090 Osnabrück, juan.saborio@dfki.de, christoph.tieben@dfki.de, kai.lingemann@dfki.de, hendrik.meemken@dfki.de, joachim.hertzberg@dfki.de
[3] Universität Osnabrück, Institut für Informatik, Wachsbleiche 27, 49090 Osnabrück, konstantin.nahrstedt@uni-osnabrueck.de, thomas.jarmer@uos.de https://orcid.org/0000-0002-4652-1640
[4] Bernard Krone Holding SE & Co. KG, Produktinformatik, Heinrich-Krone-Straße 10, 48480 Spelle, franz.kraatz@krone.de
[5] Universität Osnabrück, Institut für Geographie, Seminarstraße 19 a/b 49074 Osnabrück, gabriele.broll@uni-osnabrueck.de

expert knowledge more accessible by computing large amounts of input data and producing a recommendation that helps the farmer simplify complex situations.

Many tools can support a human decision-maker by providing a series of organizational and analytical resources. We propose the use of a DSS that combines expert knowledge encoded as inference rules and exploits various types of information to generate suitable recommendations that follow a field's description, legal considerations and the principles of logic (such as coherence and consistency). Prior work suggests a DSS has the potential to increase yield and quality by optimizing the harvest date [Ha17], with examples ranging from crop-growing-models to statistical approaches [Ro18; Ha17].

In this paper, we utilize a more mature version of the DSS prototype discussed in [Ti22], but instead focus on an evaluation methodology in the context of pasture harvesting. Our results suggest that this approach has the potential to support farmers and secure high-quality fodder.

2 Material and methods

The DSS is based on the SEMPR framework, suitable for inference and semantic web tasks [Ni21]. Inference rules are written in a formal description language and were modelled from interviews with experts and literature research. Given a set of rules and the description of a field, the DSS infers all possible harvesting and management options while observing relevant restrictions, such as the weather conditions automatically obtained from the German weather service (DWD). In the vegetation period of 2021, the recommendations were first tested on two fields and their results were used to further tune the DSS [Ti22].

In order to find an appropriate harvesting date of silage, we consider a dry period of two days before and three days after a potential harvest date. If the dry period extends to two days before and seven days after the cutting day, hay harvesting is possible. A dry day is defined as less than 2 mm of rain per day. We then compare the recommendations from the DSS across four additional days (after each data collection date) with the weather thresholds.

Additional results include whether the harvest form "hay" or "silage" is possible, and whether the more significant part is grass or legumes. Both options can be recommended if possible, so the farmer can decide based on his needs. This requires information about the growth stage of grass and legumes, plant height and legume rate. These values are compared with specific thresholds for silage and hay. The DSS always uses the latest possible data.

- For silage harvesting:
    - Plant height must be ≥ 25 cm or
    - The growth stage of grass either "before ear emerging" or "after tillering",

- The crude fibre content must be ≤ 22%
- For hay harvesting:
  - plant height must be ≥ 25 cm and
  - grass growth stage at "flowering" or later.

The crude fibre content c_t at time t is computed by a simple linear growth model [Be11]:

$$c_t = 0.3\,(d_t - d_v) \tag{1}$$

where d_t is the current date and d_v is the vegetation start date.

In 2022, 13 farmers collected data from 29 fields, from which 9 are managed as organic. 26 fields are harvested in the form of silage, the rest in the form of hay. 13 fields are permanent grasslands and 16 are integrated in the crop rotation. The altitude over sea level ranges from 0 to 364 m. Sand, clay and loam soils are present. This represents different locations and environments across West and Northwest Germany. Between February 25th and July 28th, a total of 198 measurements were made with a frequency of 7 to 21 days. Each farmer received instructions ahead of data collection to ensure consistency. The following data were collected by them: growing stage of grass and legumes, plant height, legume rate, harvest date and abnormalities. Fields are managed in an "intensive" or "extensive" way, where we defined extensive as harvest after May 31st 2022.

The recommendations of the DSS were compared with the decisions of the farmers, considered the experts in their own respective farm and fields. All statistical analyses were computed in the software environment R (V4.0.1). Differences in means between subsets (hay and silage, extensive and intensive managed) are estimated with a Wilcox Test (α=0.05). Coefficient of determination (R^2) and a linear model are computed between harvest date of the farmer and harvest date recommended by the DSS for different subsets (all data, hay, silage, extensively and intensively managed). As a measure of prediction error, the means of the root mean square error (RMSE) was used:

$$\text{RMSE} = \sqrt{\frac{1}{N}\sum_{i=1}^{N}(d_{s,i} - d_{f,i})^2} \tag{2}$$

where, for each field i, d_s is the harvest date recommended by the DSS and d_f the farmer's, for a total of N fields.

3 Results

The farmers provided 52 harvest dates, out of which 14 correspond exactly with the DSS. The differences in days between the farmers and DSS have a minimum of 0 and maximum of 49 with a median of 3. The maximum differences are shown in Tab. 1. The highest accuracy shows the subset of intensively managed fields with an R² of 0.891 and RMSE of 3.2. The hay subset shows a lower R² of 0.426 and higher RMSE of 20.45.

The linear regression between farmer and DSS harvest dates are shown in Fig. 1, which demonstrates an overall underestimation of the time until harvesting and also a higher accuracy for the recommendation for intensive managed fields.

Dataset	R²	RMSE	Mean differences in days (±Standard deviation)	Max. differences in days
All	0.746	7.83	7.84 (±11.92)	49
Silage	0.792	5.85	5.97 (±10.11) a	41
Hay	0.434	20.45	20.45 (±15.29) b	49
Intensive	0.891	3.20	3.20 (±5.95) A	28
Extensive	0.748	22.60	22.60 (±14.03) B	49

Tab. 1: Coefficient of determination (R²), root mean square error (RMSE), mean differences in days (±Standard deviation) and maximum differences in days between farmers' decision and DSS recommendation for different subsets. Lowercase indicates significant differences between silage/hay fields, uppercase letters indicate significant differences intensive/extensive fields.

The differences between farmers and the DSS are significantly higher for extensive fields than for intensive fields, and also higher for hay fields than for silage fields. The recommended harvest form was the same as harvested. In many cases the DSS suggests both options.

4 Discussion

The 14 out of 52 exact matches suggest the DSS is more risk averse than the farmers, often recommending to harvest one or two days later with less rain. Another source of disagreement might be the gaps in data acquisition, since the DSS uses the latest available data, but this may be improved with crop simulation models [Ro18; Ha17]. Further, implementation of UAV-based images can also increase the accuracy of growing models [In19].

The DSS shows an appropriate accuracy with R² of 0.746 and RMSE of 7.83, but a maximum difference of 49 days with respect to farmers is not suitable in practice and may impact optimal yield and quality. This occurs primarily in "hay harvest" and "extensive" fields, without which the R² improves to 0.891 and the RMSE falls to 3.2. The differences in days are significantly smaller for intensive fields than for extensive fields. For hay, a higher amount of crude fibre than silage is needed so hay fields are harvested later. Some fields belong to programs for environmental protection and have restrictions for the harvest time. In this case, the DSS recommends a harvest date much earlier and in form of silage, because the agronomic parameters were suitable.

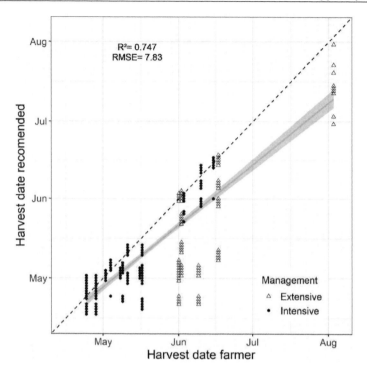

Fig. 1: Linear regression between farmer and DSS harvest dates. Shapes indicate the intensity of the field management. Solid line is the regression line with confidence interval of 95%. Dashed line is the 1:1 line (i.e., x = y). N=381.

It is important to remark that in its current form, the DSS makes inferences only at the level of fields, not farms. In practice, a farmer must often consider additional factors such as construction, equipment and the management of other crops and livestock, which may influence their chosen dates, although generally all fields of a farm share the same harvest date. Field-level suggestions can nevertheless contribute to farm-level decision making. Harvest forms were suggested correctly, often both "silage" and "hay" due to weather conditions. In such cases the farmers can simply use this information according to their specific needs.

In terms of knowledge representation, important rules are those weather-based, which determine harvest conditions, and those that determine optimal harvest quality from grass height, a measurement strongly correlated with quality parameters like protein content and digestibility [Sk09]. The growth stage is an important addition. The crude-fibre model, however, is too simplistic and is not representative, so perhaps a dynamic model may yield better accuracy. For one field, a big gap of 49 days occurred. In this case, the field was harvested in June as hay. A higher threshold for growing height could improve the recommendation for hay.

5 Conclusion

Our results show that despite some disagreements, the DSS recommends suitable harvest dates for pasture, the best results coming from intensively managed fields used in dairy farming. Currently, data collection in the field is sufficiently easy and fast but implementing growth models or estimating plant height via remote sensing could further relieve the farmer and contribute to higher quality measurements. Future work on the DSS includes improving result presentation and explanations, which may provide additional insight into field and farm management. With suitable refinements, a DSS has the potential to support a farmer and secure high yields and good quality even under conditions of uncertainty.

Acknowledgements: The Agro-Nordwest project is supported by funds of the Federal Ministry of Food and Agriculture (BMEL) based on a decision of the Parliament of the Federal Republic of Germany via the Federal Office for Agriculture and Food (BLE) under the innovation support programme. The DFKI Niedersachsen (DFKI NI) is sponsored by the Ministry of Science and Culture of Lower Saxony and the VolkswagenStiftung.

Bibliography

[Be11] Berendonk, C.: Ermittlung der Schnittreife im ersten Aufwuchs. https://www.landwirtschaftskammer.de/landwirtschaft/ackerbau/gruenland/ermittlung-schnittreife.htm. (accessed 2020.11.30), 2011.

[Ha17] Hanrahan L. et al.: PastureBase Ireland: A grassland decision support system and national database. Comput. Electron. Agric. Vol. 136, 2017.

[In19] Insua J.R. et al.: Estimation of spatial and temporal variability of pasture growth and digestibility in grazing rotations coupling unmanned aerial vehicle (UAV) with crop simulation models. PLoS One Vol. 14, No. 3, 2019.

[Ni21] Niemann N. et al.: Wissensverarbeitung in der Landwirtschaft mit regelbasierten Inferenzsystemen und Begründungsverwaltung, in Meyer-Aurich et al.: *Informations- und Kommunikationstechnologien in kritischen Zeiten, Lecture Notes in Informatics (LNI)*, 2021, Vol. P-309, pages 229–234.

[Ro18] Rotz, C A. et al.: The Integrated Farm System Model, Session 2018.

[Sk09] Skládanka J. et al.: Influence of preparatory cut and harvest date on the yields and quality of perennial grasses, in Cagaš et al.: *Alternative functions of grassland. Proceedings of the 15th European Grassland Federation Symposium*, 2009, Vol. 14, pages 242-245.

[Ti22] Tieben C. et al.: Auf dem Weg zu einem Entscheidungsunterstützungssystem zur Pflege und Ernte von Grünlandflächen, in Gandorfer et al: *Künstliche Intelligenz in der Agrar- und Ernährungswirtschaft, Lecture Notes in Informatics (LNI)*, 2022, Vol. P-317, pages 289-294.

Datenfluss bei der Applikation der Bodenbeprobung mit dem mobilen Feldlabor „soil2data"

Vadim Riedel[1], Andreas Möller[2], Matthias Terhaag[3], Thomas Meyer[3], Daniel Mentrup[4], Hendrik Kerssen[4], Elena Najdenko[5], Frank Lorenz[5], Tino Mosler[6], Heinrich Tesch[6], Walter Peters[7], Stefan Hinck[1] und Arno Ruckelshausen[1]

Abstract: Die Digitalisierung des Bodenbeprobungsverfahrens mit einer automatisierten Generierung einer Düngeempfehlung auf Grundlage der analysierten Bodennährstoffgehalte – direkt nach Beendigung der Bodenbeprobung auf dem Acker – ist ein übergeordnetes Ziel bei der Nutzung des mobilen Feldlabors „soil2data". Neben den Bodennährstoffanalyse-Ergebnissen sind für die Umsetzung einer automatisierten generierten Düngeempfehlung weitere Informationen notwendig. Die Quellen dieser Informationen haben einen unterschiedlichen Ursprung. Es sind Daten aus verschiedenen Quellen vom Bewirtschafter, von Dienstleistern und vom mobilen Feldlabor, welche miteinander verknüpft und synchronisiert werden müssen. Für einen automatisierten Prozessablauf zur Generierung einer Düngeempfehlung ist die Datenorganisation eine essenzielle Voraussetzung. Die Grundlage der Empfehlung sind die Tabellenwerke der offiziellen Düngeempfehlung, die bei den für die Düngung zuständigen Behörden der Bundesländer vorliegen. In dieser Publikation werden die notwendigen Daten und der Prozessdatenfluss für die Bodenbeprobung und Düngeempfehlung-Generierung beschrieben und grafisch dargestellt.

Keywords: mobiles Feldlabor soil2data, Bodennährstoffanalyse, Digitalisierung Bodenbeprobung, automatisch generierte Düngeempfehlung, Prozessdaten

1 Einleitung

Für ein optimiertes und effektives Düngemanagement im Pflanzenbau sind Informationen über den – teilflächenspezifischen – Bodennährstoffstatus eine wichtige Berechnungsgröße, neben weiteren Einflussgrößen wie z. B. das – teilflächenspezifische – Ertragspotenzial [HMK13] oder die Bodenart [LWK22]. Gegenwärtig werden bei der Bodennährstoffanalyse die Bodenbeprobung und Nährstoffanalysen in zwei getrennten Verfahren durchgeführt: 1. Bodenprobenahme auf dem Feld und 2. Analyse im Labor. Von der Beprobung bis zum Vorliegen der Analyseergebnisse können bis zu mehrere Wochen vergehen. Somit liegen die Ergebnisse nicht zeitnah zum Düngezeitpunkt vor. Mit dem mobilen Feldlabor soil2data (Forschungsprojekt „soil2data") ist die Möglichkeit

---

1 Hochschule Osnabrück, Postfach 1940, 49009 Osnabrück, v.riedel@hs-osnabrueck.de
2 ADVES GmbH & Co. KG, Eschstraße 23, 49424 Goldenstedt-Lutten, a.moeller@adves.one,
3 ANEDO GmbH, Hülsmeyerstraße 35, 49406 Eydelstedt, m.terhaag@anedo.de,
4 iotec GmbH, Albert-Einstein-Straße 30, 49076 Osnabrück, hendrik.kerssen@iotec-gmbh.de,
5 LUFA Nord-West, Jägerstraße 23-27, 26121 Oldenburg, frank.lorenz@lufa-nord-west.de,
6 MMM tech support GmbH & Co. KG, Weigandufer 18, 12059 Berlin, tino@mmm-tech.de,
7 Bodenprobetechnik Peters GmbH, Bahnhofstraße 36, 49635 Badbergen, peters@bodenprobetechnik.de,

geschaffen worden, die Bodenproben direkt auf dem Acker zu sammeln, aufzubereiten und zu analysieren [Ts19]. Damit eröffnet sich die Option, das Bodenbeprobungsverfahren zu digitalisieren und eine Düngeempfehlung automatisiert zu generieren. Dieses setzt ein spezifisches Datenmanagement mit definierten Eingangsdaten und Prozessschritten voraus. Im laufenden Projekt „prototypes4soil2data" wird unter anderem ein Datenmanagement für eine automatisch generierte Düngeempfehlung entwickelt und umgesetzt. Der Aufbau des mobilen Feldlabors aus dem Forschungsprojekt „soil2data" ist zu einem modularen Aufbau weiterentwickelt worden. Entsprechend sind auch im Datenmanagement die Schnittstellen zwischen den einzelnen Modulen zu implementieren.

Um die Bodennährstoffanalyse direkt auf dem Acker durchführen zu können, ist ein Konzept entwickelt worden [Hi22; Hi18]. Es sind die einzelnen Prozessschritte der beiden Hauptarbeitsprozesse „1. Bodenproben auf dem Acker sammeln" und „2. Nährstoffanalyse im Labor" analysiert und in Teilprozessschritte unterteilt worden. Das modular aufgebaute Feldlabor „soil2data" (s. Abb. 1) besteht aus 5 verschiedenen, aufgaben-spezifizierten Applikationsmodulen (App): app2field, field2soil, app2liquid, liquid2data und data2app [Ri22]. Dabei ist jedes einzelne Modul als eigenständige App in der Lage, die spezifizierte Einzelaufgabe autark zu erfüllen, d.h. jedes Modul kann einzeln unabhängig vom Gesamtaufbau genutzt werden. Allerdings wird die volle Funktionalität durch das Gesamtkonzept erreicht. Für die Umsetzung der automatisierten Düngeempfehlung sind mehrere unterschiedliche Eingangsdaten und Messdaten notwendig. Die Eingangsdaten kommen aus verschiedenen Quellen, z. B. vom Bewirtschafter, von Dienstleistern und vom mobilen Feldlabor, und sind miteinander zu verknüpfen.

Abb. 1: Mobiles Feldlabor „soil2data"

2 Material und Methode

Die Datengrundlage, Datenquellen und Datenströme des mobilen Feldlabors sind für ein gesamtheitliches Datenmanagement analysiert worden. Die Schnittstellen für die einzelnen Module mit deren Eingangs- und Ausgangsgrößen sind zu definieren und im Gesamtsystem zu integrieren. Die erforderlichen Daten für die automatisierte Generierung der Düngeempfehlung sind zu definieren, zu verknüpfen und ggf. im Prozessablauf zu synchronisieren. Erforderlich sind folgende Daten: Flächeninformationen (Name, Lage etc.), ggf. Teilflächen, Bodenart, Humusgehalt, Bodenfeuchte, angebaute Kultur und Ertragserwartung sowie die Analyseergebnisse des Bodens. Es ist ein Softwaremodul notwendig, um die zuvor kurz skizzierten Aufgaben eines Datenmanagements im Gesamtsystem auszuführen. Dieses Modul übernimmt das Datenmanagement mit Schnittstellen für externe und interne Datenflüsse. Des Weiteren gilt es ebenso externe und interne Daten zu verknüpfen und zu synchronisieren.

3 Ergebnisse und Diskussion

Abbildung 2 zeigt den Datenfluss bei der Applikation der Bodenbeprobung mit dem mobilen Feldlabor „soil2data". Das Modul data2app mit der Komponente „data hub" ist konzipiert für das spezifische Datenmanagement des mobilen Feldlabors „soil2data". Es können externe Bewirtschaftungsdaten als Eingangsdaten in den Prozess integriert und für die entsprechenden Teilprozessschritte bereitgestellt werden. Für die Generierung der Düngeempfehlung werden externe Informationen über die Flächen, ggf. Teilflächen, Bodenart, Humusgehalt, Bodenfeuchte, angebaute Kultur und Ertragserwartung benötigt.

Die Flächenangaben sind notwendig, um die Analyseergebnisse und die Düngeempfehlungen Flächen oder Teilflächen zuordnen zu können. Die Angaben über Bodenart, Humusgehalt, angebaute Kultur und Ertragserwartung sind notwendige Daten für die Erstellung der Düngerempfehlung, da die Düngemenge eine Abhängigkeit zu diesen Kriterien aufweist. Diese Informationen werden im weiteren Prozessablauf mit den vom mobilen Feldlabor erhobenen Analyseergebnissen verknüpft. Die Datengrundlage für eine Düngeempfehlung stellt der Projektpartner LUFA Nord-West mit der LUFA-Plattform (https://kundenportal.lufa-nord-west.de/) bereit. Ein Datenabruf zur Bewertung der vorliegenden Analyseergebnissen mit den dazugehörigen Informationen wird vorgenommen. Als Ergebnis sendet die LUFA-Plattform die Düngeempfehlung an das Modul „data2app" bzw. über den „data hub" an die/den LandwirtIn mit den Analyseergebnissen zurück. Im Rahmen des laufenden Projekts erfolgt die Anbindung an die LUFA-Plattform, darüber hinaus besteht die Möglichkeit, weitere externe Datenquellen bzw. Plattformen an die data2app mit dem data hub anzubinden.

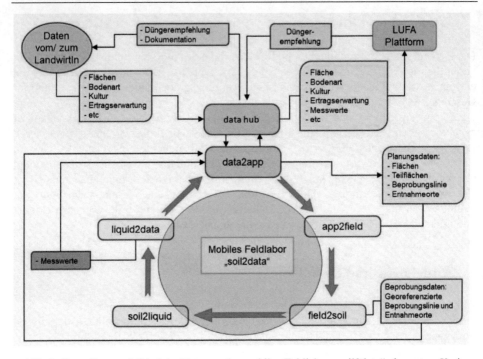

Abb. 2: Datenflussmodell bei der Nutzung des mobilen Feldlabor „soil2data", der untere Kreis sympolisiert das mobile Feldlabor mit den 4 Apps mit dem Datenfluss während der Bodenbeprobung, im oberen Bildbereich wird der Datenfluss der externen Daten zum Feldlabor, der Datenfluss vom Feldlabor zur LUFA-Plattform und der Datenfluss von der LUFA-Plattform zum Landwirt über die data2app mit dem data hub skizziert

Für den Arbeitsprozessablauf Bodenbeprobung und Analyse werden unterschiedliche Informationen für die eigentliche Durchführung der Bodenbeprobung benötigt. Es werden unter anderem Planungsdaten für die eigentliche Bodenbeprobung über die zu beprobenden Flächen und ggf. über eine Unterteilung in Teilflächen sowie über das Vorliegen von Beprobungslinien und Entnahmeorte benötigt. Die Planungsdaten werden an das mobile Feldlabor gesendet und für die Nutzung mit Hilfe des Moduls „app2field" visuell bereitgestellt. Diese flächenbezogenen Informationen helfen dem/der FahrerIn sich räumlich zu orientieren, z. B. zur visuellen Navigation zur Fläche sowie während der Beprobung als Orientierung innerhalb der Fläche. Bei der Beprobung werden die Entnahmeorte während der Bodenprobenmaterialentnahme georeferenziert von dem Modul „field2soil" in Kombination mit dem Modul „app2field" gespeichert. Ebenso wird die Beprobungsspur vom ersten bis letzten Entnahmeort einer Mischbodenprobe aufgezeichnet und gespeichert. Beide Informationen – Entnahmeorte und gefahrene Beprobungsspur – stehen für eine spätere Dokumentation und zukünftige Weiternutzung zur Verfügung.

Nach Beendigung des Sammelns des Bodenprobenmaterials wird das Bodenmaterial an das Modul „soil2liquid" für die Bodenaufbereitung weitergeleitet. Für ein korrektes Mischungsverhältnis von Extraktionsmenge und Bodenprobenmenge muss die Menge an Bodenprobenmaterial bekannt sein. Anhand der Anzahl der durchgeführten Einstiche kann eine Ableitung des vorliegenden Bodenprobenmaterials vorgenommen werden. Die getätigte Einstichanzahl wird vom Modul „field2soil" an das Modul „soil2liquid" übermittelt.

Die Bodenaufbereitung ist an den LUFA-Standard zur Bodenaufbereitung angelehnt und erfolgt zweistufig. Nach jeweils der ersten bzw. zweiten Aufbereitungsphase erfolgt die Übergabe der Bodensuspension mit der Information erste bzw. zweite Aufbereitungsstufe an das Modul „liquid2data". Nach Beendigung der zweiten Aufbereitungsphase bzw. der Analyse dieser Suspension werden die Analyseergebnisse vom Modul „liquid2data" an das Modul „data2app" übermittelt. Für den Arbeitsprozessablauf Bodenbeprobung und Analyse ist die aktuelle Beprobung beendet und eine neue Beprobung kann starten.

Die erhobenen Bodenanalysergebnisse werden – wie oben erwähnt – mit den zusätzlichen Informationen verknüpft und an die LUFA-Plattform für die Generierung der Düngerempfehlung gesendet. Neben der Düngeempfehlung und den Analyseergebnissen erhält der/die LandwirtIn eine Dokumentation über die Beprobung. Ebenso werden die Beprobungsspur mit den Entnahmeorten gespeichert und können für Dokumentationszwecke sowie für zukünftige Bodenbeprobungen oder Wiederholungsmessungen genutzt werden.

4 Zusammenfassung

Das mobile Feldlabor „soil2data" kombiniert die Arbeitsprozesse „Bodenbeprobung" und „Bodenanalyse" auf dem Acker. Die volle Funktionalität des mobilen Feldlabors wird durch Kombination aller Module erreicht. Doch kann jedes Modul als eigenständiges Modul unabhängig vom Gesamtaufbau genutzt werden. Im Vergleich zu anderen bestehenden Systemen zur Nährstoffanalyse auf dem Feld [Hi22; Hi18] bietet das mobile Feldlabor insbesondere durch die Generierung der Düngerempfehlung einen deutlichen Mehrwert für die AnwenderInnen.

Es wird eine Bodenprobe gesammelt und direkt auf dem Acker analysiert. Die Analyseergebnisse werden mit Hilfe des Moduls „data2app" mit dem „data hub" zur LUFA-Plattform gesendet und der Boden verbleibt auf dem Acker. Unmittelbar nach dem Ende der Beprobung wird automatisiert eine Düngeempfehlung generiert. Der Prozess „Bodenbeprobung" wird mit der Anwendung des mobilen Feldlabors „soil2data" digitalisiert. Die automatisch generierte Düngeempfehlung und die Analyseergebnisse lassen sich in nachfolgende Arbeitsprozesse integrieren. Mit der Nutzung des mobilen Feldlabors ergeben sich weitere neue Anwendungsoptionen, z. B. die Verifizierung der aktuellen Analyseergebnisse mit vorliegenden Ergebnissen und ggf. eine sofortige Wiederholung der Beprobung bei unklaren Ergebnissen. Weiter eröffnet das mobile

Feldlabor das Potenzial, sehr flexible und dynamische Messungen durchzuführen, z. B. die Beprobungsdichte aufgrund von aktuellen Ergebnissen zu erhöhen.

Förderhinweis: Das Projekt prototypes4soil2data wird vom Bundesministerium für Ernährung und Landwirtschaft (BMEL) und der Bundesanstalt für Landwirtschaft und Ernährung (BLE) gefördert.

Literaturverzeichnis

[Hi22] Hinck, S., Möller, A., Terhaag, M., Mentrup, D., Kerssen, H., Najdenko, E., Lorenz, F., Mosler, T., Tesch, H., Peters, W., Nietfeld, W., Riedel, V., Ruckelshausen, A.: Analyse-to-go on the field: prototypes4soil2data. Präsentation auf dem 22nd World Congress of Soil Science (WCSS 2022), Glasgow, Schottland, im Druck, 2022.

[Hi18] Hinck, S., Möller, A., Mentrup, D., Najdenko, E., Lorenz, F., Mosler, T., Tesch, H., Nietfeld, W., Scholz, C., Tsukor, V., Ruckelshausen, A.: soil2data: Concept for a mobile field laboratory for nutrient analysis. Proceedings of the 14th ICPA (unpaginated cd-rom). Montreal, Canada, 2018.

[HMK13] Hinck, S., Mueller, K., Emeis, N.: Part Field Management: Comparison of EC-value, soil texture, nutrient content and biomass in two selected fields. In Proceedings of the 3rd Global Workshop on Proximal Soil Sensing, Potsdam, "Bornimer Agrartechnische Berichte", Heft 82, S. 270-277, 2013.

[LWK22] Düngeempfehlung Grundnährstoffe der Landwirtschaftskammer Niedersachsen, https://www.lwk-niedersachsen.de/services/ download.cfm?file=22858, letzter Aufruf: 27.10.2022.

[Ri22] Riedel, V., Möller, A., Terhaag, M., Mentrup, D., Kerssen, H., Najdenko, E., Lorenz, F., Mosler, T., Tesch, H., Peters, W., Nietfeld, W., Hinck, S., Ruckelshausen, A.: Prototypes4soil2data: Modular designed mobile field laboratory for standardized soil nutrient analysis directly on the field. In Proceedings 20th International Commission of Agricultural and Biosystems Engineering (CIGR 2022), Kyoto, Japan, im Druck, 2022.

[Ts19] Tsukor, V., Hinck, S., Nietfeld, W., Lorenz, F., Najdenko, E., Möller, A., Mentrup, D., Mosler, T., Ruckelshausen, A.: Automated mobile field laboratory for on-the-go soil-nutrient analysis with the ISFET multi-sensor module. In Proceedings 77th International Conference on Agricultural Engineering (AgEng 2019), VDI-Reports 2361, Düsseldorf, Germany, S. 377-382, 2019.

A data quality assessment tool for agricultural structured data as support for smart farming

Christof Schroth[1], Patricia Kelbert[1] and Anna Maria Vollmer[1]

Abstract: In the field of precision farming or smart farming, more and more sensors are used and produce a massive amount of data. Examples are machinery, weather stations, or georeferenced data, which can be used, among other things, by Artificial Intelligence decision support systems to improve or facilitate farmers' daily work tasks. Even if there are no issues in transferring (Internet of Things) sensor data from machines to farm management information systems, data still contain errors such as missing, implausible, or incorrect data values. In this paper, we present an automated data quality assessment (DQA) tool based on the ISO25012 standard. We describe the process of how we developed this tool with support from practitioners who produce agricultural data in the context of the EU Horizon 2020 project DEMETER. Additionally, we highlight some of the requirements we collected for such a tool and briefly discuss how we addressed them. For example, we learned that in the context of developing smart farming services, the data quality dimensions Accuracy, Completeness, Consistency, and Credibility are the most important ones for practitioners such as farmers, digital service providers, or machine suppliers. Therefore, we included them in the DQA tool and implemented it in Python. It is released under the open-source Apache 2 license. Individual parameters can be provided as input for calculations (e.g., thresholds or time lengths) to meet different users' needs. The output of the DQA is provided in machine-readable JSON format and can be used for further analysis, e.g., to improve the quality of the data collection or the follow-up data analysis. This can help practitioners develop more valuable smart farming services.

Keywords: precision farming, smart farming, data quality, open source, structured data

1 Introduction: motivation for the data quality assessment tool

The aim of the EU Horizon 2020 project DEMETER[2] is – among other objectives – to increase performance in farming operations through digital means by improving interoperability among different information and information communication technology devices.

The Internet of Things and Big Data have the potential to improve the efficiency of farming through sensors or satellite data using Artificial Intelligence and image processing [NCP20]. Not only the technology is heterogeneous, but so are the use cases in the field of smart farming or agriculture 4.0, e.g., autonomous agricultural machinery or trustworthy food supply [Li21]. Hence, it is challenging for practitioners to adapt to these

---

[1] Fraunhofer Institute for Experimental Software Engineering IESE, Department Data Science, Fraunhofer-Platz 1, 67663 Kaiserslautern, Germany {christof.schroth, patricia.kelbert, anna-maria.vollmer}@iese.fraunhofer.de
[2] https://h2020-demeter.eu/

different technologies when developing data-driven use cases. An automated assessment of data quality is beneficial to improve farming businesses that depend on a complex set of connected Internet of Things devices.

Data quality (DQ) has been a common concern in many domains over the past decades [SI11]. In the context of geospatial data, several approaches have been developed to answer specific questions and detect outliers in sensor data [Sa20]. The causes of DQ issues can be, for example, sensor faults, lack of GPS positioning accuracy, or wrong manual entries by farmers. A more detailed discussion on sensor data quality in general and geospatial machinery data for precision farming in particular can be found in [TKW20] and [AS22]. However, practitioners do not only need to detect poor data quality but also find explanations for its causes.

There are some problems in data that can be detected easily, for example in the case of a technical issue like a sensor stuck on zero, which affects the whole dataset. But other problems cannot be detected so easily, e.g., outliers or semantic errors. However, corrupted, inaccurate, implausible, or invalid data can have a massive impact on the success of analyses based on Machine Learning algorithms or decision support systems: the "garbage-in garbage-out"-principle applies here.

To our knowledge, quality problems of the data itself (unlike problems in acquiring data) are not much discussed in the field of smart farming. Therefore, we investigated DQ in the DEMETER project in two use cases containing structured georeferenced data from farming machine sensors and developed an automated data quality assessment tool. In the following, we will describe the process we applied to develop this tool and how this can help farmers or software developers of farming solutions.

2 Bottom-up development of the data quality assessment tool

The starting point for a quality assessment are the quality needs, which strongly depend on the use case and its requirements. Based on the latter, the concept of data quality can be broken down into several quality aspects of varying importance. The ISO standard 25012:2008 "defines a general data quality model for data retained in a structured format within a computer system" [IS22]. It defines dimensions (called "characteristics" in the standard; in literature usually known as "dimensions" [TKW20]), as a "category of data quality attributes that bears on data quality". In its data quality model, this ISO standard defines 15 quality dimensions: Accuracy, Completeness, Consistency, Credibility, Currentness, Accessibility, Compliance, Confidentiality, Efficiency, Precision, Traceability, Understandability, Availability, Portability, and Recoverability. For each dimension, measurements (basically, mathematical functions) are available in the ISO standard 25024 to calculate the data quality for specific purposes.

During a series of interviews and workshops conducted between 2019 and 2022, we discussed with three groups of experts which data quality dimensions are more likely to be relevant for georeferenced agricultural data. We focused on two data-driven use cases defined within the DEMETER project, both conducted in the area of precision farming. One use case with a focus on arable farm processes (spraying and fertilizing of crops) is developing both an automated job cost calculation system for a given field to support the farmers' daily decisions [AS22] and an automated job documentation system. The other use case focuses on monitoring agricultural machinery data like engine oil temperature or engine pressure. In the following, we will describe the steps of how we obtained the DQ assessment tool from a bottom-up approach:

Step I): To enable a deeper investigation of DQ, we – together with experts from the project partners – assumed that there are no problems in transferring data from sensors or machines to databases. Consequently, our discussions revealed that there was no need to investigate system-dependent dimensions such as Availability, Portability, or Accessibility. The experts also stressed that metadata (or at least specific application knowledge) is highly relevant for the analysis of shapefiles. For example, metadata is necessary to check that the actual measurement units fit the expected units (e.g., kilometers vs. miles or acres vs. hectares). Based on the prioritization of the remaining (system-independent) 12 dimensions, we additionally learned from the experts that they are mainly interested in Accuracy, Completeness, Consistency, and Credibility.

Step II): We implemented an initial version of the DQ assessment tool containing DQ measurements for the top dimensions. The first version returned a report in a .docx format, with map illustrations, a graphical representation of the data repartition, and textual information describing the mapping (presence/absence) of metadata. The discussions with our experts revealed that it was not easy to strictly categorise DQ measurements into one specific dimension. We also found out that it is essential to provide a configuration of the different measures that can be edited by the user (e.g., machine supplier or technology provider) to provide individual parameters.

Step III): The tool was presented to the experts, and they were asked to provide feedback on the produced outputs. The follow-up discussions quickly showed that a .docx format would not be suitable for large amounts of data. In parallel, within the DEMETER project, a new ontology (the DEMETER Agriculture Information Model, AIM[3]) was created for exchanging agricultural data through a common vocabulary of different homogeneous data sources. We agreed to further develop the DQ assessment tool to output a JSON file that is both machine- and human-readable and can be easily mapped to the AIM ontology later on. The experts also expressed the need to obtain a detailed list of problematic events to facilitate the identification of the causes of poor DQ. Indeed, this first version only allowed getting an overview of the percentage of problematic data, but to remedy it (to check the data itself or clean it up for further analysis), it is necessary to also have the indices of the affected data (e.g., the line number of the dataset table) in order to find suspicious events. However, the experts valued the graphical representations of the field maps with the highlights of problematic values.

---

[3] http://agroportal.lirmm.fr/ontologies/DEMETER-AIM, https://h2020-demeter.eu/technical-components/#aim

In a second round, we refined the DQ assessment tool and simplified its use: a user interface was added, the configuration options pre-filled, and the documentation extended. As of today, 17 measurements have been implemented to assess the DQ of structured data. The individual steps described above regarding the development of our DQ assessment tool are illustrated in Fig. 1.

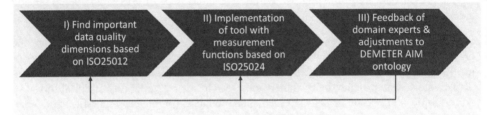

Fig. 1: Overview of the methodology

3 Functionality of the developed data quality assessment tool

The data quality assessment tool is built as a REST API using Python. It fulfills the OpenAPI specification[4]. This means that both humans and computers can easily discover and understand the capabilities of the tool and use it. To handle data privacy concerns (e.g., if the data is not allowed to leave the company), the tool has been dockerized[5] and can run on premise or be accessed remotely.

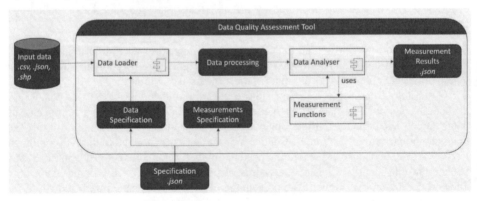

Fig. 2: Visualisation of the functionality of the data quality assessment tool

---

[4] https://spec.openapis.org/oas/latest.html
[5] https://www.docker.com/

The tool takes as input a specification file, where the user defines two major sets of parameters: a) where to find the files to analyse, and b) on which criteria these files should be checked. It accepts structured data: comma separated files, e.g., sensor measurements; JSON, e.g., metadata; and shapefiles, e.g., field boundaries or field application data. These sets can either be accessed remotely or locally (see Fig. 2).

Four groups of measurements can be distinguished: a) Completeness functions, such as detection of missing values, detection of time gaps, detection of zero-GPS points (latitude and longitude are zero), and event identification when the sensor measurements are stuck at zero; b) Credibility functions, such as domain conformance, zip code analysis, detection of zigzags in the tramlines or guidance lines, and coordinate reference system validation; c) Accuracy functions, such as range analysis, outlier detection; d) Consistency functions, such as verification of the chronological order and distinct values measurements.

Users can not only specify which parts of the dataset should be analysed, but can also make their own adjustments, such as a reference Z-Score value for outlier detection, lower and upper values for range analysis, etc. The simplicity of using the JSON configuration lies in the fact that it is solely based on a key-value system and can be easily edited using any text editor (see Fig. 3).

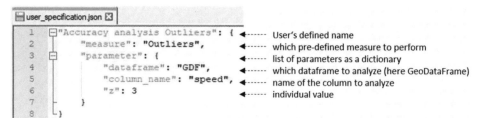

Fig. 3: Example of the JSON specification file as configuration for the tool

Since the software meets the OpenAPI specification, it is possible to use it in the command line, in an automated way, or manually via a web browser. The data quality assessment tool is released under the open-source Apache 2 license. It can be used in conjunction with other solutions developed within the DEMETER project (e.g., for the visualisation and assessment of driving data from agricultural machinery) and can be easily extended to fit the settings of a different use case (e.g., by adding new measurements).

4 Conclusion and next steps

Experts see new advantages of the DQ assessment tool, yet they have to decide what to do with the results of the data quality assessment (e.g., rules for sorting out a file or missing values imputation) since the tool does not perform any corrections or data cleaning. Furthermore, they need to understand the measurements in order to interpret the results correctly: indeed, a result of 0% is not necessarily bad, just as a result of 90% can be very critical. For example, if the GPS points are outside the boundaries of a field but the values of AppliedRate are zero (i.e., nothing was spread outside the field), this has no major consequences.

Also, if larger fleets are equipped with the DQ assessment tool, extrinsic dimensions (e.g., Availability, Accessibility) will need to be considered. For real-time applications, new measurements or updated functionalities may be needed to reflect the behaviour of data streams, e.g., to define suitable data chunks and thresholds and calculations across them. Finally, the question of how to effectively communicate the results to farmers (who usually own the equipment used to collect the data) remains open. These points are future work that motivate us to further investigate DQ in the context of smart farming and to continue refining the DQ assessment tool.

Acknowledgments: This paper was funded by the EU Horizon 2020 project DEMETER, grant agreement No. 857202. We also thank Jens Henningsen for his valuable comments on this article and the experts involved for providing valuable feedback on our tool.

Bibliography

AS22 Abdipourchenarestansofla, M.; Schroth, C.: The importance of data quality assessment for machinery data in the field of agriculture. In (VDI Wissensforum GmbH Hrsg.): LAND.TECHNIK 2022: The Forum for Agricultural Engineering Innovations. VDI Verlag, Düsseldorf, pp. 495-500, 2022.

IS22 ISO: ISO/IEC 25012:2008. https://www.iso.org/standard/35736.html, Access: 10/24/2022.

Li21 Liu, Y. et al.: From Industry 4.0 to Agriculture 4.0: Current Status, Enabling Technologies, and Research Challenges. IEEE Transactions on Industrial Informatics 6/17, pp. 4322-4334, 2021.

NCP20 Navarro, E.; Costa, N.; Pereira, A.: A Systematic Review of IoT Solutions for Smart Farming. Sensors (Basel, Switzerland) 15/20, 2020.

Sa20 Safaei, M. et al.: A Systematic Literature Review on Outlier Detection in Wireless Sensor Networks. Symmetry 3/12, p. 328, 2020.

SI11 Sadiq, S., Yeganeh, N.; Indulska, M.: 20 Years of Data Quality Research: Themes, Trends and Synergies. In (Heng Tao Shen; Yanchun Zhang Hrsg.): Australasian Database Conference (ADC 2011). ACS, Perth, Australia, pp. 153-162, 2011.

TKW20 Teh, H. Y.; Kempa-Liehr, A. W.; Wang, K. I.-K.: Sensor data quality: a systematic review. Journal of Big Data 1/7, p. 1645, 2020.

Active-learning-driven deep interactive segmentation for cost-effective labeling of crop-weed image data

Freddy Sikouonmeu[1] and Martin Atzmueller[1,2]

Abstract: Active learning has shown its reliability in (semi-)supervised machine learning tasks to reduce the labeling cost for large datasets in various areas. However, in the agricultural field, despite past attempts to reduce the labeling cost and the burden on the labeler in acquiring image labels, the load during the acquisition of pixel-level labels for semantic image segmentation tasks remains high. Typically, the respective pixel-level masks are acquired manually by drawing polygons over irregular and complex-shaped object boundaries. In contrast, this paper proposes a method leveraging the power of a click-based deep interactive segmentation model (DISEG) in an active learning approach to harvest high-quality image segmentation labels at a low cost for training a real-time task model by only clicking on the objects' fore- and background surfaces. Our first experimental results indicate that with an average of 3 clicks per image object and using only 3% of the unlabeled dataset, we can acquire pixel-level labels with good quality at low cost.

Keywords: deep learning, active learning, deep interactive segmentation, real-time semantic segmentation, crop-weed detection, data annotation

1 Introduction

In the field of agriculture, learning under supervision or partial supervision (supervised or semi-supervised learning) still provides highly competitive results in comparison to their counterparts whereby learning is done without any label. In a classic supervised learning paradigm, images are labeled for training a task model to achieve satisfactory results. This becomes tedious and expensive when dealing with a large pool of images. Several approaches like active learning (AL) have been applied to reduce the overall labeling cost. They either focus on the selection of informative and diversified images or on the selection of cost-effective images to be labeled. These approaches reduce the labeling effort or burden on the labeler by reducing the overall images to be labeled; however, this effort essentially remains high during labeling while acquiring pixel-level masks for semantic image segmentation tasks. These pixel-level labels are typically acquired manually by drawing polygons over object instance boundaries, i.e. clicking around an object boundary. In the agricultural field, objects such as leaves, harvesters, and stones are complex, and irregular in shape, and may necessitate several labeler clicks if labeled this way. Therefore, this leads to an increase in difficulty and the overall annotation cost needed to label an image in the dataset.

---
[1] German Research Center for Artificial Intelligence (DFKI), Osnabrück, 49090, freddy.sikouonmeu@dfki.de
[2] Osnabrück University, Semantic Information Systems Group, Osnabrück, 49090, martin.atzmueller@uos.de

This paper proposes a method to reduce the annotation cost using click-based deep interactive segmentation (DISEG) in an active learning approach for (semi-)automating the labeling process. A DISEG model is used to acquire pixel-level label masks for objects or regions in images selected through AL by only using the labeler's fore- and background clicks. We use the acquired labels to train the task model. For this, we focus on real-time crop-weed semantic image segmentation (RT-seg) to evaluate our approach.

2 Related work

Interactive segmentation has been around for a long time but has typically been implemented using classical graph-based techniques to interactively segment the foreground from the background using low-level image features and labeler inputs as guidance. Given the limitation of such an approach, the authors in DIOS [Xu16] proposed using a deep convolutional neural network (CNN) that predicts an object label mask based on the labeler clicks (fore- and background clicks). These clicks are encoded as image distance maps and fed into the deep learning model with the original image for predicting the clicked object label mask. When using DIOS for pixel-level labeling, the predicted label mask for an object on the first click might not be accurate enough, therefore in such cases the labeler adds further fore- and background clicks to adapt the predicted object mask until being satisfied with the results. Based on the work of DIOS [Xu16], several variations of their initial idea were proposed. Our work leverages the work of [SPK21], where the previous object mask is further provided as input for extra guidance to the model. AL focuses on the intelligent selection of samples from a pool or stream of images to be labeled, in particular, in contexts where labeling could be expensive and time-consuming [Se95]. AL in agriculture has been applied in various subfields, e.g., for crop-weed detection in [Sh20]. Related to this paper is the work of DIAL [Ga22] for remote sensing, which applied AL to train a single multiclass DISEG model to segment objects on an image. In contrast to our work, their DISEG model plays both the role of the annotation model and the task model. However, this approach is tied to the domain being investigated since their DISEG model expects each click to be assigned to a specific class during training. This is in contrast to our method which separates the DISEG model from the specific task model. Our DISEG model is not required to have any knowledge of an object class and focuses on differentiating an object's foreground from its background by using a labeler click.

3 Approach

Our approach uses two separate CNNs in its pipeline: the annotation model (DISEG) and the task model. The annotation model is responsible for automating the labeling process by assisting the labeler during labeling, while the task model is the target model that learns from the labeled images acquired in the labeling stage. The task model is also responsible for selecting the informative images based on their uncertainty from the pool of images to be labeled by the labeler. Our DISEG architecture is the well-known High-Resolution Network HRNET18 as used in [SPK21]. For our task model, we chose the FASSDNet architecture [Ro21] due to its satisfactory results during our experiments on small devices like NVIDIA Jetson NX and AGX. This is then small and fast enough to be deployed on mobile devices like robots and harvesters. We note that our proposed approach is not model and hardware specific and can be used with any other model.

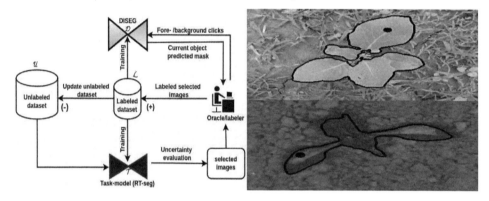

Fig. 1: Active-learning-driven pipeline (left image). The predicted mask for cauliflower (top right) and sugar beets crop predicted mask (bottom right) using only one labeler click (foreground click)

We show an overview of the complete pipeline in Figure 1 (left). Given that during AL the task model is uncertain at early iteration stages (cold-start), we first randomly choose an initial small seed set of images to be labeled manually. The seed set is used to initially train the DISEG model (D) and task model (T). During our experiments, we instead revealed the provided label masks for images in the seed set. The loop in Figure 1 starts as follows: After initially training D and T on the seed set, the task model is used for selecting a batch of informative images from the pool of unlabeled images by estimating each image's uncertainty. The images with the highest uncertainties are selected and passed to the labeler, and he/she uses the DISEG model to label each object or region on these images. The acquired labels are then collected and added to those from previous iterations to train the task and the DISEG model. The cycle is repeated with the selection of the next batch by calculating the uncertainties of images in the unlabeled pool until the set budget is exhausted e.g., time, the maximum number of iterations, or the number of images.

4 Results and discussion

For a fast and large-scale evaluation of our approach, we simulated the labeling process i.e., the acquisition of the labeled masks by randomly generating labeler clicks on objects surfaces. To simulate a labeler click interaction, we iterate over each object or region in an image at a time. For an object, we first add a random foreground click point on its surface as a normal labeler would have done. The click point and the image are passed to the DISEG model, which predicts a mask for the selected object (Fig. 1 top left). We compare the predicted label mask to that of the manually acquired labels provided by the dataset authors. In case the Intersection over Union (IoU) of the predicted object mask label is lower than a given IoU threshold, we randomly add further fore- or background clicks to adapt the predicted mask. Similar to [SPK21], we limit the total number of randomly generated clicks to be added during labeling an object to 20. The maximum number of clicks represents the set point at which the model is believed to be unable to predict a satisfiable mask with an IoU equal to or greater than the set threshold. In case the model is incapable during the simulation of predicting an object label mask with an IoU greater or equal to that of the set threshold, this object mask label is simply ignored.

We apply two publicly available crop-weed datasets with different sizes to evaluate our approach: the sugar beets dataset [Ch17] and the CWF-788 dataset [Li19]. The former consists of 10K crop-weed images, whereas the CWF-788 (Crop in the weedy field) is a relatively small dataset consisting of 755 Cauliflower images. We split each dataset into a train (70%), validation (20%), and test set (10%). Only the training split is used as the unlabeled dataset for active learning image selection, labeling, and training. We ran our experiments by selecting the most informative images from the unlabeled pool based on their uncertainties. Four different AL uncertainty query functions were used for the sampling of the next batch of images to be labeled in our experiments: margin, entropy, random, and Monte-Carlo dropout. We sample at each iteration 32 and 16 images with the highest uncertainties from the sugar beets and CWF-788 dataset respectively. As a baseline, we train our task model (without AL) on the complete training set. For experiments on the sugar beet dataset, we set the image size at 512x1024 and trained for 100 epochs using the stochastic gradient descent as an optimizer combined with a cyclic scheduler. We use the bootstrap loss function and set the batch size to 16. For our experiments on the CWF-788 dataset, we use similar hyperparameters as in our sugar beets experiments except for the image size, optimizer, and loss function, which is set to 128x128, adam, and cross-entropy, respectively. During all our experiments the DISEG annotation model is trained for 100 epochs, using the adam weight optimizer with a progressive decreasing learning rate initially set at 0.0001 as in [SPK21].

As a proxy metric for evaluating the performance of our DISEG model, we use the average number of clicks (NoC) capped at 20 needed to reach a threshold IoU of 80% (NOC20@80) and 90% (NOC20@90) while annotating object instances on the test set. This aligns with previous related works [Xu16] and [SPK21] that set the maximum number of clicks that could be randomly sampled to reach a set IoU during a click simulation to 20. We notice that on the CWF-788 our DISEG model needs an average of 3 and 4 clicks per object in an image to predict a label mask with an IoU of at least 80% and 90% respectively, that of the manually provided label i.e., NOC20@80=3, and NOC20@90=4. This could already serve as coarse semantic labels for the dataset. In some use cases, these coarse segmentation masks are sufficient for training a task model. Similarly, we observed that on the sugar beets test set our DISEG model adapted throughout the learning process could reach a NOC20@80 =3 and a NOC20@90 =12.

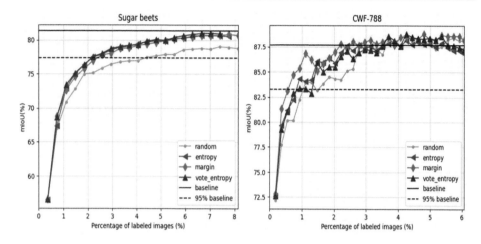

Fig. 2: Percentage of labeled images for different AL query functions – sugar beets and CWF-788

Figure 2 shows the result of 3 average runs on both the sugar beets and the CWF-788 datasets for each query function. We notice that in our experiments, we can reach 95% of the performance of the baseline model by only using a limited set of data, i.e., less than 3% of the set-aside train datasets to be labeled. Furthermore, in all our experiments all query functions (entropy, margin, MC-dropout) performed better or slightly better than the random sampling query function, even in some cases (CWF-788) surpassing the baseline. We argue that these query functions heavily contribute to reducing the annotation cost by selecting highly informative (highly uncertain) images for labeling. Their selection focuses on images with classes where the task model is at most uncertain, which leads to the labeling and training of difficult images. Therefore, we did not only observe that AL further helps in reducing the annotation cost by reducing the overall number of images to be labeled but that in some cases it even causes the task model to surpass the baseline model. Finally, our DISEG model revealed to be struggling while predicting the masks of small objects like small leaves and weeds at the early growth stages of the crop plant. This was observed in the sugar beets dataset requiring on average 12 clicks to predict a mask with an IoU larger than 90% i.e. NOC20@90 =12. A potential reason may be the fact that the DISEG model is having difficulties capturing the context and edge boundary information around small objects during training, making it difficult for the model to predict a mask for such object instances during testing.

5 Conclusion

In this paper, we proposed an approach combining click-based DISEG with active learning to further reduce the annotation cost. This approach leverages the power of a DISEG model to acquire pixel-level labeled masks for images selected through AL at a low cost to train a real-time crop-weed segmentation model. We evaluated our approach on the sugar beets dataset and the CWF-788 cauliflower dataset regarding the proposed method. Overall, our experiments showed satisfactory results in reducing the acquisition of pixel-level masks. On average, only 3 clicks per object or region in an image are required in both datasets to reach an IoU of 80% of an object label provided by the authors' datasets. Further experiments also showed that combining both concepts not only contributes in reducing the number of clicks required to label a complete image but also in reducing the overall number of images to be labeled. Furthermore, by applying our method, we could reach 95% of the performance of our baseline model using less than 3% of the overall unlabeled dataset at an average of 3 clicks per object instance on an image. These first experimental results indicate the usefulness of combining both DISEG and AL to enable a (semi-)automatic annotation process for acquiring pixel-level image labels at low cost.

Acknowledgements: The resKIL project is funded by the Federal Ministry of Food and Agriculture under grant No. 28DK102D20. The DFKI Niedersachsen (DFKI NI) is sponsored by the Ministry of Science and Culture of Lower Saxony and the VolkswagenStiftung.

Bibliography

[Ch17] Chebrolu, N. et.al.: Agricultural robot dataset for plant classification, localization and mapping on sugar beet fields. The International Journal of Robotics Research, 36(10):1045-1052, 2017.

[Li19] Li, N. et.al.: Real-time crop recognition in transplanted fields with prominent weed growth: a visual attention-based approach. IEEE-Access, 7:185310-185321, 2019.

[Ro21] Rosas-Arias, L. et.al.: FASSD-Net: Fast and Accurate Real-Time Semantic Segmentation for Embedded Systems. IEEE Transactions on Intelligent Transportation Systems, 2021.

[Se95] Settles, B.: Active Learning Literature Survey. Science, 10(3):237-304, 1995.

[Sh20] Azubi, L. et.al.: Gradient and log-based active learning for semantic segmentation of crop and weed for agricultural robots. In: 2020 IEEE International Conference on Robotics and Automation (ICRA). IEEE, pp. 1350-1356, 2020.

[SPK21] Sofiiuk, K.; Petrov, I.; Konushin, A.: Reviving iterative training with mask guidance for interactive segmentation. arXiv preprint arXiv:2102.06583, 2021.

[Xu16] Xu, N. et.al.: Deep interactive object selection. In: Proceedings of the IEEE conference on computer vision and pattern recognition. pp. 373-381, 2016.

[Ga22] Gaston, L. et.al.: DIAL: Deep Interactive and Active Learning for Semantic Segmentation in Remote Sensing. IEEE Journal of Selected Topics in Applied Earth Observations and Remote Sensing, 15, 3376-3389, 2022.

Evaluierung eines Funktionsmusters für ein Tracking-Referenzsystem in der Rinderhaltung

Katrin Sporkmann[1], Heiko Neeland[2], Christiane Engels[3], Maria Trilling[4], Marten Wegener[5], Steffen Pache[6] und Wolfgang Büscher[7]

Abstract: Im Rahmen des Experimentierfelds *CattleHub* wird eine Spezifikation für ein Tracking-Referenzsystem entwickelt, welches Vergleichsuntersuchungen von kommerziellen Trackingsystemen für Milchkühe ermöglicht und mit dem weitere neue Anwendungsfälle für die Praxis erschlossen werden sollen. Für eine erste Untersuchung im Stall ohne Tierpräsenz wurden statische und dynamische Messreihen mit dem Funktionsmuster eines solchen Systems durchgeführt. Die statischen Messreihen erzielten eine mittlere Positionsgenauigkeit von 50,7 cm mit einer Präzision von 4,6 cm und einem Offset von 50,5 cm. Die Positionsgenauigkeit des bewerteten Systems wurde hauptsächlich von einem hohen Offset für die y-Koordinate bestimmt. Die dynamischen Messreihen zeigten eine durchschnittliche Standardabweichung von 8,8 cm vom Mittelwert für die Strecken in y-Richtung und von 14,4 cm für die Strecken in x-Richtung. Die Bewegungsverläufe konnten durch das System zeitlich gut abgebildet werden. Die nächsten Erprobungsschritte des Referenzsystems erfolgen mit Prototypen am Tier.

Keywords: Assistenzsysteme, Tracking-Referenzsystem, OpenCattleHub, Reverse TDoA, DRMS

1 Einleitung

Mit stetig wachsenden Tierbeständen in der Milchviehhaltung steigt der Bedarf der Tierhaltenden an effizienten Werkzeugen zur Bewältigung des Herdenmanagements. Bedingt durch den technologischen Fortschritt bei gleichzeitigem Preisverfall für industrielle Echtzeit-Lokalisierungssysteme in den letzten zehn Jahren wuchs auch das Interesse an Trackingsystemen für die Milchviehhaltung. Neben der Positionsbestimmung ermöglichen Trackingsysteme eine kontinuierliche Tierbeobachtung und daraus resultierend die Erfassung von Tieraktivitäten, die wertvolle Verhaltensparameter für die tierhaltenden Betriebe liefern. Beispielsweise wird seitens der Forschung versucht, aus

---

[1] Thünen-Institut für Agrartechnologie, Bundesallee 47, 38116 Braunschweig, at-lit@thuenen.de
[2] Thünen-Institut für Agrartechnologie, Bundesallee 47, 38116 Braunschweig, heiko.neeland@thuenen.de
[3] Universität Bonn, Institut für Landtechnik, Nußalle 5, 53115 Bonn, christiane.engels@uni-bonn.de
[4] Landwirtschaftskammer Nordrhein-Westfalen, Haus Düsse 2, 59505 Bad Sassendorf, maria.trilling@lwk.nrw.de
[5] Technische Universität Chemnitz, Professur Schaltkreis- und Systementwurf, Reichenhainer Str. 70, 09107 Chemnitz, marten.wegener@etit.tu-chemnitz.de
[6] LfULG – Lehr- und Versuchsgut Köllitsch, Am Park 3, 04886 Köllitsch, Steffen.Pache@smekul.sachsen.de
[7] Universität Bonn, Institut für Landtechnik, Nußalle 5, 53115 Bonn, wolfgang.buescher@uni-bonn.de

den Positionsdaten auf das Sozialverhalten von Milchkühen zu schließen [MFL21], was genaue und valide Positionsdaten notwendig macht. Gleichzeitig entstand mit dem steigenden Angebot von kommerziellen Tierortungs- bzw. Trackingsystemen in der Milchviehhaltung der Wunsch nach einer Bewertung der Funktions- und Positionsgenauigkeit. Andere Studien bewerten Trackingsysteme manuell oder verwenden Methoden der Bildanalyse [Po14; Me18]. Im Gegensatz dazu ist ein Ziel im Experimentierfeld *CattleHub* die vergleichende Untersuchung mit Hilfe eines mobilen Tracking-Referenzsystems auf Funkbasis, als *OpenCattleHub* bezeichnet. Zur Überprüfung der Qualitätsanforderungen unter praxisnahen Bedingungen wurde das Funktionsmuster des Systems ohne Tierpräsenz in einem Abteil eines Milchviehstalls untersucht. Ziel dieser Untersuchung war der Funktionstest des Systems in einer Stallumgebung unter Berücksichtigung der Einflussfaktoren Funktionsbereich, Tag-Höhe und Tag-Nummer.

2 Material und Methoden

Zur Evaluierung des Funktionsmusters als Tracking-Referenzsystem wurden statische und dynamische Positionsmessungen in einem Stallabteil des Milchviehstalls des Versuchs- und Bildungszentrum Landwirtschaft Haus Düsse ohne Tierpräsenz durchgeführt (vgl. Abb. 1).

Abb. 1: Verwendetes Stallabteil ohne Tierpräsenz zur Evaluation des Funktionsmusters des Tracking-Referenzsystems (hier ist die Durchführung der dynamischen Messreihen zu sehen) (Quelle: Thünen-Institut)

Das Funktionsmuster besteht aus stationären Ankern (Satlets) und im Projekt entwickelten Transpondern (Tags). OpenCattleHub ist für den mobilen Einsatz in unterschiedlichen Stallumgebungen konzipiert. Zur Positionsbestimmung wird Ultrabreitband-Technologie (UWB) nach dem Prinzip des „Reverse TDoA" verwendet, welches Eigenlokalisierung bei einer nahezu unendlichen Anzahl von Tags auf Grund geringer Auslastung des Funkkanals ermöglicht. Die räumliche Auflösung beträgt 10 cm und die Samplerate 3 - 5 Hz. Zur Datenübertragung vom Transponder zum Rechner wurde Bluetooth Low Energy (BLE) eingesetzt.

Für alle Versuche wurden wie in Abbildung 2 dargestellt sechs Anker (Satlets) im Stallabteil verteilt in einer Höhe zwischen 3,07 und 3,67 m angebracht. Für das Einmessen der Anker, der Messpunkte (M) und der Wegstrecken (R) wurde ein Laserdistanzmesser GLM 120 C (Robert Bosch Power Tools GmbH, Deutschland) verwendet.

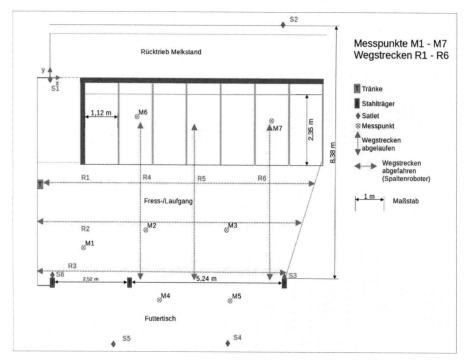

Abb. 2: Stallabteil mit Messpunkten für statische Messreihen und Wegstrecken für dynamische Messreihen.

Die statischen Messreihen erfolgten anhand sieben ausgewählter Messpunkte (s. Abb. 2) jeweils in den Höhen 75 und 152 cm, entsprechend der durchschnittlichen Höhe der Transponder am Halsband von liegenden und stehenden Kühen, vgl. [Hi20]. Für jeden Messpunkt und jede Höhe wurden drei baugleiche Tags nacheinander mit jeweils einer Wiederholungsmessung für eine Messdauer von je 2:30 min platziert. Die dynamischen Messreihen wurden auf drei Längsstrecken auf dem Laufgang (s. Abb. 1 und Abb. 2,

R1 - R3) mit einem Spaltenroboter abgefahren und auf drei Querstrecken vom Fressgitter bis in die Liegebox (s. Abb. 2, R4 - R6) von einer Person abgelaufen. Eine Schnur diente als Spurführung sowohl für die Längsstrecken als auch für die Querstrecken.

Zur Bewertung der Genauigkeit des Systems wurden die nach Maalek und Sadeghpour [MS13] beschriebenen Kennzahlen „Distance Root Mean Squared (DRMS)", „Präzision" und „Offset" mit SAS 9.4 (SAS Institute Inc., Cary, North Carolina, USA) in cm berechnet. Die Präzision spiegelt die Streuung der Position um einzelne Messpunkte herum wider und der Offset ist ein systematischer Messfehler, der die Genauigkeit in Form einer Abweichung bestimmt. Für die Bewertung der dynamischen Messreihen wurde eine gleichförmige Bewegung entlang der Schnur angenommen und die Streuung orthogonal zur Bewegungsrichtung in Form der Standardabweichung berechnet.

3 Ergebnisse

Das Funktionsmuster der *OpenCattleHub*-Spezifikation erzielte für die statischen Messreihen im Mittel eine Positionsgenauigkeit von 50,7 cm (DRMS) mit einer Präzision von 4,6 cm und einem Offset von 50,5 cm (Tab. 1). Damit liegen 63,2 % (95 %) der Messwerte in einem Radius von 50,7 cm (87,7 cm) um den tatsächlichen Messpunkt.

Kennzahlen in cm	Tag-Höhe[1]		Funktionsbereich[1]			Tag-Nummer[1]		
	75 cm	152 cm	Liegebox	Laufgang	Futtertisch	1	2	3
DRMS	50,1	51,5	63,4[a]	45,8[b]	43,9[b]	49,4	50,4	52,3
Präzision	5,2[a]	3,8[b]	4,4	4,5	4,8	5,0	3,9	4,9
Offset	49,8	51,2	63,3[a]	45,6[b]	43,6[b]	49,2	50,2	52,0

Tab. 1: Positionsgenauigkeit in Abhängigkeit der Kategorien Tag-Höhe, Funktionsbereich und Tag-Nummer anhand der Kennzahlen DRMS, Präzision und Offset für 77 Messreihen ([1]unterschiedliche Kennbuchstaben (a, b) unterscheiden sich signifikant auf dem 5%-Niveau)

In Tabelle 1 sind die Ergebnisse zu den Kennzahlen DRMS, Offset und Präzision für die Kategorien Tag-Höhe, Funktionsbereich und Tag-Nummer dargestellt. Auffallend ist der niedrigere DRMS bzw. der höhere Offset in der Liegebox, der sich signifikant von den Funktionsbereichen Laufgang und Futtertisch unterscheidet. Der höchste Offset von 69,6 cm wurde in der Liegebox in der Höhe 152 cm erfasst, der sich für nahezu alle untersuchten Kategorien auf einen hohen Offset der y-Koordinate zurückführen lässt. Die Messwerte waren im Mittel um 43,6 cm in y-Richtung verschoben (vgl. Abb. 2). Für die x-Richtung beträgt der Offset im Mittel 2,1 cm. Die höchste Positionsgenauigkeit mit 41,8 cm (DRMS) wurde im Laufgang in der Höhe 152 cm erreicht, die niedrigste in derselben Höhe mit 69,7 cm in der Liegebox. In einer Höhe von 75 cm ist die Präzision mit 5,2 cm signifikant niedriger als in der Höhe 152 cm (3,8 cm). Die höchste Präzision mit 2,7 cm wurde in der Höhe 152 cm auf dem Laufgang erzielt, wohingegen die niedrigste Präzision ebenfalls auf dem Laufgang mit 5,6 cm in der Höhe 75 cm gemessen wurde. Alle drei untersuchten Tags verhalten sich sowohl in der Präzision als auch im Offset ähnlich.

Die dynamischen Messreihen der abgelaufenen Strecken R4 - R6 in y-Richtung zeigten mit einer Standardabweichung von 8,8 cm eine deutlich geringere Streuung im Vergleich zu den abgefahrenen Strecken R1 – R3 in x-Richtung mit einer Standardabweichung von 14,4 cm.

4 Diskussion und Fazit

Das untersuchte Funktionsmuster erreichte eine Positionsgenauigkeit von $\leq$ 100 cm für 95 % der Messwerte. Die im Projekt geforderte Positionsgenauigkeit von $\leq$ 50 cm wurde für 63,2 % der Messwerte, die in einem Radius von 50,7 cm um den tatsächlichen Messpunkt liegen, fast erreicht. In [Hi20] wurde ein annähernder Wert von 50 cm für eine Tag-Höhe von 150 cm ohne Tierpräsenz erreicht. Mit Tierpräsenz erreichten [Po14] eine Genauigkeit von 51,5 cm und 90 % der Messwerte lagen in einem Radius von 97 cm (Ubisense). Bei [Wo17] lag die Positionsgenauigkeit bei 122 - 180 cm (Smartbow) und [RBH21] erreichten einen Wert von 39 cm mit einer Streuung von 62 cm (Eigenentwicklung).

Die gleiche bzw. bessere Positionsgenauigkeit (DRMS) des bewerteten Systems wird durch den hohen Wert des Offsets für die y-Koordinate bestimmt, während die Präzision mit <10 cm als sehr gut für ein Tracking-Referenzsystem einzuschätzen ist. In den Untersuchungen von [En22] wurde ein ähnlicher Effekt mit einem gleichen Funktionsmuster festgestellt, der aber sowohl für die y-Koordinate als auch die für x-Koordinate zu beobachten war. Obwohl eine Sichtverbindung von mindestens vier Ankern auf alle Tag-Positionen gegeben war, wurden ortsabhängige Offsets festgestellt. Für die Höhe 152 cm in der Liegebox war dieser auffällig hoch. Ein Fehler durch den Einfluss der Stalleinrichtung und Stahlkonstruktion kann in der hier vorliegenden Studie als minimal angesehen werden, da dieser Offset für Funktionsbereiche Laufgang, Futtertisch und verstärkt für die Liegebox auftrat. Eine Erklärung dafür kann weder aus der Kollision der Funkwellen mit der Stalleinrichtung noch aus Fehlern beim Einmessen abgeleitet werden.

Die dynamischen Messreihen unterscheiden sich jeweils für die x- und y-Richtung. Die Laufstrecke in Richtung y ist sehr präzise, die Standardabweichung in x-Richtung ist hingegen nahezu doppelt so hoch. Da für beide Richtungen nur jeweils ein Träger (Versuchsperson bzw. Roboter) aktiv war, müssen in geplanten Folgeuntersuchungen beide Bewegungsarten für beide Richtungen genauer untersucht werden. Wünschenswert wäre dabei ein verbessertes 2D-Referenzverfahren bzw. Spurführung für die Wegstrecken, damit die Abweichungen bei der Versuchsdurchführung minimiert und zurückgelegte Wegstrecken erfasst werden können.

Zusammenfassend lässt sich festhalten, dass das Funktionsmuster von OpenCattleHub als mobiles Tracking-Referenzsystem für die Rinderhaltung geeignet sein kann. Die hohe Präzision sowohl für dynamische als auch für statischen Messreihen und zudem gute

Positionsgenauigkeit bestätigen das. Weitere Untersuchungen zur Optimierung des Offsets und der Validierung des Tracking-Referenzsystems sowie der Einflussfaktor Tier sollen bei Folgeuntersuchungen für eine Vielzahl von Tags berücksichtigt werden.

Danksagung und Förderhinweis: Für die freundliche Unterstützung bei den Untersuchungen im Milchviehstall bedanken wir uns bei den Mitarbeiter*innen des Versuchs- und Bildungszentrums Landwirtschaft Haus Düsse.

Die Förderung des Vorhabens erfolgt aus Mitteln des Bundesministeriums für Ernährung und Landwirtschaft (BMEL) aufgrund eines Beschlusses des deutschen Bundestages. Die Projektträgerschaft erfolgt über die Bundesanstalt für Landwirtschaft und Ernährung (BLE) im Rahmen der Förderung der Digitalisierung in der Landwirtschaft mit dem Förderkennzeichen 28DE108E18 (Experimentierfeld *CattleHub*).

Literaturverzeichnis

[En22] Engels, C., et al.: OpenCattleHub: A portable reference system for indoor tracking in livestock farming. PRECISION LIVESTOCK FARMING '22, S. 602-609, 2022.

[Hi20] Hindermann, P., et al.: High precision real-time location estimates in a real-life barn environment using a commercial ultra wideband chip. Computers and Electronics in Agriculture, Art.-Nr. 105250, 2020.

[Me18] Meunier, B., et al.: Image analysis to refine measurements of dairy cow behaviour from a real-time location system. Biosystems Engineering, S. 32-44, 2018.

[MFL21] Melzer N., Foris B., Langbein J.: Validation of a real-time location system for zone assignment and neighbor detection in dairy cow group. Computers and Electronics in Agriculture, Art.-Nr. 106280, 2021.

[MS13] Maalek, R.; Sadeghpour, F.: Accuracy assessment of Ultra-Wide Band technology in tracking static resources in indoor construction scenarios. Automation in Construction 30, S. 170-183, 2013.

[Po14] Porto, S. M. C., et al.: Localisation and identification performances of a real-time location system based on ultra wide band technology for monitoring and tracking dairy cow behaviour in a semi-open free-stall barn. Computers and Electronics in Agriculture, S. 221-229, 2014.

[RBH21] Ren K., Bernes G., Hetta M., Karlsson J.: Tracking and analysing social interactions in dairy cattle with real-time locating system and machine learning. Journal of Systems Architecture, Art.-Nr. 102139, 2021.

[Wo17] Wolfger B., et al.: Technical note: Evaluation of an ear-attached real-time location monitoring system, Journal of Dairy Science S. 2219-2224, 2017.

Wann, wo und wie? Ein softwarebasiertes Mehrebenen-Informationssystem zur Optimierung von Beweidungssystemen

SMILe

Astrid Sturm [1], Oliver Schöttker [2], Karmand Kadir[3] und Frank Wätzold[4]

Abstract: Wir präsentieren den Prototyp eines **S**oftwarebasierten **M**ehrebenen-**I**nformationssystems für **L**andwirt**e** (SMILe) für die Berechnung optimierter Weideproduktionssysteme im Grünland. Anhand der im SMILE zur Verfügung stehenden Daten können moderne und nachhaltige Weideproduktionssysteme dargestellt und optimiert werden. Aus den verarbeiteten ökologischen und agronomischen Daten werden Aussagen über den Zustand von Weideflächen, daraus folgend das Beweidungspotential für bestimmte Flächen abgeleitet und eine Empfehlung an Nutzer:innen präsentiert. SMILe unterstützt Nutzer:innen bei der Planung und Umsetzung „virtueller Zäune" als Alternative zu physischen Zäunen.

Keywords: Beweidung, Grünland, Weideproduktionssystem

1 Einleitung

Dauergrünland stellt einen zentralen Bestandteil landwirtschaftlicher Nutzfläche weltweit dar und spielt eine wichtige Rolle in der extensiven Tierhaltung [HI22]. Es ist aber auch von großer Bedeutung für das Tierwohl und dient darüber hinaus dem Schutz der Artenvielfalt [SZ22]. Das Verhalten von Weidetieren hilft dabei, die Heterogenität ökologischer Strukturen zu fördern mit positiven Auswirkungen auf die Bereitstellung von Ökosystemdienstleistungen und die Artenvielfalt [Ha22; HI22]. Aufgrund ihrer betriebswirtschaftlichen Vorteilhaftigkeit findet die moderne Nutztierhaltung jedoch heutzutage zu großen Teilen in Form von intensiver Stallhaltung statt [Ki22], wodurch die Bewirtschaftung von Grünlandflächen vielfach zu einer intensiven und ökologisch nachteiligen Futtermittelproduktion herabgestuft wird [HI22].

Zur Erreichung einer ökologisch und agronomisch nachhaltigen Weidewirtschaft und um die wachsende Nachfrage nach weidebasierten Produkten erfüllen zu können [SZ22], ist es daher wichtig, das Weidemanagement insgesamt zeit- und kosteneffizienter zu machen.

---

[1] Brandenburgische Technische Universität Cottbus-Senftenberg, Environmental Economics, Erich-Weinert Str. 1, 03046 Cottbus, sturm@b-tu.de, https://orcid.org/0000-0002-7424-4484
[2] oliver.schoettker@b-tu.de, https://orcid.org/0000-0002-5768-9860
[3] kara.kadir@win.tu-berlin.de
[4] waetzold@b-tu.de

Um diese Zielstellungen zu erreichen, ist eine Digitalisierung und Einbindung moderner Sensortechnik in die Weidewirtschaft notwendig [Ba22; Ma22]. Die Verwendung spezieller Softwaretools kann dabei nützlich sein und Nutzer:innen umfangreiche Informationen und Entscheidungshilfen liefern [St18]. Wir stellen in dieser Arbeit das „Softwarebasierte Mehrebenen Informationssystem für Landwirte (SMILe) vor, welches im Rahmen des interdisziplinären Forschungsprojektes „GreenGrass" entwickelt wird (greengrass-project.de). „GreenGrass" untersucht verschiedene Aspekte produktionstechnischer, ökologischer und sozio-technischer Innovationen im Rahmen nachhaltiger Weidewirtschaft. Kernelement ist die Entwicklung einer Tierlenkungstechnologie unter Einsatz sogenannter „virtueller Zäune". Weidetiere werden dabei – statt mittels herkömmlicher physischer Zäune – mithilfe eines Halsbandes geortet und über virtuell definierte Weidegrenzen auf den Weideflächen eingezäunt. Die Tiere senden und erhalten Signale über ein Halsband, welches sie zudem daran hindert, bestimmte zuvor definierte Weideflächen zu verlassen oder andere Flächen zu betreten (z. B. besondere ökologische Schutzbereiche). Die Weidefläche selbst ist nicht physisch eingezäunt, der Zaun ist virtuell.

2 Material und Methoden

2.1 Datengrundlage

In „GreenGrass" werden Daten aus verschiedenen Bereichen – z.B. Fernerkundungsdaten aus Drohnenbefliegungen und Satelliten (z. B. [BH21]), ökologische Feld- und Modelldaten – im Landschaftskontext erhoben, modelliert und miteinander verknüpft.

SMILe integriert diese Daten mit jeweils unterschiedlichen Datensätzen (z. B. Bilder, Höhenmessungen, Grünlandzahl, Daten zu Biomasse und Biomassequalität, und Artenzahl pro Fläche) mithilfe speziell definierter Datenerfassungsrichtlinien und Schnittstellen. Die räumlich unterschiedlich aufgelösten Daten werden in SMILe auf eine gemeinsame Untersuchungseinheit innerhalb eines 2,5 m x 2,5 m Rasters aggregiert und verarbeitet. Die zeitliche Skala der Datenerfassung unterscheidet sich für die unterschiedlichen Datenquellen. Während Daten aus ökologischen Modellen 3-mal jährlich auf Basis von Feldbegehungen bereitstehen, werden Fernerkundungsdaten auf Basis von Sentinel-2-Satellitendaten in einem 5-tägigen Rhythmus bereitgestellt. Agronomische und ökologische Modellrechnungen ergänzen die Datengrundlage in SMILe. Der Datenfluss in die Software erfolgt über eine Datenbank (Abb. 1). Die gespeicherten Daten werden von SMILe verarbeitet, um Aussagen über den Zustand und das Beweidungspotential bestimmter Flächen treffen zu können.

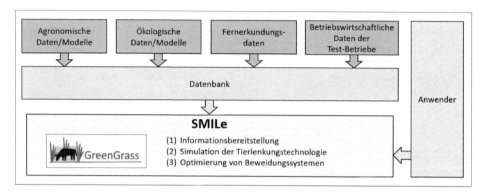

Abb. 1: Datenfluss innerhalb von SMILe

2.2 Funktionalität von SMILe

SMILe umfasst im Wesentlichen drei Funktionen:

(1) Informationsbereitstellung: Agronomische und ökologische Informationen zu den betrieblichen Grünlandflächen werden visuell aufbereitet und Nutzer:innen zeitnah zur Verfügung gestellt (Abb. 2). Dies erlaubt es, einen detaillierten Überblick über den Zustand der betrieblichen Grünlandflächen – aktuell und im Zeitverlauf – zu erhalten und betriebliche Abläufe (wie etwa die Planung von Beweidungsstrategien) an der aktuellen Datenlage auszurichten.

(2) Simulation der Tierlenkungstechnologie: SMILe bietet Nutzer:innen die Möglichkeit, virtuelle Zäune zu planen (Abb. 2). Hierdurch können die Auswirkungen einer geplanten Beweidungsstrategie auf Teilflächen des Betriebs simuliert sowie agronomische und ökonomische Betriebsparameter abgeschätzt werden. Darüber hinaus können ökologische Wirkungen der virtuellen Zaunplanung simuliert werden (z. B. der Einfluss von Beweidung auf die Vegetation). Die Zäune können gezielt zum Ausgrenzen bestimmter Teilflächen der Weide benutzt werden, um so Areale vor Vertritt und Beweidung zu schützen, z. B. Vogelgelege. Die geplanten Zaunverläufe können anschließend in der zugrundeliegenden Datenbank hinterlegt sowie aus SMILe zur weiteren Verwendung in Tierlenkungstechnologien exportiert werden. Es ist grundsätzlich möglich, neben der „GreenGrass"-eigenen Technologie bereits am Markt befindliche virtuelle Zaunsysteme mit SMILe-Exporten zu beliefern, oder alternativ die geplanten Zaunverläufe zur Grundlage manuell zu setzender, physischer Zäune zu machen.

(3) Optimierung von Beweidungssystemen: SMILe soll es Nutzer:innen ermöglichen, den Einsatz der Tierlenkungstechnologie im Rahmen einer Beweidungsstrategie zu optimieren (Abb. 3). Diese Optimierung soll sowohl mit Blick auf agronomische und ökonomische Betriebsparameter als auch auf ökologische Zielgrößen möglich sein. Ziel der Optimierung ist es, durch Simulation von Beweidungsstrategien eine Beweidung zu berechnen, so dass relevante Zielgrößen maximiert werden (z. B. die durch Beweidung

einzelner Flächen zur Verfügung stehende Energie aus Biomasse), unter der Nebenbedingung der Wahrung und/oder Erreichung weiterer betrieblicher Zielgrößen (z. B. Erreichen bestimmter Artenschutzvorgaben oder Milchleistungen).

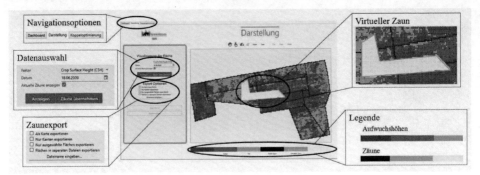

Abb. 2: Darstellung agronomischer und ökologischer Zustandsinformationen im Zeitverlauf in SMILe am Beispiel des „GreenGrass" Testbetriebs in Relliehausen (Niedersachsen), sowie Darstellung der Planung eines virtuellen Zauns auf der Testfläche (gelbe Markierung)

SMILe wurde in einem Co-Creation-Prozess fachübergreifend innerhalb des Projektes und mit Nutzer:innen entwickelt. In „GreenGrass" findet eine enge Begleitung der Forschungsarbeiten durch die Einbindung von Praxisakteuren aus mehreren Reallaboren statt. Diese Praxisakteure liefern wertvollen Input für die Entwicklung von SMILe z. B. durch die Unterstützung bei der Parametrisierung und Plausibilitätsüberprüfung von in SMILe verwendeter Werte sowie bei gewünschten Funktionalitäten der Software.

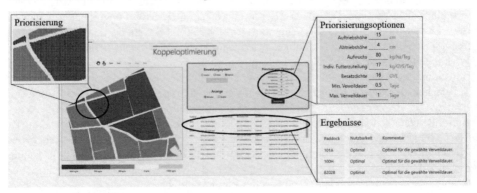

Abb. 3: Simulations- und Optimierungsrechnungen von Beweidungssystemen in SMILe

3 Ergebnisse, Diskussion und Schlussfolgerung

Weidehaltung im Grünland ist sowohl aus Tierwohl- als auch aus Biodiversitätsaspekten wünschenswert und notwendig. Um Weidehaltung nachhaltig, effizient und zukunftsfähig auszugestalten, ist eine Digitalisierung mit Einbindung von Daten aus moderner Sensor- und Fernerkundungstechnik vielversprechend. Um diese Daten nutzerfreundlich und problemspezifisch zu verarbeiten und darzustellen, bedarf es neuer Softwarelösungen wie dem hier vorgestellten Entscheidungshilfetool SMILe. SMILe unterstützt Nutzer:innen bei der Umsetzung moderner und innovativer Weidemanagementsysteme. Wichtiger Bestandteil ist die Möglichkeit der Planung und Simulation „virtueller Zäune". SMILe trägt so zur Digitalisierung und Effizienzsteigerung moderner Beweidungssysteme bei.

Der aktuelle Entwicklungsstand von SMILe ist ein Prototyp einer grünlandorientierten Entscheidungshilfesoftware mit geplanter weiterer Entwicklung zusätzlicher Features. Für einen zukünftigen Produktivbetrieb ist eine hohe Verfügbarkeit der entsprechenden Daten sowie eine hohe Robustheit der verwendeten Modelle unerlässlich. Derzeit ist insbesondere die Erfassung drohnenbasierter Fernerkundungsdaten mit der notwendigen Auflösung mit hohen Kosten behaftet, welche jedoch zukünftig aufgrund technischen Fortschritts sinken dürften [Sc22]. Die Befliegungen können entweder durch geschulte Anwender oder eigens beauftragte Dienstleister durchgeführt werden. Zukünftig sind zudem geplante und teil-autonom durchgeführte Befliegungen mit minimalem Personalaufwand denkbar. Die Sentinel-Daten stehen bereits jetzt kostenlos zur Verfügung und stellen eine solide Datenbasis für die Entscheidungsprozesse dar bis Drohnendaten flächendeckend realisierbar sind. Die Anschaffung von Halsbändern zur Verwendung einer virtuellen Zauntechnologie verursacht derzeit hohe Kosten [Ki22].

Die fortschreitende Digitalisierung in der Landwirtschaft verursacht große Herausforderungen, aber bietet auch Potentiale mit Blick auf betriebliche Wirtschaftlichkeit und Effizienz wie auch bezogen auf Nachhaltigkeit und ökologische Rahmenbedingungen. Die Funktionalitäten von SMILe liefern in dem Zusammenhang einen innovativen Beitrag zur Gestaltung einer modernen und zukunftsfähigen Weidewirtschaft, einer Verbesserung des Tierwohls sowie zur Förderung weiterer Ökosystemleistungen.

Förderhinweis: Die vorgestellten Arbeiten sind als Teil des Projektes „GreenGrass" entstanden, welches vom Bundesministerium für Bildung und Forschung (BMBF) im Rahmen der Förderlinie „Agrarsysteme der Zukunft" gefördert wird (Fördernummer 031B0734).

Literaturverzeichnis

[Ba22] Bahrs, E.: Wie wird die Digitalisierung unsere Landwirtschaft verändern? Umweltzeitung,5, 12-14, 2022.

[BB20] Bloch, R., Bellingrath-Kimura, S.: Smart Farming – Eine Chance für nachhaltige Agrarsysteme? In: M. Göpel et al.: Die Ökologie der digitalen Gesellschaft. Jahrbuch Ökologie 2019/2020. Stuttgart S. Hirzel. S. 110-116, 2022.

[BH21] Bareth, G, Hütt, C.: Upscaling and validation of RTK-direct georeferenced UAV-based RGB image data with Planet imagery using polygon grids for pasture monitoring. Int. Arch. Photogramm. Remote Sens. Spatial Inf. Sci., XLIII-B3-2021, 533-538, 2021.

[Ha22] Hamidi, D. et al.: Heifers don't care: no evidence of negative impact on animal welfare of growing heifers when using virtual fences compared to physical fences for grazing. Animal 16 (9), 2022.

[HI22] Horn, J., Isselstein, J.: How do we feed grazing livestock in the future? A case for knowledge-driven grazing systems. Grass and Forage Science 77 (3), 2022.

[Ki22] Kiefer, A., et al.: Beurteilung des ökonomischen Potenzials des virtuellen Zaunsystems in der deutschen Milchviehhaltung am Beispiel Brandenburgs". In: M. Gandorfer et al. (2022): Künstliche Intelligenz in der Agrar-und Ernährungswirtschaft, Lecture Notes in Informatics (LNI), Gesellschaft für Informatik, Bonn, 2022.

[Ma22] MacPherson, J., et al.: Future agricultural systems and the role of digitization for achieving sustainability goals. A review. Agronomy for Sustainable Development 42 (70), 2022.

[Sc22] Schöttker, O., et al.: Monitoring costs of result-based payments for biodiversity conservation: Will UAV-based remote sensing be the game-changer? MPRA Working Paper No. 112942. https://mpra.ub.uni-muenchen.de/112942/

[St18] Sturm, A., et.al.: DSS-Ecopay – A decision support software for designing ecologically effective and cost-effective agri-environment schemes to conserve endangered grassland biodiversity. Agric. Syst., 161, 113-116, 2018.

[SZ22] Stampa, E., Zander, K.: Backing biodiversity? German consumers' views on a multi-level biodiversity-labeling scheme for beef from grazing-based production systems. Journal of Cleaner Production 370(10), 2022.

Analyse ausgewählter digitaler Lösungen zur N-Düngung

Erkenntnisse aus dreijährigen Feldversuchen

Beat Vinzent[1], Franz-Xaver Maidl[1] und Markus Gandorfer[1]

Abstract: Auf Basis dreijähriger Feldversuchsdaten wurden in Parzellenversuchen an einem niederbayerischen Hochertragsstandort verschiedene digitale Düngesysteme analysiert. Die Variation der einzelnen N-Düngegaben der getesteten Systeme war insgesamt nicht sehr ausgeprägt. In der Gesamtschau konnten durch die zusätzlichen Informationen zur N-Bemessung mit den digitalen Düngesystemen keine signifikant höheren N-kostenfreien Leistungen im Vergleich zu Referenzsystemen erzielt werden. Hinsichtlich der Kosten aber auch Serviceaspekte unterschieden sich die Lösungen deutlicher voneinander.

Keywords: Precision Farming, teilflächenspezifische N-Düngung, Fernerkundung, Düngesysteme

1 Einleitung

Seit längerem werden digitale Lösungen wie beispielsweise traktor- und handgetragene Sensoren als Instrumente für eine Verbesserung der Nährstoffeffizienz in der Landwirtschaft entwickelt. Entgegen den Erwartungen haben diese Technologien bis heute keine stärkere Marktdurchdringung erreicht [GG22], wenngleich die Anforderungen an eine effiziente N-Düngung in der Landwirtschaft für einen nachhaltigen Ackerbau steigen. Bei korrekter Anwendung effizienter Düngealgorithmen können positive Umwelteffekte erreicht werden [Ar22; Ma22], zudem reizt aktuell die Möglichkeit, bei passender Düngestrategie kostensparend zu düngen. Eine bedarfsgerechte Bemessung bzw. Umverteilung der N-Düngermengen ermöglicht eine Reduzierung positiver N-Salden zumindest auf Teilflächen mit niedrigem Ertragspotential. Im günstigsten Fall kommt es zu einer Absenkung des Düngeniveaus ohne Ertrags- und Qualitätsverluste [Ma22; Mi22]. Digitale Düngesysteme können Anwender dabei entlasten, den eingesetzten Dünger teilflächenspezifisch sinnvoll zu verteilen, außerdem sind sie bei Vorhandensein zielführender Algorithmen in der Lage, die absolute Höhe der Düngermenge festzulegen [Ma12; Vi19]. Hier stellt sich unter anderem die Frage, ob es mittlerweile kostengünstige und anwenderfreundliche Alternativen zu den bekannten traktorgebundenen Sensorsystemen gibt. So gibt es seit einigen Jahren zunehmend Lösungen, die beispielsweise fernerkundungsgestützte Daten verwenden. Ein Vorteil dieser Düngesysteme – die in der Regel als Mapping-Ansatz zu charakterisieren sind – ist, dass die N-Düngung vor dem Befahren des Feldes geplant wird. So kann bei der Planung

---

[1] Bayerische Landesanstalt für Landwirtschaft, Institut für Landtechnik und Tierhaltung, Kleeberg 14, 94099 Ruhstorf, beat.vinzent@lfl.bayern.de, franz.xaver.maidl@lfl.bayern.de, markus.gandorfer@lfl.bayern.de

auf rechtliche schlagbezogene Restriktionen bei der Düngung reagiert werden. Bisher gibt es wenig Erfahrungswerte dazu, ob digitale Lösungen zur N-Düngung auf Satellitendatenbasis oder Sensoren als Handgeräte dieselben Effekte wie die traktorgebundene Sensortechnik hervorrufen können. Die Versuchsfrage lautete dabei: Können digital gestützte Düngeempfehlungen dem Nutzer einen agronomischen Mehrwert bei der N-Düngung in Winterweizen bieten?

2 Material und Methoden

2.1 Versuchsaufbau

Auf Basis dreijähriger Feldversuchsdaten in den Untersuchungsjahren 2020 bis 2022 wurden zur Beantwortung der Versuchsfrage Kleinparzellenversuche an einem niederbayerischen Hochertragsstandort im unteren Rottal durchgeführt. Als Varianten wurden mehrere digitale Düngesysteme in einem lateinischen Rechteck mit 4 Wiederholungen analysiert. Die qualitätsbetonten Winterweizensorten waren Impression bzw. Asory mit der Vorfrucht Zuckerrübe in jedem Versuchsjahr und späten Saatterminen zwischen Ende Oktober und Mitte November. Für eine zusätzliche Prüfung des teilflächenspezifischen Umverteilungseffektes werden zukünftig separate Versuchsanlagen angestrebt. In die Untersuchungen wurden neben der Fernerkundung auch statische Düngesysteme der Offizialberatung, Handsensorik und eine Landwirt-Variante miteinbezogen. Abschließend wurde nicht nur die agronomische Leistung ermittelt, sondern ebenso die Kosten der einzelnen Systeme sowie die Datenverfügbarkeit während der Düngesaison betrachtet. Die Berechnungen der N-kostenfreien Leistung gründen auf fünfjährigen Durchschnittspreisen (2018-2022) für Getreide und Betriebsmittel.

2.2 Geprüfte Varianten

- Ungedüngte Kontrolle

- DSN

    Das Düngeberatungssystem Stickstoff (DSN) stellt die Düngeempfehlung der Offizialberatung dar. Es bildet die Basis für die schlageinheitliche N-Düngungshöhe, dient aber zugleich als Basis für einige digital gestützte Düngesysteme. Vom N-Sollwert der Kultur (A-Weizen mit 9 t Ertragspotential) werden Abschläge beispielsweise für den N_{min}-Gehalt im Boden und den Einsatz organischer Dünger sowie weitere Standort- und Managementfaktoren getätigt, um letztlich zu einer absoluten N-Düngeempfehlung zu gelangen [LfL22].

- Landwirt-Variante

  Diese Variante fungiert als betriebsübliche Referenz. Der Landwirt orientierte sich in der Höhe der Gesamtdüngung zwar an DSN, beschränkte die Düngegaben allerdings auf zwei Gaben ohne Spätdüngung, da er aus eigener Erfahrung stets eine späte hohe N-Mineralisierung erwartet hat.

- FarmFacts N Manager pro

  Die absolute N-Düngermenge für die drei Düngetermine wird grundsätzlich in Anlehnung an DSN vorgegeben. Auf Basis von Modellrechnungen zur Ertragsbildung, die durch eine Kombination aus Pflanzenwachstumsmodell und historischen bzw. aktuellen Satellitenaufnahmen der Biomasseentwicklung erfolgen, wird die zu düngende N-Menge bei hoher Ertragserwartung nach oben und bei geringer Ertragserwartung nach unten korrigiert.

- Yara N-Tester Bluetooth

  Es wird eine absolute N-Düngeempfehlung gegeben, dabei sind Angaben zu Ertragsziel, Weizensorte und Bestandesentwicklung notwendig. In den Versuchen wurden die ausgebrachten N-Mengen wie folgt bestimmt: die erste N-Gabe zu Vegetationsbeginn über die photometrische Biomassebestimmung mittels Smartphone-App; die zweite und dritte N-Gabe wurden über das Handgerät N-Tester Bluetooth ermittelt. Die teilflächenspezifische Verteilung mittels aktueller Satellitenkarten der Biomasseentwicklung über Yara atfarm wurde nicht geprüft.

Im Versuch wurden noch weitere Düngetools untersucht, die hier jedoch aus systematischen sowie Platzgründen nicht dargestellt sind. Tabelle 1 gibt einen Überblick zu den ausgebrachten N-Mengen der geprüften Varianten.

	Verteilung 2020	Verteilung 2021	Verteilung 2022	N-Düngungshöhe im 3-Jahres-Schnitt (kg/ha)
Kontrolle	0/0/0	0/0/0	0/0/0	0
DSN	50/60/48	68/50/60	60/55/50	167
Landwirt	90/60/0	80/90/0	80/88/0	163
FarmFacts	53/52/53	68/56/61	75/45/62	175
Yara	70/34/29	110/20/54	95/35/43	163

Tab. 1: Dreijährige Mittelwerte der ausgebrachten N-Mengen aller geprüften Varianten

3 Ergebnisse

In allen Versuchsjahren waren die Düngeversuche auf sehr homogenen Flächen angelegt. Die Homogenität der Schläge wurde empirisch durch mehrjährige NDVI-Karten sowie durch die Erfahrungswerte des Landwirts verifiziert. Die N-Düngungshöhe im 3-Jahres-Schnitt der geprüften Varianten wich nicht sehr von der durch DSN empfohlenen Menge für den Schlagdurchschnitt ab, wobei sich größere Unterschiede in den Teilgaben zeigten (Tab. 1).

Bei der Betrachtung der mehrjährigen Versuchsdaten fällt auf, dass das Ertragspotential am Standort hoch ist. Im Schnitt der Jahre wurden selbst in der ungedüngten Kontrolle Kornerträge von mehr 6,6 t erzielt, die gedüngten Parzellen erreichten Kornerträge zwischen 9 und 10 t. Durch die N-Düngung konnten Mehrerträge zwischen 40 und 45 % erzielt werden, wobei sich abgesehen von der ungedüngten Kontrolle die einzelnen Düngesysteme im Kornertrag nicht signifikant voneinander unterschieden (Abb. 1, relativ dargestellt).

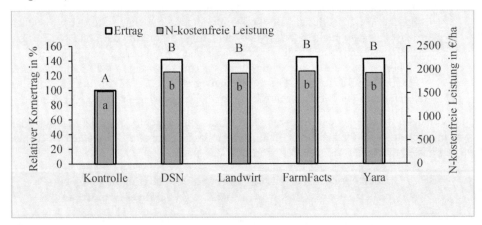

Abb. 1: Dreijährige Mittelwerte der relativen Kornerträge in Bezug zur ungedüngten Kontrolle sowie der N-kostenfreien Leistung; Anova und Tukey-Test für α = 0,05

Zur Berechnung der N-kostenfreien Leistung wurde die erzielte Marktleistung den Kosten für die N-Düngung einschließlich dem Aufwand für die zwei bzw. drei Überfahrten zur Düngung gegenübergestellt. Unterschiedliche Proteingehalte wurden monetär bewertet. Es ergibt sich analog zur Ertragssituation ein einheitliches Bild über alle gedüngten Varianten (Abb. 1).

Eine wesentliche Voraussetzung für die Höhe der absoluten N-Düngeempfehlung wie auch für die teilflächenspezifische Verteilung der Düngung, die auf „In-Season" Informationen beruht, ist die Verfügbarkeit aktueller Fernerkundungsdaten zur Bestandesentwicklung. Im günstigsten Fall ist dieses Kartenmaterial maximal fünf Tage alt oder jünger. Die folgende Tabelle zeigt für jedes Versuchsjahr die Anzahl der verfügbaren Daten mit Satellitenbildern für den Parzellenversuch im Zeitraum von

01.04.-10.06. eines Jahres, die Zeit, in die normalerweise alle drei N-Düngergaben fallen. Theoretisch findet alle 3-5 Tage der Überflug eines Satelliten statt, sodass im besten Fall kontinuierlich Kartenmaterial für die Bestandscharakterisierung zur Verfügung steht. Aus der Tabelle ist ersichtlich, dass die Zahl der verfügbaren Satellitenbilder ohne störende Umwelteinflüsse (Bewölkung) jedoch deutlich geringer war. In einzelnen Jahren betrug die Zeit zwischen zwei verwertbaren Überfliegungen bis zu vier Wochen (Tab. 2).

Versuchsjahr	Termine mit verwertbaren Satellitenkarten für die Düngeplanung					
2020	08.04.	16.04.*	23.04.	28.04.	18.05.	02.06.
2021	08.04.*	23.04.	28.04.	08.05.	07.06.	
2022	28.04.	03.05.	18.05.	23.05.		

Tab. 2: Termine in den Versuchsjahren, zu denen bei den Anbieter FarmFacts und Yara verwertbare Satellitenkarten für die Düngeplanung zur Verfügung standen; *gilt nur für FarmFacts

Die Kosten der beschriebenen digitalen Düngesysteme unterschieden sich zwischen den Anbietern stark. Um ein Gefühl für diese Kosten zu entwickeln, wurde von einem Rottaler Marktfruchtbetrieb (repräsentiert die Gegend der Feldversuche) mit 90 ha Ackerfläche und 50 % Winterweizenanteil in der Fruchtfolge ausgegangen, auf denen die Düngesysteme zum Einsatz kommen. Durch die Nutzung des Yara-Ansatzes entstehen Kosten von 12,96 €/ha. Dem Nutzer bietet dieser Anbieter die Möglichkeit, auch aktuelle Fernerkundungsdaten mit Informationen über die Biomasseentwicklung der Pflanzenbestände abzurufen. Außerdem sind mit dem N-Tester absolute N-Düngeempfehlungen möglich. Im Jahr 2022 betrugen die Kosten der atfarm-Variante für Landwirte im Rahmen einer Unterstützungsaktion [To22] aufgrund hoher N-Düngerpreise 0 €/ha, dies mag sich aber auch wieder ändern. Die Kosten für den FarmFacts N Manager pro betragen für das betrachtete Szenario 40,20 €/ha (Kombination aus Betriebspauschale und flächenabhängiger Servicegebühr). Bei der Einordnung dieser Kosten ist anzumerken, dass es sich bei diesem Ansatz um eine aufwändige Kombination von Satellitendaten sowie einem Pflanzenwachstumsmodell handelt und nutzerfreundliche, einsatzbereite Applikationskarten inkl. Beratungsleitung angeboten werden. Bei Yara müssen die Applikationskarten selbst erstellt und exportiert werden.

4 Diskussion

Mit den getesteten digitalen Düngetools hätte ein unerfahrener und ortsfremder Anwender im mehrjährigen Durchschnitt hohe Erträge und Qualitäten erzielen können. Sowohl für die Bestimmung der absoluten Menge einer N-Düngergabe als auch für die teilflächenspezifische Verteilung gibt es unterschiedlich komplexe Angebote. Der mögliche Vorteil, der speziell in Niedrigertragsbereichen durch die teilflächenspezifische Umverteilung der N-Düngung erreicht werden könnte, wurde in der vorliegenden

Versuchsanlage nicht geprüft, dies sollte aber in weiteren Untersuchungen zukünftig geschehen. Eine schwer zu kalkulierende Tatsache bestand in der Verfügbarkeit tages- oder zumindest wochenaktueller Fernerkundungskarten zur N-Versorgung der Pflanzenbestände, weil die Satellitendaten aufgrund ungünstiger Witterungsverhältnisse zwischen der zweiten März- und der zweiten Junidekade mehrere Wochen alt sein konnten. Es ist zu diskutieren, inwieweit bei solchen Unsicherheiten selbst einfach zu handhabende oder finanziell niederschwellige Angebote dann überhaupt den Erwartungen an eine bedarfsgerechte N-Düngung nachkommen können. Die getesteten digitalen Düngetools hatten für den Fall des „gap filling" verschiedene Kompensationsansätze: Die N-Düngeempfehlung des Anbieters Yara konnte durch den N-Tester direkt im Pflanzenbestand bestimmt werden. Die Variante des FarmFacts N-Manager pro arbeitete dagegen mit einem Pflanzenwachstumsmodell, das auch ohne aktuelle Fernerkundungsdaten oder bei schwach entwickelten Pflanzenbeständen Düngeempfehlungen geben kann.

Literaturverzeichnis

[Ar22] Argento, F.; Liebisch, F.; Anken, T.; Walter, A.; El Benni, N.: Investigating two solutions to balance revenues and N surplus in Swiss winter wheat. Agricultural Systems Vol. 201. 2022.

[GG22] Gabriel, A.; Gandorfer, M.: Adoption of digital technologies in agriculture – an inventory in a European small-scale farming region. Precision Agriculture, 1-24. DOI: 10.1007/s11119-022-09931-1, 2022.

[LfL22] Landesanstalt für Landwirtschaft: Düngebedarfsermittlung für landw. Kulturen, https://www.lfl.bayern.de/duengebedarfsermittlung, abgerufen am 23.10.2022.

[Ma12] Maidl, F.-X.: Voraussetzungen für eine sensorgesteuerte teilflächenspezifische N-Düngung. In: Informationstechnologie für eine nachhaltige Landwirtschaft. 32. GIL-Jahrestagung, S. 199-202, 2012

[Ma22] Maidl, F.-X.; Kern, A.; Kimmelmann, S.; Hülsbergen, K.-J.: Sensorgestützte teilflächenspezifische Stickstoffdüngung mit wissenschaftlich begründeten Algorithmen. Kongressband VDLUFA (im Druck) 2022.

[Mi22] Mittermayer, M; Maidl, F.X.; Nätscher, L.; Hülsbergen, K.J.: Analysis of site-specific N balances in heterogeneous croplands using digital methods. European Journal of Agronomy 133, 126442. DOI: 10.1016/j.eja.2021.126442, 2022.

[To22] Top Agrar: Jetzt kostenlos: Yaras digitale Plattform Atfarm + N-Tester Yara, https://www.topagrar.com/acker/news/jetzt-kostenlos-yaras-digitale-plattform-atfarm-n-tester-yara-12866478.html, abgerufen am 23.10.22.

[Vi19] Vinzent, B.; Maidl, M.; Münster, S.; Gandorfer, M.: Überbetrieblicher Einsatz eines Sensorsystems zur teilflächenspezifischen Stickstoffdüngung. Referate der 39. GIL-Jahrestagung in Wien, A. Meyer-Aurich et al. (Hrsg.), S. 263-268, 2019.

Räumliche Erfassung des organischen Kohlenstoffgehaltes von Böden einer landwirtschaftlichen Intensivregion aus Sentinel-2-Daten

Lucas Wittstruck[1], Heike Gerighausen[2], Annelie Säurich[2], Markus Möller[2], Knut Hartman[3], Michael Steininger[4], Simone Zepp[5] und Thomas Jarmer[1]

Abstract: Der Gehalt und die räumliche Verteilung organischen Kohlenstoffs in Böden stellen eine wesentliche Information zur Bewertung des Bodenzustandes dar. In der vorliegenden Arbeit wurde daher eine quantitative Schätzung des organischen Kohlenstoffs aus räumlich hochaufgelösten multispektralen Satellitendaten in einem landwirtschaftlich geprägten Gebiet nahe der Stadt Köthen (Sachsen-Anhalt) vorgenommen. Die Grundlage bildete ein Bodenkomposit, welches aus mehrjährigen Sentinel-2 Daten (2017-2022) unter Anwendung von Vegetations- und Bodenindizes berechnet wurde. Ergänzend wurde ein digitales Geländemodell der Shuttle Radar Topography Mission (SRTM) berücksichtigt. Die Ergebnisse der Studie haben gezeigt, dass durch die Kombination von optischen Fernerkundungsdaten mit einem Geländemodell robuste Schätzungen des organischen Kohlenstoffs erreicht werden konnten ($R^2 = 0{,}83$, RMSE $= 0{,}23$ und RPD $= 2{,}46$), welche mit Resultaten aus hyperspektralen Fernerkundungsdaten vergleichbar waren.

Keywords: Fernerkundung, Maschinelles Lernen, Präzise Landwirtschaft, Organischer Kohlenstoff, Sentinel-2

1 Einführung

Der Gehalt an organischem Kohlenstoff (C_{org}) in landwirtschaftlich genutzten Böden liefert wichtige Informationen über den Zustand der Böden und deren Potenzial zur Kohlenstoffspeicherung [Pr09]. Aufgrund der räumlichen und zeitlichen Variabilität des Kohlenstoffgehaltes bedarf es für eine präzise und nachhaltige Bewirtschaftung hochaufgelöste Bodenkarten. Studien haben gezeigt, dass insbesondere die Kombination aus Laboranalysen und flugzeuggestützten hyperspektralen Fernerkundungsdaten zur präzisen Abbildung räumlicher Bodeneigenschaften beitragen kann [Hb12]. Die geringe Verfügbarkeit dieser Daten sowie die hohen Kosten durch Befliegungen und eingesetzte Sensortechnik erlauben nur eine geringe Anwendbarkeit für größere Gebiete. Aus diesem

---

[1] Universität Osnabrück, Institut für Informatik, D-49090, Osnabrück, lwittstruck@uni-osnabrueck.de, thomas.jarmer@uos.de.
[2] Julius Kühn-Institut, Institut für Pflanzenbau und Bodenkunde, D-38116 Braunschweig, heike.gerighausen@julius-kuehn.de, annelie.saeurich@julius-kuehn.de, markus.moeller@julius-kuehn.de
[3] EOMAP GmbH & Co. KG, D-82229 Seefeld, hartmann@eomap.de
[4] Mitteldeutsches Institut für Angewandte Standortkunde und Bodenschutz, D-06114 Halle, m.steininger@bodensachverstaendige.de
[5] Deutsches Zentrum für Luft und Raumfahrt, Deutsches Fernerkundungsdatenzentrum, D-82234 Weßling, simone.zepp@dlr.de

Grund kommen frei verfügbaren multispektralen Fernerkundungsdaten wie Sentinel-2 (Copernicus) eine große Bedeutung zu, da diese Sensoren die Erdoberfläche mit hoher räumlicher und zeitlicher Auflösung erfassen.

Das Ziel dieser Arbeit war die Ableitung des Gehaltes an organischem Kohlenstoff auf Basis von multispektralen Sentinel-2-Daten sowie frei zugänglichen Geländeinformationen. Die Ergebnisse wurden dabei mit einer bereits vor Ort durchgeführten Studie von Kanning et al. [KSJ16] verglichen, die einen hyperspektralen Befliegungsdatensatz zur Schätzung des C_{org}-Gehaltes verwendete.

2 Material und Methoden

2.1 Untersuchungsgebiet

Das Untersuchungsgebiet (11°54′E, 51°47′N) befand sich in der Köthener Ebene zwischen den Städten Köthen und Bernburg (Saale) im Bundesland Sachsen-Anhalt. Die Region wird intensiv landwirtschaftlich genutzt, was auf die sehr fruchtbaren Lößböden und Braunerden in der Region zurückzuführen ist [Bu22].

Die örtliche Niederschlagsmenge beträgt 500 mm jährlich bei einer mittleren Geländehöhe von 70 Metern über dem Meeresspiegel [Dw22]. Das Relief ist eher eben und zeichnet sich durch sanfte Bodenwellen aus. In einigen Bereichen kann eine humose Oberbodenschicht von bis zu 40 cm Tiefe auftreten [KSJ16].

2.2 Bodenanalytik

Zur Schätzung des organischen Kohlenstoffs wurden insgesamt 210 Bodenproben berücksichtigt, die aus den oberen 2 cm des Bodenprofils mehrerer Felder im Untersuchungsgebiet entnommen wurden. Die exakte Position jeder Probe wurde mit einem differenziellen GPS-Gerät erfasst. Für die Laboranalysen wurden die Proben luftgetrocknet und von groben Pflanzenresten befreit. Des Weiteren wurden die Proben zerkleinert, gesiebt und anschließend gemörsert. Im Labor wurde der Gehalt des organischen Kohlenstoffs über die Messung des Glühverlustes (DIN 18128:2002-12) bestimmt.

2.3 Fernerkundungsdaten

Für die Ableitung des Gehaltes an organischem Kohlenstoff wurde ein Bodenkomposit aus optischen multispektralen Sentinel-2-Daten erstellt. Dies erfolgte unter Verwendung der Google Earth Engine, einer von Google bereitgestellten Entwicklerplattform. Für die Berechnung des Bodenkomposites wurden zunächst alle Sentinel-2-Daten (Level-2) innerhalb des Untersuchungsgebietes im Zeitraum von 2017 bis 2022 selektiert. Dabei wurden lediglich Szenen mit einer maximalen Wolkenbedeckung von 10 % berücksichtigt. Wolken wurden anhand des Sentinel-2 Wolkenwahrscheinlichkeitsdatensatzes (s2cloudless) identifiziert und anschließend in den Bilddaten maskiert. Wolkenschatten sind anhand der Wolkenprojektion sowie Pixel mit niedriger Reflexion im nahinfraroten Spektralbereich entfernt worden.

2.4 Methodisches Vorgehen

Für die Auswahl repräsentativer unbedeckter Bodenpixel wurden verschiedene Boden- und Vegetationsindizes sowie empirisch bestimmte Schwellenwerte angewendet. Zur Identifizierung von vegetationsbestandenen Bildpixeln eignet sich der in der Fernerkundung weit verbreitete Normalised Difference Vegetation Index (NDVI). Zudem wurde der Bare Soil Index (BSI) berechnet, welcher die Identifizierung von unbedeckten Bodenflächen und Brachflächen verbessert.

Für alle genutzten Indizes wurden empirische Schwellwerte getestet, sodass möglichst komplett unbedeckte Bodenpixel ohne Störgrößen ausgewählt werden konnten. In der Folge wurden die validen multi-temporalen Bodenpixel im Untersuchungsgebiet bandweise zu einem Wert zusammengefasst, indem für jedes Pixel der Median aus den verfügbaren Bodenreflexionswerten berechnet wurde. Als Ergänzung wurden aus dem Komposit neben dem NDVI und dem BSI die Boden- und Vegetationsindizes Soil Adjusted Vegetation Index (SAVI) sowie Normalized Burn Ration 2 (NBR2) für die anschließende quantitative Analyse berechnet.

Als weitere Modellgrößen wurden Terrainvariablen aus dem digitalen Geländemodell von der Shuttle Radar Topography Mission (SRTM) extrahiert, welche eine räumliche Auflösung von 30 Metern aufweisen. Neben der absoluten Höhe wurde die Hangexposition, die Hangneigung sowie der Topographische Feuchte Index (TWI) berücksichtigt. Alle Datenlayer wurden zu einem Stack zusammengefasst und auf zehn Meter räumlicher Auflösung resampled.

Die Modellierung erfolgte mit einer Random Forest Regression, welche die gemessenen C_{org}-Gehalte der entnommenen Bodenproben anhand ihrer korrespondierenden Bildspektren prognostizierte. Für eine unabhängige Validierung des Modells wurden die Daten in zwei Drittel Trainings- und ein Drittel Testdaten aufgeteilt. Zur Modellbewertung wurden das Bestimmtheitsmaß (R^2) und der mittlere quadratische Fehler (RMSE) berechnet. Darüber hinaus wurde der RPD-Wert bestimmt, indem der RMSE durch die Standardabweichung der Messwerte geteilt wurde.

3 Ergebnisse und Diskussion

Die Laboranalytik der untersuchten Böden ergab einen durchschnittlichen C_{org}-Wert von etwa 1,8 % (Tab. 1). Insgesamt variierten die Konzentrationen im Untersuchungsgebiet deutlich, wobei Proben mit geringem C_{org}-Gehalt überrepräsentiert waren.

	Anzahl	Min.	Max.	Mittelw.	Std.
C_{org} [%]	210	0,83	4,09	1,78	0,66

Tab. 1: Laboranalytik für den organischen Kohlenstoff

Die Ergebnisse der Modellierung zeigen, dass sich der organische Kohlenstoff mit hoher Genauigkeit anhand des auf Basis von Satellitendaten berechneten multispektralen Bodenkomposites sowie der Integration der Geländeparameter prognostizieren ließ (R^2 = 0,83, RPD = 2,41 und RMSE = 0,41) (Abb. 1). Geringe Schätzfehler traten überwiegend im höheren C_{org}-Wertebereich auf, wobei es zur Unterschätzung dieser Werte kam.

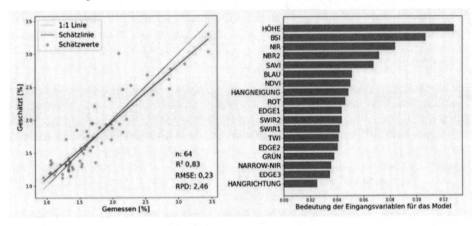

Abb. 1: Modellvalidierung (links), Wertigkeit der Modellvariablen (rechts)

Die Wichtigkeit der einzelnen Modellvariablen ist in Abbildung 1 rechts dargestellt. Dieser Darstellung ist zu entnehmen, dass neben der absoluten Höhe sowohl die Bandinformationen als auch die berechneten Indizes zum guten Ergebnis des Modells beitrugen. Insgesamt war ersichtlich, dass die Multispektraldaten und die Geländeinformationen unterschiedliche, aber sich ergänzende Informationen liefern konnten.

Die Anwendung der Modelle auf die Bilddaten zeigte kleinräumige Trends auf (Abb. 2). Konzentrationsunterschiede des organischen Kohlenstoffs orientierten sich hierbei insbesondere im nördlichen Teil des Untersuchungsgebietes am Relief, wodurch die hohe Wertigkeit der absoluten Höhe für das Modell zu erklären war. Kleinräumig konnten zum Teil große Konzentrationsunterschiede festgestellt werden, welche auch in der Farbgebung des Bodenkomposites zu erkennen waren. Dies mag auf Fehler im Komposit zurückzuführen sein, wie möglicherweise unmaskierte Wolken oder Wolkenschatten. Die prognostizierten Werte im Untersuchungsgebiet entsprachen in etwa den Konzentrationsbereichen der Laboranalytik.

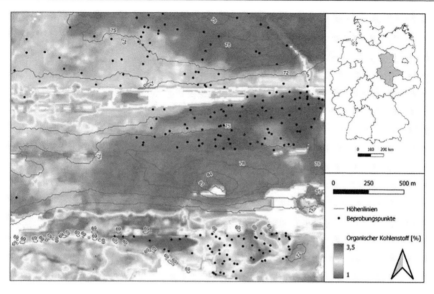

Abb. 2: Räumliche Schätzung des organischen Kohlenstoffs

In der Vergleichsstudie von Kanning et al. [KSJ16], bei welcher flugzeuggestützte Hyperspektraldaten (aisaDUAL) zur Modellierung genutzt wurden, konnte für das Untersuchungsgebiet ein R^2 von 0,89 erreicht werden. Insbesondere Spektralwerte im sichtbaren und nahen Infrarotbereich erwiesen sich für das Modell als relevant. Dies konnte auch in dieser Arbeit festgestellt werden, wobei auch wichtige Informationen aus dem kurzwelligen Infrarotbereich (SWIR) vorlagen.

Kanning et al. [KSJ16] zeigten in der räumlichen Anwendung ihres Modells die deutliche Abhängigkeit der C_{org}-Konzentration vom Relief. Auch dies konnte in dieser Arbeit gezeigt werden. Schätzfehler ließen sich unter anderem auf Bildfehler (Bildstreifen) zurückführen, welche durch die Erhebung der Daten entstanden. Derartige Einflussgrößen waren in dieser Arbeit nicht zu erwarten, da aus einer Vielzahl an Satellitendaten ein Mediankomposit berechnet wurde, wodurch Bildfehler reduziert werden sollten. Der mögliche Einfluss von Wolken und Wolkenschatten sollte hier dennoch erwähnt werden.

Insgesamt konnte mit dieser Arbeit jedoch ein vergleichbares Ergebnis erzielt werden. Damit bietet der vorgestellte Ansatz ein großes Potenzial zur Erfassung von Bodenparametern, insbesondere da die verwendeten Daten frei verfügbar sind und nur wenige Vorverarbeitungsschritte benötigen.

4 Schlussfolgerungen und Ausblick

Die Ergebnisse dieser Arbeit haben gezeigt, dass sich der organische Kohlenstoffgehalt mit einer hohen Schätzgenauigkeit mit Hilfe von multispektralen Satellitendaten und

Geländeinformationen prognostizieren lässt ($R^2 = 0{,}83$). Die Modellgüte unterscheidet sich von der Studie mit hyperspektralen Eingangsdaten nur geringfügig. Somit kann festgestellt werden, dass die Kombination aus multitemporalen Satellitendaten sowie Geländeinformationen fehlende spektrale Informationen kompensieren kann. Die räumliche Übertragung der Modelle ermöglichte die Erfassung kleinräumiger C_{org}-Konzentrationsunterschiede im Untersuchungsgebiet, wodurch die Grundlage für ein angepasstes Bodenmanagement geschaffen wurde. Darüber hinaus lässt sich der vorgestellte Ansatz für größere Gebiete und fortlaufend unter Berücksichtigung weiterer Geodaten anwenden. Dieses Vorhaben wird aktuell im Verbundprojekt SOIL-DE angestrebt, wo deutschlandweite Karten des Kohlenstoffgehaltes landwirtschaftlich genutzter Böden (Oberboden) auf Basis verschiedener optischer Fernerkundungssysteme (Landsat/Sentinel 2) entwickelt werden [u.a. Mö22, Ze21].

Förderhinweis: Die Förderung des Projektes SOIL-DE (Förderkennzeichen 281B301916) erfolgte aus Mitteln des Bundesministeriums für Ernährung und Landwirtschaft (BMEL) aufgrund eines Beschlusses des deutschen Bundestages. Die Projektträgerschaft erfolgte über die Bundesanstalt für Landwirtschaft und Ernährung (BLE).

Literaturverzeichnis

[Pr09] Prechtel, A. et al.: Organic carbon in soils of Germany: Status quo and the need for new data to evaluate potentials and trends of soil carbon sequestration. Journal of Plant Nutrition and Soil Science, 5/172, S. 601-614, 2009.

[Hb12] Hbirkou, C. et al.: Airborne hyperspectral imaging of spatial soil organic carbon heterogeneity at the field-scale. Geoderma, 175-176, S. 21-28, 2012.

[KSJ16] Kanning, M.; Siegmann, B.; Jarmer, T.: Regionalization of Uncovered Agricultural Soils Based on Organic Carbon and Soil Texture Estimations. Remote Sensing, 927/8, 2016.

[Bu22] Bundesamt für Naturschutz - Landschaftssteckbriefe Köthener Ebene, https://www.bfn.de/landschaftssteckbriefe/koethener-ebene, 27.10.2022.

[Dw22] Deutscher Wetterdienst, Climate Data Center, ftp://ftp-cdc.dwd.de/pub/CDC/observations_germany/climate/monthly/kl/historical/, 27.10.2022.

[Mö22] Möller, M. et al.: Scale-Specific Prediction of Topsoil Organic Carbon Contents Using Terrain Attributes and SCMaP Soil Reflectance Composites. Remote Sensing, 10/14, 2022.

[Ze21] Zepp, S. et al: Estimation of Soil Organic Carbon Contents in Croplands of Bavaria from SCMaP Soil Reflectance Composites. Remote Sensing, 16/13, 2021.

Entwicklung eines automatischen Monitoringsystems für die Geburtsüberwachung bei Sauen

Martin Wutke[1,2], Clara Lensches[1], Jan-Hendrik Witte[3], Johann Gerberding[3], Marc-Alexander Lieboldt[4] und Imke Traulsen[1]

Abstract: Die Überwachung des Abferkelungsverlaufs ist in der Schweinehaltung von großer Bedeutung, um auftretende Geburtsstörungen frühzeitig erkennen und geeignete Maßnahmen ergreifen zu können. Da eine zeitnahe Geburtserkennung und -betreuung aufgrund intensivierter Haltungsbedingungen oftmals nur schwer zu erzielen ist, war das Ziel der vorliegenden Studie, die Eignung neuronaler Netzwerke zur automatischen Identifikation des Geburtsmomentes zu untersuchen. Anhand einer YoloV5-Netzwerkarchitektur bestimmten wir auf Basis der Detektion unterschiedlicher Körperteile der Muttersau den potentiellen Geburtsbereich innerhalb der Abferkelbucht und identifizierten den Moment der Geburt des ersten Ferkels anhand der Objektdetektion des Ferkels innerhalb des Zielbereichs. Wir validierten unser Analysemodell durch zweistufigen Ansatz und erreichten einen Precision-, Recall- und MAP-Wert von 0.982, 0.989 und 0.993 im Rahmen der Objektdetektion sowie einen Accuracy-, Recall- und Precision-Wert von 0.9, 0.8 und 1 bei der Bestimmung des Geburtszeitpunktes.

Keywords: Geburtsüberwachung, maschinelles Lernen, Deep Learning, Videoanalyse

1 Einleitung

In der Ferkelerzeugung sind eine hohe Anzahl lebend geborener Ferkel je Sau und Jahr, geringe Aufzuchtverluste sowie das Hervorbringen gesunder, uniformer und marktkonformer Ferkel essentiell für den wirtschaftlichen Erfolg eines ferkelerzeugenden Betriebes [HGK16]. In den vergangenen Jahren hat sich die Anzahl der gesamt geborenen Ferkel je Sau und Wurf stark erhöht, wobei gleichzeitig ein gesteigertes Auftreten von Totgeburten und frühen postnatalen Verlusten beobachtet werden konnte [Le03]. Diesbezüglich hat der geburtsnahe Zeitraum große Auswirkungen auf die Überlebensfähigkeit neugeborener Ferkel [vv04], wobei als eine der häufigsten Ursachen für Geburtsstörungen und Ferkelverluste die perinatale Asphyxie bei der Geburt anzuführen ist [Ed02]. Eine Asphyxie während des Geburtsvorgangs kann entweder direkt zu einer Totgeburt oder zu Ferkeln mit herabgesetzter Vitalität und geringerer Anpassungsfähigkeit an das extrauterine Leben führen [He96]. Als wesentliche Risikofaktoren für das Auftreten perinataler Asphyxie gelten hierbei vor allem in der Wurfreihenfolge später geborene Ferkel, die Wurfgröße und die Dauer der

---

[1] Georg-August-Universität Göttingen, Systeme der Nutztierhaltung, Albrecht-Thaer-Weg 3, 37075 Göttingen, martin.wutke@uni-goettingen.de, clara.lensches@uni-goettingen.de, imke.traulsen@uni-goettingen.de
[2] Fachhochschule Südwestfalen, Statistik und Data Science in der Agrarwirtschaft, Lübecker Ring 2, 59494 Soest, wutke.martin@fh-swf.de
[3] Carl von Ossietzky Universität Oldenburg, Department für Informatik, Ammerländer Heerstr. 114-118, 26129 Oldenburg, jan-hendrik.witte@uni-oldenburg.de, johann.gerberding@uni-oldenburg.de
[4] Landwirtschaftskammer Niedersachsen, Geschäftsbereich Landwirtschaft, FB 3.7, Mars-la-Tour-Straße 6, 26121 Oldenburg, marc-alexander.lieboldt@lwk-niedersachsen.de

Abferkelung, sowie verlängerte Geburtsintervalle zwischen der Geburt aufeinanderfolgender Ferkel [He96; va05]. Aus diesen Gründen kommt der Überwachung der Geburtsverläufe eine hohe Bedeutung zu und ist essentiell, um frühzeitig geeignete Maßnahmen bei der Erkennung von Geburts- und Gesundheitsstörungen ergreifen zu können. In diesem Zusammenhang zeigen die jüngsten Fortschritte im Bereich des maschinellen Lernens das Potential überwachter Lernalgorithmen bei der Erkennung von Problemsituationen und der automatisierten Auswertung großer, unstrukturierter Datenmengen [Ga20; Ki21; Wu21]. Insbesondere im perinatalen Zeitraum können Systeme des Precision Livestock Farmings eine Unterstützung von LandwirtInnen und MitarbeiterInnen ferkelerzeugender Betriebe im Hinblick auf das Vermeiden von Ferkelverlusten leisten [Oc16]. Zwar fanden ML-Algorithmen im Rahmen des Geburtsmonitorings bereits in früheren Studien Anwendung, allerdings fokussierten sich diese Arbeiten entweder auf die Untersuchung von Verhaltensmerkmalen der Sau vor der Geburt [Kü20] oder auf die Analyse der Ferkelvitalität [HTK21]. Ziel der vorliegenden Studie war die Entwicklung und Bewertung eines solchen Unterstützungssystems zur automatisierten Geburtsüberwachung und Erkennung von Problemsituationen. Hierfür analysierten wir Videoaufnahmen von 52 Abferkelungen und trainierten ein convolutional neural network (CNN) zur Objektdetektion, um das Tierverhalten innerhalb der Abferkelbucht kontinuierlich überwachen zu können und den Zeitpunkt des Geburtsbeginn automatisiert zu identifizieren und zu dokumentieren.

2 Material und Methoden

Die Videodaten wurden im Rahmen des Verbundprojektes „Experimentierfeld DigiSchwein" (Förderkennzeichen: 28DE109F18) im Zeitraum von Mai 2021 bis Oktober 2022 erhoben [Li21]. Hierfür wurden RGB-Kameras vom Typ Axis 3206LVE 3 m senkrecht über Einzelabferkelbuchten installiert, welche die stattfindenden Geburtsvorgänge mit einer Auflösung von 1920 x 1080 Pixeln sowie einer Rate von 20 Bildern pro Sekunde aufzeichneten. Für das Modelltraining wurden 750 Einzelbilder vor und nach der Geburt des ersten Ferkels zufällig ausgewählt und manuell annotiert. Für die Bildannotation wurden vier Objektklassen definiert (Kopfregion, Hinterteilregion, Schwanz, neugeborene Ferkel) und mittels eines Bounding-Box-Ansatzes markiert. Um den Informationsgehalt in den Daten im Rahmen des Modelltrainings zu erhöhen, wurde jedes Bild durch Verwendung einer horizontalen Drehung, einer vertikaler Drehung und einer zufälligen Rotation augmentiert, wodurch sich der Gesamtdatensatz auf 3000 Bilder erhöhte.

Abb. 1: Die in Graustufenbilder umgewandelten Videoframes zeigen die Abferkelbucht bei Tageslicht (A) und bei Nacht (B).

Abschließend wurden die annotierten Einzelbilder in einen unabhängigen Trainings- und Testdatensatz unterteilt, wobei wir dem Vorgehen früherer Studien folgten [Kc21; SM18; Th19] und 90 Prozent der Daten für das Modelltraining und 10 Prozent der Daten für die Modellevaluation nutzten. Die Abferkelbuchten sowie die annotierten Objektklassen sind beispielhaft für zwei Videoframes in Abbildung 1 dargestellt.

2.1 Modellimplementierung

Das vorgestellte Analyseframework folgt einem zweistufigen Ansatz, bei dem zunächst die annotierten Körperteilpositionen geschätzt werden. Basierend auf diesen Körperteilinformationen wird in einem nachgelagerten Schritt die Orientierung der Sau in der Bucht sowie der Geburtsbereich nahe dem Hinterteil als Zielregion bestimmt. Über die Detektion konsistenter Ferkelpositionen innerhalb des Zielbereichs und der entsprechenden Videoframenummer wird darauf aufbauend der Zeitpunkt des Geburtsbeginns identifiziert und als Information zur weiteren Verarbeitung abgelegt. Die Einführung der Zielregion hat sich als empirisch vorteilhaft erwiesen, da Ferkeldetektion in angrenzenden Buchten und falsch-positive Klassifikationen im Rahmen des Detektionsprozesses frühzeitig identifiziert und von der weiteren Analyse ausgeschlossen werden können. Zur Detektion der Körperteil- und Ferkelpositionen folgten wir dem Vorgehen früherer Studien [INK21; Ya21] und verwendeten ein CNN mit einer YoloV5-Architektur [Jo20]. Während des iterativen Trainingsprozesses wurde das CNN über 100 Iterationen darauf trainiert, für jedes Eingangsbild die Objektpositionen in Form der Bounding-Box-Koordinaten, des Boxmittelpunkts und der zugehörigen Klasseninformation zu generieren. Nach dem Modelltraining kann das trainierte CNN dazu verwendet werden, die Objektklasse und Position für bisher unbekannte Bilder zu schätzen.

3 Ergebnisse und Diskussion

Zur Eignungsbeurteilung des vorgestellten Ansatzes zur Geburtsüberwachung und Bestimmung des Geburtszeitpunktes haben wir unser Analyseframework in zwei Stufen evaluiert. Die erste Evaluationsstufe zielt darauf ab, die Leistung des Detektionsmodells zur Bestimmung der Körperteilpositionen zu bewerten. Hierfür wurden die 300 manuell annotierten Bilder des Testdatensatzes verwendet und die Precision, Recall und Mean Average Precision (MAP) Metrik berechnet. Die Ergebnisse der ersten Evaluationsstufe sind nachfolgend in Tabelle 1 aufgeführt.

Objektklasse	Häufigkeit	Precision	Recall	MAP
Kopf	300	0,997	0,998	0,995
Hinterteil	300	0,988	0,993	0,992
Ferkel	151	0,968	0,99	0,995
Schwanz	176	0,977	0,974	0,99
Alle	927	0,982	0,989	0,993

Tab. 1: Evaluationsergebnisse des Detektionsmodells für den Testdatensatz

Wie in Tabelle 1 zu erkennen ist, zeigt das Detektionsnetzwerk für alle Objektklassen durchgehend Leistungswerte im hohen 90er-Bereich auf. Vor allem die Objektklassen Kopf und Hinterteil mit einem Recall-Wert von 0,998 und 0,993 verdeutlichen, dass in Situationen, in denen diese Objektklassen zu erkennen waren, das CNN diese korrekt lokalisiert und klassifiziert hat. Die geringste Detektionsgüte wurde bei den Klassen Ferkel und Schwanz erzielt, was durch die Verteilungshäufigkeit im Trainingsdatensatz erklärt werden kann. Im Unterschied zu den Objektklassen Kopf und Hinterteil, welche in jedem Videobild vorhanden waren, waren die Klassen Ferkel und Schwanz nicht in jedem Bild sichtbar und somit im Datensatz unterrepräsentiert.

Für die zweite Evaluationsstufe überprüften wir, ob die vorgestellte Methodik einerseits in der Lage ist, den Moment der Geburt des ersten Ferkels verlässlich zu bestimmen und andererseits in Phasen ohne Geburtsaktivitäten keine Falschmeldung zu generieren. Für diesen zweiten Evaluationsschritt wurden insgesamt 20 zehnminütige Videosequenzen mit und ohne Geburtsvorgang unterschiedlicher Sauen ausgewählt. Zur Validierung wurde jedes Video durch einen Experten manuell gesichtet, welcher binär klassifizierte, ob eine Geburt im betrachteten Zeitraum stattfand. Darüber hinaus wurde der Geburtszeitpunkt sowie die zeitliche Abweichung des automatisch identifizierten Geburtszeitpunktes vom manuell bewerteten Zeitpunkt bestimmt. Zur Beurteilung der binären Klassifikation folgten wir dem Vorgehen früherer Studien [De19; Mo19] und bestimmten die richtig-positiv-Rate (TP), die falsch-positiv-Rate (FP), die richtig-negativ-Rate (TN) und die falsch-negativ-Rate (FN) und berechneten die Accuracy-, Recall- und Precision-Werte. Die Ergebnisse der zweiten Evaluationsstufe sind in Tabelle 2 aufgeführt.

Datensatz	Anzahl Videos	Geburten erkannt	Abweichung (in Sek.)	Accuracy	Recall	Precision
Mit Geburt	10	8	11,5	-	-	-
Ohne Geburt	10	0	-	-	-	-
Alle	20	8	11,5	0,9	0,8	1

Tab. 2: Evaluationsergebnisse für die zweite Evaluationsstufe zur Erkennung des Geburtszeitpunktes

Das vorgestellte Analyseframework zeigt sowohl bei der Identifizierung als auch bei der Überwachung von Phasen ohne Geburtsereignisse gute Ergebnisse. Von den zehn ausgewählten Videosequenzen mit Geburtsverlauf konnte der Zeitpunkt der ersten Ferkelgeburt in acht Fällen korrekt bestimmt werden, wobei die automatische Bestimmung im Durchschnitt 11,5 Sekunden später erfolgte als der von einem menschlichen Beobachter ermittelte Zeitpunkt. In zwei Videosequenzen wurde der Blick auf das neugeborene Ferkel durch den Ferkelschutzkorb und die Muttersau verdeckt und war auch für den geschulten Beobachter nur bedingt als Geburt erkennbar. Das Problem verdeckter Ferkel kann in diesem Zusammenhang als limitierender Faktor für den kontinuierlichen Praxiseinsatz eingestuft werden, welcher bei längeren Phasen der Verdeckung die Modellleistung wesentlich beeinflussen kann. Zur Adressierung dieser Limitation könnten Vorhersagemodelle aus dem Bereich des Objekttrackings eingesetzt werden, welche über die Schätzung zukünftiger Objektpositionen den Einfluss von falsch negativen Detektionen reduzieren könnten [Cu22]. Darüber hinaus untersuchten frühere Studien wie Küster et al. [Kü20] Veränderungen im Verhaltensbild der Sau, um beispielsweise verstärktes Nestbauverhalten zu identifizieren. In Problemsituationen und zur Erhöhung der Robustheit des vorgestellten Ansatzes zur

Bestimmung des Geburtszeitpunktes könnten solche Verhaltensmerkmale als zusätzliche Informationsquelle eingesetzt werden und somit den Mehrwert der vorgestellten Methodik steigern. In der Gruppe ohne Geburtsereignisse lieferte die vorgestellte Methodik konsistente Ergebnisse ohne Fehlklassifikationen.

4 Zusammenfassung und Ausblick

Die zunehmende Intensivierung der Schweinehaltung führt im Bereich der Abferkelung einerseits zu einer hohen personellen und zeitlichen Inanspruchnahme von LandwirtInnen und stellt andererseits einen wesentlichen Zeitpunkt zur Sicherstellung des Tierwohls dar. Ziel dieser Studie war es deshalb, die Eignung moderner maschineller Lernmethoden aus dem Bereich der neuronalen Netzwerke zur Überwachung des Geburtsprozesses eingehender zu analysieren. Durch die Detektion unterschiedlicher Körperregionen und neugeborener Ferkel konnte die Orientierung der Muttersau in der Abferkelbucht sowie ein potentieller Geburtsbereich bestimmt werden, in dem bei wiederholter Erkennung neuer Ferkel abschließend der Geburtszeitpunkt bestimmt werden kann. Durch diesen automatisierten Prozessschritt ist es möglich, eine zeitnahe Erstkontrolle der Ferkel durchzuführen und bei Auftreten von Geburtsstörungen geeignete Maßnahmen einzuleiten. Darauf aufbauend soll das vorgestellte Geburtsüberwachungssystem im Rahmen zukünftiger Arbeiten durch Einbeziehen der individuellen Geburtsintervalle, einer Unterscheidung zwischen lebend und tot geborenen Ferkeln sowie einer Ausweitung des Analyserahmens auf unterschiedliche Buchtensysteme ergänzt werden.

Literaturverzeichnis

[As21] Ashhar, S. M. et al.: Comparison of deep learning convolutional neural network (CNN) architectures for CT lung cancer classification. International Journal of Advanced Technology and Engineering Exploration 74/8, S. 126-134, 2021.

[Cu22] Cui, Y. et al.: Remote Sensing Object Tracking With Deep Reinforcement Learning Under Occlusion. IEEE Transactions on Geoscience and Remote Sensing 60, S. 1-13, 2022.

[De19] Debelee, T. G. et al.: Classification of Mammograms Using Texture and CNN Based Extracted Features. Journal of Biomimetics, Biomaterials and Biomedical Engineering 42, S. 79-97, 2019.

[Ed02] Edwards, S.: Perinatal mortality in the pig: environmental or physiological solutions? Livestock Production Science 1/78, S. 3-12, 2002.

[Ga20] García, R. et al.: A systematic literature review on the use of machine learning in precision livestock farming. Computers and Electronics in Agriculture 179, S. 105826, 2020.

[He96] Herpin, P. et al.: Effects of the level of asphyxia during delivery on viability at birth and early postnatal vitality of newborn pigs. Journal of animal science 9/74, S. 2067-2075, 1996.

[HGK16] Hoy, S.; Gauly, M.; Krieter, J.: Nutztierhaltung und -hygiene. Verlag Eugen Ulmer, Stuttgart, 2016.

[HTK21] Ho, K.-Y.; Tsai, Y.-J.; Kuo, Y.-F.: Automatic monitoring of lactation frequency of sows and movement quantification of newborn piglets in farrowing houses using convolutional neural networks. Computers and Electronics in Agriculture 189, S. 106376, 2021.

[INK21] Islam, M. M.; Newaz, A. A. R.; Karimoddini, A.: A Pedestrian Detection and Tracking Framework for Autonomous Cars: Efficient Fusion of Camera and LiDAR Data: 2021 IEEE International Conference on Systems, Man, and Cybernetics (SMC). IEEE, S. 1287-1292, 2021.

[Jo20] Jocher, G. et al.: yolov5. Code repository, 2020.

[Kc21] Kc, K. et al.: Evaluation of deep learning-based approaches for COVID-19 classification based on chest X-ray images. Signal, image and video processing 5/15, S. 959-966, 2021.

[Ki21] Kim, M.-J. et al.: Research and Technology Trend Analysis by Big Data-Based Smart Livestock Technology: a Review. Journal of Biosystems Engineering 4/46, S. 386-398, 2021.

[Kü20] Küster, S. et al.: Usage of computer vision analysis for automatic detection of activity changes in sows during final gestation. Computers and Electronics in Agriculture 169, S. 105177, 2020.

[Le03] Leenhouwers, J. I. et al.: Stillbirth in the pig in relation to genetic merit for farrowing survival. Journal of animal science 10/81, S. 2419-2424, 2003.

[Li21] Lieboldt, M.-A. et.al.: Experimentierfeld DigiSchwein. In (Meyer-Aurich, A., et al., Hrsg.): 41. GIL-Jahrestagung, Informations- und Kommunikationstechnologie in kritischen Zeiten. Lecture Notes in Informatics (LNI)-Proceedings, Volume 309, Gesellschaft für Informatik, Bonn, S. 391-396, 2021.

[Mo19] Mobeen-ur-Rehman et al.: Classification of Diabetic Retinopathy Images Based on Customised CNN Architecture: 2019 Amity International Conference on Artificial Intelligence (AICAI). IEEE, S. 244-248, 2019.

[Oc16] Oczak, M. et al.: Automatic estimation of number of piglets in a pen during farrowing, using image analysis. Biosystems Engineering 151, S. 81-89, 2016.

[SM18] Shallu; Mehra, R.: Breast cancer histology images classification: Training from scratch or transfer learning? ICT Express 4/4, S. 247-254, 2018.

[Th19] Thian, Y. L. et al.: Convolutional Neural Networks for Automated Fracture Detection and Localization on Wrist Radiographs. Radiology. Artificial intelligence 1/1, e180001, 2019.

[va05] van Dijk, A. J. et al.: Factors affecting duration of the expulsive stage of parturition and piglet birth intervals in sows with uncomplicated, spontaneous farrowings. Theriogenology 7/64, S. 1573-1590, 2005.

[vv04] van Rens, B. T. T. M.; van der Lende, T.: Parturition in gilts: duration of farrowing, birth intervals and placenta expulsion in relation to maternal, piglet and placental traits. Theriogenology 1-2/62, S. 331-352, 2004.

[Wu21] Wutke, M. et al.: Detecting Animal Contacts-A Deep Learning-Based Pig Detection and Tracking Approach for the Quantification of Social Contacts. Sensors (Basel, Switzerland) 22/21, 2021.

[Ya21] Yap, M. H. et al.: Deep learning in diabetic foot ulcers detection: A comprehensive evaluation. Computers in biology and medicine 135, S. 104596, 2021.

[YLM22] Yang, N.; Li, Y.; Ma, R.: An Efficient Method for Detecting Asphalt Pavement Cracks and Sealed Cracks Based on a Deep Data-Driven Model. Applied Sciences 19/12, S. 10089, 2022.

Overview of control systems for robotic harvesting of sweet peppers and apples

Mostafa Shokrian Zeini[1], Redmond R. Shamshiri[1,2], Volker Dworak[1], Jana Käthner[1], Nora Höfner[1], Eduardo Navas[1,3] and Cornelia Weltzien[1,2]

Abstract: Automated harvesting systems are becoming a crucial part of digital agriculture. Substituting time-consuming and laborious manual harvesting with a continuously automated operation would result in reduced human efforts, which contribute to higher field efficiency. This could be achieved by means of robotic harvesting which comprises robot manipulators, gripping and grasping mechanisms, software implementations. However, the inadequate design of control strategies could cause the agricultural production loss. This paper reviews some of the latest achievements in control systems of agricultural robotics and more specifically in robotic harvesting. The employed robot arms, their degrees of freedom (DOF), and the crops are also considered in this review study. While the control algorithms are being developed with high robustness and fast-response properties, our conclusion is that the performance of controllers could be drastically affected by different parameters such as the number of DOF, estimation accuracy of the robot pose during visual servoing and failure of robot's inverse kinematics solver.

Keywords: agricultural robotics, automated harvesting, robot manipulator, control algorithms

1 Introduction

Robotic automated harvesting of fruits and vegetables has been developed during the last decade due to the lack of farm workers and its costs' growth [Sh18]. Scaling up in agriculture and saving labor are essential in solving these problems. Robotic harvesting can enhance productivity by decreasing manual human resource and costs of production, increasing yield and quality, and providing superior control over environmental implications. However, adaptive (to high crop variability), robust systems are required for the complexity of agricultural environments along with the high production needs.

Fruit harvesting robots are mainly composed of a fruit detection system, a fruit picker, a manipulator, a control system, and a traveling device [Bu05]. Two major challenges need to be considered and solved during robotic applications development for harvesting horticultural products. The first one is the detection of a target fruit location. The second is the precise end-effector's movement towards the mentioned location so that the harvest

---

[1] Leibniz-Institut für Agrartechnik und Bioökonomie e.V. (ATB), Technik im Pflanzenbau, Max-Eyth-Allee 100, 14469 Potsdam, Deutschland
[2] Technische Universität Berlin, Fachgebiet Agromechatronik, Straße des 17. Juni 135, 10623 Berlin, Deutschland
[3] Centre for Automation and Robotics, UPM-CSIC, Carretera CAMPO-REAL Km 0.2, Arganda del Rey, 28500 Madrid, Spanien

action could be performed. There are multiple solutions for each of these challenges. The robot parts design should be adapted to a distinct type of fruit as different crops have different physical properties and characteristics, e.g. in contrast to tomato, sweet peppers' leaves are not picked and mostly cover the fruit, making the fruit hardly detectable and difficult to localize [BHV16]. Moreover, sweet pepper crops sometimes grow in clusters, rendering it complex to access, and pick each single fruit without damaging. Also for apple crops, the fruit is rotated (not pulled) until the detachment of fruit peduncle from the branch [Bu05]. Therefore, the manipulator, the end-effector and the control algorithms should be designed based on the harvesting procedure, guaranteeing suitable robot adaptation to the crop type. Control algorithms are designed by using both control theory and control engineering principles, and constitute the control system which drives the desired movement of the harvesting robot.

This paper provides an overview of control systems as one of the main parts of robotic harvesting for two different crops. The reviewed researches have been selected based on their precise indication of the implemented control systems. The designed control schemes in automated sweet pepper harvesting are described in Section 2. Section 3 reviews three different control strategies for robotic apple harvesting, followed by the conclusion remarks in Section 4.

2 Sweet pepper harvesting

A simulation approach in V-REP software, Robot Operating System (ROS) and MATLAB software has been carried out in [Sh18]. The research has been conducted in two phases: (i) the creation of the simulated workspace in the virtual robot experimentation platform (V-REP), and (ii) the development of communication and control architecture using ROS and MATLAB. An exact replica of the 6 DOF Fanuc LR Mate 200iD robot manipulator, models of sweet pepper fruit and plant system, and different vision sensors were created in V-REP to form the simulated workspace. Two control schemes were developed and evaluated; the first one was based on joint velocity control and the second one based on joint position control. A Proportional-Integral-Derivative (PID) control law was applied to both of the designs in order to minimize the offset error between the center of the camera frame and the image position of a detected fruit. Results demonstrated that the robot could self-adjust so that its tip RGB sensor displays maximum possible view of the largest detected fruit and fast stabilization. The stability was achieved in 2.5 seconds without overshoot and oscillations.

A flexible modular framework for eye-in-hand sensing and motion control in robotic sweet pepper harvesting was provided in [BHV16] as a standardized approach. In contrast to specialized software, the framework suggested goals to support various agricultural applications, hardware and extensions. A set of ROS nodes was created to guarantee modularity and separation of concerns, implementing functionalities for application and robot motion control, image acquisition, fruit detection, visual servo control and simultaneous localization and mapping (SLAM). Baxter robot was selected for its native

ROS support and the ability of publishing the pose of the end-effector and all joints and also running a ROS master core to which an internal controller publishes and executes target joint angles. The objective of the experiment was to demonstrate that the robot could find and access the fruit. The final pose of the end-effector was always centered with the fruit, except for cases where a solution of the joint positions could not be found due to the failure of robot's inverse kinematics (IK) solver. These instances were specified by the robot arm already being fully extended to its limits, but not yet horizontally or vertically aligned with the fruit.

In 2017, harvesting experiments were conducted in a sweet pepper crop located in a commercial greenhouse [Ba17]. Figure 1 provides an overview of the harvesting robot which was developed as part of the research project CROPS "Clever Robots for Crops". The manipulator module of the platform (Jentjens Machinetechniek BV, the Netherlands) included a 9 DOF custom-made manipulator, end-effector and air compressor for its pneumatics, and a cabinet containing computers and electronics. The motion planner of the robot calculated a straight path through the workspace, i.e. point-to-point planning. IK were then solved to realize the motion by using an algorithm developed in [Ba13], capable of exploiting the redundant DOF. The results of failure analysis for four different testing conditions showed that the contribution of manipulator error to total failures was of 3% for the Fin Ray and of 6% for the Lip-Type end-effectors. Furthermore, the number of DOF influenced the maneuverability around obstacles. In this application, planned motions were relatively simple and fewer DOFs had not a strong influence on the result. However, in other applications, DOFs could play an important role.

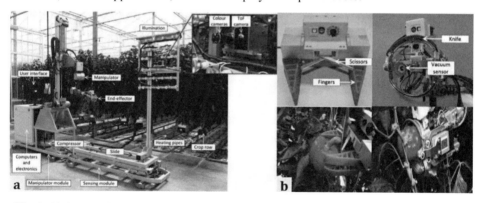

Fig. 1: (a) An overview of the CROPS project harvesting robot [Ba17] and (b) Fin Ray (left) and Lip-type end-effectors (right)

3 Apple harvesting

An apple harvesting robot was developed in [Bu05] by using a feedback controller and machine vision for the manipulator. As the detected fruit had to be in the image center in order to measure for its distance from the camera, the camera was mounted on the manipulator and had to be specifically positioned. Two feedback control strategies using machine vision have been implemented and simulated for this positioning procedure.

The first design was a three-position on-off controller for moving the camera at a constant step and have the machine vision monitor the position of the fruit until the fruit is at the image center. In order to avoid instability or oscillations, the constant step's value had to be set to a minimum. Consequently, the response time for the system to position the fruit in the image center is affected. The second scheme was a proportional (P-) controller with variable gain for moving the camera with a value proportional to the error. The controller was tuned in three steps. The camera is moved at a determined step distance at first. Then, the pixel change in the image is computed, and finally, the proportional gain is calculated using the defined step distance and the pixel change. Numerical results showed that both controllers were capable to move the manipulator to position the fruit in the image center, which proved the feasibility of applying machine vision as a feedback sensor and also, the faster response time of the P-controller compared to the three-position controller.

A reliable low-cost robot for automatic apple harvesting has been developed and evaluated in [De11]. The robotic setup included a manipulator, end-effector and image-based VSC system. In order to obtain a quasi-linear behavior and to simplify the control design, a geometrically optimized manipulator with a 5 DOF Prismatic Revolute-Revolute-Revolute-Prismatic (PRRRP) structure was implemented (Fig. 2. a). The control system was composed of an industrial computer and an AC servo driver. The image-based vision servo (IBVS) control algorithm was used in the robot control system in order to perform the localization and achieve the picking motion for the target fruit (Fig. 2. b).

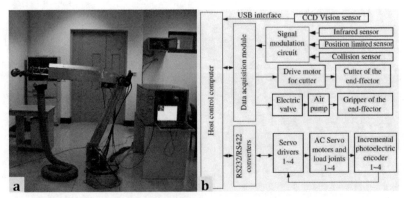

Fig. 2: (a) PRRRP 5 DOF manipulator [De11] and (b) Hardware structure of apple harvesting robot control system

The performance of the prototype robotic setup was demonstrated by laboratory tests and field experimental evaluations. 100 laboratory picking tests were performed in 10 different positions, resulting in 86 successful and 14 failed pickings (success rate 86%) and 14.3 seconds for average picking time of one apple. Continuously picking field experiments were carried out in an orchard with a complex environment. Overall, the mean recognition time was 15.4 seconds and the picking success rate was 77%, proving the performance of the prototype harvesting robot and the designed control system.

A fast and precise scheme with a Single Shot MultiBox Detector (SSD) was developed in [On19] to detect the position of fruit and achieve an automated harvesting using a 6 DOF UR3 robot arm made by UNIVERSAL ROBOTS. The joints angles and the route of the robot arm are calculated by IK at the detected position, followed by the robot arm movement towards the target fruit. The robotic harvesting is then performed by twisting the hand axis. Experimental results indicated the detection of more than 90% of the apples in 2 seconds and the harvesting of an apple in 16 seconds. Moreover, the suggested apple harvesting scheme is assumed to be applicable for near species of apple.

The reviewed harvesting robots and control strategies as well as their corresponding camera and/or sensor(s) are summarized in Table 1.

Crop	Manipulator	DOF	Controller	Camera/Sensor	Reference
Sweet Pepper	Fanuc LR Mate 200iD	6	PID	Logitech C920 HD Pro USB/proximity Hokuyo URG04LXUG01	[Sh18]
Sweet Pepper	Baxter	7	ROS actionlib service	USB CMOS color Autofocus Camera (DFK 72AUC02-F, TheImagingSource)	[BHV16]
Sweet Pepper	CROPS	9	IK-based	VRmMS-12; CamBoard nano/ SR4000; Prossilica GC2450C	[Ba17]
Apple	Multi-joint vertical manipulator	4	Machine Vision Feedback P-based	color CCD camera/ laser ranging sensor	[Bu05]
Apple	PRRRP Structure manipulator	5	IBVS	color CCD camera/ infrared double photoelectric cells	[De11]
Apple	UR3	6	IK-based	ZED	[On19]

Tab. 1: Summary of reviewed harvesting robots, control strategies and their camera/sensors

4 Conclusion

The design of a low-cost and efficient harvesting robot requires collaboration in areas of horticultural engineering, machine vision, sensing, robotics, control, intelligent systems, software architecture, system integration, and greenhouse crop management. In this study, we reviewed different harvesting robot manipulator components with an emphasize on control systems and considering carried out numerical and in-field experimental results in literature. As such, we could conclude that future researches should consider advanced and adaptive nonlinear control algorithms. These control strategies are robust to the unknown fruit motion caused by wind gusts and the dynamical robot modeling uncertainties. Consequently, they could overcome the undesirable fruit motion that might influence the automatic harvesting efficiency. Also, the reviewed VSC systems relied on high-gain feedback for disturbance compensation. However, it is well-known that the performance of high-gain feedback controllers could be significantly compromised in the presence of measurement noise. Therefore, future research activities should be focused on the design of optimized robust nonlinear control algorithms for disturbance compensation.

Bibliography

[Bu2005] Bulanon, D. M . et al.: Feedback Control of Manipulator Using Machine Vision for Robotic Apple Harvesting, ASAE Annual Meeting, paper number 053114, 2005.

[BHV16] Barth, R., Hemming, J., & van Henten, E. J: Design of an eye-in-hand sensing and servo control framework for harvesting robotics in dense vegetation, Biosystems Engineering, vol. 146, 71-84, 2016.

Ba17] Bac, C. W. et. Al.: Performance Evaluation of a Harvesting Robot for Sweet Pepper, Journal of Field Robotics, 34(6), 1123-1139, 2017.

[Ba13] Baur, J. et. al.: Dynamic modeling and realization of an agricultural manipulator. In Proceedings of the XV International Symposium on Dynamic Problems of Mechanics, Buzios, Brazil, 1-7, 2013.

[De11] De-An, Z. et al.: Design and control of an apple harvesting robot. Biosystems Engineering, 110(2), 112-122, 2011.

[On19] Onishi, Y. et. al. : An automated fruit harvesting robot by using deep learning. ROBOMECH Journal, 6(13), 2019.

[Sh 18] Shamshiri, R. R. et. al.: Robotic Harvesting of Fruiting Vegetables: A Simulation Approach in V-REP, ROS and MATLAB. In (Ed.), Automation in Agriculture - Securing Food Supplies for Future Generations. IntechOpen 2018.

GI-Edition Lecture Notes in Informatics

P-299　M. Gandorfer, A. Meyer-Aurich, H. Bernhardt, F. X. Maidl, G. Fröhlich, H. Floto (Hrsg.)
Informatik in der Land-, Forst- und Ernährungswirtschaft
Fokus: Digitalisierung für Mensch, Umwelt und Tier
Referate der 40. GIL-Jahrestagung
17.–18. Februar 2020,
Campus Weihenstephan

P-300　Michael Felderer, Wilhelm Hasselbring, Rick Rabiser, Reiner Jung (Hrsg.)
Software Engineering 2020
24.–28. Februar 2020
Innsbruck, Austria

P-301　Delphine Reinhardt, Hanno Langweg, Bernhard C. Witt, Mathias Fischer (Hrsg.)
Sicherheit 2020
Sicherheit, Schutz und Zuverlässigkeit
17.–20. März 2020, Göttingen

P-302　Dominik Bork, Dimitris Karagiannis, Heinrich C. Mayr (Hrsg.)
Modellierung 2020
19.–21. Februar 2020, Wien

P-303　Peter Heisig, Ronald Orth, Jakob Michael Schönborn, Stefan Thalmann (Hrsg.)
Wissensmanagement in digitalen Arbeitswelten: Aktuelle Ansätze und Perspektiven
18.–20.03.2019, Potsdam

P-304　Heinrich C. Mayr, Stefanie Rinderle-Ma, Stefan Strecker (Hrsg.)
40 Years EMISA
Digital Ecosystems of the Future: Methodology, Techniques and Applications
May 15.–17. 2019
Tutzing am Starnberger See

P-305　Heiko Roßnagel, Christian H. Schunck, Sebastian Mödersheim, Detlef Hühnlein (Hrsg.)
Open Identity Summit 2020
26.–27. May 2020, Copenhagen

P-306　Arslan Brömme, Christoph Busch, Antitza Dantcheva, Kiran Raja, Christian Rathgeb, Andreas Uhl (Eds.)
BIOSIG 2020
Proceedings of the 19th International Conference of the Biometrics Special Interest Group
16.–18. September 2020
International Digital Conference

P-307　Ralf H. Reussner, Anne Koziolek, Robert Heinrich (Hrsg.)
INFORMATIK 2020
Back to the Future
28. September – 2. Oktober 2020,
Karlsruhe

P-308　Raphael Zender, Dirk Ifenthaler, Thiemo Leonhardt, Clara Schumacher (Hrsg.)
DELFI 2020 –
Die 18. Fachtagung Bildungstechnologien der Gesellschaft für Informatik e.V.
14.–18. September 2020
Online

P-309　A. Meyer-Aurich, M. Gandorfer, C. Hoffmann, C. Weltzien, S. Bellingrath-Kimura, H. Floto (Hrsg.)
Informatik in der Land-, Forst- und Ernährungswirtschaft
Referate der 41. GIL-Jahrestagung
08.–09. März 2021, Leibniz-Institut für Agrartechnik und Bioökonomie e.V., Potsdam

P-310　Anne Koziolek, Ina Schaefer, Christoph Seidl (Hrsg.)
Software Engineering 2021
22.–26. Februar 2021,
Braunschweig/Virtuell

P-311　Kai-Uwe Sattler, Melanie Herschel, Wolfgang Lehner (Hrsg.)
Datenbanksysteme für Business, Technologie und Web (BTW 2021)
Tagungsband
13.–17. September 2021,
Dresden

P-312　Heiko Roßnagel, Christian H. Schunck, Sebastian Mödersheim (Hrsg.)
Open Identity Summit 2021
01.–02. Juni 2021, Copenhagen

P-313　Ludger Humbert (Hrsg.)
Informatik – Bildung von Lehrkräften in allen Phasen
19. GI-Fachtagung Informatik und Schule
8.–10. September 2021 Wuppertal

P-314　Gesellschaft für Informatik e.V. (GI) (Hrsg.)
INFORMATIK 2021 Computer Science & Sustainability
27. September– 01. Oktober 2021, Berlin

P-315 Arslan Brömme, Christoph Busch,
Naser Damer, Antitza Dantcheva,
Marta Gomez-Barrero, Kiran Raja,
Christian Rathgeb, Ana F. Sequeira,
Andreas Uhl (Eds.)
BIOSIG 2021
Proceedings of the 20th International
Conference of the Biometrics
Special Interest Group
15.–17. September 2021
International Digital Conference

P-316 Andrea Kienle, Andreas Harrer,
Jörg M. Haake, Andreas Lingnau (Hrsg.)
DELFI 2021
Die 19. Fachtagung Bildungstechnologien
der Gesellschaft für Informatik e.V.
13.–15. September 2021
Online 8.–10. September 2021

P-317 M. Gandorfer, C. Hoffmann, N. El Benni,
M. Cockburn, T. Anken, H. Floto (Hrsg.)
Informatik in der Land-, Forst- und
Ernährungswirtschaft
Fokus: Künstliche Intelligenz in der Agrar-
und Ernährungswirtschaft
Referate der 42. GIL-Jahrestagung
21.–22. Februar 2022 Agroscope, Tänikon,
Ettenhausen, Schweiz

P-318 Andreas Helferich, Robert Henzel,
Georg Herzwurm, Martin Mikusz (Hrsg.)
FACHTAGUNG SOFTWARE
MANAGEMENT 2021
Fachtagung des GI-Fachausschusses
Management der Anwendungsentwicklung
und -wartung im Fachbereich Wirtschafts-
informatik (WI-MAW), Stuttgart, 2021

P-319 Zeynep Tuncer, Rüdiger Breitschwerdt,
Helge Nuhn, Michael Fuchs, Vera Meister,
Martin Wolf, Doris Weßels, Birte Malzahn
(Hrsg.)
3. Wissenschaftsforum:
Digitale Transformation (WiFo21)
5. November 2021 Darmstadt, Germany

P-320 Lars Grunske, Janet Siegmund,
Andreas Vogelsang (Hrsg.))
Software Engineering 2022
21.–25. Februar 2022, Berlin/Virtuell

P-321 Veronika Thurner, Barne Kleinen, Juliane
Siegeris, Debora Weber-Wulff (Hrsg.)
Software Engineering im Unterricht der
Hochschulen SEUH 2022
24.–25. Februar 2022, Berlin

P-322 Peter A. Henning, Michael Striewe,
Matthias Wölfel (Hrsg.))
DELFI 2022 Die 20. Fachtagung
Bildungstechnologien der Gesellschaft für
Informatik e.V.
12.–14. September 2022, Karlsruhe

P-323 Christian Wressnegger, Delphine
Reinhardt, Thomas Barber, Bernhard C.
Witt, Daniel Arp, Zoltan Mann (Hrsg.)
Sicherheit 2022
Sicherheit, Schutz und Zuverlässigkeit
Beiträge der 11. Jahrestagung des
Fachbereichs Sicherheit der Gesellschaft
für Informatik e.V. (GI)
5.–8. April 2022, Karlsruhe

P-325 Heiko Roßnagel,
Christian H. Schunck,
Sebastian Mödersheim (Hrsg.)
Open Identity Summit 2022
Fachtagung vom 07. - 08. July 2022,
Copenhagen

P-327 Masud Fazal-Baqaie, Oliver Linssen,
Alexander Volland, Enes Yigitbas,
Martin Engstler, Martin Bertram,
Axel Kalenborn (Hrsg.)
Projektmanagement und
Vorgehensmodelle 2022
Trier 2022

P-328 Volker Wohlgemuth, Stefan Naumann,
Hans-Knud Arndt, Grit Behrens,
Maximilian Höb (Editors)
Environmental Informatics 2022
26.–28. September 2022,
Hamburg, Germany

P-330 Informatik in der Land-, Forst- und
Ernährungswirtschaft
Fokus: Resiliente Agri-Food-Systeme
Referate der 43. GIL-Jahrestagung
13.–14. Februar 2023 Osnabrück

All volumes of Lecture Notes in Informatics
can be found at
https://dl.gi.de/handle/20.500.12116/21.

The titles can be purchased at:

Köllen Druck + Verlag GmbH
Ernst-Robert-Curtius-Str. 14 · D-53117 Bonn
Fax: +49 (0)228/9898222
E-Mail: druckverlag@koellen.de